The Great
Zapruder Film Hoax

Also by James H. Fetzer

Author

Scientific Knowledge: Causation, Explanation, and Corroboration

Artificial Intelligence: Its Scope and Limits

Philosophy and Cognitive Science

Computers and Cognition

Philosophy of Science

Co-Author

Glossary of Epistemology/Philosophy of Science

Glossary of Cognitive Science

Editor

Foundations of Philosophy of Science: Recent Developments

Principles of Philosophical Reasoning

Science, Explanation, and Rationality

The Philosophy of Carl G. Hempel

Aspects of Artificial Intelligence

Sociobiology and Epistemology

Epistemology and Cognition

Probability and Causality

Consciousness Evolving

Murder in Dealey Plaza

Assassination Science

Co-Editor

Program Verification: Fundamental Issues in Computer Science

Philosophy, Language, and Artificial Intelligence

Philosophy, Mind, and Cognitive Inquiry

The New Theory of Reference

Definitions and Definability

THE GREAT ZAPRUDER FILM HOAX

DECEIT AND DECEPTION IN THE DEATH OF JFK

Edited by

James H. Fetzer, Ph.D.

CATFEET
PRESS
Chicago

This book and others from CATFEET PRESS® and Open Court
may be ordered by calling 1-800-815-2280.

PRESS

CATFEET PRESS® and the above logo are trademarks of
Carus Publishing Company.

Front cover drawn from Jack White's color-photo section in
Murder in Dealey Plaza (2000) *with frame 335 of the fake Zapruder film.*
Back cover photograph of the editor by Janice E. Fetzer.

© 2003 by James H. Fetzer, Ph.D.

First printing 2003
Second printing 2004 (corrected and updated)
Third printing 2005 (with corrections)

Printed and bound in the United States of America

Library of Congress Cataloging-in-Publication Data
The Great Zapruder film hoax : deceit and deception in the death of JFK
    / edited by James H. Fetzer.
        p.   cm.
Includes bibliographical references and index.
ISBN: 0-8126-9547-X (trade paper : alk. paper)
    1. Kennedy, John F. (John Fitzgerald), 1917-1963—Assassination.
    2. Kennedy, John F. (John Fitzgerald), 1917-1963—In motion pictures.
    3. Zapruder, Abraham. 4. Amateur films—Texas—Dallas—History—20th
Century. 5. Amateur films—Forgeries—United States—History—20th
Century. 6. Impostors and imposture—United States—History—20th
Century. I. Fetzer, James H., 1940–

E842.9.G67 2003
364.152'40973'09046—dc22

                                                            2003055736

Jack White
for showing the way

*The most dangerous and vicious of all forgeries are those
committed on behalf of a cause—the cause of a nation,
of an institution, or of a leader—and intended
to bring about a permanent falsification of history.*

— Allan Nevins, author of the Foreword to
John F. Kennedy, *Profiles in Courage* (1956)

CONTENTS

Epilogue

Appendices

Index

Acknowledgments

Contributors

Preface

. . . we always kept coming back to New York to study the Zapruder film [which was then in the possession of Life]—the single most important piece of evidence. Quite obviously, the Zapruder footage contained the nearest thing to "absolute truth" about the sequence of events in Dealey Plaza.
                                        —Josiah Thompson, *Six Seconds in Dallas* (1967)

Perhaps no greater debate has raged in the history of the study of the death of JFK than has arisen over the authenticity of a 27-second home movie of the assassination, known as "the Zapruder film". According to Abraham Zapruder, a local businessman from Dallas, after whom it has been named, he used a fully-wound, spring-loaded, hand-held Bell & Howell camera to film the Presidential motorcade as it passed through Dealey Plaza on 22 November 1963. (See his statement below.) This footage has been described as "the most significant amateur recording of a news event in history".

Some students of the crime take it as the absolute foundation for understanding what actually transpired. Others are not so sure. Questions have been raised about virtually every aspect of the film and its contents, including inconsistencies between eyewitness reports and the contents of the film, differences between the alleged "camera original" and other copies, discrepancies between the film and other photographs and films, and a host of other issues, even extending to whether Zapruder really took the film that bears his name. And there are good reasons to ask.

The Zapruder film is a piece of a rather large and complex puzzle over the true causes of the death of Jack Kennedy. According to the official account, a lone gunman named Lee Oswald fired three shots from the sixth floor of the Texas School Book Depository with an obscure Italian World War II-vintage Mannlicher-Carcano 6.5 mm carbine and scored two hits, with one miss, as the following photograph displays. Abraham Zapruder was standing on a 4-foot concrete pedestal at the location shown below, which gave him a comprehensive view of the plaza and a suitable position for taking his film, even though a freeway road sign would partially block his view.

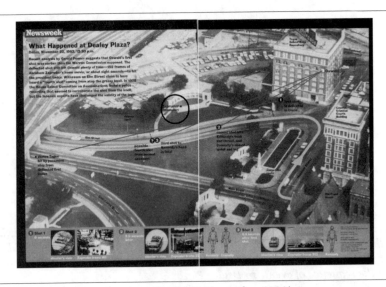

Newsweek *(22 November 1993)*
with the location of Abraham Zapruder identified

According to this depiction, the first shot hit the branch of a tree and was deflected to the west, where it struck a curb and injured a distant bystander. The second allegedly struck Jack at the base of the back of the neck, transited his neck without hitting any bony structures and exited just above his tie, then hit Governor John Connally near his right armpit, shattering a rib and exiting his chest, then impacting with his right wrist and being deflected into his left thigh. The Warren Commision also claims that this bullet was found—in virtually pristine condition—on a stretcher at Parkland Hospital, and it has come to be known as "the magic bullet" (the Prologue). The third shot hit Jack in the head and killed him.

As every serious student of the assassination is well aware, there are good reasons to question almost every aspect of this official account, apart from the description of the wounds to Governor Connally, as *Murder in Dealey Plaza* (2000) has shown (Appendix A). What even serious students of the assassination may not have noticed, but as David W. Mantik, M.D., Ph.D., has observed, this diagram shows the third hit occurring 30–40 feet further down Elm Street than is shown in frame 313 of the Zapruder film! Which means that, if *Newsweek* is right, then the film must be wrong; and if the film is right, then *Newsweek* must be wrong. (Compare it with the Moorman photograph below.)

Of course, magazines can make mistakes. But, as Mantik explains in his discussion of this peculiar inconsistency in *Murder in Dealey Plaza* (2000), this downhill location is rather strongly supported by early reenactments of the assassination as well as by data tables and documents, all of which the Warren Commission ignored. The case against Oswald was riddled with inconsistencies, which by now have become well-known. This has been amply demonstrated by studies published in many books, which range from Harold Weisberg's *Whitewash* (1965) and Mark Lane's *Rush to Judgment* (1966) to Noel Twyman's *Bloody Treason* (1997) and Stewart Galanor's *Cover-Up* (1998), to cite just a few.

The "Out-of-Camera" Original

What is most intriguing from the point of view of the film, however, is the possibility that those early reenactments, data tables, and documents were correct, which would mean that something is seriously wrong with the film. If frame 313 has been faked, then the film is a fraud. And if the film is a fraud, then what our government has been telling us has been an enormous lie, a form of deception and deceit on a grand scale that no one should continue to deny. Previous studies published in *Assassination Science* (1998), in *Murder in Dealey Plaza* (2000), and elsewhere have raised these questions. This book settles them. The frame has been faked and the film is a fraud.

To be more precise, distinctions must be drawn between different ways in which this film or any other film might or might not be subject to change from what is called the "out-of-camera" original. One is the removal of individual frames or of sequences of frames. This form of editing can be effected simply by splicing the film. No one doubts that the extant film—in most of its versions, at least—has been spliced. When its frames are numbered from 1 to 486, there are well-know splices at frames 154–157 (where frames 155 and 156 are missing) and at frames 207–212 (where frames 208, 209, 210, and 211 are missing).

What may come as more of a surprise is that the version of the film that is most widely supposed to represent the state of the art, MPI's "Image of an Assassination" (1998), is not only missing these six frames, whose omission from many versions of the film is a matter of public record, but has frames 331 and 332 out of order and does not include frames 341, 350, and 486 (the final frame in the film)! This is especially surprising and disappointing if you know that there is at least one version of the film, Robert Groden's "pristine" version, which includes all of these frames—and in their proper order! But omissions and commissions of these kinds do not affect the film's authenticity.

Moreover, as John Costella, Ph.D., has observed, the MPI version, which includes the sprocket holes, still suffers from multiple additional defects due to aspect ratio problems (which stretch out each frame horizontally, compared to the original) and poor resolution caused by repeated resizing of and rotation of each image (which caused the images to be more blurred than necessary, even on the DVD version). It also suffers from the pincushion distortion of the Zapruder camera (which stretches each image outward at the corners). Research on the film has been undermined by the failure to have access to images that are close approximations to—much less improvements upon—what would have been the "camera original" if Zapruder's camera had taken the film.

MPI Frame before (left) and after (right) pincushion and aspect ratio corrections (with ghost panels added and sprocket holes masked)

Costella's work establishes a new standard for research on the film that incorporates corrections for the kinds of distortions that have created obstacles to research in the past. To advance the frontiers of knowledge, science, education, and inquiry, it is available on my web site, *www.assassinationscience.com*, without charge. Selected frames from this new version, which we call "the Costella combined cut", appear in the color-photo section of this book. This version is far superior to anything previously available. Yet it is important to emphasize that none of the improvements that are reflected here affect the question of the authenticity of the film. That is another matter entirely, which concerns the content of the film far more than the presentation of its images.

Moorman photograph with Zapruder circled,
The Sydney Morning Herald *(25 November 1963)*

This distinction has been a source of profound confusion, especially in the public mind. When the Assassination Records Review Board (ARRB) determined the Zapruder film was "an assassination record" on 24 April 1997, it solicited professional assistance in order to ascertain the compensation that should be accorded the Zapruder family. An expert from Kodak, Rollie Zavada, was commissioned to study the film and ascertain whether or not it was the "camera original". It was Zavada's conclusion that the extant film had indeed been taken with a camera of the very kind Zapruder was supposed to have used and that certain kinds of "anomalies" that had raised doubts over the authenticity of the film were predictable effects of the camera's mode of operation (Appendix B).

A longer version of his study, known as "The Zavada Report", was submitted to the ARRB and became a part of its formal records. While Zavada's work has resolved some of the issues that have been raised in research regarding the "ghost images" and claw marks that were discussed by Mantik in *Assassination Science* (1998), for example, Zavada does not appear entirely willing to come to grips with the serious possibility that copies of the film in the National Archives might not really be "first day copies", as Mantik explains in *Murder in Dealey Plaza* (2000). Most importantly, Zavada's work substantiates that the film strip is authentic Kodak celluloid but does not vouch for its contents, which, as he himself concedes, is a question that lies beyond his competence. Nevertheless, his work represents an important contribution to Zapruder film research.

Events at the NPIC

The technical requirements for film alteration impose contraints on the time within which alteration could have taken place. Zavada's research may possibly have invalidated the hypothesis that Mike Pincher, J.D., and Roy Schaeffer advanced in *Assassination Science* (1998)—namely, that the original was in the hands of the National Photographic Interpretation Center (NPIC) run by the CIA already on Friday night, 22 November 1963, where it underwent extensive editing to create a new "original" and three copies that were flown back to Dallas the following morning—without also eliminating alternatives that provide a more generous time frame while it was in the hands of *Life*. But they appear to have been right about the NPIC. [*Editor's note*: See Lifton's chapter for "Hawkeyeworks".]

For example, as Costella has observed, it would not have been difficult to have imposed some edits on the film before it was shown to a small group of newsmen on Saturday morning before *Life* purchased the film. That what was shown appears to have been different from what we have available now is reflected by Dan Rather's famous report, broadcast shortly after he had seen the film, of having watched the President fall forward—"his head . . . went forward with considerable violence"—rather than back-and-to-the-left as we see today. A transcript of Rather's report may be found in Richard Trask, *Pictures of the Pain* (1994), pp. 85–90, where Trask explains that Rather was allowed to watch the film only once and to take no notes.

Moreover, ARRB interviews with Homer McMahon, who was in charge of the color photo section for the NPIC at the time, substantiate that he was brought a home movie of the assassination by Secret Service Agent William Smith. McMahon had been instructed to review the film and prepare a briefing board displaying the impacts of bullets on bodies for an unspecified government offical. McMahon reported that, after ten or more viewings of the film, it was his opinion that President Kennedy was shot six to eight times from at least three directions, which, of course, is even more strikingly at variance with what can be observed in the film today (Appendix C).

The medical evidence published in *Assassination Science* (1998) and *Murder in Dealey Plaza* (2000) provides ample support for four shots to JFK—a shot to his back from behind; a shot to his throat from in front; and two shots to the head, one from the back and one from in front—and possibly as many as three to Connally, raising the prospect that McMahon may have meant six to eight impacts on bodies in the vehicle, since four plus three equals seven, a number between six and eight. But what is most important here is the striking difference in the film that McMahon studied at the NPIC that night and the film that we have available to us today.

McMahon was told by Smith that the film had been developed at Rochester, the location of Kodak headquarters. Films do not need to be developed twice. According to Noel Twyman's chronology (Appendix D), the original was developed at Eastman Kodak in Dallas and three prints were made at Jamieson Film Company that day. He reports that the "first copy" was purchased by oilman H. L. Hunt. It has long been known that the film identification numbers display a gap: the original is #0183 but the copies are #0185, #0186, and #0187. Hunt might have received #0184 or, as David Healy has proposed, #0184 may have been taken to Rochester as a negative and turned into a positive, which was then taken to NPIC. There could have been many "copies".

FEDERAL BUREAU OF INVESTIGATION

Date December 4, 1963

ABRAHAM ZAPRUDER, 3909 Marquette Street, Dallas, advised that on November 22, 1963, he was standing in the park area north of Elm Street and just west of the intersection of Elm and Houston Streets. He had taken this position in order to take 8 millimeter movie film of the President and the Presidential motorcade as it passed by him. He stated he had with him a Bell and Howell 8 millimeter zoom-lens camera, which was either a 1962 or 1963 model. He advised he had loaded this camera previously with a 25-foot roll of 16 millimeter film, which in effect affords 50 feet of 8 millimeter film. He had shot the first 25 feet earlier and had reversed the roll and shot a few feet on November 22, 1963, at the park area of some girls who work in his office, prior to the arrival of the Presidential motorcade. He stated his camera was fully wound, was set, manually, on maximum zoom-lens. The camera was set to take normal speed movie film or 24 frames per second. The control buttons for the zoom-lens were not touched once he started taking photographs of the Presidential motorcade.

ZAPRUDER stated that he first picked up the motorcade as it made the turn on to Elm Street from Houston Street. The motorcade then passed behind a street directional sign and from that point on until it disappeared from sight to his right, or the west, he was taking moving pictures of the President's car. He stated he had started taking pictures prior to the first shot being fired and continued taking pictures until the motorcade disappeared to his right. ZAPRUDER advised he could not recall but having heard only two shots and, also, stated that he knew that from watching through the viewfinder that the President had been hit. He stated he took the exposed film immediately to the Jamieson Film Company on Bryan Street, Dallas, and stayed with the film through its entire processing. He had the original print and three copies made. The film was in color. The original is on 16 millimeter film, and according to Mr. ZAPRUDER is much clearer than those appearing on 8 millimeter film. He subsequently turned over two copies to the United States Secret Service and sold the original and one copy to Life Magazine.

Mr. ZAPRUDER turned over to Special Agent ROBERT M.

2

BARRETT his Bell and Howell 8 millimeter zoom-lens camera described above. He requested that the camera be returned to him after it had served its use to the FBI. He advised this camera had been in the hands of the United States Secret Service Agents on December 3, 1963, as they claimed they wanted to do some checking of it. He, also, stated he had received a call from the Bell and Howell Company who stated they wanted to place the camera in their archives and would replace the camera with a new one.

on 12/4/63 at Dallas, Texas   File # DL 89-43

by Special Agent ROBERT M. BARRETT /gmf   Date dictated 12/4/63

The film was developed at Eastman Kodak but the prints were made at Jamieson. The camera had three settings: single frame, normal speed (16 fps), and slow motion (48 fps). A "setting" of 24 fps would result from shooting at 48 fps but then only printing every other frame.

Other Eyewitness Reports

Other eyewitness reports are equally telling in different ways. More than fifty-nine witnesses have said that the limousine either slowed dramatically or came to a complete stop after bullets began to be fired, which Vince Palamara has collated in *Murder in Dealey Plaza* (2000). The most plausible explanation for those reports, of course, is that *the limousine slowed dramatically as it came to a complete stop*. Some witnesses were distracted by what was going on and heard or saw different parts of the action. But it was such an obvious indication of Secret Service complicity that it had to be taken out.

A French investigative reporter, William Reymond, and an independent student of the crime, Rich DellaRosa, have both reported viewing another version of the film. In the case of DellaRosa, he has seen it on three different occasions (Appendix E). They both describe the events presented as more vivid and detailed, including the turn from Houston onto Elm, the driver bringing the limo to a halt—and jostling the passengers—after bullets began to be fired, and the driver, William Greer, only accelerating after the President had been hit twice in the head, from behind and from the front. And, in *Assassination Science* (1998), Mantik has discussed the reports of others who have also seen a different, more complete film.

There exists such striking evidence of fraud and fabrication in the death of JFK, not merely in relation to the photographic record but throughout this case—including the fabrication of X-rays, the substitution of a brain for that of JFK, the reshooting of the autopsy photographs, the destruction of the limousine, the substitution of a windshield, the alteration of photographs, planting of a palmprint, and the suppression of evidence—that it is difficult to imagine why anyone would want to defend the position that the film could not have been altered. Given the manipulation of evidence in almost every other respect, it makes more sense to presume that it probably has been faked.

Some students of the assassination, however, have placed such emphasis upon the film as the most basic evidence in this case that they appear to be unwilling to relinquish that position, seemingly without regard for the evidence. Such an attitude contradicts the most basic principle of scientific reasoning, *the requirement of total evidence*, which insists that, in the search for truth, reasoning must be based upon all the available relevant evidence. Evidence is relevant when its presence or absence (or its truth or falsity) makes a difference to the truth or falsity of the hypothesis under consideration, which in this case, of course, is that of the authenticity of the Zapruder film.

No one exemplifies this attitude better than Josiah Thompson, whose classic book, *Six Seconds in Dallas* (1967), was based upon a study of the Zapruder film. Since I organized and moderated the first Zapruder Film Symposium at the JFK Lancer Conference in 1996, which brought together a dozen of the best experts on the film, he has been adamant that it is authentic—possibly threatened by the prospect that his work was based on a fake film—and that no credible evidence to the contrary exists. That appears to me to be a remarkable claim, but when I have challenged him by enumerating a dozen or more indications of fakery, he has dismissed them, contending that the photos and films "fit together" because they are genuine. But they might "fit together" because they have been altered for that purpose. They might "fit together" by design. He begs the question when the problem is figuring out which photos and films are genuine and which are not.

There are disturbing indications that *Life* was profoundly involved in this whole affair. A stunning article by Paul Mandel in *Life's* Memorial Edition (undated but early December 1963) offers an exact description of the shot sequence, with distances and times that correspond to notes from the NPIC, which were discovered by the ARRB and published in *Murder in Dealey Plaza* (2000), pp. 323–324. This hints at a close working relationship between *Life* and the CIA. Worse, this piece even attempts to explain away a shot to the throat with a shooter from behind, claiming, "the 8mm film shows the President turning his body far around to the right as he waves to someone in the crowd. His throat is exposed—toward the sniper's nest—just before he clutches it"! Since nothing of this kind occurs in the extant film, unless its own "original" had already been altered, *Life* was clearly lying, which establishes its complicity in the cover-up.

Falsification vs. Verification

More important than our numerous encounters is the apparently perfect articulation Thompson provides of the underlying rationale that resists the very idea that the film has been faked. During his testimony to the ARRB on 2 April 1997, he raises a crucial question about the film's significance, which he then answers to his own apparent satisfaction:

> Why is this film important? It is enormously important. If you want to know what happened in Dealey Plaza, this film shows you, as much as any film can. How could it be used by the research community? Well, there have been certain quibbles about the authenticity of this film. I have no doubt that it is authentic, but that can be proven, that can be shown. All queries and challenges to the authenticity, if this film is in government hands, remains in government hands, can be satisfactorily overcome. When that is done, this film then becomes a baseline for all additional studies for what happened in Dealey Plaza.

> For example, the medical evidence. There have been many claims of extra autopsies, faking of autopsy photos, et cetera, et cetera. If the medical evidence does not match what you see on the Zapruder film, then you might have cause to challenge that sort of evidence. Evidence of other films could be compared against this film as a baseline. If they match, fine. If they don't match, you know that something is wrong. Much more importantly, of course, is the deduction of trajectories and ultimately, of firing points, which can only be done with great precision by using the most resolved copy of the film available. (Appendix F)

As a point of logic, proving that the film is authentic poses far more daunting challenges than proving that it is not. *A single frame in which a specific event is not portrayed as it occurred in Dealey Plaza* would be sufficient to impugn the film's integrity. Showing that it is authentic, by comparsion, would require proof that, in each of its 486 frames, *every feature of every frame portrays events in Dealey Plaza exactly as they occurred!* But how could anyone possibly know exactly how every event actually occurred in Dealey Plaza? The very idea boggles the mind. It can't be proven and it can't be shown.

For Thompson's claim to make sense, even remotely, it would have to be possible—not just logically or physically, but historically possible—to possess independent knowledge of every event that transpired in Dealey Plaza to compare that knowledge with events as portrayed in the film. But that is a fantasy. If it were possible to possess independent knowlege of every event that transpired in Dealey Plaza, it would not be necessary to compare it with the film: we would already know what we wanted to know and we would not need to rely upon the film at all!

Whether or not the film remains in government hands surely does not affect the logical properties that distinguish verification from falsification. Moreover, placing such absolute reliance upon a strip of celluloid contradicts the principles of evidence that obtain in cases of this kind. As *McCormick on Evidence*, 3rd edition (1984) observes, "*a photograph [or film] is viewed merely as a graphic portrayal of oral testimony and becomes admissible only when a witness has testified that it is a correct and accurate representation of the relevant facts personally observed by the witness.*" Witnesses take precedence over photographs and films.

Zapruder would vouch for his film in a court of law on 13 February 1969, long before serious questions had been raised about its authenticity. He would explain that the film had been developed at Eastman and then taken to Jamieson for prints. But he would also say that he could not tell if it might be missing frames and that he could not vouch for the film's chain of custody. Today, there might be experts on both sides to address the question of authenticity, which would require a hearing of its own to settle the issue. Given the studies published in this book, I doubt very much that the film would be admissible, except perhaps as a subject of litigation.

Obstacles to Understanding

In a series of lectures, articles, and posts, which range from a presentation at the JFK Lancer Conference on 20 November 1998 entitled "Why the Zapruder Film *is* Authentic" to a report about a discussion following the performance of a play, "Frame 312", at the Alliance Theater in Atlanta on 25 October 2002, Josiah Thompson persists in defending the film's authenticity and attacking those who challenge it. (For a striking illustration, see the reviews of *Assassination Science* (1998) and of *Murder in Dealey Plaza* (2000) he has posted on Amazon.com.) He advances three lines of argument, however, that have to be taken seriously by everyone who cares about this question.

Thompson's first line of defense is that the chronology of the possession of the original would not have allowed it, which he summarizes with the observation that, "At no time during this hectic weekend did the original of the film ever leave the custody and control of Abraham Zapruder and *Life* magazine". The Healy conjecture that the first negative, #0184, may have been flown to Rochester, turned into a postive, and then taken to NPIC, however, renders that argument unsound. And, as Costella explains here, the extant film cannot have been constructed out of the original Zapruder film. If there were additional negatives or additional films used in constructing the expanded film—including the missing Gordon Arnold film—then a chronology of the Zapruder original does not track them. The first argument therefore fails.

Thompson's second line of defense is that frames were published by *Life* in its issue of 29 November 1963, which imposed severe constraints on alteration, especially since it was in production already the weekend of the assassination. But, as Costella has also observed, that issue includes only 31 frames out of 486, and they appear to have been carefully selected to minimize their informational content. They are poor quality, black and white prints, which do not include any frames from frame 269 to frame 323—three whole seconds of film (half of Thompson's "six"). None of the published frames, moreover, includes Jean Hill, Mary Moorman, Charles Brehm, Joe Brehm, or Beverly Oliver. Such ommisions would lend additional fliexibility to faking the film. The appearance of these frames does impose constraints upon the fabrication process, but they are weak ones and would not have severely constained the product. This argument is therefore likewise not compelling.

Thompson's third line of defense—his "clincher" argument—is that the Zapruder film would have had to have been altered to conform to other photographs and films that had yet to be developed! But that assumes the alteration would have had to have been complete within 72 hours, for example. This imposes an unnecessary constraint on the alteration process, but it does raise the important point that changes to the Zapruder film would have dictated alterations to other films, such as the Nix and the Muchmore films. The studies published here support the conclusion that the fabricated Zapruder film—and a few photographs, such as the Moorman and perhaps the Altgens—were used as a guide for introducing other changes into the photographic record. Indeed, as Richard Trask, *Pictures of the Pain* (1994), pp. 590–591, reports, the FBI was still collecting photographs and films weeks after the assassination. It happened the other way around.

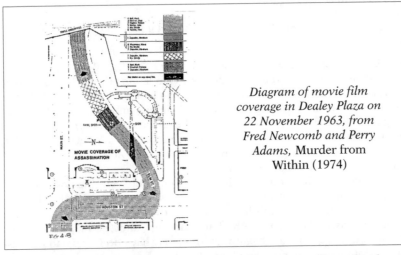

Diagram of movie film coverage in Dealey Plaza on 22 November 1963, from Fred Newcomb and Perry Adams, Murder from Within *(1974)*

The situation we encounter resembles that of detectives confronted with a corpse. They can know that the body is dead without also knowing exactly how, when, and why the death occurred. Earlier work by Daryll Weatherly, Harrison Livingstone, David S. Lifton, Duncan MacRae, Roy Schaeffer, Mike Pincher and others, especially Jack White and David Mantik, has provided evidence that something was wrong with the film. We now know, beyond reasonable doubt, that the film is a fabrication. The entire photographic record has thereby become suspect, which should usher in a new era of research reinvestigating one of the most fascinating aspects of the cover-up, including many other photographs and films, such as the Muchmore, Willis, Betzner, Altgens, and Moorman, studies of which are published here. That Zapruder did not take "the Zapruder film" overwhelmingly substantiates the conclusion established by *Assassination Science* (1998) and *Murder in Dealey Plaza* (2000) that JFK was killed by an extensive conspiracy concealed by a meticulous cover-up.

Thompson has attacked me personally for for having observed, on the occasion of the 1996 Zapruder Film Symposium, that an "historical turning point" had been reached because alteration had been established by the evidence presented and for suggesting that those who continue to disagree are displaying irrationality of belief. But *rationality of belief* obtains when you accept, reject, and hold beliefs in suspense in proportion to the available relevant evidence. Objective logical relationships obtain between specific evidence and specific hypotheses. Those who ignore the evidence and continue to hold beliefs that have been falsified are indeed "irrational" in proportion to their familiarity with the evidence. If anyone doubts that sufficient proof was presented at the first symposium, let them consider the results of the second Zapruder Film Symposium, as they are reported on the pages of this book.

What the Evidence Tells Us

If we want to know what happened in Dealey Plaza, then this film is only one piece of evidence and has to be treated cautiously, like other evidence in this case. So much of the evidence has been changed, altered, or faked that it would be naive in the extreme to assume—to simply take for granted!—that the film is genuine. (See the Prologue.) Its authenticity has to be tested and measured against the eyewitness reports, medical findings, other photos and films, and the rest of the evidence whose authenticity has been established on independent grounds. Approached with great caution, however, it can provide important information about the conspiracy and cover-up.

Some of the most important indications that the Zapruder film has been faked include the unresponsive spectators, the impossible frame 232, the Stemmons Freeway sign's inconsistencies, differences in lamppost verticality between the film and Dallas Police Department photographs, the missing limousine stop, the Greer backward head-turn in frames 302–303, the disappearing blood spray in frames 313–314, the "blob" of gushing brains, the Greer forward head-turn in frames 315–317, the absence of tissue debris on the limousine's trunk, the missing Connally left turn, and the "full flush left" problem.

Questions about the film's authenticity are anything but "quibbles". That the film has been altered in various respects has been established beyond reasonable doubt on the basis of internal anomalies, physical impossibilities, eyewitness testimony, and other forms of proof. In conjunction with other evidence, however, authentic features of this film can be identified, which substantiate other findings. Frame 225, for example, shows a hole in the windshield. Frames 313–316 show motion of the President's body, back-and-to-the-left. Frame 330 shows a "solar flare". Frame 374 shows a blow-out to the back of the President's head. These are major findings that help us to unravel the case.

Frame 225 substantiates eyewitness testimony of a through-and-through hole in the windshield that is also visible in the Altgens photograph. It supports the study of Doug Weldon, J.D., that the shot to the throat originated from the front and to the left. When the phony "blob" and fake blood spray have been sorted out, frames 313–316 support a shot to the right temple from the right/front, as many students have alleged. Frame 330 substantiates a shot that impacted the chrome strip above the windshield, which may have been fired by a Mannlicher-Carcano but whose trajectory is almost horizontal. Frame 374 not only shows the back-of-the-head wound reported by some 40 witnesses but substantiates that autopsy X-rays and photographs have been altered or reshot.

So, when approached with caution, the film *can* help with firing points and trajectories. Frame 330, for example, suggests that the Dal-Tex Building rather than the Book Depository was the origin of this shot. Yet even these findings have to be treated with caution. A more complete analysis of frame 313 suggests a highly complicated deception that ties together the Moorman photograph with the Zapruder film to create a false impression of the location at which the right temple shot occurred, where *Newsweek*—for reasons unknown—may have got it right. The blood spray and the bulging blob of brains and gore appear to be special effects that were introduced to conceal the true causes of death. Shifting the location at which the fatal shots were inflicted was no doubt an additional measure to confuse and confound those who would ever attempt a systematic reconstruction of events in Dealey Plaza, which was surely the most important reason for faking the film in the first place.

Participants in the Zapruder Film Symposium, *Duluth, MN (10 May 2003)*
Back: Jack White, Jim Fetzer, John Costella, and Gary Severson;
Front: David Mantik, David Healy, and Jeremiah Haynes

The rationale for faking the film has become obvious. By taking for granted a false depiction of the sequence of events in Dealey Plaza, it becomes logically impossible to systematically reconstruct what actually happened on 22 November 1963. No wonder so much dedicated research on the film has encountered dead ends. The article of faith—"All queries and challenges to [its] authenticity . . . can be satisfactorily overcome"—is now exposed as a sham. The very idea of using it as "a baseline for all additional studies of what happened in Dealey Plaza" stands revealed as a hoax. The fake film has functioned as the backbone of the cover-up for nearly forty years. Shattering the illusion allows us to carry the case forward, confident that, by satisfying the basic scientific requirement that we must take into account all the available relevant evidence in arriving at conclusions in the search for truth, we can finally comprehend what happened to President John F. Kennedy and thereby contribute to a better understanding of one of the darkest chapters in our nation's history.

J.H.F.

Prologue

Fraud and Fabrication in the Death of JFK

James H. Fetzer, Ph.D.

[*Editor's note*: The duplicity of *The Warren Report* (1964) is nowhere more manifest than in its contention that, "Although it is not necessary to any essential findings of the Commission to determine just which shot hit Governor Connally, there is very persuasive evidence from the experts to indicate that the same bullet which pierced the President's throat also caused Governor Connally's wounds." According to its own report, one shot—which must have been the first—missed. That shot cannot have hit Governor Connally. Another hit the President in the back of the head, killing him. That shot cannot have hit Governor Connally. The only shot that could have hit him—unless there were more shots, more shooters, and a conspiracy—had to have been the shot the Commission claimed had hit the President in the back of the neck, which is provably false and even anatomically impossible.]

Those who continue to support *The Warren Report* (1964) display the tendency to take their position for granted as though it were obviously true. If it were true, of course, then the "magic bullet" hypothesis—that a bullet entered the back of the President's neck, transited his neck without hitting any bony structures, exited his throat right at the knot of his tie, entered John Connally's back, shattering a rib, exiting from his chest, damaging his right wrist and then entering his left thigh—has to be true (Figure 1). If the "magic bullet" hypothesis is false, then *The Warren Report* (1964), *The HSCA Report* (1979), *Case Closed* (1993), and every other position that incorporates it must be false. And if it is false, then those who have rejected that hypothesis—the "conspiracy theorists"—have been right all along!

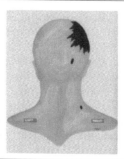

Figure 1. Warren Commission diagrams of JFK's wounds

1

So how can we determine whether or not the "magic bullet" hypothesis is true? It would obviously be false if the bullet had not entered the base of the back of the President's neck, if it had not transited his neck without hitting any bony structures, or if it had not exited from his neck at the level of the knot of his tie. If any of those claims is false, then *The Warren Report, The HSCA Report, Case Closed,* and every other position incorporating it must be false. (This may sound just a bit repetitive, but I don't want anyone to lose their way in tracking the structure of the argument as others may have failed to track the trajectory of the "magic bullet".) So is this theory true?

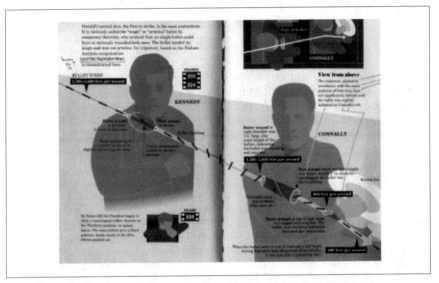

Figure 2. Gerald Posner's depiction of the "magic bullet" theory

Even Gerald Posner's own diagram (Figure 2) appears to shift the location from the official diagrams. The physicians who conducted the autopsy at Bethesda did not actually dissect the neck to determine the trajectory that this bullet is supposed to have taken but determined it as a matter of "inference". Thus, on page 4 of the autopsy report, which may be found in *Assassination Science* (1998), p. 433, the following critical sentences may be found:

> 2. The second wound presumably of entry is that described above in the upper right posterior thorax. . . . The missile path through the fascia and musculature cannot be easily probed. The wound presumably of exit was that described by Dr. Malcolm Perry in the low anterior cervical region.

Notice, in particular, that the entry and exit locations were matters of "presumption", which Humes defended on the basis of an "inference" drawn *after the body had been removed from the morgue* for preparation for the funeral. After conversations with Parkland that allegedly only took place on Saturday, he belatedly realized that the wound to the back must have been the entry for the wound to the throat as its exit! Also notice that the description of "the upper right posterior thorax", which is the upper-right portion of the chest cavity, does not quite place the wound where it has to be if the "magic bullet" hypothesis is true. Yet that is the basis for the theory!

Fortunately, we have other reports from physicians who were in the position to make the relevant observations, including Admiral George Burkley, the President's personal physician, who was with the body in Dallas, accompanied it on the flight back, and was present during the autopsy. According to his death certificate, which has also been reprinted in *Assassination Science*, p. 439, "a second wound occurred in the posterior back at about the level of the third thoracic vertebra" (Figure 3). Burkley's death certificate may also be found in Gary Shaw, *Cover-Up* (1976/1992), p. 65, and in Stewart Galanor, *Cover-Up* (1998), Document 8, which both include most of the evidence that matters here.

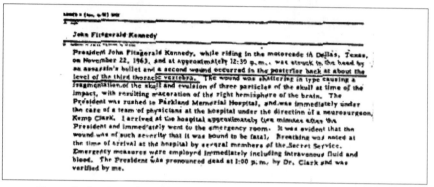

Figure 3. Section of Burkley's Death Certificate for President Kennedy

The third thoracic vertebra, however, is too low to have been the entry location for a bullet fired from above and behind that could possibly have exited from the President's throat at the level of the knot of his tie. Anyone who may be in doubt should consult Gary Shaw, *Cover-Up* (1976/1992), p. 65, which includes a diagram that identifies that location specifically (Figure 4) and, provides a diagram of the trajectory that the "magic bullet" had to take if it entered at the location specified by Admiral Burkley and exited at the location specified by Commander Humes, which has been widely ridiculed in the conspiracy literature. So which of them is right? Did the bullet enter high enough for the hypothesis to be true?

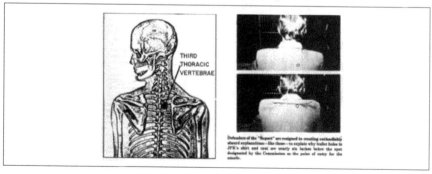

Figure 4. The location of the 3rd thoracic vertebra

Many books on the assassination, including Josiah Thompson, *Six Seconds in Dallas* (1967) and Gary Shaw, *Cover-Up* (1976/1992) have observed that damage may be found in the President's shirt and jacket that substantiate the lower entry point. Photographs of the shirt and jacket may be found, for example, in Thompson's *Six Seconds*, p. 48, Shaw's *Cover-Up*, p. 64, and many other sources, including Stewart Galanor, *Cover-Up* (1998), Documents 6 and 7 (Figure 5). As Gary Shaw observes, moreover, the claim that the shirt and jacket were bunched appears to be rather difficult to sustain.

Figure 5. Photographs of the President's Shirt and Jacket

One reason is that photographs and films taken during the assassination do not show the jacket to be bunched-up, as this defense requires. More importantly, however, observations of the wound itself provide independent confirmation for the location supported by the shirt and jacket. This includes the autopsy diagram drawn by J. Thornton Boswell, Hume's assistant, which may be found in Shaw's *Cover-Up*, p. 62, and in Galanor's *Cover-Up*, Document 5, which, like the shirt and jacket, show the wound to be about 5 or 6 incles too low to be the point of entry for a bullet that exited at the President's throat (Figure 6). Boswell's diagram, moreover, was verified by Admiral Burkley!

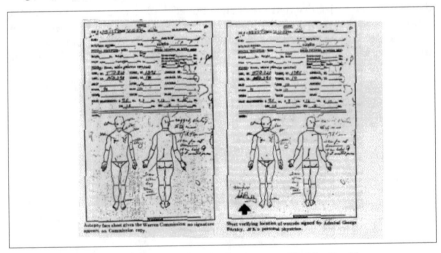

Figure 6. Boswell's autopsy diagram, verified by Burkley

Another diagram was prepared by FBI Special Agent James W. Sibert, who observed the autopsy at Bethesda, and may be found in Noel Twyman, *Bloody Treason* (1997), p. 100. It plainly demonstrates the paradox confronted by the "magic bullet" hypothesis even in relation to its most elementary assumptions, since the back wound is clearly too low to be the entry point for a bullet that exited from the throat, if the bullet was fired from a position above and behind the President (Figure 7).

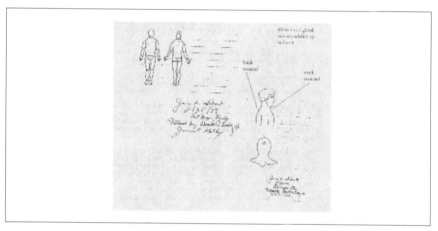

Figure 7. Agent Sibert's diagram of the location of the wounds

So, unless Lee Oswald was actually, say, firing from inside the trunk of the Lincoln limousine, this trajectory cannot be sustained. It also shows that Warren Commission diagrams of this wound are hopelessly inaccurate. Sibert attended the autopsy with another agent, Francis X. O'Neill, subsequently submitting a report of their observations at the time (Figure 8). Dated 9 December 1963, it reads, in part, as follows (in relation to a missing "total body X-ray"):

> A total body X-ray and autopsy revealed the bullet hole located just below shoulders to right of spinal column and hand-probing indicated trajectory at angle of 45 to 60 degrees downward and hole of short depth with no point of exit. No bullet located in body.

An excerpt of their report, which includes this passage, may be found in Mark Lane, *Rush to Judgment* (1966), Appendix IV. They also reported the conclusion that the bullet had worked its way out of the body during cardiac massage at Parkland Hospital. Further discussion of this wound, including diagrams, may be found in Robert Groden, *The Killing of a President* (1993), pp. 78–79.

No doubt, the estimate of the degree of downward trajectory as falling between 45 and 60 degrees cannot be rendered more exact, since it was done by an autopsy physician using his finger to probe the wound! A precise determination of the location from which the missile had been fired would also require knowledge of the position of the body in the vechicle, of the vehicle in the street, and of the inclination of the street as relevant variables. But this report nevertheless clearly substantiates that the wound was at a downward angle, that there was no point of exit, and that the bullet was not in the body.

1
DL 89-43
KCB: rmb

RESULTS OF AUTOPSY ON JOHN F. KENNEDY

On November 23, 1963, an autopsy was performed on the
body of former President JOHN F. KENNEDY at the National Naval
Medical Center, Bethesda, Maryland. A total body X-ray and
autopsy revealed one bullet hole located just below shoulders
to right of spinal column and hand-probing indicated trajectory
at angle of 45 to 60 degrees downward and hole of short depth
with no point of exit. No bullet located in body.

A second bullet entered back of head and thereafter emerged through top of skull. Two metal fragments removed from
brain area, the first 7 x 2 millimeters and the other 3 by 1
millimeters in size.

The above two metal fragments were turned over to
Agents of the FBI for delivery to the FBI Laboratory.

A piece of skull measuring 10 by 6.5 centimeters had
been flown in to Bethesda from Dallas hospital and this disclosed
minute metal fragments where bullet emerged from skull.

With respect to the bullet hole located in the back,
pathologist at National Naval Medical Center was of the opinion
this bullet worked its way out of the victim's back during cardiac
massage performed at Dallas hospital prior to transportation of the
body to Washington.

With respect to this situation, it is noted that
Secret Service Agent RICHARD JOHNSON turned over to the FBI
Laboratory one 6.5 millimeter rifle bullet (approximately .25
caliber), copper alloy, full jacket, which he advised was found
on a stretcher in the emergency room of the Dallas hospital to
which the victim was taken. JOHNSON was unable to advise whether
stretcher on which this bullet was found had been used for the
President.

The above information was received by communication
from the Baltimore Office, dated November 23, 1963.

CD 5

Figure 8. The Sibert and O'Neill Report

As though this evidence left any room for doubt, reconstruction photographs demonstrate that the location they support was in fact *taken to be correct* for the purpose of reenactment of the crime. A photograph from the FBI reenactment, for example, may be found in Galanor's *Cover-Up* as Document 4 (Figure 9). Observe where the large round white patch is located!

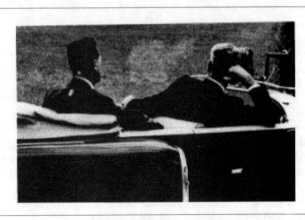

Figure 9. FBI reenactment photograph

And a similar photograph (Figure 10) even appears on the inside front cover of *The New York Times* Bantam paperback edition of *The Warren Report* (1964)!

Figure 10. The New York Times *reenactment photograph*

The best of all is a photograph of the author of the "magic bullet" hypothesis, Arlen Specter, using a pointer to demonstrate the trajectory that the bullet must have taken, when the marking patch is visible several inches below his hand (Figure 11), also found in *Assassination Science*, p. 34! Which means that a photograph intended to illustrate the "magic bullet" theory actually refutes it.

Figure 11. Newsweek *(22 November 1993) reenactment photograph*

Readers who are unfamiliar with this case may wonder how in the world, given all of this evidence, *The Warren Report* (1964) could have concluded that JFK was hit at the back of the base of the neck. But, thanks to the good work of the ARRB, we know the answer to that question. Gerald Ford, a member of the commission, had the description of the wound changed from "his uppermost back" to "the back of his neck", a discovery that was among the first of the ARRB's important releases. The following *The New York Times* (3 July 1997) story appears in *Assassinatation Science*, p. 177 (Figure 12). *The Times* considered it unimportant enough to print on p. A8, insuring that most readers would miss it!

Ford Made Key Change In Kennedy Death Report

WASHINGTON, July 2 (AP) — Thirty-three years ago, Gerald R. Ford changed — ever so slightly — the Warren Commission's main sentence on the place where a bullet entered President John F. Kennedy's body when he was killed in Dallas.

Mr. Ford's change strengthened the commission's conclusion that a single bullet passed through Kennedy and wounded Gov. John B. Connally, — a crucial element in the commission's finding that Lee Harvey Oswald was the sole gunman.

Mr. Ford, who was a member of the commission, wanted a change to show that the bullet entered Kennedy "at the back of his neck" rather than in his uppermost back, as the commission originally wrote.

Mr. Ford said today that the change was intended to clarify meaning, not alter history.

"My changes had nothing to do with a conspiracy theory," he said in a telephone interview.

Figure 12. The New York Times *(3 July 1997) report on Gerald Ford*

In 1992, a private investigator, Joe West, interviewed Thomas Robinson, who had prepared the body for the funeral. Robinson told him that, in addition to a large gaping hold in the back of the head, there was a small wound in the right temple, and a wound on the back, 5 to 6 inches below the shoulder, to the right of the spinal column, and that there was no discoloration to the face, indicating that the President had died instantly. His important notes from their conversation on 26 May 1992 (Figure 13) include the observation of "small shrapnel wounds in face", which David W. Mantik, M.D., Ph.D., believes were caused by tiny shards of glass from the bullet that passed through the windshield.

Under these circumstances, it appears to be "piling on" to note that Dr. Mantik has also demonstrated that no bullet could have entered the President's neck in the vicinity of the location implied by the magic bullet hypothesis and exited at the location of the wound to the throat (construed as a wound of exit) because cervical vertebrae intervene, as Galanor's *Cover-Up*, Document 45, and *Murder in Dealey Plaza* (2000), pp. 3–4, both explain. Mantik found a patient with chest and neck dimensions similar to those of JFK and took a CAT scan cross-section of his neck on the appropriate plane. By performing the simple experiment of drawing a line connecting the Commission's own entry and exit locations, he ascertained that such a trajectory was anatomically impossible (Figure 14). Arlen

Specter had obscured this critical anatomy through the use of hypothetical questions that took for granted the throat wound was a wound of exit and the bullet hit no bony structures, as Charles Crenshaw, M.D., observed in *Assassination Science* (1998), p. 58.

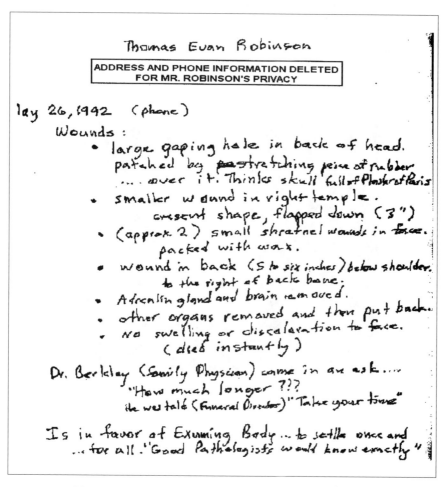

Figure 13. Joe West's interview notes with Tom Robinson

Nor does it appear necessary to add that Malcolm Perry, M.D., who performed a tracheostomy in a vain attempt to save the President's life, described the wound to the throat as an entry wound three times during a press conference held at Parkland beginning at 3:16 PM. His observation was widely broadcast over radio and television that day—the transcript of which may now be found in *Assassination Science* as Appendix C—and even published in *The New York Times* (23 November 1963), p. 2, which may also be found in *Assassinatation Science*, p. 15. This wound description has been confirmed by Charles Crenshaw, M.D., in his work and diagrams, which may also be found there.

If the bullet did not strike the back of the neck, then *The Warren Report* (1964), *The HSCA Report* (1979), *Case Closed* (1993), and every other work taking it for granted cannot possibly be true. It follows that the throat wound and the damage to John Connally must have been caused by separate shots and could not have been inflicted by a lone assassin. But if this most elementary assumption is false, then it is not conspiracy theorists who have been indulging in flights of fancy in support of their untenable hypotheses but those who support the government's official account.

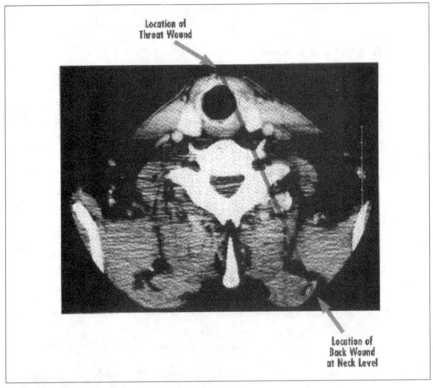

Location of
Throat Wound

Location of
Back Wound
at Neck Level

Figure 14. Mantik plotted the trajectory on a CAT scan.

Contrary to *The Warren Report*'s explicit declaration, precisely which shot hit Governor Connally is essential to its most fundamental findings, namely: that a lone assassin fired three shots with a Mannlicher-Carcano carbine, scoring two hits with one miss. The shot that missed cannot have hit the Governor. And the shot that hit the President in the back of the head and killed him cannot have hit the Governor. The only shot that could have hit him was the shot the government claims hit the President at the base of the back of the neck. That contention is not only false but provably false and not even anatomically possible. The wound to the President's throat and the wounds to Governor Connally must have been caused by other shots and other shooters, which not only proves that the President was killed as the result of a conspiracy but that the Commission took pains to cover it up. *There was no "magic bullet".*

Indeed, studies published in *Assassination Science* (1998) and in *Murder in Dealey Plaza* (2000) have established that JFK was hit at least four times: once in the back from behind (a shot that appears to have been fired from the roof of the County Records Building); once in the throat from the front (a shot that appears to have been fired from the south end of the Triple Underpass); and twice in the head, once from behind (a shot that appears to have been fired from the Dal-Tex Building) and once from the front (a shot that appears to have been fired from the north end of the Triple Underpass). I suspect that most of these shots were with silenced weapons. [*Editor's note*: Many witnesses reported that the first shot sounded like a firecracker. Jim Lewis has fired shots through windshields of junked cars, demonstrating that it is possible to hit a dummy in the throat from 200 yards and that the windshield "crack" sounds like a firecracker.]

Other medical fabrications

The monstrous deception perpetrated on the American people by *The Warren Report* (1964) was crucially dependent upon two enormous fabrications: one, the so-called "magic bullet" theory; the other, the Zapruder "home movie" of the assassination. The "magic bullet" theory receives its appropriate burial—hopefully, once and for all—in this chapter. The Zapruder "home movie" receives its last rites—let us pray, with no prospect of resurrection—in this book. But the evidence in this case is littered with other alterations to the evidence, which range across the medical evidence and the physical evidence through the film record, up to and including motion pictures that were taken in Dealey Plaza on 22 November 1963.

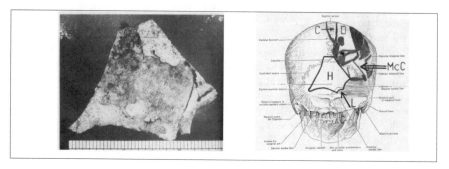

Figure 15. The Harper Fragment and a diagram of the human cranium

Saturday afternoon, 23 November 1963, a medical student named Billy Harper found a fragment of skull bone on the grass opposite the grassy knoll. He took it to his uncle, Jack Harper, M.D., on the staff at Methodist Hospital, who shared it with the Chief Pathologist, A. B. Cairns. He and three others identified it as occipital bone from the back of a human cranium. They took photographs of this piece of bone, which is known as "the Harper fragment", before turning it over to the FBI, which was a good thing because, like other evidence in this case, it was "misplaced". David W. Mantik, M.D., Ph.D., has identified the location on the back of the President's skull from which it was blown out, as *Murder in Dealey Plaza* (2000) has explained. Not all of the evidence in this case was altered, fabricated, or otherwise faked. Some of it was simply "lost".

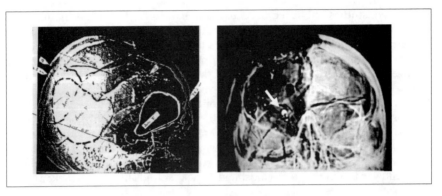

Figure 16. The right lateral cranial X-ray and the anterior-posterior X-ray

Although autopsy X-rays are usually considered to be "the best evidence" of the true causes of death, in the case of our 35th President, that turns out not to be the case. David W. Mantik, M.D., Ph.D., who is Board Certified in Radiation Oncology, which is the treatment of cancer using radiation therapy, and who makes life and death decisions affecting his patients' health and welfare on virtually a daily basis, has visited the National Archives and subjected (what are officially classified as) the original X-rays to simple tests using a technique from physics (known as "optical densitometry") and has discovered that the right-lateral cranial X-ray has been altered by imposing a patch to conceal a massive blow-out to the back of the head (delineated here as "Area P") and that the anterior-posterior X-ray has been changed by the addition of a small, metallic slice (indicated by the arrow) that just happens to be the same 6.5 mm diameter as the Mannlicher–Carcano.

Mantik's original studies may be found in *Assassination Science* (1998), pp. 153–160 (on the right lateral cranial X-ray) and pp. 120–136 (on the anterior-posterior X-ray). He has recently ascertained by independent evidence that the left lateral X-ray is also not an original X-ray. These X-rays were used to discount more than forty eyewitnesses who reported observing a major defect to the back of the President's skull (in the case of the right lateral X-ray) and to connect the President's death with an obscure World War II Italian Mannlicher-Carcano carbine. A brilliant synthesis of the medical evidence and what it tells us about the death of JFK may be found in one of his chapters in *Murder in Dealey Plaza* (2000), where the alteration of the X-rays is also discussed in the Prologue as "Smoking Gun #7".

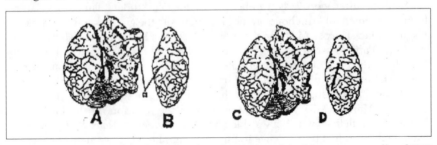

Figure 17. Brain drawings stored in the National Archives purportedly of JFK

The brain itself is missing, but there are photographs and drawings in the National Archives, which, according to the official government account, are those of JFK. Robert B. Livingston, M.D., a world authority on the human brain who was also an expert on wound ballistics, studied the reports of the numerous physicians at Parkland Hospital in Dallas who observed massive damage to the brain, including loss of copious quantities of cerebral and cerebellar tissues extruding from the skull. In Livingston's opinion,

> It simply cannot be true that the cerebellum could have been seen extruding from the occipital-parietal wound—by several experienced and thoroughly competent physicians—and for the same brain to be seen in superior and lateral photographs and depicted in a diagram (superior view) showing the cerebellum as being apparently intact. A conclusion is obligatorily forced that the photographs and drawings of the brain in the National Archives must be of some brain other than that of John Fitzgerald Kennedy.

Livingston's report may be found in *Assassination Science* (1998), pp. 161–167. New documents and records released by the Assassination Records Review Board (ARRB) have disclosed that the Naval medical officers who conducted the autopsy conducted two supplemental brain examinations, the first on 25 November 1963, the second a week or so later. The first was with JFK's brain, the second with the substitute. A chapter devoted to this matter by Douglas Horne, the ARRB's Senior Analyst for Military Records, may be found in *Murder in Dealey Plaza* (2000), pp. 299–310, a stunning confirmation of Livingston's conclusion.

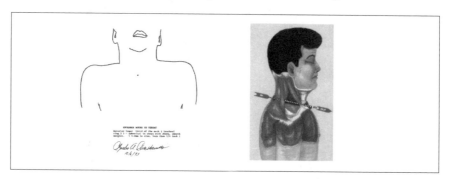

Figure 18. Crenshaw diagram of throat wound versus government diagram

Charles Crenshaw, M.D., was a resident at Parkland Hospital when JFK was brought into Trauma Room #1. He was present during the vain effort to revive the moribund President and was the last physician to observe the body before it was prepared for transportation to Bethesda Naval Hospital, including closing the eyes of the deceased. He authored a chapter about his experience for *Assassination Science* (1998), pp. 37–60. At my request, he also drew the wounds he had observed for its four-part Appendix A. If the throat wound was a neat, small wound of entrance, the Commission's diagram showing the throat wound as a wound of exit must be wrong, as this chapter has already shown.

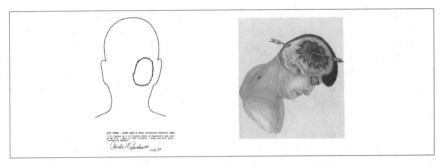

Figure 19. Crenshaw diagram of head wound versus official diagram

Crenshaw also drew the massive blow-out to the back of the head as he observed it at Parkland, which bears striking similarity to a similar diagram approved by another physician who was present at the time, Robert McClelland, M.D., as well as reports by more than forty eyewitnesses who described a similar wound at the back/right of the head. Crenshaw's original diagrams may be found in *Assassination Science* (1998), pp. 414–415. The McClelland diagram may be found in *Murder in Dealey Plaza* (2000), p. 180, where a chapter on the medical evidence by Gary Aguilar, M.D., pp. 175–217, may be found along with that by David Mantik, M.D., Ph.D., pp. 219–297.

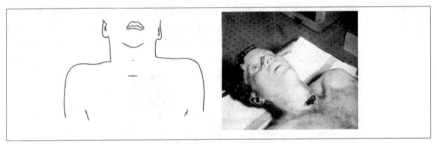

Figure 20. Crenshaw diagram of post-tracheostomy versus official autopsy photo

Crenshaw also observed a neat horizontal incision performed by Malcolm Perry, M.D. During a press conference held at Parkland Hospital after the President's body had been removed, Dr. Perry three times described the wound to the throat as a wound of entry. This important evidence was not made available to the Warren Commission on the alleged ground that it was part of some 200 hours of television video, which would take time to review and classify. But when you consider that this would have been some of the first footage taken that day, it becomes apparent that this was merely a flimsy pretext for excluding evidence. It has finally been published as Appendix C to *Assassination Science* (1998). The large, gaping wound to the throat visible in autopsy photographs has led to speculation that the body may have been subject to alteration en route from Parkland to Bethesda, as David Lifton, *Best Evidence* (1980), has proposed. It seems fair to say that, if the body was not altered, then the photograph was faked, but both could be the case. (Note the open eyes!)

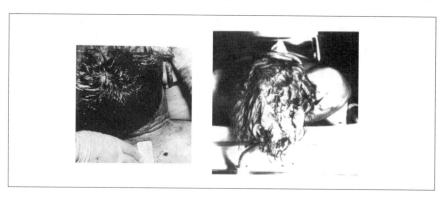

Figure 21. Comparison of purported autopsy photographs of John F. Kennedy

The incoherence of the autopsy photographs becomes apparent from comparing these examples, in one of which the President's hair is rather short and well kept, the other in which the President's hair is longer and matted with mucky matter. Because of these discrepancies, when the ARRB deposed Commander James Humes, USNMC, who had been in charge of the autopsy at Bethesda Naval Hospital, Jeremy Gunn of the ARRB asked him if the pathologists had given the deceased the equivalent of a shampoo and a haircut during the autopsy (since these are supposed to be photographs of the same autopsy subject):

> Gunn: No cleaning, no combing of the hair or anything of that sort?
> Humes: No, no, no, no, no, ...

Humes' deposition, with fascinating commentary by David Mantik, may now be found in *Murder in Dealey Plaza* (2000) as Appendix G. The quoted exchange occurs on page 447.

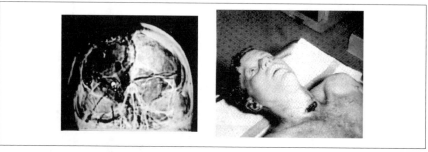

Figure 22. Comparison of anterior-posterior X-ray with autopsy photograph

During an X-ray exposure objects of greater density absorb more radiation and therefore leave the photographic plate less exposed (white or transparent), while those that are less dense absorb less of the radiation and therefore leave the photographic plate more exposed (dark or opaque). Darker areas thus represent less dense material, while whiter areas represent denser material. Virtually the entire right-front of JFK's cranium appears to be missing in the skull X-rays.

Yet in the autopsy photographs, that region appears to be intact. They cannot both be authentic, though they could both be fake. Jackie observed that from the front, he looked just normal, but that the back of his head had been shattered, confirming what other witnesses reported.

Figure 23. Malcolm Kilduff's announcement of the President's death

At 1:30 PM on 22 November 1963, Acting Press Secretary Malcolm Kilduff announced the President was dead and that it had been a simple matter of a bullet right through the head, while pointing to his right temple and attributing this finding to Admiral George G. Burkley, USNMC, the President's personal physician. This wound and the wound to the throat were widely broadcast on radio and television that day. When it was announced that the lone assassin had been firing from above and behind, some TV commentators remarked, "How could the President have been hit from in front from behind?", which became the principal problem the Commission had to cover up. Wounds of entry to the throat and to the right temple became wounds of exit, through the simple expedient of reversing trajectories—with a little help from friends such as Gerald Ford, Arlen Specter, and their "magic" bullet.

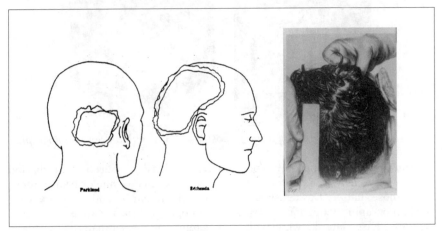

Figure 24. Divergent representations of the head wound in the medical record

Anyone who is aware of the enormous disparity in the description of the wound to the back of the President's head must comprehend that something is wrong. At Parkland, physician after physician reported a massive defect to the right/rear, with extruding cerebral and cerebellar tissue. At Bethesda, the autopsy physicians described a much larger wound that extended forward into the top and right of the cranium. Given the relationship between them, the Parkland description may be said to resemble a "heel" relative to the Bethesda description as a "footprint" including it. Astonishingly, the HSCA not only reconstituted the back of the head but moved the wound four inches higher than the location specified by Bethesda—to the crown of the head. As David Lifton, *Best Evidence* (1980) has emphasized, no matter how much the evidence changed, the conclusion still remained the same.

Framing Lee Oswald

Figure 25. Lt. Day with the Mannlicher-Carcano from the Book Depository

What is most interesting about this photograph is the clip (circled), which should not be present. Unlike the M-1, which retains its clip until the last round has been fired, the Mannlicher-Carcano ejects its clip when the last round is chambered. If this photo were authentic, it should not show the clip still in the weapon, which would only occur if the clip were sprung in such a fashion that it could not have properly held the bullets to be loaded into the weapon at all. The clip appears to have been added to the photograph by conspirators who were unfamiliar with the weapon. An excellent article on the clip by Walter F. Graf and Richard R. Bartholomew, "The Gun that Didn't Smoke", may now be found on the electronic research journal, *assassinationresearch.com*. See the related "Smoking Guns" #3 and #4 in the Prologue to *Murder in Dealey Plaza* (2000).

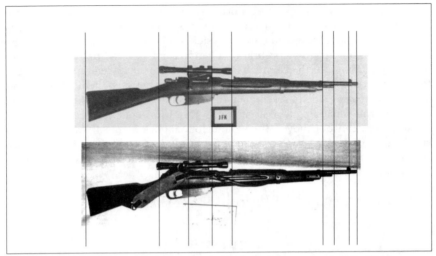

Figure 26. Comparison of weapon in Dallas with weapon in Washington

A Mannlicher-Carcano was photographed by the Dallas Police Department (bottom) and a Mannlicher-Carcano was photographed by the FBI (above) when it was received into evidence. They are not the same. Obviously, the same weapon would have the same features in the same relative positions. But that is not the case. The telescopic sights, for example, are not in the same relative positions. These are different weapons, raising the question of which if either is authentic. They cannot both be "the weapon found in the Book Depository" but they could both have been drawn from a collection of weapons used to frame Lee Oswald for a crime he did not commit. Jack White discusses *three* different weapons alleged to have been "Oswald's rifle" in the chapter that follows.

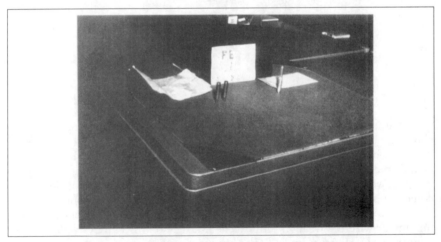

Figure 27. Official FBI "Evidence Photograph" showing two spent shell casings

Observe that this FBI "evidence photograph" shows only two spent and one unspent cartridge casing, where it should show three spent casings. The problem is that Oswald was alleged to have fired three shots, scoring two hits with one miss. That means a shell casing is missing. A third spent casing was later produced, but it had an indentation that would have prevented it from holding a bullet. Even Josiah Thompson, *Six Seconds in Dallas* (1967), offers reasons for believing this casing was a plant. That should come as no surprise, since all the shell casings appear to have been planted to frame Oswald. Other evidence of two spent shell casings may be found in Noel Twyman's *Bloody Treason* (1997), pp. 111–116.

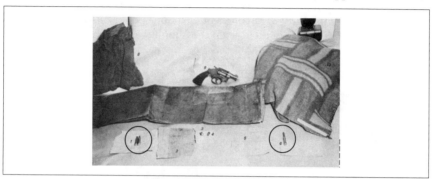

Figure 28. Dallas Police "Evidence Photograph" featuring a paper bag

Another photograph featuring two spent shell casings and one unspent casing may be found in Jesse Curry's *JFK Assassination File* (1969), pp. 88–94, which includes copies of the FBI's formal acknowledgement of receipt thereof. The paper bag with which Oswald is allged to have carried his Mannlicher-Carcano into the Book Deposition is especially interesting, since it looks like new paper purchased for the purpose of a display. I invite anyone to take a weapon of this kind—assembled or disassembled—and try carrying it in a bag like this without tearing, ripping, or otherwise damaging the bag. This is simply another aspect of the elaborate deception intended to blame a patsy for the crime.

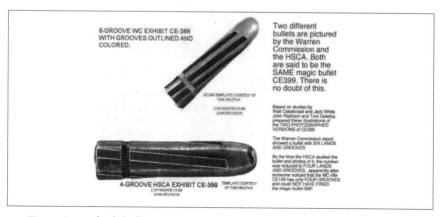

Figure 29. Which bullet is the "magic bullet"? The Warren bullet or the HSCA?

In the early 1990s, Jack White and Walt Cakebread noticed that the "magic bullet" of *The Warren Report* (1964) is a different bullet from the "magic bullet" of the HSCA. The first has six lands and grooves, while the second has only four! This deception is paralleled by the substitution of shell casings from the Tippit shooting. As Robert Groden, *The Search for Lee Harvey Oswald* (1995), pp. 138–141, has observed, the four spent shell casings found at the scene of the shooting of Officer J. D. Tippit were of two different brands, two from Western, two from Remington-Peters, while the slugs themselves were three of one brand, one of the other. The four casings had been ejected from an automatic, moreover, while Oswald was armed only with a revolver, but a substitution was later made. It is rather difficult to imagine that anyone would shoot a police officer four times on a public street and then obligingly open the chamber of his revolver to remove the incriminating shell casings.

Figure 30. The Life *photo that incriminated Oswald in the public mind.*

The authenticity of the "backyard photos" has been subject to serious dispute, where an excellent discussion may also be found in Groden's *The Search for Lee Harvey Oswald* (1995), pp. 90–95. Groden observes that the chin is not Oswald's rather pointed chin, that the shadows under the nose and behind the subject seem to be inconsistent, and that there appears to be an insert line just below the lower lip and above the chin. Jack White noticed that the communist newspapers he is holding have known dimensions. Using them as an internal ruler, he has determined that the subject in the photos was only about 5'6" tall, much too short to be Lee Oswald, who was about 5'10". Either the subject is too short or the papers are too large. Oswald had said that this photograph was a fake, which with time it would be possible to prove. He was right.

The Photographic Evidence

Figure 31. The Altgens windshield versus the Secret Service windshield

An image from one of the most famous photographs taken in Dealey Plaza during the assassination (here on the left) shows a small, while, spiral nebula with a dark hole at the center, where JFK's left ear would be were it visible. He is holding his throat from a shot from the front, which has just passed through the windshield en route to its target. The limousine would be taken back to Ford Motor Company in Michigan and completely rebuilt on 25 November 1963, the day of the formal state funeral, where it would be outfitted with a new windshield. The Secret Service would subsequently produce yet another windshield (here on the right) that displayed a very different kind of damage. That there had indeed been a shot through the windshield is confirmed by frame 225. A shot through the windshield from the front implies a conspiracy.

Figure 32. Windshield of the Presidential limousine seen at Zapruder frame 225

Figure 33. Frame 232 published in Life *with physically impossible features*

As a principle of optics, stationary features of a scene in a photograph should be blurred by the same amount, and uniformly moving features of a scene in a photograph should be blurred by the same (different) amount. When what would become frame 232 was published in *Life* in its (undated) Memorial Edition, however, it displayed physically impossible properties. As specific examples, a real spot in the stationary bush is not blurred, just as a real spot on the moving limousine is not blurred, which could not happen with an authentic frame. John P. Costella, Ph.D., has analyzed this phenomenon, which is one of several proofs that the film was completely fabricated and not merely subjected to alteration. As his chapter explains, this glitch appears to have occurred by rushing the first color frames into print before the process was complete. It reflected a stage in fabricating the film.

Figure 34. Blunder made in putting the Stemmons Freeway sign into the film

John Costella has also discovered that a blunder occurred in introducing the Stemmons Freeway sign into the fabricated film. Authentic frames are pulled out at the edges due to the optical properties of the lens system, which creates the phenomenon known as "pincushion distortion". The sign itself appears to be surprisingly square and vertical, because the fabricators introduced it without correcting for the pincushion distortion. That meant that, if pincushion distortion correction were now applied, it would reveal the deception by a kind of "twitching" of the sign, illustrated here by the differences displayed by vertical lines as imaginary extensions of the sign's properties. This is yet another indication that the film has not simply been subjected to alteration but was fabricated using film and techniques that did not require any Zapruder footage.

Figure 35. The"blob" and "blood spray" were added on to frame 313.

As Noel Twyman, *Bloody Treason* (1997), p. 160, explains, Dr. Roderick Ryan, a retired scientist from Kodak and a special effects expert, told him that the "blob" appeared to have been painted in. David Healy has suggested that the blood spray may have been added to the film using a glass painting technique, where the spray was painted onto a piece of glass and imposed over the original film in creating a new version. Costella has now subjected the blood spray to a meticulous mathematical analysis and has discovered its rate of dissipation is actually faster than a lead weight in free fall, far too rapid to be genuine. That complements David Mantik's analysis of the film, which suggests that frame 313 is a composite or merge of two shots to the head—one from behind and one from the front—which Mantik believes took place some 30–40' further down Elm Street than the film displays. Several chapters of *Murder in Dealey Plaza* (2000) bear on this issue.

Anyone who has watched the extant version of the Zapruder film has been struck by the forcible impact of at least one bullet upon the President's head that drives him back and to the left—*back and to the left!*—as Oliver Stone's film, "JFK", emphasizes. What many Americans may not know is that, when these frames were originally published in the 26 volumes of "supporting evidence", frames 314 and 315 were reversed, which greatly reduced the dramatic force with which this event occurs. David S. Lifton made this observation and had a friend write J. Edgar Hoover, who confirmed it. In 1975, Groden induced Geraldo

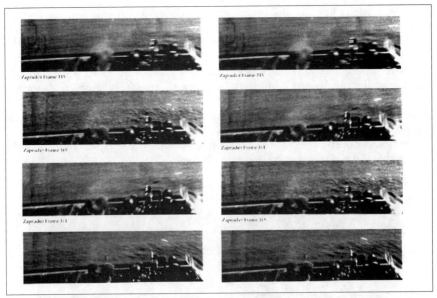

Figure 36. Frames 313, 314, 315, and 316 were published in the wrong order.

Rivera to show the film—for the first time to the nation on television—which led to the creation of the House Select Committee on Assassinations and its 1977-78 reinvestigation. This led to its conclusion (strongly based upon acoustical evidence) that there had been a second shooter on the grassy knoll but the shooter had missed.

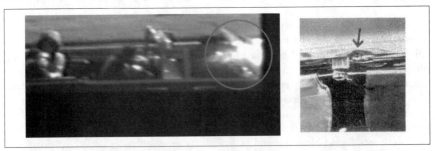

Figure 37. A hit to the chrome strip was even recorded by frame 330.

The Warren Report (1964) acknowledged that one of the shots had missed, which must have been the first (see above). Several other shots also appear to have missed, including one that hit the chrome strip over the limousine's windshield. Frame 330 captured the moment of impact, which created an image like that of a "solar flare". Mike Pincher, J.D., and Roy Schaeffer were the first to make this observation in their chapter in *Assassination Science* (1998), pp. 221–238. Photographs of James Tague, who was slightly injured by the first shot that missed, and of the indentation in the chrome strip may be found in Robert Groden, *The Killing of a President* (1963), p. 41. The display of the flare suggests that it was probably fired from the Dal-Tex Building rather than the Book Depository.

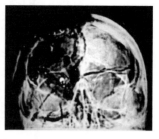

Figure 38. Comparisons between X-rays and frames extremely revealing

A comparison of the anterior-posterior X-ray with frames such as 335 which feature the "blob" appears to be extremely revealing of a pattern of interlocking deceptions. If we assume that the "blob" was painted in, as Roderick Ryan observed, and that the anterior-posterior X-ray was altered to show the right/front of the skull was missing, then that was no doubt to reinforce the impression that the President had been hit in the head from above and behind. If JFK had been hit from above and behind by a high-velocity bullet, the damage that those images reflect might have been the kind of damage such a high-velocity shot would have brought about. While he may have been hit in the back of the head by a bullet fired from the Dal-Tex Building with a Mannlicher-Carcano, it would have been unlikely to cause damage this extensive in kind, since the Mannlicher-Carcano is not a high velocity weapon.

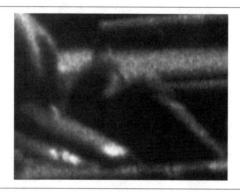

Figure 39. The fabricators made mistakes in creating the fake Zapruder film.

Costella estimates that 95 percent of the film is flawless, while 4 percent is sloppy and the remaining 1 percent gives the game away. As he explains in his chapter on the film, the necessary alterations were so extensive that the entire film had to be recreated. No omission can quite compare with frame 374, however, in which the massive blow-out to the back of the President's head is visible. Notice how closely it corresponds with Crenshaw's drawing, McClelland's drawing, and Mantik's "Area P". In order to perpetrate the fraud, it was essential to patch this blow-out and substitute someone else's brain, which takes us back to Figure 1, where we began.

Additional Evidence of Alteration

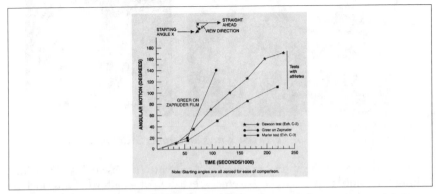

Figure 40. Greer's forward head turn occurs between frames 315 and 317.

Many kinds of deception were employed in fabricating this film. One was the exclusion of whole frames and series of frames. Noel Twyman noticed, for example, that the driver, William Greer, looks backward at Jack Kennedy in frames 302–303, which is an angular rotation of about 105° in a single frame (officially, about 1/18th of a second), which is as fast as the blink of an eye, the fastest human reflex, which is not humanly possible. He also noticed that, between frames 315 and 317, Greer turns forward in another extraordinarily fast turn. He tested his hypothesis that this turn was also too fast to be humanly possible and discovered that it should have taken about twice as much time as the film shows. That may not sound like much until you realize that that would turn a four minute mile into a two minute mile! His studies, which prove that frames have been removed from the film, may be found in *Bloody Treason* (1997), Exhibits C-1 through C-4.

Before the shooting started, Governor Connally had been facing toward the crowd on the right. He started to turn toward the left and suddenly felt a blow on his back. The Governor had been hit by a bullet which entered at the extreme right side of his back at a point below his right armpit. The bullet traveled through his chest in a downward and forward direction, exited below his right nipple, passed through his right wrist which had been in his lap, and then caused a wound to his left thigh. The force of the bullet's impact appeared to spin the Governor to his right, and Mrs. Connally pulled him down into her lap. Another bullet then struck President Kennedy in the rear portion of his head, causing a massive and fatal wound. The President fell to the left into Mrs. Kennedy's lap.

Figure 41. Connally's left turn has been removed from the extant film.

Governor Connally was always insistent that he had not been hit by the same bullet that hit JFK. Even from his hospital bed, he explained that he had heard a shot, knew that something was going on behind him, and turned to his right. Unable to see the President, he turned back to his left—and that is when he felt a doubling-up in his chest! *The Warren Report* (1964) was at least vaguely consistent with his descriptions—no doubt, because he was still alive and would have been outraged at serious distortion—but was resourceful in downplaying its significance. Its page 46 reports, "Unable to see the Preesident as he turned to the right, the

Governor started to look back over his left shoulder, but he never completed the turn because he felt something strike him in the back." Using the phrase, "he started to look back over his left shoulder", is a nice example of half-truth. Although some have speculated he was shot from the County Records Building, when his left turn is taken into account, it appears more likely that he was hit from the Book Depository, not from the "sniper's nest" but from a window on its west side.

> I also asked him to describe what he saw at the instant of the fatal head shot. His answer was very descriptive. He said he saw Kennedy's head suddenly whip around to the left (counter-clockwise). I also asked him if he saw the explosion of blood and brains out of the head. He replied that he did. I asked him if he noticed which direction the eruption went. He pointed back over his left shoulder. He said, "It went this way." I said, you mean it went to the left and rear? He said yes. Bartholomew then asked him, "Are you sure that you didn't see the blood and brains going up and to the front?" Swartz said, "No; it was to the left and rear." We went over this several times with him to be certain that he was clear on this point. He was very clear.

Figure 42. Erwin Swartz observed brain matter blown out to the left/rear.

An associate of Abraham Zapruder, Erwin Swartz, viewed the film in (what may have been) its original state at Eastman Kodak, where it was developed. Nearly sixty witnesses have reported that the limousine slowed dramatically or came to a complete halt, as Vincent Palamara has explained in a chapter of *Murder in Dealey Plaza* (2000). When Noel asked him about the limo stop, he was vague and could not recall. But when Noel asked him about the effects of the fatal head shot, Swartz was quite specific and very graphic. He said that he had seen Kennedy's head suddenly "whip around to the left", that he had seen an explosion of blood and brains from the head, and that it had blown out "to the left and rear". Twyman pressed him on this crucial point, but Swartz was emphatic. His account may be found in *Bloody Treason* (1997).

> VINCENT J. GULLO, Jr.;
> [Gullo: 8/27/98 letter to Vince Palamara---I wrote "Sam [Kinney] told me that a) he found the piece of the right rear of President Kennedy's skull on the C-130 while en route back to AAFB after the tragedy and b) that one of you guys got sick from seeing the rear of the limouisne with all the blood and goredo you remember any of these specific events?"Gullo responded: "I am totally familiar with the facts as you outline themThis was a bench mark in my life and I have shared my thoughts on this incident with few individuals---mostly federal agents. I am sure you can understand my reluctance to entertain your questions given the sensitivity of the matter even to this date."(emphasis added); Gullo did not respond to my follow-up letter:1

Figure 43. Secret Service agents observed blood and brains on the trunk.

Further confirmation of the blow-out to the left/rear comes from Secret Service agents, such as Sam Kinney and Vincent Gullo, Jr. Vince Palamara, who is the leading assassination expert on the Secret Service, wrote to Gullo to explain that Kinney had to told him of his discovery of a piece of the right-rear of the President's skull in the limousine during the flight back to Washington, D.C., and that another member of the detail had become nauseated from observing the blood and gore on the limousine trunk. Gullo confirmed Kinney's statements to Palamara, saying that he "was totally familiar with the facts as (Palamara) outlined them", but that he was reluctant to go any further. No doubt, since this provides further confirmation that this shot was fired from the right/front, which by itself establishes the presence of more than one shooter and the existence of a conspiracy. The completely clean trunk of the limousine as seen in the extant film also indicates that this part had to be "tidied up" lest it contradict the government's position.

- just prior to the headshot(s) the limo stops (not slows but stops)—the occupants of the limo are jostled as the car comes to a sudden stop. In my opinion. JFK was hit in the head by a shot from the rear. Bill Greer turns around and looks directly at JFK. Just as he does, the exploding headshot occurs as if on cue—clearly fired from the front, with blood and brain matter splattering to the left rear—very graphic. Greer then turns back around and the limo lurches forward. The stop lasted maybe three or four seconds. (I believe that Greer stopped the limo in response to a signal being given from someone along the curb.)

Figure 44. Other reports confirm both multiple shooters and the limo stop

Homer McMahon, who was in charge of the Color Photo Section at the National Photo Interpretation Center run by the CIA, has told the ARRB that he was brought a film the night of the assassination and asked to prepare a briefing board that displayed the shot sequence and their impacts upon passengers. He watched the film at least ten times and concluded that Jack had been hit six to eight times from at least three directions. We have discovered that Jack was hit four times and that Connally may have been hit as many as three. The sum of these numbers equals seven, which is between six and eight, suggesting that he was describing the number of impacts on bodies in the limousine. (See Appendix C.)

Others who have seen a more complete film include William Reymond, a French investigative journalist, and Rich DellaRosa, who moderates the *JFKresearch.com* forum. Both have stated that the film they saw included a limo stop that may have lasted as long as 3 to 4 seconds, during which Jack was hit in the back of the head from behind and fell forward; then, as Jackie was easing him back up and looking right into his face, he was hit by the shot that entered his right temple, which blew his brains out to the left and rear. (See Appendix E.) The indications of multiple shooters and of Secret Service complicity were so overwhelming they had to be taken out, which was done by creating a fabricated film.

Jim Fetzer
presenting at the
Zapruder Film Symposium,
Duluth, Minnesota
10 May 2003

Part I

Which Film *is* "The Zapruder Film"?

James H. Fetzer and Scott A. Lederer

[*Editor's note:* From a logical point of view, the phrase, "the Zapruder film", implies the existence of one and only one thing of the kind thereby named or described. If there were either less than one or more than one film of that "Zapruder" kind—which we might describe as "film of the assassination of President John F. Kennedy taken in Dealey Plaza from the vicinity of the pergola in Dealey Plaza"—then that phrase would not properly apply. The discovery that there are different versions of the film known by that name thus raises the question addressed here, "Which film *is* 'the Zapruder film'?"]

There are at least four versions of "the Zapruder film" currently available to the public or to students of the film. One is David Lifton's "'Z' Film" (undated). Another is on the Macmillan CD, "JFK Assassination: A Visual Investigation" (1993).

Lifton Frame 1

Macmillan Frame 1

Groden Frame 1

MPI Frame 1

29

A third—several versions, actually—is found in Robert Groden's video, "The As-sassination Films" (1995). The fourth—in digitally enhanced form—is presented in MPI's "Image of an Assassination" (1998). If they had all and only the same properties, they would be four prints of the same film.

MPI Frame 1
Groden Frame 1
Macmillan Frame 1
Lifton Frame 1

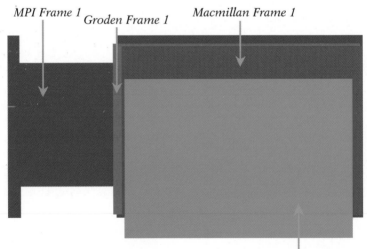

MPI Frame 1
Groden Frame 1
Macmillan Frame 1
Lifton Frame 1

A systematic comparison of their visual fields after digitizing the images and scaling them to the same size, reveals they are not the same. As the results pre-sented display, the Lifton images include less than those on the Macmillan ver-sion, which include less than those shown on the Groden ("pristine") version, which include less than those shown on the MPI version. If we take the MPI ver-sion, which provides the most information, as 100 percent for the purpose of comparison (79 percent in the frame, 21 percent in the sprocket area), then Groden's presents 73.9 percent, Macmillan's 69.8 percent, and Lifton's only 54.3 percent as much information, suggesting that the MPI version is the best available cut.

	Lifton	MacMillan	Groden	MPI Frame	MPI Sprocket Area	MPI Total
Width (pixels)	620	645	674	671	273	
Height (pixels)	360	445	451	484	317	
Area (pixels)	223200	287025	303974	324764	86541	411305
Percentage of MPI	54.3%	69.8%	73.9%	79.0%	21.0%	100.0%

These calculations weigh in favor of taking the MPI version as the research standard—as the most complete for the purposes of investigation—which is how it has been promoted and marketed. The back cover of the VHS version, for example, says that, "In 1997, the LMH Company and the MPI Media group worked together to create a state-of-the-art digital reproduction of the camera original— a copy that will serve researchers for years to come." Leaving aside the claim that this film represents "the camera original", which is the focus of research presented elsewhere in this book, this claim can also be disputed on other grounds.

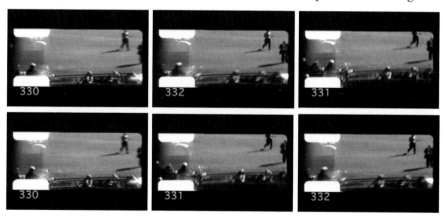

The MPI sequence (above) versus the correct sequence (below).

In spite of the expertise that was applied to the production of this enhanced version, we have discovered, as others—including John Costella, Ph.D.—have found, several significant shortcomings. Specifically, the MPI version (a) has reversed the order of frames 331 and 332 ; (b) does not include (what ought to be) frames 341, 350, and 486; (c) does not include frames 155 and 156; and (d) does not include frames 208, 209, 210, and 211. These deficiencies became apparent in multiple comparisons with the Groden "pristine" version, which includes the missing frames.

Frames 339-340 as seen on MPI video tape

Note the position
of this man's feet
as he runs forward

Groden Frame 341 does not
appear to show up in the
MPI version

Frames 341-342 as seen on MPI video tape

Frames 347-348 as seen on MPI video tape

Note how much of the
rear wheel can be seen
compared to MPI frame
348 and 349

Groden Frame 350 does not
appear to show up in the
MPI version

Frames 349-350 as seen on MPI video tape

Frames 482-483 as seen on MPI video tape

Groden Frame 486 does not
appear to show up in the
MPI version. MPI ends on
what they number as frame 483
which corresponds to Groden's
frame 485

Note the position of the
tree branches in the
Groden frame 486

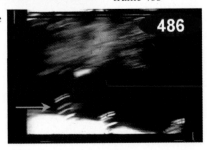

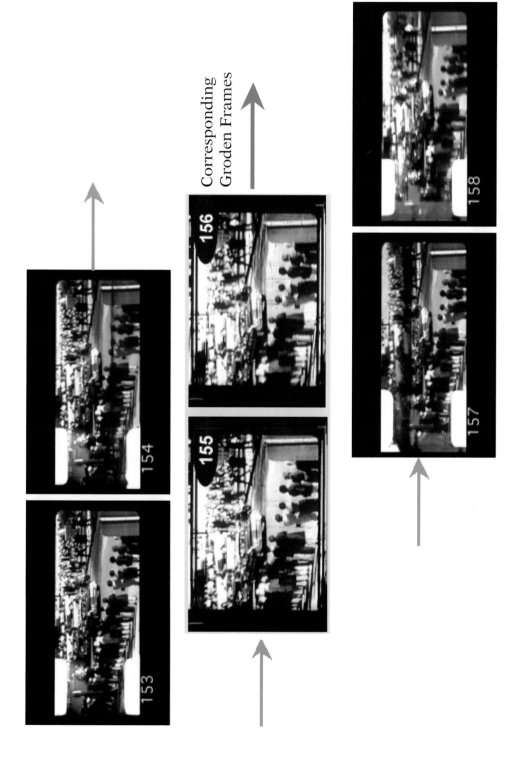

Corresponding
Groden Frames

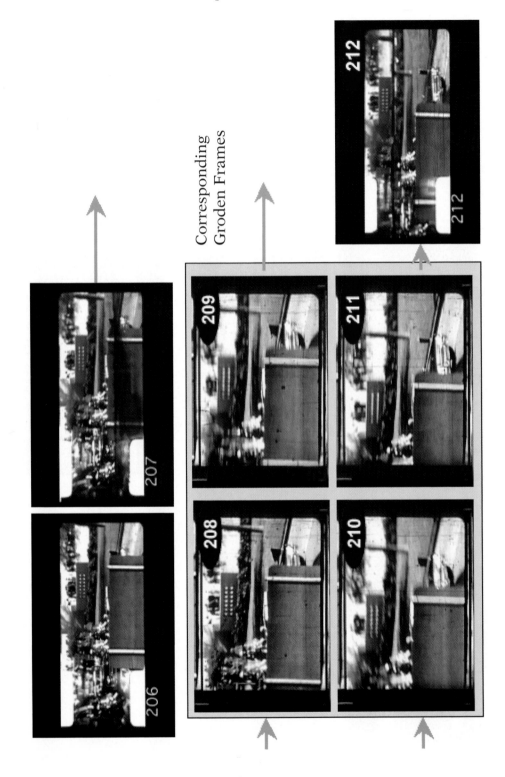

Corresponding
Groden Frames

The Costella Combined Edit

With frames out of order, with three missing frames, and with two series of two and four missing frames, respectively, it becomes rather difficult to appreciate the depiction of the MPI digital version as a "state-of-the-art reproduction". Because its frames provide more information than do those of the other films, the obvious prospect that deserves consideration is to correct these imperfections by (a) correcting the order of frames 331 and 332; (b) restoring those three missing frames, 341, 350, and 486; (c) restoring frames 155 and 156; and (d) restoring frames 208, 209, 210, and 211, in order to create a substantially improved version.

We therefore drew missing frames from the "pristine" Groden version for this purpose and presented the complete version (call it "the Fetzer edit") at the Duluth conference. We soon discovered, however, that John Costella had not only identified the shortcomings that we were addressing but had gone further by enhancements in the form of (i) correcting for pincushion and for aspect ratio distortion; (ii) including so-called "ghost panels" with fragments of information from sequential frames; and (iii) masking the open sprocket holes to make them less visually intrusive.

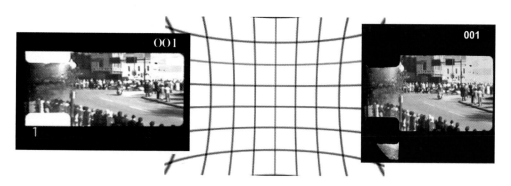

MPI Frame before (left) and after (right) pincushion and aspect ratio corrections (with ghost panels added and sprocket holes masked)

The corrected version thus represents a new standard for Zapruder film research, which we call "the Costella combined cut" or, for short, "the Costella combination". As Costella observes elsewhere in this book, however, another of the oddities of the MPI version is that the quality of the MPI frames, even on the DVD, is no better than what was previously available. Other than with respect to the areas immediately surrounding JFK, no high-resolution scans of frames are to be found in the MPI version, which means that the other versions we have discussed retain research value. While selected frames are published here, the entire film—all 486 frames in their corrected versions—is being made available to the public without charge at **www.assassinationscience.com**. In the rest of this color-insert section, selected frames of special importance to the issues dealt with here appear, along with other images, whose presentation in color appears most appropriate within this context.

The Combined Edit / John Costella, Ph.D.

[*Editor's note*: As Scott Myers has observed, a 50-foot roll of 8 mm film begins as a single roll of 16 mm film, which is 33 feet long. Four feet at each end allow for threading and running the fogged leader/trailer. The useable film is 25 feet long. After the first half (one side) has been exposed, the roll is turned over, thus producing 50 feet of 8 mm film. 50 feet x 12 inches per foot divided by 0.150 inches per frame equals 4000 frames. Each side thus has 2000 frames, which should yield (a) 2000 frames at 1 frame per trigger squeeze; (b) 125 seconds of film at 16 fps; (c) 41.67 seconds of film at 48 fps; where (d) 486 frames shot at 16 fps would take 30.375 seconds; and (e) 486 frames shot at 48 fps would take 10.125 seconds. The speed officially attributed to Zapruder's camera was 18.3 fps, which should yield a 486 frame film that runs 26.56 seconds. Phil Guliano notes that the Bell & Howell 414 is spring driven. According to Richard Trask, *Pictures of the Pain* (1994), pp. 58-59, when fully wound, it has 73 seconds of running power. At 18.3 fps, that would yield about 1336 frames.]

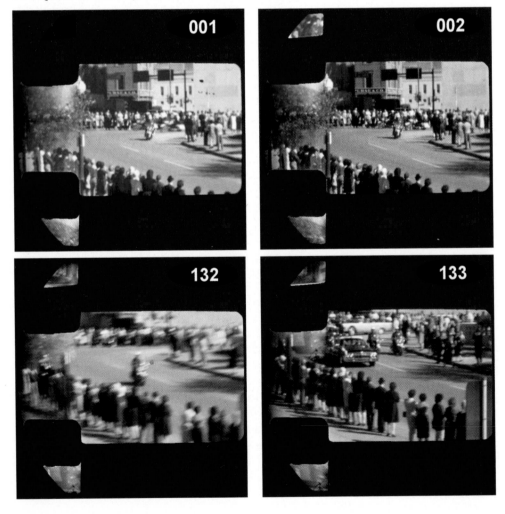

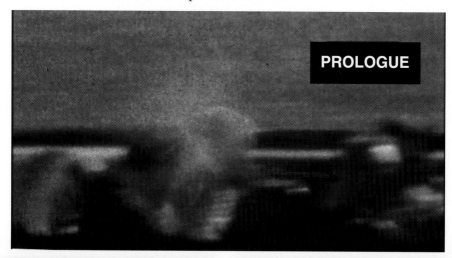

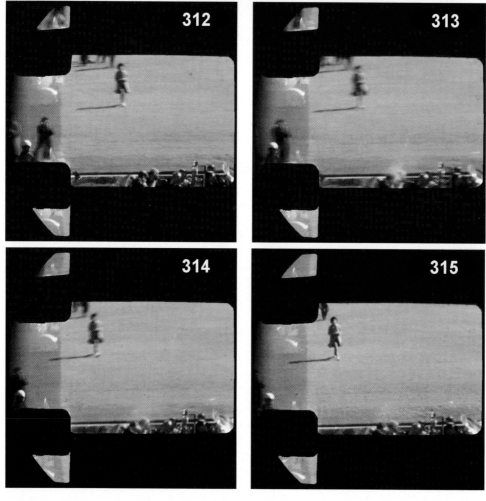

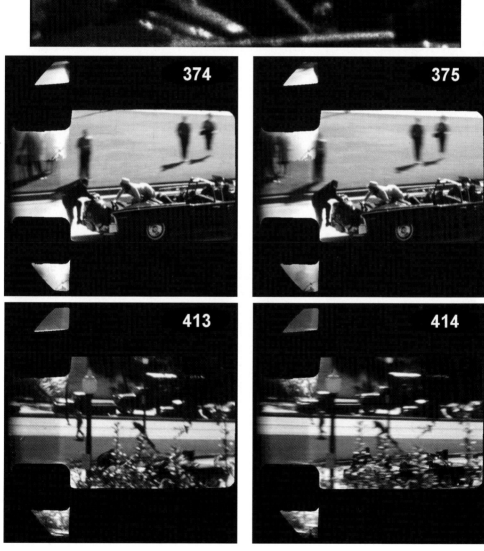

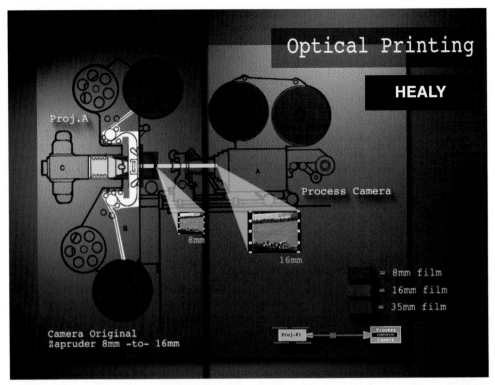

WHITE

Betzner seems to show, with the same "clarity" as Zapruder and Sitzman, another man standing on an extension of the same wall, behind the bush. His right hand seems to be holding a camera to his eye. Is this the source of the "other" film?

Lampposts altered

In 1963 the lampposts were 16' tall, and next to the curb. After the assassination lampposts were moved away from the curb and changed to 14' height to make photo replications much harder.

14-foot pole is in location of Zfilm lamppost

WHITE

WHITE

The FBI-210 photo from the pedestal overlaid over composite of DPDeast and White/Costella panorama

Same shoes?

WHITE

Mary wore black penny loafers. Jean wore black canvas boat shoes. Zapruder shows both with WHITE shoes.

Zapruder Film vs. Zavada Test Frames

The "full flush left" (and even "beyond full flush left") intersprocket images seen at left are representative of all frames in the so-called original Zapruder film, using the MPI DVD, "Image of an Assassination" (1998), as the source. The DVD contains accurate images of frames made directly from the original film at the National Archives. Seen at the right are frames from the test film exposed by Kodak consultant Rollie Zavada in cameras identical to Zapruder's. The inability to consistently replicate this phenomenon inside the test cameras suggests that the Zapruder film in the National Archives is not a camera original—that it was not exposed in Zapruder's Bell & Howell 8 mm camera. Another difference between the "original" and the Zavada test film is apparent: the exaggerated "light bleed" from lower right hand corner of each sprocket hole in the Zavada test film is markedly different than the Zapruder frames from the "original". (Caption text by Doug Horne and David Lifton.)

*James H. Fetzer
and
Scott A. Lederer*

29 June 2003

Mysteries of the JFK Assassination:
The Photographic Evidence from A to Z

Jack White

[*Editor's note:* The alteration of the film has sometimes been supposed to be too complicated a task to have been undertaken, even if there was a conspiracy! In this chapter, the legendary photoanalyst presents his findings and discoveries about photographs and films related to the death of JFK. Some of his conclusions—including his identification of the third "tramp" as E. Howard Hunt as opposed to Chauncey Holt—remain controversial to this day, perhaps none more so than his belief that there were two "Oswalds", one of whom may still be alive. These unsettled aspects of the case, some of which I expect to be illuminated by John Armstrong's *Harvey and Lee* (2003), suggest that research on many of these matters may be expected to endure. The full-color slides Jack presented at the conference are represented here by black-and-white reductions (but also see the color-insert section).]

The films must be studied in the context of all other evidence of the assassination, because not just the Zapruder film is suspect. Many images and much evidence can be shown to be altered by the conspirators. If it can be proved that unknown parties altered, faked, or created many of the evidentiary images of the JFK murder, then the Zapruder film itself can be seen as just a part of a much larger effort by the government to tell a false story of the assassination.

Other photos and images can be used to verify the authenticity of not only the Zapruder film, but also *all* films and photos, as well as other evidence in the assassination. Proof that any photo or evidence does not represent the truth may help convince skeptics that if much other evidence was faked, then the Zapruder film is not exempt from tampering. So let us look at many assassination images from A to Z to see what they tell us about the JFK assassination in general and the Zapruder film in particular. Alteration of the Zapruder film becomes much more believable when proof is offered that many other images were tampered with, or in some cases, altogether created or substituted. All films and evidence must be in agreement. The full significance of some of the things seen in the Zapruder film can be understood more easily through comparison of Z frames with other images and evidence, which I have accumulated during 40 years.

The brief summary which I am presenting at this symposium is the result of many years of research and culminates in what I refer to as *"The Great Zapruder Film Hoax."* What follows is a very abbreviated summary of some of my study of all images and evidence of the JFK assassination—from A to Z.

A is for Altgens...5 and 6

Altgens exposure 5 as limo turns from Main to Houston and exposure 6 as limo passes TSBD on Elm Street. Both raise important questions and answers.

Let's start the alphabet with A—for Altgens. AP photographer James Altgens took these two exposures critical to study of the Z film—his exposures 5 and 6. Altgens 5 shows the turn from Main to Houston. Altgens 6 shows the limo halfway down Elm after shots have been fired. I believe these Altgens exposures are genuine and can be used for comparisons with the official story depicted by Zapruder.

A is for Altgens...5 full frame

Here is the full frame of Altgens 5. Of key evidentiary value is its depiction of the spectators along Houston Street—especially the apparent image of Joseph Milteer in the crowd. Milteer, a right-wing extremist, just before the assassination, predicted the Dallas assassination scenario to a police informant in Miami. The HSCA denied that Milteer was in Dallas.

A is for Altgens...5 Milteer, crosswalk

Altgens 5 shows the CROSSWALK PEOPLE and Joseph Milteer.

It is important to study the Altgens people in the crosswalk as well as the group which appears to contain Joseph Milteer.

Altgens 5 also shows, in addition to Joseph Milteer, the people standing in the crosswalk of Elm at Houston. This is important because the Zapruder film also shows these persons at almost the same moment.

A is for Altgens...5 Milteer closeup

The man seen by the curb in Altgens appears to be Joseph Milteer.

If Milteer is standing along Houston Street as the Altgens photo seems to show, the government version cannot be true.

A is for Altgens...crosswalk people

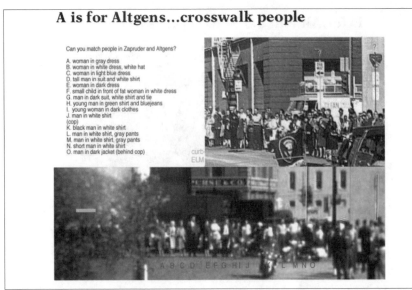

Can you match people in Zapruder and Altgens?

A. woman in gray dress
B. woman in white dress, white hat
C. woman in light blue dress
D. tall man in suit and white shirt
E. woman in dark dress
F. small child in front of fat woman in white dress
G. man in dark suit, white shirt and tie
H. young man in green shirt and bluejeans
I. young woman in dark clothes
J. man in white shirt
(cop)
K. black man in white shirt
L. man in white shirt, gray pants
M. man in white shirt, gray pants
N. short man in white shirt
O. man in dark jacket (behind cop)

A comparison of the crosswalk people in Altgens with the corresponding individuals in Zapruder at the same moment in time shows that the people are entirely different. If we assume that the Altgens photo shows the people who were in the crosswalk as the limo arrived, then those shown in Zapruder cannot reflect reality.

A is for Altgens...crosswalk people

Not a single person can be seen who is the same. A close look at Zapruder shows, for instance:

A. a woman in white coat and white coat and white hat—not seen in Altgens.
B. a very big tall man in suit and white shirt—not seen in Altgens.
C. a small boy in a white shirt—not seen in Altgens.
D. a man in suit, white shirt and necktie—not seen in Altgens.
WS. four men in white shirts—not seen in Altgens.

In addition, Altgens shows a large number of black persons. Zapruder shows none.

A is for Altgens...man in doorway

Altgens' image of a man in the doorway of the Book Depository was the first photo to raise questions about the veracity of the official story. Marguerite Oswald wondered whether the man was LHO. The government claimed the image was of Billy Nolan Lovelady—because if it shows Oswald, the whole Warren scenario collapses. The question has never been answered definitively.

A is for Altgens...windshield hole

Altgens 6 seems to show a bullet hole in the windshield by the rearview mirror. Could this be from a frontal shot?

Several witnesses saw a bullet hole in the windshield. The official story denies it. But Altgens 6 seems to show a hole, which from the south knoll, lines up perfectly with JFK. A shot from the front disputes the official story and the Zfilm. [*Editor's note:* This feature of the photo is discussed in *Assassination Science* (1998), pp. 142–144, and Doug Weldon, J.D. in *Murder in Dealey Plaza* (2000), pp. 128–150.]

A is for Altgens...8 shows Zapruder?

The last exposure taken by Altgens was number 8. It seemingly shows Zapruder just dismounting from the pedestal—but the man, whose foot is on the bottom step, is just barely taller than the 4-foot tall pedestal. A person just behind him in dark clothes appears to be a short lady with dark hair. But Marilyn Sitzman was very tall and wearing light clothing. Is this really Zapruder and Sitzman? Or is this image altered to fit the official story?

A is for Arnold...in Moorman?

Gordon Arnold   Badgeman   Hardhatman

Gordon Arnold, a soldier who said he was filming the motorcade from atop the grassy knoll in front of the picket fence, is not seen in any photos except the Moorman Polaroid in the analysis seen above. Questions: (1) What happened to his film? (2) Was he removed from other photos because those controlling the images dared not show an unknown person filming, whose footage might surface at a later time? If Gordon Arnold's story is true, the official story is false.

B is for Babushka/Beverly Oliver

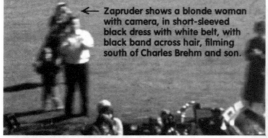

← Zapruder shows a blonde woman with camera, in short-sleeved black dress with white belt, with black band across hair, filming south of Charles Brehm and son.

Numerous other photos show this woman in a long tan raincoat and a scarf over her head. She was called the Babushka Lady for many years until she was identified as Beverly Oliver.

Zapruder frames show several spectators along Elm, including a woman standing south of Charles Brehm. Sho appears to be filming with a movie camera. Zapruder shows the woman to have blond hair with a black band across the top, and wearing a short-sleeved black dress with a white belt. Comparing these Zframes with numerous other photos of the same woman by Wilma Bond and others, we see that the woman was really wearing a long tan raincoat and a headscarf. For many years she was called The Babushka Lady until she was identified as an entertainer named Beverly Oliver, who was acquainted with Jack Ruby. Beverly says her undeveloped film was confiscated by the FBI. Her image is obviously altered in Zapruder according to what we see in other photos—and the government has suppressed her important movie of the motorcade, which was taken from her by an FBI agent. Does this one image from the Zfilm prove fabrication?

B is for Backyard...faked photos

The so-called Backyard Photos were a crude attempt to frame Oswald. I will not show *all* the dozens of proofs of fabrication, which I have already shown in my video *Fake*. I will just list a few proofs, such as:

B is for Backyard...faked photos

*same LHO face on 3 bodies
*chin is square, not pointed
*fingers are chopped off
*shadows are wrong
*left arm is too short
*rifle is wrong length
*body is out of balance
*newspapers are wrong size
*rifle swivels are in wrong place
...and many, many more!

These backyard photos are definite fabrications. Why would the Zfilm be exempt from fabrication then?

B is for Badgeman...Moorman gunman

In 1982 Gary Mack and I discovered an image in the Moorman photo which seems to show a gunman in a police uniform. This figure has become known as Badgeman. There also seem to be two other persons in the shadows—Gordon Arnold, as previously mentioned, and a man standing near Badgeman's left shoulder, who seems to be wearing a hardhat.

B is for Badgeman...enlargement

The image of badgeman became very clear when I bracketed copy exposures to obtain optimal tonal range. The above negatives are not enhanced in any way. In my opinion, there is no disputing that the image shows a man in a police uniform.

B is for Badgeman...close-up

Hair
Forehead
Eyebrows
Eyes
Nose
Ear
Cheek
Puff of smoke
Shoulder
Shoulder patch
Left arm
Badge on chest

When viewed close-up, the features are clearly seen—hair, eyes, eyebrows, nose, cheek, ear, uniform with shoulder patch and badge, and left arm in rifle-firing position. The government had the Moorman photo in its possession—but it was *not published* in *The Warren Report* (1964). Perhaps they noticed the presence of Badgeman, and could not afford for the public to see a gunman on the knoll. If they would withhold evidence like this, they would not hesitate to alter the Zfilm and other evidence.

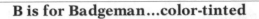

B is for Badgeman...color-tinted

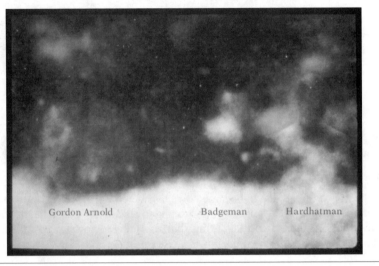

Gordon Arnold   Badgeman   Hardhatman

Because some people had difficulty discerning the Moorman people in black and white, I used photo-tint transparent oil paint to tint a black and white print so everyone could see the three people on the knoll. These images apparently presented great difficulty for the commission—so they suppressed them.

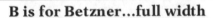

B is for Betzner...full width

Hugh Betzner took this little-studied black and white image of the assassination. Can it tell us anything about Zapruder and the Zapruder film? Perhaps. At least half a dozen researchers have said they have seen *another movie* of the assassination from a similar viewpoint as Zapruder. Is it possible that the Betzner photo shows another photographer near the pedestal?

B is for Betzner...another camera?

Betzner seems to show, with the same "clarity" as Zapruder and Sitzman, another man standing on an extension of the same wall, behind the bush. His right hand seems to be holding a camera to his eye. Is this the source of the "other" film?

Close examination of Betzner shows what could be another movie photographer. He is the same size as Zapruder and seems to be holding a camera to his face. If this is another photographer, his position is only about ten feet away from Zapruder's pedestal. He could be the source of the "other" film seen by several researchers.

B is for Betzner...studying spectators

Betzner is also a useful photo to study the curb people seen in Zapruder. It can be seen that nine people in Zapruder cannot be seen in Betzner, apparently hidden by the secret service men. Such comparisons of one photo to another is essential to determine authenticity.

B is for Betzner...Zapruder & Sitzman

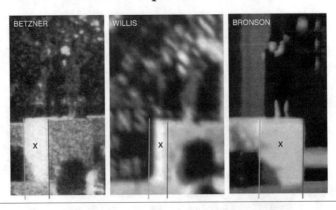

Betzner is a useful photo for studying Zapruder and Sitzman, their location on the pedestal, and what they were wearing. Comparing Betzner to Willis, the couple look very similar. But when both pictures are compared to the Bronson slide taken at the same instant, they are radically different. The Bronson slide is believed to be genuine—so are both Zapruder and Sitzman *altered* in Betzner and Willis? And how were they dressed?

Both Betzner and Willis show Sitzman in a *light* dress, but in Bronson she wears a dark dress with light sleeves. Is this evidence of alteration? Or were the persons on the pedestal not Zapruder and Sitzman?

B is for Betzner..."limo stopped"

From the deposition of Hugh Betzner:

watching the crowd, ...
I walked down toward where the President's car had stopped.
.... I don't know

"I walked down toward where the President's car had stopped."

...but Zapruder does not show the limo stopping.

Betzner gave a deposition in which he said that the JFK limo stopped, which agrees with statements by many other witnesses. If the limo stopped—the Zfilm is faked, since it depicts continuous motion.

B is for Betzner...or empty pedestal?

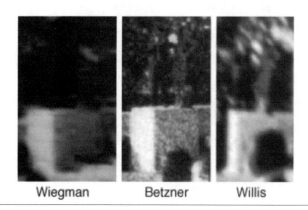

| Wiegman | Betzner | Willis |

Or was anybody on the pedestal? Just a few seconds after the Betzner and Willis photos, a frame from the Dave Wiegman film shows *nobody* on the pedestal despite the images of Betzner and Willis.

B is for Betzner...retouched!

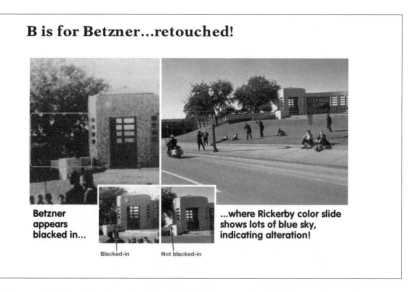

Betzner appears blacked in...

...where Rickerby color slide shows lots of blue sky, indicating alteration!

Blacked-in   Not blacked-in

This may be the clincher. A color slide by Art Rickerby from almost the same line of sight as Betzner shows blue sky west of the pergola. Betzner's sky is obviously blacked in. If they bothered to retouch Betzner, would they leave the Zfilm unaltered?

B is for Bond...shows Willis retouched?

Wilma Bond's trains behind the pergola.

What was going on in the train yard? Bond's photo from Houston Street shows the train cars the same size as the Murray photo above from behind the fence.

Where is the train in the window? Bond's photos show a train car through the pergola windows. But the Willis photo at bottom, from the same elevation and a similar viewpoint shows NO TRAIN through any of the windows. This may be an indication of alteration of the Willis photo.

I will touch on just once on Wilma Bond's important slides. As shown above, Bond's photos show passenger train cars behind the pergola. From the same elevation and a similar viewpoint the Willis 5 slide shows no train. Do the Bond slides show alteration of the Willis slide? If Willis is altered, would they leave Zapruder unaltered?

B is for Bothun...Umbrellaman photo

Dick Bothun photographed the two guys, Umbrellaman and Cuban.

Dick Bothun's photo gives us one of the best views of the mysterious *Umbrellaman* and his companion I call "The Cuban." Other photographers like Towner, Bond, and Grant also took photos of these strange characters, and I will discuss them more later.

B is for Brehm...impossible moves?

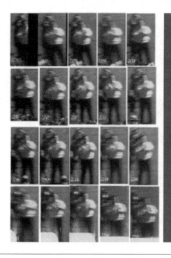

Zapruder shows Charles Brehm clapping his hands four times in one second.

Zapruder shows Brehm's son suddenly appearing within only four frames.

If either of these actions is physically impossible, then the Zapruder film is faked.

B is for Breneman...Z frames disappear

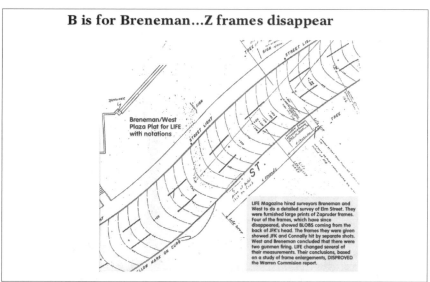

Breneman/West Plaza Plat for LIFE with notations

LIFE Magazine hired surveyors Breneman and West to do a detailed survey of Elm Street. They were furnished large prints of Zapruder frames. Four of the frames, which have since disappeared, showed BLOBS coming from the back of JFK's head. The frames they were given showed JFK and Connally hit by separate shots. West and Breneman concluded that there were two gunmen firing. LIFE changed several of their measurements. Their conclusions, based on a study of frame enlargements, DISPROVED the Warren Commision report.

Dallas surveyors Chester Breneman and James West were hired by *Life* Magazine to survey and draw plats of the plaza, with locations correlated to Zapruder frames. *Life* furnished them with 11x14 enlargements of numerous Z frames. Their survey, using the photos as reference, was to locate where various gunshots occurred. According to Breneman, four of the frames showed *blobs* emerging from the rear of JFK's head, but those frames were not among the ones published by *The Warren Report (1964)*. Breneman reported that JFK and Connally were hit by separate shots. If Breneman and West were furnished with frame enlargements which are not in the extant film, *the Z film is altered.*

B is for Bronson...the full slide

Charles Bronson took this slide from atop a pedestal at Main and Houston. It depicts most of the important players in Dealey Plaza on 22 November.

B is for Bronson...the Elm St. players

From the left we see the Newman family, Moorman and Hill, Toni Foster, two unknown twin women, identically dressed, Charles and Joe Brehm, the Umbrellaman and Cuban, two unknown boys, the Chism family, a group of wildly waving women, and the JFK limousine, all captured in an important panorama. Cropped out at left are Zapruder and Sitzman.

B is for Bronson...how about Zapruder?

What about Zapruder/Sitzman on the pedestal?

Although the pedestal is in FULL SUNLIGHT, Zapruder and Sitzman
are obscured in deep shadow in Bronson. Fortunately when I had the
Bronson original in my possession, I made black/white negatives of
the slide at bracketed exposures. To my surprise, the two figures on
the pedestal are quite clear with enough exposure.

So, what about Zapruder and Sitzman? The Bronson slide seems not to show
them, since that area is very dark, even though the pedestal is in full sunlight.
Fortunately, when I had the Bronson original in my possession, I made black
and white negatives using bracketed exposures, and found that the people on the
pedestal are quite clear.

B is for Bronson...Zap unobscured

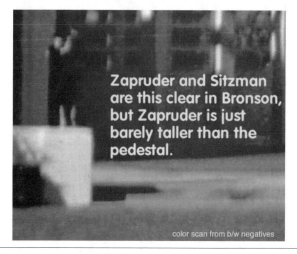

Zapruder and Sitzman
are this clear in Bronson,
but Zapruder is just
barely taller than the
pedestal.

color scan from b/w negatives

Here is what the black and white negatives reveal—two people on the pedestal, but if they are Zapruder and Sitzman, then the Bronson slide proves that
Zapruder could not have shot the Zfilm.

B is for Bronson...the Zapruder waltz

COULD ZAPRUDER FILM THE JFK LIMO?

ZAPRUDER & SITZMAN WALTZ IN BRONSON... but she blocks his view to limo!

TO LIMO

Zapruder and Sitzman are facing each other, as if waltzing. His camera is aimed at her chest, and he cannot see the limousine, since she blocks his view. Does this prove that the film attributed to Zapruder was not shot by him?

B is for Bullets...6 or 4 grooves?

6-GROOVE WC EXHIBIT CE-399 WITH GROOVES OUTLINED AND COLORED.

CE-399 TEMPLATE COURTESY OF TOM GELETKA

COPYRIGHT© 7/1/98 JOHN RITCHSON

Two different bullets are pictured by the Warren Commission and the HSCA. Both are said to be the SAME magic bullet CE399. There is no doubt of this.

Based on studies by Walt Cakebread and Jack White John Ritchson and Tom Geletka prepared these illustrations of the TWO PHOTOGRAPHED VERSIONS of CE399.

The Warren Commission report showed a bullet with SIX LANDS AND GROOVES.

By the time the HSCA studied the bullet and photos of it, the number was reduced to FOUR LANDS AND GROOVES...apparently after someone noticed that the MC rifle CE139 has only FOUR GROOVES and could NOT HAVE FIRED the magic bullet 399!

4-GROOVE HSCA EXHIBIT CE-399   TEMPLATE COURTESY OF TOM GELETKA

COPYRIGHT© 7/1/98 JOHN RITCHSON

The famous "stretcher bullet", which prompted the famed *Single Bullet Theory*, was pictured in the Warren Report. Not until the early '90s did Walt Cakebread and I notice and prove that the Warren Commission photo of CE-399 has *six* lands and grooves. Walt knew that the Mannlicher-Carcano rifle had *only four* lands and grooves. He obtained enlargements from the Archives of CE-399 as shown by the Warren Commission and also as later published by he HSCA. The HSCA bullet properly has *four grooves*. In the intervening years, someone had *counterfeited* a four-groove bullet and substituted it for the six-groove Warren Commission bullet in the Archives. Who had access? Only the FBI.

B is for Bush...on scene of crime?

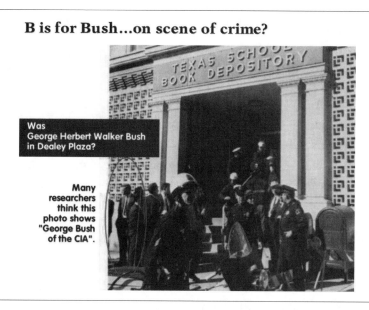

Was
George Herbert Walker Bush
in Dealey Plaza?

Many
researchers
think this
photo shows
"George Bush
of the CIA".

Chief Jesse Curry published this photo in his *JFK Assassination File* (1969). Numerous researchers believe that it shows George Bush of the CIA standing in front of the TSBD. Bush later became president. Others who may have became president because of what they knew about the JFK assassination were Johnson, Nixon, and Ford.

C is for Cancellare...important photo

Life photographer Cancellare captured this scene within first 20 seconds. Note the pickup truck.

Frank Cancellare shot this important photo within about 20 seconds after the gunshots ended, as can be determined by things in the scene. Note the pickup truck in the rectangle.

C is for Cancellare...Pickupman & bed

THE MAN AND THE PICKUP BED

Zapruder frames, left, show a pickup truck which has a COVER over the bed at the rear, with no opening. About 20 seconds later, Cancellare photographed the same truck, and it has NO COVER over the bed, and a man we refer to as Pickupman appears to be sitting inside the pickup bed. Both photos cannot be true.

C is for CIA...false defector program

CIA False Defector program

THE
FORT WORTH
CONNECTION

WWII was just over. The CIA wanted to send false defectors to Russia. CIA agent David Atlee Phillips lived in the same westside Fort Worth neighborhood as widow/divorcee Marguerite Ekdahl, who had three small children to support and needed money. They no doubt had common friends. He likely appealed to her patriotism to LEND THE IDENTITY of her youngest son Lee Harvey Oswald, to the government for a small monthly payment. LEE's identity was furnished to a CIA program which had NOTHING to do with the assassination.

World War II was just over in the late 1940s. The CIA came up with a program to send false military defectors as spies to the Soviet Union. In Fort Worth Texas, CIA agent David Atlee Phillips lived in the same westside neighborhood as Marguerite Ekdahl, a widow/divorcee with three small children to support. Possibly through common acquaintances, he met Marguerite and appealed to her patriotism and need for some easy money to simply lend the identity of her youngest son Lee to this secret government defector program. Thus was born the myth of Lee Harvey Oswald. This was the secret the Warren Commission had to hide at all costs.

C is for Conein...the ugly American

Col. L.Fletcher Prouty long claimed that this veteran agent was the chief planner of the JFK assassination, and that he was in Dealey Plaza.

LUCIEN CONEIN of the CIA

Lou Conein was famed for his CIA exploits in Southeast Asia. His long-time co-worker Col. L. Fletcher Prouty said that Conein was a genius at planning the details of operational scenarios. Prouty claimed that the JFK assassination had all the complex marks of being an operation planned by Conein. Records exist that Conein was in Fort Worth on 21 November. Prouty claimed that Conein was in Dealey Plaza the next day to see his plan in action.

C is for Conein...in Dealey Plaza!

Altgens photographed Lucien Conein in Dealey Plaza, smiling as JFK passed by.

It appears that Prouty was right. The Altgens photo above shows at the corner of Main and Houston a man who is the spitting image of Conein. He was not the only operative there to see the plan carried out.

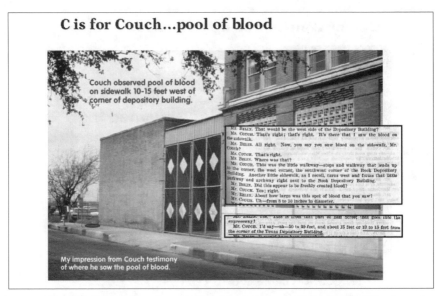

C is for Couch...pool of blood

Couch observed pool of blood on sidewalk 10-15 feet west of corner of depository building.

My impression from Couch testimony of where he saw the pool of blood.

Photographer Mal Couch reported that he saw a pool of fresh blood on the sidewalk 10 to 15 feet from the southwest corner of the depository building. He described it as being 8 to 10 inches in diameter. This is one of the unsolved mysteries of the assassination. Was this pool of blood related to several reports of a Secret Service man being killed?

D is for Dillard...important pic ruined

The high regard of the government for JFK photo evidence:

Press photographer Tom Dillard took two important negatives of the TSBD during the shooting. In the course of "studying" the original negative, the FBI DESTROYED it as evidence. Why?

Would they show any reluctance in destroying other photo evidence, such as Zapruder, Nix, and the others?

Irreparable damage done to the Dillard negative frame #24 during the course of the SRI study

Would the government destroy important evidence? Yes. For example, one of Tom Dillard's original negatives was destroyed while the FBI "studied" it. This is inexcusable and must have been deliberate.

D is for Dorman...Towners and RRman

Elsie Dorman's movie from a window in the Depository shows several significant things, including the frame above, which shows Jim and Tina Towner, Tina's blond friend, a stool near the curb, and a man in railroad cap and overalls. They should all be seen in the Zapruder film.

D is for Dorman...Jim,Tina, RRman

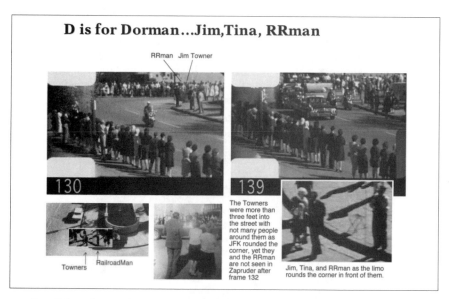

Careful analysis of many images, including Tina Towner's movie, shows that Tina and Jim were standing far off the curb, both filming, as the limo first appears in Zframe 133, and therefore should be seen in the Zapruder film. Dorman's film shows that the only person close to the Towner group of three was a railroad man. Between the Towners and the railroad man is a folding stool. Zapruder at this moment shows a larger crowd on the corner, and it does not include Jim, Tina, the blond, the railroad man, or the stool. Jim and the railroad man, however, were visible in frame 130, just 9 frames before the frame shown above.

D is for DPD...important photos

2 DPD photos crucial to proving Zfilm is fake!

On Monday following the assassination, the Dallas Police took the above two photos from the pedestal. Many years later researchers discovered that these photos are crucial to proving the Zfilm is fake. Of interest in the top photo are the Stemmons signboard at center and the lamppost at right. The bottom photo clearly shows the size and location of the odd yellow curb stripes on the Elm curb. Since two of the curb stripes also are clearly seen in Zapruder this is very important—especially since the actual stripes were later lengthened in an attempt to make photo replications difficult.

D is for DPD...Stemmons photo vital

This photo can be overlaid with Zapruder frames to show that the Zapruder sign and the lamppost are are not placed correctly. Dr. John Costella has done an extensive scientific analysis of the Stemmons sign and declares it the most important "smoking gun" of Zapruder film alteration. His study also shows that the lamppost, as seen in Zapruder, is placed at the wrong angle.

D is for Dulles...visits LBJ ranch

Kennedys to See Lot of People,

The Fort Worth Press, just before the president's visit, published a front page photo of the fired CIA chief visiting the ranch of Vice President Lyndon Johnson.

The Fort Worth Press, a few days before the JFK visit, published a front page photo showing Allen Dulles at the LBJ ranch. I believe this visit to the vice-president by the fired CIA chief was to finalize plans for the Dallas coup, which would make Johnson president and gain revenge for Dulles.

E is for Ekdahl...over 6 feet tall

FROM PAGE 21, VOL. XI

Mr. Jenner: Describe Mr. Ekdahl, please.

Mr. Pic: Rather tall. I think he was over 6 feet. He had white hair, wore glasses, very nice man.

OVER 6 FEET?

Then how tall is Marguerite?

It appears from this photo that Marguerite Ekdahl was at least 5'7" tall...and rather slim, and in all photos of her she smiles broadly. The Marguerite we know from 11-22 was 5'2".

John Pic, oldest son of Marguerite, testified about his stepfather Ekdahl that he was over six feet tall. This photo of Ekdahl shows that Marguerite was only about 5 or 6 inches shorter—perhaps 5'7". The historic Marguerite was short—only about 5'2" tall.

F is for False Defectors...Lee, Harvey

In 1959, Lee, below, obtained a passport to leave the country.

But Harvey, above, used the passport a few days later to begin the LHO defection to Russia.

Marguerite Oswald, when her son Lee was very young, volunteered his identity to a long-range government program for training young men to become false defectors to Russia. From grade school through high school, and then through the Marine Corps, Lee and his surrogate *led parallel lives* for more than ten years as they trained for the top secret assignment—*which had nothing to do with the assassination* that happened years later. The two photos above show that despite a superficial resemblance, the two men have different shaped heads.

F is for FBI...makes a counterfeit bullet

The FBI counterfeits, photographs and substitutes a FOUR-GROOVE bullet for the original SIX-GROOVE bullet.

Opposite sides of CE399 "stretcher bullet" in photo taken by FBI for the Warren Commission Report.

Opposite sides of CE399 "stretcher bullet" in photo taken by FBI for the report of the House Committee on Assassinations.

The original magic bullet had six grooves when it should have had four. So the FBI counterfeited a replacement with four grooves, photographed it and switched it with the original in the Archives.

Hoover's FBI apparently had the assignment to eliminate *inconvenient evidence*, whether it was photographs, testimony, or physical evidence. The bureau conducted a dragnet of all photos immediately after the coup. All photos which were tampered with were in their possession. Testimony of witnesses was changed by agents. Evidence in the possession of the bureau which was found to be inconvenient to the official story was lost or changed. *Only* the FBI had access to this evidence.

F is for FBI...LHO W2 form forgeries

Among LHO possessions were found two W-2 income withholding forms. John Armstrong thought the employer ID numbers seemed too close together for companies which were founded MANY YEARS APART. Research proved him correct. Only the FBI had possession of these forms.

THE FBI FAKED THESE FORMS!

John Armstrong obtained originals of 4 LHO W-2 forms from the government and researched them. From 3 different companies and 2 different years, he found the employer ID numbers were issued fraudulently, and that all of them were proved to have been typed on the SAME IBM TYPEWRITER.

The research of John Armstrong has uncovered much FBI malfeasance. First, he discovered that the bureau obtained school records of young Lee Oswald in Fort Worth and destroyed these records when they conflicted with the school records of Harvey Oswald in New Orleans at the same time.

He also discovered that the bureau forged income tax forms for young LHO in New Orleans. He noted that two W2 forms allegedly found in Oswald's possession had employer ID numbers very close together *even though the two companies were started many years apart*.

He checked, and found that the ID numbers were false. He then located in government files other LHO tax forms, and found that they were fraudulent also—and had all been typed on the *same IBM typewriter*, according to IBM scientists. Only the FBI had possession of these records.

F is for Foster...the running woman

Many frames of the Zapruder film show a woman in a tan coat and gray pants running across the grass in Dealey Plaza. I always thought she looked strangely tall compared to Jean Hill and Mary Moorman in the foreground. The woman has been identified as Toni Foster, who is said to have been about 5'2" tall.

F is for Foster... giant running lady

Costella frame shows Toni Foster to be 6'5" by Jack's measuring rod at lampposts.

Acting on my suspicion that Toni Foster seemed much too tall, using the known height of two lampposts in the plaza, I conducted many studies, and to my amazement Toni appeared in Zapruder to be about seven feet tall!, based on the 14-foot height of the lampposts. John Costella, noting minor errors in my studies caused by lens distortion of frame 310, corrected for the distortion, and I redid my study with the corrected frame. The resulting composite above shows the corrected Toni is about 6'5" tall—at least 15 inches taller than her actual height. This perhaps indicates that whoever fabricated these frames *enlarged the background* considerably from the curb upward.

F is for Franzen family...in Zapruder

In several Zapruder frames, most very blurry except a few like this, a family of three persons is seen. They are Jack Franzen, his wife, and son Jeff. Study of them in Zapruder and other images produces contradictory and puzzling results.

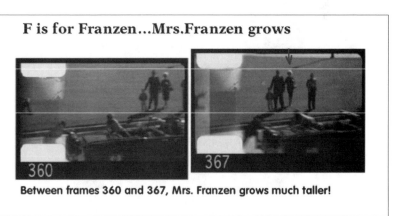

F is for Franzen...Mrs.Franzen grows

Between frames 360 and 367, Mrs. Franzen grows much taller!

Comparison of Zapruder frames 360 and 367 shows that in just seven frames, less than half a second, Mrs. Franzen has grown half a head taller while Jack and Jeff remain the same height. There is no explanation which could cause this—except alteration.

Standing just west of Mrs. Franzen is a lone man that researchers have dubbed "Ginandtonicman," who seems to hold a glass in his right hand.

F is for Franzen...mystery woman

...in Nix replaces Mrs. Franzen

It is essential to compare Zapruder frames to other films to determine authenticity of either or both. Here I check Zapruder frame 369 with a comparable frame in Nix, to check the Franzen family and the Ginandtonicman, seen clearly in Zapruder. We find that in Nix, Mrs. Franzen (3) *disappears* from her position holding her husband's left elbow. He and son Jeff , as well as the Ginandtonicman, are in the same position in Nix and Zapruder. But in Nix, a new *mystery woman* (?!) appears west of the Ginandtonic man (4). She clearly is not Mrs. Franzen. Something is wrong with one or both of these films.

Carrying research further regarding the mystery lady seen in the Nix frame, I assembled a group of 15 Nix frames and found that in Nix, the mystery woman is present, but the ginman is not. When studied carefully in sequence, it is seen that the ginman suddenly appears from nowhere, morphing out of the image of the mystery woman. This cannot be photographically correct unless the Nix film has been altered!

G is for Ginandtonicman...gin or signs?

Ginandtonicman or Signman?

Zapruder, left, shows a man who seems to hold a glass of gin and tonic in his right hand.
But Cancellare, enhanced below, shows the same man seemingly holding several large retangular signs with lettering on them.
Both images cannot be right.

As mentioned, Zapruder shows a lone man by the south Elm curb who seems to hold a glass in his right hand. Some researchers have named him the Gin And Tonic Man. However, a few seconds later, the Cancellare photo shows the same man clutching several large signs to his chest. If he was holding signs instead of a glass, where are the signs in Zapruder? If he was holding signs, Zapruder has been altered.

G is for Grant...shows Cuban best.

Grant gives best look at Umbrellaman and Cuban

Note the eyeglasses and cap worn by the Cuban, and the large bulge under his jacket.

G is for Greer...impossible head turn

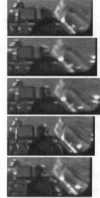

Limo driver
Greer looks
forward
in frame 301
and to rear in
frame 305

...while at
the same
time agent
Kellerman is
seen using a
radio/phone

Greer head turn and
Kellerman on phone
clearly seen in Costella
enhancements of
frames 301-305.

The Zapruder film shows SS limo driver making a turn of his head to look over his shoulder in 5 frames—about a quarter of a second. This is believed to be physically impossible. If impossible, the Zfilm is faked. These same frames show SS agent Kellerman on the limo's radio telephone. There is no record of Kellerman's radio transmission from the limo.

H is for Harrelson...arrested in plaza

Charles V. Harrelson,
convicted hitman,
under arrest as
a tramp in Dealey
Plaza, without
any doubt.

Considerable evidence, too lengthy to detail here, shows that convicted hitman Charles Harrelson was one of the three tramps arrested and marched through Dealey Plaza, as seen above. Harrelson, serving a life sentence for the murder of a federal judge, himself admitted to participating in the plot to kill the president. You must admit that his presence at the scene of JFK's murder is suspicious.

H is for Harvey...and Lee

Here we see the passport photo of Lee, and the DPD arrest photo of Harvey. They are sized so that the distance between the pupils of the eyes are the same. Though many facial features are similar, the shape of the head clearly identifies two different men. Lee has a head which is almost oval in shape. Harvey's head is more triangular in shape. Lee's head is longer than Harvey's. Lee and Harvey are obviously different people.

H is for Harvey...eleven days apart

These two Oswald photos were taken only twenty-one days apart in 1959. They seem to be of two different persons, and both were taken just prior to his defection. The latter photo is part of a faked composite.

H is for Harvey...Marina's husband

Harvey and Marina, 1962

Harvey in New Orleans, 1955

The Oswald who attended Beauregard Junior High School in New Orleans is obviously Harvey. Note the similarity to the Oswald who was married to Marina. At the time Harvey was attending Beauregard, Lee was attending Stripling Junior High in Fort Worth. Lee's Stripling records were confiscated by the FBI and have disappeared.

H is for Hill...standing in the street

Jean Hill, the lady in red

...from November 22 till she died, Jean Hill steadfastly said that she and Mary Moorman were standing in the street when the Moorman photo was taken. Note her statement in the Friday Dallas Times-Herald at right. She and Mary never wavered that they were standing in the street...yet the Zapruder film shows both of them standing TWO FEET SOUTH OF THE CURB ON THE GRASS. If the girls were standing in the street as both always insisted, the Zfilm is FAKE!

DALLAS
ASSASSINATION

Candid Sn

Picture of

A Dallas woman snapped a candid picture of President Kennedy —then heard the scream, "My God, he's been shot."

The Polaroid snapshot taken by Mary Moorman, 2832 Ripplewood, shows the President of the United States slumped over the seat of his limousine. His young wife was ~~leaning toward him.~~

Standing in the street at the triangle west of the Houston and Main street intersection, Jean Hill, of 9402 Bluff Creek, and her companion were eyewitnesses to the shooting of President Kennedy n Dallas Friday.

Both heard a sequence of shots, saw the President slump over toward his wife, heard the piercing

scream

They i run up from the motorca running The s diately with fig mass to motorca dent an Connally with sir "The were lo the seat down at "Then

The Dallas Times-Herald on the day of the assassination interviewed witness Jean Hill. She told them that she and her friend Mary Moorman were *standing in the street* when they took a Polaroid snapshot of the assassination. The Muchmore frame above shows them standing in the street. Mary, in the black coat has just taken the photo. But the Zapruder film shows both Jean and Mary *on the grass*, two feet south of the curb, despite evidence to the contrary. If they were in the street and not on the grass, the Zfilm is proved to be fake.

H is for Holt...not a tramp

Chauncy Holt, admitted CIA operative, came forward in the 90s claiming to be the old man tramp. Photoanalysis shows his claim is bogus.

Chauncey Holt, 1990s   Old Man Tramp, 1963

In the 1990s, Chauncey Holt came forward claiming to be one of the three Dealey Plaza tramps, and to also be a former CIA agent. Extensive photoanalysis, too lengthy to discuss here, proves that his claims were disinformation.

H is for Hunt...the old-man tramp

The old tramp gets a face transplant.

However, another former CIA agent, E. Howard Hunt, does fit the description of the Old Man Tramp. His facial features, when overlaid precisely, are an exact match. Hunt also was deeply involved in many facets of the assassination plot. A CIA agent arrested in Dealey Plaza had to be covered up at all costs. No arrest records were kept, and no investigators were interested in the tramps. Holt—no. Hunt—yes.

I is for Invisible...photo artifact?

456 ↑ Lamppost disappears.
A photographic anomaly?

Some seeming anomalies in the Zfilm are difficult to analyze. In frame 456 seen here a lamppost becomes completely invisible, so that the rear of the limo as well as Clint Hill on the trunk are seen through the area where the post should be. Is this a result of panning blur? I don't know. This may or may not be important—but all anomalies should be explained.

I is for Itek...studied Zfilm for CBS

...and the photographic analysis firm reported that the Zfilm verified the Single Bullet Theory and the rest of the Warren Report. Itek assumed the film was genuine.

Itek Corporation, a major government contractor, was hired to analyze the Zapruder film, the Nix film, and other images. Itek obediently said the films verified *The Warren Report* (1964).

J is for Jackie...and Jean's white dog.

At Love Field, Jackie holds in her left hand a small toy dog or sock hand-puppet Lambchop apparently given to her by someone in the crowd. This is what Jean Hill identified as a small white dog in the limo.

Jean Hill said that as limo approached her on Elm, she saw the president and his wife looking at a small white dog between them.

If the Zapruder film shows NO DOG, it is altered!

Jean Hill, one of the closest witnesses to the shooting, was ridiculed for many years for her statement that as the limo approached she saw JFK and his wife looking at a small white dog between them. Of course no dog was in the limo. But researchers have discovered at least two photos, above, which show Jackie holding a small toy Lambchop hand puppet which someone gave her at Love Field. Evidently Jean saw Jackie holding up the puppet as the limousine drew near, and mistook it for a small dog. Jean did not imagine this. It happened—and should be seen in the Zfilm, but is not.

K is for Kennedy...autopsy fake pix

The president himself was not exempt from body alteration—or at least photographic alteration. Photos of JFK's wounds clearly do not match witness descriptions, especially the huge exit hole in the occipital, which above is shown with undamaged scalp.

L is for Lampposts...changed up

Lampposts altered

In 1963 the lampposts were 16' tall, and next to the curb. After the assassination lampposts were moved away from the curb and changed to 14' height to make photo replications much harder.

14-foot pole is in location of Zfilm lamppost

At some point after the assassination, all the curbside lamposts in Dealey Plaza were moved to different locations and/or replaced with poles of different height. Researchers think this was part of a coverup plan to confound and confuse attempts to replicate photos in the plaza.

L is for Lansdale...in Dealey Plaza

Gen. Ed Lansdale of the CIA was identified in this photo by his friend Col. Fletcher Prouty as being in Dealey Plaza. Prouty thought that Lansdale was one of the planners of the assassination.

Col. L. Fletcher Prouty, who worked daily at the Pentagon with Ed Lansdale of the CIA, noted that Lansdale was photographed in Dealey Plaza in one of the tramp pictures. Several other Lansdale friends, when shown the photo, also recognized him. Prouty said that Lansdale and Lou Conein may have planned the details of the Dallas operation together.

L is for Lee...and Harvey

To repeat—Lee Oswald, on the left, at an early age loaned his identity to the CIA for use in a false defector program. Harvey, at right, learned to be Oswald, and he and Lee led parallel lives for more than ten years. His agency controllers sacrificed Harvey as the patsy to take the fall for the JFK hit. Lee, however, may still be alive today, living under another name.

L is for Lee...both were in Marines

Lee in a Marine photo found in the files of naval intelligence. Note the 13-inch head, found in many intelligence personnel photos.

Most of the official photos of LHO in the Marines are of Lee, not Harvey. This photo of Lee, which could not be found by HSCA investigators, was located by John Armstrong in the files of Naval Intelligence. As I told the HSCA, he has a head 13" long, which I later discovered was a peculiar identifier of photos of intelligence personnel.

L is for Lee...Lee/Harvey merge

Lee

graduated from
Marine boot camp...
but Harvey also was
in Marines, creating a
confusion of multiple
records.

It was in the Marine Corps that the personas of Lee and Harvey were merged, creating a confusion of multiple records. Researcher John Armstrong, by composing timelines of all LHO records, has separated Lee and Harvey into distinct persons in different locations at the same time.

L is for Lee...Lee/Harvey confusion

Some of the images of Oswald do not fit either Lee or Harvey. At left is a fat-faced Oswald. At right is a very thin-faced Oswald photo said to be found in Oswald's wallet. Neither looks like the man arrested for the shooting of the president.

L is for Lee...Lee and faked Lee

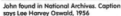John found in National Archives. Caption
says Lee Harvey Oswald, 1956

New version found by James Richards

Different version alleged to be
found in LHO possessions

The two photos at left are clearly pictures of Lee. The photo at right was altered in an apparent attempt to make it look more like Harvey, who had a thinner face. It allegedly was found in Harvey Oswald's wallet, but was not really a photo of Harvey. Some researchers think this is a photo of *Robert* Oswald, though the government says it is LHO.

L is for Lee...Lee fake defection pic

When the time came for Harvey to switch with Lee and defect to Russia, there were plenty of *official LHO* photos which could have been used to release to the news media. But those photos were mostly of *Lee*, and someone might notice that the defector, *Harvey*, did not match the photo. So the official defection photo released to *Associated Press* was a highly retouched version of a fuzzy small snapshot of Lee at Atsugi. It is vague enough that it doesn't look like either Lee or Harvey.

M is for Marguerite...more than one

How many Marguerites?

The Warren Report says that Marguerite worked at Paul's Shoe Store in Fort Worth. John Armstrong located the manager who ran the store at that time, and he had an 8x10 glossy photo which showed Marguerite (above). The problem with this is that at that same time period...

...the Marguerite shown above was living in New Orleans where the Warren Report says she lived while young Lee Harvey Oswald attended junior high school and she worked in a department store on Canal Street. Two women, two Marguerites, two cities. Who are the women above?

This is the Marguerite most people are familiar with in 1963. Is she the same person shown in the other two photos just a few years earlier?

Many photos exist of Marguerite Oswald—but many look like different women, as seen here. The one on the right is the one known to history as Marguerite. But left and center are two other Marguerites, photographed in 1955. The one at left was working in Fort Worth at Paul's Shoe Store at the same time that the one in the center was working in a department store and as a barmaid in New Orleans.

M is for Marguerite...how many?

Many Marguerites

The younger woman at left is believed to be the original Marguerite Clavier, who married Pic, Oswald, and Ekdahl in later life, and bore three sons. Which of the photos above depict the same woman many years later?

So how many Marguerites were there? Well, there was the original Marguerite Clavier Pic Oswald Ekdahl, who had three sons. But after enlisting young Lee in the false defector program, the real Marguerite sometimes gave way to various stand-ins in a manner not yet fully understood. But it is clear that each child, *Lee* and *Harvey*, had to have mothers, because the deception began when each child was very young.

M is for Marguerite...moms aplenty

Lee and Harvey both had to have mothers

Lee's mom, 1947, Fort Worth

Lee's mom, 1955, Fort Worth

Harvey's mom, 1955, New Orleans

Harvey's mom, 1963, Fort Worth

Lee's mother in 1947 in Fort Worth was Mrs. Ekdahl. Lee's mom in 1955 was a Fort Worth woman whose identity is not certain. Harvey's mother during the same period in 1955 was a New Orleans woman whose identity is not known. Harvey's mother during the 1960's assassination period was the historical Marguerite. Her true identity is unknown. Whether there were other Marguerites is also unknown. It is very likely that some of these women were CIA operatives.

M is for Marina...fake babydoll photos

Marina, Lee and the faked BabyDoll photographs.

A remarkable series of four photos from Minsk show Marina, Lee, and what appears to be a stiff doll figure. All the pix have been proved to be FAKE photo composites. The purpose of such fakes is unfathomable.

During the period Oswald was in Russia, he married Marina and had a child. Several strange snapshots of Marina, "Lee" and the baby exist. The baby looks like a stiff doll in the photos, and all the photos are provably faked composites. In the upper left, Oswald is clearly pasted in, and in the bottom photo, Marina is pasted over the older woman. My two articles on these peculiar faked photos were published in *the Fourth Decade*. I can think of no reason for this odd charade.

M is for Marines...photos confusing

A number of Marine photos of Oswald exist. Only John Armstrong knows whether they show Lee or Harvey, because each photo must be associated with a timeline.

Since a large number of photos exist during the period *both Oswalds* were in the Marines, the only way to determine whether Lee or Harvey is depicted is by comparative timelines which show LHO locations where and when. Until John Armstrong's book is published, only John can really say for sure which is which.

M is for Moorman...her Polaroid photo

Seen here is the famous Polaroid photo of the assassination taken by Mary Moorman and her friend Jean Hill. It has long been believed to be one of the few photos from Dealey Plaza that is untampered. The lines-of-sight in this photo can determine within inches exactly where Mary was located when she snapped the shutter.

M is for Moorman...where was she?

Zapruder shows
Mary 2 feet south
of Elm curb
on the grass.

What difference does it make where Mary was standing? Because the Zapruder film shows a precise spot two feet south of the curb where she stands as she shot the photo, that's why! If her photo can tell us exactly where she stood, it either proves or disproves the authenticity of the film. *If she is not standing on the grass two feet south of the curb, this is the only proof needed that the film is faked!*

M is for Moorman...reference cross +

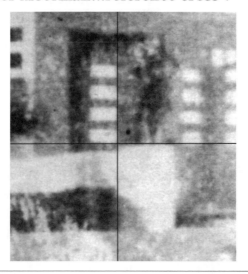

One day I was in Dealey Plaza with a copy of the Moorman photo looking for anything which might reveal exactly where Mary stood. I knew that Zapruder showed her standing two feet south of the curb. I zeroed in on the pedestal, and noticed that the edges of the pedestal and the edges of the window in the background formed a perfect juncture as seen here—a big cross which is very easy to locate from memory, over and over again.

So I tried to locate the cross. I stooped lower and lower, till finally I was on my knees, with my eyes only about 40 inches off the ground—*much too low for a standing adult*! I had found proof that the Zfilm was faked.

M is for Moorman...in the street

Mary on the spot.

I conducted many experiments and photographed them. I established beyond any doubt Mary's line of sight. By taking photos along the line of sight, I was able to replicate the correct line of sight with my camera two feet north of the curb and 54 inches above the pavement. I spray painted a yellow circle on the spot. Taking into account the asphalt buildup since 1963, I calculated that the height was just right for Mary's lens. Later, Dr. Fetzer and Dr. Mantik did a careful scientific replication of my experiment, using a surveyor's transit. They agreed that Mary *could only take the photo by stepping off the curb*.

M is for Moorman...the difference

What difference does it make?

About this much.

What difference does it make? If Mary was in the street, she would be four feet closer to Zapruder and approximately a foot lower. In Zapruder, she would look about like the image at right. Her feet would be hidden by the limousine.

M is for Moorman...Mary a midget?

Little Mary with Jim, Stewart, and David

...with big Mary in the street

Here are Jim and David finding the exact line of sight with the transit as Stewart Galanor looks on. I have overlaid images of Mary from Zapruder on the line of sight both two feet south of the curb and two feet north of the curb. You can see that she is normal size in the street, and a midget on the grass, since her lens must be just 41.5 inches above the grass.

M is for Moorman...shoes, Mary&Jean

Same shoes?

Mary wore black penny loafers. Jean wore black canvas boat shoes. Zapruder shows both with WHITE shoes.

Because a film from the knoll would have hidden the shoes of Mary and Jean behind the limo, the fabricators of the film had to guess at their shoe colors. When they moved them onto the grass, the animators gave both women *white shoes*. Earlier snapshots that day showed them to be wearing *black shoes*—another proof of fakery.

M is for Muchmore...in the street!

Marie Muchmore's movie also shows Jean and Mary in the street. Muchmore frames show their feet hidden north of the curb. I have overlaid here a Muchmore frame on a Bond slide from near the same location. Compare Jean, in red, standing on the grass moments later, with Jean standing off the curb in Muchmore.

N is for Nix...knoll frames blacked-in

Nix frames blacked-in

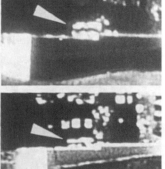

Edges of sloppy retouching are clearly seen around car top.

One of my earliest studies showing film fakery was with these frames from the Nix film, which were published in *The Fourth Decade*. It is very obvious that frames showing the knoll area have been blacked in. The retouching was so sloppy that the edges of the blacked-in area are clearly visible. Note also the train windows seen above the car top in the bottom frame have been blacked out in the upper frame. If the Nix film was retouched, why would the Zapruder film be left unretouched?

N is for Norton...check eyes and nose

Is Norton the original Oswald?

Norton today **Young Norton**

The late JFK researcher Mae Brussell corresponded with a young man named Donald O. Norton from Akron Ohio. Norton told Mae that he was *the real Lee Harvey Oswald*. Researchers John Judge and Bill Kelly met this man in Mae's presence once at the University of Toledo. Other researchers later determined that Norton was still living, and obtained a photo of young Norton. Later he moved to Florida, and an older photo of him was obtained as he looks today. His left eye, in particular, as well as the nose, looks very much like the Marine photo of Oswald.

N is for Norton...writing looks same

Signature comparisons of Oswald and Norton

Lee Harvey Oswald

Lee H. Oswald

Donald O. Norton
Donald O. Norton

wald Osw L e
wald Os H e
nald On N o

LETTERFORMS and SLANT

Handwriting exemplars of Donald O. Norton and Lee Harvey Oswald were compared and found to be very similar, as shown here—especially the WALD and NALD. Is Norton really Oswald? I do not know. But it is a very curious story, especially given that a CIA agent named Donald P. Norton was discovered during the Garrison investigation.

O is for Oliver...connections

When Beverly Oliver married underworld character George McGann, best man was Jack Ruby's best friend R.D.Matthews at right. Before the assassination, Ruby gave Bev a green dress with white polkadots and told her to wear it on Friday to watch the JFK motorcade. Because of possible rain, the dress was covered by a raincoat.

Why was a teenage friend of Jack Ruby in Dealey Plaza with a movie camera to film the motorcade and told to wear a green dress with white polkadots?

Teenage Beverly Oliver worked as a singer in a club next to Jack Ruby's Carousel Club. She knew Ruby well, and also his underworld friend R. D. Matthews. Through them she met another underworld character, George McGann, and married him. Matthews, seen here, was McGann's best man. Why was a teenager acquainted with mobsters in Dealey Plaza filming the assassination with a camera given to her by another acquaintance, Larry Ronco? Why did Ruby tell her to wear a green dress with white polkadots? This is all too strange to be totally innocent.

O is for Oliver...blue or tan?

Zapruder frames show Beverly Oliver in a blue low-cut dress with a white belt and a black band over her blonde hair, at right. ——>

At the same moment, Muchmore shows her in a tan raincoat with hair covered by a scarf, as do all other photos of her.

Beverly appears in numerous photos. All except Zapruder show her in a tan raincoat with a headscarf over her head. Zapruder shows her with a low-cut blue dress with a white belt and no raincoat. Zapruder shows her blonde hair with a black band across the top, not a head scarf. Both cannot be correct. Zapruder has her dressed wrong!

P is for Paines...agents or pawns?

Ruth and Michael Paine are truly mystery characters in the assassination. That they were deeply involved with Marina Oswald is without question. The research of John Armstrong shows that they knew both Harvey Oswald and Lee Oswald. They were clearly involved in some sort of intelligence operation. But that does not translate into their being involved in the assassination plot. Like many others, such as Marguerite and Robert Oswald, were they unwittingly drawn into a murder plot which they did not expect?

P is for Phillips...CIA mastermind

My opinion is that David Atlee Phillips, acting at the behest of fired CIA director Allen Dulles, planned the assassination scenario and was intimately involved with all phases of implementation. It is my opinion also that his participation began in the late 1940s with the recruitment of young Lee Harvey Oswald to participate in the agency's false defector program. He continued until his death to direct the post-assassination coverup. His agency specialty was—*propaganda*.

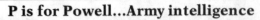

P is for Powell...Army intelligence

Army intelligence officer James Powell was standing at the corner of Elm and Houston taking photographs of the motorcade. He took this photo of the depository immediately after hearing the shots. I have several questions regarding Powell. Was he on assignment there? Was this photo taken to incriminate Oswald? Where are the other slides which he took, and why have they never been made public?

Q is for Questionable Evidence

- There are questionable movies, including Nix and Zapruder.
- There are questionable people, including several Marguerites, two Oswalds, the Paines, and many others.
- There are questionable documents—many fabricated by Hoover's FBI.
- There is questionable testimony and changed testimony.
- There are questionable investigators, including the FBI, Dallas Police, and congressional committees.
- There are questionable investigations, from the Warren Commission to the HSCA.
- And there are questionable conclusions, such as the Single Bullet Theory

So far I have shown you some of the Questionable Evidence. There are many faked photos. ID photos, backyard photos, bullet photos, Russian photos, Marine photos. Beyond question—there are many unanswered questions.

R is for Rickerby...blue sky

Rickerby color pic above is taken from a similar viewpoint as Betzner, but slightly lower. But note in Betzner, at bottom, a large rectangular black shape where blue sky is seen in Rickerby.

Life photographer Art Rickerby took several important Dealey Plaza photos—but this color slide was withheld until recently, when I discovered it on the internet. It is important because it is a clear color shot of the Umbrellaman and Cuban. But it is also important because it shows bright blue sky behind the pergola where Betzner and Nix are blacked-in.

R is for Rickerby...Cuban, Uman

Rickerby took two important photos of the Umbrellaman...but investigators ignored them, even though in the color photo at left the Cuban appears to have a walkie-talkie to his left ear.

Rickerby took these two photos of the Umbrellaman and The Cuban. The color photo seems to show the Cuban with a radio device held to his left ear. Despite these and other photos of this interesting pair, investigators ignored them completely.

R is for Rifle...found in TSBD, no clip

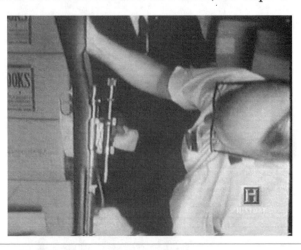

Lt. Carl Day of the DPD is shown removing a Mannlicher-Carcano from under a stack of boxes on the sixth floor of the TSBD. But it was also identified as a Mauser. Still later the Dallas Police and the Warren Commission showed various photos, all said to be the same gun that Day is handling here. Later photos show a clip protruding from the bottom of the rifle. No clip is seen here. No clip was on the evidence list of the Dallas Police. The rifle could not be fired without a clip—so conveniently a clip later shows up.

R is for Rifle...forged serial number

The forged serial number C2766 ...a clumsy FBI mistake.

Wrong serifs on C, 2, and 6.

Position wrong in relation to fixed points on rifle.

Close study of the serial number shows that the same number was photographed on two different guns. One was evidently counterfeited by the FBI, and rather ineptly. The serifs on the "C" and the numbers do not match in the two photos. The spacing does not match. The location related to a fixed point does not match. Why were there two Mannlicher-Carcanos with the same serial number?

R is for Rifles...3 guns said to be same

As shown above, in one of my exhibits prepared for my HSCA testimony, it is clearly seen that at least three different guns appear to have been identified at various times as the same gun. The top rifle D was photographed by the Dallas police. It seems to have a much shorter stock. Middle rifle A was photographed by researcher Fred Newcomb in the National Archives. Bottom rifle W is CE-139 as photographed by the FBI for the Warren Commission. Even though all three guns had the same serial number, it appears that the photos show different guns.

R is for Rifles...connection to LHO?

M-C rifle CE139 is NOT the gun in the backyard photos!

The backyard photos were used by the Warren Commission to connect Oswald to the Mannlicher-Carcano rifle found in the TSBD. But the fabricators of the back-yard fake photos *used a different rifle* than the one from the scene of the crime. This is easy to see because the backyard rifle had *bottom-mounted* sling rings—and CE-139 has *side-mounted* sling rings. So even if LHO owned the gun shown in the backyard photos, it is *not the same gun said to have been used to shoot the president*—therefore the backyard photos are exculpatory—not incriminating! If they faked photos and substituted guns, would they fail to alter the Zfilm?

R is for Robert…and SS mysteryman

In newly discovered photo below, Robert Oswald is escorted from Parkland on 11-24-63 by Mysteryman.

Moments after the shooting in Dealey Plaza on 11-22-63 Mysteryman in hat and dark glasses watches as Charles Brehm tells Jimmy Darnell what he witnessed. The glasses appear to be the same. The nose, mouth, and right ear appear to be the same. The Secret Service had charge of the Oswald family, but there were NO SS men on the ground in Dealey Plaza… or were there? This man's identity MUST be determined.

Recently discovered on the internet is the photo at upper left of Robert Oswald on 24 November being escorted from Parkland Hospital by a Secret Service man in sunglasses and a snapbrim hat. In a well known photo of Charles Brehm in the plaza, the same man is seen standing behind Brehm in the crowd. Only the man's hat is a different style in the two photos. Even the sunglasses appear to be the same. Officially there were no Secret Service men on the ground in Dealey Plaza, so who is this unknown mysteryman?

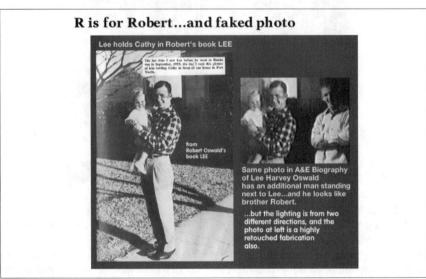

R is for Robert…and faked photo

Lee holds Cathy in Robert's book LEE

The last time I saw Lee before he went to Russia was in September, 1959, the day I took this picture of him holding Cathy in front of our house in Fort Worth.

from Robert Oswald's book LEE

Same photo in A&E Biography of Lee Harvey Oswald has an additional man standing next to Lee…and he looks like brother Robert.

…but the lighting is from two different directions, and the photo at left is a highly retouched fabrication also.

A full-page photo in Robert's book, *Lee,* shows Lee holding Robert's daughter Cathy. The photo is clearly retouched, with the shadows and grass painted in. In a bizarre twist, when the same photo was shown in an A&E documentary, Robert was added into the photo at right. The A&E photo is obviously faked, because the sunlight is from two different directions. There can be no innocent explanation for faking these photos.

R is for Robert...did he know both?

Did Robert and Pic and wives know both Lee and Harvey?

At right is a photo taken by Robert when he took Lee hunting. Above, Thanksgiving at Robert's house. I cropped out all three wives, Marge, Vada and Marina.

Robert's book LEE shows both Harvey and Lee. He had to know both.

I am often asked—"Did Robert Oswald know that there were two Lee Harvey Oswalds?" My answer is *"Yes, he had to know."* In his book, *Lee,* Robert has photos of both of them. At left is the Thanksgiving photo including John Pic and Harvey. At right is Lee, when he and Robert went hunting. Lee and Harvey are *obviously* different persons in these two pictures.

R is for Roscoe...in LHO snapshot

This snapshot allegedly was found among Oswald possessions. At center it seems to show a fellow marine, ROSCOE A. WHITE.

Allegedly found by Dallas police among the possessions of Oswald was this snapshot which apparently shows Roscoe White, who confessed to being part of the JFK assassination plot. The photo is the same format as the Imperial Reflex camera. The other Marines are unidentified, as is the location.

R is for Roscoe...beach photo proof

BEACH PHOTO shows Roscoe second from left.

Comparison with LHO photo shows Roscoe is the same man photographed by LHO.

Roscoe's broad square chin in both photos seems to be the same as seen in backyard photo 133A, only one of the reasons I believe Roscoe posed for the faked photos.

ROSCOE ON BEACH

ROSCOE IN LHO PIC

133A

Roscoe White, who made a deathbed confession of involvement in the assassination, is shown at top with some fellow Marines in swimsuits When Roscoe in that photo is compared with the photo taken by LHO, it is seen that the two men pictured appear to be the same. Not only that, the chin of Roscoe in both photos appears very similar to the chin of Oswald in the backyard photos.

R is for Roscoe...whose chin?

The backyard chin...LHO or Roscoe?

Here is a comparison of photos of Roscoe comparing his chin to Oswald's chin and to the backyard chin. I believe that Roscoe posed for the backyard photos and substituted Oswald's face above the chin. Roscoe was said to be expert in "trick photography". I believe that Roscoe was "placed" within the DPD by the CIA.

Zapruder's companion on the pedestal, Marilyn Sitzman is depicted in many photos wearing a tan dress. However, the Bronson slide shows her in a dark-colored dress with light-colored sleeves. And all images show her at least a foot or more taller than an extremely short Zapruder.

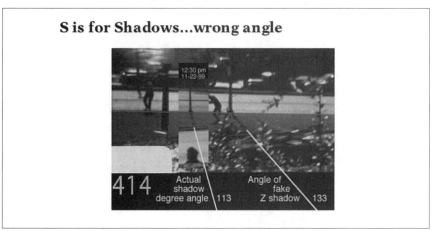

Here is a composite of Zapruder frame 414 with a photo I took at a time calculated to match the sun's position on 22 November at 12:30 pm. The angle of the shadow of the same lamppost shows that the shadow in Zapruder is 20 degrees farther west, as it would have been about 30 minutes earlier. This suggests to me that the faked Zapruder film was based on a reference film taken earlier from the pedestal, before the crowd gathered. An earlier film could have been used as a *guide film* for animators.

S is for Stemmons...smoking gun!

This photo taken from the pedestal by the Dallas police is the smoking gun when it comes to proof that the Z film is fake. It can be shown scientifically that the back view of the Stemmons sign *does not match the Zapruder film*—absolute proof of fakery!

S is for Stemmons...image mismatch

The FBI-210 photo from the pedestal overlaid over composite of DPDeast and White/Costella panorama

DPD Stemmons sign does not match Zapruder or FBI photo

Here is one of my studies comparing the signs. In the background is a composite panorama of the DPD photo overlaid over a present-day color panorama. Overlaid over that is an FBI photo taken from the pedestal—which shows a clear mismatch between the FBI photo and the DPD photo. This mismatch is similar to the Zapruder mismatch.

S is for Stemmons...Zapruder wrong

Here is one of my early studies of the Stemmons sign overlaid over the DPD photo. I sized Zframe 34 to exact scale of the lamppost and the Houston intersection. Then, at the same scale, I overlaid Zframe 194 so that the concrete wall in the background matched. I found that the sign was both too large and not in the correct location. Dr. John Costella has refined and improved on my analysis with great precision. Dr. Costella is an expert in physics and optics, and he considers the sign mismatch the ultimate proof of alteration.

T is for Towner...Cuban walkie-talkie

JIM TOWNER took this important pic which shows the Cuban and umbrellaman. It seems to show the Cuban talking on a walkie-talkie radio.

About 25 years ago I had the opportunity to copy the original Jim Towner slide seen here. One of the things I noticed was that the Cuban is talking on a radio device. On the original, as well as a computer enhancement at bottom, an antenna protrudes behind his head. In 1963, walkie-talkie devices were not commonplace except to the military. Several other images also seem to show the radio device.

U is for Umbrellaman...and his friend

The two mystery men of Dealey Plaza... were officially ignored

The closest spectators to Kennedy when he was shot were two curious men—one holding an open umbrella and the other raising his right fist during the shooting. Instead of running away like most spectators, the two sat down close together. The dark man I call the Cuban is photographed talking on a radio. Other photos show them eventually walking away in opposite directions. It is amazing that official investigations showed no interest in finding and identifying these men.

V is for Van...Altgens vs Zapruder

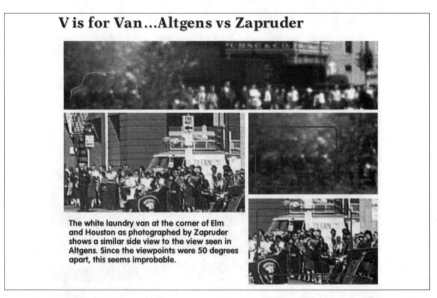

The white laundry van at the corner of Elm and Houston as photographed by Zapruder shows a similar side view to the view seen in Altgens. Since the viewpoints were 50 degrees apart, this seems improbable.

A white laundry van appears parked at the corner of Elm and Houston. Towner, Altgens and other photos show the van. Oddly, it is seen in Zapruder partially obscured by a tree—but it appears to be seen at the same angle as seen in the Altgens photo taken from the Main Street intersection.

W is for Waltz...Zapruder & Sitzman

The Dealey Dance Floor Pedestal and the Six-second Zapuder Waltz

Betzner	Willis	Bronson	Nix	Moorman	Groden
Zap...under 5' Sitz...about 5.5'	just over 5' about 6'	about 5' nearly 6'	just over 5' about 5.5'	5.5' about 6'	

The various images of Zapruder and Sitzman on the pedestal show them drastically moving around and changing sizes and directions. I call this "the Zapruder Waltz." Note that here the pedestals are all sized the same, but the heights of the persons change radically. For comparison 6'2" Robert Groden is on the pedestal at right with a pole marked in feet. These comparisons indicate that most images show Zapruder to be only about five feet tall.

W is for Wiegman...NO Zapruder!

Wiegman shows NOBODY on Zpedestal!

In Wiegman clear frame, one person in dark clothes is on ground. Sitzman, in light clothes, is not seen. This is before limo enters underpass.

NBC photographer Dave Wiegman jumped from the press convertible as soon as he heard the first shot, and started running down Elm Street, his camera rolling. The jerky film has very few clear frames. But one clear frame shows the Zapruder pedestal—*with nobody on it*, though a person seems to be crouching *behind* the pedestal. A few frames later, he captures another clear frame which clearly shows that the limo has not yet reached the underpass. Since the Zfilm shows the limo at this same point, about to enter the underpass, Mr. Z must be on the pedestal still filming—*but the pedestal is empty*!

W is for Whodunnit?...coup command

Dulles
Johnson Nixon Hoover
Phillips Hunt Lansdale Conein
Assorted CIA Assets/Agents
Pentagon/Joint Chiefs
Secret Service   Dallas Police
Others as necessary

So far you have seen lots of faked evidence to cover up the assassination. About this time I usually am asked who was behind it all. I believe the arrogant Allen Dulles presided over the coup. Before proceeding, he had to insure against exposure, so he checked first with those who obviously might search for the plotters—the successor and possible later successor, along with the chief investigator. Dulles then enlisted four of his most trusted colleagues to plan and execute the coup. These four used their vast network of assets to carry it out, including agents, Cubans, informants, Mafia and right-wing fringe elements. One of these assets was Lee Harvey Oswald, who was framed for the crime. The Joint Chiefs of Staff had to be compromised as well as the Secret Service and Dallas Police. There are some indications that George Herbert Walker Bush also may have been involved, especially given his family's close ties to Nixon. The above, in my opinion, is the chain of command of the coup structure.

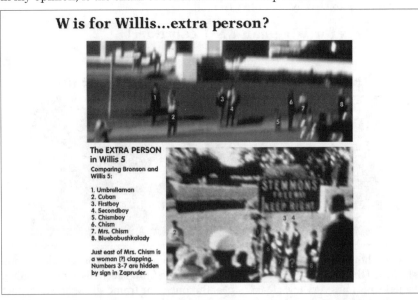

W is for Willis...extra person?

The EXTRA PERSON in Willis 5

Comparing Bronson and Willis 5:

1. Umbrellaman
2. Cuban
3. Firstboy
4. Secondboy
5. Chismboy
6. Chism
7. Mrs. Chism
8. Bluebabushkalady

Just east of Mrs. Chism is a woman (?) clapping. Numbers 3-7 are hidden by sign in Zapruder.

Phil Willis took a series of important slides during the assassination. Some of them seem to be tampered with. The Bronson slide, top, shows the main players along Elm Street. Willis seems to show, just east of Mrs. Chism, a woman who is clapping. She is not seen in Bronson.

X is for X-rays...JFK autopsy fakes

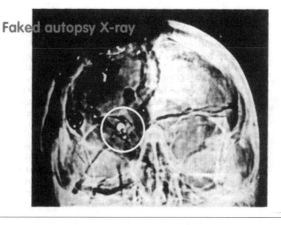

Faked autopsy X-ray

Dr. Mantik has proved with an electronic densitometer that many of the president's autopsy X-rays were altered by darkroom manipulation. Why did someone feel the need to alter this important evidence? Who did the alteration? If the X-rays were altered, why would the Zapruder film be left unaltered?

Y is for Yellow curb stripes...altered

Yellow curb stripes in Elm Kill Zone
The DPD photo above is the only record we have of the Elm yellow curb stripes as they appeared on Nov.22, 1963. After the assassination, these mysterious stripes were repainted nearly twice the length, apparently to confuse comparisons with later photos, such as left (compare red line with yellow).

On 22 November 1963, several freshly painted yellow curb stripes were photographed on the south curb of Elm Street. At least two of these stripes appear in Zapruder frames. The photograph above was taken by the Dallas Police Department Monday after the assassination and shows the stripes were about two feet long. The color photo was taken in the 1990s, showing the stripes had been lengthened to about 40 inches. The purpose of these stripes is unknown—but what *is* known is that after the assassination, the stripes were lengthened, perhaps to frustrate efforts to replicate photographs. These stripes appear to have beem originally painted by the assassination team and later were repainted as part of the cover up.

Y is for Yellow paint on Oliver shoes

the yellow paint on Bev's shoes.

Beverly Oliver, who had been shooting movies near the south curb, later noticed that she had stepped in yellow paint that day. It was all over the soles of her shoes. She tried to get the paint off, but could not get it all off. She put the shoes away with some paint still on them, and never wore the shoes again. The shoes are identical to the ones here.

Later on 22 November, Beverly noticed that the shoes she had worn that day had yellow paint all over the soles. She had stepped in some wet yellow paint. She tried to get the paint off, but could not. The shoes, which she still has, are identical to those in this photo of her. The paint color is identical to the yellow paint on the south curb of Elm.

Z is for Zapruder...my conclusions:

1. Did not take extant film
2. Did not fake extant film
3. Was an intelligence asset
4. Was unwitting participant
5. Was an opportunist
6. His $25,000 lie
7. His $16,000,000 leverage
8. The "Zapruder film" a fraud

Despite the fame of his film, Abraham Zapruder's exact role in the assassination is still quite a mystery. The Dallas dress manufacturer burst on the scene the afternoon of the assassination being interviewed by Jay Watson at WFAA-TV. He claimed to have shot an 8mm movie film of the assassination and wanted to get it developed. Thereafter, two stories began to emerge—the official version and the version uncovered by researchers. You know the official story. Kodak developed the film, Jamieson made 3 copies, Dan Rather viewed the movie, and *Life Magazine* bought all rights to the film for $25,000, which Zapruder gave to charity. The film was then locked away for many years.

But researchers over the years developed a version full of mystery and at odds with the official story. Zapruder was a member of the Dallas White Russian community and had possible ties to intelligence, Lyndon Johnson, H. L. Hunt, Gordon McClendon and Jack Ruby—a suspicious background for a man who just "happened" to shoot the most famous film of the assassination. Let's look beyond the mystery.

I believe that Zapruder could not have taken the extant film, as I have demonstrated. The Bronson slide alone shows he was not able to photograph the limousine from the pedestal, because Sitzman was blocking his view of Elm Street. There are many other proofs.

Zapruder was a dress manufacturer. He was not a photographer. He could not have faked the film. So where did the fake film come from?

Researchers over the years have developed indications that Zapruder likely was an asset of an intelligence agency. As a member of the White Russian community and an acquaintance of George DeMohrenschildt, he had ties to many players in the assassination. As a member of the Jewish community, he was acquainted with Jack Ruby. Ruby's Carousel janitor, who testified to the Warren Commission, was a former employee of Zapruder. DeMohrenshildt's wife Jeanne LeGon was employed by Zapruder as a dress designer.

I do not think Zapruder was a part of the plot to kill the president. I do not think he knew that JFK would be killed. I do think he was persuaded to be in Dealey Plaza with his camera by an intelligence agency which was planning to film the assassination and needed an *amateur photographer* willing to claim he took the movie, if necessary. I think Zapruder did shoot film that day—*but not the existing Zapruder film.* Here are my opinions.

Abe was a shrewd businessman. He had been handed authorship of the most famous film in history, whether or not he shot it. The first thing he did was consult his attorney and draft legal papers. Then he went through the official motions he had been assigned, getting the film developed and establishing himself as the photographer. But he also realized he had been *set up* to be an unwitting accomplice to the killing of the president, so he had to be careful.

He set about *getting rid of the film.* Perhaps part of his assignment was to sell it to *Life* magazine. Perhaps part of his assignment was to show it to Dan Rather of CBS, who apparently saw a different version than the extant film. Zapruder claimed untruthfully that *Life* paid him only $25,000, which he donated to charity. In actuality, his contract with *Life* was for $150,000 plus one half of all future world-wide rights, making him a wealthy man. But Zapruder could not shake the nightmares of his unwitting participation in the president's murder. So I believe that he set about to protect himself and his heirs.

I believe that Zapruder stashed away with persons unknown *materials known only to himself* as protection and leverage. What this might be is not known, but we can speculate. Perhaps it was *the film he really shot*, before editing and alteration. Perhaps it was footage edited out of the film. Perhaps it detailed who asked him to be a decoy photographer. It was perfect material for blackmail.

I speculate that whatever it was that he stashed away enabled these persons unknown at an appropriate time *to apply Zapruder's secret leverage and get* $16,000,000 *from the government* for the tiny strip of film *which they never actually possessed* while retaining all the copyright income potential.

I believe there is no doubt that the so-called Zapruder film is a fake. I believe that Zapruder himself knew it, and protected himself from involvement in the plot by keeping certain unknown secret materials which were later used to obtain $16,000,000 from the government for the fraudulent film.

I have shown you many proofs that the extant Zapruder film is not a genuine depiction of what happened on 22 November 1963. If the Zapruder film is not genuine, a very powerful force produced the fake film. What entity is that powerful?

Just think about it. Someone murdered President Kennedy on Elm Street in 1963. Forty years later it is clear that the official story of a lone assassin is untrue. I have shown you much JFK evidence which was provably altered or counterfeited to support the official story. It is clear that an intelligence agency asset known as Oswald was framed for the crime of which he was only a fringe player.

Think about it:

—If someone was brazen enough to execute the president on a public street

—If someone was heartless enough to frame an innocent man for murder

—If someone was cruel enough to kill a policeman as part of the plot

—If someone was confident enough to fabricate evidence against the patsy

—If someone was powerful enough to continue the coverup for forty years

Then why would they hesitate to fabricate the Zapruder film?

Jack White
presenting at the
Zapruder Film Symposium,
Duluth, Minnesota
10 May 2003

Part II

Technical Aspects of
Film Alteration

David Healy

[*Editor's note*: The first to hear the news of the assassination in Saigon, where he was stationed with the US Army Military Advisory Group, David Healy has spent more than thirty years in video and film production and post production. The film "feels wrong" to him, which has led him to consider the question of whether it could have been edited with the technology and expertise available in 1963. John Costella, who has now emerged as the leading authority on the film, describes Healy's presentation as the most important to be given during the Zapruder Film Symposium held in Duluth on 9–11 May 2003.]

Over the past six months or so, I have designed graphics to look into the question, "*If the Zapruder film has been altered, how was it done*? Were the technology and operators that would have been required available at the time?"

For the purpose of orienting my discussion, consider the following image of an optical printer, which has considerable detail. My hope is that novices to film processing and optical printing equipment amongst us will be able to grasp what in fact (I believe) was done to the JFK-assassination camera-original film. [*Editor's note*: See also the color-photo section.]

Film traveling mattes and counter-mattes can be a confusing issue, which means that my challenge is to show the process in plain old *English* rather than the kind of doublespeak that surrounds "the Zapruder film" and how it appears to have been done.

It's my opinion that we will *never* know the historical fate of the Zapruder 8mm camera original (double 8mm-split) film, where by "*the*" camera original, I thereby encompass Zapruder's and *others* that may have been taken at the time! I suspect that Zapruder's original never got out of Dallas. [*Editor's note*: Homer McMahon's experience at the NPIC establishes that at least one film of the assassination made it across country that night, whether or not it was Zapruder's.] Then again it could be in a thousand fragments at the bottom of a landfill somewhere in Southern California.

An optical-printer operator's job description

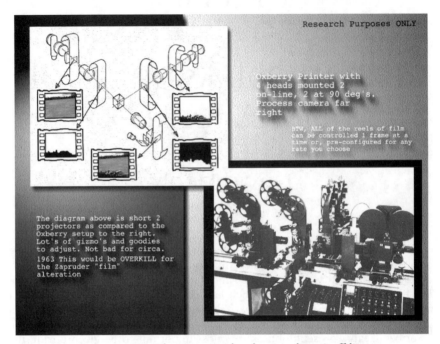

Oxberry 1200 Film Printer, 4 heads - 2 in-line, 2 off-line
set at 90° with aerial image optics (circa 1964)

The job requirements for a "Film Optical Printer Technician" are relevant here. I ran across this job description on a website dealing with post-production issues in the commercial film industry. Various forms of this photographic craft have been around, by the way, since the 1890s.

So we're *not* talking rocket science here. Nevertheless, it can be a confusing medium, precisely because there are so many different ways to arrive at the same film *product*. Here is that job description:

1. Sets up and operates optical printers and related equipment to produce fades, dissolves, superimpositions, and other optical effects required in motion pictures, applying knowledge of optical effects printing and photography:

2. Reads work order and count sheet to ascertain optical effects specifications and location of subject material on original photography film.

3. Analyzes specifications to determine work procedures, sequence of operations, and machine setup, using knowledge of optical effects techniques and procedures.

4. Loads camera of optical effects printer with magazine of unexposed film stock. Mounts original photography film in transport and masking mechanism of optical-printer projector and moves film into designated position for optical effect, using counter and film markings to determine placement.

5. Adjusts camera position, lens position, mask opening, lens aperture, focus, shutter angle, film transport speed, and related controls, using precision measuring instruments and knowledge of optical effects techniques to determine settings.

6. Selects designated color and neutral density filters and mounts in filter holder to control light and intensity.

7. Sets controls in automatic or manual mode, moves control to start camera, and observes printer operation and footage counter during filming.

8. Adjusts controls during filming operation when operating in manual mode, and stops camera when designated counter reading is observed.

9. Moves controls to rewind camera film and original photography film and repeats select portions or entire operation number of times necessary to produce designated effect. Sets up and operates animation and matte cameras and related equipment to photograph artwork, such as titles and painted mattes.

10. Sets up and operates single pass optical printers when enlarging or reducing film or performing related operations.

11. Sets up and operates subtitle camera and related equipment to photograph film subtitles.

12. Examines frames of film exposed with different combinations of color filters (wedges) to select optimum color balance based on experience and judgment.

Considerations of this kind are preliminary to and even presupposed by the desire to know which frames in Zapruder were altered, around what date, and by which means (in relation to different processes). [*Editor's note*: John Costella has proven why the whole film has to be a fabrication, given that the ghost images link each frame with its predecessor and successor frames. Which raises the possibility that the known "splices" were introduced to create breaks in the ghost images that did not have to be explained.]

An old hand in the TV and film industry

It may be useful to offer some background about myself. I'm one of those who has been there/done that with television for more than thirty years. The first camera I used in TV work that didn't roll around on a ton and a half pedestal was the CP-16 16mm film camera used for shooting news when I was at an ABC "O and O" station.

I have operated virtually *every* handheld camera made for the broadcast industry at one time or another since then, up to and including today's Panasonic and Sony's new 16:9 High Definition hand-held camera systems. I was an FCC licensed broadcast engineer for 15 years (after three license renewals, I didn't bother anymore). I could field strip any camera, handheld or studio-head, repair it and have it up and running again in a few hours, provided I had access to the manuals, scopes and spare parts.

My first film edit was on a Moviola Flatbed in 1967 and my first electronic edit was in 1968 on two Ampex 1200's running 2" videotape with Editec function (more commonly known then as "Punch On" crunch editing). And I have been editing ever since. When I wasn't engaged in editing over the next 15 years, I was shooting tape or film for all three national networks and a few television stations in the 5th rated market place in the country.

Getting the news-camera bug out of my system, in 1982 I began doing programming for myself instead of depending upon others. I also engineered, designed and built two television production studios, engineered, designed, and built two editing facilities, and field tested ENG news camera packages for a camera manufacturer.

You couldn't buy American then. RCA had abandoned the business, but their old TK-76 3 tube Plum-i-con was a great handheld camera—they sold a ton of them. During the past 18+ years, I've produced, directed, edited, and operated camera on more than 300 pieces for various clients (companies, corporations, and or governmental agencies, including NASA).

For 13 years, my specialty has been video post production for Silicon Valley high tech corporations and a few other Fortune 500 companies (but not their ad agencies) with heavy emphasis on using a film/video/digital media *compositing* program called "Adobe After Effects", a program which, with it's current widespread usage, has probably put most of the film industry's high-end optical printing houses out of business.

So do I know a little about this industry? Yes. Can I draw parallels between how things were done in the film optical business of 1961–64 and video composing post-production today? Yes, I can.

My interest in the JFK assassination

My father was a union president in Boston, MA, for many years, In fact, that's where I was born. He knew JFK personally and campaigned for him during his statewide elections. My father was invited to his Presidential inauguration.

I was in the US Army and served from 2/63 thru 2/64 with the Military Assistance Advisory Group (MAAG/Vietnam). It was my Commander-in-Chief who was murdered in Dallas in November 1963.

My interest in this has endured for some time now. I first saw the Zapruder film around the Geraldo showing in 1975. It was a bootleg copy that some cameraman had come across. The first time I saw it, perhaps five or six other television cameramen were with me and, to a man, we felt it was very peculiar.

Every man in the room had combat-zone camera experience and their comments can be summed up as follows: either Zapruder knew what was coming down or he was stone-cold deaf. Anyone who was unaware of what was about to transpire and was forward of any muzzle blast—especially within 50 feet to his rear, as he reported—would have been off that pedestal in a flash.

My knee-jerk summation of the Zapruder film? JFK had to have been shot by more than one rifle and from more than one direction—possibly three directions, but certainly at least two. I don't give much credence to the so-called *jet effect*. [*Editor's note*: See the study of the "jet effect" by Ronald F. White, Ph.D., in *Assassination Science* (1998).]

My more considered opinion? At least two guns from the rear, where, at my gut level, I surmise two from the right rear and one from the front, probably as an insurance policy (from the limo driver's front-facing perspective). [*Editor's note*: For further discussion of the number of shooters and shots, see the Prologue.]

Some problems with the standard chronology

The final uptake: while Zapruder has it in the can—the film as it sits in the camera, before it gets to Kodak in Dallas—is the last time we can know for sure that it's in its original state. All bets are off once that film enters Kodak .

We're told Kodak can't do the optical prints. Fine. Jamieson Film Company can do them. That's the first *red* flag for me: Kodak doesn't have any Double 8mm *print* stock available! Now let me get this straight: Kodak only sells film and film processing, that's their corporate mission, their lifeblood even. And no print film is available for the film of the *century*?

A question that may provoke a little interest is why camera-original film was used for the Zapruder optical prints. Could bumping from 8mm to 16mm produce a lot better film if it's coming off of Kodacolor camera stock? Of course, it would!

And, by the way, over the years we've been told about emulsion side-out stuff regarding the Zapruder film: you can't this, you can't that . . . ! Maybe one of these photo experts on the non-alterationist side of the aisle would provide me with the proper definition of bipack film printing, which is more commonly called "emulsion to emulsion" printing.

One could make *any* camera original duplicate in a bipack setup look exactly like the original—with the emulsion side out for the edge numbers. I hope this doesn't come as too much of a shock, but some film is manufactured *without* edge #s and footage-count indications.

It's back and forth between Jamieson and Kodak and eventually we end up with three *unsplit* Double 8mm optical prints on Kodak Double 8mm camera stock. Let's stop right here. A conspiracy may be unfolding, but I think it starts in earnest here. Imagine what one extra (4 total) Double 8mm Unsplit optical print from Jamieson would do to the official equation. The Secret Service gets its two copies, *Life* gets its plus the camera original; everyone is making copies and making stills off of 8mm frame blowups; the NPIC is looking over the film for Soviet involvement; everyone in Washington has a lupe in their hand checking for this and checking for that!

Of course this is making any film alteration timetable look horrible, because there's no time for this and no time for that: officially, all copies are accounted for—which, in my opinion, is an unwise conclusion. [*Editor's note*: See a chronology of the film recording (more or less) its official history in Appendix D.]

Maybe Richard Stolley of *Life* never got the camera original. Maybe he got a camera stock optical print: how would he know the difference? Maybe he did, but that's beside the point, which is the possibility that the Zapruder camera original never left Dallas, even to this day! [*Editor's note*: The evidence weighs in favor of copies of films of the assassination having made their way out of Dallas, as the Prologue explains.] But, either way, the official story of four Double 8mm optical prints and the camera original can still be disseminated. Nothing has to change as we know the story up until today.

Just give me four matte artists, two optical-printer journeymen, one effects director, some 8mm Kodacolor camera stock, 16mm and 35mm camera *and* print stock, one 4-projector head optical/aerial printer with bi-pack option, one Step Printer for making travelling mattes and then you can swing by in fourteen days and pick up your order. *Then what?*

Well, it's Christmas season. You just have to make four deliveries to exchange the two Secret Service copies and *Life's* Unsplit version (that undoubtedly has already been split) and the first-day issue *Life* "camera-original". You may say, "Somebody's going to know!" *Life* published a few frames, but so what? The few who saw the 8mm film only remember Kennedy's brains on the street—whether it was at frame 313 or at 613 with a stopped limo or not, they could care less.

The perpetrator was caught within 12 hours, was dead within 48 hours, and the goverment has the film! It's over and done with. Except find a hiding place for a couple of *extra* copies of the altered Zapruder film, then *burn* the *actual* camera original. [*Editor's note*: Which scenario for creating the fake was employed does not matter as much as that several alternatives were available.]

As evidence in a muder trial for the conspirators, the authentic original film from Dealey Plaza could and most probably would have meant execution, where, in its absence, the matter is open to speculation. In my estimation, there'll never be closure regarding this murder, not even with a confession, because the Zapruder camera original *never* left Dallas and was destroyed nearly forty years ago.

How was the film edited?

Why edit it? A simple question, isn't it? *Why?* It wasn't that someone wanted to cover up the deed itself; hell, it was done in front of *God and everyone*. It might be something as simple and obvious as editing out incriminating scenes and frames.

Was the film altered (#1)?

Yes! Why? Possibly to remove any indication that the Secret Service as an *agency* had anything to do with any assassination plot. It's my firm belief that the SS did *not* plot and/or plan this crime, but may have been lax and screwed up their job that day.

I think that the SS as an agency did *not* conspire to murder the President. Quite frankly, I think it (as an agency) was as much a victim of this murder as were we the citizens of the USA. But as individuals? There may have been an agent or two who could have been persuaded to join a group that planned to ouster the President. [*Editor's note*: See Vince Palamara's chapter on the Secret Service in *Murder in Dealey Plaza* (2000).] So what was removed?

A. The limo left turn problems: probably 100-140 frames.

B. The limo stop (momentarily or extended): 10-40 frames.

What're the totals? Say, six seconds to eight seconds of material, out immediately before any other considerations are made. No big deal, easily accomplished, take about an hour; but what's the rush? The only thing we need here, if an alteration is under way, is a frame count and that is very easy to provide.

Was the film altered (#2)?

To create a lone-nut killer! Why? We really don't need an assassination conspiracy at this time to go along with all the other problems we have on an international scale (Communism in general; Moscow in particular; Castro in Havana specifically). So remove any frames that show indications of another discharged weapon in the plaza. So what was removed?

A. These frames could be found in the *limo stop* extracted frames above.

Was the film altered (#3)?

To prove the lone nut scenario! How? First, any indication that might prove the film was altered during "kill zone" frames had to be eliminated. (Think about it: what had to be eliminated? Anything that did not move in the "background layer" of the limo in direct photo coverage of Zapruder's lens.) From the Zapruder camera's point of view (POV), what wasn't moving can be converted into a point of reference. The traffic on the other side of the lawn, for example, wasn't moving.

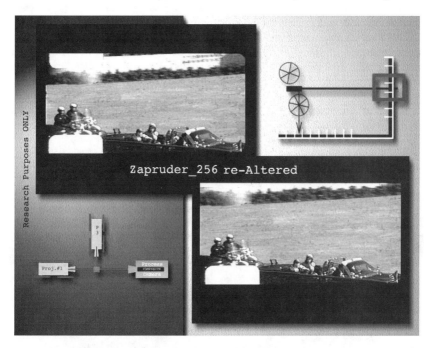

Zapruder frame #256 original (left) same frame background
enlarged/foreground no change (right)

The image above on the left is a reconstituted Z-256. As you can see, when it comes to optical printing *nothing* is sacred and that certainly includes sprocket hole areas.

The left side image is in four elements—background and foreground and two mattes (male and female or matte/counter-matte). It appears normal with the exception of cleaning up the lawn! Look at the image on the same image on the right and you'll notice the background area has become smaller.

"How would you do that on a optical printer?", you might ask. It's very simple, actually. The projector that has the background loaded is moved in just a little, nothing else: just slide it in on it's guide rails, and it's done!

Move projector #1 to the right and the background gets bigger; back to the left, it gets smaller. It can be done automatically over any number of frames you want in real-time or the operator can control it, one frame at a time. You might ask, "How do they get this stuff lined up?" That's simple, too.

There's a viewfinder at the side of the process camera just beside the shutter gate that shows all the elements in composite form (put together to create a single image, i.e., one full frame such as you see in this graphic). The viewfinder is at the far right (follow the line from "Proj#1" to the "Process Camera").

A test for those interested in Z-250, 251, and 252: put all three in sequential order (one on top of the other); then rotate through them as quickly as you can (maybe 4 or 5 cycles), paying particular attention to the left side of the frame and noticing the rear of the limo as it rotates about 5 degrees around the y-axis; in other words, it swings a bit to the right-center.

This may be an entry point for a optical effect that is coming, namely: enlarging the grassy area for whatever reason was deemed important. What amazes me is this is 2nd year film school stuff! There are plenty of so-called "experts" on the other side of the fence who should know better than to suggest this stuff can't be done!

You may also want to check out Raymond Fielding, *The Technique of Special Effects Cinematography* (1965). It's not at your typical bookstore, but you'll probably find it at your neighborhood University Library. [*Editor's note*: David W. Mantik has a copy, to which he has made reference in both of his chapters in *Assassination Science* (1998).]

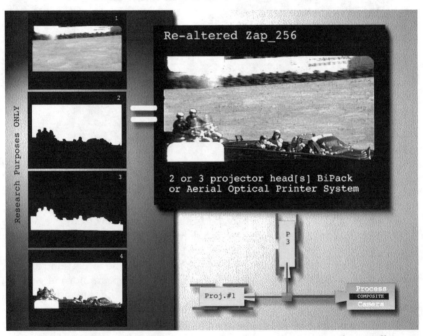

Matte elements on left with composed make-up image on right, in effect separating foreground from background (composed image on the right)

Primary elements (mattes left and background right)

Primary elements in combined form

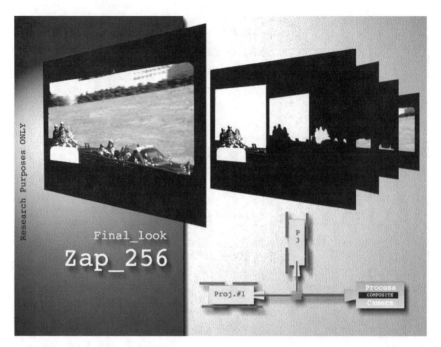

Another view of matte elements (image on left side is final composed image)

The elements on the left make up the image on the right! Use 2 laced up bi-pack heads and there it is! Add another projector head and we'll have enough to do some blood spray and a skull flap! Not all of the 486 frames of the Zapruder film have to be altered to get the desired effect, of course.

And that effect, in my opinion, was to cover up a massive exit wound at the rear of JFK's head. A best case scenario: 120 frames needed changing (not including excised frames, which, by the way, is easier to accomplish than enlarging the background area of Z-256, simply being done using a step printer. [*Editor's note*: As John Costella obseres in his chapter on the film, simple frame excision could have been used for films to be projected on Saturday, 23 November 1963, with travelling mates and other effects used to create the final published frames.]

I now understand why Oliver Stone is so vilified by the lone-nutter camp; he knows how simple it would have been! It's really no more complicated than that.

This is the last we'll see of Z-256 for awhile. The main idea here is to display four separate film elements (notice I'm not using the term "8mm" here; I'll deal with that later) combined to make a composite image. Shortly, I'll be displaying six elements.

Next, the primary graphics are completed for images producing 8mm, Double 8mm Split, and 16mm definitions. I'll follow the processing trail of the Zapruder Film in Dallas that day. This isn't going to be minute by minute account. It'll be general so that novices like myself can really get a handle on the film's chain of events immediately after the shooting.

I'll be expressing personal opinions and raising issues that deal with the Zavada Report as well. [*Editor's note*: He refers to Rollie Zavada, a retired Kodak expert consulted by the ARRB in the process of obtaining the film as an official "assassination record". See Appendix B.]

After the processing trail and film definitions are completed, I'll then attempt to take some of the voodoo out of film editing and printing. I'm sure there are many readers who already understand how this is done, but this is for those among the uninitiated.

Developing the film

Let's assume: the deed in Dallas has been done, history has been made; now we have to develop that history. Zapruder's camera is on the left (the picture is from NARA). [Editor's note: For more on the camera, see Appendix B.]

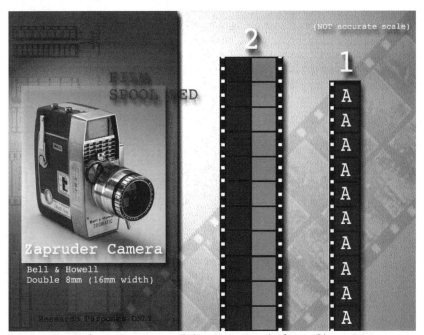

Zapruder 8mm camera (left), #1 8mm split frame film strip,
#2 double 8mm non-split film strip

No. 1 is a depiction of standard 8mm film, where the standard roll is 50' long and lives on a spool. In general, you would have to load the film in a dark area and correctly thread the film up, although on some camera makes and models this is an automatic threading process.

Can things can go wrong? Yes, most certainly, they can and do; but after you do this a few times, it does get easier. When you are finished shooting the 50' of film, it's back to a darkroom or other dark place—possibly even a camera bag— to remove the exposed film and send it for processing.

No. 2 is a bit more confusing. In its final form, it will be two strips of 8mm film, but as the depiction shows, it's shown in its original Double 8mm (16mm) Unsplit configuration. What's Double 8mm (16mm)? It's actually the same kind of film but with a twist.

See the top frame in #1, with an "A" in it? That's a single frame of 8mm film, where its entire frame width is 8mm. In number #2, look at the top darker and lighter frame. These two 8mm frames, side-by-side, represent a total of 16mm size in width. Because you have two 8mm frames side by side, it's called *"Double"* 8mm. Because the total width measures out to 16mm, that's where the film description *"Double* 8mm Unsplit (16mm)" originates.

The Double 8mm film in the magazine is 25' long (plus a few extra). When the 25' has been exposed, you pop out the magazine, turn it over, put it back in, windup and shoot for another 25'. When that's done, you pop the magazine out and send the film magazine to the processor. Bingo! No more need for dark and dirty places to load film.

Now I'll deal with film processing in Dallas, where the "split" angle will be defined and start down the road on how a Double 8mm Unsplit film of this kind physically became the infamous 8mm Zapruder film. [*Editor's note*: assuming, of course, that there was such a film taken by Zapruder, a matter discussed by John Costella in a later chapter.]

Processing the film

Zapruder camera original film Kodak-processed (Dallas, Texas) number #0183 double 8mm non-split film

After the assassination, it appears Zapruder used some common sense by leaving the film in the camera. When Zapruder and associates showed up at the front door of Kodak in Dallas, Phil Chamberlin and Richard Blair (both of Dallas-Kodak) maintain that that was when the film was removed from the camera. I shall assume here it was *still* in its Double 8mm Unsplit format, since, based upon what I have read, it *was*.

The film was then processed (developed) at Kodak-Dallas in its Double 8mm (16mm width) configuration. Of course, all interested parties waited around: none of this, "Drop it off and we'll call you when it's ready!" stuff. The developed Zapruder Double 8mm filmstrip was given Kodak perforation ID #0183, where the perforation number may be found at the head end of the film.

Zapruder also wanted 3 copies (but at whose request?–which raises interesting questions) in Double 8mm (16mm width) configuration and was told by Chamberlin, "Nope, not here! It'll have to go to Kodak-Rochester, NY." No one was going to stand for that, so Pat Pattist of Kodak-Dallas contacted Jamieson Film Company of Dallas and made arrangements for Jamieson to make three copies of Zapruder Double 8mm Unsplit.

(I want to explain something here. Making copies of a motion picture film, in its purest form, means one thing and one thing only: optical printing! It doesn't matter how many copies—they are optically printed one at a time, in this case using the Camera Original Double 8mm Unsplit (16mm width) as the "non-destructive" Optical Print.)

Bell & Howell camera (left frame) and camera original film (#0183) with three optical film prints with Kodak control numbers assigned

Jamieson Film Company agreed to do the deed. It had handy a 2-or-3 Optical Printer (one of which is presented in the graphics above) with a 16mm width gate assembly for the Zapruder Double 8mm Split 16mm. So, all of this can be done right here in Dallas.

And they did. Dallas-Kodak's Richard Blair provided Zapruder with three rolls of Kodacolor II Type A camera original film to be used for print stock. [*Editor's note*: and possibly even more.]

So now the Zapruder camera original is in the hands of Jamieson Film Company in Dallas. The company does not exist today, by the way, though it did at least up until 1998.

Well, now everyone is there at Jamieson Film Company in Dallas. The whole group of them—all these people. I know, I know, it's the chain of evidence stuff. (It is amazing how seriously they took the film. It would have been nice if the authorities had taken the same care with the other evidence!)

The Double 8mm Unsplit processed Zapruder Film Kodak perf. #0183 has arrived at Jamieson. Three prints were then struck but *not* processed at Jamieson, which raises several important questions in my mind:

1) Why only three (3) copies? Why not five, six, a dozen? Are not more even better?

2) They are numbered #0183, #0185, #0186, and #0187. So what happened to #0184?

I understand Kodak-Dallas did free processing for any assassination related photos that day and perhaps thereafter. So, if the perf. #1084 was assigned to someone else's film, who was it and what film? [*Editor's note*: As the Preface notes, David Healy has suggested that #0184 may have been flown back to Rochester en route to the NPIC.]

Well, it's time for the parade to move back to Kodak-Dallas for processing the three optical prints of the Zapruder Double 8mm Unsplit 16mm width camera original. The unprocessed prints are processed and assigned perforation numbers #0185, #0186, and # 0187. I have heard, but been unable to confirm, that an affidavit exits somewhere about alleged problems with one of these numbers, which, I believe, was #0187. [*Editor's note*: Getting something like this into the record may have been a way to obfuscate the existence of #1084 by creating a certain degree of ambiguity.]

At this time, the Zapruder Double 8mm film and the Double 8mm 16mm width prints were compared and declared to be "close enough for government work," as the phrase has it. Now we're going to SPLIT the Double 8mm_Split 16mm width camera original. [*Editor's note*: See the Twyman chronology concerning their "official" distribution.]

For old time argument's sake, I posit that four (4) optical prints were struck at Jamieson Film Company. [*Editor's note:* By the way, where was Abraham Zapruder during this time? Maybe at the television station? Should he not have been protecting his film?]

Incidentally, Zavada's report also reports—after further conversation with Jamieson Film Company—that the 3 optical prints of Zapruder's Double 8mm Unsplit 16mm width were not actually created on Jamieson's 3-head optical printer, but were in fact created on Jamieson's Bell & Howell Model J optical printer. How many people know Bell & Howell got an Academy Award for technical achievement in the creation of a *color* optical printer for the film industry in 1962?

I understand from Jim Fetzer that Roland Zavada is not supportive of Zapruder film alteration based upon assumptions he has made about editing time factors and such. Nor, I understand, is Mr. Jamieson. [*Editor's note*: Zavada's position appears to be based upon assumptions regarding the time line that are not embraced by the contributors to this book.]

Zapruder "Unsplit" double 8mm film on the left,
same film "split and spliced" on the right

To resume, we are back at Kodak-Dallas just a couple of hours after the assassination has gone down. Optical prints have been made and processed. None has yet been split. The Secret Service has blessed the prints as copies that are good enough for their purposes, both as evidence for their assassination investigation and for making futher copies on their own, which means at least one of their copies will have to be split at some time. So what's left to be done about this film business at Kodak-Dallas? Well, let's *split* Zapruder's film.

It's done! I think the accompanying graphic is all of the technical explanation anyone need to understand the results of splitting the Double 8mm film. But I would add just a few notes. Side A of the Zapruder film is what could be classified as "around the home filming".

There are a few affidavits or film content notes around regarding just what is on this A-side of the Double 8mm Split film, but to the best of my knowledge no one has recently seen that footage nor all of the footage that comes before the assassination footage on Side B, which may be more than we think. 50 feet of the most viewed film footage in the history of film and nobody gives a damn what's on half of it! Incredible!

Let's recapitulate the official depiction of the situation in Dallas on 22 November 1963:

(a) Zapruder inadvertently films the assassination of the 35th President of the United States;

(b) Zapruder and film go to Kodak-Dallas; the camera-original film is assigned perf. #0183

(c) Zapruder and film then go to Jamieson Film Company; three optical prints are struck;

(d) Zapruder and film and Optical prints return to Kodak-Dallas, where the optical prints are assigned perf. #0185, perf. #0186, and perf. #0187 (all in the time span of a few hours).

So we are left with some tantalizing questions about the distribution of the prints:

(1) who has perf. #0185?

(2) who has perf. #0187?

(3) what is and who has perf. #0184?

where the third of these questions may easily be the most important among them.

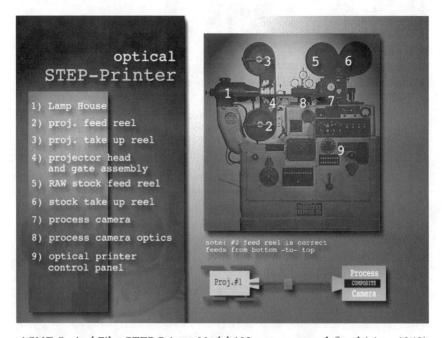

ACME Optical Film STEP Printer-Model 103 components defined (circa 1960)

That about rounds this out. Now I'll turn to the simple and not so simple optical film printing stuff and how basic printers work. Forget all the esoteric nonsense and voodoo about film printing. You only have to remember one thing, namely: One (1) film projector (transmitting) is aimed (by various means) into another film camera (receiving), where the receiving camera is commonly called a "process camera". And I'll make a few comparisons with your home VHS deck and camera along the way.

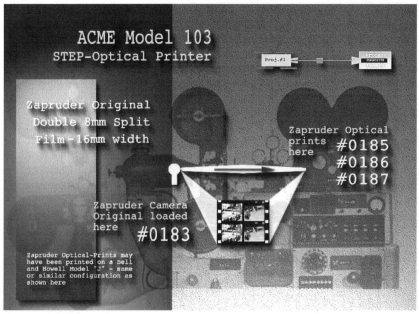

Sample: print process creation of the three Zapruder optical prints

So, where are we?

Out of the gate, so-to-speak! Film editing has been around virtually since the first picture was taken. (It seems as though we can't stand real images. We simply have to change them to make them more palatable—perhaps as our own creations—for whatever reason.) But something I'm not going to do here is to provide a history of film editing. Libraries have been written about the craft.

As you can tell by now, I'm not a writer. Videotape production is my game, with lots of 2D and 3D computer-generated graphics and lots of editing. Things have changed quite a bit over 30 years in going from16mm/35mm film to 2 inch reel-to-reel videotape, 1 inch reel-to-reel videotape, then to 3/4 inch, and on to 3/4 inch SP cassette videotape, then to 1/2 Beta and Beta SP cassette tape, and now DVCams, DVT and Mini-DV (about 1/8th of an inch) digital videotape cassette tapes.

The acquiring media may change over the years but techniques stay the same. The game of editing is all about taking information from one media source and transferring it to another similar source or a different source, via light/optics, BNC cables—NTSC video RF cables, SCSI cables and finally Firewire cables. All these cables and such are doing only one thing, namely: providing a conduit for transferring information in a non-destructive editing mode, from one source (playback machine) to another source (recording machine).

An example of non-destructive editing

What's "non-destructive" editing? Here's an example. Your are on a family outing at the park and you have your mini-DV VHS camera with you and are taking some pictures of the kids doing their thing. When you got to the park, you noticed that the tape in the camera had about 15 minutes of footage recorded on it already. It's a 60 minute tape, so you have 45 minutes to play with.

You've been recording for about 10 minutes and suddenly a fire alarm goes off. The park office is on fire. You look after the safety of your family then go tape (record) some of the fire. Fire trucks show up, you got some of that; ambulances take away the injured, you got some of that, too; people told you what they saw, you got some of that; and so on and so forth.

The event is over. Finally, the TV news ENG remote truck arrives. It's too late, the fire is out! Then someone tells them you have a lot of tape of the fire and surrounding events. You have something they'll never get and they need it! You've got it. So they make an offer to buy and you agree to sell. You name a price and they agree, with the condition you will get your tape back in the same shape you gave it to them in. They guarantee it.

Here's what *they* do. Your VHS tape is taken to the studio and inserted into a VHS deck for playback. The VHS video/audio output ports are connected via cable to the BetaSP video/audio input ports. They load the tape up in a VHS deck, fast forward to where the fire footage starts (15:00 minutes from the head of the reel), put the deck in pause, set up a record BetaSP deck, put a videotape in the deck, hit play, record and pause. Then hit pause again on *both* decks and watch the transfer till completion.

They will edit this later to conform to the story as related on the newscast. In short, a non-destructive transfer/edit of electronic data from one videotape to another via a simple cable hook-up has been performed, which, I might add, is from one videotape format to another (VHS to BetaSP).

So, who got what? TV Station got an exact duplicate of what you shot for the six o'clock news. You got a few bucks and your tape back with all of the footage intact, *exactly* as you gave it to them. Facts being what they are, you can't even tell that they *used* your videotape, because there are *no signs* and *no clues*.

If this were film, we have just witnessed an optical print being struck (made or created). In the video trade, it's called making a "dub".

Now, for the *real* reason we are here. Let's say you were using an 8mm camera instead of the videocamera while at the park with the family. (They hold seconds of unexposed film as compared to tens of minutes of re-usable videotape stock.) You were lucky because, in this instance, you got the most exciting 10–15 seconds of footage during the fire—so lucky in fact the TV station wants it really bad.

Well, you have to get the film developed (it's Double 8mm Unsplit) and then processed and *then* split. Then strike a print to 16mm for the TV station's usage and, for good measure—after all, you are an astute businessman—you ask the station to have the optical print house make a print from 16mm to 35mm.

Why not? Who knows? Maybe Hollywood will be interested. This is beginning to sound familiar.

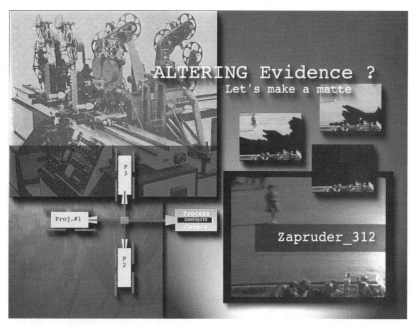

Creating a scenario with traveling mattes

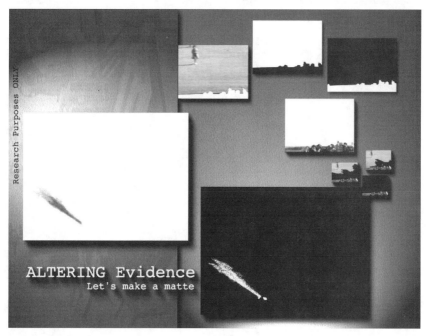

Determining the elements necessary to "fit" the scenario

The processes involved in altering a film

Creating individual mattes required for alteration of the film

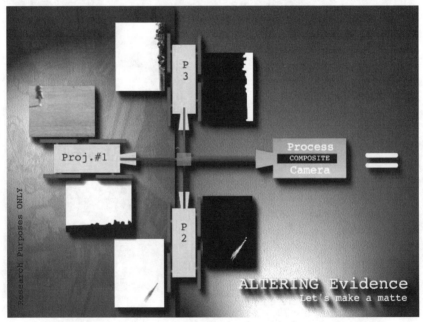

Assigning created elements to projector positions on optical printer

Well, here we are. We are going to look at a few graphics that cover's *how* this film alteration could have been pulled off. We're dealing with a piece of 8mm film roughly 25 feet in length, give or take a foot or two.

Our area of interest, the assassination footage, covers about 14+ feet, so we're not talking about a whole lot of footage here. I consider it a short cut actually.

Last year, for example, I did 32 effects-inserts totaling 9.5 minutes of finished material into one 44 minute documentary for television (video). Of course this is now nearly 40 years after the *deed*.

Things have changed for us with the advent of computers, but the techniques have not changed and, for experienced optical printer operators, this is a piece of cake, provided of course they have a mapped-out plan of attack, which, by the way, comes with the territory in this kind of trade.

Assume it's 7:00 PM on 22 November 1963. Zapruder has in his possession:

One (1) Split 8mm Camera Original of the assassination; and,

Three (3) Unsplit 8mm (16mm width) Optical prints of the above; then around 10:00 PM that night, he visits the Secret Service office and drops off two (2) of his Un-Split 8mm (16mm width) copies.

The next morning he cuts a deal with Richard Stolley of *Life* magazine and turns over either his one (1) 8mm split Camera Original of the assassination or his remaining one (1) 8mm Unsplit 16mm width Optical print.

There a little confusion about this on Erwin Swartz's part. (Swartz was Zapruder's business partner.) He recollects that either the camera original itself or the optical print was delivered to Stolley on the 23rd. In any case Stolley and *Life* received one or the other on 23 November 1963, where the other followed a few days later.

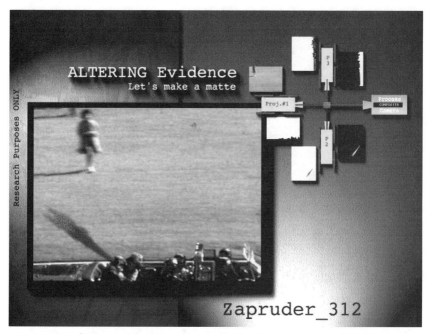

Final composition (creating a new head shot on frame Z-312)

That left Zapruder with what was legally and technically nothing—evidently the "A" side of the film, the family footage, was not part of the film package! (Well, not exactly nothing! He received some $25,000 initially plus payments that would total another $125,000, not to mention what his estate has cleared when the government paid $16,000,000 in compensation for declaring the film to be "an assassination record".)

(An aside about the time-line objection to alteration: "Editing time factors are too short; it couldn't have been done; there's not enough time; . . .". Yadada, yadada, yadada. Nonsense. In my estimation, there was about two months to get this job done. With 1963 equipment and standards and techniques, it should have taken between two to three weeks of lab time at the maximum. We are not doing a 300-minute version of "Doctor Zhivago" here.

What exactly do you need to control? Four (4) pieces of celluloid, two (2) in Secret Service control, the other two (2) in the hands of *Life* magazine. What's the big deal? *Life* dribbles out a few frames here and there. And those who saw the film first-hand when it was shown on Friday and Saturday will remember nothing but JFK's massive head wound. [*Editor's note*: For more on objections to the very possibility of film alteration, see the Preface and Costella's first chapter.])

Let's assume I have my hands on an 8mm Split first-generation Zapruder optical print from the group of three above that were created from the camera original. What then?

First, I'd destroy side "A". Then I would fully map out the film and its frames (assassination, side B) top to bottom—on paper with a frame count. Then I'd wait for instructions on what the producer/director wanted to accomplish with the finished piece of new film. Or I'd wait to be told exactly what to do.

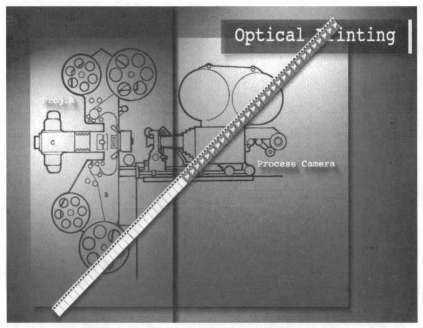

Optical Printing Diagram A: Double 8mm "Split" and "Spliced"

When the word came to prepare for an edit with some optical effects, I'd figure out which system at my disposal is the best for the job, which is what you see in Optical Printing Diagram A. This is a straight across optical printer with a bi-pack facility (which we won't use, but who knows whether it not might come in handy later on: I'm talking about those two extra film reels in the back of the projector on the left).

Let's look at Optical Printing Diagram B. The projector on the left is where the Zapruder 8mm optical print will be laced up, fed from the bottom to the top or, in optical-printer's lingo "heads up". The *white* overlay depicts the 8mm film path. The process camera on the right is where we'll be going next, as we will see shortly.

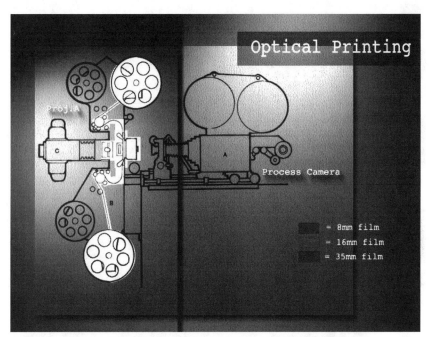

Optical Printing Diagram B: Going from 8mm to 35mm

Now for Optical Printing Diagram C. Let's get the 8mm intermittent—that's the film gate assembly, claw, et cetera, and correct sprocket stuff—set up on the projector head on the left. That's the white overlay there. Lace up the 8mm Zapruder assassination optical print, represented by the color green. [*Editor's note*: A colorized version is in the color-photo insert section.]

You could look at this as if your going to make a VHS copy of a movie you just rented from the video rental store. Over to the process camera, load a 16mm film magazine, represented by the color blue, with film and we're just about ready to go.

Nothing fancy here, we are just making a 16mm optical print (a 16mm copy if you will). Note that this will be the last time 8mm will be touched until the answer print is delivered to the client, whomever that might be.

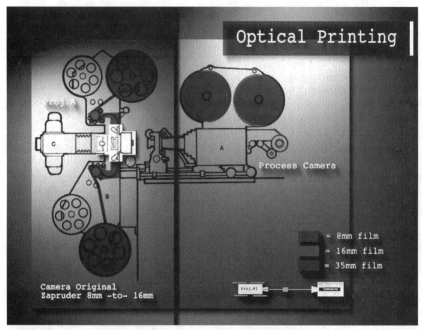

Optical Printing Diagram C: 1st pass set up

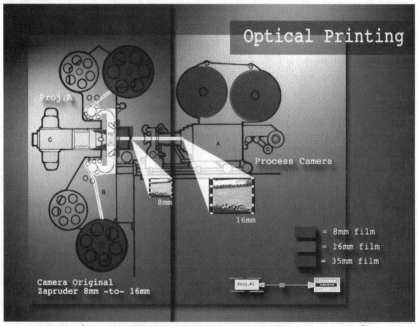

Optical Printing Diagram D: 1st pass—8mm to 16mm transfer

Consider Optical Printing Diagram D. The 8mm film is loaded and ready on Projector A. The process camera on the right is set and ready to film ("record", if you will, for all you video buffs). Turn on the projector light on A on the left and roll the process camera on the right. Then in 20 seconds of real time, we have a 16mm copy of the assassination.

The 16mm negative goes into the soup. (You may decide to make another 16mm copy for backup. After all, who knows which way the wind is going to blow?) Process your print and view it for quality. If the quality is good, then move forward.

Consider Optical Printing Diagram E. We're going to make a 35mm print of the 16mm print we just got out of the soup and dryer. We'll do the same process again but now with the 16mm we have just made. Lace it up in the projector on the left (of course, replacing the 8mm intermittent with the 16mm intermittent, the projection lens stuff). Turn the projector light back on and roll both machines—it's not even necessary for, "All quiet on the set."

20 seconds later, we have a 35mm optical print and maybe a backup 35mm, too, of the 16mm optical print of the 8mm optical print that was made in Dallas at Jamieson Film Company from the Zapruder camera original. Quality? If it's set up right, with the right filter pack and the proper light housing set ups and proper film gamma settings, you could not distinguish any of these new "prints" from the camera original.

Consider Optical Printing Diargram F. For your general information, this graphic demonstrates going from 35mm directly to 8mm (back to the original Zapruder film size), where we're bypassing the 16mm stage.

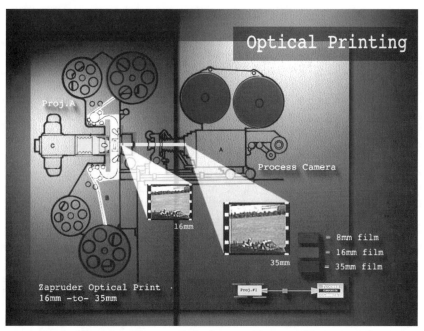

Optical Printing Diagram E: 2nd pass—16mm to 35mm transfer

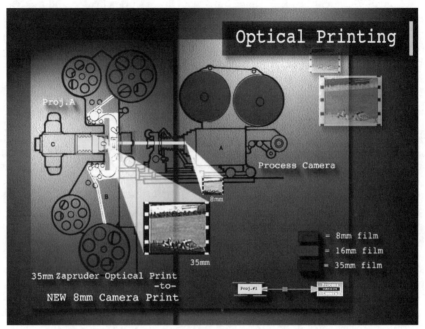

*Optical Printing Diagram F: 3rd pass—35mm to 8mm transfer
(after all optical effects have been applied to the 35mm film)*

An historically fascinating photographic composite

Well (see opoosite), what is this kind of photo/picture doing here? Over the past 10 years or so, there have been many comments regarding the possibility of alteration: Was the equipment available? Did the level of talent required for an alteration of the Zapruder film exist, if, indeed, an alteration was possible at all?

Throw in for good measure the anti-alterationists' theory that "any technique employed in an alteration attempt would have been spotted at once", which means it's also foolish to even attempt it! So it couldn't be done with any reasonable hope for success.

Well, take a good look at this picture I submit for consideration. What is this here for? It's called "Fading Away", by Henry Peach Robinson. This is a composite image. There are ten (10) separate images that collectively make up this composite. During Robinson's era this was called "a modern photographic technique—combination photography."

I'm sure Jack White has seen some of these images. They are in my estimation prime examples for most modern day photographic techniques, both still and motion. In fact, motion picture optical printing is one of the direct results of this type of composite photographic experimentation.

No cut lines are visible ("matte lines" in today's language). The film density is uniform across all 10 distinct image pieces making up this one image. That was quite a feat for those days. Yet Zapruder alteration would require the mixing of only five or perhaps six sources (maximum).

Composite image? If so, how many layers?

You wondered if we had the technology, techniques, craftsmanship and the folks that could pull off the Zapruder film alteration during 1963–64? Well, the picture you're looking at was composed four years prior to the Civil War! That's correct, in 1858!

How the Zapruder film may have been altered

Well here we are, off and running with the mystical kludges called "optical printers". The name includes *all* the printers in the family. So take a look at the next image (following page), which displays some equipment.

The diagram on the left shows the big machine on the right, where it looks as though the operator might be making opening or closing credits on Panavision film (or it could be 65mm film), which is called "The Oxberry" aerial-image animation stand. This is the real thing, not a mock up, not a figment of someone's imagination—the real deal!

Weighing in around 5,000 pounds, usually bolted into a concrete floor, the projector head that sits on the floor is usually resting on an old machine lathe assembly, which is rock solid, not to mention the fact you can control the in-and-out positions closer to the mirror on the floor—which makes the image in the process camera above larger as a simulated zoom lens effect, if you will—of the projector within 0.001 of an inch. When you are dealing with lens openings as small as we're dealing with in optical printing, there is virtually *no* room for size tolerances and differences. It's either right on or it doesn't work.

Note the camera on the stand on the left (marked #1) or the process camera. I've spoken about these cameras before, where they have the film that the new content is going to be photographed on (like a blank videocassette before you make a dub of the Blockbuster movie you are not suppose to dub) and the projectors on the floor are *controlled* by a synchronized motor that advances each assembly one frame at a time (more if required).

It's critical that you understand that these two sources work in complete synchronicity with one another. The whole contraption is controlled by that roll-around control panel in inset-B. The thing sticking up that looks like a cane in inset-B is the actual frame counter.

So what is "aerial image" printing? For that matter, what's the definition of "aerial image"? Suppose you set up a projector in your back yard and got power to it. Hang a sheet between two trees, getting it all nice and taut. Load some film in the projector, aim it at the sheet and turn it on.

The image is displayed on the sheet: focus up and enjoy, but only for a second. Freeze the projector and its image on the sheet: What do you see? Just a single frame frozen on the sheet, nothing happening, no movement, nada. Now, leaving the projector as it is with a frozen image being projected onto the sheet, take the sheet down. Yes, take the sheet down.

What's where the sheet was? Nothing, right? No. There's an aerial-image there. You can't see it but it's still there. For that matter, hang a mirror (at a angle) where the sheet was and you can bend the light. If you actually have a strong enough light in the projector, hang enough mirrors, put a few strategically placed prisms to bend the light . . . Well, you get the idea.

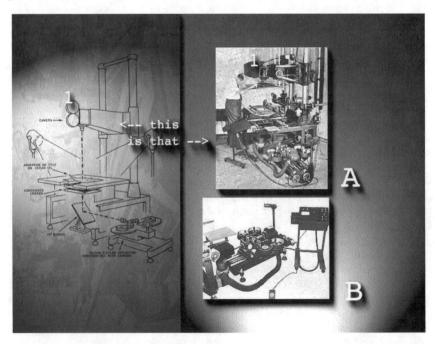

Oxberry Animation Stand used for composing 35mm matte segments

Getting the system up and runnning

Here's a quickie test to see if this system is up and running. System test? What's all this about? Consider the following diagram. You're going to make a composite 35mm film clip of an action scene that has one film element that was shot on the west side of town (see BB), which I'm going to call the "foreground scene", and some outdoor background imagery that was shot 10 days ago on the east side of town (see AA) which I'll call the "background scene". The object here is to combine both scenes into one scene that looks natural.

Here's the ingredients. 2 ea. 35 mm film clips, each 15 second duration, 2 ea. stacks of mattes (mattes and counter-mattes). How many mattes? One for each frame of the 15 second clips (see A and B below). Do the math. At 24 frames a second—well, that's 360 mattes for 15 seconds. Impossible? No, a piece of cake. It takes about 2.5 hours to do one pass, so we'll be done in about 6 hours. Bear in mind one crucial point here: the Zapruder film only has about 15 effective seconds of footage. Let's start.

Load the 15 seconds of background footage AA on #1 (the floor projector). Load up the process camera #3 with about 1:00 minute of 35mm raw stock (advance this about 3 feet—that's a good starting point). Turn on the sync motor (remember that it controls both the process camera #3 and the floor projector #1 motors and advances both of them one frame at a time).

Now on #2, the animation stand, put the first matte A on the table (see the holes at the top of the matte; they can only go one way). The director has given you the outline of how the shot is to be composed. You frame up #3 to fit the right composition, which is usually nothing more than moving the camera up or down a little. Once you are all framed up, the process can begin.

1. *Zero* the frame counter for the process camera #1;

2. First frame of projector cued up AA on #1;

3. Turn on the sync motor;

4. First matte A in place on #2;

5. Frames 1–360 expose sequence: expose #3, advances #1 and #3, change#2, expose #3, advance #1 and #3, change #2, . . . (until all 360 cycles are completed).

Then rewind #3 to the first frame on the counter (remember the one you zeroed out as the very first step in the process). Load up film clip BB in #1 (after you remove the other film, of course). Get it all cued up to its first frame. *Do not change anything on the process camera.* Don't even touch it! Mount the first counter-matte B on #2—then start the process till the 360 mattes are completed.

Once your all set up, each cycle—720 in total—should take about 5 seconds each. You can do the math. [*Editor's note*: 720 x 5 seconds = 3600 seconds, which is 60 minutes.]

When all the frames have been exposed, then remove the film magazine from #3 and process the exposed film. What you will receive back from the lab will be a composite positive or negative, depending on what type of film you shoot in #3.

This process describes how some think certain parts of the Zapruder film were in fact altered, a process that creates the illusion of the foreground-most element (layer) "floating" over the background elements

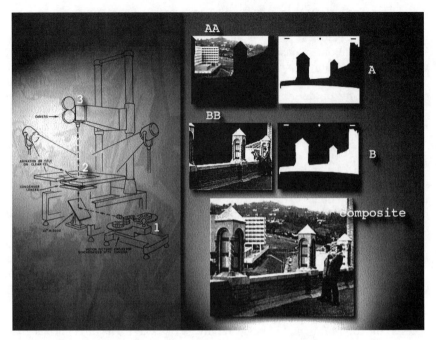

Oxberry Animation Stand with elements for the composition

Everything that I'm showing falls into the category known as "optical film effects": altering existing or primary camera footage in *some* way to accomplish a script's, director's, producer's, or studio's aims, objectives, or goals. In many situations, such effects are performed to correct errors made by inexperienced cameramen, mechanical defects, or to accomplish a shot for film that the budget would not cover.

Such is the case with this problem. Supppose we need 1000 people escaping multi-story buildings—rushing from a burning city into the water nearby. Our problem is we've only got the budget for 250 extras and a couple of single story buildings! The scene lasts for 10 seconds or 240 frames. What's this got to do with Zapruder?

Here's what I'd do as director. Build the single story city set on the bank of a river. Build a camera platform high and away looking down on the site at a 45 degree angle from a distance of 300 yards. Have the stage manager or 2nd director organize the 250 extras to the right side of the city (stage left) at the base of a single story building, get the camera in its fixed position, then lock it down and do not touch it for the duration of these shots.

Roll the film. Have the 250 (stage left) make their escape to the water's edge and beyond. Stop the camera. Move all the folks to the stage right side of the building and do exactly the same thing. Stop the camera. Move everyone to the center stage area and 50 percent of the folks up the street a bit between the buildings and do exactly the same thing. All three areas are showing mass confusion and chaos, exactly as you would expect for the fleeing population of a city.

All right, now we've got a total of 30–40 seconds of finished film (the 3 cuts below that are numbered 1-2-3). The film is processed. This is what they look like. You are happy, and this is what happens next.

You tell the creative director you want the optical printing lab to give you matted sequences (the corresponding matte sequences are numbered 1a, 2a, 3a) of the best 8–10 seconds of each area escape (left, center, right).

Then have the studio's artists put together a matte sequence with brushes (in other words, do a painting—a very realistic one, I might add—that includes second, third, and fourth stories for the buildings in the scene comprising the upper third of the frame).

The smoke and other effects are done with another pass on the printers. We could even simulate with optical printing the effects of the ground shaking from an earthquake or an explosion, if we wanted.

This sequence, by the way, really happened, in a Hollywood production from the early 1950s. Anyway, throw them all together with their mattes and then gaze at the final images, where the drop shadows are in place to give more definition to how the full frame composition is put together.

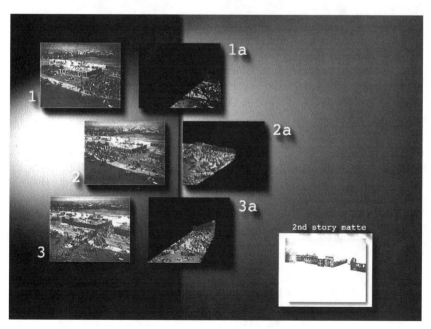

Creating a four-element matte sequence (circa 1955)

So what does this have to do with the Zapruder film? Nothing other than the fact that, if an optical print technician and matte artist wanted to do simple frame removal, frame squeezes, slow down or speed up of the action, minor glass painting or matte painting, and such, the Zapruder film would have offered no serious challenges to professional, hands-on, optical film printing technicians. No challenge at all.

The "final" composite—what's real, what's not real?

My purpose has not been to assert that the 8mm "camera original" Zapruder film has been fabricated, but rather to explain why any claims that the Zapruder film could not have been altered because of limited time, lack of necessary equipment, or inadequate knowledge or expertise are claims made out of ignorance. A valuable resource for confirmation are the technical newsletters of that period published by the Society of Motion Picture Engineers (1915–54) and by the Society of Motion Picture and Television Engineers (1955–2003) newsletters. Sophisticated alteration of the kinds that I have described could have been done in 1963–64.

"Yes, Virginia, ..."

David Healy
presenting at the
Zapruder Film Symposium,
Duluth, Minnesota
10 May 2003

A Scientist's Verdict: The Film is a Fabrication

John P. Costella, Ph.D.

[*Editor's note*: John Costella, Ph.D., is one of the most recent additions to the assassination research community. After graduating top of his class in Honors degrees in both Electrical Engineering and Science from the University of Melbourne, Australia, he completed a Ph.D. in theoretical physics, specializing in high energy physics, Einstein's theory of relativity, and classical electrodynamics—the detailed mathematical description of the motion of objects, and the light they emit. As John describes below, his initial goal was to apply advanced computer techniques to extract details from the photographic record of the assassination–but what he found led him to question, and then finally help to disprove, the authenticity of the Zapruder film itself. His account of his visit to Dealey Plaza in May 2003, prior to the Zapruder Film Symposium, is itself both remarkable and revealing.]

Introduction and Motivation

By any measure, I am a newcomer to the assassination. In 2000 I had the same vague knowledge of the event that most Australians my age would have; I hadn't even managed to find time to sit down and watch Oliver Stone's decade-old movie *JFK*. Some years earlier, the younger brother of a friend had borrowed Robert Groden's picture book *The Killing of a President* (1993) from a public library, and had shown me several images from it. Even earlier, I remember seeing a news item on television that stated that advanced computers had been used to dispel the idea that there was a gunman in the bushes on the infamous "grassy knoll"; and I had also seen a mock trial of Lee Harvey Oswald that concluded that, had he lived, he still would have been convicted of the two murders. But American Presidents generally do not feature in History classes in Australian schools (indeed, Australian Prime Ministers rarely rate a mention themselves), and I was almost completely ignorant about this crucial period in modern history.

Of course, everyone knew that there had been a conspiracy in the assassination of JFK. This may reflect a difference of outlook between Australians and Americans. I know that this is not simply a consequence of my relative youth, and hence that of my regular acquaintances (I wasn't born until the second anniversary of Earl Warren's presentation of his Report to President Lyndon B. Johnson), because I have yet to meet an Australian who was of mature age in 1963 who swallowed the U.S. government's account of the crime either. Of course, distrust of public officials is a fundamental part of the Australian psyche, developed, no doubt, from our convict origins. But by all accounts the same level of skepticism was held throughout continental Europe, and other parts of the world.

145

It would seem that there was ample evidence that something was amiss from the very beginning, but that in the early 1960s many ordinary Americans still had such a degree of faith and trust in their government that they largely took the Warren Commission's findings at face value. And hence the very seed of destruction of this faith was sown.

My own active interest in the assassination was awakened when I stumbled back across Groden's book in the public library, while looking for some light reading material for the summer vacation in December 1999. The details of the assassination, and the cover-up, were intriguing in themselves; but what really piqued my interest was the collection of photographs and film frames that were shown. It was evident that there really was a scarcity of photographic evidence of the actual shots themselves; but, moreover, what photographic evidence did exist was often blurred. Not because the cameras used were not focused correctly—they generally were—but because the photographer had moved the camera during the exposure, or because they hadn't panned their camera to follow the motion of the presidential limousine.

Deblurring the images

Moving the camera involuntarily during such a period of crisis is completely understandable, of course. But I was surprised that no computer methods had been used to try to remove the resultant blurring. I well remembered sitting through seminar after seminar in the early 1990s as visiting astronomers would wring their hands about the Hubble Space Telescope being sent up with an incorrectly designed lens. (This was in the days before the rescue mission was sent up to put corrective "spectacles" on it.) I was amazed by how much detail could actually be recovered by using modern computers to apply advanced mathematical tricks to the images. The reason is that the Hubble Space Telescope lens was "perfectly wrong": it was perfectly formed, but to the wrong "prescription". Astronomers were able to make use of this knowledge to recover a large portion of the information lost to blurring—not as good as having a corrective lens installed, but at least producing results that were superior to any ground-based telescope.

Blurred photographs and film frames represent a physically similar situation, even if the camera is correctly focused and the blurring is due to the motion of the camera. So why hadn't the photographic record of the assassination been put through the same process?

After doing some research, I found that there were several apparent reasons. Firstly, knowledge about the computational techniques needed was relatively scarce, and indeed there appeared to be an active process of suppression. (It is of strategic military importance in the processing of satellite imagery taken through the atmosphere: both of images taken by satellites of the ground, and images from ground telescopes of the satellites themselves!) Secondly, the required computational power put the technique beyond the reach of most researchers until the late 1990s. (Some small portions of some Zapruder frames were processed at Los Alamos in the late 1970s, which was only possible because of the huge processing power available at the facility.) And thirdly, most assassination researchers had no idea that such techniques were possible; indeed, even today many experts in the field of image processing still believe that "deblurring" is impossible!

While doing this research, ideas had come to mind for methods of performing this "deblurring" in a new way. From my Engineering studies, I was well familiar with the Fourier filtering theory used for most existing techniques, but I believed that the computing power necessary to carry them out could be applied in a much more direct "brute force" approach. Over the next year and a half I toyed with several ideas—using images scanned from Groden's book as test cases—and eventually perfected a computer program that could extract quite good results in a reasonable period of time.

The Zapruder film

While this work was proceeding, I decided that it was about time that I rented a copy of Oliver Stone's movie *JFK* from the video store and actually sat down to watch it. (I have a bad habit of not watching blockbusters when they come out; I didn't see *Star Wars* until 1989.) It was only when watching the courtroom scenes near the end of the movie that I realized that, contrary to my mistaken impression, the frames of the Zapruder film itself had not been subject to any systematic deblurring by computer.

I asked on several public Internet newsgroups dedicated to the assassination for assistance in getting hold of digital images of the frames. The hope, of course, was that I might be able to use my new program to extract new evidence in the case—shadowy figures lurking on the infamous grassy knoll, for instance—that might have previously evaded assassination researchers.

Through these queries, I became aware that a company called MPI had released a DVD of the Zapruder film in 1998 that included the best digital copies of the frames yet available to researchers. A number of researchers generously emailed me digital "captures" of all of these frames. Others assisted me in making sense of the images themselves, which had been the subject of intense criticism and controversy.

A comedy of errors

The MPI saga seemed to me to be a bizarre one—but in time I realized that it fit neatly into the pattern of supposed incompetence with which the entire assassination had been whitewashed, by those ascribing to the U.S. government's official view of the crime.

The first problem was that MPI had ostensibly been somewhat at a loss in preparing their material for video reproduction. Images had obviously been resized and reframed a number of times, resulting in a loss of clarity. And, in the end, the images were produced with the wrong dimensions: images of complete frames were overstretched, horizontally, compared to the real frames; highly zoomed images of JFK, in contrast, were compressed horizontally.

The second problem was that MPI had, somehow, completely omitted three frames of the film (including the very last frame!), resulting in incorrect numbers being allocated to the last 143 frames shown, including two frames that were also interchanged in two of the sequences, but not in the others.

The resulting DVD was, perhaps, of suitable quality for an average home video collection. I was flabbergasted to discover that it was also intended to be the final "reference" digitization for assassination researchers of the camera-original Zapruder film, before the latter was sealed and locked away in the National Archives. Apart from a small region surrounding JFK in a number of frames (shown in a highly zoomed sequence on the DVD), the resolution of each image was *inferior* to that published in *Life* magazine just two weeks after the assassination, as well as that already available from other sources!

Suspicions aroused

But events were starting to get even stranger. After I contacted (completely at my initiation, out of the blue) a world expert in image processing, and mentioned in passing the Zapruder film, the said expert casually told me that all frames of the film had already been deblurred, and that he himself held a copy of the computer tapes of the full-resolution versions of MPI's digital scans of the original film, locked away in his personal vault! This was remarkable, because I had not mentioned the MPI project to him at all, and the presence of these high-resolution full-frame digital scans was an issue that I was only just starting to wonder about.

I relayed this remarkable news to Gary Mack, curator of the Sixth Floor Museum at Dealey Plaza, which today ostensibly holds the rights to reproductions of the Zapruder film (providing that it is a genuine film taken by Abraham Zapruder, rather than a work of the U.S. government or commissioned by it, which is explicitly excluded from copyright protection under U.S. copyright laws). I was astounded to be met with indifference.

Attack on the "alterationists"

At the same time, those assisting me with my study of the film, over the Internet, drew my attention to the evident "pincushion distortion" in the film frames: an optical effect, common to telephoto lenses, that causes objects to be slightly pulled towards the corners of the image. My assistants then provided a highly scathing account of an analysis by someone called David Mantik in a book about the assassination that had apparently been published, pointing out that Mantik had found the Stemmons Freeway sign to widen as it passed into the sprocket hole region of the film, but had jumped to the erroneous conclusion that this was evidence that the film was a complete fake—rather than realize that it was the expected effect of the pincushion distortion!

What? A fake? I couldn't believe what I was hearing. I had never heard the charge that the Zapruder film was a forgery. I had, by that stage, studied the motion blurring in the film for many months, and I knew that the blurring of the background together with the blurring of the moving limousine always seemed to add up to the correct motion of the limousine during the time of the frame's exposure, to within reasonable uncertainties. How on Earth could anyone fake that, for an entire film?

I was determined to investigate this claim in greater detail, by analyzing the pincushion distortion in the film. One of my Internet assistants provided me with a figure from the patent for the lens system used in Zapruder's camera: "about three and one-half percent" of distortion. Precision measurements on several frames allowed me to get a handle on the distortion, and it turned out to be 3.6% at the corners of the designed image area. I wrote a simple computer program to remove the distortion. After this correction was made, image features became consistent, the Stemmons Freeway sign stayed constant in width, and indeed the blurring of background objects became consistent across the entire field of view. I wrote to my Internet assistants, stating confidently that, in my view, the film was completely self-consistent, and it would be essentially impossible to create frames with such internal self-consistencies in the time period allowed by the published chronologies of the film's history that they had provided me with.

The intrigue continues

Another of my Internet assistants, who was adept at writing computer programs for image analysis, could not agree with my pincushion correction results. After extensive discussions it emerged that he was using an equation for the distortion that differed fundamentally, but subtly, from my own. I tried to explain why the equation he was using was impossible on physical grounds (and it also disagrees with every other analysis of correction of pincushion distortion available in the literature, and indeed on the Internet itself), but he failed to accede.

He also continued to digress into detailed discussions of higher-order corrections to the distortion that were clearly and demonstrably of negligible importance—digressions that, to my mind, were a waste of time. He sent me volumes of equations, graphs, and analyses, and source codes for his computer programs. I was appreciative of his enthusiasm and generosity, but rapidly recognized that the material could easily sidetrack me for months, if not years, if I were not careful. It almost felt like I was being sidetracked on purpose.

I seemed to be encountering obstacles wherever I looked. For six months I had—again completely on my own initiative—been in contact with Robert Groden, renowned expert on the Zapruder film, and author of the book that I had first used as my reference for the assassination. Groden had promised to send me digital scans of the "missing" frames of the film—those reportedly damaged and destroyed by *Life* magazine during its ownership of the film—from the best quality digital tapes he had in his vault. The only problem was that the process of obtaining these images seemed to be going nowhere, for no good reason. (Eventually, another researcher simply sent me a copy of the CD of Groden's video release, *Assassination Films* (1998), which contained copies of the "missing" frames. A year to the day after my last communication with him, Groden replied by e-mail—as if the twelve-month delay had never occurred—asking, "Now which frames were you after, again?")

A semi-private Internet forum: a false start

Soon after this—around October 2001—I was invited to participate in a semi-private forum on the Internet, dedicated to the assassination, which allowed the convenient uploading of images. I was surprised to learn of the existence of this site: why hadn't I been told about it at the start of 2001, when I first called for assistance on the public newsgroups, and when my assistants had offered their services? It struck me as a rather strange omission. But I joined the group, and publicly offered the opinions I had voiced in private about the authenticity of the film.

I started to upload some of the first results of my deblurring work with the film, but was met with complaints from the person running the group, stating that "enhanced" images of all the important frames had already been posted! When I checked, it turned out that all that had been uploaded were images from the MPI DVD: no "enhancements" had been done at all.

Things were getting stranger by the day. I was engaged in a number of public discussions, in which bizarre theories about optics were put forward as the gospel truth. It took some time for me to dispel these strange beliefs. It was only after this that I was introduced to breaking news in assassination research: a free-for-all fight between "Tink and Fetz", and their respective followers, over a veritable assassination holy war that was referred to as "Moorman in the street".

Moorman in the street

By this stage I was almost punch-drunk with assassination intrigues. "Tink", as it turned out, was Dr. Josiah Thompson, author of one of the earliest books on the assassination; and "Fetz" was Professor Jim Fetzer, editor of two volumes *Assassination Science* and *Murder in Dealey Plaza*, published just before the turn of the century. "Moorman in the street" referred to an analysis in the latter volume by researcher Jack White, where it was claimed that the lines of sight inherent in Moorman's fifth Polaroid located her camera position precisely—at such a low height that she must necessarily have been standing on the roadway of Elm Street—whereas the Zapruder film shows her standing on the grass some feet behind the curb. Because Jack White believed in the authenticity of the Moorman Polaroid, this discrepancy (together with numerous others) necessarily led him to conclude that the Zapruder film was itself a fraud.

Why hadn't I been made aware of these two volumes? Or of this active debate in the assassination research community? I scarcely had time to ponder those two questions before being hit with another remarkable discovery: there was yet another semi-private forum on the Internet, JFKresearch.com, dedicated to the assassination. But even more extraordinarily, most members of this other group believed wholeheartedly that the Zapruder film was a complete fabrication!

My Internet assistants warned me against visiting this other newsgroup. They described its members as fanatical and irrational, and liable to tear apart anyone who dared disagree with their views. However, the treatment I was getting at the first group was itself less than acceptable. And when Professor Fetzer himself posted a humble apology to the first group, for some moderately intemperate comments he had made elsewhere regarding some researchers investigating the "Moorman" issue, I decided that the members of *JFKresearch.com* might not be ogres after all. And so I decided to visit *JFKresearch.com*.

And changed my history with the assassination irreversibly.

Another semi-private Internet forum: the real thing

The first thing I noticed on *JFKresearch.com* was that there were many more people contributing, and many more discussions. And they were definitely vociferous. I discovered that I had been associating with many researchers whose loyalties had been questioned, and that my public association with them had been carefully cultivated. The appearance of someone with a Ph.D. in physics, with this background of suspect contacts, smelt like a rat. What research was I going to "debunk"?

I must admit that I walked blindly into the first trap. I had been carefully prepared for the "Moorman in the street" issue, and it was the only topic of discussion that most researchers wanted to discuss. Jack White, Jim Fetzer, and David Mantik had taken measurements in Dealey Plaza during the 38th remembrance of the assassination, in November 2001, which appeared to confirm Jack's conclusions. Members of the opposing "team" had made their own measurements, in the preceding week, and had come to the opposite conclusions. Clearly, someone was doing something wrong somewhere.

I weighed into the debate. I analyzed Jack White's images, and concluded that, whilst there was a slight "gap" in the alignment he had made, this gap only shifted the Moorman lens position up by just over two inches, which was insufficient to invalidate Jack's overall conclusions. Jack himself refused to agree to the existence of any "gap". But many were overjoyed to see the work vindicated. Others were suspicious, expecting me to later do a back flip and destroy the conclusions. To them, that was the reason why I was introduced to the case: to destroy Jack's research.

Costella the villain

Unfortunately, their worst nightmare seemed to become a reality. In May 2002, the opposing "team" published a detailed report, including images from a new drum scan of a negative of the original Moorman Polaroid. It was this scan that caused me to reassess my analysis: not because it showed anything new about the day of the assassination, but because it suggested that I had misunderstood the geometry of the "Zapruder pedestal" itself. I went back over the images Jack White had posted, that I had used in my analysis. I couldn't understand why the drum scan was showing something subtly different. I then did something I should have done in the first place: *I asked for modern photographs of the "Zapruder pedestal" from the approximate Moorman position.* Several researchers posted such photos, including Jack himself. They confirmed my worst fears. I had made a monumental blunder.

The worst part of it all is that I could have avoided it, if I had asked for those modern photos in the beginning. Two crucial edges, that I believed were parallel, were not. Why did they appear to be parallel in the images I had analyzed? Ironically, I discovered that it was because of the JPEG compression that was applied to them before they were posted on the Internet—the very medium that allowed me to partake in the research in the first place. Images posted to the group were only accepted in compressed format, for logistical reasons. Compression implies a loss of information; and, in this case, the compression algorithm decided to approximate the two non-parallel edges by two parallel edges. The effect is so subtle that it is unnoticeable to the naked eye—that's how image compression works—but when magnified and analyzed to high precision, it led me to completely erroneous conclusions. It was something that I should have realized—with my background in digital systems and signal theory, I had no excuse at all for ignorance. But it simply never occurred to me.

I posted my concession. Needless to say, those who suspected my entry just six months earlier felt their doubts confirmed. I had, they concluded, been introduced as a stooge to agree with Jack's conclusions, only to drag him down months later when my own work was shown to be erroneous.

That may well have been the end of the story, had I decided to suffer the ignominy in private, and withdraw from assassination research. But I realized that I had not actually played my role according to plan. The "team" had expected me to dig my heels in, to steadfastly refuse to accept that I had made a mistake, and then continue to escalate the weight and respectability of their own research until they had proved beyond any doubt whatsoever that I had used incorrect assumptions, by which time my reputation in the assassination research community would be in tatters—and, by association, those who believe that the Zapruder film is a fraud. But I didn't follow the script. By rapidly realizing—and acknowledging—that the "team" had pinpointed shortcomings in my work, I foiled their plan. But more surprises were to come.

The Zapruder Film Symposium, Duluth, Minnesota, 9–11 May 2003

Flying into Duluth with Jack White on Friday, 9 May 2003, after our eight-hour wait in Minneapolis–St. Paul, the fog was almost thick enough to force us to turn around and make the twenty-minute flight back again. Fortunately, there was just enough visibility for us to land—and to prevent me from seeing much of Lake Superior in the minutes I had to spare over that weekend. The weather was still chilly the next morning as Jim Fetzer picked us up from the hotel—a contrast to the 90-plus degree days I'd enjoyed in Dallas (see the Appendix). But each suited my purposes almost ideally: sunny warmth for work in Dealey Plaza; cool comfort for long and fascinating sessions in a lecture theater.

Arriving at the venue, I could see immediately that David Healy and Rick Janowitz had clearly put in many hours getting the audiovisual recording gear set up perfectly, and Pauline Nuhring had all the presentation equipment exactly where we needed it. When the record of the Symposium is released on DVD, some who weren't in attendance may wonder whether it was necessary to cut out segments where equipment did not work, and so on—but, remarkable as it may sound, there was no glitch throughout the entire two days that lasted longer than five or ten seconds, despite the wide variety of presentation formats used. It was as if the Symposium were charmed—as if it were meant to be.

Jim Fetzer

The Symposium was formally opened by the host, Jim Fetzer. After welcoming attendees and outlining the program and procedures, Jim proceeded to provide a wonderful introduction to what the Zapruder film actually is. He displayed the complete film in various formats that have been made available to researchers over the years, and outlined the details of several other formats that he did not display. By this time, even those members of the audience who had not studied the film in any detail had a good feel for what it looked like, what it showed, and how the different versions of it varied in quality, color, and format.

Jim then emphasized a point that is, again, well-known to researchers of the film, but which may not be obvious to the newcomer: the various formats made available over the years show vastly different amounts of the total image area available on the film. One reason why this is so crucial in the case of the Zapruder film is that the Zapruder camera's design was such that, when used in telephoto mode, much of the film area between the sprocket holes was also exposed with imagery—sort of a continuation or extension, on the left side, of what was designed to be shown on a projector. But, somewhat perversely (and quite likely purposefully), this "extra" imagery was, until the mid-1990s, only available in a very few places: in poor-quality black and white images in Volume XVIII of the Warren Commissions Exhibits (shown for less than a third of the film), and but a few dozen frames printed in color in *Life* magazine in 1966.

This changed with the release of the MPI video and DVD in 1998, which showed the (almost) complete film together with the sprocket hole regions, in color, digitized anew from the "camera-original" film. Because of this, the MPI frames show almost the maximum amount of image area possible. (The four edges of each frame are cropped off very slightly, which is both an annoyance and a hindrance to precision photographic analysis, but it does not amount to any substantial loss of area when considered as a percentage.)

Thus, for most of the thirty years before 1998, a sizeable portion of the film—that hidden in the sprocket hole regions—could not be studied in detail by researchers at all. Moreover, those "complete" film versions that *were* available generally did not even show the entire region in the area of the film designed to be projected. Jim presented figures summarizing the proportion of the total film area displayed in each of the various formats—the variations of which may surprise even some of the more experienced researchers of the film.

One important point that was made, however, was that *all* extant copies of the film do show exactly the same content for each of the 486 individual frames. In other words, every extant copy of (say) Frame 250 shows the same content as every other copy of Frame 250, to within reproduction uncertainties, damage, and mold infestation of the original film (which is evident on MPI's digitization).

An exciting development—for me—during the Symposium itself was the discovery of the *only* exception I know to this rule. It appears that the slide of Z-323 sent to Stewart Galanor by the National Archives—published in the back of his book *Cover-Up*—is *missing* the bright object in the grass that can be seen moving across the field of view, beginning in Z-313. This is highly significant, because the same object was missing in the black-and-white copy of Z-323 published by *Life* magazine on the weekend of the assassination—*but it is present in every other copy of Z-323 that I have ever seen*. Before the discovery of the Galanor frame, it had been argued that this merely represented a retouching job at *Life* for publication purposes (as well as in two other frames in the same issue that should have also shown the object in the grass). Although investigations are continuing as I write these words, it seems highly probable that *the National Archives has—or had—a version of Z-323 that differs from all others*, which was the source of the Galanor frame, and which, somehow, must have had the same parentage as the *Life* image on the first weekend. This would imply that *there are two different extant versions of Z-323 in the National Archives*.

Although it might seem that this small difference is almost negligible compared to the wholesale fabrication of the film itself, one must look at its import *for people who still believe the Zapruder film to be genuine*. Such skeptics must now try to explain just exactly how, when, and where this modification could have been made. Adding to their difficulty is the fact that *the "camera original" film on the MPI disc appears to show the "puddle" where the object has been retouched out, as well as the object itself!* In other words, this seems to imply some sort of process of alteration and "un-alteration". Once one accepts the evidence for this tampering with the *original film*, any confidence one might have had in it must surely evaporate.

Returning to Jim's presentation, other fascinating aspects of the MPI project are, at first, disturbing, but on closer inspection are completely typical for anything related to the assassination. MPI obviously could not digitize the six frames that were destroyed on the original film, simply because they *were* destroyed. But it is well known that there were 486 frames in the Zapruder film, before the splices were made, which means there are now 480 frames remaining (which, coincidentally, makes it exactly six feet long). But, somehow, MPI only managed to find 477 of these frames. It was determined soon after the MPI release that Z-341 and Z-350 were, inexplicably, skipped altogether. However, for a number of years it was not known—or not widely advertised, at any rate—where the third lost frame was.

Last year I went through the entire film, comparing it frame by frame with other known versions, and was flabbergasted to find that it is *the very last frame of the film* that was somehow missed by MPI. Jim also found the same thing, by the same painstaking process. How is this possible? Even if one allows the possibility of skipping Z-341 and Z-350 through sloppy, unprofessional work, surely the very *last* frame cannot get "lost in the crowd"?

Another long-known anomaly with the MPI disc is that, in the sequences that show the sprocket hole regions, Z-331 and Z-332 are interchanged. The "innocent explanation" for this is that Zapruder appears to have actually panned *backwards* slightly during the transition from Z-331 to Z-332, which would make one place the two frames in the wrong order if one were arranging them simply by watching how background objects progress across the field of view. There is nothing physically impossible with having Zapruder pan backwards for a frame, of course: he was free to jiggle his camera as he liked. But consider the enormous implication of this "innocent explanation": it implies that MPI *actually had a pile of loose images that they had to put into the correct order*. Could anyone possibly defend this sort of process? Why were the images not produced carefully, sequentially, like a well-ordered production line? *Is it then any wonder that they "lost" three of the frames?* In any case, this is another of the many anomalies that Jim independently verified.

But there is yet another quirk with the MPI project: *none of the images has the correct aspect ratio (shape)*. Those showing sprocket hole regions are stretched horizontally; those zoomed in are compressed horizontally. Careful measurements by numerous researchers have (independently) found the factors necessary to correct these mistakes.

Now, if one were to buy the MPI disc or video, would one see these mistakes listed on an Errata sheet? One would not. Rather, every researcher who begins to make use of the MPI material must learn of these mistakes the hard way. Until now. Jim's careful documentation of these errors, shown and described explicitly in his presentation, should hopefully bring this continued confusion to an end. [*Editor's note:* See the color photo section, "Which Film *is* 'The Zapruder Film'?"]

Following this, Jim made note of the two splices apparently made in the original film. The more famous of these was already obvious when the Warren volumes were published: the apparent destruction of four frames, and a crude splice performed, around Z-207 through Z-212. The second, less well-known splice occurred around Z-155 and Z-156. Although it is likely that these splices were added to the film precisely for the purpose of making the rest of the film look genuine, and for getting researchers excited about a red herring—after all, if the whole thing is a fabrication, why else would you then destroy some and put in a crude splice, if not subterfuge and disinformation?—it is still necessary for anyone who wants to research the film to understand why there are frames missing in the MPI version.

Jim then went through the entire film, frame by frame, showing the MPI version where it was available, replacing it with a Groden frame where it was not, and indicating how MPI frame numbers over 330 must be carefully modified if one is to refer to the correct frame number. When it is released on DVD, this will be an invaluable reference for future researchers trying to make any sense of this mess.

Jack White

Jim then introduced legendary researcher Jack White, a lifelong resident of Fort Worth, Texas, who has over the past few decades done more of the "background" work on the photographic evidence than any other single person.

What do I mean by this? One has to try to turn one's mind back to the time when none of the evidence of the assassination was even familiar to any researcher, let alone intricately understood. Jack was one of a very small number of researchers who looked at the photographic evidence, in some sort of totality, and *instinctively* realized that things were not correct. His enormous visual memory and processing ability served him well in his own career in photographic and graphic arts work, of course, but it also meant that he could discern discrepancies intuitively, visually, without needing to perform calculations or making measurements (as I generally need to do to check what he already sees).

There are times, of course, when Jack has been fooled by a genuine optical illusion; not everything he discerns with the naked eye turns out to be truly indicative of fabrication. Moreover, some of his most tenaciously held but erroneous conclusions have been caused by physical evidence in Dealey Plaza having been subtly modified since 22 November 1963—such as the modification of the yellow curb stripes that led him to believe that the background of the Zapruder film was magnified. In Duluth I likened Jack's research to the task faced by a marathon runner trying to run through gravel roads containing hidden pits of quicksand.

So if he gets things wrong so often, why is Jack White *the* researcher who made all of the rest of this work possible? *Because he has visually processed the vast photographic record of the assassination and has detected that subset of it that contains potential evidence of fabrication.* Asking why some of his findings have later turned out to be mistaken is to completely and absolutely miss the point. Jack is like the sieve that puts to one side, for our inspection, things that do not look right. *Ask why it is that almost every smoking-gun proof of fabrication has arisen from some aspect of the photographic evidence that Jack has identified as being anomalous.* Then you might understand what we owe this man.

Jack and I work well together, precisely because we *don't* work the same way—although it was only after being able to spend a week together in Dallas and Fort Worth that we most fully understood each other. I watch carefully where Jack has "sniffed out" something that is not quite right. (I have no choice—it would take me about 500 years to go through all the photographic evidence and see what he sees already!) I then try to find something in there that provides a *clean proof*, violating the laws of physics, with as few uncertainties, as few undetermined variables, as possible. Most of the time, something doesn't tie down tightly enough—there is enough uncertainty that a devil's advocate (or, more to the point, a disinformation agent) could "weasel out" of an airtight conclusion, based on a scientific *possibility* (even if it's not at all a likely *probability*). But once in a while all of the pieces of the jigsaw puzzle slide together without even a molecule of weasel room, and then I bring the jaws of the bear trap together and *that's it—hasta la vista, Baby—you're out*—and that's the end of the game, my friend, the end of the lie. It happens as quickly as that.

Jack usually doesn't understand why I ignore most of his great findings, and pick up on just one or two of them and run with them like they're the end of the Universe. What he usually doesn't realize is that *it is indeed the totality of his findings that tells me, as a gut feeling, where and how the fabrications have been created*. Because I know only too well that, even if there is a small or even a reasonable possibility that any one finding could be wrong, there is *absolutely no chance at all that they are all wrong*. As a corpus, they tell me exactly, in my bones, what has been done to the photographic evidence. *That* is what I—and many others—never would have had a chance of doing, had there been no Jack White. Most of the pieces of evidence can't be picked out and held up as irrefutable, individually; indeed, refuting them, individually, out of context, away from the corpus, is what the disinformation agents spend most of their energies on. I see my job as putting before them the individual gems—perfect, flawless, self-contained proofs of fabrication—as objects truly worthy of such energetic efforts. The extent to which a researcher avoids the gems, and returns to the easy target of picking out Jack's less watertight observations one by one for focused attack, tells me what their true agenda is.

So what did Jack present in Duluth? Over a period of two and a half hours he presented a wonderful overview of the corpus of his evidence that tells me, and any other thinking and genuine individual, that the photographic record of the assassination is a sham. That some of these items were seized on by other presenters and buffed up to be sparkling gems in their own right, *even while the Symposium was in progress*, is a marvelous illustration of exactly what I have tried to convey above. I guess the simplest way to say it is that *Jack White provides us the raw material from which we mold our proofs*.

It would be an injustice were I to try to list or summarize this photographic tour de force in any sort of printed form, so I will not do Jack a disservice by making such an attempt. The DVD of his presentation—containing his extensive comments on each slide—will be the best reference anyone could have on the corpus of the photographic evidence. [*Editor's note:* See the color photo section.]

David Healy

The next speaker faced the unenviable task of moving from behind the cameras—which he was running with just a single assistant, Rick Janowitz—to present on the other side of it. The only consolation of such a huge workload, I guess, would be the prospect of being able to edit your own presentation if anything didn't work out right.

But it did work out right—and wonderfully so. David Healy launched into a carefully crafted defense of his publicly stated opinion, based on his vast experience in the film and television industry, that the technical ability, know-how, and equipment was *more than sufficient* in 1963 to carry out the editing of the Zapruder film necessary to produce what we now have before us today.

At times in his presentation, the Symposium host, Jim Fetzer, expressed concern that David was skipping over some of the slides in his presentation—that he may not be explaining things "from the ground up", for those not already familiar with his arguments. But David was working to a plan, in his own inimitable way, and was laying the groundwork for what must be realized as *the* definitive exposition of the state of the art of film editing and fabrication in 1963, that will serve as a reference work for all researchers in this field for years to come. One consequence of this was that some of the more pedagogical parts of his task came later in his presentation, rather than earlier. But, after two and a half hours, it was all there.

David began by explaining carefully the literature *already in print* in 1963, or that published in the years afterwards that described the period up to 1963, that dealt with film editing technologies and methodologies. As he explained, this literature didn't even describe the state of the art at that time, because the field *was* literally a "black art", with practitioners reluctant to divulge their secrets except through what was effectively a traditional trade apprenticeship system; what appeared in print effectively represented that basic level of skill that had, by the time of publication, become commonly known.

He then described the various pieces of equipment that then existed, in particular "optical printers", that could be used to very quickly copy a film with selected frames omitted. (This was important for my own presentation, because I believe that one of the two "parallel paths" of the editing of the film involved the creation of quickly edited films for the purposes of projection over the weekend of the assassination, that could have been created very rapidly by the simple excision of frames or groups of frames by means of an optical printer.)

He then moved on to explaining the various levels of *editing* of frames that could be carried out in 1963. This represents a modification of the contents *within* a frame, rather than the simple excision of complete frames, which could be carried out rapidly using an optical printer.

As David explained it, the simplest form of editing involves "glass painting", whereby additional content is painted onto a piece of glass, through which the original film is projected and the combined image exposed onto a new piece of film. Such techniques could, for example, have been used to create the infamous "blob" on the President's head following Zapruder frame 313, as well as the "blood spray" in Frame 313 itself. (In my own presentation I provided data demonstrating why this spray could not possibly be a real spray of bloody matter; essentially, it disappears within a frame, which violates the laws of physics.)

The next level of sophistication involves "mattes". This is basically just a highly sophisticated form of the "cutting and pasting" that pre-school children carry out every day. David emphasized that it is quite possible to bring each frame's contents up to a much larger format, carry out the editing in the larger format, and then reduce the results down the intended final format (in the case of the Zapruder film, eight millimeter). A nice by-product of such a process is that, after reduction, any small imperfections in the "cutting" process in the large format are not visible, because the grain size of the final film provides an ulti-mate limit to resolution that will *automatically* smooth out the imperfections.

David then provided an overview of the techniques that can be used to "cre-ate" additional content, to fill in any "holes" in the images after foreground ob-jects have been cut out. (Part of this overview has already been published in a previous issue of *assassinationresearch.com*.) Such methods are more time-con-suming, and become prohibitively difficult if one does not already have the "raw material" corresponding to the imagery one wants to create. (This is one reason why it is highly likely that there were films of the assassination *other than* an "original" Zapruder film: it would be too difficult to create imagery of the motor-cycle escort, for example, because in such an "original" film such images would have been contained only in the sprocket-hole regions, which would have been spoiled by the "ghost images" from adjacent frames.) But if one has a "back-ground" or "pilot" film of Dealey Plaza, as Jack White has for some time sug-gested, together with footage of bystanders (waiting for the President to arrive, as Jack has also suggested), as well as actual footage of the limousine and its occupants during the assassination, then one has all the "raw ingredients" that one needs to fabricate the Zapruder film. The trajectories of objects can be cal-culated by a "mensuration expert" or "photogrammetrist"; motion blur can be simulated perfectly by moving the enlarger during an extended low-intensity exposure. These are the high-quality images that one would publish in *Life* maga-zine and in the volumes of the Warren Commission, which would withstand scientific analysis for authenticity—*provided that no mistakes were made.*

By the time that one gets to this level of sophistication, one is essentially performing a *photographic* fabrication, rather than a film fabrication: after all, a film strip is nothing more than a sequence of photographs, that will be displayed rapidly one after the other to give the appearance of continuous motion. David finished his presentation by displaying a photographic fabrication, made up of *ten* different individual photographic elements, seamlessly joined together with perfectly matched brightness and contrast. The real question was: could this sort of film mastery have been created in 1963? David answered the question with the simple observation that the fabrication he showed had been created *in 1858*, more than a century before the assassination.

John Costella

The bulk of my own presentation is described in detail in the sections below. I began my presentation by providing a short description of the optics that one needs to understand in order to study the Zapruder film with precision: ideal imaging systems; the effects of pincushion distortion; the behavior of perspec-tive in images, when one changes the direction of view; and so on. I then moved on to the results to be described shortly, making use of David Healy's explanation of the techniques and equipment that would have been used to carry out the actual fabrication of the film. I finished with the "best guesses" I provide below for the timeline in creating the film.

David Mantik

David Mantik did a wonderful job of lifting the pace and refreshing our minds. He began with an eye-opening overview of the history of film fabrication—and particularly for the purposes of propaganda. Together with David Healy's presentation of the technical means, this review put the fabrication of the Zapruder film into perfect historical perspective: means, motive, and opportunity. To my mind, the most important part of his work was his re-analysis of the extant Zapruder film by the method of "jiggle analysis" used by the Nobel-prize-winning physicist Luis Alvarez in 1975, which was published in the *American Journal of Physics* in 1976. David didn't use the same method as Alvarez, but instead used another method that should lead to the same conclusions, *if the Zapruder film were a genuine film*.

Although the squiggly graphs he showed on the screen probably meant nothing to anyone else in the audience, when I saw them my jaw almost dropped to the floor. The squiggles represented the "jiggling" of the Zapruder camera as Abraham Zapruder ostensibly filmed the assassination. (If Zapruder had "panned" his camera around to follow the limousine perfectly, the curves on David's graph would have been perfectly smooth.) David identified a number of areas of this "jiggling" that were slightly more violent than the others, which one would, using the Alvarez philosophy, assume to represent gunshots, or else something else that startled Abraham Zapruder.

As such, one might wonder where David was going with all this. Why would anyone want to re-do Alvarez's analysis, almost thirty years later, on the basis of a film which one knows *is a complete fabrication*?

The answer lies in the fact that neither David nor I would take any notice of such results, in terms of trying to figure out what actually happened on 22 November 1963. Rather, what was "on trial" here was *Alvarez's methodology*. David highlighted the fact that he had identified periods of "more violent" jiggling at times *that were different from what Alvarez found*.

Already, this tells us that someone is seriously wrong with the Alvarez study. The reason is that Alvarez's graphs (distributed on paper to all members of the audience at the start of David's presentation) show *very clearly* the periods of "jiggling" that Alvarez identified as gunshots, or other equally startling stimuli. They stood out in Alvarez's graphs like a few trees in an otherwise open, cleared field. How could David find evidence for "trees" in *different* locations?

The answer—which was evident to me the moment he put up his results—is that David's graph *showed "jiggling" right throughout the film*. In some places, the jiggling was a tad more violent; in others, a tad less violent. Trying to pick out "the" jiggles—the supposed responses to startling stimuli—was like trying to find the tallest trees in a *forest* of almost-equal-sized trees. But the analogy is not quite perfect: the task is *even more difficult* than this, because the "jiggles" oscillate about a central line, and what one wants to find is not necessarily the tallest "peak" or "trough" (although this would be a good hint as to where to start) but rather the greatest amount of "violence" of oscillation, which must take into account *a number* of oscillation cycles.

In my time I have sat through many a physics seminar where data this "noisy" had been presented, and where a "signal" for something had been claimed. Although there are a number of mathematical tests that one can apply to test for significance of such a "signal", any physicist seasoned in experimental data can look at such graphs and immediately recognize whether something significant has been found, or whether one is simply looking at the natural statistical fluctuations inherent in any piece of random noise. Looking at David's graphs, I knew that I was mostly looking at noise.

So how on earth did Alvarez present such "clean" data? He appears to have simply ignored any signs of blurring, except in those frames in which he thought he detected a large amount of blur. By taking frame-to-frame differences of these blur measures, he magnified them in size, apparently without taking into account that the uncertainties inherent in his method of ignoring other frames would likewise be magnified. Without quantifying these errors, he made the most elementary blunder that even first-year physics students are taught to avoid, all the while professing to offer a model of pedagogical instruction. [*Editor's note*: That a physicist of his caliber would commit such a blunder suggests that it must have been intentional, where submitting this piece as an example of teaching methodology was probably intended to circumvent the ordinary peer-review process and avoid being required to correct it.]

What this means is that the "jiggle analysis" performed by Luis Alvarez in 1975 is completely erroneous, extremely misleading, and bereft of any scientific justification. Which may explain the curious fact that his paper, by a highly respected Nobel laureate, has never been cited in a single professional physics journal—not once in the twenty-seven years since it first appeared! Its publication, moreover, which was accompanied by an editorial statement prohibiting further debate of this issue, has to qualify as the single most shameful action ever taken by the *American Journal of Physics* during its entire history—even rivaling the abuse of the *Journal of the American Medical Association* in the early 1990s. [*Editor's note*: See *Assassination Science* (1998), Part I.]

A by-product of David's analysis was the recognition that, throughout the extant Zapruder film, the pattern of the ostensible "jiggling" of the camera from frame to frame is fairly well consistent with what one expects for a human holding a hand-held camera, namely, it has a "power spectrum" that peaks at around three oscillations per second. Ironically, this result relies on other research that Alvarez himself performed—in 1962, in conjunction with Bell and Howell in developing methods for eliminating "jiggle" in hand-held cameras. Whether one should take this research at face value is, I guess, now open to question; but in any case the "jiggling" does provide a nice touch to what was, by any account, a technical *tour de force* in fabricating the Zapruder film. I have myself always felt that the "jiggling" throughout the film was introduced in order to ensure that it is difficult to follow the action with the naked eye, and to furthermore ensure that there were very few frames available in which images of either the foreground or the background were perfectly clear; this degree of blurring allows one a little more latitude in one's editing work. Getting this "jiggling" to match the typical behavior of a man holding a Zapruder camera, however, is a feat that would require a degree of research—or simulation (as was reported to have occurred extensively in Dealey Plaza in the weeks following the assassination).

David then presented a nice final touch to this research: he had performed the same sort of "jiggle analysis" on the *Muchmore* film. And the results surprised him— and me—greatly: his graph for the frame-to-frame movement of the Muchmore camera showed a beautifully smooth curve, without *any* apparent jiggling. Referring to the Alvarez interpretation, David joked that "maybe Muchmore was deaf"— she apparently hadn't been startled by any gunshots at all. In reality, of course, almost every presenter had emphasized the fact that, given that the Zapruder film is a fabrication, by necessity the short portions of the Nix and Muchmore films showing the limousine on Elm Street must *also* be fabrications. (The task is much easier for these films, being of much lower resolution, much shorter, and of an even more dubious chain of custody than the Zapruder film.) A caveat with the Muchmore analysis is that Marie, being behind the white concrete "peristyle" structure next to the reflecting pool on Houston Street, may have attained some degree of stability by perching her elbows on the "ledge" of the peristyle; but against any such explanation is the fact that she had ostensibly rushed over from her previous position in order to film the presidential limousine, and missed the start of its descent down Elm Street, which would seem to negate any possibility of her setting herself up in a "stable perch".

David Lifton

The next morning, I was eagerly looking forward to the presentation by David Lifton. David's account of being drawn into the investigation of the assassination in 1965, and to eventually figure out a large portion of the truth about the medical evidence, had stopped me from getting enough sleep last year when night after night I couldn't put down his book *Best Evidence* (1980, republished 1988). That he was still investigating the assassination nearly 40 years later was almost unbelievable to me; giving my presentation with Jack White and David Lifton in the audience reminded me of the story Richard Feynman told about having to give a nuclear physics seminar, as a young physicist, to find Niels Bohr, Wolfgang Pauli, and Albert Einstein all sitting in the audience. (For those less interested in physics than me, all four were Nobel laureates—Feynman not until 1965, however.)

Having said that, I had been a little apprehensive about David's late addition to the program. I was aware of several points of potential disagreement between David and other presenters—particularly over the subject of his most recent research, Lee Harvey Oswald—and, given the disruption to the Symposium caused by the withdrawal of retired Kodak scientist Roland Zavada (which by his own admission was caused by the fact that he would have no useful evidence to present in favor of his own opinion that the Zapruder film is authentic), I was keeping a very careful watch over any untoward developments.

But David did not disappoint. The potential points of contention evaporated into nothingness, and his presentation made my jaw drop—literally—many times. He tied up so many of the "loose ends"—of where things could have been done, and how, and why—things that I had no hope of ever knowing enough about to offer an opinion—that for the first time I felt we had a complete picture of what probably happened. Not that we know, for certain, all of the details; rather, we now know how the whole thing *could have been done*, with essentially no "gray" areas.

Again, not having taken any notes (knowing I could rely on the video when released), it would be impossible for me to try and reconstruct David's presentation from memory; the fact that he crammed what could easily have been a three-hour exposition into the bare one and a half hours that he had been able to be given makes any such thought infinitely more impossible. But highlights, for me, were a cogent explanation of why the (optically printed) rapidly edited versions of the film would have been sent to Rochester for developing, and his opinion as to where the more sophisticated photographic work would have been performed.

David put forward his own theory of where Abraham Zapruder fit into the whole process, which I do not personally agree with, but which nevertheless is a reasonable alternative that deserves to be considered alongside the more usual scenario. David believes that Zapruder was an innocent bystander drawn into the assassination by accident: that he just happened to take a film from the concrete pedestal in Dealey Plaza, exactly as he described, and that the planners of the assassination then realized that this film was a fly in the ointment, that needed to be dealt with urgently—which allowed the shrewd businessman Zapruder (and now his family) to secure a handsome profit. Personally, I believe that the filming of the assassination was planned all along; that, if the assassination had gone according to plan, the film may well have been able to have been shown on television within days; that the Zapruder pedestal was actually used for the coordinator of the assassination (it is the *only place in the whole of Dealey Plaza* that is in visual contact with every key location in the assassination, including the entire motorcade route, the upper floors of the Texas School Book Depository, and over the picket fence and through the windows of the pergola into the parking lot and railroad yard); and that Abraham Zapruder had been told what to do, perhaps by contacts within the intelligence or White Russian communities.

But as I sat there during David's presentation, I realized that we had passed a milestone. *No longer were we debating whether the Zapruder film was a fake*—we had finished with that question, and had passed into the domain of trying to figure out precisely *how* it was done, and what part it played in the entire assassination. Perhaps, five or ten years from now, answers to such questions may be known with the same certainty of proof that we now have for the fabrication of the Zapruder film. But for now, they are still open questions, and the greater the variety of *possible* scenarios under consideration, the greater the likelihood that progress will be made sooner rather than later.

Panel discussion

Following David Lifton's presentation (when he had to leave in order to catch a plane) there was a panel discussion hosted by Jim Fetzer. The first portion consisted of Jim asking questions of Jack White, David Mantik (until he also had to leave to catch a plane), and myself, which allowed us to present a "broad brush" overview of where the Zapruder film fabrication fits into the assassination as a whole. This overview was vitally important, because in any sequence of presentations concentrating on cutting edge research, it is always difficult to put the work in context—to stitch it together with what is already known to experts, but may not be known to those viewing the presentation.

Following that, Jim opened up the panel to questions from the audience. This allowed a more complete discussion of a number of issues raised during the Symposium. A highlight for me was the suggestion from Gary Severson that the first shot, deflected by the windscreen into the President's throat, was meant to be *the* shot—to the head—which would have occurred behind the Stemmons Freeway sign. Such an outcome would have allowed a film taken from the Zapruder pedestal (quite possibly by the coordinator of the assassination himself, according to my theory) to be shown to the public immediately: the President would have gone behind the sign alive, and come out the other side dead. This would also tie in with Jack White's observations (in *Murder in Dealey Plaza*) that "Zapruder" appears to be filming early on (as seen in the Willis and Betzner photos—if they are genuine in this region, of course), but as the limousine proceeds down Elm Street he seems to stop filming (as seen in the Bronson slide, the Moorman Polaroid, and the Nix film, in which he is apparently filming but then flinches away—again, assuming these to be genuine, in at least this region). If this had happened, there would have been no need for further shots, and a different patsy than Lee Harvey Oswald could have been implicated in a location in front of the President. Or Oswald could have been implicated, provided that the head wound was not demonstrably inconsistent with a shot from the Depository. Or conspirators could have been jointly implicated with Oswald.

Again, what was most heartening about this suggestion was the realization that *researchers were now considering what scenarios were possible given that the Zapruder film tells us absolutely nothing about the truth.* We had stepped out from behind the shadow of what was surely the greatest photographic hoax of all time.

The Hoax of the Century

The Stemmons Freeway sign and the lamppost

One of the most mysterious objects in the extant "Zapruder" film of the assassination is the Stemmons Freeway sign. There are so many curious aspects to its presence in the film that researchers have long suspected it to be the "weak link" in the fabrication of the film.

First, of course, is the question of why Abraham Zapruder would have chosen a filming location that would have placed the sign directly in his view as the motorcade traveled down Elm Street. Indeed, in his testimony, he was quite confused when viewing "his" film, being quite sure that he had actually filmed the entire procession down the street (and, in addition, had not missed the turn from Houston onto Elm). Early analyses of the film purportedly located a shot to the President around Frame 210—when the sign obscures the view completely! Visiting Dealey Plaza, it was patently clear that standing *next to* the Zapruder pedestal would have given a view that was almost as good; but, moreover, standing in the "Black Dog Man" position behind the white "retaining" wall would have given a far *superior* view—with no blockage by the sign at all!—all the way from the top of Elm down to the Triple Underpass, with the further benefits that one would not have to perch oneself atop a tall, narrow pedestal, but instead would have the ability to use the top of the white wall to prop one's arms on top of to give even more stability to one's filming.

Secondly, there are reports that the sign itself was taken down in the days following the assassination, subsequently replaced, and then finally removed altogether in the years following. But photographs taken by the Dallas Police Department on the Wednesday following the assassination show the sign in place. The question has remained: was the sign even taken down in the first days, and, if so, when was it replaced? It is quite possible that the story of the removal of the sign was deliberately introduced into the folklore of the assassination for disinformation purposes—to obfuscate the problems inherent in the sign's depiction in the "Zapruder" film. Alternatively, the removal and reinstallation of the sign may have been used as a means to try to hide mistakes made in the Zapruder film.

Thirdly, the very appearance of the sign seems to make no sense. Down each side of the back of the sign, in the extant film, are visible "panels" of lighter material. As researcher Jack White has pointed out, it was not possible to splice together the boards used to create the signs without a metal frame, and in any case it would seem to be of no purpose to splice such narrow pieces to each end of the sign.

When was the Stemmons Freeway sign locked into place?

Before studying the Stemmons sign further, it is worth asking when it was irreversibly "frozen" into place in the extant film. The answer lies in the 29 November 1963 issue of *Life* magazine, which was most likely rolling off the presses within two days of the assassination. Three of the images shown in that issue show parts of the Stemmons sign, including the bizarre "panels" down the edges (see Figure 1). These three images essentially fixed the Stemmons sign in place, as far as the "Zapruder" film is concerned, because they show the left, right and top edges of the sign, together with the supporting poles; the public distribution of millions of copies of this issue of *Life* removed the possibility of revising the depiction of the sign at any future time.

Figure 1. The three images published in the 29 November 1963 issue of Life *magazine (created and printed on the weekend of the assassination) that show the Stemmons Freeway sign.*

The square and level sign

The Stemmons sign shown in this early issue of *Life* has an additional noticeable property, over and above those already noted: it appears to be essentially "square on" to the Zapruder camera, as shown by the fact that the top and side edges of the sign are essentially at right angles. This "squareness" of the sign is somewhat perplexing, for several reasons.

Pincushion distortion

Firstly, if one examines the frames of the extant film, one finds (as described in the Introduction above) that there is a classical "pincushion" distortion, that effectively "pulls the corners" of each image out. This is most obvious when one views the top edge of the white wall in the background, which should (for an ideal imaging system) be perfectly straight, but in fact appears to bow out towards the corners of each frame. (See Figure 2.)

Figure 2. Frame 249 of the extant Zapruder film, showing the correct effect of pincushion distortion of the lens system of the Zapruder camera. The edges of the white wall in the background are straight in the real three-dimensional space of Dealey Plaza, which means that they should be straight in any image from an ideal imaging system. The very noticeable curvature of the white wall represents the effect of pincushion distortion: the "pulling out of the corners" of the frame.

When one examines the patent for the lens system used on the Zapruder camera, one finds that the designed degree of distortion matches exactly what is seen in the extant film. The reason that such distortion was essentially unavoidable, even for such a state-of-the-art domestic film camera, is that the lens system was designed for color imaging, over an adjustable range of zoom (wide angle or telephoto) for which the main goals are to avoid colored fringes on objects, as well as avoiding any loss of focus or other aberrations; to achieve these goals to a high degree of precision requires a trade-off in pincushion distortion, which is especially noticeable at maximum zoom.

As such, the extant film therefore exhibits a phenomenon—pincushion distortion—that *would* be expected for a genuine film shot through the Zapruder camera. But the problem is that the Stemmons Freeway sign should *also* have been consistently subjected to this pincushion distortion: it should bend and sway in the raw footage, for the same reason that the straight wall edge in the background is bent into a curved shape.

Removing the pincushion distortion

In its raw form, it is difficult to tell whether the extant film does show the correct pincushion distortion of the Stemmons sign. Fortunately, it is quite simple to use a modern digital computer to actually *remove the pincushion distortion* from the frames of the extant film. This is illustrated in Figure 3 for the raw frame shown in Figure 2. By removing the pincushion distortion, many other subtle artifacts of the pincushion distortion are also repaired, such as the "fattening" of the motorcycle cops in the original distorted image above.

Checking the distortion of Stemmons Freeway sign

We now need to check whether the Stemmons Freeway sign is also correctly affected by this pincushion distortion. There are two ways that we could con-

Figure 3. The same frame as shown above, but with the pincushion distortion removed by digital computer. Note that the edges of the white wall in the distance are now straight, as expected for an ideal imaging system. (Laying a straight edge against the image is the quickest way to verify the straightness of the edges; the curved frame edge creates something of an optical illusion.)

ceivably check this. The first option would be to examine the raw frames, as they exist in the extant film. As the sign passes across the field of view, the pincushion distortion should make it bend slightly towards the nearest corner of each film frame. Alternatively, we might examine the frames that have had the pincushion distortion removed. In these corrected frames, the sign should stay *exactly the same shape* and in *exactly the same orientation* as it passes across the field of view. Relative to the background, the sign as a whole might move left or right slightly, or up or down slightly, by the "parallax effect" caused by any movement of Zapruder's camera as a whole as he (ostensibly) filmed the motorcade—but that is the only possible variation of the sign, if the film were genuine. (To see the effects of parallax yourself, close one eye and hold your finger out in front of your face. Now move your head around. Your finger appears to shift left or right, or up or down, as you move your head, but your finger's *shape* and *orientation* relative to the background do not change.)

Frame 193   Frame 228

Figure 4. Two frames of the extant Zapruder film that may be used to check whether the Stemmons Freeway sign is self-consistent when pincushion distortion is taken into account.

Frame 193 *Frame 228*

Figure 5. After pincushion distortion has been removed and camera perspective brought to a common direction of view, the backgrounds of the two frames can be brought into exact alignment. However, when this is done, the right pole and right edge of the back of the Stemmons sign "flip-flops" in position and direction. This is impossible for a real sign photographed on a genuine film.

Frame 193 *Frame 228*

Figure 6. The same images as in Figure 5, with illustrative lines overlaid. Two of the vertical lines represent the alignment of the white wall in the background, and two the right pole and right edge of the sign. A movement of the Zapruder camera between Frame 193 and Frame 228 could shift the lines sideways, by the "parallax" effect, but it cannot change the angle, as seen here. This establishes the fabrication of the Stemmons sign on the extant film. (See color photo section.)

Clearly, it is simpler to follow the second option—provided that the effects of pincushion distortion *can* be removed (as it can by using a modern digital computer). The simplest way to perform the comparison is to analyze one side of the sign in two different Zapruder frames, one frame showing the sign near the bottom right of the frame, and the other frame showing it near the far left of the frame. For this purpose, Frames 193 and 228 of the extant "Zapruder" film serve our purposes admirably. (See Figure 4.) To compare these two frames, it is desirable to not only remove the effects of pincushion distortion, but also to take into account the fact that the Zapruder camera was pointing in two slightly different directions when the two frames were exposed; this latter effect is small, but should be accounted for in precision tests. Fortunately, it is again possible to use an advanced mathematical algorithm on a digital computer to transform the perspective of each image (after pincushion distortion has been removed) to represent what an ideal camera would have photographed when its center of view is pointed in a *common* direction. For definiteness, we take this common direction to be the top of the corner of the white wall in the background. (By "center of view" we mean the center of the part of the frame intended to be viewed through a projector, i.e., not including the region between the sprocket holes.)

After this is done, it should be possible to overlay the fixed objects of the two images exactly, if the film frames are genuine. Positioning and orienting the two backgrounds in this way yields the results shown in Figure 5. It can be seen that, whereas the two backgrounds can be aligned precisely, the Stemmons sign in the foreground appears to "bend" in opposite ways. This is made clearer when indicative lines are overlaid on the two images, as shown in Figure 6. The behavior of the Stemmons sign in the extant film is completely impossible for a real object in Dealey Plaza photographed through the Zapruder camera.

The Stemmons Freeway sign is fake

The inescapable conclusion is that *the Stemmons Freeway sign as seen in the extant "Zapruder" film is a fabrication*. It does not represent a physically real object that was present during the assassination. Rather, it has been inserted into the film after the event.

This is, of course, a remarkable confirmation of a long-held suspicion: that the Stemmons Freeway sign is the "weak link" in the fabrication of the extant film. But can we go further? Having determined that the Stemmons sign does not fit in with the physical objects in the background of the film, can we determine just *how* and *when* it was introduced into the film? Is it possible to glean some information about the fabrication process by studying this mismatch in more detail?

Indeed it is. But to do so we must first understand all of the effects of the pincushion distortion in greater depth, and understand how it has misled researchers in various ways in recent years.

Correct effects of pincushion distortion in the extant film

Firstly, we must recognize that the extant film *does* correctly exhibit a number of effects of the pincushion distortion of the Zapruder camera lens. We have seen in Frame 249, shown above, that the distortion has "bent" the straight edges of the white wall in the background, by exactly the amount that would be expected on the basis of the technical specifications listed in the patent to the lens system itself. Such correct distortion effects are seen throughout the extant film.

Another product of the pincushion distortion is the stretching of objects near the corners or edges of each frame, as noted above for the "fattening" of the motorcycle cops in Frame 249. Very many examples of this can be easily found throughout the extant film. All that one needs to do is compare the image of a fixed background object when it is near the edge of a frame, to the same object shown near the center of another frame. One invariably finds that the object appears to grow, as it gets further away from the center of the frame. This is a completely correct effect of the pincushion distortion of the lens system in the Zapruder camera.

"Background magnification"

This phenomenon has, however, been responsible for a mistaken hypothesis about the extant film: "background magnification". The reason for this illusion is subtle, but straightforward. The extra area of the film between the sprocket holes is (as viewed in normal orientation) to the left of the main frame area. Because this sprocket hole region is further from the center of view of the camera than any other part of each frame, the stretching effects of the pincushion distortion are most noticeable there. Now, on the whole, the extant film pans to the right as the motorcade proceeds down Elm Street. This means that background objects are continually being swept from the main frame area into the sprocket hole area, where they are enlarged noticeably by the pincushion distortion. In trying to match up frames to form a complete panorama—without realizing the effects of the pincushion distortion—researchers have, in the past, found it necessary to increasingly enlarge frames as the film pans further and further to the right. This has led to a mistaken hypothesis that the grassy background of the film was progressively enlarged after the last background objects disappeared from view.

In fact, there is no background enlargement, as will be shown shortly. This illusion is completely an artifact of the pincushion distortion.

Ironically, the *width* of the Stemmons Freeway sign itself obeys this magnification effect quite precisely—even though the *angles* of the sign edge and lamppost are not correct. As discussed in the Introduction, this was discovered when following up on work carried out by researcher David Mantik and published in *Assassination Science*. Mantik measured precisely the width of the sign on frames found in Volume XVIII of the Warren Commission *Exhibits* (1964), and discovered that the width of the sign grew subtly but increasingly rapidly as it moved into the region between the sprocket holes. This was taken to be evidence of alteration, but at the time of his measurements the large effects of pincushion distortion in the Zapruder camera were not realized. When the same measurements are performed after the pincushion distortion is removed (or, equivalently, when Mantik's measurements are corrected for this distortion using a relatively simple mathematical formula), it is found that the width of the sign stays completely constant, to within measurement errors, in all frames.

But this may seem quite perplexing. How can the Stemmons Freeway sign *correctly* exhibit one manifestation of pincushion distortion—the stretching of its width as it gets further from the center of the frame—but *not* exhibit *another* manifestation of the same effect—the bending of its edges towards the corners of each frame? This curious fact is, in fact, the key to determining when and how the Stemmons Freeway sign was inserted into the film.

A fake sign pasted onto a genuine background

Clearly, at least one genuine film of Dealey Plaza taken from the "Zapruder pedestal" (the concrete block Zapruder is said to have stood on with Marilyn Sitzman when taking his film) was available to the fabricators of the film, because even the images published in *Life* on the first weekend exhibit lines of sight that can only be correctly obtained from such a vantage point. The correct effects of pincushion distortion are also evident in the extant film as we now have it. These extant frames are compatible with those published in that early issue of *Life*, but it is difficult to determine whether the *Life* images *by themselves* are sufficient to demonstrate the correct pincushion distortion: the frames are sufficiently cropped (and of sufficiently poor quality) that there is nothing physical for which the distortion can be objectively and reliably verified. (For example, not enough of the white wall shown above is visible to determine its curvature.)

But we do have three first-weekend images in *Life* that show the back of the Stemmons Freeway sign (see Figure 1). These three frames determine the positions of the edges and poles of the sign relative to the background. *Any further frames of the "Zapruder" film that were produced had to show the sign in the same position as in these three published images.* The creators of the film must have realized this constraint as soon as they allowed these three images to be released to the public.

The blunder of the century

So where did the creators of the film go wrong? *They placed their version of the Stemmons Freeway sign onto the background imagery after the background was already pincushion distorted!* This is why the sign appears to be so beautiful and rectangular in the raw extant film frames: it was created that way! And this is why the sign's edges aren't pulled towards the corners like everything else in the extant film—indeed, as all real objects in Dealey Plaza *must* behave.

An interesting question is *why* this mistake arose. If, instead, the Stemmons sign had been pasted into the film *before* the pincushion distortion was applied, then the resulting fabrication would have been almost perfect (at least as far as the Stemmons Freeway sign is concerned). It is difficult to guess as to the exact reason why this was not done. It is possible that some of the footage used was already correctly distorted (possibly actually filmed through the Zapruder camera or one with similar characteristics), and the sign had to be repositioned at a late stage, just before publication of the first-weekend issue of *Life*. Alternatively, it is possible that the sign *was* in original draft images created in the first hours, but a decision was taken to move it after the pincushion distortion had already been applied. It has even been suggested that there is no evidence that the Stemmons Freeway sign actually existed at all in Dealey Plaza before the time of the assassination—in which case it may have been inserted into the film as a complete fabrication, in order to provide a "hiding place" for the first shot, and that a real sign was only erected in Dealey Plaza afterwards in order to agree with the film!

Testing the "pasted-in sign" hypothesis

The answer to the question of *why* the Stemmons Freeway sign was incorrectly added to the film may only be known when the full facts of the assassination are finally revealed. But it is important to at least check that the extant film does, in fact, support the hypothesis that the Stemmons Freeway sign was added to a background that was already pincushion-distorted. If this hypothesis were correct, we would expect to find the sign appearing to have a constant and consistent shape in the *raw* frames of the extant film, i.e., in the frames that have *not* had the pincushion distortion removed.

As can be seen in Figure 7, this is precisely what is found. Our hypothesis about the fabrication process has been confirmed: the image of the Stemmons Freeway sign seen in the extant film was pasted into the film after pincushion distortion was already in place, and hence never passed through the lens of the Zapruder camera. No evidence of the fraudulence of the "Zapruder" film is more unequivocal than this.

Frame 193   Frame 228

Figure 7. The raw versions of the frames analyzed above, without any removal of the pincushion distortion. The wall and bushes in the background are stretched horizontally in Frame 228, a correct manifestation of the pincushion distortion. The Stemmons Freeway sign, on the other hand, is identical in both frames, and aligns vertically with the background wall and bushes. This confirms that the Stemmons Freeway sign was pasted into the film after the pincushion distortion was already in place.

Hitting a raw nerve

After the analyses above were originally performed, questions were raised in some quarters—those described in the Introduction above—about the validity of the mathematical algorithms employed to remove the pincushion distortion and adjust the perspective direction of view of the images concerned. Although there seemed to be little justification for this attack—pincushion distortion being a well-understood and widely analyzed feature of photographic systems—it nevertheless led to a degree of uncertainty in the assassination research community, many of whose members simply lacked the background in mathematics or physics necessary to determine who was telling the truth.

Veteran researcher Jack White realized that what was needed was a more powerful and unequivocal test of the mathematical algorithms and computer programs that had been used. He traveled to Dealey Plaza in July 2002 and took a sequence of sixteen overlapping photographs from a precise height above the Zapruder pedestal, at approximately 10 degree intervals, which together panoramically covered the entire part of Dealey Plaza featured in the extant "Zapruder" film. (One of these images is shown in Figure 8.) The challenge was then laid down: use the computer programs to create a seamless panorama of Dealey Plaza, using only the sixteen images taken from the Zapruder pedestal.

Figure 8. One of the photographs taken by researcher Jack White in July 2002 to panoramically cover the view from the Zapruder pedestal.

Jack White's panoramic images of Dealey Plaza

The job of creating a seamless panorama was daunting, but feasible. After the small distortion of White's lens system was removed, the orientation of each photograph was adjusted to produce a consistent horizontal, the perspective of each was adjusted to yield a horizontal camera direction of view, and each resultant image was then mapped onto a sphere surrounding the camera position, making use of topographical information of Dealey Plaza, together with the overlap regions of adjacent photographs (about a third of each photograph on both the left and right sides). Because the effects of these transformations are intertwined, an iterative process was employed that rapidly converged on a self-consistent solution. The resulting spherical map surrounding the camera position was then mapped to a modified Mercator projection in which the meridians represent compass bearing from the camera location, and the equally spaced parallels represent the angle of depression from the camera height.

Over a hundred identifiable points on the resulting image were then compared with bearing and depression coordinates calculated on the basis of the
topographic survey drawn up for the House Select Committee on Assassinations.
The coordinates were found to agree with those calculated to generally better
than a tenth of a degree. A low-resolution version of the full panorama is shown
in Figure 9.

*Figure 9. A low-resolution version of the full panorama created
from the photographs taken by researcher Jack White in July 2002.
The full-resolution image is of about the same quality as that shown
in Figure 8; to reproduce it here would require an image ten times
as wide and ten times as tall as here shown.*

The critics silenced

After the construction of this panoramic view demonstrated the power of the
algorithms employed, it was asked whether it might be possible to construct a
similar panoramic view from the Zapruder pedestal *as it appeared in 1963.* To
this end, two photographs taken by members of the Dallas Police Department on
the Wednesday following the assassination were analyzed, together with a photograph later taken by the FBI's Lyndal Shaneyfelt (Shaneyfelt Exhibit #33 in the
Warren Commission volumes). These are shown in Figure 10.

*Figure 10. Three photographs that provide a view from the Zapruder pedestal
in late 1963. The first two photographs were taken by members of the Dallas
Police Department on the Wednesday following the assassination (wreaths and
memorials are visible). The third was taken by the FBI's Lyndal Shaneyfelt some
time after the assassination. Together, the three photographs almost completely
cover the view shown in the 2002 panoramic image above.*

Creating the 1963 panorama

Mapping these three historical photographs into the three-dimensional space
of Dealey Plaza was more challenging than those taken by Jack White in 2002,
because so few images were available, and because it was not known if any of
these views were cropped. However, detailed measurements taken from the pho-

tographs allowed an estimate of the lens distortion of the cameras used, and cropping was estimated by means of an iterative process of correcting the perspective of each image, mapping the result onto a sphere surrounding the Zapruder camera position, and then comparing the result with the 2002 panorama.

After these steps were performed, a "1963 panorama" from the Zapruder pedestal was created, by overlaying the mapped images over the 2002 panorama. (See Figure 11.) Alignment of all of the fixed objects seen in both panoramas was achieved, excepting only a discrepancy of the height of a the section of the Elm Street curb closest to the Zapruder position: the 1963 curb appears several inches lower than the 2002 curb. As the curb height may have been altered by road surfacing works in the intervening 39 years, the meaning of this discrepancy, if any, is not yet clear.

Figure 11. A low-resolution version of the panorama created from the three photographs shown above, mapped onto a sphere surrounding the Zapruder camera location, and overlaid on the 2002 panoramic image. This provides a "1963 panorama" of the view from the Zapruder pedestal.

A Zapruder panorama

After the successful creation of this "1963 panorama", it was asked whether the same might be done using the frames of the extant "Zapruder" film itself. To this end, forty-five such frames were chosen, that between them covered the entire panoramic view, with substantial overlap between adjacent frames to enable precise calibration and registration of fixed objects. Attached to many of these frames were the "ghost panels" representing the exposure of the region of film between the sprocket holes of adjacent frames from light allowed through the camera gate for the frame in question. These images were then corrected for pincushion distortion, perspective-adjusted for their direction of view, and again mapped onto a sphere surrounding the Zapruder camera position. A low-resolution version of the resulting image is shown in Figure 12.

Figure 12. A low-resolution version of the "Zapruder panorama", created from 45 different frames of the extant film, and mapped onto a sphere surrounding the Zapruder camera position.

This panoramic view of the extant "Zapruder" film was then overlaid on the "1963 panorama" shown above, which itself was overlaid on the "2002 panorama". This is shown in Figure 13. The ability to construct this panoramic version of the extant film, and overlay it on the 1963 and 2002 panoramic views, had several crucial ramifications.

Figure 13. The "Zapruder panorama" above, overlaid on the "1963 panorama", which itself is overlaid on the "2002 panorama". This reconstruction answered a number of outstanding questions regarding the extant film and its correspondence with real objects in Dealey Plaza.

Understanding the background of the extant film

Firstly, the Zapruder panorama provided the final proof that the phenomenon of "background magnification" was, indeed, an illusion of the pincushion distortion of the Zapruder lens, together with the direction of panning of film as the motorcade proceeded down Elm Street, as described above. Had there been any actual magnification of the background, it would not have been possible to "stitch" the Zapruder frames together and overlay the result on the other panoramas.

Secondly, it allowed the various bystanders seen in the extant film to be located in context in Dealey Plaza—a process that is difficult to perform with the raw frames of the extant film, because of the maximum zoom setting of the lens of the (presumed) Zapruder camera.

Most importantly, however, the Zapruder panorama overlay allows us a chance to again examine the Stemmons Freeway sign, as it appears in the extant film. When one examines in detail that part of the overlay showing the sign, one finds that the backgrounds of the two panoramas can be overlaid precisely, but *the Stemmons Freeway sign itself is completely inconsistent* (see Figure 14). Of only minor consequence is the fact that the sign appears to be too far to the left in the extant film: this could easily be produced by the "parallax effect" if the Zapruder camera were moved around somewhat during filming. Most damning, rather, is the fact that it is *too wide* in the extant film, and that *the angles of its edges are wrong*. Indeed, the Zapruder panorama shows somewhat blurred edges for the Stemmons sign, because of its inconsistencies from frame to frame under the removal of pincushion distortion, as analyzed above. But even allowing an "average", blurred image of these edges, its incorrectness is still manifest.

The sign is wrong in every respect

To investigate this discrepancy in detail, it is again worthwhile separating the two panoramic images and viewing them side-by-side. This is shown in Figure 15.

*Figure 14. Enlargement of a portion of Figure 13. The background of
the extant film matches the "1963 panorama", but the Stemmons Freeway
sign does not.*

This comparison confirms a discrepancy that has been recognized for many years:
that between the extant film and the Dallas Police Department photographs taken
five days after the assassination. But defenders of the authenticity of the film
have an explanation for this discrepancy: for reasons unknown, the Stemmons
Freeway sign was (according to the explanation) removed following the assassination, then re-erected before the Dallas Police Department photographs were
taken, only to be removed again afterwards, and then re-erected by the FBI when
they re-created the scene photographically for the benefit of the Warren Commission.

*Figure 15. Corresponding portions of the "Zapruder panorama" and the
"1963 panorama". All background objects in the two images are aligned, but
the Stemmons Freeway sign is different.*

The lamppost separates the wheat from the chaff

Refuting such a scenario (however bizarre) is difficult, especially as it seems
to have become a part of the folklore surrounding the assassination. Fortunately,
however, the tale focuses on just the Stemmons Freeway sign, and ignores one
further "foreground" object to the right of the sign: the *lamppost* on Zapruder's
side of Elm Street, that the motorcade passes behind just before passing the
Charles Brehm, his son, and Beverly Oliver. Comparing this lamppost in the two
panoramas allows us to determine whether the tale can be believed.

Such a comparison is shown in Figures 16 and 17. Again, the actual *position* of the lamppost—to the left in the extant film compared to the "1963 panorama"—can be explained by the parallax effect if the Zapruder camera was in a slightly different position. *But the angle of the lamppost cannot be changed by parallax.* This tells us that *both* the lamppost *and* the Stemmons Freeway sign were improperly added to the extant film. (See the appendix below describing my visit to Dealey Plaza in May 2003 to see the lengths gone to in order to discredit any work that analyzes the angle of the lamppost.)

Figure 16. The lamppost in the "Zapruder panorama" and the "1963 panorama". Again, all background objects in the two images are aligned, but the lamppost is on a different angle in the extant "Zapruder" frame than it was just days later. There are no reports of the lamppost also being broken out of the concrete sidewalk and replaced on a different angle within days of the assassination. It, like the Stemmons Freeway sign, was positioned improperly in the fabrication of the film.

Figure 17. The angle of the lamppost in the extant film is wrong by about 1.5 degrees, as illustrated by the overlaid lines. The photograph taken by the Dallas Police Department shows the lamppost to be perfectly vertical, as seen from the Zapruder pedestal (the panoramas have been constructed to keep vertical objects vertical). The extant "Zapruder" film shows the lamppost leaning slightly to the right; it makes an angle of about 1.5 degrees with the vertical.

Inconsistencies leave no doubt about alteration

In summary, it is important to realize that the Dallas Police Department photograph—and indeed the entire 1963 panorama—is *not* needed to demonstrate that the extant Zapruder film is a hoax. As shown above, the Stemmons Freeway sign's depiction is *internally inconsistent* in the frames of the extant film: that it does not suffer from the pincushion distortion of all other real objects tells us at which stage it was inserted in the fabrication of the film. What the 1963 photograph *does* provide is an alternative view of Dealey Plaza from the Zapruder pedestal—and this view provides additional damning evidence, not just for the falseness of the depiction of the Stemmons Freeway sign, but also of the lamppost to its right. Together, these analyses remove any doubt that the extant "Zapruder" film is a fraud—a hoax—that was most carefully crafted from real footage taken both before and during the assassination, and was almost—*but not quite*—technically perfect.

The Moving Limo that isn't Moving

To date, one of the apparently strongest pieces of evidence of the non-genuineness of the extant "Zapruder" film had been an observation in Noel Twyman's *Bloody Treason* by Dr. Roderick Ryan, an Oscar award winner for technical contributions to the motion picture industry, regarding Frames 302 and 303. (See Figure 18.) After examining the differently blurred backgrounds in the two frames, Dr. Ryan concluded that the limousine was moving in Frame 302, but was stationary in Frame 303. Unfortunately, this conclusion, apparently obtained on visual grounds, does not hold up under detailed scrutiny.

If one removes the pincushion distortion from Frames 302, 303, and 304, and then overlays them precisely, one finds that the limousine moves 0.53° to the right in each frame period, relative to the background, as measured at the Zapruder lens position. Now, the shutter of Zapruder's Bell and Howell 414PD camera is open for a time equal to about 45 percent of the period between exposures, which means that the limousine should move about 0.23° while each frame is being exposed. This calculation is completely independent of the actual speed of the camera.

Frame 302　　　　　　　　　　　　　　Frame 303

Figure 18. Two frames of the extant film that have mystified researchers.

Understanding the blurs within a single frame

Let us first understand what this figure for the motion of the limousine means in the context of an arbitrary Zapruder frame.

Imagine the camera were to be held absolutely stationary, relative to the background, during the exposure of a frame. In that case, the background would not be blurred at all, and the limousine would be blurred left–right by an amount equivalent to an angle of 0.23° at the Zapruder camera position. (The motion of the limo is approximately left–right for these frames, as oriented in the extant film.)

Now imagine that the camera were to instead pan along perfectly with the limo. In that case, the limo would not be blurred at all, but the background would be blurred left–right by 0.23°.

Now consider the case when the camera partially follows the limousine, but not by the full amount of 0.23°. Let's say it only pans right by 0.10° during the frame exposure, relative to the background. This would mean that the background would be blurred by 0.10°, and the limo would be blurred by 0.13°, because the limo moves relative to the moving camera by this amount during the exposure of the frame. One can see that, for this camera motion, the blur of the limo plus the blur of the background must add up to 0.23°.

But these cases do not exhaust the possibilities. The camera can, of course, move up or down as well, but even excluding such motion for our current discussion, and restricting our attention to left–right panning, there are two further possible cases. Firstly, if the camera were to actually pan *to the left* relative to the background, by (say) 0.10° during the frame exposure, then the background would be blurred by 0.10°, and the limo would be blurred by 0.33°. You can still understand this as "adding up to 0.23°", if you take the background blurring to be a "negative" blurring (even though "negative" and "positive" blurring actually look identical, unless something in the background is moving upwards or downwards).

Finally, if the camera were *panning to the right faster* than the limousine's motion, say by 0.43° during the frame exposure, then the background would be blurred by 0.43°, and the limo would be "negatively" blurred by 0.10°.

The blurs in Frames 302 and 303

Let us now examine the actual amount of blurring in each of Frames 302 and 303. This can be estimated most easily if we have available a point-like object: the length of the line that such an object is blurred into is a good estimate of the amount of blurring during the exposure of the frame. The specular reflections from the bubbletop attachment bar on the limousine provide four convenient point-like objects for the limo itself, and can be checked against other features of the limo. Alternatively, we can examine the gradual transition of intensity and color, in the blurred image, of what should be a relatively sharp edge between two solid regions in real life.

When we do this, on a good quality copy of the frame, we find that in Frame 302 the limousine is blurred by about 0.14°, and the background objects are blurred by about 0.37°. *This is consistent with the Zapruder camera panning faster to the right than the limo's motion.* It causes the background to be excessively blurred, and the limo slightly blurred in the "negative" direction (the limo is moving backwards in the field of view of the camera, because the camera is panning too quickly to the right).

For Frame 303, we now find that the limousine is blurred by about 0.13°, but the background is blurred by only 0.10°. The background is far sharper than it was in the previous frame, yet the limousine's blur is essentially unchanged. At a first visual glance, this looks highly anomalous. But note that *the blurs again add up to 0.23°*. This is consistent with the Zapruder camera panning to the right at a rate that is *slower* than the limousine's motion. The total blur of 0.23° is almost divided evenly between the limo and the background, and provides one of the sharpest overall frames in this segment of the film. *But it does not violate the laws of physics.* It is for this reason that Dr. Ryan's conclusion cannot be supported.

This is not to say that Frames 302 and 303 are genuine. If one examines these frames in detail, one finds that some objects appear to be sharper than they should be; for example, the driver Greer, and the two "flaps" above the windscreen, are all sharper in Frame 303 than the specular reflections. This discrepancy is not completely unexpected, given the other anomalies that can be found in these frames (to be discussed shortly).

Blurring in other frames

Given the loss of the "smoking gun" of Frames 302 and 303 (as far as the blur is concerned, at least), one might wonder whether all frames of the extant film survive the same analysis. Of course, it is not practical to perform the analysis on all objects in all 486 frames of the extant film. However, one would expect that frames published most rapidly after the assassination would be most subject to mistakes— especially since some of the details of the timing of the film (and hence the speed of the limo) may not have been finalized. And this is, indeed, what we find.

Too much haste

The Memorial Edition of *Life*, published just weeks after the assassination, provides the first really high quality, color images of the Zapruder film. Two of these images, in particular, are of remarkable clarity. But on closer examination, one finds that they are simply *too* clear: both the background *and* the limo are not subject to any motion blur, yet—according to the film we now have—the limo was indeed moving at the time. The cleaner of the two images to analyze is shown in Figure 19. It corresponds to what we now refer to as Frame 232 of the Zapruder film.

Figure 19. Image from the Memorial Edition of Life. *Note the point-like highlights in the bushes, and the tree leaves against the tree trunk. Note also the point-like reflection below Kellerman's door handle. Comparison with other frames establishes that these point-like objects are not imperfections in the film.*

An analysis of modern copies of Frames 231, 232, and 233 establishes that the limousine moved by 0.28° in each frame period, which implies that it moved by 0.13° during the exposure of Frame 232. This distance is shown in Figure 20.

By the same arguments as used above to explain the self-consistency of Frames 302 and 303, the blurring of the background *plus* the blurring of the limousine and the motorcycles must add up to *at least* 0.13°. But clearly there are many features and edges in the image that rule out any such conclusion. Most conspicuous are various point-like highlights, both in the background and on the limousine, which other frames establish as ostensibly genuine objects in Dealey Plaza, rather than artifacts or imperfections in the film or its reproduction. (The particular spot on the limousine pointed out in Figure 20 can be seen on clear photographs of the limousine unrelated to the Zapruder film; see, for example, the image on the front cover of *Assassination Science*. This is important, because if it were simply a reflection of an object not connected with the limousine, it would not establish the anomalous nature of the blur in the image.)

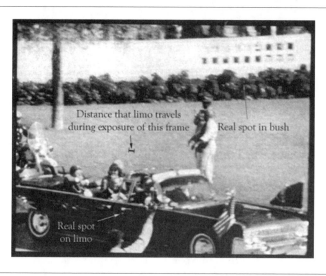

Figure 20. The same image as Figure 19, with the distance the limo moves during the exposure of the frame indicated, and two examples of point-like objects highlighted. If the image were genuine, either the entire limo or the entire background would be blurred by the amount shown, or some combination of the two. (See the color photo section.)

Evidence of complete fabrication, not simply alteration

The existence of this impossible image in *Life*, within a matter of weeks of the assassination, demonstrates that the film was completely *fabricated*, rather than simply *altered* (as was established by the fraudulence of the Stemmons Freeway sign).

Objects were not simply added to or deleted from the film; frames were not simply excised before the final film was created. Rather, *the entire film is a creation*. To be sure, it is "based on a true story": actual pieces of footage of Dealey Plaza, of the bystanders, and of the presidential motorcade were most certainly used. But these film elements were edited together, before publication in *Life*, and elsewhere.

It is reasonable to assume that the image in Figures 19 and 20 was published before the timeline of the film—and hence the putative speed of the limo—had been finalized. It, together with its counterpart shown in Figure 21, provides a crucial snapshot of what can only be generously described as "work in progress".

Figure 21. Another impossibly sharp image from the same page of Life.

When is a hole not a hole?

Answer: When it's a sprocket hole in the "Zapruder" film!

It is usually assumed that the first published images of the "sprocket hole areas" of the Zapruder film were the black and white images published in the Warren Commission *Exhibits* in November 1964. But contained within the color images published by *Life* for their 2 October 1964 issue on the Warren Commission *Report* (presented to President Lyndon Johnson on 24 September 1964) is a small glimpse of one sprocket hole, which may provide a crucial insight into the processes used to fabricate the film.

It has been reported that at least three different versions of the Warren Report issue of *Life* were published—and to this day their chronological order remains a point of contention. In at least one of those versions appears a portion of what would later be determined to be Frame 347 of the extant Zapruder film (see Figure 22).

Apart from the strange appearance of Secret Service agent Clint Hill's right forearm, this image is unique because it appears to show the top-right corner of the lower sprocket hole. No later issue of *Life* showed the edge of any sprocket hole. (A small part of one edge of a sprocket hole was published in the Memorial Edition in early December 1963, but does not shed any light on the fabrication of the film. The 24 November 1966 issue, that showed the inter-sprocket region of many frames, had black masks applied in the shape of sprocket holes, which overlapped and covered the actual edges of the holes.) [*Author's note*: The 25 August 2003 issue of *Life*, "100 Photographs that changed the world", published

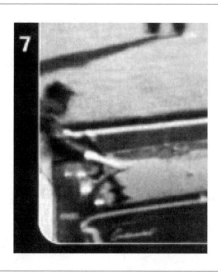

Figure 22. Part of an image in one version of the 2 October 1964 issue of Life, *showing what appears to be part of the lower sprocket hole, together with a "ghost" image from the next frame exposed through the gate of the camera.*

since this chapter was written, shows frame 313 with sprocket holes. Unlike the familiar photo of LBJ being sworn in, however, it did not make the "Top 100".]

The sprocket hole shown above presents something of an enigma. Stretching up towards Clint Hill's right armpit is a bright white "ghost" image, which has been explained as part of the exposure of Frame 348, shining through the gate of Zapruder's Bell and Howell 414PD camera into the inter-sprocket area of Frame 347 (which at that time had already been exposed and wound on). Below this, at about the level of the top of his hip, the top-right corner of the sprocket hole itself can be seen curving around. But what is remarkable is what happens when the edge of the hole crosses the ghost strip: instead of the interior of the hole being completely white—as would be expected when a hole (i.e. an absence of film) is exposed to light—we instead see a *pale blue strip* (when the image is viewed in color) beside the ghost strip!

This behavior makes no sense if we assume that the curved line does indeed represent the edge of the sprocket hole; a hole is a hole: it cannot be anything other than white. To check that we are not misinterpreting this curve, we can overlay the *Life* image on the same frame published on DVD by MPI in the late 1990s (labeled as Frame "346" by them; see the summary of Jim Fetzer's Symposium presentation above). (See Figure 23.) Reference to the full MPI image establishes that the curved line does, indeed, represent the putative edge of the sprocket hole. But now we see something utterly remarkable: the curved edge of the sprocket hole, which in the *Life* image clearly cuts across the ghost strip, has now been subtly but unmistakably bent around to give the impression that it continues on as the *left* line—which in the *Life* image is merely the continuation of the ghost strip!

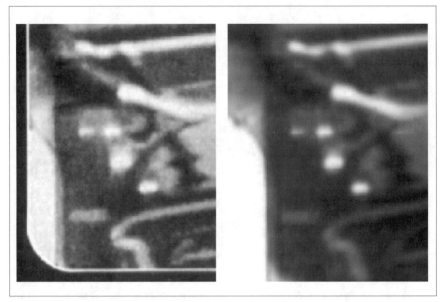

Figure 23. Comparison of the sprocket hole shown in the 2 October 1964 issue of Life *with that published on DVD by MPI in 1998.*

A double exposure rather than a real hole

What does this change mean? Clearly, it was a mistake that *Life* were unwilling to repeat: never again were the edges of sprocket holes shown for Zapruder frames. [*Author's note*: until this year!] It is noteworthy that, in both (color) versions of the image, the "overlap" region is a lighter blue color, matching the appearance of the adjacent chrome areas of the limousine. This suggests that it may be a double exposure: the deep blue of the limousine subsequently exposed with a white sprocket-hole shape. The brighter (apparently white) area to the left of this lighter blue strip—which in the MPI version is unmistakably meant to represent the "true" sprocket hole—seems to represent the *triple* exposure of the deep blue limo, the white sprocket hole shape, and the bright "ghost" image through the gate in the next frame's exposure.

If this analysis is correct, it provides crucial information about how the film was fabricated. It implies that the entire film, *including images of "sprocket holes"*, was fabricated as a complete whole, most likely in a format much larger than 8 mm, and that this was then transferred to a genuine Kodak 8 mm film of the correct vintage.

Such a scenario has been put forward in recent years by researcher David Healy, and was at variance with my own earlier hypothesis that the edited scene imagery may have been re-photographed through Zapruder's actual camera to induce the correct lens distortion and ghost imagery. Healy's scenario would simply require the fabricators to obtain an analysis of the image characteristics of the Zapruder camera, and replicate them with optical elements. Such effects were well within the capabilities of 1963 technology.

Sprocket hole haloes

Supporting Healy's scenario is an observation made by David Mantik in *Assassination Science* that the sprocket holes of the extant film (as examined by him personally in the National Archives) often appear to have "haloes" around them. Such an effect can be understood if the "sprocket holes" were originally added to the fabricated film by simply exposing sprocket-hole shapes of white light. At first, it may have been believed that all that would ever need to be produced were enlarged *copies* of the film showing inter-sprocket regions, for which such an artifice would be more than sufficient. But at some point it was clearly recognized that an actual 8 mm "camera original" film would need to be produced. Although the sprocket holes in the double-8 film stock used followed quite tight tolerances, it is understandable that small registration errors were unavoidable; in other words, the *real* holes in the strip of 8 mm film did not perfectly align with the sprocket hole-shaped areas projected onto it from the fabricated film.

The existence of these haloes also provides a possible explanation for why the MPI images of the film are so relatively dark: the haloes are so much less obvious when the contrast between them and the background (often the limousine itself) is set to such a low level. Even the image shown above—which has itself been brightened to make it more comparable to the *Life* image—still leaves a halo region that may not, at first, be noticed. Fortunately, the extremely bright image in *Life* highlights the anomaly for us.

The disappearing blood spray

In the wider context of the assassination, the most incongruous feature of the extant "Zapruder" film is arguably the depiction of a single, fatal shot to the President's head, which appears to blow out the entire right temple area, leaving a massive "crater". (See Figure 24.)

The obvious inconsistencies between this imagery and the wounds to the President when he arrived at Parkland Hospital are enough to convince any serious student of the assassination that this section of the film is a complete fabrication. (Author David Lifton seems to be the first person to have made this observation in print, in his 1980 book *Best Evidence*.) But even leaving aside this "medical" evidence of alteration, the film itself can be examined for physical inconsistencies that would not occur if it were genuine, but which may have been overlooked if created as a work of "special effects".

The "explosion" in Frame 313

The bright red "explosion" shown in Frame 313 of the extant film appears to be a completely spurious addition. Recall that this "explosion" is not a ball of flame (as it would be if it were a special effect for an action movie), but rather is supposed to represent bloody matter ejected from the President's head. Now, whereas flame is caused by the emission of light upon the combustion of some material (which will subside when the fuel is spent), the red "spray" shown in Frame 313 ostensibly represents the reflection of light from the bloody matter, which would persist while this matter remains in the field of view.

The question, then, is how long one would expect the "bloody spray" to remain in the field of view, if the film were genuine.

Figure 24. Taken from Frames 304 through 326 of the extant Zapruder film. Note that the "explosion" (which is red when viewed in color; see the color insert section) almost completely disappears by the next frame.

The most obvious explanation for its quick disappearance is that it is somehow being carried along, at supersonic velocities, by the shock wave generated by the bullet in the President's head. But a simple matter of timing rules out any such explanation. The reason is that Frames 313 and 314 (in wider view) show some sort of projectile ejected upwards and forwards from the President's head—which has been presumed to be a spinning piece of bone, because of the way it appears at regular intervals in each of the frames (i.e., with a piece of it "glinting" in the sunlight as it spins). An analysis of the motion of this projectile in the two frames—which shows that it has traveled about twice as far by the end of Frame 314 as by the end of Frame 313—reveals that the bullet must have impacted just after the end of the exposure of Frame 312, which is about half a frame before the start of the exposure of Frame 313. (The Zapruder camera exposes each film frame for about 25 milliseconds, and spends about 30 milliseconds winding the film on for the next exposure, so that the shutter is open nearly half of the time; this ratio is fixed, *regardless* of whether the actual operating speed of the camera was 18.3 frames per second or some other value.) Since any other object traveling at high velocity from the impact of the bullet must trace back to the same time of impact, the distance traveled by the end of Frame 314 can only be about twice that traveled by the end of Frame 313. Thus, it is quite impossible that the "blood spray" that is seen just barely emerging from the President's head in Frame 313 could disappear almost completely by the end of Frame 314.

Disappears faster than a lead ball

The next most plausible explanation is that the "spray" quickly falls into the limousine, or below the side of the limousine, out of view. But if one does the calculations, one finds that even a *lead ball* would take half a dozen frames to drop out of view, if dropped from the epicenter of the "explosion" seen in Frame 313. A spray of bloody matter droplets would take even longer, because of air resistance; indeed, it would most likely "hang" in the air for an appreciable time (on the time scale here being considered).

The final way out of the dilemma is to suggest that, as the "spray" disperses after Frame 313, it becomes less noticeable against the other objects seen in the scene—in other words, that it is still contained within the following frames, but is simply not visible to the naked eye. Such an explanation seems quite reasonable; but, moreover, it can be tested by explicitly analyzing the color components of each frame of the extant film. Such an analysis is complicated slightly by the unreliable adjustments to the brightness of the film made by MPI, on a frame-by-frame basis, after they digitized the film, but it is possible to normalize out these adjustments by means of careful measurements.

The graphs in Figure 25 show the total red, green, and blue components of each of the frames shown in the figure above. Smooth changes to these totals would be expected as the President and Mrs. Kennedy change their position, and as the perspective of the limousine itself changes as it passes the Zapruder position. The excess in all three channels that starts at Frame 313 and rapidly dies off (within six frames) corresponds to the whitish "haze" surrounding the head shot.

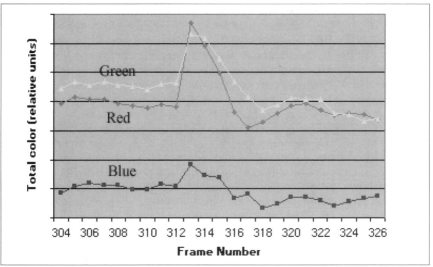

Figure 25. Graphs showing the total amount of red, green, and blue in each of the frames shown in the previous figure (relative units, zero suppressed).

In addition to this is an excess in the red channel concentrated on Frame 313—in other words, the "blood spray" itself disappears within a *single* frame.

A work of special effects

These results confirm that what is visible to the naked eye is not just an optical illusion. The "spray" that appears in Frame 313 starts to disappear immediately, and far too rapidly, to represent physically real matter: it has essentially disappeared completely within six frames—which is, recall, the time needed for a lead weight to drop out sight!

The inescapable conclusion is that the head shot depicted in the extant film is a work of special effects. Indeed, when the above frames are viewed as a continuous video clip, the head wound seems to morph into different shapes, with the infamous "blob" moving around for no apparent reason (as has been noted by analysts of the film for many years).

The Mysterious Object in the Grass

Another of the most noticeable properties of the extant Zapruder film is the scarcity of background reference objects in the portion of the film purporting to show the fatal shot to the President's head. This was quite possibly by design: access to the grassy region between Elm and Main Streets may have been relatively restricted in the hours before the assassination. Clearly, restricting the number of bystanders in the background would make any film editing work much easier to accomplish.

The black and white images in the issue of *Life* that was rolling off the presses on the weekend of the assassination provide a fascinating insight into the status of the work in progress in those early days, especially when compared to what was later presented as the "Zapruder film". We are to believe that three seconds of footage surrounding the fatal shot were not used at all; that it was decided that any images used would be cropped to completely exclude the Brehms, Beverley Oliver, Mary Moorman, and Jean Hill from view—they do not appear in any frames in this first-weekend issue (indeed, Moorman and Hill never appeared in *any* issue of *Life*); and that poor-quality images, clearly many generations removed from any original footage, would be used by the new owners of the camera-original film. Such actions would make little sense if *Life* were genuinely reporting their "scoop" evidence of the assassination, but they make perfect sense if one assumes that the process of fabricating what we now know as the "Zapruder" film was still in progress, and options had to be kept open until it was sure that all other photographic evidence of the event had been rounded up and analyzed. (Recall that Beverley Oliver was filming—her film was reportedly taken and never seen again—and that Moorman took a photo with a Polaroid camera—which was quickly seized by authorities after the assassination.)

But is there an even more specific message in these eccentricities of the first-weekend issue of *Life*? The three-second gap surrounding the head shot suggests that the details of this fatal injury were being kept open (indeed, the text accompanying the images states that the President "collapses" onto his wife's shoulder—no mention of a shot at all!). But more than this, the lack of any bystanders in the background and the poor quality of the reproductions make it completely impossible to estimate *the speed of the limousine* in this crucial period of time.

The speed of the limousine is tied to image blur

Why were these image properties necessary to mask the speed of the limousine? Because if there had been any identifiable object in the background—such as a bystander—the relative blurring of the limousine and the bystander would have allowed the speed of the vehicle to be estimated fairly accurately. And even without bystanders, if the image quality had been better—even only as good as Groden's bootleg copies, or what has been published by MPI in the 1990s—then bumps and other undulations in the grass itself would have been sufficient for an estimate of speed to be made. By avoiding or eliminating bystanders, and degrading the quality of the reproductions sufficiently, the speed of the limousine around the time of the fatal shot was left open.

These observations gain in importance when juxtaposed with the disagreement between the extant Zapruder film and witnesses to the event as to whether the limousine stopped or not. Witnesses of "other" (as yet publicly unreleased) films of the assassination have reported that the limousine actually stopped—in agreement with the majority of eyewitnesses—and that there were two clearly separate shots to the President's head. The extant Zapruder film, in contrast, shows the limo slowing only slightly, with a single explosive shot to the President's head. Because this extant footage is internally inconsistent, it is highly likely that the eyewitnesses presented a more faithful representation of the assassination.

The missing object in the grass

Moreover, there is one feature of the extant film that seems to seal its fate. Beginning in the same frame—Frame 313—that the heat shot impacts, a bright, small object in the grass in the background can be seen entering the field of view. This object moves across the field of view over succeeding frames, and provides a firm indication of the vehicle's motion. Indeed, the object is correctly blurred, in various directions and by various amounts, in concert with the apparent tracking error speed of the "Zapruder" camera.

The only problem is that this object is completely absent from the images published in that first-weekend issue of *Life*, as noted by David Mantik in *Assassination Science*, and this absence has left proponents of film authenticity stumped for a reasonable answer. (See Figure 26.) If it were missing from just one frame, one might argue that it had been retouched for the purpose of publication, being mistaken for a photographic blemish. But there are many other spots and other artifacts clearly visible in the published images, which have *not* been edited out. Why would *Life* edit this one object in the grass, and leave all the other blemishes, if the goal was to clarify the poor-quality images they were working with? And why were their images so poor anyway, when they supposedly owned the original film?

More importantly, the object is actually missing from *three different frames* published on the same page of *Life*! Thus, if one assumes that staff members at *Life* were actually in possession of frames of what appeared to be a genuine film, then they must have realized that the object was not a photographic defect, but rather represented some real object in Dealey Plaza. This would imply that *Life* actively *edited the film* prior to publication, which is hardly helpful to those who believe that the film is genuine and above suspicion. Why would *Life* edit out this one object, and no others? Did they perhaps believe it to be a bullet lying in the

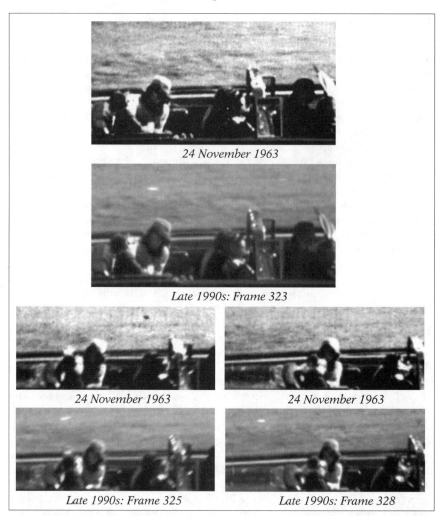

24 November 1963

Late 1990s: Frame 323

24 November 1963

24 November 1963

Late 1990s: Frame 325

Late 1990s: Frame 328

Figure 26. The three frames published in the 29 November 1963 issue of Life (printed on the weekend of the assassination) in which the "object in the grass" is missing, juxtaposed with their modern counterparts from the MPI DVD.

grass? How could we then place any faith in the evidence provided by this rapid publication of frames by *Life*?

The simplest explanation is that the object in the grass was probably added at a later date, to explicitly give the impression that the limousine was moving (at a speed of something up to ten miles per hour) at the time that the President received a single shot to the head.

A retouched object, later added back in?

Whether or not there was *actually* an object in the grass at that position is difficult to ascertain. The version of Frame 323 published in that first issue of

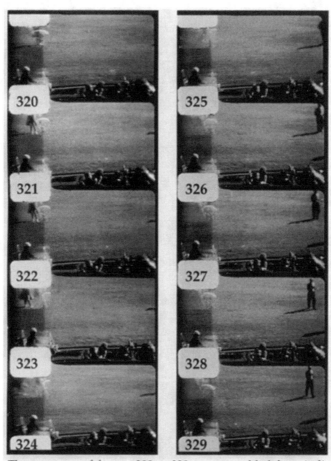

The sequence of frames 290 to 329 was assembled from individual slides stored in the National Archives.

Figure 27. From page 170 of Stewart Galanor, Cover-Up *(1998).*
The original is in color.

Life (which was reproduced in a larger format than the other frames published) seems to show a faint but visible "puddle" in the area where the object should be, which, at first glance, seems to represent a rough job of retouching. Amazingly, however, the modern version of this same frame—apparently taken directly from the camera-original Zapruder film—seems to show the same "puddle", but superimposed with the mysterious object! (This may be just discernible in the reproductions shown above.) Thus, unless we are to believe that *Life* altered the camera-original film in just this way, making no other changes (a bizarre suggestion that *no* assassination researcher has proposed!), this apparent evidence of retouching simply provides more questions—and doubts—than answers.

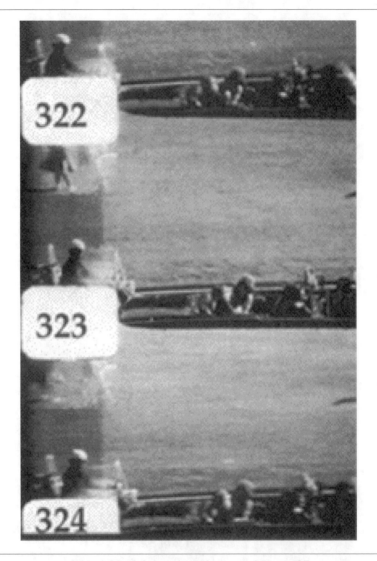

Figure 28. Enlargement of a part of Figure 27.

The amazing find in Galanor's book Cover-Up

As described above, one of the most exciting advances made *during* the Zapruder Film Symposium in Duluth, Minnesota was the discovery that this same
object in the grass appears to be missing from Frame 323 *in the National Archives*. Stewart Galanor ordered a set of slides from the Archives, which he published in the back of his book. In every frame other than Frame 323, the object in
the grass is clearly visible. (Frame 322 is a repeat of Frame 321—an error known
to Galanor but due to reasons that are still not clear to me, at the time of writing—but every other frame published shows the object in its correct position.)

But remarkably, Frame 323, which has the same color, brightness, and contrast as every other frame, *does not show the object in the grass*, in exactly the same way as the *Life* issue published on the first weekend. (See Figures 27 and 28.)

Although still under investigation at the time of writing, this find seems to be of monumental importance: there appear to be *two different versions of Frame 323 in the National Archives*. Anyone who wishes to cling to the idea that the Zapruder film has not been altered needs to first address this issue—and then consider all of the other evidence presented in this book.

Greer's Impossible Head Turns

One of the biggest mistakes made in the creation of the film was the depiction of the driver of the presidential limousine, Secret Service agent William Greer. In his book *Bloody Treason*, researcher Noel Twyman investigated in detail the two impossible head turns of Greer—one just before the putative head shot to the President, and one just after it. In each case Greer appears to turn his head almost completely around, within a time of just a single Zapruder frame—0.055 seconds—which is physically impossible.

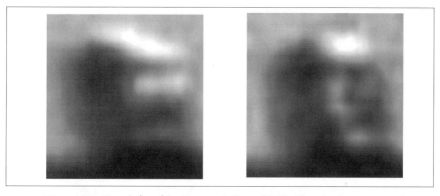

Figure 29. Greer's head in Frames 302 and 303. The shadow across the bottom portion of his face is the top of Kellerman's head. These are from the MPI DVD.

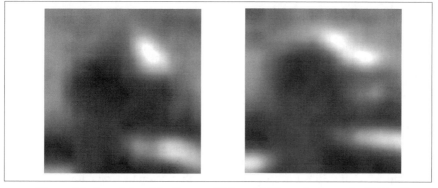

Figure 30. Greer's head in Frames 316 and 317, again from the DVD. The bright stripe across the lower right of his face is the top of Kellerman's head.

Do we have clear images of these anomalies?

In Figures 29 and 30 I show enlargements from the MPI DVD images of the four crucial frames in question. One might think that these images—obtained from the original film, not a copy—should be superior in quality to those published by Twyman, which were reprinted from a copy of the film. But in a sad indictment on the entire MPI saga, one finds that *the quality is no better* in the MPI images. The reasons for this have been described in the Introduction above. No high-resolution scans of any portion of any frame, other than the area immediately surrounding JFK, were published on the DVD.

Nevertheless, the point at issue remains well established: Greer's head appears to turn 100°–120° within the space of a single frame.

Twyman employed two professional athletes to try to replicate Greer's apparent feat. When allowed to swing around on a stool, the minimum time required was *double* that shown in the Zapruder film; when forced to sit on a fixed seat, the minimum time was *three times* that shown in the film.

Replicating the Twyman experiment at home

I decided that it would be simple enough to replicate this experiment for myself—and, indeed, it is not too difficult for most people to perform. (Twyman makes this very suggestion in his book.) All one needs is a regular domestic video camcorder, plugged directly into a VHS video tape recorder that allows "frame by frame" playback of stills, displayed through a regular television.

The first task is to hold a stopwatch up to the camera, and record it for some number of seconds. Playing back the video, one can then count the number of "frame advances" that occur per second. For a high-quality video recorder, this will be equal to the number of fields per second of broadcast television (i.e. 50 frame advances per second in Australia and Europe, or 60 frame advances per second in North America). If this is confirmed, one essentially has a 50- or 60-frame-per-second measurement device. (If the camera has a "high-speed shutter" setting, such as 1/500th or 1/1000th of a second, use it. In this case, you may need to use a reading lamp to illuminate the object being filmed, because such a short exposure time is usually only appropriate for outdoor sunlit scenes.)

The next step is to simply set up a chair or stool in front of the camera, and get volunteers to attempt the head turning feat. Twyman used professional athletes, in order to try and obtain people most likely to have the strongest yet most flexible neck muscles. I didn't go quite that far, but I hazarded a guess that ordinary people should be able to perform almost as well (after all, it's not a skill that athletes—or Secret Service agents—specifically train for). Test subjects were my fifteen-year-old tennis-playing stepson, my thirty-five-year-old self, and my wife Robyn. To more closely replicate the situation in the limousine, we used a fixed seat, rather than a stool.

Our own experimental results

As expected, after some warming up, my stepson and I both replicated the seated athlete's performance: about 0.160 seconds to turn through the angle shown in Frames 302 and 303 above, or three times that taken by Greer. It was relatively straightforward to determine this time fairly accurately, because at 50 frames per second the motion took about eight frames. (The entire front-to-back turn took longer than this, of course: the timing was taken for the roughly 100°–120° angle of rotation shown in the film.) My wife Robyn was a little slower, but not much—about 0.200 seconds—but had the dual excuses of both a long ponytail flapping behind her, as well as a history of chronic neck and back problems that made her wary of snapping her head around as fast as humanly possible. Regardless, it seemed like that there was a fairly narrow band of times in which a young adult human (let alone a 54-year-old human) could most rapidly snap their head backwards.

I encourage anyone who has any doubts about this feat to perform this very experiment for themselves. Not only to verify that a time of 0.160 seconds is about the fastest that can be achieved on a fixed seat, but also to take note of the physical effects of such a rapid head turn. When really pushing oneself to the limit, to try to achieve that final reduction from (say) 0.180 seconds to 0.160 seconds, one finds that the entire snapping motion really leaves one feeling dizzy, and for a second or so it is not easy to focus one's sight on anything. Of course, Greer not only snapped his head, but moreover was *driving the limousine*. I urge anyone considering doing this experiment whilst driving a motor vehicle to reconsider, unless doing it in a large unpopulated field!

The dizzying effect and g-forces

After noting this dizzying effect (and trying not to think about how many millions of brain cells I killed while doing the experiment), I realized that there should be a relatively simple way of understanding it on physics grounds. Rotating one's head puts one's brain and eyes under a centripetal acceleration. How large is this acceleration? A relatively simple high school formula is sufficient to make an estimate. A quick measurement reveals that the distance from the front of one's brain (and eyes) to the axis of rotation of the head is about four inches. Turning one's head through an angle of 105° in a time of T seconds then yields an acceleration a that is approximately given by

$$a = (0.034/T^2) \, g$$

where 1g is the normal acceleration of gravity. (This ignores the rotational acceleration needed to get the head spinning, and then to get it back to rest again, but the centripetal acceleration is a good rough estimate of the accelerations involved; the rotational effects will "scale" in the same way as described below.)

Nine times the force

For a time $T = 0.160$ seconds, we find $a = 1.3 \, g$, which is a reasonable acceleration that could cause a little dizziness. For Greer's apparent Zapruder film feat of $T = 0.05$ seconds, on the other hand, we find $a = 11.2 \, g$! As highlighted by Twyman, a rotational speed that is *three* times as fast implies a force that is *nine times as great*. Conversely, this explains why a large increase in effort (in trying to spin one's head around as quickly as possible) only has a small effect on performance: a 50 percent increase in force only decreases the time taken by 22 percent. (Compare Robyn's time and my time: not having neck and back problems, I probably put an extra 50 percent of force into my effort.) Again, it is clear why we are unlikely to see any human able to replicate Greer's apparent Zapruder film feat in our lifetimes.

Is There Evidence of Hidden Cameramen?

Once one comes to grips with the fact that the extant Zapruder film is a complete *fabrication*, rather than simply an *alteration* of an original film, the question then naturally arises: where could the other films of the assassination, used to provide the raw footage for the fabrication task, have come from?

Other films

This question is difficult to answer definitively. The problem is that, if the "best" photographic evidence of the assassination—the Zapruder film itself—is fraudulent, how can we possibly place our faith in any of the *other* films or photographs?

The answer, of course, is that we can't. It may well be that some *are* genuine and unaltered, and that what remains has been crafted to fit in with these reference points. But it may also be the case that *nothing* that has survived to the modern day is trustworthy.

Nevertheless, we must at least take a look at the available photographic evidence, and keep an open mind as to what we might find.

The Betzner photograph

The third photograph taken by Hugh Betzner, Jr. in Dealey Plaza on 22 November 1963 shows the presidential limousine and the Secret Service follow-up vehicle traveling down Elm Street at about the time that the shots are believed to have started (see Figure 31). As noted by researcher Jack White in *Murder in Dealey Plaza*, a very short "Abraham Zapruder" and a very tall "Marilyn Sitzman" can be seen on the concrete pedestal in the background. At the left of the white "retaining" wall is the famous "Black Dog Man" shape.

Figure 31. From Betzner's third photograph.

But it is the pergola shelter to the right of and behind "Zapruder" and "Sitzman" that seems to be hiding a new surprise. In studying a high-resolution computer scan of the Betzner photograph from the 24 November 1967 issue of *Life*, researcher Alan Healy discovered what appears to be a tripod-shaped object barely visible in the darkness of the shelter doorway. (See Figure 32.) Once noticed, this shape can be discerned with the naked eye on the original issue of *Life*. Independent verification is obtained from the lower-quality print of the Betzner #3 photograph contained on page 161 of Trask's *Pictures of the Pain*, in which the shape is just barely discernable to the naked eye.

 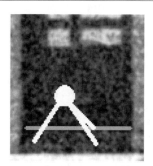

Enlargement of pergola doorway   *Sketch of the broad features visible*

Figure 32. Enlargement of the doorway of the pergola shelter behind Zapruder and Sitzman, as seen in the Betzner photograph of Figure 31. This "tripod" shape can be seen with the naked eye in both the Life *publication of the image, as well as in that published in Trask's* Pictures of the Pain.

Support for the thesis that this tripod-shaped object was "really" present in Dealey Plaza at the time that the photograph was taken, and is not merely an artifact of the photographic reproduction, is supplied by the other barely discernable line apparent in the shadows of the pergola shelter: the join between the floor of the shelter with the rear wall. On the other hand, the fact that this line *can* be seen through the "legs" of the tripod tends to rule out the existence of any person being behind the tripod; at best, such an "operator" could only be off to one side of it.

Comparison with the Willis slide

What are we to make of this apparent shape in the shadows? The seventh slide taken by Major Phillip L. Willis in Dealey Plaza that day—at almost the same time and from almost the same place as Betzner—shows a well-lit pergola shelter with nothing inside. The tripod shape in Betzner then suggests that one (or both) of these two photographs has been altered. It is easier to believe that the Willis slide was altered to remove the contents of the shelter (and that the Betzner was thought to be too dark to reveal the object), than that the Betzner was altered to insert phony evidence of a bogus tripod.

But researcher Jack White has also highlighted the prominent bright circular "blob" or "dome" above the top left of the shelter doorway in all copies of the Betzner #3 photograph, which is not apparent in any other photographic evidence of the assassination. The problem, as always, is to decide whether to trust the Betzner photograph to the exclusion of the other evidence, or to reject the Betzner as the "odd man out".

Would the Betzner tripod position even be of use?

One might ask whether a camera located on the apparent tripod would even have any use in filming the assassination. Despite apparent disadvantages, the answer must be "yes". Calculations have shown that being lower than the "Zapruder" camera position would have allowed a shelter tripod camera to film the presidential limousine *underneath* the Stemmons Freeway sign—in drastic contrast to the Zapruder position.

On the other hand, reconstruction films taken recently by researcher Rick Janowitz have confirmed that the view of such a camera would be blocked by the "Zapruder pedestal" itself by the time the limousine reached a position roughly corresponding to where the fatal head shot occurs on the extant Zapruder film. Thus, a film shot from the shelter tripod would be useful in *contributing* footage of the assassination, in conjunction with other films, but it could not, by itself, provide a basis for the synthesis of the entire extant Zapruder film.

Where is the negative of Betzner photograph #3 today?

Given these questions, an analysis of the original negative of Betzner photograph #3 would be highly desirable. But according to Trask, in 1976 the House Select Committee on Assassinations could not locate it. It is not known whether *Life*, who purchased the negative in 1967, now has it, whether Betzner retained it, or whether it is truly "lost".

A remnant of a later photo shoot?

An alternative explanation for the tripod object seen in the Betzner photograph is that it represents a real object in Dealey Plaza at the time the photograph was taken—but that this was not on 22 November 1963, but rather some later date. How could this be possible? It's not difficult to imagine. Consider the fact that the Betzner photograph was only "discovered" by *Life* investigators in 1967—four years after the assassination. Moreover, the 24 November 1967 issue, in which the photograph appears, claims that the photo had never been published before. How, then, are we to be assured of its authenticity? Clearly, we cannot.

It is quite possible that this—and other—photographs were created some time after the assassination, to "fill in" the otherwise rather empty photographic record of the event, especially where the photographers themselves had described the photographs that they took. In this example, two FBI reports on Hugh Betzner, Jr. are extant. The first, written 23 November 1963, describes the three photos he took, and the fact that, after the shooting, Deputy Sheriff Eugene L. Boone requested that he turn over the camera including the undeveloped film, which he did. The second, dated 20 December 1963, states that Betzner "loaned" to the FBI his roll of negatives, on 22 November, and that it was returned to him "after developing" on 25 November. As the late Harold Weisberg noted in *Photographic Whitewash*, there are *no* copies of the Betzner pictures in the Warren Commission's files, and he was never called as a witness. Why, then, should we suddenly trust *Life*'s 1967 "discovery" as being genuine? (Interestingly, this issue of *Life* containing 23 photographs from nine assassination witnesses—*all previously unpublished*—appeared shortly after the self-publication of Weisberg's book, apparently "answering" the question of what these photographs—discovered by Weisberg after sifting through the Warren Commission's files—actually showed!)

If there was indeed a later "photo shoot", it may explain why the background of the extant Betzner photograph shows a tripod: it may simply have been equipment left in the pergola shelter at the time! (The foreground objects would, of course, have been pasted in from actual photographs taken during the assassination.) If this were the case, the "tripod" would not have any bearing on the question of additional film cameras at the time of the assassination, but would instead form part of the story of the fabrication of these later photographs.

The troublesome Mr. Altgens

If some of the extant photographs of the assassination were created at a later date, one might hope to discover documentary evidence revealing the subterfuge. Fortunately, there is a document in the files of the Warren Commission that, together with testimony in the Warren Commission *Hearings* themselves, provides such crucial evidence.

Some background is helpful here. A photograph of the motorcade traveling down Elm Street published in *The Saturday Evening Post* shows, in its background, a person standing in the doorway of the Texas School Book Depository, who looks remarkably like Lee Harvey Oswald, but who (it was argued) was actually another employee of the Depository, Billy Lovelady. The story of this controversy is well known to students of the assassination. Less well known is the story of the man who allegedly took the photograph, veteran Associated Press photographer James W. "Ike" Altgens.

Although the controversy erupted very shortly after the assassination, official identification of the AP photographer who actually took the photo was much slower. On 23 January 1964, Don Schanche, managing editor of *The Saturday Evening Post*, sent to J. Lee Rankin, chief counsel for the Warren Commission, a full-negative print of the Lovelady–Oswald photograph, as well as several extreme blow-ups. Rankin responded coolly—five weeks later, on 28 February, only days after researcher Jones Harris and his lawyer had visited the Warren Commission armed with blow-ups of the same photograph. On the day of Jones's visit, Rankin wrote J. Edgar Hoover relating the incident. Hoover wrote back on 9 March, still skirting the issue of who actually took the photograph.

It was only in the 24 May 1964 issue of the *New York Herald Tribune* that Dom Bonafede reported that Altgens "recalled shooting the picture". The next day, *Chicago American* columnist Maggie Daly pointed out that it was "odd" that neither the FBI nor the Warren Commission had ever interviewed Altgens. This was, apparently, enough criticism to generate some action. On 1 June, Hoover wrote Rankin, enclosing two copies of the *Tribune* article, and offered this remarkable comment:

> It would appear from the above article that Mr. J. W. Altgens, Associated Press Photographer, is the individual who took the picture in question and efforts are being made to locate and interview him.

Fortunately, the might of the FBI was brought to bear on the question of Altgens' location: he was in the Dallas office of the Associated Press, a short walk from the FBI, and his home phone number was listed in the directory.

The FBI interviewed him on 2 June, and on 5 June produced a six-page report on the Bonafede–Daly saga (slightly less than half of which was actually dedicated to Altgens' statements). This FBI report is Commission Document 1088, and, while perhaps solving any outstanding problems the Commission had with the Lovelady incident, it was apparently overlooked by those involved in creating and rewriting the history of the assassination.

Let us consider what the FBI reported. After biographical information of Altgens, we have the following:

> ALTGENS advised that on November 22, 1963, he was assigned by Associated Press to take up a position along the motorcade route for the purpose of obtaining pictures of the President and the Presidential motorcade. ALTGENS related he left his office at 11:15 A.M. and proceeded to the triple overpass above Elm and Main Streets where he intended to take his pictures. He said he arrived there about 11:25 A.M. and was advised by uniformed police officers that, even though he had his press credentials, he would not be permitted to take photographs from the triple overpass. ALTGENS stated he then went to the intersection of Main and Houston Streets, arriving there at approximately 11:40 A.M. He said he remained at this location until the motorcade arrived.

> Just before the Presidential limousine passed, ALTGENS stated he stationed himself in the intersection on the southwest side and took a picture of President and Mrs. KENNEDY as their limousine turned onto Houston Street. ALTGENS advised he then ran diagonally (northwest) downhill over the grassy area that separates Main and Elm Streets, stopping on the south side of Elm Street, across the street from the stairs leading down from the colonnade located on the north side of Elm Street, to get in front of the motorcade again. ALTGENS stated it was from this position that he took the photograph of the Presidential car and the motorcade scene. He said this picture also depicts an individual standing in the doorway of the entrance of the Texas School Book Depository who resembles LEE HARVEY OSWALD. ALTGENS related he was standing about thirty feet from the President when he took this photograph. He recalled that at about the instant he snapped the picture, he heard a burst of noise which he thought was firecrackers. He advised he does not know how many of these reports he heard since they had no significance to him at the time, and he was unaware of what was happening.

> After taking the above photograph, ALTGENS stated he then turned the film in his camera, adjusted the focus to 15 feet and was raising his camera to eye level when he heard another report which he recognized as a gunshot. He said the bullet struck President KENNEDY on the right side of his head and the impact knocked the President forward. ALTGENS stated pieces of flesh, blood and bones appeared to fly from the right side of the President's head and pass in front of Mrs. KENNEDY to the left of the Presidential limousine. ALTGENS stated Mrs. KENNEDY grabbed the President and ALTGENS heard her exclaim, "Oh, no!" as the President slumped over into her lap. ALTGENS said he also observed blood on the left side of the President's head and face. ALTGENS stated he was staring in utter disbelief at what he had just witnessed and was so

aghast that he froze and did not snap the picture. ALTGENS advised he was about fifteen feet from the President at this time, was sure the shot came from somewhere behind the President, and is positive this was the last shot fired. He said the President's car was proceeding at about ten miles per hour at the time.

ALTGENS advised he did not know Governor CONNALLY had also been shot since his attention was focused on the President. He said he learned from the wire services that Governor CONNALLY had been shot.

ALTGENS stated the driver of the Presidential limousine apparently realized what had happened and speeded up toward the Stemmons Expressway. At this point, ALTGENS advised he took a photograph which depicted a Secret Service man standing on the back of the Presidential limousine, left side, assisting Mrs. Kennedy back to her seat. ALTGENS stated the whole area seemed to be utter confusion. Police came from everywhere as the President's car disappeared from sight.

ALTGENS advised that as the President's car disappeared he observed some Secret Service Agents and police officers with drawn guns on the north side of Elm Street running in the direction of the top of the triple overpass. He said he thought they were chasing someone who had fled from somewhere behind the President. ALTGENS stated he also ran in this direction. After proceeding across Elm Street and up toward the triple underpass, ALTGENS stated he met the police officers returning. At this juncture, ALTGENS advised he then ran to a nearby telephone and informed the office that the President had been shot and that he had witnessed it. He then sprinted to his office in the Dallas News Building with the pictures he had taken. ALTGENS stated the pictures showing the President slumping in his seat with Mrs. KENNEDY bending over him "moved" on the Associated Press Wirephoto Network at 12:57 P.M., which was seventeen minutes after the first news bulletin was sent out by Associated Press.

ALTGENS advised the above three pictures he took were all turned in to Associated Press, and received wide publication and circulation, both in the United States and abroad. ALTGENS said he used a 35 mm Nikkorex camera with a 105 mm lens (telephoto lens). He said the camera was loaded with Eastman Kodak Tri-X film.

The remainder of the report discusses telephone calls to Altgens from Bonafede, John Gold of the *London Evening News*, and other information about the Daly article.

What a remarkable report! An entire chapter could be written on Altgens' reported statements: that he was not permitted to photograph from the triple overpass (but railway workers were permitted to stand there?); that he made a remarkable 75-yard sprint through the crowds to get back in front of the motorcade; that this 26-year veteran AP photographer had no idea of distances (stating he was thirty feet from the President when, in fact, he was more than sixty feet from him); that the President pitched *forwards* after the fatal head shot; the "Secret Service Agents" that appeared (none, apparently, stayed in Dealey Plaza); and so on.

Figure 33. Three photographs, widely published after the assassination, reasonably credited to Associated Press photograph James "Ike" Altgens.

But what is more important for us here is the clear description of the three photographs that Altgens took: one as the limo made the turn from Main onto Houston; one looking up Elm Street towards the front of the limo (showing Lovelady–Oswald in the doorway of the Depository); and one looking down Elm towards the back of the limo, showing Clint Hill on the rear foothold of the car. Indeed, the FBI summary, "ALTGENS advised the above three pictures he took were all turned in to Associated Press, and received wide publication and circulation, both in the United States and abroad," is an accurate one: these three photographs (see Figure 33) *were* widely published following the assassination. (The third was published in the Melbourne *Herald* on 23 November 1963—the day of the assassination, Melbourne time—but, remarkably, did not show any of the background objects that would allow the location to be pinpointed; and what would later become the base of a lamppost was identified as Kennedy's head!)

Testimony before the Warren Commission

Seven weeks later, on 24 July 1964, Altgens testified before the Warren Commission. His testimony clarifies further for us his actions on the day.

Mr. LIEBELER. Houston and Main?

Mr. ALTGENS. Yes; Houston and Main. When the caravan reached Houston and Main I made at least one shot—one picture—I don't have the roll of film with me now so I don't know exactly, but I know I had made an additional one or two pictures of the caravan coming down Main Street prior to that, but I got the one picture with the President waving into the camera. Mrs. Kennedy was looking at me at the time, just as I got ready to snap it the north wind caught her hat and almost blew it off, so she raised her left hand to grab her hat and I did not get her looking into the camera, but I got the Governor and Mrs. Connally and the President with the President waving into the camera.

Mr. LIEBELER. This was as they turned?

Mr. ALTGENS. This was as they turned into the sunlight.

Mr. LIEBELER. Turning into Houston Street; is that right?

Mr. ALTGENS. Turning right; headed toward the Book Depository Building.

Mr. LIEBELER. All right.

Figure 34. Two other photographs that may reasonably be taken to be the "additional one or two pictures of the caravan coming down Main Street" described by Altgens in his testimony before the Warren Commission.

Mr. ALTGENS. I thereupon grabbed my gadget bag that I carry my extra lenses in and ran fast down across the Dealey Plaza to get down in front of the caravan for some additional pictures and I took this one picture—

Altgens then describes the famous photograph he took which shows Lovelady-Oswald in the doorway of the Texas School Book Depository.

This testimony establishes that Altgens took one or two photographs of the motorcade as it traveled down Main Street, prior to his taking the photograph showing the limousine turning the corner onto Houston—even though the extant films show Jackie *never* looking at Altgens!. The photographs shown in Figure 34 may be reasonably assumed to be these two additional photos of the motorcade on Main Street.

Later on in his testimony, Altgens describes his final photograph, of Clint Hill on the back of the limousine:

The car never did stop. It was proceeding along in a slow pace and I stepped out in the curb area and made another picture as the Secret Service man stepped upon the rear step of the Presidential car and went to Mrs. Kennedy's aid and then after that I immediately crossed the street and once again I was looking to see if I could find anything in this area of Elm and Houston Streets that would suggest to me where the shot came from.

Altgens then describes in greater detail than in his FBI report what he did on the other side of Elm Street. (The "slow pace"—slow enough for Clint Hill to simply "step up" onto the rear step—is itself an interesting contrast to what we see in the extant Zapruder and other films.)

Altgens retrospectively takes two more photographs

What is the problem with these accounts of Altgens' activities on 22 November 1963? Nothing—until we move some decades into the future! Somehow, at some time, two extra photographs were added to Altgens' assassination collection. (See Figure 35.)

There are many problems associated with these photographs—not the least of which, of course, is that Altgens' own testimony, under oath, makes both of them impossible!

*Figure 35. Two other photographs that Trask claims Altgens took—despite
contradicting Altgens' report to the FBI, his testimony before the
Warren Commission, and denials by Altgens to Trask himself.*

The first additional photograph (allegedly the fourth in the sequence overall)
purports to show the Presidential limousine progressing down Houston Street
towards Elm Street. The problem is not simply that Altgens did not describe this
important photograph of the limousine—which shows the limo approaching the
Texas School Book Depository, the supposed location of the assassin. Of greater
significance, rather, is the fact that, *had* Altgens taken such a photograph, he
would have had far less time to make the 75-yard dash through the crowds to the
bottom of Elm Street, in order to take his most famous photograph (showing
Lovelady–Oswald in the background). This is something that Altgens would have
well remembered; he testified that it was his plan all along to make the dash to
Elm Street to get another shot of the motorcade from the front.

But the second additional photograph (allegedly the seventh and last in the
sequence overall) is even more problematical. This purports to show Abraham
Zapruder and Marilyn Sitzman walking away from the "Zapruder pedestal", with
the Hesters crouched on the ground nearby. If genuine, it would be the clearest
photographic evidence actually showing Abraham Zapruder in Dealey Plaza at
the time of the assassination—albeit from behind. (See Figure 36.)

The problem with this additional photograph is that Altgens explicitly states
what he did after taking his photo of Clint Hill on the back of the limousine: he
crossed to the north side of Elm Street! Yet a detailed analysis reveals that this
extra photograph was taken from the *south* side of Elm Street. Altgens also described in detail for Liebeler *everything* he observed after the assassination, including "a couple of Negroes looking out of a window" on the fifth floor of the
Texas School Book Depository. Does he describe Zapruder and Sitzman, or the
Hester couple crouched on the ground—a sight he apparently thought worthy
enough to take a photograph of? Absolutely not. In fact, he describes the *only*
people he saw on the ground:

> After that I made a good look through this area to see that no one
> else had been hit. I noticed the couple that were on the ground over
> here with their children, I saw them when they went down and they
> were in the area and laid there some time after the Presidential car
> had disappeared.

Figure 36. An enlargement from the second extra photograph ascribed to Altgens by Trask, purporting to show Abraham Zapruder and Marilyn Sitzman after they climbed off the "Zapruder pedestal" (seen in foreground). This photograph, denied to have been taken by Altgens himself, seems to have been first published in Josiah Thompson's book Six Seconds in Dallas *(1967).*

Mr. LIEBELER. They threw themselves on the ground in this grassy area that I have just described previously where you ran across after this last shot?

Mr. ALTGENS. Yes; but they were not hit. I looked at them and they weren't hit by a bullet, so I took another long look around before I started my dash back to the office, and as it turned out, my report was the first that our service had of the assassination and my pictures were the only pictures that we had available for a period of about 24 hours.

So where were Zapruder, Sitzman, and the Hesters? Why don't they rate a mention at all in any of Altgens' testimony?

Trask's version of history

It is revealing to see what Trask has to say about Altgens' movements on 22 November 1963. In his book *Pictures of the Pain,* he devotes an entire chapter to Altgens, titled "The AP Man". Some of the story is quoted from Altgens; other parts seem to be "interpolated" by Trask himself. Most damning, however, is the following paragraph:

    In later years Altgens became unsure of the number of photographs he took that day of the assassination, and has been reluctant to acknowledge authorship of all seven since he is very adamant about not wanting to take credit for someone else's work. In discussions with him, it is evident that he is sure or reasonably sure that he took five of the photos, but admits to leaving things to AP's judgment. In testimony six months after the shooting, he did mention that he made one or two pictures of the caravan coming down Main Street, but with the length of intervening years and the fact that he possibly never saw in print form all his pictures before the negatives were sent to New York, this [sic] explains some of his caution about authorship of the photos.

In other words, *Altgens categorically denied taking seven photographs!* Trask's attempt to dismiss his denial as simply due to the senility of a 73-year-old witness, some 29 years after the event, does him no credit at all. Why not simply refer to Altgens' contemporaneous testimony, as a strapping young 45-year-old? (Trask was, after all, 47 years old himself at the time he dismissed Altgens' account of events.)

Trask's "proof" of his version of events, in the very next paragraph of his book, is most revealing:

    An examination of the negative sequence, however, shows quite conclusively that these seven pictures are Altgens's, a fact first noted by researcher Richard E. Sprague, who found the individually cut negatives at AP in New York. The film is of the same type (Tri-X), is numbered sequentially, is chronological, and taken from the same vantage points at which Altgens is known to have been located. Mr. Altgens's personal caution is refreshing but in light of the evidence, not problematical to the evidence.

Trask would have been a perfect addition to the staff of the Warren Commission! To discount completely the adamant statements of the witness himself, and instead trust completely and wholeheartedly a set of individually cut negatives "found at AP in New York", is breathtaking. It is fortunate that the Altgens photographs were never required to be admitted into evidence.

It is amusing to note Trask's findings when wishing to actually verify this proof of Altgens' untruthfulness:

    The original Altgens negatives which were created on November 22, 1963, are deposited with other negatives on the subject within the vast Wide World Photo operations in New York City. Some of the original seven negatives have had copy negatives in cropped format created, while others of this historically valuable set unfortunately appear to be misidentified, misplaced, or even missing.

Need I say more?

How the film was fabricated

In the previous sections I have presented what I believe to be the best evidence that the extant "Zapruder" film is, beyond any doubt at all, not a pristine, authentic record of the assassination. There are many other observations I could have mentioned in support of this conclusion, of various degrees of certainty and reliability; but once one has irrefutable proof of fraud, there is little point in debating arguments that may not be quite as watertight. Rather, it is more important to understand how the fabrication could possibly have been carried out, and what its implications are for the assassination as a whole.

I must emphasize from the outset that the evidence tells us what the extant film *cannot* be, but it doesn't uniquely tell us what it *really is*. The latter must necessarily be a best guess, based on one's broad knowledge of the assassination in general, the technology available in 1963, and the evidence presented in the film itself. In making such a best guess, I will generally tend towards the simplest explanation that is consistent with all of the facts available to us. It may well be that, in some respects, a more complicated scenario did, in fact, occur; it is inevitable that some of my guesses will be too conservative. But I strongly believe that, should the full truth about the film's creation ever be revealed, it will broadly agree with what I present here.

A complete fabrication

Firstly, it is straightforward to see that the extant film cannot be considered to be "slightly altered", in the same way that it is impossible for a woman to be "slightly pregnant". If all we had to worry about was the inconsistent depiction of the wound to the President's head, we might be able to believe that some amount of retouching was performed. Or if we were to simply add in the lack of pincushion distortion for the Stemmons Freeway sign, we might believe that a larger version of the sign was carelessly pasted, photographically, over the top of the original sign, perhaps to widen it or raise it in order to hide details of the shot to Kennedy's throat. Such alterations would, of course, be highly important in the context of the crime; but they would not change the fundamental story that a film of the assassination was taken by Abraham Zapruder and was ultimately (after such alterations) revealed to the public.

But we no longer have the luxury of subscribing to such a "slightly altered" scenario. Consider the images published in *Life* that showed no motion of the limousine or the motorcycles. Imagine that these were based on genuine film frames. How could this be possible? There are several possibilities that spring to mind. Firstly, the limousine and motorcycles may have been moving much more slowly at the times that these frames were exposed. But the exposure time of the Zapruder camera is a *fixed proportion* of the time between frames (about 45 percent). Thus, *regardless of the actual speed of the camera*, if the motorcade were actually moving so slowly that there would be no noticeable blur of either it or the background, then the following frame should show the motorcade having advanced only a very small distance along Elm Street. But this is not what is seen in the film frames published by the Warren Commission.

What way could there be out of this dilemma? We might hypothesize that there were many more frames originally in the film—either with a much more slowly moving motorcade, or, more likely, with the Zapruder camera running in triple-speed mode—and that (say) two out of every three frames were skipped when the original film was copied. This is still a "fairly limited alteration" scenario. Or we might hypothesize that a different camera altogether was used, which had a much faster exposure time relative to the period between frames.

These explanations would suffice for just the one or two frames shown in *Life*, but they are completely untenable when the film as a whole is considered.

For there are many other frames of the film—in fact, the vast majority of them—in which the blurring of foreground and background *is* completely consistent with the motion of the motorcade, together with the characteristics of the Zapruder camera. But what is not always appreciated is that *this blurring is not something that can be applied to a sharp frame as a whole*. Indeed, even with a modern computer it is impossible to produce the motion blurring seen in even one single frame, unless one first carefully (digitally) "cuts out" each set of objects that is moving with a particular speed, and applies the direction and length of blur that is appropriate to that particular speed. And even so, joining up the edges of objects moving with different speeds is even more intricate—because they overlap and "bleed into" each other in the blurring process. Such a procedure is possible, but time-consuming. It would also have been possible using film techniques in 1963—but it would have been even more intricate.

We have, of course, lost any sight of a "slightly altered" scenario.

Most frames required substantial editing

We are left with no alternative but to conclude that the film was substantially edited. One might think that, at a minimum, frames were deleted from the original film, and the remaining frames had blurring applied to the objects inside them, as described above, to make the motion of the limousine from one frame to the next self-consistent. And that a new Stemmons Freeway sign was pasted over the old. And that the lamppost was removed, and pasted back on a slightly incorrect angle. (For what purpose? A good question!) And that the wounds to the President were altered. So is *this* the minimum amount of alteration that we can assume?

It is not.

Most of the extant film is technically self-consistent

Ironically, the most powerful constraints on any alteration of the film come not from what is *wrong* with it, but rather what is manifestly *right* with it.

Recall, from the Introduction above, that I originally believed these properties of the film so self-consistent and interlocking that I could not see any possible way that it could have been altered, short of a complete work of fabrication that simply was incompatible with the published chronology of its existence. These properties remain as correct today as when I first marveled at them; the only difference is that I am now aware of *mistakes where they were not correctly applied*.

The worst of these mistakes I have described in the previous sections; but one might get the wrong impression if one simply read through those sections and thought that I had selected them at random from various parts of the film, almost without much thought. Rather, what one finds when going through the film frame by frame is that, time after time after time, the properties are, generally, completely self-consistent. If I were to make an estimate, I would guess that, if I had listed every property of every object that I measured in frames of the film, about 95 percent of the time all of their interlocking properties would have been absolutely consistent. For most of the remaining 5 percent of the list, properties sometimes appeared to be a little perplexing, and difficult to interpret—and often just plainly seemed wrong; but they could generally be subsumed in the general self-consistency of the film when uncertainties and measurement errors were allowed. Absolutely impossible phenomena, such as have been described in the previous sections, would make up much less than 1 percent of the list.

In other words, the mistakes that I have cataloged above are not phenomena that repeatedly appear throughout the film—that may, to a skeptic, represent some sort of misunderstanding that I might have of the camera, or of its optical properties—but rather represent those very few *exceptions* to the rule of absolute and undeniable self-consistency. And as any good student of Science knows, it is the *exceptions* to well-tried and well-trusted laws that provide the key to progress.

The properties of the film that rule out any simple editing

So just what *are* these self-consistent and interlocking properties of the film? They are, essentially, three in number: pincushion distortion, motion blurring, and "ghost images".

Pincushion distortion and motion blurring have been dealt with in depth above. "Ghost images", on the other hand, are a fascinating yet powerful consequence of the particular camera that Zapruder ostensibly used, together with the mode he used it in. Their study has generally only been possible since the late 1990s, when MPI released their DVD of the "original" film—*including the region between the sprocket holes*. This region was shown for hundreds of frames in the volumes of the Warren Commission Exhibits, but the quality of the reproduction was generally not sufficient to allow much study of this region. Several researchers in the 1990s were able to study this "intersprocket region", as it is generally called, only by examining slides in the National Archives; David Mantik's chapter in *Assassination Science* contains a summary of these early observations.

The remarkable "ghost images"

Having the entire set of frames available for extended perusal, it becomes clear that the "ghost objects" seen in the intersprocket region actually "belong" to the frames exposed immediately before and immediately after the frame in question. [*Author's note*: See Zavada's description in Appendix B.]

The explanation is that the gate (opening) in the Zapruder camera, which is designed to ensure that only the frame in question receives any light during the exposure time, needs a "taller" opening in the intersprocket region to allow the film-winding arm to progress the film between exposures. Of course, the camera was never designed to expose film in the intersprocket region—which is never normally projected—in the first place; this is just a curious property of the particular camera design used. Moreover, because of the way the lens system works, the circle of light coming through the lens system is smallest for wide-angle filming, moderate for normal settings, and widest at maximum telephoto zoom— which is the setting ostensibly used for the extant film. (The field of view in the extant film *is*, in fact, compatible with this setting, and the Zapruder lens system, as determined by detailed calculations, and explicitly by an analysis of footage taken with an identical model camera by researcher Rick Janowitz.)

The net result is that, while (for example) Frame 304 was being exposed, imagery off the top and to the left of the frame area was being exposed just above the lower sprocket hole in Frame 303's piece of film, and imagery off the bottom and to the left of the frame are was being exposed just below the upper sprocket hole in Frame 305's piece of film.

Attaching the "ghost images" to the frames they belong to

When understood in this way, these "ghost images" lose much of their initial mystery, and indeed the "panels" of adjacent frames can be attached to each frame in order to sometimes have an extra glimpse at objects above or below the level filmed in the frame area proper. ("Ghost" objects are only visible, and recognizable, if they are sufficiently bright compared to the background.) This is illustrated in Figure 37 for Frame 305 of the extant film.

So why are these "ghost images" of such crucial importance in understanding possible alteration scenarios for the film? There are several reasons.

Figure 37. An example of how "ghost panels" can be attached to a frame to provide a glimpse of objects above or below the designed frame area. Here, Frame 305 has had attached the "ghost panel" from just above the lower sprocket hole of Frame 304, and the "ghost panel" from just below the upper sprocket hole of Frame 306. Pincushion distortion has also been removed. The circular mask represents the approximate circle of light exposed onto the film during Frame 305. The top edge of the top panel and the bottom edge of the bottom panel represent the extremities of the "gate" that covers the film. Note that the peristyle structure can be seen in the top "ghost panel", and the rear back corner of the limo in the lower "ghost panel". The peristyle, in particular, aligns precisely when placed into the Dealey Plaza panorama shown in Figure 13.

The "ghost images" have correct pincushion distortion

Firstly, the light forming the exposure of Frame 305, as seen in Figure 37, was ostensibly subject to pincushion distortion as it traveled through the Zapruder lens—*including the light that bled into the intersprocket regions of Frames 304 and 306.* In order to reconstruct the image shown above, it is necessary to first attach these "ghost panels" to Frame 305, and then to correct the pincushion distortion of the entire image. When this is done, it is found—*without exception*—that identifiable objects, like the peristyle structure, match up *precisely* with the panoramic images constructed of Dealey Plaza (to the extent that such objects can be identified, of course). The particular image shown above is doubly impressive in this regard: the peristyle lines up *and Mary Moorman is on exactly the right bearing established in the "Moorman in the street" debate.* (Both sides of the debate agreed on her compass bearing; what was in contention was her lens height.)

What is important here is that *if pincushion distortion is not taken into account, these alignments simply do not work*: not only are objects incorrectly placed, but they are moreover incorrectly sized, and on the wrong angle. (Note that the effects of pincushion distortion are close to maximal for the "ghost panels", being farthest from the center of the designed image area of any of the light exposed.)

We thus have two crucial properties of the Zapruder camera—pincushion distortion and "ghost images"—interacting in precisely the right way in the frames of the extant film.

The "ghost images" are correctly blurred

But this is not all. The frame shown above has a relatively unblurred background. What happens when we throw in some motion blur? *Without exception, the motion blur of each "ghost images" matches that of the frame in which it was exposed*, as would be expected if these "ghost images" were, indeed, genuinely created when Abraham Zapruder shot his film. This holds true even for those few frames in which the motion blur is not completely straight: where the camera ostensibly "curved" a bit during its jerky motion. And moreover, objects in the intersprocket region "beneath" any ghost images have the correct motion blurring of the frame that *they* belong to. In other words, in many cases one can see the effects of *three different* sets of motion blurring: that of the frame before, that of the frame after, and that of the frame itself, all appropriately shown in the one intersprocket region.

"Ghost images", blurring, and pincushion distortion

But the *piece de resistance* is yet to come. When I was first investigating these ghost images—in the image deblurring work I did early in the piece—I found that the motion blurs were not always completely consistent with the frames that they came from: they were often slightly too large, and the angles were a little bit wrong. But this was before I was made aware of the pincushion distortion of the Zapruder lens. When this distortion is corrected, as in the image above, all of the motion blurring became completely correct! In other words, *three crucial phenomena are correctly and inextricably linked on the extant film: "ghost images", motion blurring, and pincushion distortion.*

It was a realization of the incredible complexity of these interactions that first led me to believe that any editing of the film was impossible in the short timeframe (just hours or days) that the published chronology of the film seemed to allow.

However, we know, without any shadow of a doubt, *that the film is fraudulent*. It is no good to try to argue that these subtle optical effects are so complex and intertwined that the film could not have been edited—we know that it was! So what does this tell us about the way in which the film could possibly have been altered? It is only by staring at this problem for weeks and months that the scales start to drop from one's eyes, and the true story of the Zapruder film begins to emerge.

We know that events were deleted from the film, and yet the surrounding frames were seamlessly stitched back together to give the impression of a single continuous film. As far as imagery to the right of the sprocket holes is concerned, this is, as noted above, a time-consuming job, but it is possible. But what about the intersprocket region? Clearly, we have to extract the "ghost panels" from each frame, attach them to the frames they came from, edit and re-blur these images, and then combine them back together to form a new intersprocket region, compatible with the edited film.

We have to extract the "ghost panels" . . . .

Double exposures

Parts of the intersprocket region are double exposures. In the example shown in Figure 37, the top of the image is a double exposure of Frames 305 and 304; the bottom of the image is a double exposure of Frames 305 and 306. The middle section is a single exposure of Frame 305. The editors of the film had to extract the two exposures from each doubly exposed area of film.

There is only one problem. *It is impossible to undo a double exposure!* Anyone who has had the misfortune to have had two irreplaceable photos merged through a camera malfunction will know how heartbreaking this is. (The first roll of film I ever took in my life had one of these—of my Grade One class—and I'll never forget it!) Unfortunately, even though modern computers can perform digital magic in many shapes and forms, they are absolutely unable to help at all with this apparently simple task.

The impossibility of separating a double exposure

Why is it impossible to undo a double exposure? It's not difficult to understand, fundamentally, why this is so. In a double exposure, each photographic grain is literally exposed to light added together from two different images: the total intensity (of each wavelength, if you want to be pedantic) is just the sum of the intensity at that position from each source image. It's not unlike asking someone to add together 19 and 23: they will rapidly tell you that the answer is 42. The photographic grain (or charge-coupled device for that pixel of a digital camera or camcorder) responds to the total amount of light hitting it: the light from the first image plus the light from the second image.

Now imagine asking someone the following: "Two numbers add up to 57. What are the numbers?" The problem is, of course, impossible. There are an infinite number of possible answers. If we made the further restriction that each number cannot be negative (as is true for light intensities), the range of possible answers would be restricted (each number must be somewhere between zero and 57, inclusive), but there are still an infinite number of possible answers. There is no way to reconstruct the two individual numbers, if all you have is their sum.

The same is true for a double exposure. All we have is the sum of the two images. It is fundamentally and absolutely impossible to extract the two original images. That information has been irretrievably and irrevocably lost.

So how the hell did they do it for the Zapruder film?

They didn't. It is impossible.

There was no Zapruder film.

There was no Zapruder film.

There was no Zapruder film. It takes a while to sink in.

Oh, sure, it's possible that Abraham Zapruder was in Dealey Plaza on 22 November 1963, and that he took a film—even though the evidence would tend to point to the contrary. *But the extant "Zapruder" film cannot simply be an edited version of any such film.* Why? Because, if such a film *did* exist, then the entire intersprocket region would have to have been thrown away, and a new one created. *Out of what?* Not an original Zapruder film itself—the peristyle, and the bottom of the limo, and the grass–curb edge of the grassy knoll, and the buildings in the background at the start of the film in the upper ghost panel—none of these things could have been shown in an original film; or not if filmed at maximum telephoto zoom, anyway. Could he have filmed on a "normal" setting, rather than telephoto? No, not possible: in such a mode, his camera could not possibly have captured the degree of detail seen on the extant "Zapruder" film. Which means that *other* footage was needed.

Something other than an "original Zapruder film" is needed

In other words, the extant "Zapruder" film contains imagery that came from somewhere other than an "original" Zapruder film.

Now recall how much effort would be required to edit frames of an "original" Zapruder film anyway: objects moving at different speeds need to be cut out, blurred appropriately, and then pasted back together.

But what if the original images were blurred? How could this blurring have been removed, so that the new blurring could be applied?

Deblurring was impossible in 1963

In 1963, it couldn't. Deblurring is something that is just, and only just, possible using modern digital computers. The "computers" available in 1963 were no more sophisticated than a modern calculator; raster graphics had not even been invented! And deblurring is impossible by photographic means.

So it was crucial that the "original" Zapruder film have images that were not blurred. *But if the limousine was moving, this is impossible.* Either the motorcade, or the background, had to be blurred—the Zapruder camera simply had an exposure time that was too long to take sharp images of moving objects. Perhaps it could have been used in triple-speed mode: that would reduce the blurring in each frame by a factor of three. But then Abraham Zapruder would have been a patent liar; and surely anyone who viewed such a film in the first days would have realized it was running in "slow motion" mode (for example, Rosemary Willis would be bounding along like she was on the Moon).

And so we are again returned to the same point: it is conceivable that Abraham Zapruder took a film with his camera as he claimed—and he may or may not have even known what events were taking place around him—but *such a film, if it existed, contributed only tangentially to what is now known as the "Zapruder" film.*

Blueprint for a complete fabrication

We can now finally make progress in understanding how the extant film was created—fabricated, completely. Film was clearly needed of the broad panoramic sweep of Dealey Plaza, as seen from a camera perched atop the "Zapruder pedestal", because the panorama created from the extant film (shown in the previous sections) demonstrates how precisely it matches the expected topography. Whether this was an actual "pilot film" taken from that position, as has been suggested by Jack White, or whether it was constructed from still photographs, cannot be determined (although the erroneous angle for the lamppost to the right of the Stemmons Freeway sign perhaps suggests that a limited number of still photographs was employed—perspective correction not being easily available to the creators of the film at the time). Whether this background imagery was obtained before the assassination, or after it, cannot be determined either; there clearly was ample opportunity for either. (Before it, because no one would have taken any notice of anyone filming in Dealey Plaza; after it, because there would be nothing out of the ordinary in the authorities taking photographs of the scene of the crime.)

Next, footage of real bystanders needed to be supplied. This was almost certainly done by filming up Elm Street from a position somewhere near the Zapruder pedestal, prior to the motorcade entering Dealey Plaza, and after it did enter. The exact Zapruder position was not necessary, because these bystanders would be pasted onto the accurate "pilot film" background anyway. And the timing of some of the footage can be estimated by noting how little attention the bystanders actually pay to the appearance of the President and the First Lady! Why is this? *Because they were still waiting for them to arrive!* That is why the bystanders to the left of the Stemmons Freeway sign continue to stand around patiently, rather than wave to the limo (or even turn to follow it with their heads!). That is why the two men to the right of the tree continue to look up towards the corner of Houston Street, rather than pay any attention to the motorcade. To be sure, some of the footage of bystanders was taken while at least some vehicles passed—the people stepping back off the street, and so on—but this is most certainly in the minority.

Where are Moorman and Hill, and other bystanders, in Life?

Now, what about the Brehms, Beverly Oliver, Jean Hill, Mary Moorman, and so on?

Here the work was much more delicate—more intricate—and required more time. So when *Life* published images on the weekend of the assassination, they simply ensured that these people were not shown at all!

By the time the Memorial Edition was being finalized—probably a couple of weeks later—it was known that Beverly Oliver's confiscated film would not be used at all, and so it was permitted that she be shown, albeit blurred, on the edge of one frame.

Mary Moorman, on the other hand, *never* appeared in *any* issue of *Life*—nor did her friend, Jean Hill. Why? Moorman was probably omitted because she had a camera, and one of her Polaroid photographs (or, quite possibly, a modified version of it) was being used to round out the photographic record of the event, and very careful measurements needed to be taken to ensure that the position of Moorman's camera, inherent in the published Polaroid, would be consistent with her position in the Zapruder film. Jean Hill, on the other hand, who one would suspect to be the most photographically conspicuous bystander of all (wearing her bright red dress), also seems to have caused some difficulties for the animators (she only ever has two different head postures: back towards the motorcycle cop, who was apparently her boyfriend; and towards the President, at the last moment before the fatal shot), and as a result did not feature at all in *Life*.

Films of the actual motorcade

On top of this, of course, was needed actual footage of the motorcade during the turn from Houston onto Elm, and traveling down Elm Street.

There have been numerous reports of "other films" of the assassination, which some researchers claim are so clear, stable, and graphic that they appear to have been professionally filmed on 16 mm. As I have never viewed any of these "other films", I can only hazard a guess that some of them may be genuine; but, even if they are all themselves additional forgeries, it does not change the fact that at least one film of the actual event was needed—preferably multiple. This raw material was then reworked into a "sanitized" version (recall, no blood, except for the artificial spray in Frame 313, and the bizarre "blob" that moves around the President's head) that was photographically pasted in over the background, together with the bystanders.

The Zapruder story

Finally, it would have been desirable to actually *have* an "original Zapruder film" taken of the assassination from the Zapruder pedestal. Not to provide much raw material for the final product, of course—for the reasons described above—but merely to provide a rough guide as to how it should all look. Moreover, it would be desirable to actually have someone up on the purported filming pedestal, with a film camera, if that was going to be the cover story for the unofficially official film of the assassination!

Whether Zapruder was co-opted for the job, whether someone else did it for him, or whether anyone was actually up on that pedestal at all is still an open question. Certainly, there is no hard photographic evidence placing Abraham Zapruder in Dealey Plaza that day: as Jack White has shown here and in *Murder in Dealey Plaza*, what images *do* exist of him are highly dubious, and more confusing than helpful—it's hard to find one that actually shows him filming at *any* time!

Could the film have been fabricated without knowing *in advance* that Zapruder would be up on that pedestal, filming with the camera he did film with?

It's possible—all of the other footage could well have been obtained during or after the event—and it may explain why there were such problems with the Stemmons Freeway sign (if it did, indeed, get removed on the afternoon of the assassination because of a bullet hole), as well as the adjacent lamppost. But it's difficult to guess one way or the other.

As noted above, following my visit to Dealey Plaza in May 2003 I have been of the opinion that whoever stood on the Zapruder pedestal was the "coordinator" of the assassination, being in visual contact with every important position in Dealey Plaza that has been implicated (and especially the parking lot behind the picket fence on the grassy knoll). My best guess is that whoever was there possibly *did* take a film of the motorcade, at least for the first half of the presidential limousine's descent down Elm Street. After the assassination, such a "coordinator" could quite easily have become one of the false Secret Service agents on the knoll who aided in turning away those bystanders who raced up the knoll, looking for the assassins.

What about the known chronology of the Zapruder film?

Now the most important question of all: how could such a sophisticated fabrication process have been possibly carried out, given the known history of the film?

Actually, the constraints are not as severe as one would believe. Once one understands that the film is a complete *fabrication*—a *creation*—one's perspective changes drastically.

Firstly, we need to deal with those people—unrelated to and unaware of its fabrication—who saw the film on the weekend of the assassination itself. Whether we need to include Abraham Zapruder in this list of people is an open question; but it does not hurt to assume that he was an innocent stooge.

What, then, did these people view in those first hours and days? A film, certainly, and an 8 mm one at that; one that was probably taken from the Zapruder pedestal; and one that probably had a fairly accurate depiction of actual events.

So why didn't these people realize that what was eventually shown as "the Zapruder film" was different to what they saw?

There are several answers to this.

Early viewers of the film describing things "wrongly"

The first is that, in some respects, they did.

Dan Rather's famous "incorrect" comments about Kennedy's reaction to the fatal shot (pitching forwards, rather than "back and to the left") was most likely an accurate recollection of a shocking and gruesome event he had just witnessed on film. (Note that Altgens and others gave the same description—apparently so shocking that it made him freeze, and miss taking his photograph.)

Others reported seeing blood and brain matter ejected from the back of the President's head, which again was most likely true.

The difficulty of comprehending from just a few viewings

The second answer is that it is difficult to realize how little can be comprehended on the first viewing, or first several viewings, of a film of this nature.

I can appreciate this because it is only a few short years since I first saw the film in detail. For a long time, I couldn't make much out of anything. Groden's book talked about movements of people that I simply couldn't see, no matter how hard I looked. It even took me a long time to actually *find* Abraham Zapruder in the Willis photo, despite the caption that told me he was there. After viewing the film over and over and over, hundreds or even thousands of times, and after examining it frame by frame in minute detail, one's visual comprehension of the contents of the film is almost infinitely more detailed than what one gets on a first viewing.

Consider the fact that these first viewers of the film didn't even have the first inkling about what had actually happened; and that the film they did see was probably far more gruesome than what we have available today. I could imagine that one's eyes would be riveted to the President's head, no matter if the film were replayed fifty times.

A good test of this principle arose recently, in connection with the "Moorman in the street" controversy. After many months of heated debate, it struck me that there were people heavily involved in the debate who had actually seen the "other" film—some on a number of occasions. So I asked the question, "OK, you've seen the 'other' film. Tell me: did Mary Moorman step onto the street, or not?" Without fail, none could remember. (I don't count here a report of a viewing of the "other" film *after* the Moorman controversy arose, because in that case the viewer knew what they were looking for.) And that's exactly what I would expect. After all, if you had a limited opportunity to see what may well be the *genuine* film of the assassination, would you direct your gaze to Moorman's shoes? Jean Hill's dress? Charles Brehm's shirt? Of course not!

Two parallel lines of work: moving pictures and stills

And so it is quite possible that there were two parallel lines of work taking place after the assassination.

On the one hand, the original Zapruder film (assuming he took one—or some film taken from that area, if not) was being processed, and perhaps had events removed immediately. Deletion of frames with an optical printer carried no risk of detection at that stage—all that was needed was a film that could be projected; no one was going to sit there with a magnifying glass examining the blurring in the sprocket hole area! Projected at full speed, even quite a rough job of event deletion would largely go unnoticed.

On the other hand, work was being rapidly undertaken to create publishable images from "the 8 mm film of the assassination", as it was called for some time. These were to be contained in the *Life* issue that was probably rolling off the presses on Sunday, 24 November.

Flexibility the key

The name of the game at this stage was *flexibility*. Images had to be rapidly produced, which gave a broad overview of the assassination scene, but, once published, they could never be retracted.

So it was ensured that what *was* published was optical mud—poor quality reproductions, clearly many generations removed from any original imagery, and black and white. Images of the motorcade near the top of Elm Street could be essentially genuine: bystanders are relatively clear. For reasons yet unclear to me, a new version of the Stemmons Freeway sign was pasted in. (Or, again, did this sign really exist before the assassination? Was this its first incarnation?)

Images further down Elm Street, however, were more conservative. Little was shown other than the limousine, its occupants, and the curb and grass behind it. The President was shown holding his throat in several similar images.

And then the three-second gap.

Well, it's three seconds' worth if we go by the extant film. In reality, it represents a huge gap in the photographic record. The next we see is that the President is sort of slumping over towards his wife. The text says that he "collapses" on her shoulder. No actual mention of a shot to the head.

Again, flexibility.

We see more today than what was really published

Today, with the benefit of having seen all of the frames that were created to fill in the gap *between* these images, we can see the President's head wound—sort of—in this first issue of *Life*. But with a different set of images in between, almost anything could be imagined.

It is difficult for many students of the assassination to really grasp how a different scenario of the assassination could have been painted, given the images published so quickly by *Life*. This is more so, the longer the said researcher has viewed and re-viewed the film as we now have it. In one sense, I am therefore fortunate to have been such a recent inductee to the research community: the film was still new to me at the time that I was made aware that it could well be fraudulent, and I had not had much opportunity to view it as a motion picture— something that is much more powerful, psychologically, than simply viewing individual, disconnected frames. It is inevitable that as new researchers come on board, *with the assumption that the film is as tainted as the rest of the evidence in this case*, the hurdle of overcoming the reluctance to part with what for a long time seemed to be the primary evidence for conspiracy and cover-up will subside.

John Costella and Jim Fetzer at the Zapruder Film Symposium,
Duluth, Minnesota, 9–11 May 2003. (Photograph by Jan Fetzer)

But there were still mistakes

Despite the very minimal amount of information contained in the first-weekend images in *Life*, and despite the best efforts of the fabricators, some of the images caused serious headaches and constraints in fabricating the rest of the film: the men looking up at Houston Street ignoring the limousine; the Stemmons Freeway sign; the moving "blob" on the President's head; the missing object in the grass, and so on.

But the page was still essentially left blank: there were many ways in which the details could be filled in.

The need for high quality images

Within the next couple of weeks, however, the first serious images needed to be released. Those published in the Memorial Edition of *Life* are high quality, and in color. (Indeed, as noted above, they are *too* high quality—motion blurs had not yet been properly calculated.)

Key frames in the creation of the film had been locked into place. The general timeline for the assassination had been established. The story was quickly determined: one lone nut assassin, three shots, Kennedy/Connally/Kennedy.

A strange article was even published near the end of the Memorial Edition, in which the three hits had been identified visually from the film (something which researchers still cannot agree on forty years later!), and the number of frames between each one had been counted. (Moreover, all three bullets had been recovered: the first, which had entered the President's throat, was recovered at the autopsy! It also reported that the Oswald feat had been replicated using an identical rifle with an identical site at targets at the identical distances and moving at the same speeds!) This article was written by Paul Mandel, who is an inhabitant of the list of "suspicious deaths"—he died in early 1965.

A role for NPIC?

Documents from the CIA's National Photographic Interpretation Center (NPIC), obtained originally under Freedom of Information suits (see Appendix C) suggest that the emerging Zapruder timeline formed another serious constraint on the creation of the film. Especially noteworth is that NPIC had the ability to directly enlarge frames by a factor of 40—an 8mm frame the size of your little fingernail becomes an 8- by 10-inch photograph (*ready for editing*) in a single step!

Certainly, the final film produced needed to at least allow the *Life* analysis to be a *reasonable* estimate—if not as definite as originally made out to be. The removal of the limo stop allowed less freedom in developing what turned out to be the "missing three seconds" of the first-weekend images.

The obvious splices in the film

To this point, I have not discussed the most obvious form of "alteration" of the extant film, namely, the splices that appear in what is sometimes still called the "camera original" film. The most famous of these occurs between frames 208 and 212 at just the point where the President's limousine is passing behind the Stemmons Freeway sign as it pans across Zapruder's view. Another, less well-known splice occurs between frames 155 and 157—earlier than the selection of frames published by the Warren Commission. [*Editor's note*: These splices and the missing frames are discussed and illustrated in the color photo section of this book, "Which Film is 'The Zapruder film'?"]

Early researchers were stunned by the preposterous suggestion that *Life* had allowed the film to be damaged and then crudely "hot spliced" back together, which was not even remotely credible, or that the remnants of the damaged frames would have been casually discarded as though they were of no value, even in that condition. So what was the purpose of these "splices"? Why were they introduced at all? One possibility is that they were deployed as a "red herring" to outrage and mislead students of the film and thereby lend specious credibility to its authenticity—rather in the same fashion that school children create "authentic" looking aged maps using tea stains and burnt corners.

Another possibility is that, when the fabricated frames were being transferred to a genuine strip of Kodak celluloid, a mistake that might have revealed the forgery was detected after the first 150–200 frames had been created. Rather than start again, it may have been prudent to introduce another genuine strip of Kodak celluloid and splice them together, possibly even creating the subtle impression that "alterations" should take the form of splices like these! [*Editor's note*: These considerations also appear to have ramifications for the conclusions of Zavada's studies of the film (Appendix B).]

Perhaps the most likely explanation derives from the observation that *the ghost panels below frames 207–211 would have shown the bystanders visible under the left edge of the Stemmons Freeway sign*. This sequences pans across the sign in such a fashion that removing even a few of these frames eliminates those ghost images from consideration. [*Editor's note*: Indeed, since the ghost images are the links that tie these frames together, the interruptions in the sequence at 154–157 and at 207–212 raises the possibilily that the film itself might have been created from three separate segments, one that lasted from 1–154, another from 157–207, and the third from 212–486, which undermines any claims that Zavada's studies have "proven" the film's authenticity.]

[*Editor's note*: For a film to be advertised as "a state-of-the-art digital replication of the camera original—a copy that will serve researchers for years to come"— when it is missing the ghost panels, frames 155-156, 208-211; reverses frames 331 and 332; and omits frames 341, 350, and (even) 486(!) ought to be considered to be a scandal, possibly even justifying legal action for false advertising or consumer fraud. Other evidence of deceit and deception in the preparation of the MPI DVD, "The Image of an Assassination" (1997), may now be found in the new Appendix I.]

When was it finished?

So when was the entire film complete?

Obviously, the set of frames published by the Warren Commission in late 1964 tells us that the most important "central" part of the film was complete within a year. Is that a reasonable time frame to create a couple of hundred frames, including the intersprocket regions? I believe it is.

Certainly, the film as a motion picture had to be in a fairly consistent form by the time members of the Warren Commission viewed it, at the end of January 1964. But, again, one must ask the question: what, really, had to be "right" with the film? Of main concern was getting the content pretty well right. There is no suggestion that members of the Warren Commission sat down with the original strip of film and measured blurs and ghost images in the intersprocket region, as David Mantik was to do in the 1990s. The transparencies later made for the identification of bullet hits, again, needed to match what we now have today only insofar as a visual recollection would allow. Until the actual publication of the twenty-six volumes of Exhibits in November 1964, fine details were still, essentially, malleable. (It is striking that *Life* was still using the same frames in its Warren Report issue of 2 October 1964 as it had in its Memorial Edition.)

It is more difficult to determine whether the rest of the film—before about Frame 160, and after about Frame 340—was also completed in detail by the end of 1964. Certainly, the film as a complete entity didn't really need to exist until Garrison subpoenaed it for the Clay Shaw trial in the late 1960s. The intersprocket regions of the frames not published by the Warren Commission didn't really need to exist until the 1990s. Whether these even less restrictive deadlines are meaningful, or unnecessarily generous, is not clear.

Early bootleg copies at Life

And what of reports that many copies of the "original" film were made by *Life* even before the end of 1963?

Clearly, the process of fabricating the film would have been in dire jeopardy, had there not been in place a mechanism for ensuring that no *genuine* footage ever saw the light of day! Given the careers of several *Life* executives, it is difficult to argue with the proposition that anyone who *did* have a copy of anything other than the final "release" version of the Zapruder film would be made fully aware of the consequences of it escaping into the wild.

Possessors of "other" films

Certainly, those who claim to have seen "other" films of the assassination report an extremely high degree of caution amongst those possessing them— that they literally owe their life to maintaining its confidentiality. This behavior is consistent with the knowledge that the extant film was actually a fabricated creation.

Of course, those who participated (knowingly or unwittingly) in its creation and cover-up in the 1960s may well have been convinced that it was necessary on the grounds of national security; it is unfair to apply today's standards to what was a very insecure and uncertain time in global politics. But whether they ever tell us the full story, or not, remains to be seen.

John Costella
presenting at the
Zapruder Film Symposium,
Duluth, Minnesota
10 May 2003

Appendix: Weird experiences en route to Duluth

[*Editor's note*: John Costella's odd experiences en route to Duluth may sound bizarre, but they are perfectly consistent with the history of the conduct of reasearch in Dealey Plaza. The City of Dallas may well be the only one in America to have removed street signs, relocated street lamps, and resurfaced a major thoroughfare without removing the old asphalt (producing a build-up of four to six inches higher than in 1963) in an evident effort to thwart inquiry into the death of JFK, as I know from personal experience. It is common knowledge that the plaza is under surveillance by a camera mounted to the Book Depository. A few years ago, I was in the plaza and sat down on the curb to quietly remove some flakes from the yellow curb stripes that appear to have marked "the kill zone" to compare them with remnants of paint on Beverly Oliver's shoes, which was acquired when she stepped on the freshly painted marks. A few weeks later, I asked Jack if he could return to the plaza for some more samples. He reported that, to his utter astonishment, the remaining remnants of those stripes had been sandblasted off, after having gradually deteriorated for more than 35 years! Some vaguely plausible denial, no doubt, will be forthcoming, but what Costella reports is really not a stretch, when you know the history. (See the Epilogue.)]

In the sections above, I have provided what I consider to be the "best evidence" that the Zapruder film is a complete fabrication. From my investigations, I have absolutely no doubt at all—none whatsoever—that it is a fake. There are literally hundreds of problems with the film that I could point to that suggest that one aspect or another is flawed to various degrees of certainty. But what I have presented here are those absolutely undeniable mistakes in the film that prove, *beyond any doubt*, that it is, first, demonstrably *altered*, and, secondly, a complete *fabrication*. I would willingly take the stand in a court of law and swear to these conclusions.

Following those crucial pieces of evidence, I have offered other indications of where mistakes have occurred. Finally, I have provided my best guess as to how the film was actually fabricated—the "means", if you like, of the forgery process. Details of this I cannot, of course, be certain of, because there are many possible ways that it could have been done. But what is important is that it could have been done. Now that I have described the results of my research, I must now relate my experiences in actually visiting Dealey Plaza for the first time-after my research was essentially complete—in May 2003.

Visiting Dealey Plaza: May 2003

As my work on the Zapruder film was progressing in 2002, Professor Jim Fetzer invited me to speak at a Zapruder Film Symposium to be held in Minnesota in May 2003. The Headmaster of Mentone Grammar at the time, Neville Clark, enthusiastically approved my absence for a week, with the only proviso that being that I give a lecture to the History class on my return, describing the state of knowledge in this most important phase of modern history—of which he had a keen interest and knowledge. (He had himself been awarded a Military Cross—the seventh highest military award available in this country—for outstanding bravery in the Vietnam War, and was aware that my wife Robyn's uncle had been posthumously awarded the highest, a Victoria Cross. Most Australians, of course, would have much preferred that they had never had the chance to earn their medals in the first place, had President Kennedy been able to fulfill his plan withdraw all troops by the end of 1965. "All the way with LBJ" was a boast that was later to haunt the Australian Government in infamy, culminating in their loss of office to the Labor Party in 1972 after 23 continuous years in office, at which time the new Prime Minister Gough Whitlam immediately withdrew all Australian troops.)

The Dallas stopover

Shortly after receiving the invitation to speak at the Symposium, there were calls from some members of the JFKresearch.com forum for me to abstain from making any final pronouncement on the "Moorman in the street" issue unless and until I was able to visit in person the site of the assassination, Dealey Plaza, in Dallas, Texas, in order to investigate the issue first-hand.

My planned visit to the United States in May 2003 seemed too good a chance to pass up to fulfill this challenge. Tightening up the itinerary with a fairly hectic set of flights, we found it possible for me to spend about two days in Dallas before flying up to Minnesota for the Symposium, and still be back in Melbourne within the week.

And so it was that on 7 May 2003, I made the trip from Melbourne to Los Angeles and through to Dallas—the International Date Line allowing me to arrive in Dallas just a few apparent hours after leaving my home in Narre Warren, a suburb about 25 miles south-east of the center of Melbourne. I was fortunate, while in Dallas, to stay at the Lawrence Hotel (formerly the Paramount), just a couple of blocks from Dealey Plaza, and even more fortunate that legendary researcher Jack White, a lifelong resident of Fort Worth, was my most generous and selfless host—and "research assistant"—during my visit.

During those two days, I was treated to the most thorough assassination tour one could imagine—far better than some of the tawdry offerings I have seen advertised on the Internet. I had not set a huge agenda of scientific measurements to make—Jack had already provided everything I had previously asked for; all I needed was to verify some of the particulars. Rather, I wanted to spend the time getting the sort of thorough "feel" for Dealey Plaza—and Dallas in general—that one can only get by being there in person. In addition to retracing Oswald's alleged movements on the day of the assassination in Jack's car, and seeing where the famous "backyard photographs" were taken, we scoured almost every square yard of Dealey Plaza and its surrounds, and discussed the various theories that had been put forward over the decades as to where shooters may have been located.

And we stumbled across objects that, whilst humorous at the time, provide profound questions to anyone who doubts the ongoing cover-up of the assassination.

A device on the Airports sign

After some hours spent investigating Dealey Plaza and its surrounds on that first day, Wednesday, 7 May, Jack and I were walking along the Elm Street sidewalk adjoining the "grassy knoll", up from the Triple Underpass. We stopped at the back of the Airports sign (that is in roughly the same position as the Fort

Worth Turnpike sign was in 1963; see Figure 38) to discuss the metal framework that covered the back of the sign.

Figure 38. The Airports sign on the grassy knoll, down near the Triple Underpass, as it appeared (from the front) on Wednesday, 7 May 2003

Our interest in this relatively obscure aspect of Dallas road sign architecture stemmed from earlier discussions on JFKresearch.com about the appearance of the back of the Stemmons Freeway sign in the Zapruder film. Down the sides of that sign there appears to be some strange sort of "panels", which have a different color to that of the rest of the back of the sign. Jack had noted that, because the signs were (in those days) made out of plyboard, there was no way to join panels of this nature onto the sign without the use of metal framework, which was clearly not shown in the film.

Although I had seen such a framework on the Airports sign in photographs taken from the overpass, the resolution from that distance was never sufficient for me to examine the framework in detail. Standing right behind the sign, in person, gave me that opportunity.

I thought I should take a photo of the framework so that I could study it in greater detail on my return to Melbourne. (See Figure 39.) After taking the photo, Jack was pointing out to me that the sign was indeed made out of plyboard– because some researchers had doubted that plyboard signs even existed. I was examining the side of the sign, and was considering whether I could take a decent photo of the "grain" (interior structure) of the plyboard itself from the side, when I noticed something strange.

I asked Jack, "What's *that*?" Jack took a look at the small white plastic device I was pointing to, affixed near the left edge of the sign (as seen from the back), about two-thirds of the way down the sign from the top. (See Figure 40.) He had no idea what it was. Although we are both about 6'2" tall, the device was too far above our heads to get a good look at it. After some stretching and straining, we could make out the text on the side of the device: "Wireless RainSensor(tm)", with an FCC number (required for all wireless radio communications devices used in the United States) in small print below it.

Figure 39. The back of the Airports sign as it appeared on 7 May 2003

We had a good laugh about this device, assuming it to be something used by the Dallas Weather Bureau for measuring rainfall throughout the city. Why choose the infamous grassy knoll as a measurement point? In any case, it provided us with some light humor.

Figure 40. An enlargement of a portion of Figure 39. Note that the device is completely shielded from rain angling in from the east—by the sign itself. Note also the two "shelves" above the device, created by the metal framework, which would prevent any rain angling in from the south from reaching the device either

Something curious in hindsight

It did not hit me at the time (perhaps the thirty-odd hours of travel I had just completed had dimmed my brain a little), but this Wireless RainSensor was mounted in a curious position. Being mounted flat on the back of the sign, two-thirds of the way down, even the slightest breeze from the east would cause any falling rain to hit the front of the sign itself, rather than enter the RainSensor. Moreover, the metal framework itself—the reason I had stopped to take a photograph in the first place—formed two effective "shelves" that ended right above the RainSensor, so that even the slightest breeze from the south would *also* cause the falling rain to be blocked before it could enter the RainSensor.

Why choose such a silly location for a RainSensor? It was, indeed, wireless—the wire hanging down from it was clearly the radio antenna—so it could have been mounted anywhere. Why not on the lamppost that can be seen in the background of Figure 39? Or, for that matter, on the lamppost that can be seen in the background of Figure 38? Or if the sign was the desired position, why not mount it on a bracket that protruded some distance from the edge of the sign, to allow the rain to actually enter the device?

As noted, none of this ran through my mind that Wednesday afternoon in Dallas. We thought it was something to do with the Weather Bureau, not realizing that such sensors were often also used for irrigation systems. Ironically, Jack had previously noticed a plastic-topped pop-up sprinkler up near the steps, not too distant from the sign, embedded in the edge of the grass of the knoll, but it appeared to be caked with dirt and no longer functional, and he commented at the time that he had never noticed any sprinkler system running in any of his visits to Dealey Plaza. Had we put the two observations together, and given them any significance, we might have made a logical connection. But that would have thrown a spotlight on the central question: why put a RainSensor in a location that would prevent it measuring rainfall?

But we didn't make the connection; we continued on with our tour of Dealey Plaza, were refused entry to the Observation Tower for dinner because a dress code had been in force for ten minutes, and ended up at the Spaghetti Warehouse in the West End, where Jack accused me of "inhaling" a bowl of soup, a "Turin Trio" covered with mozzarella and mushrooms, and a piece of cheesecake. (My father, who was born in Turin, would have been proud.)

The next day

Jack and I had decided that I would spend the morning of Thursday, 8 May visiting the Sixth Floor Museum and the Conspiracy Museum, and completing my own verifications of the photographic data that Jack and others had provided to me over the preceding eighteen months.

I wanted to make the most of my only full day in Dallas, and was already walking down from the Lawrence Hotel to Dealey Plaza by about 7:30 AM. I stopped to read the plaque mounted behind the peristyle, near the north reflecting pool along Houston Street. The Plaza was completely empty, save for a man near the corner of Elm and Houston whom I had seen selling Robert Groden's newsletters the day before.

Less than a minute later, I could hear two men talking not far behind me. One was saying to the other, "So the motorcade came down that street, and turned there, and . . .", and the man other was disagreeing with him, pointing out a different, equally incorrect route. I turned, and noticed that the two men were wearing expensive suits and sunglasses—but neither of them was holding any sort of map or guide that could form the basis of their disagreement. They certainly didn't look like any sort of tourist I had ever seen in my life.

Trying to hide a wry smile, I turned to the men, and pointed out the motorcade route for them. I turned back to the plaque to continue reading. One of the men then said to the other, "So Oswald was up there at the time." I again turned, to see him pointing directly at the correct window of the former Texas School Book Depository—but again without any form of map or photograph to guide his apparent guess. I thought it time to bring the game to an end. I walked up to the men, pointed to first floor of the building, looked each of them in the eye, and said, "No, Oswald was probably right in there, eating his lunch."

The two men looked at me, and then rapidly walked off towards the corner of Elm Street. For the next fifteen minutes, as I went about my business in the Plaza, I could see them separately pacing backwards and forwards inside the pergola on the grassy knoll, deep in conversation on their cellphones.

For the first time I entertained the thought that, if *this* was the best that U.S. intelligence could serve up, then maybe the 9/11 terrorist attack was the result of intelligence incompetence after all.

A productive afternoon

After my extensive tour of the Sixth Floor Museum (where I learnt how to edit and selectively display the film and photographic evidence of the assassination in order to make the Warren Commission's version of events sound vaguely plausible) and the Conspiracy Museum (where I was amused to find that a new "Aliens" exhibit had opened in the basement the day I arrived in Dallas—consisting of two small posters, a video player and about ten videotapes about aliens– which I obviously had no time to watch), as well as a return to Dealey Plaza to verify the panoramic photographs that Jack had taken from the Zapruder pedestal the previous July, I ran back to the lobby of the hotel to make my 1:30 PM rendezvous with Jack for our afternoon's work.

We made the short walk back to Dealey Plaza along Houston Street. At the corner of Main and Houston, we started to take a shortcut across the grass towards the Mary Moorman position. Looking up, I suddenly stopped, turned to Jack, and asked, "OK, tell me why you need *two* RainSensors in Dealey Plaza?" Jack followed my line of sight to the lamppost on Main Street just five or ten yards from where we were standing, and spotted the white device protruding from the side of the lamppost, mounted on a bracket. We had another good laugh, and I had Jack pose for a photo under the second of these devices that, for us, were acquiring celebrity status in their own right. (See Figure 41(a).)

On checking the display on the back of the digital camera that the photo had come out well, I noticed something strange. I looked up, across the street, at the lamppost directly on the *other* side of Main Street—and confirmed with my own eyes what the digital camera had shown: there was *yet another* Wireless

RainSensor mounted only fifteen yards or so from the one Jack had just posed beneath. (See Figure 41(b).)

(a) *(b)*

Figure 41. The discovery of two more Wireless RainSensors on Thursday, 8 May. (a) Jack White poses for a photo beneath a RainSensor mounted on a bracket attached to a lamppost on the north side of Main Street. What is now the Federal Building looms in the background. (b) Another RainSensor is found, mounted on the lamppost located symmetrically on the south side of Main Street, some fifteen yards away. It can also be seen in the background of (a).

This discovery really was too much for us. Regardless of their ostensible purpose, it was clear that there was absolutely no sense at all in having two such sensors only fifteen yards apart—and this was even before we had considered the bizarre placement of the device on the back of the Airports sign. Jack and I had another hearty laugh about the need to measure the rainfall at three different points of one small plaza—that the weatherman on the radio could announce that it was raining on the north side of Main Street, but not on the south side.

After Jack had cracked a few more jokes about such strange precipitation patterns in Dealey Plaza ("Maybe it was raining on the Umbrella Man but not on anyone else"—a reference to the infamous man who appears to pump an umbrella in the extant Zapruder film, standing next to the Stemmons Freeway sign), I started to think more seriously about the implications of our latest find. It was patently obvious that the devices were not RainSensors—or, more to the point, they may *well* be genuine RainSensors, but being employed for other purposes. Even if it was alleged that they were used for a watering system, the distance between them was much less than the distance of *either* of them to any possible radio receiver—which, one would presume, would actually control the sprinklers. Thus, the transmission distance of each *must* necessarily be large enough that one of them is clearly redundant: even if two separate watering systems were needed, for the two symmetrical sections of grass between Main, Elm, and Commerce, each base station could obviously receive the signal from a *single* RainSensor.

My thoughts then turned immediately to surveillance. I considered the possibility that each of the devices had small cameras installed. But I quickly rejected this possibility. Firstly, there already was a "surveillance" camera in Dealey Plaza: the 24-hour web-cam operating from the "sniper's nest" in the Sixth Floor Museum (on the Internet at www.earthcam.com/jfk). Secondly, the white building directly behind the Plaza, which in 1963 was the Post Office building, is today the Federal Building, complete with armed guards on the entrances, and a permanent guard on the parking lot atop the south grassy knoll (on the other side of Dealey Plaza from the more infamous north grassy knoll). If national security demanded video surveillance of Dealey Plaza, then surely it would be much simpler for the FBI to point a telephoto lens or two out of one of those many windows overlooking the Plaza—or simply log on to the Sixth Floor Museum's webcast.

And thirdly, I ran across Main Street to take some close-up photographs of the third RainSensor: this one was not quite as high off the ground as the others, and by holding the digital camera above my head, I could get a reasonable photo of it. (See Figure 42.) It looked to me as if there was probably no suitable location for a camera lens (the "holes" through the top section went right through— probably where the water flows out of the genuine rain sensing device at the top; the bottom canister was sealed, and clearly would have to contain the battery and the radio transmitter, to which the antenna was connected).

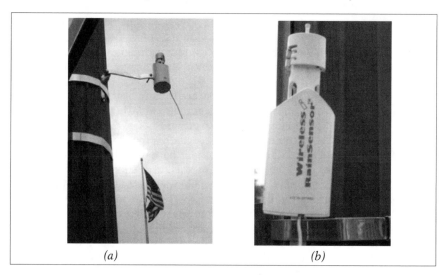

(a) *(b)*

Figure 42. Close-up views of a Wireless RainSensor. (a) Photo showing how the device was mounted to the lamppost on the south side of Main Street. American flag in the background welcomes me to the supposed Land of the Free. (b) Close-up view of the device obtained by holding the camera up at full arm-stretch.

Audio surveillance, on the other hand, is a different question. If one wants to listen to a conversation from a great distance, one can point a highly directional microphone at the person in question, and in many cases one can pick up audio that most people would usually assume to be completely impossible to hear from such a distance. But such a procedure requires one to be tracking the person visually to begin with, and would be more difficult to carry out if the person was shielded by one of the many concrete structures in the Plaza.

A highly sensitive microphone mounted *within* Dealey Plaza would avoid these problems: it would be able to "listen" to the whole Plaza, at all times, without needing to track people, and concrete obstacles would be no problem. But such a microphone would itself pick up a lot of background noise: traffic, trains screeching around the corner on the railway overpass, and so on.

How can one eliminate such noise? Spectral filtering can help, but only to a certain point. Rather, what is needed is *an array of microphones* at precisely known positions. Fairly simple electronic (or digital) techniques can then be used to compare the signals, and cancel out most of the extraneous noise—especially any noise that is external to Dealey Plaza.

Remarkably, that seemed to be exactly what we had found: two devices placed symmetrically, on either side of Main Street. However, the third device, down on the back of the Airports sign, seemed to be the "odd man out". Together with the first two, it would provide a much more substantial cover of those parts of the Plaza where researchers tend to congregate, being very much closer to the Zapruder pedestal, and particularly the picket fence. But its location still created an asymmetry, which would reduce somewhat the efficacy of any noise-reduction algorithm.

A lack of symmetry leads to the next discovery

As these thoughts ran through my mind, my eyes immediately turned to the Airports sign's mirror-image location, down on the south knoll, near the Triple Underpass, that we had explored (after crossing over the overpass) just the day before. And as if on cue, to some hidden script, there appeared the sight shown in Figure 43.

The presence of this fourth device answered many of the questions I had. Firstly, it completed the almost precisely symmetrical layout that I had known would be most efficient at eliminating background noise. As can be seen from Figure 43(b), which looks somewhat northeast rather than due north, the fourth RainSensor is located a little further west than that on the back of the Airports sign. But why? Either from the viewpoint of noise reduction, *or even as a set of genuine rain sensors*, it would have made much more sense to simply mount the sensor on the north grassy knoll on the lamppost that is symmetrical with that of Figure 43—the one that is seen in the background of Figure 38. After looking at Figures 41, 42, and 43, it *cannot possibly* be argued that the person who mounted the RainSensors didn't have brackets for mounting them on lampposts, or didn't realize that if they wanted them to be actually exposed to the rain, that they had better not be shielded by an object like a sign and its metal framework.

As I ran back to where I had left Jack on the north side of Main Street (almost getting killed by a truck in the process—traveling on the wrong side of the road, as vehicles in the U.S. are wont to do), I scoured the rest of the Plaza, playing a

(a)   (b)

Figure 43. The fourth Wireless RainSensor, found located in an almost mirro-image position to that of the Airports sign. (a) Position of the lamppost on the south grassy knoll, near the Triple Underpass. (b) Looking back from behind the lamppost. The Airports sign, pergola structure, and former Texas School Book Depository can be seen in the distance. (The strange paint job is unexplained.)

game of "spot the RainSensor". But it seemed that the four we had found were the only ones—or the only obvious ones, in any case. So my thoughts returned to the "odd man out" device on the back of the Airports sign. Why not just put it on the lamppost like the other three?

Standing in the middle of Dealey Plaza, the answer was obvious: of the four symmetrical locations, the lamppost on the grassy knoll *was the only location that would be obvious to researchers studying the Zapruder film*. It was the only location on the grassy knoll itself; it was the only location visible on the Zapruder film, and hence on any recreations of it; and it was by far the closest location to the concrete pedestal on which Zapruder allegedly stood when shooting his film. The only reason to put the device on the back of the Airports sign was blindingly obvious: concealment.

Having determined, to my satisfaction, the reason for the existence of the devices, I gave them no more thought during my visit to Dallas. Even before the incident with the two "suits", I had expected to be under surveillance; and, although the RainSensors added a new twist for American citizens visiting Dealey Plaza (photographs taken by Jack White demonstrate that the devices have been there for at least a year, perhaps far longer), as a foreign national I didn't have any reason or inclination to complain about rights that I most likely didn't have in the first place.

But I made sure I greeted the north Main Street RainSensor with "Hi, spooks!" and a wry grin towards the Federal Building, every time I walked down to the Plaza from my hotel.

The adjustable lamppost

One would think that I had had enough excitement for one day in Dealey Plaza. But no sooner had Jack and I started returning to our intended destination of the Mary Moorman position, on the south side of Elm Street, than we stumbled across yet another surprising find.

Jack had known for years that many of the lampposts in Dealey Plaza had been shifted from their original positions, and our precision work in 2002 had detected an even greater number of small changes. Some of the major changes had allegedly been made in the name of safety—lampposts located on the curb had been moved up onto the grass, apparently to prevent motorists from colliding with them as they took a look at the infamous grassy knoll. Other changes had been made for no obvious reasons. But it was often tacitly assumed that those lampposts that *were* present in the modern Dealey Plaza would remain in the same place from day to day, month to month, year to year.

As I have already explained, one of the mistakes made in the fabrication of the Zapruder film was the orientation of the lamppost seen in the middle section of the film, behind which the presidential limousine passes: it is wrong by a couple of degrees, compared to photographic evidence taken by the Dallas Police Department just days after the assassination. Unfortunately for the fabricators of the film, this sort of mistake cannot be ascribed to uncertainties in the camera position or orientation: the angle of the lamppost relative to the background, after the camera optics and perspective are accounted for, is something that does not and cannot change.

So how would one go about covering up such a mistake? One way would be to ensure that there is a plethora of photographic evidence showing that a lamppost can apparently change its orientation in different photographs. But if this is physically impossible, how can one generate such apparently unimpeachable examples? Simple: *ensure that one has a lamppost whose orientation can be changed by a couple of degrees, one way or the other, by a simple procedure that can be carried out overnight*.

If I had made such a suggestion at any time before visiting Dealey Plaza, I would have surely been labeled a paranoid "crackpot" spinning far-fetched theories involving non-existent agents of obfuscation, by those wishing to assert the Zapruder film to be uniquely resistant to the sort of tampering so prevalent with most of the other evidence in this case. But just minutes after completing our investigation of the Wireless RainSensors, I noticed that the lamppost directly opposite the "Zapruder pedestal"—the location from which Abraham Zapruder allegedly took his film—had an odd protrusion near its base: two thick washers. (See Figure 44.)

I pointed them out to Jack, who, again, had not noticed them before. He conjectured that the washers had been placed under the lamppost when it was installed to balance it up, to ensure it was acceptably vertical. But as he examined the washers from the south, I went around to the north side of the lamppost, and by lying on the grass running downhill from the lamppost to the curb of Elm Street (with my feet just latching over into the gutter) I was able to get a

(a)   *(b)*

Figure 44. Discovery of washers underneath the lamppost directly opposite the Zapruder pedestal. (a) The lamppost as seen "from behind", looking north towards the grassy knoll. (b) Close-up view of the washers seen in (a).

good view of the underside of the entire lamppost. Far from being something added to just one side (as one would expect for a balancing-up object), *the entire base of the lamppost* was propped up by small stacks of washers, by about an inch. On one side, however, the stacks had an extra small washer, which raised the lamppost by an extra quarter of an inch or so. (See Figure 45.)

There is clearly no useful purpose to raising a lamppost by an inch off its concrete base, using such stacks of washers. If it required balancing up, by (say) the height of one of the small washers on one side, then one would simply need to place a few of these washers between the lamppost and the concrete base!

Raising it *all* by an inch, however, is a clever strategy. After my return to Australia, Jack and I have separately found evidence for such washers in photographs taken in Dealey Plaza going back at least two years. Anyone discovering these stacks of washers, and claiming it to be evidence of foul play, could thus be quickly dismissed, once it was realized that these washers were not a recent addition. But these older photographs do not show all of the stacks, in the detail shown in Figure 45, simply because no one was lying on the grass with their feet in the gutter trying to photograph them, as I was. So how can we know that the stacks were arranged the same way in the past as they were on 8 May 2003?

Of course, we *can't*. It would be a relatively simple task to have a few men visit Dealey Plaza in the early hours of morning, lift the lamppost a few inches, rearrange the stacks of washers, and lower the lamppost again. Even adding the extra small washers seen in Figure 45 would change the angle of the lamppost by

Figure 45. The base of the lamppost shown in Figure 44, as seen from Elm Street, looking south, as it was on Thursday, 8 May 2003. On this particular day, the west side of the lamppost's base was raised one inch by the washers, and the east side by an extra quarter of an inch, which would tilt the lamppost by about two degrees compared to its orientation if it were uniformly raised by one inch.

around two degrees. This would be unnoticeable to the naked eye, but it would evident in precision comparisons of photographs taken on different days, months, or years—*and it would be of sufficient size to discredit any findings regarding the incorrect lamppost orientation in the Zapruder film.*

Unless, of course, you get caught.

More fun and games

One might think that, after these discoveries, the rest of my trip in the U.S. would necessarily be an anticlimax. But nothing could be farther from the truth.

Jack and I flew together from Dallas-Fort Worth to Minneapolis-St. Paul on Friday, expecting to take a quick connecting flight to Duluth for the Symposium. Our first surprise involved the gentleman in a suit who was sitting in front of Jack throughout the flight. He dropped his seat back as far as it would go–but instead of resting, he spent the entire time listening attentively to our discussions, and even tried to join in as we entered Minnesota. When the plane came to a rest at the terminal, Jack decided that we might as well wait until the rest of the passengers deplaned, as we had one and a half hours to wait anyway. It surprised both of us when the nosy gentleman also stayed—even when all of the rows around us were empty. After we started looking at him curiously, he reluctantly got up, and walked out.

But he hadn't gone. Five minutes later, when we finally made our way to the front of the plane ourselves, I spotted the man talking to the Captain about airspeed and altitude, and that sort of thing. But just as we passed him, he interrupted the Captain mid-sentence, saying, "Sorry—gotta go," and followed us out.

Intrigued, I dawdled somewhat as we entered the main terminal. The gentleman had no choice but to go past us again. We quickly spotted our immediate goal: the restrooms. As we walked, five or ten yards behind our suited friend, I thought to myself, "If that guy stops in front of those television screens until we walk past him, I'm not imagining this." As if on cue, he stopped, examined the lists of flights, and as soon as we passed continued on behind us.

After a while, I lost sight of the man, and after a snack we continued to our gate for our connecting flight.

It was only an hour later, after a runway was closed, our flight canceled, the bad news given that we would be stuck in the airport for seven more hours, and all of the credit card payphones failed, that I again spotted our friend hovering around. I wrote Jack a note, starting with "Don't look now ...", but after Jack asked me out loud, "Which guy?" he disappeared, never to be seen again.

Strange animals used for luggage inspections

After eventually getting to Duluth late at night, checking into the hotel, and going through our presentations one last time, we knew we faced a busy day ahead. Interviews planned for Friday afternoon had been postponed to the next evening, making an already full day even more overloaded.

After I had already hit the sack, I realized that I needed to iron the shirts that had been somewhat crumpled in my luggage for the previous four days. Dragging myself back out of bed at 1:30 AM, I set up the ironing board from the hotel room's wardrobe and took out my shirts.

I was flabbergasted to find small puncture holes near the left under-arm of each shirt. It almost looked as if some sort of animal had clawed them repeatedly. I managed to hide the worst of the holes with some serious ironing work, but wondered what else would be thrown my way before the weekend was out.

Vale, loyal shaver

I didn't have long to wait to find out. Not too many hours later, after showering myself back into consciousness, I opened the case for my electric shaver. I went to switch it on, but the switch seemed to be half-on already. As I flicked it all the way up, the machine came to life, and then died. I then noticed that the small cleaning brush had been packed in a different place to where it belonged: under the shaver, in the molded foam, where it should not be. I swore, realizing that the shaving case must have been searched during our eight-hour delay in Minneapolis-St. Paul, and that the luggage inspectors must have left the thing switched on, flattening the battery.

Grabbing the American-Australian power adaptor from the digital camera's bag, I plugged the shaver into the wall. It again came to life when I switched it on.

And then died.

Forever.

I was starting to get sick of these games. With less than half an hour until we were to be spirited off to the Symposium venue, I had to find a quick way to make myself respectable. Fortunately, I had a cheap disposable shaver in a travel pack. Unfortunately, I hadn't used a blade for twenty years, the disposable was really cheap, and I had no shaving foam. For a while there seemed to be more blood on my face than appears on the entire extant Zapruder film.

But everything came together brilliantly in the end.

Photos that almost weren't

After my return to Melbourne, I discovered that it was lucky that I hadn't tried to use the digital camera in Duluth. When grabbing the power adaptor for the electric shaver, I had noticed that the digital camera bag was *also* packed differently to how I had packed it in Dallas, but by that time I didn't give it a second thought.

Back in Melbourne, however, I wanted to clear off the 64 MB memory card so that the next user of the school's camera could start afresh. I noticed that the docking station was excessively scratched on one side—it was essentially new when I left Melbourne. And when I turned on the camera, it kept complaining that the memory card needed initialization.

Eventually, I realized that it, too, was dead.

Fortunately, my backup-mentality had served me well in Dallas. Each evening I had downloaded all of the day's photos to my laptop, and burnt a few copies of them to appropriately stashed CDs. On Wednesday I had wiped the memory card so that I could take a full quota of up to 98 full-resolution images on Thursday. But on Thursday evening I decided to leave the day's photos on the camera, as an additional backup. Little did I think that that action may well have saved the other copies of the photos: the inspected memory card was destroyed, quite possibly in the belief that doing so would destroy the only photos of the Wireless RainSensors, and washers under the lamppost.

The teacher that didn't

Back in Melbourne after a week of jet setting (41 hours in the air, 23 hours waiting in airports), I expected to find my classes in good hands. I had spent two hours in my classroom the previous Friday explaining everything to the replacement teacher.

Unfortunately, his story was just as bizarre as the rest of my trip. I was already a little uneasy when speaking to him before I left. Despite having apparently lived in Melbourne for seventeen years, his American accent had no traces of local effects. When I told him I was going to a Symposium in Duluth, Minnesota, he told me that that was where he came from; when I was incredulous, he said, "Minnesota, I mean." He had trouble understanding my Australian accent, which made no sense for someone who had lived here for even a year, let alone the best part of two decades. (I had spent three months in the U.S. in 1992, so was familiar with the problems Americans have adjusting to our accent.) Despite excusing myself for having a head cold and coughing often, he stood very close to me, looking me square in the eye as if he were inspecting my soul, rather than taking over a few Mathematics classes for a week.

When I returned, his bizarre story had been completed. He had only lasted one day—three hours of teaching, in fact—before apparently securing a whole term of work elsewhere, leaving the school to find another teacher at short notice. Reliable students swore that he spent almost the entire time searching my drawers, rather than teaching or assisting students. When asked by the students about my JFK work, he smiled, saying, "Oh, that's just propaganda. It sells books." (Just a few days earlier he was very interested.) After giving them an ultra-right-wing propaganda lecture, telling students how much better America is than Australia, one of the more astute students got him talking about American sports, which seemed to relax him. The student then quickly asked, "What do you think about John Howard?" "Oh, yes, we've heard a lot about him in the States recently." Which was true—John Howard had, only weeks earlier, been a special guest of President George W. Bush at his Texas ranch as reward for his alliance in the second Gulf War—but he had also been a Federal politician since the late 1970s, Federal Treasurer in the early 1980s, Leader of the Opposition in the late 1980s, and Prime Minister of the Commonwealth of Australia since 1996. A strange answer for someone who had allegedly spent the past seventeen years living in Australia.

Acknowledgments

There are so many people who have helped me with this work, directly and indirectly, that it is difficult to know how I can possibly thank them all. My only chance is to list just those without whose help I would simply not have been able to make any contribution at all, and to hope that those I have omitted will understand my difficulty.

I have been most fortunate to have had the wonderful support of my colleagues at Mentone Grammar: from Neville Clark, the former Headmaster; Tim Argall, the current Headmaster; Mal Cater, Warwick Dean, and, formerly, Ian Webster, the Deputy Headmasters; Brian Morphett, my immediate boss, the Head of Mathematics, chief sounding board, *de facto* advertising manager and fan club president, and the man responsible for getting me permission to do things that teachers normally don't have the chance of doing; David Lee, the Head of ICT Resources, the man responsible for keeping my technology running like clockwork, together with his infinitely generous and helpful colleagues, Dimi Tzitzivakos, David Chioda, and, formerly, Peter Margaritas; Jamie Robertson, the Head of History, who not only lent me a mountain of background resources from his senior JFK unit, as well as an invaluable set of clippings published within hours of the assassination in my own local newspaper, the Melbourne *Herald*, but also spent innumerable hours explaining post-War history to me; Hugh Green, the Chief Librarian, who overlooked the overdue notices on all the JFK videos I had borrowed on Jamie's recommendation, and who together with his colleagues always provides invaluable and patient assistance to me; Craig Hewett, our maintenance man, who had my Year 12 class in fits of laughter when he smuggled a genuine spy-camera circuit board into my room in his pocket when replacing a faulty fluorescent tube, and nonchalantly tossed it to me from the top of the ladder, pretending to have taken it out of the light fitting, knowing that I would analyze the circuit and realize it was really a camera; and all of the other colleagues who have chatted with me about the research, proof-read early drafts of this chapter, or simply *made me realize that this crime continues to bring angst and anguish to anyone who cares where this world is heading, even forty years after the fact*. Their ongoing concern and interest, and their enthusiasm for my own small part in its resolution, helps keep me going.

My students, who almost to a man would prefer to spend every class talking about JFK and the Zapruder film than learning trigonometry or calculus, remind me constantly of Einstein's complaint that learning is always fun, excepting only when you are forced to do it. I guess if I could get the History teacher to teach Mathematics as a digression, we'd have a great way of ensuring 100 percent enthusiasm for every class. In any case, I'm proud to be contributing to the broader and more rounded education that Mentone Grammar prides itself in—preparing our men for life, not just for a university lecture theater.

Assistance from the assassination research community is almost impossible to describe. It truly is a case where I can simply repeat Sir Isaac Newton: "If I have seen further it is by standing on the shoulders of giants." I have been infinitely fortunate to be in the right circumstances, at the right time, with the right background, to tie together some loose threads in the vast tapestry of what is, in my opinion, the greatest investigation of a crime in the history of mankind—*performed almost completely by individual civilians*. In completing one chapter of the story of the photographic evidence, I am only too well aware of the enormous legacy left by the early researchers, such as Harold Weisberg, who has already passed on; through the thread of doubt about the Zapruder film maintained in the intervening decades by those such as Jack White and David Lifton, whom I am overawed in having had the chance to collaborate with; through to the ballooning number of researchers who, in the 1990s, turned their energies to discovering the flaws in this six-foot length of celluloid that was once considered to be the Holy Grail of the assassination evidence, and is now, almost begrudgingly in some quarters, being recognized as the Hoax of the Century—researchers such as David Mantik, Harrison Edward Livingstone, Noel Twyman, Greg Burnham, Scott Myers, Rick Janowitz, and all the many others; to the man who has provided the "missing link" in the proof of alteration of the Zapruder film—the detailed technical knowledge of film and photographic alteration techniques and its history, David Healy; to the selfless saint of a man, Rich DellaRosa, who single-handedly and at considerable cost to himself and his own health, through his JFKresearch.com forum, has provided the only means by which I could have ever participated in this research in the first place; and of course to the editor of this volume and its two prequels, Professor Jim Fetzer, who has unarguably driven the research community through the apparently insurmountable obstacles placed before it by those who would like us *to simply all go away*, who like to obfuscate and prevaricate and bloviate, and finish every debate with the smug conclusion, *"We will probably never know."*

We will probably never know?

We *will* know. Not every detail, to be sure; but enough.

The continued existence of our civilization demands nothing less.

The most thanks of all, of course, must go to my family. As anyone who has invested a part of their life in this case knows, there are times when the black hole almost pulls you inside the event horizon, and I can only imagine that, without a loving family to ground you back in the real world, it would be tough to resist. Fortunately my sons Micka, Mark, Andy, Matthew, and Jack, and my Mum, Helena, are very supportive, even when my time has been stretched; my young sons Matty and Jack love the small models of Air Force One that I brought back from the States, without yet fully realizing the connection with the mission I was on—or the cruel irony that I was helping to investigate the crime that sent Big Jack to St. Matthew's in that saddest of funeral processions, almost forty years ago.

And to my beautiful wife Robyn, for putting up with me and being herself.

Part III

Was Mary Standing in the Street?

Jack White

[*Editor's note*: Few incidents in the history of the study of the death of JFK have provoked such strenuous disputation as that over Jack White's observation that certain structural features of the Dealey Plaza pergola provided a line of sight present in the Moorman that should permit a determination of Mary's location at the time she took her famous photograph. These features are the left-hand side and the top of the pedestal from which Abraham Zapruder was allegedly taking his film and the bottom and right-hand side of the window behind them. These features create two points in space that are located approximately 35 feet apart, generating an imaginary line to the lens of her camera about 100 feet away. A minor structural indentation at the top of the pedestal has misled some to think that the intersection of these lines is indeterminate, but that is a mistake. Observations and measurements based on these features have been repeated many times and provide powerful evidence that Mary was in the street.]

In the main body of my Duluth presentation, it was not possible in the brief amount of time to include much relevant information about the Mary Moorman Polaroid. I showed that it is possible, using a line of sight internal to the photo, to establish that Mary was standing *in the street* when she snapped the photo, not two feet south of the curb *on the grass* as seen in Zapruder. I showed that Mary and her friend Jean Hill are both presented by Zapruder to be wearing white shoes, while other Polaroids they shot that morning have them wearing black shoes.

I gave you a brief look at one of the many tests establishing the line of sight, all of which show it to be much too low for Mary to be standing on the grass. I also showed that the Moorman Polaroid reveals persons on the knoll that I have identified as Badgeman, Hardhatman and Gordon Arnold. I also showed that the picture seems to show two persons on the pedestal purported to be Abraham Zapruder and Marilyn Sitzman.

But I did not, in my presentation, tell many interesting and relevant details about my Moorman studies. For instance, I addressed the probability that many photos and films of the assassination have been altered. But I did not address the *authenticity of the Moorman photo* itself. If the Moorman photo is altered like much of the other filmed evidence, then are my analyses still relevant? Before I address that, I will give a brief history of my study of the photos Moorman took that day and of my observations.

In 1982 JFK researcher Gary Mack noticed what he thought to be the image of a gunman behind the fence on the knoll in a Moorman slide copy given to him by Robert Groden. Mack asked whether I could copy the image, enlarge and enhance it. By copying the slide at great enlargement and using a wide range of exposure f-stops, I was able to derive a number of optimum exposures which show in clear detail the face of a man whose chin is obscured by a puff of smoke, in a rifle-firing pose. He seems to be wearing a Dallas police uniform, complete with shoulder patch and badge. Considering the original image is smaller than an eighth-inch square, the image is extremely sharp. This image was later confirmed by computer photoanalysts at Massachusetts Institute of Technology and Jet Propulsion Lab, but neither would go public because of political considerations.

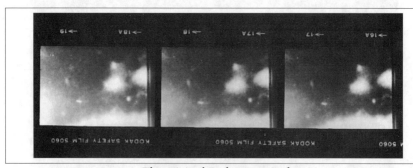

The original Badgeman study

Having confirmed that "Badgeman" was indeed in the Moorman photo, I did much additional study over the years that located two additional persons, which I hand colored with transparent oils here for ease of identifying them on the otherwise black and white picture. To the left of Badgeman seems to be a man in a T-shirt wearing a construction helmet. I named him "Hardhatman". About twenty feet in front of Badgeman seems to be a man in an Army uniform, complete with overseas cap, holding a camera to his eye. This image was matched with the story of a Dealey Plaza witness named Gordon Arnold.

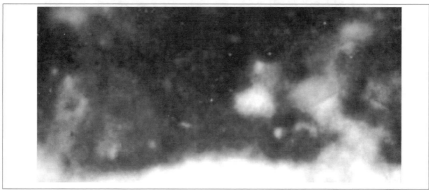

The other knoll characters

In the mid 1980s I was able to meet Mary Moorman, and she allowed me to make photocopies of the two original prints which she had kept in her safe deposit box since 1963. They were very faded. I copied both the fronts and backs, as you see here. The first, number 3, was of a motorcycle cop friend of Moorman and Hill, riding in the motorcade vanguard group of policemen. The second, number 5, is the famous photo of the limo after JFK has been shot. Mary and Jean explained that the missing number 4 photo was of another motorcycle cop that they also photographed and gave the print to. He claims to have lost or misplaced the number 4 photo. Having had access to the original Polaroid prints became very important to my study and understanding of what Mary and Jean did that day.

In the late 1980s I met Jean Hill, Mary Moorman's friend. Jean had kept the first two Polaroid photos they shot on 22 November. They had come downtown to photograph two motorcycle cop friends in the motorcade. They parked Mary's Ford Thunderbird on Houston by the Old Red Courthouse, at the corner of Main. They walked to a nearby store and bought a roll of film and returned to the car to load it, after which they photographed each other to make sure the camera was working OK and to have a record of themselves on that memorable day. Mary is standing in the left photo, and Jean is seated in the right photo. Note Dealey Plaza and the Book Depository in the background. You can see that the photo of Jean sitting in the car was taken first, because Mary is holding it in the second photo. Jean brought the two pictures to my office and let me photocopy them. Also note that in the photos, both are wearing *black* shoes—whereas the Zapruder film shows both of the girls in *white* shoes—a significant proof of alteration.

Collecting Moorman prints

During the course of our studies, a search was made to find the highest quality prints of the Moorman 5 photo. We obtained prints from Josiah Thompson, Associated Press, Harold Weisberg and others, collecting more than a dozen good copies. In addition, I had the copies I made from Mary's faded originals. Many of the prints had only minor variations. They were of varying quality and contrast. Two were clearly superior for studying the Badgeman image. These were Thompson number 1 and Weisberg. Each of these showed Badgeman very clearly, which was our interest at that time. Most of the prints we obtained had the pedestal area cropped out, which I always thought curious.

Early Publication

Mary had allowed her photo of the president to be copied that afternoon, and within hours it had been circulated worldwide by wirephoto services and published within hours. The version seen here was printed by the Sydney, Australia *Morning Herald* on 25 November 1963, and is obviously highly retouched by the newspaper. Nothing sinister is implied by such local media retouching. Despite such minor changes, the various published copies are remarkably consistent, showing that material changes such as point-of-view were not affected by retouching. Because of the speed of publication, the small size of the original, the copying the same afternoon, and the internal consistencies even when retouched, I had for many years considered that the Moorman Polaroid 5 was *genuine*, given the near impossibility of alteration under the circumstances.

But I had been looking in the wrong places for changes. I had studied the Badgeman position. I had studied the car occupants. I had studied the acoustics gun position behind the fence. I had studied the three men on the steps. I had studied the "cartop gunman" area. But I had never really had occasion to study the Zapruder pedestal. In this early version, upper right, *only one person* is seen on the pedestal. In most early versions, the pedestal and anyone atop it were totally cropped out. It is the pedestal area which the conspirators were worried about.

The necessity of alteration

This Sydney, Australia version and some other versions give an indication that the conspirators had a problem with the pedestal and its occupants. The official story was that Abraham Zapruder filmed the assassination with his secretary, Marilyn Sitzman, standing behind him, both atop the 4-foot-tall structure, whose top surface measures only 30.5" x 46.5"—a very small area, much narrower than an average doorway (32"). This wireservice Sydney version shows an indistinct image of a man's torso and legs, but *no woman*. Later studies would show that the Moorman 5 photo was likely retouched because of *what was on top of the pedestal*. I will demonstrate later why this is obvious.

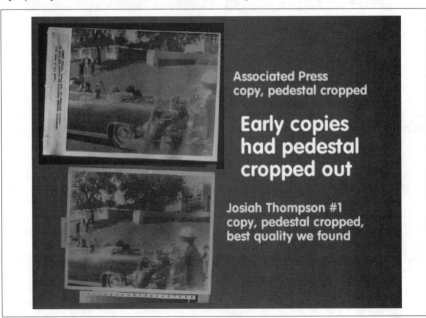

AP and Thompson prints

Having collected numerous copies of Moorman 5, I studied them intensively, making hundreds of photocopies, enlargements, and darkroom enhancements. I noticed that in virtually all the prints collected, the pedestal area was not visible, apparently having been cropped off. We obtained about a half dozen different prints from author Josiah Thompson, and his print that we called Thompson #1 was an extremely sharp copy—better than any other we found (at bottom in illustration above). By far the most common version we found was the Associated Press wireservice print at top (above).

When I had good quality prints, such as this Weisberg, I copied them in full and with many close-up details.

The Weisberg print and others

The second best quality print we located was from JFK researcher/author Harold Weisberg. Since we had to return all prints we obtained, while I had them I copied them both in full and in many close-up details, which proved very beneficial to my studies and which continue to be a great resource many years later.

The Zippo print

The Moorman version alleged to be the copy made on the afternoon of the assassination is the so-called *Zippo print* because of the Zippo lighter standing next to the small Polaroid "original". This copy does not have the prominent *fingerprint* which is seen in most later copy versions and the present original. Therefore it was always assumed that the Zippo print and copies made from it were *closest to the original*, since they are the only copies without the fingerprint. However, if we now assume that perhaps the upper right corner *had to be altered*, we then also have to assume that the Zippo print you see here had to be altered, because it seems to show both Zapruder and Sitzman on the pedestal. Recent studies suggest that Zapruder and Sitzman may not have been on the pedestal.

The "mystery Zippo print"

Among the many prints collected was this one. I do not even remember the source of it, but it clearly appears to be a *different* version of the Zippo print, so I call it the "mystery Zippo print". The pedestal area is slightly different. A dark object appears in the Pergola window, and "Sitzman" is hardly visible behind "Zapruder".

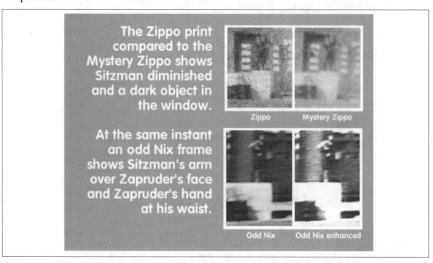

Pedestal comparisons

When seen in closeup, the differences between the original Zippo and the Mystery Zippo are apparent. Sitzman can hardly be seen in the mystery print, and a dark object is in the window. Obviously the two Zippo prints are from different sources. Almost simultaneously with the Moorman exposure, Orville Nix was filming the same pedestal scene as Mary, from a similar line of sight—but their images are radically different in this odd Nix frame. A very tall Sitzman seems to have her right arm wrapped around Zapruder's head, with her hand in front of his face. His right hand, holding his camera, seems to be down by his waist. Such inconsistencies raise doubts that Zapruder could have filmed the movie attributed to him.

Locating the line of sight

One memorable summer day several years ago I was in the plaza trying to determine exactly where Mary was standing. (The day was especially memorable because I met Kelly O'Donnell of NBC News, who was in the plaza as a tourist.) I had with me a copy of the Zippo print, and from the south side of Elm, I looked for points in the photo which lined up and which would still be the same more than 30 years later. Almost immediately I spotted a very obvious reference point—the lineup of the pergola pedestal and window, which formed a large "+" sign. I immediately tried to find the location of Mary's lens. I stooped lower and lower and lower—till I was finally on my knees before I achieved the lineup.

It suddenly struck me: Mary could not have been this low to have taken the photo. The Zapruder film shows her standing *on the grass*. But if on the grass, she had to be kneeling. I knew I had found proof of alteration of the Zapruder film. Paul Crute was about to give Ms. O'Donnell a ride in his JFK limousine replica, and I told him about my discovery. He introduced me to her and she seemed very excited about what I had found. She gave me her business card and asked me to email her with details. I emailed her, explaining the significance of my discovery. A couple of weeks later, she replied, explaining that she had been reassigned and would not be able to follow up.

Photo taken Summer 1988 with Mary Moorman's Polaroid camera from her estimated approximate position by Geoffrey Crawley, Jack White and Gary Mack, to determine the camera's resolving power, field of view, and relative size comparison of persons standing on the grassy knoll. Taken on Tri-X film since instant film was no longer available. Crawley's scientific tests indicated the camera was perfectly capable of resolving small details of persons on the knoll, and that the persons depicted were sized correctly.

Replicating the line of sight

In the summer of 1988 I assisted in the filming of the television documentary, *The Men Who Killed Kennedy*. Leading British photographic–science expert Geoffrey Crawley and I used Mary Moorman's actual camera to take the accompanying photo. We were not really concerned with finding the actual line of sight at that time, since it had not become an issue. We were more concerned with resolving power of the lens, field of view, and sizes of persons on the knoll. Producer/director Nigel Turner posed in the Gordon Arnold position near the end of the concrete wall as we shot three exposures. It turns out that we had the line of sight accurate vertically, but were about two feet too far west horizontally. At the time, it struck me as odd (but I gave it little further thought) that Geoffrey and I had to *sit on the grass* to get the vertical line of sight correct to take the photos!

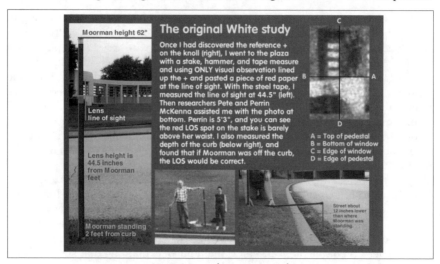

Moorman height 62"

The original White study

Once I had discovered the reference + on the knoll (right), I went to the plaza with a stake, hammer, and tape measure and using ONLY visual observation lined up the + and pasted a piece of red paper at the line of sight. With the steel tape, I measured the line of sight at 44.5" (left). Then researchers Pete and Perrin McKenna assisted me with the photo at bottom. Perrin is 5'3", and you can see the red LOS spot on the stake is barely above her waist. I also measured the depth of the curb (below right), and found that if Moorman was off the curb, the LOS would be correct.

Lens line of sight

Lens height is 44.5 inches from Moorman feet

Moorman standing 2 feet from curb

A = Top of pedestal
B = Bottom of window
C = Edge of window
D = Edge of pedestal

Street about 12 inches lower than where Moorman was standing.

My LOS study . . . original

Many times over the years I have made other attempts to replicate the photo, and found that only *one location* meets all the requirements, a spot *two feet north of the curb*. The photo cannot be replicated by an adult standing *on the grass as the Zapruder film shows*.

After locating the reference + line of sight, I made several trips to the plaza to attempt to show my discovery photographically. Using a tall wooden stake and a tape measure, I drove the stake in the ground 2 feet south of the curb on the line of sight. Using "eyeball" sighting only, unaided by magnification, I concluded the line of sight was 44.5" above ground. Researchers Pete and Perrin McKenna assisted me and took photos. Perrin, who is 5'3" posed with me beside the stake.

The line of sight I marked in red was just barely above her waist level. Pete also took a photo of me demonstrating that a spot off the curb was about a foot lower—showing that if Mary was *standing in the street*, she could have been on the line of sight. This study was published in *Murder in Dealey Plaza* (2000) but it has since been superceded by more accurate studies by me and other research-ers.

My LOS study . . . more precise

I decided greater precision was needed to convince those who thought my original visual study was not accurate enough. So using a Leica telephoto lens on a tripod, I took photos positioned on the line of sight. I hammered a white steel rebar into the ground 2 feet south of the curb on the line of sight. Position-ing the lens just over the top of the rebar stake, I then took photos to match the + line of sight reference. Once I had the exact position and took photos, I used a yardstick to measure the distance from the ground to the center of the lens. It measured 41.5 inches—three inches lower than my previous "eyeball" estima-tion! I spray-painted a yellow circle on the pavement where Mary had to have been standing. It was about a foot lower than where the camera tripod was lo-cated. I had proved that Mary must have been in the street two feet north of the curb!

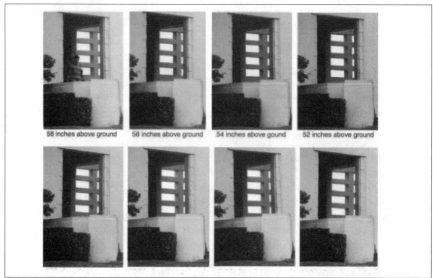

My LOS studies. . . tripod heights

While I had my camera on the tripod on the line of sight, I took the opportunity to expose a series of photos of the + reference point, using the tripod crank handle to raise the camera in two-inch increments from the original 41.5 inches. This provided a handy reference for comparison of future attempts to take photos on the line of sight from two feet south of the curb (Mary's Zapruder location). I took pictures all the way to 58 inches, which is about the height Mary's lens would be if she were standing—more than 16 inches difference.

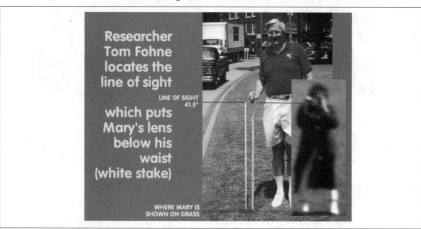

Fohne LOS study

On the internet, my Moorman line-of-sight studies provoked much discussion. One internet JFK researcher, Tom Fohne, came to Dallas on vacation and asked me to meet him in Dealey Plaza. I had my white rebar stake and hammer with me, and I asked him to replicate the LOS experiment. Visually, he found the + reference point and hammered the stake down till he was satisfied with his "eyeball" view over the top of the stake looking toward the pedestal. He then measured it with my steel tape measure. The top of the white stake was at 41.5 inches.

Janowitz/Myers LOS study

Later, another internet researcher, Rick Janowitz, came to the plaza from Ohio and met me and Dallas researcher Scott Myers in the plaza. Rick had rigged up a rifle scope with a laser on a camera tripod. Assisted by Scott, Rick aligned the laser beam spot with the corner of the pedestal and window reference cross. Scott photographed me holding a rod so the laser spot fell on the rod as I pointed to it. We measured the red laser dot at 42". Then Rick knelt two feet south of the curb so that the laser dot fell on his cheek near his ear. I photographed it, and sized Mary so her lens corresponded with the laser dot, resulting in the midget Mary in front of Rick's tripod.

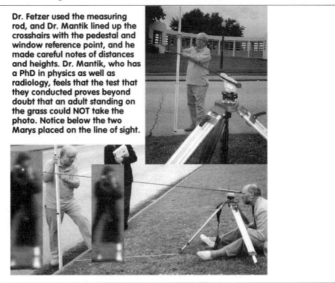

Mantik/Fetzer LOS study

Dr. James Fetzer and Dr. David Mantik both had previously visually verified my line of sight studies, each independently. But though Dr. Mantik had written about it in *Murder in Dealey Plaza*, each had only made an imprecise visual confirmation of the experiment. Both Fetzer and Mantik felt that greater precision was required, so a more scientific observation was arranged. I obtained a theodolite (surveyor's transit). Fetzer and Mantik lined up the crosshairs in the telescope with the reference point on the knoll and recorded many measurements. I photographed them making their independent observations, which both concluded provided empirical evidence that Moorman could *not* have been standing on the grass.

On the way to Duluth from Australia, Dr. John Costella stopped in the plaza in 2003 and did an informal and brief line-of-sight study. Comparing his photo with tripod photos of known heights (left) he picked 50 inches above ground as being closest to his unscientific POV observation, within an inch or two.

50 inches above ground   45.5 inches above ground

Costella LOS study . . . photo

John Costella, on his way from Australia to the Duluth conference, stopped in Dallas to make observations. He took the pedestal photo at top, standing approximately where Moorman is seen in Zapruder. He allowed for slightly more "gap" between the pedestal and window alignment than others had done. His hand-held photo was a quite good approximation of the line of sight. Comparing it to my "tripod height photos", he said he thought it was closest to my photo taken 50 inches above ground. I disagreed slightly. I thought it was closer to 47 inches—but it mattered little, since 50 inches is still way too low for Moorman to be on the line of sight as shown in Zapruder! Whether 41.5" or 50" makes little difference if Mary is lower on the line of sight than Zapruder depicts her.

Another way Dr. Costella describes his "non-scientific observations" is that the LOS corresponds approximately with the second shirt button above his belt. In the photo here, which I took of him in the Minneapolis airport, that button appears to be about 4 feet above ground. This corresponds closely to his other estimate, using the photograph he took in Dealey Plaza, of being about 50". He did not do a "scientific" experiment of the LOS because he considers the tiny size of the Polaroid pedestal/window lineup to be too small for precision measure-

John Costella's two "non-scientific" line-of-sight observations

1. Standing in the plaza, John determined that Mary's lens was "about even with the second button above his belt" (approximated by red spot). Smaller Mary is on this line.

2. Comparing a photo he took on the line of sight as he perceived it, and comparing it with photos taken/measured with a tripod, he picked 50" as closest to his photo. The larger Mary is on this line.

Costella LOS study . . . 2nd button

ment, and he points out that exposure differences between Moorman and replica photos can make measurements difficult. For instance, the bright light "bleed" at the window edges of Moorman and other various photos makes for difficult comparison. He further warns that he does not consider the line-of-sight to be very relevant, since he believes that the Moorman photo has been altered and thus is not acceptable as evidence, since not everything that was on the original is still there. Costella, who teaches math and physics, is an authority on lenses and optics.

The white rebar stake top is on the Moorman line of sight. The BBC lady is 5'1.5" tall. The red dot is the height of Mary's lens above the grass, 2 feet south of curb.

The BBC lady study

On the day that Tom Fohne was visiting the plaza and conducting his line-of-sight experiment (white stake seen here, 41.5" lens height), by chance there was a television crew in the plaza from the BBC. They were there filming a documentary on the assassination, and the lady producer asked me what Tom and I were doing. After I told her we were studying the Moorman line of sight because we believed the Zapruder film is faked, she asked to interview me and conducted a five-minute interview. Noting that she was very short (about Mary's height of 5'2"), I asked how tall she was. She said that she was 5'1.5" barefoot. I asked her to stand next to the white stake for a photograph. She agreed, provided she could turn her back to the camera. You can see that when Mary's lens is placed at the top of the white stake and her feet are on the grass two feet south of the curb, she is much too short.

Though in bright sunlight (note shadow of pedestal), Zapruder and Sitzman are totally lacking in detail found in other areas of the Moorman print, seen above.

Zapruder/Sitzman in sunlight

Another anomaly which has long puzzled me regarding the Moorman photo is the lack of clear detail of the persons on the pedestal, even though other areas of the picture are distinctly sharp. The pedestal is in *bright sunlight*, which ought to make Zapruder and Sitzman at least as detailed as the policeman or the men on the steps. But they are not even as sharp as Badgeman, who was in deep shade. The pedestal casts a shadow from the sunlight, as does the hedge at the base of the pedestal. Zapruder and Sitzman are in bright sun—but are not illuminated! This is a strong indication of retouching.

This enhanced image from the Bronson slide shows a very tall "Sitzman" facing a very short "Zapruder", as if they are dancing on top of the of the small 30.5"x 46.5" dance floor. I call this "The Zapruder Waltz". In this image, no camera is seen. Sitzman is *between* Zapruder and the motorcade, so he cannot possibly be filming. Her back is toward the motorcade, so she cannot be behind him, as seen in all other photos. Perhaps this image, like many others, has been al-

The Zapruder Waltz

tered in the pedestal area. But the weight of disparate images of what was *on the pedestal* is becoming overwhelming. I believe that something was on the pedestal *which had to remain a secret*—perhaps a professional photographer with a camera on a tripod. Images of Zapruder and Sitzman were substituted to hide whatever had been there in genuine photos. As I stated in my Duluth presentation, Zapruder and Sitzman may have been *unwitting* participants in the assassination who merely were providing a cover story for the creation of the "Zapruder" film, without realizing what they were getting into.

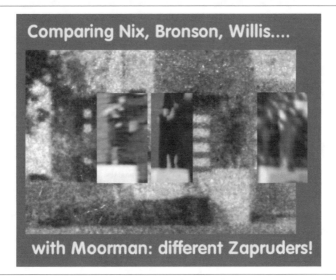

Close scrutiny of Zapruder

The many positions of "The Zapruder Waltz" become apparent when other images are compared with Moorman, all within less than 6 seconds. The various movements do not match. The people are not dressed the same. Their actions are not consistent with someone filming a smooth continuous film. A camera is not seen. The images are all blurry and indistinct. I believe that *all photos which show people on the pedestal have been altered*! It was necessary to have a citizen, Zapruder, to be author of the film. The identity of the real photographer had to be hidden or the whole charade would crumble.

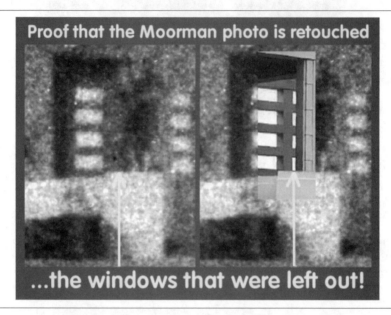

The pedestal and the window

So if all photos which show people on the pedestal have been tampered with, did that include the Moorman Polaroid? The FBI conducted a "dragnet" of all assassination snapshots and films immediately after 22 November for several months. *Every image was in government hands for periods up to three months.* Even Mary's Polaroid, which presents difficult tampering problems, was "borrowed" by the FBI and Secret Service "numerous times", Mary told researchers later. I believe that the original was enlarged, retouched *in the pedestal area*, and reduced back down with a Polaroid photocopy to appear to be an original out-of-camera print. But the retouchers made a major mistake. *Windows which should be in view of Mary's camera were left out!* The retouchers painted out whatever was originally on the pedestal, and not knowing *exactly* what to put in its place, the retouch artists just made a solid wall instead of windows! Though I had always considered the Moorman photo genuine, when I found this blunder several years ago, I knew then that the Moorman photo had been altered.

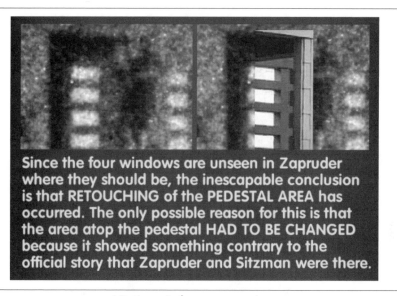

Missing windows = tampering

The conclusion is inescapable. If the four window openings which should be seen in Moorman *are not there*, the Moorman photo cannot be the genuine camera original! The only reason for such alteration is that the *real original* showed *something* atop the pedestal *contrary to the official story*. The LOS studies thus provide further evidence of the alteration of the photographic record in the death of JFK.

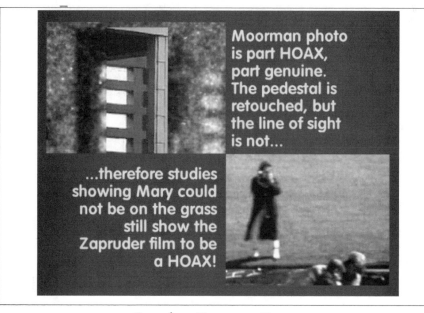

Zapruder + Moorman = Hoax

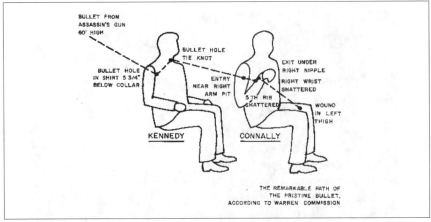

The remarkable path of the "magic bullet" when its actual entry point has been taken into account, which was appropriately lampooned in Oliver Stone's film "JFK" (Gary Shaw, Cover-Up 1976, p. 4)

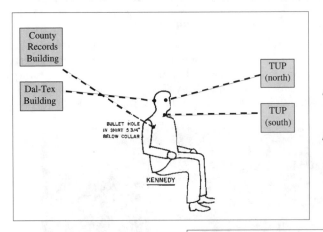

JFK appears to have been hit at least four times, once in the throat from in front, once in the back from behind, and twice in the head (once from behind and once from in front). Two shots were from the Triple Underpass (TUP).

Connally may have been hit as many as three times, once in the back, once in the wrist, and once in the thigh, where, when his turn to the left has been taken into account, these shots appear to have come from the Texas School Book Depository (TSBD), not the County Records Building.

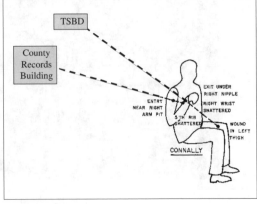

Mary Moorman
and Her Polaroids

John P. Costella, Ph.D.

[*Editor's note*: In a fascinating display of methodological brilliance, John Costella, Ph.D., initates a new dimension in JFK research by comparing information from interviews recorded in official documents with the photographic record. He dispels the myth that the Moorman was published immediately after the assassination and provides persuasive evidence that Mary's photographs were almost certainly subjected to alteration, especially in relation to the area of the pergola and the pedestal. A photographic "shell game" was at work, in the process of which three photos of the motorcade morphed into two, prompting Costella to speculate that the missing Polaroid may have been the most damaging to the government's position. Another important aspect of this study is confirmation that Jean Hill heard four to six shots, where there was a time gap between the first three and the remainder, which the authorities brushed aside on the basis that there had only been three shots and that she had to have been mistaken.]

As I observed in the introductory section to my chapter on the fabrication of the film, at the time that I first discovered Rich DellaRosa's *JFKresearch.com* Internet forum—inhabited, by and large, by numerous assassination researchers who believed the Zapruder film to be a fraud—*the* issue that everyone wanted to know about was "Moorman in the Street".

As also noted there, I jumped into the fray, didn't think long and hard enough about the compression algorithms used to send images over the Internet, and made a number of mistakes that cost me dearly.

The question still, however, remains to this day: does the line of sight inherent in Mary Moorman's fifth Polaroid necessarily place her on the street, or on the grass? If the former, then the Zapruder film is automatically and irrevocably proved to be a complete fake, without need for any additional proof.

It is this remarkable property that (rightly) has caused researchers to hope that the Moorman line of sight issue can be determined definitely, once and for all. Many believe that it is already definite; many others are waiting for words of wisdom from those who may be able to sort through all of the subtle scientific arguments, pro and con.

My own rough estimate, Dealey Plaza, May 2003

By the time I actually got the chance to visit Dealey Plaza in person, on 7–9 May 2003, I knew one thing without question: the only substantive point of contention in the Moorman in the Street issue was (whether the protagonists realized it or not) the *interpretation of the Moorman Polaroid itself*, together with other assumptions made about Mary Moorman.

I knew there was absolutely no point in my re-performing the precision measurements made eighteen months earlier by Jack White, Jim Fetzer, and David Mantik, and by numerous other researchers (on both sides of the argument) on numerous occasions over the years. The reason I knew this was because *everyone had provided photographs of their measurements that agreed with each other's*, when one compared like with like. What I mean by this is the following: if researcher X stated that they placed a camera lens Y inches above the south curb of Elm Street behind the yellow spot that Jack White had painted on the surface of the Elm Street roadway, then any other researcher Z would *not* disagree with the photograph itself. Rather, what they would be disagreeing about is whether that photograph *has any relevance to the line of sight study*. And the only reason for such a disagreement is that the two researchers are interpreting Moorman's fifth Polaroid in different ways.

Given that I had less than two days to spend in Dealey Plaza, and I knew that it would be useless replicating the measurements that *were not* in contention, I didn't plan to spend any time at all on the Moorman in the Street issue.

Well, it didn't turn out that way, of course. One reason was that Jack White was my host, and he knew that he wasn't going to let me leave Dealey Plaza until I at least had a look at the line of sight.

And so I did. Jack had (quite conveniently, I thought) brought along two copies of the Moorman. They weren't the high quality photographic copies that I hoped that I would see at his house (which I later did), but rather were related to the versions that I had originally used in analyzing the line of sight study. But it didn't really matter, because the image had been burnt into my retina anyway, and I knew exactly how much "gap" I thought there was.

What I didn't tell Jack, however, was that *I was not actually using his "cross" line of sight at all*. My reason for using a different criterion was subtle, but related to observations that Jack himself had made: basically, there is something strange happening on the Zapruder pedestal in the Moorman.

Most importantly, the edge of "Zapruder" is not clearly delineated, despite the fact that he was standing out on a pedestal in broad sunlight. Add to this the fact that there are "windows" in the pergola structure behind "Zapruder" that seem as if they should be visible—but they are hidden by something. Without a clearly visible edge to Zapruder, one must worry about the authenticity of the photograph in this region.

One might wonder why I have referred to the authenticity of the Moorman "in this region". The reason is that the Moorman was originally published *with the right edge of the image showing the Zapruder pedestal cropped off*. Whether or not this early-published image is genuine, or the extent to which it is genuine, is one issue (that I will return to shortly); but the veracity of this "extra" part of the image, not widely published until a number of years after the assassination, must necessarily have a much larger question mark around it.

In any case, I tried to make the best alignment I could, visually, as I stood in Dealey Plaza. I was mainly trying to get the vertical alignment correct, so I used the top edge of the white wall in comparison with the "windows" in the pergola behind. As a result, I didn't quite get the Zapruder pedestal in the exactly correct position, in a left–right direction, but that was not my goal (putting Mary a few inches up or down Elm Street has no fundamental significance).

The result of this attempt is shown in Figure 1. In the top image I show a particularly clear version of the Moorman, with the perspective adjusted so that the image appears as it would if Mary had pointed the center of her view directly at Jack White's "cross" line of sight. In the bottom image I show my own photograph, with perspective adjusted to again point at Jack's "cross", sized and rotated to match the top image. (I verified at Jack's house that the clearest photographic copies of the Moorman he has agree with the image I used to create Figure 1.)

Figure 1. Comparison of Mary Moorman's fifth Polaroid with the rough visual alignment I made during my visit to Dealey Plaza in May 2003. Perspective in each image has been adjusted so the camera is pointing in the same direction.

It is clear that the Zapruder pedestal needs to move a little to the right: the right edge of it shows this most clearly. However, apart from that shortcoming, I am reasonably happy that I replicated what I could see in the Moorman. (One must realize that, once the pedestal is shifted to the right, the "gap" in my photograph between the bottom edge of the lowest "window" and the top of the white wall will effectively increase, because of the relative "wedge" shape between these two edges: we will be sliding along to a larger part of the "wedge". Taking that effect into account, I believe the alignment is about right.)

Showing the photograph I took is one thing. Relating my feelings when doing it is quite another. As I stood there in Dealey Plaza, I really couldn't believe how low I had to bend, in order to get the line of sight I wanted. I once turned to Jack and said, "Damn you, Jack, I thought this line of sight business was behind me!" He was a short distance away, down Elm Street, reveling in my difficulty in getting low enough to replicate the Moorman, and snapping away on his own digital camera all the while.

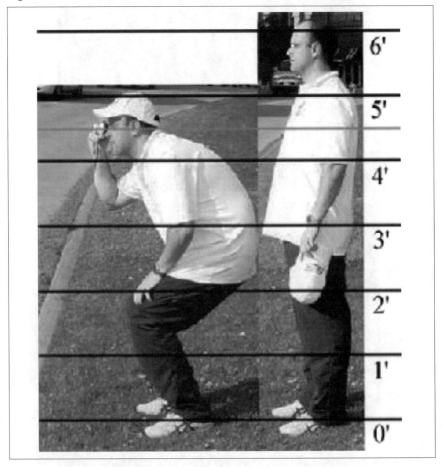

Figure 2. Photograph taken by Jack White while I took the photograph shown in Figure 1. On the right is a reference photograph of me standing up straight.

The photo Jack took when I got down to my line of sight, and took the photograph shown in Figure 1, is shown on the left of Figure 2. On the right I have placed a copy of the photograph that I asked Jack to take, immediately after I stood up straight again, so that I had a height reference (knowing that, in tennis shoes, I am about 6'2" tall).

My reason for swearing at Jack (I can't print the actual words) was that I felt that I was crouching far too low for a photo to have been taken by Mary Moorman. In Figure 2, it can be seen that my eye level is at about 4'6"; the lens (which actually took the photograph shown in Figure 1—it was a relatively inexpensive digital camera, not an SLR) is at about 4'4" or so. That seemed just ridiculously low to me at the time. *It just felt wrong.*

But that's where things start to get weird. Using the precision measurements I had made of the extant Zapruder film in my panoramic work, it is possible to determine Mary Moorman's height, and that of her lens, quite accurately. When one does the calculations, it turns out that Mary appears to be about 5'1" tall, and her lens is about 4'4" off the ground.

So what on Earth is going on here?

Figure 3. Mary and Jean (as of 1963) standing next to me. Their images have been scaled mathematically using information about Dealey Plaza and the results of my scientific studies of the Zapruder film.

The problem, to me, seems to be not that the Moorman line of sight is inconsistent with the Zapruder film, but rather that Mary Moorman *appears to be so short*. Looking at Mary and Jean on the extant film, their proportions are such that one does not think of them as being really very short. But that's exactly what the Zapruder film shows.

This can be seen most vividly by putting Mary and Jean (as of 1963) next to me in a photograph. This is shown in Figure 3. The scaling of Mary and Jean has been calculated using all of the data I have of the Zapruder film, and of Dealey Plaza. Comparing back to Figure 2, Mary's lens height can be seen to be consistent with mine.

What does this mean? It tells me that, from my own point of view, the Moorman line of sight issue is effectively dead. Mary's fifth Polaroid agrees with the extant Zapruder film.

But what it *does* do is refocus my attention on something that has always worried me: why do Mary Moorman and Jean Hill look so short? This is the enduring question that emerges from these studies.

Digging deeper into Mary's Polaroids

Another reason I had not planned to spend any time on the Moorman in the Street issue during my visit to Dealey Plaza related to my reading of Jean's and Mary's reports on and after the day of the assassination, reproduced without modification in the back of Harold Weisberg's *Photographic Whitewash*. Back in 1967, Weisberg had no choice but to read these reports in light of what was known at that time. But I ignored his footnotes, on my first reading, and pretended that I knew very little about the two girls' experiences on the day of the assassination. (In fact, at the time this wasn't far from the truth anyway.)

One crucial ingredient in this reading project was the fact that *I knew by that time that the Zapruder film was a complete fabrication*. It was easy for me to reject what I "knew" about the assassination on the basis of the Zapruder film: a sizeable proportion of my time looking into the case had already been spent in the knowledge that it was a fake. This is one time when my relative ignorance of the case worked to my advantage.

What I read shocked me, and made me realize that many good people had wasted precious time on the Moorman in the Street debate, *on the assumption that Moorman's fifth Polaroid was necessarily genuine*. I realized that *none* of Mary's Polaroids could be trusted any more than the remainder of the photographic evidence of the assassination.

Because, for most researchers, this is a new field of inquiry, and because some will not be used to considering evidence *ignoring what we "know" from the Zapruder film*, I have decided to include here a copy of each of those early reports, and make my own comments and interpretations of what I see in each one. Some of those interpretations may be incorrect, of course, but overall I cannot help but see an overall pattern of subterfuge and fraud—*detailed in the official reports themselves*—that puts Mary's Polaroids in their proper perspective.

For logistical purposes, the documents themselves are contained at the end of this section. I have ordered the documents, and my comments on them, according to the date that the witness made the report or was interviewed, not the date that the report was necessarily typed up.

22 November 1963: Jean Hill: Sheriff's Department

Document 1 is a copy of the signed and sworn statement of Jean Hill at the Sheriff's Department on the day of the assassination. (This document is not in Weisberg's book; image kindly supplied by Greg Burnham.) There are many points of interest in this document, even before we begin to scratch the surface.

The first is that Jean stated that Mary and she were the "only people in that area" on the south curb of Elm Street. This is curious, considering the fact that Charles Brehm and his son, and Beverly Oliver, were not far from them—if we believe what we see in the Zapruder film and elsewhere; other witnesses were further down Elm Street—again according to the Zapruder film and other pho-tographic evidence. Remember, however, that *Life* did not publish *any* images of Jean and Mary, the Brehms, or Oliver in the first-weekend issue.

Jean swore to what she had already stated on camera to newsmen: JFK and Jackie were looking down into the middle of the seat. Jean believed they were looking at a small dog between them (the "Lambchop" debate—about whether Jackie had a small white puppet type of toy in the limousine—is one that I will not enter; all that matters for me is that Jean saw something between then that *she thought* was a small dog). [*Editor's note:* Jackie had been given a small, toy stuffed dog or puppet.]

JFK then turned to her; two shots rang out; he grabbed his chest; he slumped forwards and to the left into Jackie's lap; and she climbed up over him and said, "My God he has been shot." There was a short pause in the shooting. The limou-sine halted for a moment. Three or four more shots rang out, and the motorcade then sped away.

Jean now says "I thought I saw some men in plain clothes shooting back but everything was such a blur". In other words, she saw men *not in any uniform* shooting—which she interpreted to be (or was convinced to interpret as) "shoot-ing back". Was this a description of some of the assassins?

Jean now describes Mary pulling her down, but the statement looks a little strange at this point: "Get down thery are shooting". But after the strange word "thery" there are *two spaces*, followed by "are", and an unusually long string of spaces to end the line. Given the compressed nature of the image I have of this document, it is not possible to tell where the editing here begins. What could this line have originally said? Quite possibly "Get down the police are shooting"? That is merely a guess, but it is something that would tie in with Jean's own impressions. On the day of the assassination, this might have seemed to be quite a reasonable thing to report—police generally *do* shoot back at the bad guys if they get a chance—but this did not tie in *at all* with later accounts. Was it per-haps felt that if *both* of them had reported seeing people shooting, it would be simply too convincing to overlook?

Jean next describes seeing a man running "towards the monument" (the per-gola structure, no doubt), and she started running up the hill, only to be turned back by "some policeman" (or was it originally "some policemen"—they "were" in the motorcade, according to the rest of the sentence?).

Already by the time she got back down the hill a Mr. Featherstone of the *Times Herald* had gotten to Mary and asked her for the picture she had taken of the President. In other words, the assassination is barely over before Mary has been asked for the picture.

Or is it just one picture? Again we have a very strange editing job: "ask her for her picture she had taken of the President", with again an *extra space* after "she". What did this originally say? Perhaps "ask her for the *pictures* she had taken of the President"?

Again we have a strange editing job right in the middle of "press room downn at the Sheriff's office". What this replaced is more difficult to guess at, but, considering the accounts later given by Jean regarding her treatment at the hands of the authorities, one might speculate that it involved more than just a friendly "press room".

22 November 1963: Jean Hill: FBI report

Document 2 is the FBI agent Lish's report of Jean Hill's recollections. This report is again intriguing. It describes Jean and Mary as standing on Elm "near the Texas School Book Depository", which is not incorrect, but not the most obvious way of describing their position.

The document defines the "Presidential party" as being the President, Jackie, and the Connallys. But it then states that Mary "took pictures of the Presidential party passing down the street". *Plural?* There is only one extant Moorman Polaroid showing any of the Presidential party, as it is here defined, at all.

Jean then heard "something like" a rifle shot, and JFK "crumpled" in his seat.

22 November 1963: Mary Moorman: Sheriff's Department

In Document 3, Mary states, "As the motorcade started towards me I took two pictures." It is necessary at this point to review the standard story about Mary's Polaroid pictures on the day.

A couple of hours before the assassination, Mary and Jean parked their car on the east side of Houston, outside the old red courthouse building. They then went to buy some Polaroid film from a local store. They returned to the car and put the film in the camera. Mary then took a test photo of Jean, sitting in the front passenger's seat of the car with the door open and one foot out; then they switched positions, with Jean taking a photo of Mary standing inside the open car door.

By the time of the assassination they were on the south curb of Elm Street. Mary took two photos of individual motorcycle officers as they drove past in the escort; the story goes that the officers were their boyfriends. The first of these photos is extant; the second was given to the officer concerned and is now lost.

Mary then took her fifth and final photo of the President, showing the grassy knoll in the background. This photograph corresponds to about Z-315 on the extant Zapruder film.

That's how the standard story goes. How much of it is genuine, and how much has been concocted to explain away evidence such as that being discussed here, is an open question.

In the context of her assassination-day affidavit, the two photographs of the motorcycle officers, #3 and #4, are clearly meant to be the "two pictures" she took "as the motorcade started towards me".

Mary then states that, as JFK was opposite her, she took a third photo (#5). As she snapped the photo, she heard a shot ring out. JFK then slumped over. Another shot rang out, and Jackie jumped up and said, "My God, he has been shot!"

This account accords well with Jean's, apart from the description of when Mary snapped her third photo (which Jean would have no direct knowledge of). There were two shots; JFK slumped over; Jackie jumped up, and made her statement.

Mary then dropped to the ground, again in agreement with Jean's account. Mary heard three or four shots in all, implying one or two more after the initial two.

Mary then states, "After the pictures I took were developed, the picture of President Kennedy showed him slumped over." This is a little surprising, given her statement that the shot only rang out as she snapped the photo, and Jean's description of JFK "jumping" a little before slumping over a moment later.

However, more surprising is the fact that Mary's statement implies that it is the *first* shot that is simultaneous with her famous #5 Polaroid. *This is so different from what we are accustomed to seeing in the Zapruder film that it is difficult to comprehend its enormous ramifications.* Either Mary and Jean were much further up Elm Street than what the photographic record indicates, or else the shooting didn't *begin* until JFK got down to somewhere near where the official account puts the *final* shot. [*Editor's note:* See the Preface.]

Mary then states that the pictures also came out "real light". This is itself a little surprising: it is usually stated that the Polaroids have faded in time, but one generally assumes that they were quite vivid on the day they were taken. It also invites the question of what she was comparing their quality to, if she had only just bought a film for testing her camera for the first time. In any case, her description implies that *all three pictures* of the motorcade came out "real light". Mary also indicated that she had turned her photographs over to officers investigating the incident.

22 November 1963: Emmett Hudson: Sheriff's Department

Document 4 is the sworn statement of the groundskeeper of Dealey Plaza, Emmett Hudson, on the day of the assassination.

Hudson's statements are most interesting because he was probably the only witness who actually knew the layout of Dealey Plaza inside-out, having tended to it day in and day out for the previous six years.

In this early statement, Hudson clearly describes *sitting* on the steps leading down what we now call the grassy knoll, with *one other man sitting on his left*. He then describes the President's car driving directly in front of them. This is curious, because in Moorman #5 we see *three* men who are *standing* on the steps.

It is worth offering a digression here. The 1967 issue of *Life* that includes previously unpublished photographs of nine bystanders shows the Betzner and the Willis photographs on opposite pages. The text accompanying these two photographs asserts that what was later called "Black Dog Man"—behind the corner of the white "retaining" wall—is actually the *third man* who appears shortly afterwards in Moorman #5. This third man is then seen to run back *up* the stairs in the Nix film. It may well be that the entire purpose of the extant Betzner and Willis photographs, and that part of the Nix film, is to account for this third man who visited briefly—whom Hudson apparently had no knowledge of at all!

Returning to Hudson's statement, we now note that he *also* reports hearing a shot, and the President falling over in his seat, when the limo was already opposite the steps!

Hudson reported hearing three shots in total—whether this was his recollection, or whether he was advised that he heard three, cannot be known. If it was his recollection, it implies that there were two further shots *after* the one that occurred when the limo was opposite his position.

He also states that the shots came from "behind and above me", which one would assume to mean somewhere over the picket fence.

22 November 1963: Mary Moorman: FBI

Document 5 is the report made on the day of the assassination by FBI agents Perryman and Gemberling regarding Mary's recollections.

The agents note that Mary took *a* photograph of the motorcade as it proceeded towards her. However, the next sentence shows clear signs of editing: ". . . and the photograph showed the police motorcycle escort [edited] the President's car." Originally there were eleven characters, not including the spaces on each end; but this has been replaced *with a different typewriter* with the nine-letter word "preceding", with two extra spaces. (See Figure 4.)

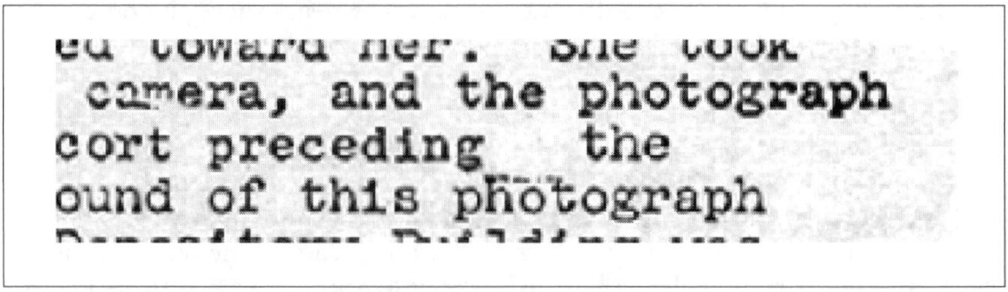
ed toward her. She took
camera, and the photograph
cort preceding the
ound of this photograph

Figure 4. An enlargement of Document 5. Note the use of a different typewriter for the word "preceding" (the 'g', for example, is different).

What could have been replaced here? Perhaps the report originally said that "... the photograph showed the police motorcycle escort *in front of* the President's car"? This would be dynamite: it would imply that there was an additional photograph *of the presidential limousine on Elm Street* that had not been published.

The report further states that the Texas School Book Depository is in the photograph. It does not state that only a portion is visible. Is this a photograph we have never seen?

The report then says, "She took a second photograph of the President as his automobile passed her . . .". This seems to confirm that *the first photograph mentioned also showed the President*.

Just as Mary snapped this second photograph of the President, she heard a firecracker sound, and shortly afterwards another. She knew that she heard two shots, possibly three. She recalled seeing JFK "sort of jump" and start to slump sideways in the seat. *How, then, did her second photograph of the President show him already slumping?* She clearly reports what Jean Hill also reported: that JFK "jumped", *after* the shot simultaneous with her photo, before slumping.

She then seemed to recall Jackie scream, "My God, he's been shot!" This is common to almost all of both Mary's and Jean's statements. She then recalls dropping to the ground with Jean but does not remember why.

Importantly, the car was moving at the time of the second photo and when she heard the shots. But then she makes a crucial statement: *"the car either stopped momentarily or hesitated and then drove off in a hurry."* Not only does this confirm the limo stop, it also places it *well after* Moorman #5.

The report then notes that, *as the presidential limousine left,* she started to leave the grassy area and was *stopped* by a Mr. Featherstone, a newspaper man with KRLD Radio and TV who questioned her. This tightens up the delay between the assassination and being "rounded up" by this Mr. Featherstone considerably.

But this is not all: the final statements are just as powerful: "the photograph she took showing the police motorcycles preceding President KENNEDY's car and also showing the Texas School Book Depository . . .". Is there any doubt that this photo showed *more than one* motorcycle, the *limousine,* and the Depository?

In any case, this first photo was given to Secret Service agents Howlett and Patterson shortly before 4:00 PM on the day of the assassination.

The "second" photo shows the President slumping sideways. She furnished *this* photo to FBI agents. Somehow, three photos have become two. The final photo always shows the President slumping.

25 November 1963: Emmett Hudson: FBI

As we now move away from the day of the assassination, we find FBI reports with an intriguing mix of new information, together with "embellishments" that clearly represent an attempt to inject aspects of the rapidly emerging "official story" into the record.

Document 6 is a report made by FBI agents Thompson and Peden on the Monday following the assassination, regarding Emmett Hudson.

The first thing we learn is that the Moorman #5 Polaroid was published in the Dallas *Times Herald* on Sunday, 24 November. Hudson apparently came to the FBI to point out that he was the middle of *three* men who were *standing* on the steps in the background of the photo. It is not explained how this is to be reconciled with his affidavit on the day of the assassination.

Hudson states that he was looking directly at JFK and saw his head slump to one side simultaneously with the loud report made by the first shot. We again have a connection: Hudson, in the background of the Moorman photo, JFK slumping, first shot.

He then heard two more shots, which came in rapid succession after the first.

The next paragraph clearly tries to mold Hudson's earlier sworn statement of shots coming from "above and behind" to introduce a new element—from the *left*—and this was then somehow extrapolated back to the Depository. But then this bizarre statement: "He again called attention to the photograph referred to above, and particularly to the corner of the Texas School Book Depository building appearing in such photograph and said the shots sounded as if they were coming from that building (Texas School Book Depository building)." What? *The Depository is not in the extant Moorman #5 photo showing the President slumping!* Moreover, Hudson had been groundsman in Dealey Plaza for six years, and so *knew* that the pergola shelter (the only structure visible in the extant fifth Moorman photo) *was not* the edge of the TSBD! Which photo could they have been possibly looking at?

Hudson further estimated that he was approximately 30 feet from the presidential limo at the time he heard the shots and immediately noticed JFK's head

270 The Great Zapruder Film Hoax

to slump to one side. This would put the limo down opposite the steps he was on, exactly as he had previously sworn—at Z-313 Hudson would have been about 80 feet away.

12 December 1963: Brown (FBI) on Moore (Secret Service)

Document 7 is a report by FBI agent Brown regarding an apparent meeting with Secret Service agent Moore.

Moore shows two Moorman Polaroids to Brown. This, already, is strange: didn't Mary give her "second" Polaroid, showing the President slumping, to the FBI on the day of the assassination? How did the Secret Service get it? Why did it then have to be shown back to the FBI? Just to generate this report?

We now find that *only the first* of the two is very light, and it is now also of "very poor quality"—as the extant version of #3 seems to be. We now explicitly learn that only a lower corner of the Depository is shown—as in the extant version of #3. We now only have *one* policeman on a *single* motorcycle—as in the extant version of #3 (excluding a small part of what is probably another motorcycle on the far left).

And now the crucial statement: "No other parts of the Presidential motorcade are seen in the photograph." As in the extant version of #3. Is this to negate the implications of the earlier report on Moorman—that the presidential limousine was visible in one of her other photos?

The "second" photo is now reported to have been sold to AP by Mary. It was a copy of the AP wirephoto that was shown to Brown (FBI, author of report) by Moore (Secret Service). Again, why is this, when the 22 November FBI report *explicitly* stated that she had turned *this particular photo* over to FBI agents?

We further learn, "The Texas School Book Depository Building does not appear in this photograph at all . . .". As in the extant version of Moorman #5. Is this to negate the previous report on Hudson, which implies that the Depository is not only visible—in whatever photo it was that he was shown—but moreover that he reportedly referred to it on the photograph explicitly?

We now also learn a crucial piece of evidence: the copy of the AP wirephoto shown by Moore to Brown has a Dallas dateline of 23 November, and a wirephoto code that translates to "AP wirephoto Saturday 3:55 pm". *We now learn that Moorman #5 was in the hands of the authorities for 27 hours before going out on the AP wire.* This completely destroys the argument that the Moorman #5 was "on the wire so quickly that no one could have altered it", as is so often stated. Twenty-seven hours is more than enough.

7 March 1964: Forrest Sorrels (Secret Service)

Document 8 is a report made by Forrest Sorrels of the Secret Service. He states that he interrogated Mary Moorman (interestingly, spelled incorrectly) at the Sheriff's Office on the day of the assassination.

She surrendered the first Polaroid, "of the Texas School Book Depository that she had taken at the time of the assassination", to Sorrels. But, according to the FBI report on Mary of 22 November, wasn't the "first" photo given over to Howlett and Patterson, shortly before 4:00 PM, not Sorrels? Are we here learning that *both* Polaroids of the motorcycles in front of the limousine—#3 and #4—were handed over to different Secret Service agents?

In any case, Sorrels claims that he wasn't sure if it showed Oswald's window so he kept hold of it. After finding out which window was the sniper's nest, on Saturday, he checked the picture again. He then suddenly realized that no details of the building, windows, or surrounding area were distinguishable anyway. *So why did he keep it in the first place?* Did he even look at the photo on Friday? Was it the same photo on Saturday? The two paragraphs make no logical sense.

On Saturday or Sunday the FBI rang the Secret Service asking for the photo. It was subsequently turned over to the FBI, believed to be Brown. But on 12 December Brown reported (see report by Brown) that Secret Service agent Moore "exhibited the following photographs in possession of the Secret Service". Does that mean that Moore showed Brown the one that Howlett and Patterson took, not the one that Sorrels gave him on the first weekend? That seems to make the most sense, but we still have the anomaly that Moore seemingly showed Brown #5, which the FBI supposedly had all along, and the Secret Service supposedly *never* had.

The paragraph describing the turning over of the photo to Brown ends with a comma—was there more? Or is this just a typing error?

Sorrels claimed that no statement was taken from Mary because of her brief signed statement to the Sheriff's Office. Why not? Was that one paragraph really sufficient? He further claimed that no report was made on the photo because it was given to the FBI and appeared to have no value.

We now learn that the "first" photo had been returned to Mary by the date of this report (7 March) and was still at that time in her possession. However, the precise date of return to her is unclear.

13 March 1964: Jean Hill: FBI

Document 9 is an FBI report by Robertson and Trettis regarding the recollections of Jean Hill, now almost four months after the assassination.

It states that Jean and Mary were standing "opposite the main entrance of the Texas School Book Depository". No one could stand in their extant positions and claim to be "opposite the main entrance": it is barely visible in the distance.

Mary "was taking photographs of the motorcade as it came into view". Despite the best work of the FBI and Secret Service, we are again returning to the idea that there were indeed *three* Polaroids made of the motorcade, not two.

Jean shouted "Hey!" to JFK, who was looking down when she shouted. JFK turned to look at Jean. The first shot then rang out; JFK "slumps" towards Jackie. More shots then rang out; the hair on back of JFK's head flew up. Jean thought that Jackie said, "Oh, my God, he's been shot!" JFK fell forward. Jean heard four to six shots in all; there was a time gap between the first three shots and the remainder. She saw a man running from the west end of the Depository.

Jean and Mary were intercepted by Mr. Featherstone, a Dallas newspaperman, before they left Dealey Plaza. He took them to the Sheriff's Office, where they were interviewed for two hours by press, Secret Service, FBI, and local law enforcement.

She was asked by a Secret Service or FBI agent what she thought when a bullet hit near her feet, raising the dust; she had no recollection of the event. Was this to place the idea in her head, putting her further down the street?

Although she recalled from four to six shots, she was told that there were three shots, three bullets.

17 March 1964: Rankin to Hoover

Document 10 is a letter from the Warren Commission's General Counsel, J. Lee Rankin, to the Director of the FBI, J. Edgar Hoover.

We are again here seeing the cementing of the idea that there were only two photos taken by Mary. According to her (according to Rankin), the "second" was given to FBI agents, and had been seen by the Commission; this must be what we now think of as Moorman #5.

We further learn that the Secret Service told Rankin that the "first" photo was turned over to the FBI (believed to be agent Brown) by the Secret Service on Saturday 23 November or Sunday 24 November, when requested. The Secret Service also told Rankin that the FBI had returned the photo to Mary.

Rankin asks Hoover whether the FBI kept a copy of it; if not, could they get it back off Mary so that the Warren Commission could look at it.

24 March 1964: Brown (FBI report)

Document 11 is a report made by FBI agent Brown, presumably on the orders of Hoover following the letter of Rankin a week earlier.

This report solidifies explicitly the idea that there were just two photographs. "Number 1" has the same descriptions as his 12 December report, which agrees with the extant version of Moorman #3. (Recall that this report contained numerous statements designed to negate statements in reports prior to 12 December.)

The report mentions that the first photo was turned over to the Secret Service on the day of the assassination, and that Mary had since had it returned to her, *without mentioning that the FBI asked the Secret Service for a photo on Saturday 23 November or Sunday 24 November and that he himself was allegedly given a photo.* "Number 2" is now unambiguously identified as the extant Moorman #5, sold to AP, but given to the FBI on the night of the assassination.

This report presents, *for the first time,* a clear statement as to how many photographs were taken, what they show, and where they went. *It represents the definition of the official reconstruction of Mary Moorman's Polaroids.*

One could hazard a guess that Hoover might have asked Rankin to make such a request in order to generate this official "paper trail". Let's see what Hoover has to say to Rankin.

27 March 1964: Hoover to Rankin

Document 12 is Hoover's response to Rankin. He ignores completely Rankin's statement that the Secret Service turned over the "first" photo to the FBI on 23 or 24 November. His response implicitly answers Rankin's question about whether the FBI kept a copy of the first photo—they did not. (Is this at all believable?) Dallas FBI agents went back to Mary and she most generously gave them both photos, which were then couriered to Washington, and thence to the Warren Commission.

We get an almost hilarious picture of agents couriering Moorman's Polaroids around the country, every time someone wants to look at one. Apparently, no one ever considered the idea of making copies of them.

31 March 1964: Rankin to Hoover

The paper trail is now complete. The Warren Commission looked at the photos for a few days, and now had no further use for them. Hoover could now courier them back to Mary in Dallas.

What is never mentioned in any of these reports

There are a number of aspects of Mary's Polaroids—as we now know them—*that are simply never addressed in these reports at all.*

First of all is the story of the "Zippo" copy being made of Moorman #5, whereby a reporter allegedly propped the Polaroid up against a "Zippo" brand lighter and took a photo of it. This allegedly represents a "smuggling out" of a copy of this photo, but the stories of Moorman's and Hill's interrogation and handing over of the photos on the day of the assassination makes this romantic story sound rather contrived. Was it a cover story concocted later in order to make the Moorman appear to have an unimpeachable pedigree? Certainly it would appear that Moorman #5 was not published until after it went out on the AP wire on Saturday afternoon. If it had truly been "smuggled out" (without the FBI, Secret Service or the Sheriff's Department officers noticing) on the night of the assassination, why wasn't it published immediately?

Secondly, the *thumbprint* that appears in all extant copies of Moorman #5 is never mentioned at all. This is prominent in *all* of the highest-resolution copies now extant, and is even faintly visible in the "Zippo". If the "Zippo" copy was, indeed, made on the night of the assassination, it would imply that the thumbprint would be quite obvious by the time all of these other agents and Commissioners were looking at it.

This is something that would surely be commented on by the FBI, had it existed at the time. They could, for instance, have identified the person who did it (they have their fingerprint!). Legend has it that Jean Hill did it in the excitement, before the finisher was applied, and that it took some time for the acids and oils from her skin to destroy the image where it had touched. But why isn't this a part of the official reports? Surely someone would want to know how such an important piece of evidence was damaged?

Thirdly, there is *no mention at all of the cropping out of the Zapruder pedestal.* Why? Who? When? If it had been cropped out on the AP wire negative, then surely that would have been obvious when the original Polaroid was viewed. Given the importance of Abraham Zapruder's film, why would no one have made mention of the fact that he could be seen?

Fourthly, there is no explanation of why one of the "first" photos should be of inferior quality to the "second", as indicated in Sorrels' report. Does this represent some poor attempt to bury the existence of *three* Polaroids showing the motorcade? Moreover, there is absolutely no explanation at all of why "both" of the "two" Polaroids should have come out "light".

Fifthly, there is absolutely no mention at all of the extant Moorman #1 and #2. Surely, if these had existed, they would have been of interest, showing, as they do, at least some parts of Dealey Plaza? At worst they could have been used to explain the *numbering* on the back of Polaroids #3 and #5 (which Robert Groden allegedly discovered *just by turning them over* in the 1970s—could the FBI really be so inept as to be unable to notice this?).

Finally, of course, there is absolutely no description of Mary's camera, other than "Polaroid"; of the settings; of the film she used; and so on. Of course, this was a common thread in this investigation, and is not restricted to Mary Moorman.

Some personal conclusions

Although it is difficult to know how to piece together this web of evidence, there are several conclusions that I have come to that, whilst not guaranteed absolutely correct, are my best guesses.

Firstly, there was clearly a 27-hour window in which what we now know as Moorman #5 could have been worked on, before going out on the AP wire.

Secondly, there is absolutely no certainty as to where Jean and Mary were standing in Dealey Plaza—remember, we can't trust the other extant photographic evidence either. Mary snapped a photo *at the time of the first shot that hit the President*. Whether this puts her further up Elm Street than previously believed, or whether this simply means that the shooting didn't occur until the limousine reached Mary's assumed location based on the extant Zapruder film cannot be known at this stage.

Thirdly, it is highly likely that the "first" photo—which started out as at least two photos and then became one—contained much more explosive content than the "second" (which became the extant Moorman #5). What these photos originally showed is anyone's guess. The fact that so much work was done to muddy their existence suggests that, in their original forms, they may well have been the most dangerous photographs of the assassination.

Fourthly, the consistent descriptions of events by Mary and Jean suggest that her last photo *should not* have shown the President already slumping. Rather, he should be "jumping up" in response to the bullet. On the other hand, it is possible that Mary did not take the photo until a fraction of a second after the first shot, in which case the "slumping" may well be genuine. In either case, *she did not take that photo after the sort of Z-313 head shot seen in the extant Zapruder film!*

This, perhaps, explains why the "blood spray" in the extant Zapruder film was made to disappear so quickly: it had to be gone within a couple of frames so that the Moorman #5 Polaroid could be matched up with the Z-313 head shot! If in reality Mary *did* snap a photo of JFK merely "slumping", as Jean's, Emmett Hudson's, and her testimony all suggest, then *there would not have been any spray or debris* in the photo. Which may mean, ironically, that the main part of Moorman #5 *may well be genuine*. Whether the Zapruder pedestal area has been altered, or whether any of the grassy knoll in the background has been retouched, would then be open questions.

What we would then have is a fascinating scenario. Jean calls to JFK—looking down into the middle of the seat—as he approaches them. He turns, and perhaps starts to wave. Mary snaps a photo *and then the first shot hits him*. He jumps, and starts to slump forward. Jackie then responds, and cries out, as Jean and Mary reported. The limo stops somewhere down *past* the steps. There are then anywhere from two to seven further shots, that inflict the remaining wounds to JFK and Connally. Jean sees the hair on the back of JFK's head flap up as his skull is blasted out. The limo speeds off. Mary is quickly intercepted and asked for her photos. She and Jean undergo hours of interrogation, after which they finally turn over the Polaroids. And the cover-up begins.

VOLUNTARY STATEMENT. Not Under Arrest. Form No. 86

SHERIFF'S DEPARTMENT
COUNTY OF DALLAS, TEXAS

Before me, the undersigned authority, on this the __22nd__ day of __November__ A. D. 19 __63__

personally appeared __Jean Hill__ , Address __9402 Bluffcreek__
__Dallas 27, Texas__

Age __32__ , Phone No. __EV1-7419__

Deposes and says:-

Mary and I were wanting to take some pictures of the President so we purposely tried to find a place that was open were no people was around and we had been standing half way down toward the underpass on Elm Street on the south side. We were the only people in that area and we were standing right at the curb. The Presidents car came around the corner and it was over on our side of the street. Just as Mary Moorman started to take a picture we were looking at the president and Jackie in the back seat and they looking at a little dog between them. Just as the president looked up toward us two shots rang out and I saw the President grab his chest and fall forward across Jackies lap and she fell across his back and said "My God he has been shot". There was an instant pause between the first two shots and the motor cade seemingly halted for an instant and three or four more shots rang out and the motor cade sped away. I thought I saw some men in plain clothes shooting back but everything was such a blur and Mary was pulling on my leg saying "Get down thery are shooting". I looked across the street and up the hill and saw a man running toward the monument and I started running over there. By the time I got up to the rail road tracks some policeman that I suppose were in the motor cade or near by had also arrived and was turning us back and as I came back down the hill Mr. Featherstone of the Times Herald had gotten to Mary and ask her for her picture she had taken of the President, and he brought us to the press room downn at the Sheriffs office and ask to stay.

Jean Hill

Subscribed and sworn to before me on this the __22nd__ day of __November__ A. D. 19 __63__

Ade... L...

Document 1. Jean Hill's Sheriff's Department statement of 22 November 1963

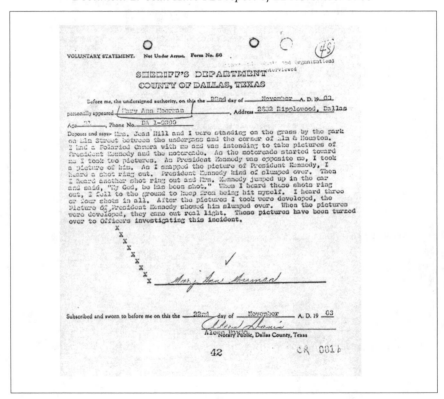

Document 2. Jean Hill's FBI report of 22 November 1963

Document 3. Mary Moorman's Sheriff's Department statement of 22 November
1963

VOLUNTARY STATEMENT. Not Under Arrest. Form No. 86

SHERIFF'S DEPARTMENT
COUNTY OF DALLAS, TEXAS

Before me, the undersigned authority, on this the __22nd__ day of __November__ A. D. 19_63_

personally appeared ___Emmett Joseph Hudson___, Address __107 South Bishop__
Dallas, Texas

Age __56__, Phone No. __WH 2-2008__

Deposes and says:- I am presently employed by the City of Dallas, Texas in
the Park Department. I have been so employed for the past 6 years. My
position is to take care of the property located on the West side of
Houston Street between Houston Street and the Tripple Underpass. I also
take care of the fountain in front of the Union Terminal. This day I
was sitting on the front steps of the slopping area and about half way
down the steps. There was another man sitting there with me. He was
sitting on my left and we were both facing the street with our backs to
the railroad yards and the brick building. At the same time the President's
car was directly in front of us, I heard a shot and I saw the President
fall over in the seat. I do not know who this other man was that was
sitting beside me. In our conversation he talked about having a hard
time finding a place to park. He also talked about working somewhere
over on Industrial Blvd. This man said lay down and we did. I definately
heard 3 shots. The shots that I heard definately came from behind and
above me. When I laid down on the ground, I laid on my right side and
my view was still toward the street where the President's car had passed.
I did look around but I did not see anything unusual, either anyone
running and I did not see any firearms at all. This shot sounded to me
like a high powered rifle.

Emmett J. Hudson

Witness, F. V. Roeder,
DSSS

Subscribed and sworn to before me on this the ___22nd___ day of ___November___ A. D. 19 _63_

Jones

Notary Public, Dallas County, Texas

*Document 4. Emmett Hudson's Sheriff's Department
statement of 22 November 1963*

FD-302 (Rev. 3-3-59)   FEDERAL BUREAU OF INVESTIGATION

                                                    Date ___11/23/63___

1

          MARY ANN MOORMAN, 2832 Ripplewood, telephone
number DA 1-9390, advises that she and a friend named
JEAN HILL, 9402 Bluff Creek, Dallas, Texas, watched
the President KENNEDY parade from the grassy area in the
parkway between Main and Elm Streets, and at approximately
12:25 p.m., as well as she recalls, she took a photograph
of the procession as it proceeded toward her. She took
this photograph with a polaroid camera, and the photograph
showed the police motorcycle escort preceding the
President's car. In the background of this photograph
she said the Texas School Book Depository Building was
visable.

          She took a second photograph of the President
as his automobile passed her, and just as she snapped
the picture, she heard what she at first thought was a
firecracker and very shortly thereafter heard another
similar sound which she later determined to have been
gunfire. She knows that she heard two shots and possibly
a third shot. She recalls seeing the President "sort of
jump" and start to slump sideways in the seat, and seems
to recall President KENNEDY's wife scream, "My God, he's
been shot"!

          Mrs. MOORMAN states that she and her companion
fell to the ground, but does not now recall what prompted
her to fall unless it was the reports and the commotion
in the President's car. She says she must have instinctively realized that there was shooting, but does not recall actually thinking about it. She states that she
could not determine where the shots came from, and her
next recollection is of people running more or less aim-
lessly, it seemed to her. She recalls that the President's
automobile was moving at the time she took the second
picture, and when she heard the shots, and has the impression that the car either stopped momentarily or
hesitated and then drove off in a hurry.

          She stated that as the President's car drove
off she started to leave the grassy area and was stopped
by a Mr. FEATHERSTONE, a newspaper man with the KRLD Radio

                                                        C D5

on ___11/22/63___ at ___Dallas, Texas___   File # ___DL 89-43___

by Special Agent __CURTIS L. PERRYMAN & ROBERT P.__ Date dictated ___11/23/63___
                    GEMBERLING/jt   36

This document contains neither recommendations nor conclusions of the FBI. It is the property of the FBI and is loaned to
your agency; it and its contents are not to be distributed outside your agency.

Document 5. Mary Moorman's FBI report of 22 November 1963

DL 89-43
2

and TV Station who questioned her concerning her observance
of the incident.

Mrs. MOORMAN advises that the photograph she
took showing the police motorcycles preceding President
KENNEDY's car and also showing the Texas School-Book
Depository Building was given by her to Secret Service
Agents JOHN JOE HOWLETT and BILL PATTERSON shortly before 4:00 p.m. November 22, 1963. The second photograph
taken at the time she heard the shots showed the President
slumping sideways in the automobile. She furnished this
photograph to Bureau Agents.

Mrs. MOORMAN advises that she saw no one in
the area that appeared to have possibly been the assassin,
and could furnish no additional information.

37

Document 5. Mary Moorman's FBI report of 22 November 1963
(continued)

David Mantik and Jim Fetzer at the Zapruder Film Symposium,
Duluth, Minnesota, 9–11 May 2003. (Photograph by Jan Fetzer)

FD-302 (Rev. 3-3-59)

Other Individuals and Organizations Involved or Interviewed

FEDERAL BUREAU OF INVESTIGATION

Date November 26, 1963

        EMMETT JOSEPH HUDSON, 107 South Bishop, Dallas,
Texas, who is employed by the City of Dallas (Park Department),
called attention to a photograph contained in the Sunday
edition, November 24, 1963, of the Dallas Times Herald,
which photograph was taken (according to information contained in the newspaper) by Mrs. MARY MOORMAN, and which photograph showed the President in a slumping condition immediately
following the impact of the shots. HUDSON called attention
to a group of three men in the photograph standing on some
concrete steps north of Elm Street and north of the position
of the Presidential car in the photograph. He pointed to the
man in the middle of this group of three individuals in the
photograph and advised, "That is me in the light colored
clothing and that is where I was standing at the time the
President was shot."

        He said he was looking directly at President KENNEDY
and saw his head slump to one side simultaneously with the
loud report made by the first shot fired by the assassin.
He said he then heard two more reports which sounded like
shots, such reports coming in rapid succession after the first
shot. He volunteered the shots were fired "just about as
fast as you could expect a man to operate a bolt action rifle,"
or words to that effect.

        HUDSON said the shots sounded as if they were fired
over his head and from some position to the left of where he
was standing. In other words, the shots sounded as if they
were fired by someone at a position which was behind him, which
was above him, and which was to his left. He again called attention to the photograph referred to above, and particularly to
the corner of the Texas School Book Depository building appearing in such photograph and said the shots sounded as if they
were coming from that building (Texas School Book Depository
building).

        HUDSON stated when he heard the shots, he turned around
and looked in the general direction of the Texas School Book
Depository building, 411 Elm Street, Dallas, Texas; however, he
did not see anyone with a rifle or firearm of any kind. He
pointed out, however, it was a matter of two or three seconds

Commission No. 5

on 11/25/63   at Dallas, Texas   File # DL 89-43

                    GASTON C. THOMPSON and
by Special Agents   JACK B. PEDEN/gm   Date dictated 11/26/63

                                30

Document 6. Emmett Hudson's FBI report of 25 November 1963

2
DL 89-43

after he heard the shots before he focused his vision on
the Texas School Book Depository building and perhaps in
that small lapse of time the assassin had stepped back
from the window.

HUDSON estimated he was approximately thirty feet
from the Presidential car at the time he heard the shots and
immediately noticed the President's head slump to one side.

He advised he did not know the identity or address
of either one of the other two men referred to above in the
three man group in the photograph. He said the only statement he remembered either one of these two men made was
that one of the men stated he worked somewhere on Industrial
Boulevard in Dallas, Texas.

*Document 6. Emmett Hudson's FBI report of 25 November 1963
(continued)*

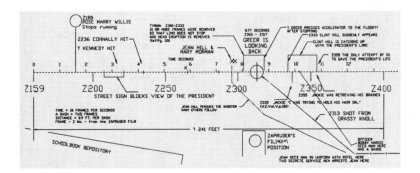

*Many students of the crime have been astonished by indications of Secret
Service complicity in setting up JFK for the hit, as the Prologue to* Murder
in Dealey Plaza *(2000) has explained. The lack of response by the Secret
Service was especially disturbing. Clint Hill, Jackie's bodyguard, was the
only agent to react by rushing forward when Jackie began to climb onto the
back of the trunk after a chunk of Jack's brains and skull. If the vehicles
were 20-25 feet apart and moving at 15-20 mph, as Emory Roberts, the
Agent in Charge, reported, then Hill performed a remarkable feat rivaling
that of world-class sprinters. As Gus Fleming, the engineer who prepared
this diagram, has observed, his run is far more plausible if the limousine
actually came to a stop, as many witnesses reported.*

FD-302 (Rev. 3-3-59)   ◯ FEDERAL BUREAU OF INVESTIGA◯N

Other Individuals and Organizations
Involved or Date   12/12/63

Special Agent ELMER MOORE, United States Secret Service,
505 North Ervay Street, Dallas, Texas, exhibited the following
photographs in possession of the Secret Service which photographs
were taken by Mrs. MARY ANN MOORMAN, 2832 Ripplewood, Dallas,
Texas, on November 22, 1963. Both photographs were made with a
polaroid camera.

The first photograph is of very poor quality, being
extremely light and exhibits a lower corner of the Texas School
Book Depository Building. No view is shown in the photograph
of the upper floors of the building and particularly the windows
on the sixth floor from which shots were fired at President JOHN
F. KENNEDY on November 22, 1963. The principal subject in this
photograph is a Dallas policeman on a motorcycle. No other
parts of the Presidential motorcade are seen in the photograph.

A second photograph taken by Mrs. MOORMAN was sold to
the Associated Press by Mrs. MOORMAN. This photograph, a copy
of which was exhibited to SA CHARLES T. BROWN, JR. by SA MOORE,
of the Secret Service, shows the automobile occupied by President
KENNEDY which photograph apparently was made shortly after
President KENNEDY was struck by a bullet fired by the assassin.
The Texas School Book Depository Building does not appear in this
photograph at all and the entire photograph is filled with the
view of the President's automobile. The photograph shows
President KENNEDY leaning slightly to the left toward the position
in which Mrs. KENNEDY is sitting in the car. This photograph
appeared in many newspapers throughout the United States and the
copy exhibited to SA BROWN by SA MOORE carries a Dallas, Texas
dateline of November 23, 1963. It is indicated to be a "(AP
Wirephoto)(zhs 71555 cer) 1963". Information appearing under the
photograph reflects the photo depicts "Kennedy hit by assassin's
bullet....photo made by Mrs. Mary Ann Moorman, wife of Dallas
plumber, with a polaroid camera."

on   12/12/63   at   Dallas, Texas   _____ File #   100-10461

by Special Agent   CHARLES T. BROWN, JR./BJD   _____ Date dictated   12/12/63

This document contains neither recommendations nor conclusions of the FBI. It is the property of the FBI and is loaned to
your agency; it and its contents are not to be distributed outside your agency.

CR 205 5-1

Document 7. FBI Agent Brown's report on
Secret Service Agent Moore of 12 December 1963

Attention: Mr. Redlich

CO-2-34,030

Inspector Kelley   March 7, 1964

SA Patterson, Dallas   —   Commission No.   486

Polaroid Picture of Assassination

        On November 22, 1963, while at the Dallas County
Sheriffs Office, Dallas, Texas, I talked to Mary Ann Mooreman, 2832
Ripplewood, Dallas, Texas. She had a polaroid picture of the Texas
School Book Depository that she had taken at the time of the
assassination which she surrendered to me for use in our investigation.
It was not known to me, at that time, exactly where the shots had come
from in that building so I could not tell if the picture was of value
or not.

        The next day I learned which window the shot had
been fired from and after checking the picture determined that the
photograph did not show this window at all. In fact, the picture
was of such poor quality that no detail of the building, windows
or surrounding areas was distinguisable.

        On the 23rd or 24th of November our office
received a call from the SAC of the local FBI office requesting the
picture and it was subsequently turned over to one of their agents,
believed to be SA Brown,

        No statement was taken from Mrs. Moorman since
she had given a signed sworn statement to the Sheriff's Office and
a copy of it was sent to this service. No report was made on the
photograph since it was given to the FBI and it appeared to have no
value in regard to the investigation.

        It has been learned that this photograph has
been returned to Mrs. Moorman and is still in her possession.

APPROVED:

Forrest V. Sorrels
Special Agent in Charge

1198.
3-10-64

Document 8. Secret Service Agent Sorrell's report
about Mary Moorman of 7 March 1964

FD-302 (Rev. 3-3-59)   FEDERAL BUREAU OF INVESTIGATION

1

Date ___3/17/64___

MRS. JEAN LOLLIS HILL, 9402 Bluffcreek, telephone
EV 1-7419, advised that she and a friend, MARY ANN MOORMAN
of 2832 Ripplewood, were in the vicinity of Main and Houston
Streets on November 22, 1963, for approximately one and one-
half hours before the arrival of President JOHN F. KENNEDY and
his party. While waiting for the motorcade to arrive at this
location, Mrs. HILL and MARY ANN walked around the parkway
area near the Texas School Book Depository Building in attempts
to determine the best vantage spot for taking photographs of
the President. Mrs. HILL said she recalls talking to a
uniformed policeman of the Dallas Police Department on the
sidewalk near the main entrance to the Texas School Book
Depository Building. While conversing with the policeman,
Mrs. HILL noticed an automobile circling the area. The windows
of the vehicle were covered with cardboard and the name "Honest
Joe's Pawn Shop" was painted on the side of the car. Mrs. HILL
made a remark about the automobile and the policeman told her
the driver had permission to drive in the area.

Just before the motorcade appeared, MARY ANN MOORMAN
and Mrs. HILL were standing on the lawn in the area between
Main and Elm Streets opposite the main entrance of the Texas
School Book Depository Building. Mrs. MOORMAN was taking
photographs of the motorcade as it came into view and when the
car occupied by President KENNEDY was passing Mrs. HILL, she
recalls shouting, "Hey!" She stated that President KENNEDY
was looking down when she shouted, and when he turned to look
at her a shot rang out and he slumped towards Mrs. KENNEDY.
Mrs. HILL heard more shots ring out and saw the hair on the
back of President KENNEDY's head fly up. She stated she thought
Mrs. KENNEDY cried out, "Oh, my God, he's been shot!" As the
President fell forward in his seat Mrs. HILL knew he had been
hit by a bullet. Mrs. HILL stated she heard from four to six
shots in all and believes they came from a spot just west of
the Texas School Book Depository Building. She thought there
was a slight time interval between the first three shots and
the remaining shots.

---

on _3/13/64_ at Dallas, Texas _____ File # _DL 89-43_

B. J. ROBERTSON and

by Special Agent _THOMAS T. TRETTIS, JR./ds_ 43 Date dictated _3/15/64_

This document contains neither recommendations nor conclusions of the FBI. It is the property of the FBI and is loaned to
your agency; it and its contents are not to be distributed outside your agency.

*Document 9. FBI Agents Robertson and Trettis's report
about Jean Hill of 13 March 1964*

2

DL 89-43

When the firing stopped, Mrs. HILL noticed that everyone in the vicinity seemed to be in a trance wondering what had happened. Mrs. HILL recalled it was then that she noticed a white man wearing a brown raincoat and a hat running west away from the Texas School Book Depository Building in the direction of the railroad tracks. She said she does not know why but she started across the street in an effort "to see who he was". In so doing she ran in front of the motorcycle escort following the President's car and was nearly hit by one of the policemen. Mrs. HILL said she lost the man from view when she looked down at what she first thought was a blood spot but later determined to be a red snow cone. She did not get a good look at this man, does not know who he was, and never saw him again. She thought the man was of average height and of heavy build.

Mrs. HILL then rejoined Mrs. MOORMAN where she had left her, and they started to leave the area. They were stopped by Mr. FEATHERSTONE, a Dallas newspaper man, who took them to the press room at the Dallas County Sheriff's Office.

Mrs. HILL stated that she and MARY ANN MOORMAN were at the Sheriff's Office for about two hours and were questioned repeatedly by representatives of the press and various Federal and local law enforcement officers. She said the Sheriff's Office was a scene of extreme confusion and it was impossible to remember what questions were asked of her by the Secret Service Agents and FBI Agents. She recalled that a man identifying himself as either a Secret Service Agent or FBI Agent asked her what she thought when a bullet hit near her feet raising the dust. Mrs. HILL told him she had no recollection of a bullet hitting near her feet. Mrs. HILL told the Agents she heard from four to six shots and heard one of the agents make the remark "there were three shots, three bullets, that's enough for now". She advised that at no time did any Federal Agent or other law enforcement officer attempt to tell her what she should say in regard to the number of shots fired or to force any other opinions upon her.

44

Document 9. FBI Agents Robertson and Trettis's report about Jean Hill of 13 March 1964 (continued)

<u>3</u>

DL 89-43

      Mrs. HILL advised that about a month ago she received
a long distance telephone call from MARK LANE, a New York
attorney, who questioned her regarding the assassination of
President KENNEDY. Mrs. HILL stated that from reading some of
LANE's statements regarding this conversation she determined
that LANE had taken some of her remarks out of context, thus
changing the meaning of her replies, had not used her full
answers to some of the questions, and had misquoted her in
this conversation. Mrs. HILL stated that LANE asked her
occupation and she replied that she was a housewife. This
point was pressed by LANE and Mrs. HILL told him she did some
substitute teaching. LANE told her this was great because
teachers made very good witnesses.

45

*Document 9. FBI Agents Robertson and Trettis's report
about Jean Hill of 13 March 1964 (continued)*

*Jack White and Jim Fetzer at the Zapruder Film Symposium,
Duluth, Minnesota, 9–11 May 2003. (Photograph by Jan Fetzer)*

MP

Jicklimer
2/3/17/04

cc: Rankin
     Willens
     Shaffer
     Redlich

MAR 18 1964

Mr. J. Edgar Hoover
Director, Federal Bureau
  of Investigation
Department of Justice
Washington, D. C.

Dear Mr. Hoover:

I refer you to SA Gemberling's report of November 30, page 37, in which there appears an interview with Mrs. Mary Ann Moorman concerning two photographs which she took of the Presidential motorcade. According to Mrs. Moorman, the second of the photographs, which is have seen, was given to agents of your Bureau. The first photograph was given to Secret Service Agents John Joe Howlett and Bill Patterson on November 22, 1963. We have received a report from the Secret Service advising us that on November 23 or November 24 this picture was turned over to an agent of your Bureau who is believed by the Secret Service to be SA Brown. The Secret Service further advises us that this photograph has been returned by your Bureau to Mrs. Moorman.

If the Bureau did obtain this photograph from Mrs. Moorman, do you have a copy in your possession? If you do not have a copy and if in fact it has been returned to Mrs. Moorman, we would like you to obtain this photograph from her with the assurance that the photograph will be promptly returned to her after it has been examined by the Commission.

Sincerely,

SIGNED

J. Lee Rankin
General Counsel

NOTE: The Secret Service letter with reference to the above is
       Commission Number 486.

Document 10. FBI Agent Brown's report
regarding Mary Moorman of 24 March 1964

FD-302 (Rev. 3-3-59)

FEDERAL BUREAU OF INVESTIGATION   MP (PHOTO)

1

Other Individuals and Organizations
Involved or Interviewed   Date   3/24/64

Mrs. MARY ANN MOORMAN, 2832 Ripplewood, made available
the following-described photographs taken by her with a Polaroid
camera on November 22, 1963:

Number 1 is a photograph of very poor quality, being
extremely light, and exhibits a lower corner of the Texas School
Book Depository Building. No view is shown in the photograph of
the upper floors of the building, and, particularly, the windows
on the sixth floor are not shown. The principal subject in this
photograph is a Dallas policeman on a motorcycle. No other parts
of the Presidential motorcade are seen in the photograph. This
photograph was the photograph Mrs. MOORMAN had turned over to the
Secret Service on November 22, 1963, and which has since been returned to her.

Number 2 is a photograph taken by Mrs. MOORMAN and was
the one sold by her to Associated Press. This photograph shows
the automobile occupied by President KENNEDY and shows him
leaning slightly to the left toward the position in which Mrs.
KENNEDY is sitting in the car. Mrs. MOORMAN advised that this
second photograph is the photograph she gave to FBI Agents on
the night of November 22, 1963, and which has since been returned
to her.

Mrs. MOORMAN advised she would appreciate these
photographs being returned to her as soon as they have served
their purpose.

_____

on 3/23/64   at Dallas, Texas   File # DL 100-10461

                                            42
by Special Agent CHARLES T. BROWN, JR./ds   Date dictated   3/24/64

This document contains neither recommendations nor conclusions of the FBI. It is the property of the FBI and is loaned to
your agency; it and its contents are not to be distributed outside your agency.   CR 897

Document 11. Letter from J. Lee Rankin to J. Edgar Hoover of 17 March 1964

OFFICE OF THE DIRECTOR

UNITED STATES DEPARTMENT OF JUSTICE

FEDERAL BUREAU OF INVESTIGATION

WASHINGTON 25, D.C.

March 27, 1964

BY COURIER SERVICE

Honorable J. Lee Rankin
General Counsel
The President's Commission
200 Maryland Avenue, Northeast
Washington, D. C.

Dear Mr. Rankin:

Reference is made to your letter of March 18, 1964, concerning two photographs taken by Mrs. Mary Ann Moorman of the Presidential Motorcade in Dallas, Texas, on November 22, 1963.

Mrs. Moorman was contacted by Special Agents of our Dallas Office, and she furnished both photographs for your information which are enclosed. Mrs. Moorman advised that photograph number one was the photograph she furnished to Secret Service on November 22, 1963. Photograph number two was the one sold by her to the Associated Press and according to your letter has been previously observed by you.

Mrs. Moorman has advised she would appreciate the return of these photographs as soon as they have served their purpose.

Sincerely yours,

J. Edgar Hoover

Enclosures (2)

Document 12. Letter from J. Edgar Hoover to J. Lee Rankin of 27 March 1964

JLR:HR:mar
2/31Mar '64

cc: Rankin
Redlich

APR 3 1964

Mr. J. Edgar Hoover
Director, Federal Bureau
  of Investigation
Department of Justice
Washington, D. C.

Dear Mr. Hoover:

I am returning herewith the two photographs taken by
Mrs. Mary Ann Moorman of the Presidential motorcade on
November 22, 1963, which you forwarded to the Commission
with a covering letter dated March 27, 1964.

You may return these photographs to Mrs. Moorman
since the Commission has no further use for them at this
time.

Sincerely,

SIGNED

J. Lee Rankin
General Counsel

Enclosures

Document 13. Letter from J. Lee Rankin to J. Edgar Hoover of 31 March 1964

*John Costella
presenting at the
Zapruder Film Symposium,
Duluth, Minnesota
10 May 2003*

Part IV

The Dealey Plaza Home Movies:
The Reel Story or the Real Story?

David W. Mantik, M.D., Ph.D.

[*Editor's note*: In this chapter, David Mantik extends his research on the photographic record, first, by analyzing the "jiggle" analysis of Luis Alvarez, which has been used in the past to support a three-shot, lone gunman scenario; and, second, by subjecting the Muchmore film to a comparison between blur analysis and jiggle analysis, which would be expected to converge in their results, with jiggles and blurs occurring at the same stages of the film. By performing his own "jiggle" analysis of the Zapruder film and comparing them, Mantik discovered that the resulting graph ought to have resembled a mass of relatively similar variations rather than a small number of striking variations, more like a forest of trees of similar height than a small number of exceptional height. This suggests that Alvarez may have employed the technique of selection and elimination by selecting data that supported a predetermined conclusion and simply omitting the rest, a practice perfected by the FBI in this case but not one to be expected from a Nobel laureate. Mantik's study of the Muchmore film is at least equally fascinating, where the results of a jiggle analysis yielded a surprisingly smooth graph, while the outcome of the blur analysis displayed striking variations. If the Muchmore film were authentic, the results of these analyses ought to converge. The argument that the Alvarez study confirms the authenticity of the Zapruder film and the inference that, if the Zapruder film had been altered, it would have been necessary to alter other films, such as Nix and Muchmore, are completely undermined by these new studies, which discredit several kinds of objections anti-alterationists have advanced.]

That is why I find the photographic record so interesting; it doesn't have the normal human failings.

Luis W. Alvarez, *American Journal of Physics* 44 (1976)

Since the birth of cinema, it has seemed ... that the major advantage of the cinema-camera for history would be to permit an exact recording of reality, to enable us to "see it as it happened." But what we get from film is only rarely an untainted and unmanipulated reproduction of the external reality at which the camera was originally pointed, and it is always a very partial reproduction of that reality.

Paul Smith, *The Historian and Film* (1976)

Introduction

Although most of the paradoxes of the John F. Kennedy (JFK) assassination are now well understood (James Fetzer, editor, *Murder in Dealey Plaza* 2000)—in particular, as evidence for conspiracy—the authenticity of the extant Zapruder home movie is still vigorously debated. This article reviews several salient pro-alteration arguments from my prior two articles (Fetzer 2000 and James Fetzer, editor, *Assassination Science* 1998) but also introduces new supporting data from the Zapruder film.

I have previously categorized the arguments against Zapruder film authenticity as follows:

- Disagreements between eyewitnesses and the film.
- Disagreements between early viewers of the film and the extant film.
- Disagreements between the film and other photographs or movies.
- Disagreements between the film and the first two enactments.
- Internal inconsistencies in the film.

The current discussion focuses almost exclusively on the final item above. New data (based on camera panning errors) are introduced and compared to the prior work of Luis Alvarez (*American Journal of Physics* 44: 813; 1976)[1] and also to similar work (G. Robert Blakey, *The Final Assassinations Report* 1979, p. 39) by the House Select Committee on Assassinations (HSCA).

The Historical Context

In a famous film from 1940, Hitler dances a jig after he descends from the railway car in which France surrendered. In fact, Hitler never danced.

With the help of a laboratory device called an optical printer, a team of patriotic British film editors was able to take an otherwise benign image of Hitler raising his leg and turn it into a diabolical little dance. Shown on the newsreel screens of all the allied nations at this psychological low point in the struggle against Nazism the footage became powerful propaganda... (John E. O'Connor, *Image as Artifact: the Historical Analysis of Film and Television* 1990, p. 11).

Almost from the day that the film projector was introduced for public use, the faking of film became a common practice. Raymond Fielding (*A History of the American Motion Picture Newsreel*, unpublished dissertation, University of Southern California 1961, pp. 5-6) reports: "Apparently there was not a single major producer in the period 1894 to 1900 that did not fake newsfilm as a matter of common practice." Paul Smith (*The Historian and Film* 1976, p. 58) adds that these early fakes consisted of re-creations of news events (using either actors or sometimes even original characters) or fabrication of events such as soldiers pretending to be in battle. These were then sold to the public as actual scenes of the Boer War. The first public discussion of the issue of faking apparently occurred in August 1900 under the title "Sham War Cinematograph Films" (Smith 1976, p. 100).

David H. Mould and Charles M. Berg describe the following scene:

Albert E. Smith and Stuart Blackton in New York, and Edwin H. Amet at Waukegan, near Chicago, used table-top seas, model ships, pinches of gunpowder and cigar smoke to restage the Battle of Santiago Bay for the camera. Most of the scenes in F. L. Donoghue's *Campaign in Cuba* were filmed on the New Jersey shore, where Thomas Edison enacted battle scenes from the Boer War. To Edison, such practices were evidence of enterprise; he claimed to have "improved the occasions" ("Fact and Fantasy in the Films of World War One," *Film and History* (September 1984), pp. 50-59).

This deception in the early newsfilm carried over to the newsreel and to the magazine film (Smith 1976, pp. 58-59). Tactics included mislabeled stock shots, staged scenes and re-enactments. Louis de Rochemont, who made *The March of Time*, did not even try to disguise this, while A. William Bluem wrote (*Documentary in American Television*): "What mattered was not whether pictorial journalism displayed the facts, but whether, within the conscience of the reporter, it faithfully reflected the facts." Smith adds that occasionally the film-maker purposefully distorted the sequence of time in order to impose his meaning on events, such as in Emile de Antonio's *Point of Order*, which included kinescopes of the Army-McCarthy hearings.[2]

On the same subject, the venerated Edward R. Murrow contributed "...one of the most famous image artifacts in the history of television documentary" (O'Connor 1990, p. 199). In "See It Now: Report on Senator McCarthy" (1954), Murrow and co-producer Fred Friendly destroyed McCarthy's credibility by selecting archival footage that showed the senator contradicting himself. In the program Murrow directly attacked McCarthy. Because it was based on real evidence the program drew great attention, but it was effective also because it employed dramatic structure (e.g., McCarthy answering himself), unflattering images of the senator, clever editing (a visual comparison of McCarthy to George Washington), and tight logical argument. Paradoxically, a significant percentage of the audience concluded that (as McCarthy intimated) Murrow was a Communist!

Astonishingly, Smith (1976, p. 99) claims: "...it is nevertheless certain that at least two-thirds of the films surviving in the archives today were anything but 'visual records.' " He adds: "... the great majority of the producers gave up almost at once any attempt at treating the camera as a 'recording machine.' " In fact, newsreel tricks were so common that MGM even made a screwball comedy, *Too Hot to Handle*, about this practice in 1938; it starred Clark Gable and Myrna Loy (O'Connor 1990, p. 213).[3]

While none of this is proof of Zapruder film alteration, it does describe an enabling climate of opinion (i.e., the reel was not required to be real), which entered cinematography from its very beginning and whose employ included many famous and powerful men. This climate of opinion, as well as actual practice, might well have facilitated similar alterations and editing of the Zapruder film. It also raises the beguiling question of whether the same editors, especially during the paranoid climate of the Cold War, had prior, or subsequent, experience with such editing of the news.[4]

Frame-to-Frame Displacement in the Zapruder Film

Daryll Weatherly suggested a technique (Harrison Livingstone, "A New Look at the 'Film of the Century,' " *Killing Kennedy and the Hoax of the Century* 1995, pp. 371-381) to assess camera panning. Essentially, it measures where the camera is pointing from frame to frame. In particular, the distance of a specific object is measured successively in each frame with respect to the frame edge. Based on the changing pattern of this distance Weatherly argued that the camera tracking could be determined in successive frames. For example, suppose (it is tacitly assumed that the limousine is moving uniformly) that the distance from the front edge of the limousine to the frame edge is smaller in one frame than in the immediately prior frame; that would mean that Zapruder's camera had moved to the left (relative to the limousine) during that particular one-frame interval. Such a shift should change the motion blur seen in imaged objects; e.g., for stationary objects, the motion blur should be less during that interval—because the camera was moving slower with respect to them, than during the prior interval. Likewise, if the camera had tracked the limousine accurately in the preceding frame, then in the examined frame some motion blur should be seen on the limousine—because the panning was now too slow for the limousine. Conversely, if the limousine edge was farther from frame edge that would mean that the camera had moved to the right (relative to the limousine) during that one-frame interval. Such inaccurate panning should be seen as increased motion blur in stationary objects—because the camera would be moving faster with respect to them. But increased blurring of the limousine should also be visible—because the camera was no longer following it accurately. In the data collected for this study, I measured Zapruder's (supposed) panning errors by measuring (with an EKG caliper) the successive horizontal distance of a specific highlight from the right edge of the frame, using the images published in the Warren Commission volumes.

The blur analysis performed by Alvarez[5] and also by the HSCA[6] identified probable sites of shots in the Zapruder film. By measuring the changing width of the blurred highlights (presumably caused by Zapruder's involuntary reaction to hearing shots) in sequential frames, the HSCA identified two such events, one between Z-189 and Z-197 and a second between Z-312 and Z-334.[7] As contrasted to the HSCA, Alvarez measured the *change in position* (i.e., the angular acceleration) from frame to frame; this technique was chosen to eliminate any gradual underlying changes in blurring that were unrelated to the hearing of a shot. He identified evidence for shots at about Z-180, Z-220, Z-290, and Z-313 (the standard headshot frame). In order to avoid a fourth shot (which would have meant multiple gunmen) he discarded the evidence at Z-290, suggesting that it was a reaction to a siren, though the evidence for that was, and still remains, unlikely. In fact, most eyewitnesses recall a siren only after Z-313.

Michael Stroscio, a Ph.D. physicist, followed up on this work (Fetzer 1998, p. 343) by noting one additional gunshot candidate, namely from Z-152 to Z-167.[8] Curiously, both Hartman and Scott, in their analysis for the HSCA, also show a possible event at about this same time (HSCA VI, p. 26).[9] Since Alvarez had available only frames published in the Warren Commission volumes, which began at Z-171, he had no opportunity to identify this additional shot. If Stroscio is right about this earlier interval—and, in my opinion, the evidence is at least as good as the other proposed times—then Oswald, faced with the minimum requirement

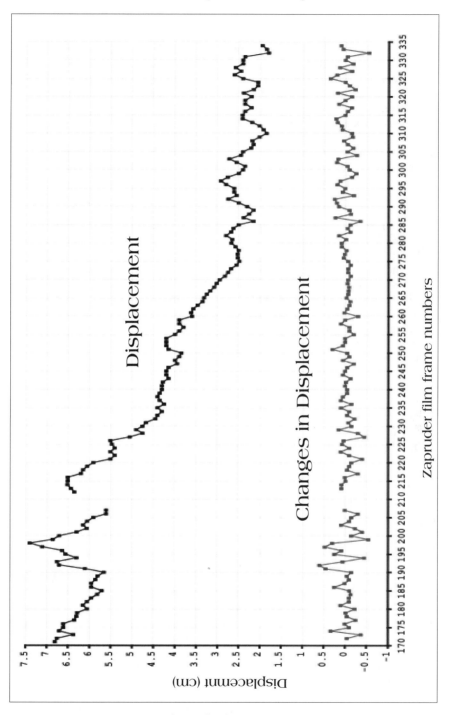

Figure 1. Frame-to-frame displacement in the Zapruder film

of getting off four shots, based simply on this evidence alone, could not have been the sole assassin.

These two techniques are not entirely identical. The blur analysis, as employed by Alvarez, utilizes the image obtained only while the shutter is open. The frame edge analysis, on the other hand, employs the entire frame cycle, i.e., about 1/18 second. Therefore, if the data from these two approaches are inconsistent they can only be explained (without invoking film alteration) by camera movement during the interval that the shutter is closed. According to Roland Zavada's report (issued by the Assassination Records Review Board), the camera is closed for about 54 percent of the cycle time; i.e., a time interval of about 54 percent x 1/18 sec = .029 sec. This is shorter than one eye blink. It seems most unlikely therefore that significant movement of the camera can occur in this extremely short time interval. Another argument, based on Zapruder's panning habits, will later be advanced to support this same conclusion.[10]

For all of the frames published in the Warren Commission volumes, I measured the horizontal distance from a specific highlight on the limousine to the right frame edge for this purpose. This data is displayed in Figure 1 (Frame-to-frame displacement in the Zapruder film). This figure also displays the *change in displacement* from frame to frame. This latter data set mimics the approach taken by Alvarez, who calculated the angular acceleration.

It should be noted that it is not possible to employ a single highlight in the image (e.g., a point on the limousine) for the entire span of frames. This is because any such site becomes obscured somewhere in the sequence. Whenever this occurs, a new point of reference must be chosen; this happened for me at several different times in the film. When this is done, however, the transition can be made essentially continuous by correlating the two measurements—so that no obvious discontinuity is seen (i.e., I pretend to reference the initial site, but the actual measurements are based on the new site).

There is one additional issue: as the limousine moves progressively to the right in the film, the perspective changes. This, by itself, changes the perceived distance of a given point (e.g., on the limousine) from the film edge. This effect can be seen in the raw data (of directly measured distances); there is a distinct trend in the size of the measurements. What is pertinent, however, as Alvarez recognized, is the *change in displacement*. Therefore these data (of changes in displacement) are also displayed.

What is first striking in the changes in displacement is the quadruple peak (even in the raw data) between Z-190 and Z-206. In the blur analysis of Alvarez, shown in Figure 2 (Zapruder blur analysis by Alvarez), a pronounced set of peaks is also seen beginning at Z-190 and continuing through about Z-197. Both approaches offer compelling evidence for an event (presumably a shot) at about Z-190.[11] Data for Z-208 through Z-211 are not shown in the present data because these frames are missing from the Warren Commission volumes. A striking feature can be seen when the present data are compared to those of Alvarez: the significant scatter of the present data, as shown here via the frame-to-frame analysis, is entirely lacking in Alvarez's presentation. His curves look remarkably smooth.

For this particular interval (Z-190 to Z-206) one other striking feature should be noted: it is the actual spacing between the peaks, which is very close to 5 frames. This would correspond to an oscillation frequency in the camera of 18.3/5 = 3.6 Hz (cycles per second). Alvarez has previously noted that the peak in the

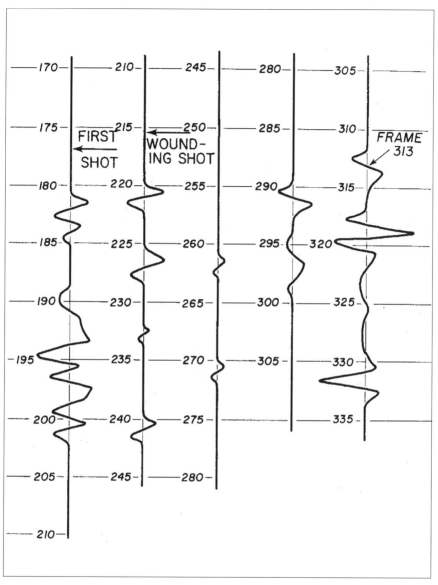

Figure 2. Zapruder blur analysis by Alvarez

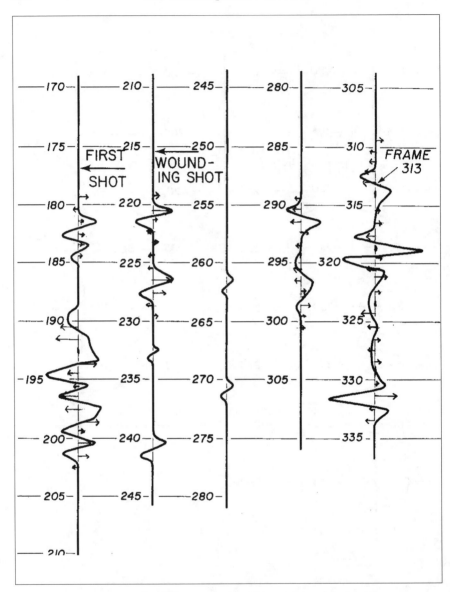

Figure 3. Directions and sizes of Zapruder's camera deflection

human power spectrum (for involuntary movement) is about 3 Hz. It is perhaps no coincidence that the hand clapping frequency he found for Brehm was 3.5 Hz. He has also emphasized that this peak frequency is essentially independent of the camera's mass and almost solely due to the internal circuits of the human nervous system. (Just for clarity it should be noted that multiple, successive peaks at intervals of 3.6 Hz are not interpreted as separate gunshots but rather as a persistent oscillation of the camera following a *single* shot.)

Although the evidence is not as compelling, two peaks may be present in the current data between Z-220 and Z-232. This seems consistent with the data of Alvarez, who described a peak beginning at Z-220, though his data suggests two possible peaks (one beginning at Z-220 and a second beginning at Z-225). Note again the separation of the two peaks: it is again about five frames. In any case, there is a fairly strong suggestion that the data obtained from these two different techniques (i.e., via Alvarez's blur analysis and via frame-to-frame analysis) are consistent with a shot at about Z-220.

Although Alvarez's data suggested a small event at Z-240, he ignored it. The present data suggest a small event at Z-247, but none at Z-240. Admittedly, the evidence for a shot here, as in Alvarez's case, is quite weak. There is, furthermore, no significant supporting data for a shot at either of these times. This time interval will therefore be ignored in further discussion here.

Alvarez noted an event (that he attributed to a siren) at Z-290, which may actually begin (according to his graph) even before this. The data presented here suggest an event beginning at Z-281 and continuing through about Z-310. As many as four peaks may be present; the intervals all seem to be about five frames again.[12] The presence of an event in this time interval seems probable, particularly since Alvarez found one, too. It should also be noted that Alvarez's graph suggests that this event persisted until just before Z-315, which might be consistent with the present data, too.

After Z-315 the data obtained in this study are more difficult to interpret as a gunshot event (or events). Distinct peaks, similar those discussed above, are not obvious. In particular, the distinct blurring noted by Alvarez (obvious even by brief inspection of the pertinent frames) at Z-318, Z-319, and even at Z-320, are nowhere seen in the present data. Instead, the frame-to-frame displacements are constant through Z-318, Z-319, Z-320, and Z-321. In fact, the entire interval from Z-314 to Z-321 shows only slight variation. This stands in striking contrast to the blur analysis of Alvarez and, in view of the standard headshot at Z-313, is quite unexpected. Instead, the most likely candidates for peaks are at minima found at Z-322, Z-327, and Z-332 (see arrows in Figure 1; these arrows were chosen to lie five frame intervals apart). In this interval, the second largest change in displacement occurs between Z-324 and Z-325, while the largest change is seen slightly later, between Z-331 and Z-332. Although not displayed in this paper, the largest *vertical* change also occurs between Z-331 and Z-332. The paradoxes raised by this abrupt transition—in two dimensions—are discussed further below.

Two significant questions remain:

(1) Are the events described by these two different techniques *qualitatively* similar? That is, are the camera deflections in the *same* direction?

(2) Are the *magnitudes* of the deflections consistent in the two techniques?

In principle, these two techniques should agree on the size and direction of camera displacement. Figure 3 (Directions and sizes of Zapruder's camera deflection) summarizes the data from these two approaches. For the frame-to-frame analysis the direction arrows describe the change in displacement *between* two adjacent frames; the size of the arrow reflects the actual measured displacement. Surprisingly, numerous disagreements are seen between the two data sets. These are discussed next.

In the interval from Z-180 to Z-185, Alvarez notes a significant event, but little change is seen in the frame-to-frame analysis. In Alvarez's analysis, the first major camera deflection after Z-191 is to the left (when the graph lies to the right of Alverez's vertical axis, the camera has moved *left*). During this time interval the frame-to-frame analysis clearly shows the camera moving to the right (left on the graph). This latter is easy to ascertain from simple inspection of the frames themselves. Alvarez's conclusions with respect to direction are discussed in detail in his article. This disagreement is the first of many to be found between these two approaches. At Z-193, however, the camera moves left in both analyses (right on the graph).

Between Z-225 and Z-228, both techniques initially show movement to the left. However, Alvarez then shows a prompt movement to the right, while the frame-to-frame data shows persistent movement to the left.

Beginning at about Z-292, Alvarez shows a large camera displacement to the left, while the frame-to-frame analysis shows a definite move to the right. Likewise, at about Z-297 to Z-298 Alvarez shows the camera moving left, while the frame-to-frame analysis shows only very small displacements, mostly to the right.

Modest agreement between the two is seen between Z-313 and Z-317.

While Alvarez shows a large movement to the left between Z-318 and Z-319, the frame-to-frame analysis shows no change at all. Between Z-319 and Z-320, Alvarez shows a large displacement to the right, whereas the frame-to-frame analysis shows a small displacement to the left.

Between Z-331 and Z-332, Alvarez shows the camera moving right, while the frame-to-frame analysis shows the largest displacement of all—but to the left!

The magnitudes of the displacements were also compared; the lengths of the arrows in Figure 3 reflect the sizes of these displacements. Since Alvarez does not offer this data in his article, pertinent changes in blur sizes (from the Warren Commission volumes) were measured specifically in the present work so that this comparison could be made.

Blur widths (horizontal and vertical) were measured (for the left-most light atop the limousine roll bar) via an EKG caliper for all frames between Z-280 and Z-334. For the horizontal direction, blur sizes ranged from 1.5 to 3.7 mm; for the vertical direction, blur sizes ranged from 1.1 to 3.1 mm. Frame-to-frame changes in blur size ranged from -1.4 to +2.1 mm in the horizontal direction (overall range = 3.5 mm) and -1.7 to 1.0 mm in the vertical direction (overall range = 2.7 mm). Differences in displacement, using the frame-to-frame technique, were determined only for the horizontal direction; these ranged from -2.0 to +2.5 mm (overall range = 4.5 mm). At least at first glance, the frame-to-frame technique seems to show a larger range of changes.

This pattern—of larger changes in the frame-by-frame displacement analysis—was repeatedly seen in a comparison between Z-280 and Z-334. In this interval, it was very common to find frame-to-frame changes in displacement of one centimeter or more while the blur sizes changed by only several millimeters. Occasionally (e.g., between Z-285 and Z-286) the frame-to-frame analysis showed a camera movement of 3.5 mm while the blur changed by only 0.3 mm (a tenfold difference). Two additional large changes in camera movement (via frame-to-frame displacement measurements) were seen between Z-321 and Z-322 (2.3 mm) and Z-324 and Z-325 (3.5 mm); by contrast, the corresponding changes in blur size were only 0.2 mm and 0.7 mm, respectively.

Conversely, on one occasion the blur size changed a great deal: 1.7 mm between Z-331 and Z-332, while the frame-to-frame shift was small, only 0.5 mm. In summary, a great deal of inconsistency in size and direction was seen when these two approaches were compared.

The Muchmore Home Movie[13]

David Lifton supplied a copy (on a reel) of this movie, which was copied from an early generation. Individual frames were first made into slides, then into individual 4 x 5 color prints. The latter were used in this study. Frames corresponding to Z-272 through Z-336 were analyzed.[14] Both blur sizes (horizontally and vertically) as well as frame-to-frame shifts were measured. The latter are shown in Figure 4 (Muchmore film: frame-to-frame displacement). Since these data show little evidence for gunshot-like peaks, the *changes* from frame to frame are not shown here (unlike the case of the Zapruder film).

With a few significant exceptions, these data appear quite smooth. But how can this be? How can these Muchmore data be so smooth when the corresponding Zapruder data is so scattered? Some possibilities include the following: (1) Muchmore was partially or completely deaf (probably not); (2) sounds were different at Muchmore's location (possibly—but were they louder or quieter?) (3) Muchmore anchored her camera against a fixed object (unknown, but probably false based on an argument below)[15]; or (4) Muchmore's central nervous system was less excitable than Zapruder's (unlikely). One noteworthy point has been made by Milicent Cranor: since Muchmore stood closer to the "sniper's nest" than did Zapruder, Muchmore's responses to gunshots should appear more dramatic than Zapruder's. Merely because the Muchmore data is so smooth, this by itself might be used as an argument that the gunshots did not all originate from the "sniper's nest." (For example, for a gunman just behind him on the grassy knoll, Zapruder would have been much closer than Muchmore.

The monotonous smoothness of the displacement data in Muchmore's film is sometimes strarkly contridicted by the grossly visible blurs. For example, the blurs seen in M-272, M-273 and M-274 (numbers are chosen to correlate with the Zapruder film) are huge, as is obvious simply from inspecting these frames. (These large blurs might be used as an argument that she did not anchor her camera against a firm object.) From M-273 to M-274 the blur increases by 5.0 mm, even though the frame-to-frame displacement changes only by 0.4 mm (more than a ten-fold difference). A similar effect occurs between M-278 and M-279: the blur increases by 3.5 mm while the frame-to-frame shift is only 0.5 mm. An opposite effect occurs between M-296 and M-297: the blur decreases by 1.0 mm whereas the frame-to-frame shift is 4.5 mm. Similar large changes in the frame-to-frame shift are seen between M-299 and M-300 (6.0 mm), between M-300 and

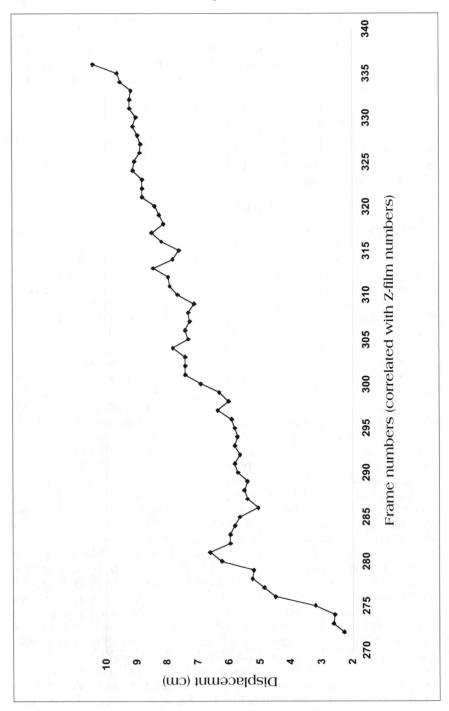

Figure 4. Muchmore film: frame-to-frame displacement

M-301 (5.0 mm), and M-335 to M-336 (8.0 mm), while blur size changes only by 1.0 mm, zero, and 0.5 mm, respectively. Likewise, in the vertical direction, the frame-to-frame change is large (4.0 mm) between M-293 and M-294, while the vertical blur undergoes no visible change at all.

Discussion

The Muchmore film is startling for the blandness of its frame-to-frame changes; even though several short-lived frame-to-frame changes are seen, no obvious gunshot events are seen. Nonetheless, the inconsistencies between the two approaches (blur analysis vs. the frame-to-frame technique) are, if anything, even more striking in the Muchmore film than in the Zapruder film. When one change is small the other is sometimes much larger, and vice versa. If the Muchmore film were authentic, this should not occur. Furthermore, these inconsistencies are found in both the horizontal and the vertical directions. These remarkable paradoxes might, of course, derive from (inaccurate) alteration of the Muchmore film.

The new data presented here for the Zapruder film are reassuring for their confirmation of two events (presumably gunshots) at about Z-190 and Z-220. Surprisingly, these data agree with Alvarez in suggesting a third event between Z-282 and Z-287. Several other investigators have proposed a shot during this same interval. I have previously cited evidence for shots during this interval (Fetzer 1998, pp. 286-288; especially see evidence items A and B). On the other hand, immediately after Z-313, the complete absence of an event, based on frame-to-frame analysis, was unanticipated and must be considered troubling. Surely if a gunshot occurred shortly before Z-313, then this event should appear in the current data, based on frame-to-frame measurements. Moreover, the suggestion in this new data of a possible event between Z-321 and Z-324 oddly occurs during JFK's most posterior excursion. This is obvious from simple inspection of the film, but may also be judged from Josiah Thompson's detailed analysis in *Six Seconds in Dallas* (1966) pp. 272-276. Prior readers of my essays may recall that I have proposed two successive head shots, with the final one (arriving from the front) at about Z-321 (Fetzer 1998, p. 285), precisely when JFK's head is erect. This conclusion was based on the remarkably consistent (and prompt) recountings by many eyewitnesses who were very close to the limousine. Some readers will also recall that this precise time matches Foster's Freeze. Toni Foster is the pedestrian in the background grass, whose position seems abruptly to freeze between Z-321 and Z-322. Therefore, the possibility of an event in this new data between Z-321 and Z-324 is intriguing and has surprising support. The absence of an event in this new data shortly after Z-313 and the contrary evidence for a possible event beginning near Z-321 was unexpected, yet surprisingly consistent with film alteration, especially as described in my prior essays.

Other than alteration, is there any plausible explanation for the inconsistencies between the two techniques? Alvarez notes that the periods of Zapruder's jitters after gunshots are very nearly five frames; therefore, this frequency of 3.6 Hz seems consistent between the two techniques. Yet even this by itself does not establish film authenticity. For example, if the original film had been exposed at 48 frames per second, but only every third frame had been retained, the camera oscillation frequency would have appeared the same as if originally shot at 16 frames per second and left unaltered.

On the other hand, if the editors had inaccurately positioned the images of individual frames (i.e., poor centering) during the alteration process (a more likely event if magnification changes had simultaneously occurred) then the frame-to-frame analysis might well bear little relationship to camera panning in the original film. In this case, the blur analysis would be the more likely of the two to be reliable. The data reviewed above (isolated from other data) then might suggest that film alteration, in the earlier frames (e.g., before Z-300[16]), either played little role or was quite regular (such as simple frame removal at uniform intervals); on the contrary, frames just before Z-313, and continuing afterward, are suspect for more extensive and irregular alteration. If true, such more extensive editing after about Z-300 would not be surprising—since the editors might well have wanted to remove the limousine stop as well as obvious debris flying backward (as was described by the early surveyors, who saw blow-ups of individual frames).

Is it possible that the inconsistencies between the two approaches can be reconciled by positing camera movement in the brief interval when the shutter is closed? If 3.6 Hz accurately characterizes the period for Zapruder's jitter, then this would seem unlikely. As measured from the current data, the peak to trough change is at most 8.0 mm over *five* frames. During the short interval (54 percent of one frame cycle) that the shutter is closed this maximum displacement would then be only about 8 mm x 54 percent x 1/5 = 0.86 mm. Such a small displacement while the shutter is closed is far too small to explain the inconsistencies between the two approaches leaves no obvious explanation for the large camera movements while the shutter is closed. To this might be added another argument: during those intervals without events Zapruder consistently pans rather well (Alvarez also notes this); therefore random effects (of unknown cause) as an explanation also seem improbable. This is especially true since many frames show paradoxes—paradoxes that beg for significant movement while the shutter is closed. Such random movements, as explanations for so many paradoxes, seem unlikely.

A specific illustration of this issue is contained in the sequential changes in Z-302, Z-303, and Z-304, which have drawn much prior discussion. In Z-303, the background pedestrian (Toni Foster) appears quite sharp. But in the surrounding two frames she is distinctly blurred. It is often claimed that the simultaneous clarity in Z-303 of both Foster (and Moorman and Hill, too) as well as the limousine, constitutes powerful evidence that the limousine was stopped in Z-303. On the other hand, if the limousine was stopped in this frame, then why the contradictory evidence of both immediately surrounding frames? In particular, if the estimated maximum camera displacement is only about 0.86 mm while the shutter is closed (based on peak to trough displacements over a five-frame cycle time, as discussed above), this would seem to leave no explanation, other than film alteration, for the sudden changes in Z-302 and Z-304.

John Costella has raised the fascinating question of whether the jiggles were deliberately inserted into the film (as would have been technically feasible), for the explicit purpose of possibly tricking viewers into identifying gunshot events. If this had been done, it would have required contemporaneous knowledge (in 1963) of human jiggles that result from unexpected and loud noises. Interestingly, the HSCA experts do not cite such prior knowledge in their own work. Perhaps even more to the point though, Alvarez does not cite such data in his paper, even though he later patented his own technique for stabilizing a camera against the typical movements triggered by the human nervous system. Another argument against such a deliberate fabrication is the presence of possible events at Z-160 and Z-290, times that are obviously inconsistent with the Warren Commission's single gunman version. Also, the Muchmore data show no such jiggles in response to gunshots. For these reasons it seems unlikely to me that these jiggles were deliberate insertions, though this cannot be conclusively ruled out. If the film was fabricated (perhaps from two or more separate films taken close together in time, as Jack White and John Costella have proposed) then time intervals in the extant film cannot be confidently calculated. It is even possible that the apparent five frame cycles seen in the extant Zapruder film are inadvertent. For example, if the extant film had been compressed in a fairly regular fashion from an original film (or films) shot at a faster speed (e.g., 48 fps) then under some conditions of fabrication, such intervals might have been conserved. Further discussion of these issues lies beyond the scope of this paper, but might be profitably explored later in more detail.

Conclusions

1. The frame-to-frame analysis in this study shows events (presumably gunshots) at about Z-190 and Z-220. Somewhat unexpectedly, it also provides strong support for an event at about Z-282 to Z-287. The present data do not examine the region around Z-160 (this precedes the images in the Commission volumes). However, both Stroscio and the HSCA experts found evidence of an event here, just as Connally begins his sudden left turn. Altogether four events are identified in the present data from the Commission volumes. This is already too many for the Warren Commission.

2. Based on frame-to-frame analysis, the evidence for a gunshot just after Z-313 is weak. This new data, however, hints at a shot near Z-321, when JFK's head was erect. If the original film had been extensively edited after Z-300 then evidence for such a Z-321 shot might have been suppressed as a byproduct of editing.

3. An oscillation period for Zapruder's camera (after presumed gunshots) is about five frames (3.6 Hz) in the extant film, consistent with the typical human cycle time. This is also the cycle time found by Alvarez for Brehm's clapping. These cycle times, although consistent with the human nervous system, cannot, by themselves, provide definite proof of film authenticity.

4. Inexplicable, often large, disagreements exist between Alvarez's study and the frame-to-frame analysis as presented here. These inconsistencies appear both in the direction and in the size of individual displacements. Furthermore, Alvarez's graph is misleadingly smooth; it does not reflect the large inherent scatter that should be seen in his data.

5. The Muchmore data are surprisingly bland, showing little of the scatter and none of the events that are seen in the Zapruder frame-to-frame data.

6. Furthermore, the blurs, both horizontal and vertical, in the Muchmore images are often inconsistent (sometimes grossly so) with the measured frame-to-frame changes. These are often so flagrant as to be evident even on simple inspection of the images.

In conclusion, the numerous irregularities and paradoxes cited here are difficult to explain in a simple and consistent manner, if these films are authentic. On the other hand, any of them might have arisen, most likely unintentionally, as a byproduct of film alteration.

Notes

1   Also see Luis Alvarez, *Alvarez: Adventures of a Physicist* (1987).

2   As a child in Wisconsin I personally watched these events live on television.

3   Although these newsreels distorted history, the reverse has also been true. O'Connor notes (O'Connor 1990, p. 229) that historians have also portrayed the movies with "... vague generalities and absurd evaluations." O'Connor then provides an illuminating quote (from historian John Garraty), which O'Connor describes as "... rather extreme in its gross inaccuracies ...". I would personally add that I have previously singled out Garraty for his simple-minded view that Oswald was the lone assassin, as portrayed in his history textbook, *The American Nation* (1966, p. 812). In both cases Garraty was probably guilty of relying too much on secondary sources rather than doing his own research, a problem that no doubt plagues many writers of history textbooks.

4   With the recent revelations about Operation Northwoods (James Bamford, *Body of Secrets* 2001, p. 82) we now know that the Eisenhower administration, with the written approval of the Chairman and all of the Joint Chiefs of Staff had devised a plan against communism that "... called for innocent people to be shot on American streets; for boats carrying ... [Cuban refugees] ...to be sunk; for a wave of violent terrorism to be launched in Washington, D.C., Miami, and elsewhere. People would be framed for bombings they did not commit; planes would be hijacked. Using phony evidence, all of it would be blamed on Castro ...". Compared to this activity, the alteration of a single piece of film footage seems rather modest.

5   Alvarez credits Harold Weisberg, *Whitewash* (1966) with the initial idea.

6   See Volume VI of the HSCA, pp. 16–31. One of the HSCA's two experts, W. K. Hartman, measured the size of the motion blur on the same object in successive frames. This is similar to the approach taken by Alvarez. However, the other expert, Frank Scott, employed frame-to frame measurements; he calculated a twenty-frame running average based on actual measurements to predict where the camera would point in the next frame; the measured (horizontal) position for this frame was then subtracted from this predicted position to obtain a new data point. If he used the frame edge as a baseline (he does not clarify this issue), his approach would be similar to the one employed here. That cameramen do respond with such characteristic jiggles was shown by a firm (Edgerton, Germeshausen and Greer) hired by CBS (Stephen White, *Shall We Now Believe the Warren Report?* (1968), p. 228).

7   Since human response times are not zero, a delay of several frames (Alvarez posited five) is usually assumed between the actual shot and the first frame with altered panning. There is also a small delay due to the finite speed of sound.

8 In striking agreement with Stroscio, the HSCA concluded from the acoustic evidence that the first shot would have reached the limousine between Z-157 and Z-161 (Blakey 1979, p. 39).

9 The HSCA noted (HSCA VI, p. 17) that "The first reaction by any of the limousine occupants to a severe external stimulus begins to occur in the vicinity of Z-162 to Z-167." Connally, previously looking left, suddenly begins a rapid movement to the right at about this time. The HSCA, however, did not consider this to be a response to a bullet.

10 In his AJP paper, Alvarez agrees with this conclusion. For example, he notes that the angular acceleration seen between Z-312 and Z-313 cannot have been caused by Zapruder's muscles, because the human nervous system cannot react that quickly. He proves his point by introducing the old parlor trick of a dropped dollar bill. The fact that it cannot be caught after being dropped by someone else (without warning) shows the relative slowness of the human reaction time; he adds that a quick response to an optical stimulus would be about 1/6 second, i.e., about 3.1 Zapruder frames.

11 Additional evidence for such a shot derives from photograph #5 by Phillip Willis, who has described precisely how his finger was triggered by hearing a shot at this time. The HSCA, by photogrammetric analysis of objects in his still photograph, determined that it was exposed at about Z-190. The evidence for a shot at about Z-190 is therefore widely accepted. Furthermore, assuming that the fatal head shot is seen at Z-313, the HSCA determined from the acoustic evidence that the second (of four gunshot impulses) would have reached the limousine at Z-188 to Z-191 (Blakey 1979, p. 84).

12 Subjecting this data to a Fourier analysis might more accurately identify the dominant frequency or frequencies.

13 The HSCA (HSCA VI, p. 19, footnote) noted that the Nix and Muchmore films were taken from distances of 2.7 and 2.1 times, respectively, farther away from JFK than the Zapruder film. They also note that initially the blur analysis was to have included the Nix and Muchmore films. They state, however, that since these films included no extensive footage prior to the head shot, this was not done.

14 The FBI determined that Muchmore's camera speed (18.5 frames per sec) was almost the same as Zapruder's (Richard Trask, *Pictures of the Pain* 1994, p. 206).

15 She shot her assassination sequence through a window in the peristyle; for her location, see the inside cover of Trask 1994.

16 Is it merely a coincidence that Alvarez found a deceleration centered at about Z-300?

David W. Mantik
presenting at the
Zapruder Film Symposium,
Duluth, Minnesota
10 May 2003

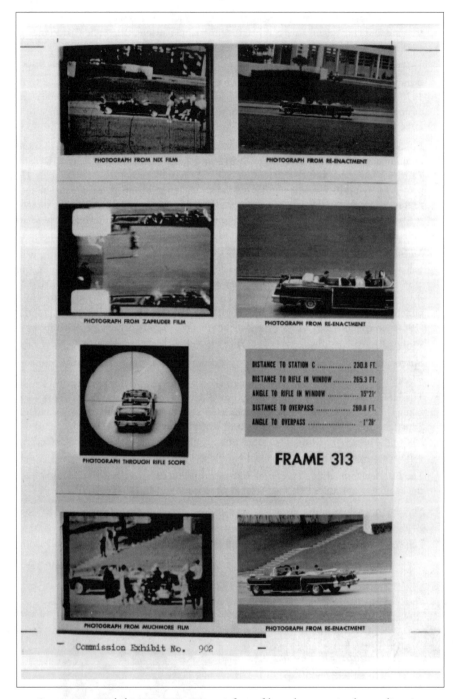

Commision Exhibit No. 902. Frames from films that required coordination

Pig on a Leash:
A Question of Authenticity

David S. Lifton

[*Editor's note*: In a captivating and personal history of his study of the death of JFK, David Lifton provides fascinating insights about many of the key players who have dealt with these issues, including Robert Groden, Harrison Livingstone, and Josiah Thompson. His early experiences with Wesley Liebeler, who had been a member of the Warren Commission staff, reflects the controversial character of the very idea that the film might have been altered *by even so much as a splice*! From his reflections on Moe Weitzman and Abraham Zapruder to The Sixth Floor Museum, he illuminates what it was like to be a student of this case when no one really understood—even remotely—the depth of the conspiracy or the extent of the cover-up. His "full flush left" theory may well prove to be the *coup de grace* to any lingering vestiges of doubt about the authenticity of the film, to which the contributors to this volume have contributed so profoundly.]

One day in the mid 1990s, I was driving toward my office in West L.A. My office consists of about three rooms, and contains about forty filing cabinets containing documents pertaining to the JFK assassination. It also contains a series of metal shelves with some rather valuable 35 mm prints and negatives—prints and negatives that I personally made—of the Zapruder film, which is the subject of much of this essay.

I don't particularly care to work in my office—I much prefer the solitude of the UCLA library, or a corner of one of several Starbucks that I like to visit—but regular visits are necessary to the office to pick up mail, check the fax machine, and so forth, and this was the way my day often started.

It was a beautiful southern California day—"another day in paradise", as we say out here in Los Angeles—when, driving down Colby, a residential street, I observed a remarkable scene. Just up ahead and over to the left a short ways, on the sidewalk, was a young man walking a rather large animal. A very large pig, it seemed.

The pig was on a leash—I remember that detail—a long verdant-green leash.

I remember blinking my eyes in disbelief. Could this really be? Surely that was some sort of dog. I drove closer. No, it wasn't. It looked just like a pig. Good Lord—it *was* a pig!

I slowed the car and pulled over to the left, rolled down the window, and called out: "Sir, is that a real pig?"

The man turned, looked directly at me, paused, and then said—rather disdainfully and very sarcastically: "No, it's a *fake* pig."

And he turned back to walking his pet.

Later that afternoon, a friend told me that pigs were very intelligent and that some people kept them as pets. But for me, my initial state of disbelief has come to be a metaphor of sorts about the Zapruder film, and the fake pig a metaphor for various aspects of my Zapruder-related adventures over the course of some 38 years, some

309

pertaining to optics, but many to money. Although the starting point is usually some theory about Dallas, the issue inevitably comes down to dealing with those who control access to that film, the money which always changes hands in connection with the film, and the issue of greed connected with that cinematic item.

The Zapruder film, as everyone knows, is a home movie of President Kennedy, his wounding, and what happened at each split second—but, when it comes to discussing and illustrating any of this publicly in connection with a book, article, or documentary film, one soon arrives at a financial crossroads of sorts, and learns that it comes down to the issue of—oink oink—money. And, depending on the exact purpose or use of the film, very substantial sums of money at that. But now serious issues have been raised about the authenticity of the film, and so that's probably why I think of the "fake pig" and the Zapruder film in the same mental picture frame.

In *Animal Farm*, Orwell made the animals the vehicle for the story about the atrocities of Stalinism.

For me, the pig on a leash has become a metaphor for much concerning the Zapruder film—from questions of authenticity to issues of pure greed.

Most people think that if there was a soundtrack on the Zapruder film it would consist of shots being fired at our late President.

I've grown rather cynical over the years, particularly in connection with the use of the film and with those who control access to this film.

So when I think of a soundtrack on the Zapruder film, I hear the sound of *oink oink*.

1965: The Z film and the JFK researchers

For most JFK researchers, the story of the Zapruder film starts in 1964, when the 26 volumes of the Warren Commission were released. We found that in Volume 18, printed two frames per page, were black and white reproductions of certain Zapruder frames. The public had seen some of these frames in *Life* magazine on three occasions, twice in color. The 29 November 1963 issue of *Life*—the first published after JFK's death—had contained a series of some 30 black and white frames. Then, on 7 December 1963, *Life* published the "John F. Kennedy Memorial Edition" which contained nine enlarged Zapruder frames, in color. The third *Life* issue to contain Zapruder frames—five small color frames on the cover, eight enlarged color frames inside—was dated 2 October 1964, and published within days of the release of the Warren Report.

People studying the case today take for granted the availability of frames from this film, either on the Internet or in VHS or DVD format. They talk of video cards, downloading a frame here or there, seeing the movie on the Internet, knowing that it was included in Oliver Stone's movie "JFK", purchasing it from MPI on DVD, etc.

None of that was the case in 1963–64. All there was were selected still frames in three issues of *Life* magazine—that was it. And the American people were very interested in those issues.

According to court documents, "The three weekly issues of *Life* and its Memorial Edition, each containing Zapruder frames, had a total distribution of over 23,750,000 copies. Weekly issues of *Life*, published outside the United States and containing Zapruder frames, had a circulation of over 3 million copies."[1]

The Zapruder film—in its entirety and as a movie film—was not available to the American public. The media reported that Abraham Zapruder—a Dallas clothing manufacturer—had sold his film to *Life* magazine for $40,000, and donated $25,000 of the money to the family of Officer J. D. Tippit, whom Oswald was accused of having shot just prior to his arrest at the Texas Theater.

It seemed like a benevolent gesture, but the story was false and a serious misrepresentation of what had actually occurred. Abraham Zapruder in fact sold the film to Time-Life for the sum of $150,000—about $900,000 dollars in today's money—in a series of payments of $25,000 per annum that began that weekend, with five additional payments being made shortly after the first of every year, starting in January 1964 and ending in January 1968.

Moreover, although *Life* had a copy of the film, it did little to maximize the return on its extraordinary investment. Specifically, it did not sell this unique property—as a *film*—to any broadcast media or permit it to be seen in motion, the logical way to maximize the financial return on its investment. In media terms, that is called "exploiting the rights". But Time-Life did no such thing.

A closer look revealed something else. The film wasn't just sold to *Life*—the person whose name was on the agreement was C. D. Jackson, a close friend of former CIA Director Allen Dulles. The issue of the film being sold to C. D. Jackson does not seem particularly significant when one first examines the Life/Zapruder contract, but appears more important later, when evidence emerges that there is something wrong with the film. Of course, that story took some time to develop.

Back in 1965, within a few months of the November 1964 release of the 26 volumes of the Warren Commission, a small number of researchers discovered that, as shown on the poor quality black and white frames printed two to a page in Volume 18, President Kennedy's head moved rapidly backwards in the frames following frame 313, depicting the impact of the fatal shot.

Several researchers went to the National Archives to see this for themselves, in motion.

They were stunned by what they saw

The Warren Commission had concluded that President Kennedy was struck twice from behind—once in the back of the neck, then in the back of the head. This basic architecture of the shooting (two rearward-striking trajectories) derived from wounds on JFK's body as reported in the Naval autopsy report (his body having been examined at Bethesda Naval Hospital the night of his murder).

Visitors who viewed the Zapruder film at the National Archives were in for a shock: the film seemed to show JFK being struck from the front, at least in the head. The rapid backward motion of JFK's head contradicted the autopsy conclusion—or so it seemed—and that was a stunner.

Thomas Stamm was one of the earliest researchers to visit the Archives, and circulated a brief written description: it was as if JFK was hit from the front by an invisible baseball bat, he said. Stamm's description made the rounds of researchers by snail mail (there being no internet in 1965). The word spread, and about that time the Archives had another visitor, Stewart Galanor.

Galanor at the National Archives

It was early 1965, and Lyndon Johnson had just been inaugurated. Galanor, who lived in New York City, was doing valuable research for Mark Lane and wanted to see the Zapruder film for himself. So he telephoned the Archives and made an appointment with Marion Johnson, the elderly white-haired archivist who at the time, handled all matters pertaining to the Warren Commission. Then he took the train to Washington.

Three decades later, in 1997, Galanor recalled what he now remembers as having been a "surreal experience."

"I was ushered into this auditorium that seats about 600 people," recalls Stewart. I was all alone. So I just walked in and took a seat in one of the first three rows.

"The film was a motion picture film, shown by a projectionist.

"All of a sudden, the lights came on the screen, and a curtain drew back.

"A voice boomed out: 'Are you ready?'

" 'Sure,' I replied."

"Then I watched this film go through, three times.

"Three times I watched as the car came down the street, the President's hands raised to his throat, and then his head and whole body were violently thrown to the rear."

Galanor had never seen anything like this. He was stunned.

The ethereal voice asked: "Would you like to see it again?"

"No," replied Stewart. "It's pretty clear what happened."

Galanor, a math major (who later taught math in New York high schools) had studied the backward motion depicted in the still frames in Volume 18. He had shown the printed exhibit to Lane, saying, "Look, this is absolute proof that the shots came from the right front." It was the same evidence that JFK researcher Ray Marcus showed me in 1965, at his home in Los Angeles (and which I wrote about in Chapter 2 of *Best Evidence*).

Lane wasn't comfortable with this kind of evidence and with an argument based on physical science. Later, he dealt with the matter briefly in his book, but it never affected him the way it did Galanor (or me, for that matter). The "headsnap" had to be seen in motion—then you believed it. Otherwise, it had the quality of an abstraction and seemed to be about debatable perceptions. When Stewart pushed the point, Lane replied, "It's arguable."

Years later, Stewart and I reflected on why our reactions differed so from that of Lane. Stewart had been a math major; I, a graduate in Engineering Physics. Stewart told me that where he saw certainty based on science (and I shared his conviction), he thought that Lane, a lawyer, saw a sticky wicket with one expert arrayed against another. "If I was a great physicist," he told me, "I could have argued it, and he would have taken me more seriously."

Stewart noted that Lane, nonetheless, started using it in lectures. He liked to build his points around an occasional joke, so he reported the backward head-motion (not easily communicated since the film wasn't available) and would say: "This is a law of physics that even applies in Dallas."

In *Rush To Judgment,* Lane wrote:

When the bullet struck the President's head, as one can see from the photographs, he was thrown to his left and toward the rear of the limousine. How could the Commission explain the sudden violent move of the President's body directly to the left and to the rear? So long as the Commission maintained that the bullet came almost directly from the rear, it implied that the laws of physics vacated in this instance, because the President did not fall forward."[2]

Years later, Stewart commented, "If *Life* magazine had let any of the major networks show that film a few days after the assassination, no one would have believed that there were shots only from the rear." And, referring to how all this was subsequently "explained" by defenders when the film was finally available, Stewart said he didn't believe any of that would have counted for much in 1963. "There wouldn't have been any 'neurological effect' or any 'jet effect,'" he said, referring to attempts years later of Commission defenders to explain this violent backward motion.

I agree. The public would have been stunned and left to ponder how Oswald could have fired a fatal shot from the rear, when the film appeared to show the fatal shot striking from the front. Immediately it would have become a very serious political problem, but *Life* never permitted that debate to occur, back in 1963 or 1964, when it would have had political consequences.

Which brings us back to the strange behavior of *Life* as a corporation, and just who it was that signed the agreement with Abe Zapruder that put the film in *Life's* possession. The contract was signed by C. D. Jackson, *Life's* publisher, and just who was he?

C. D. Jackson

The diaries of columnist Drew Pearson, published in 1974, provide day to day observations of the journalist whose *Washington Merry Go Round* column made him the nation's number one political columnist.

Pearson seemed to know about everybody and everything. In particular, he was aware of the growing influence of the CIA in the country's foreign policy, and wasn't fooled by fronts. In post-World War II Europe, for example, Pearson suspected that the National Committee for a Free Europe (NCFE), ostensibly a private organization working to roll back the Iron Curtain (in connection with which Radio Free Europe was set up), was in fact getting funding from the CIA. A July 1958 entry contains information which—when viewed from the standpoint of the events of November 1963—raises the question of whether CIA money was somehow involved in the purchase of the Zapruder film:

> *Life* magazine is always pulling chestnuts out of the fire for the CIA; and I recall that C. D. Jackson of the Time-Life empire, was the man who arranged for the CIA to finance the Freedom Balloons. ([This was] a plan to release roughly 2,000 "freedom balloons" a day, which would fly over Communist controlled countries in Eastern Europe). C. D. Jackson, Harold Stassen, and the other boys who went with me to Germany and spent money like water, while I paid my own way. I was always suspicious that a lot of dough was coming from unexplained quarters and didn't learn until sometime later that the CIA was footing the bill.[3]

C. D. Jackson, closely connected with Luce, and someone who worked closely with the CIA in the past, was the person whose name is directly connected with the purchase of the Zapruder film on 23 November 1963.

An important point must be made here. If *Life* had purchased the film, distributed it, and made a load of money off it, then the controversy (had there been one) would have concerned economic favoritism, such as whether Jackson, exploiting past government connections (his service under Eisenhower, and his friendship with former CIA Director Allen Dulles), had obtained this unique historic footage by using his government connections to out-maneuver his competitors.

But nothing of the sort occurred here and, indeed, an entirely different situation prevailed. *Life* purchased the film for $50,000 ($300,000 in 2003 money) on Saturday, 23 November—in a contract that still permitted Zapruder to sell the film as a movie (which would have permitted the public broadcast of the fatal shot, in motion) as long as he waited until *after* 29 November. But then, on Monday, 25 November, the deal changed, fundamentally. *Life* agreed to pay three times as much money ($150,000), and the contract was revised. *Life* purchased "all rights"—motion picture as well as print rights—and then assiduously followed a policy that kept the film from surfacing for another 10 years. In its own internal documents, *Life* talks of its policy of prohibiting duplication (even at the National Archives) in order to "maintain control" over the film. "Maintaining control" would have been perfectly legitimate if, by that phrase, the policy was directed at preventing *Life* from getting ripped off by competitors wanting the film for their own magazines and news broadcasts, without proper remuneration. But that wasn't the case at all.

Instead, by 25 November 1963, C. D. Jackson purchased both the actual film—as well as "all rights" to it—for nearly a million dollars (in 2003 dollars) and then failed to utilize the rights that were purchased (i.e., failed to "exploit the rights," to use standard movie-business language) in order to maximize *Life's* return on its extraordinary investment.

This was most *un*-capitalistic behavior for someone steeped in free enterprise and the American way, certainly a hallmark of *Life*, a Luce publication. Indeed, it would appear that *Life* behaved in a manner that was most unusual, if not peculiar, *Life* not being an eleemosynary—a charitable—institution. So what was going on here?

Since, as Pearson wrote, *Life* was "always pulling chestnuts out of the fire for the CIA," the question arises as to whether the Zapruder film represented such a "chestnut," and whether once again—this time in November 1963—C. D Jackson was performing true to form. An important distinction must be made at this juncture: it would be most unfair to implicate the entire *Life* operation. Reporters such as Ed Kearn and Loudon Wainright did their jobs admirably. As the contract with Zapruder makes clear, the peculiar goings-on concern the "corporate" level and the specific individual who was involved in the film's purchase: C. D. Jackson, one of former CIA Director Allen Dulles' close friends and associates.

The Changed Captions Regarding the Head Shot

When the Warren Report was released in September 1964, *Life* went to press with an issue—dated 2 October 1964—devoted to the Commission's findings. That issue was the first to contain Zapruder frames since the 29 November 1963 edition, and the *Life* Memorial Edition of early December 1963. It then became apparent that (as I reported in *Best Evidence)* something unusual was going on with regard to the captioning of the pictures.

The 2 October issue carried a selection of eight Zapruder frames, each occupying a full half page. One of them, frame 323, showed Kennedy's head and shoulders (after being driven backward) touching the rear seat of the car. It was published along with a caption saying it depicted Kennedy's head "snapping to one side", a reasonably truthful statement. Continuing from *Best Evidence*: "However, there was another version of *Life* on the stands which differed from the first only in this particular picture and caption. Frame 323 had been withdrawn, frame 313 substituted, and the caption changed to indicate it showed the head exploding 'forward', demonstrating that the shot struck from behind. To this day, it is a mystery how that last-minute change came about."

In fact, it is more than just a minor mystery. It is a mystery of the first rank. It is unheard of to "break a plate" in the middle of a press run, and the order for such a thing could only "come from corporate." Ed Kearn wrote a letter to that effect to researcher

Vincent Salandria—he didn't know how such a thing had occurred, and he worked there. Here were the two *Life* captions:

Caption for Picture 6 (when it contained frame 323):

(a) *The assassin's shot struck the right rear portion of the President's skull, causing a massive wound and snapping his head to one side.*

Caption for Picture 6, as revised (when it contained 313, showing the red blob at the front of the head):

(b) *The direction from which shots came was established by this picture taken at instant bullet struck the rear of the President's head and, passing through, caused the front part of his skull to explode forward.*

The first caption (a) referred to the head snap and (b) was subject to the possible interpretation that the President was struck from the right side, the direction of the grassy knoll. The second caption utilized the red "blob" at the front of JFK's head as evidence of exit. The way that the caption was written left no doubt about its purpose: *to establish the rearward source for this shot.*

Paul Hoch developed a matrix showing there were five different versions of *Life* on the stand, as the caption was replaced and "caught up with" the replaced picture. He also elicited a letter dated 7 December 1964, from one "Beverly Mitchell," writing "for the editors," seeking to explain the difference between the two issues by invoking a rather irrelevant matter:

> In the process of condensing Congressman Ford's article and editing it for publication, an inaccurate impression of the manner in which Lee Oswald was finally apprehended was given in the earlier version which you have. When this became evident, we stopped our presses and made the change you noted."

This was not a plausible explanation for stopping the press.

The Reversal of Two Frames in Warren Commission Exhibit 885

Shortly after the release of the 26 volumes, first generation researcher Ray Marcus discovered that (quoting from *Best Evidence*) "as reproduced in the twenty-six volumes, the two frames immediately following frame 313 were reversed. Anybody unaware of this would get confusing results if he (or she) used these reproductions to analyze the film. Several months later, I wrote a letter to the FBI which brought a reply from Director Hoover acknowledging the reversal and describing it as 'a printing error.'"

In fact, there is slightly more to the story. I was employed at North American Aviation at the time, had a security clearance, and was worried about writing the FBI about such a matter. So after drafting the letter I asked my girlfriend, Judy Schmidt, to sign it. Dated 6 December 1965, it was written in a very simple naïve style, and was addressed to "Lyndall Shaneyfelt," the FBI's photo expert.

"I have been doing some research in the 26 volumes," it said, "and recently noticed what I think is a small error in the labeling of two Zapruder frames in CE 885 in Volume 18. Since these volumes constitute an extremely important document, I thought I should bring this to your attention." I then went through Marcus' readily understood argument demonstrating the reversal.

A few weeks later, Judy came to the doorway holding an envelope between her fingers, as if were a dead bug. The return address was "Federal Bureau of Investigation" and inside, to my considerable surprise, was a letter signed "John Edgar Hoover", the

FBI Director himself: "You are correct in the observation that frames labeled 314 and 315 of Commission Exhibit 885 are transposed in Volume 18 as noted in your letter. This is a printing error and does not exist in the actual Commission Exhibit."

Well, ok; but it sure did cause confusion to anyone attempting to analyze the motion of the President's head following the impact at 313.

The Splice at Frame 212

When the 26 volumes of the Warren Commission first became available at the Government Printing Office in November 1964—about 10 weeks after the release of the Warren Report—a small but hardy band of individuals (sometimes called the "first generation researchers") began going over them with a fine tooth comb.

The first fifteen volumes contained the testimony of the 552 witnesses; the last 10—Volumes 16 through 26—were Warren Commission Exhibits, and included a wide variety of material: the entire Dallas Police File on the JFK case, State Department reports concerning Oswald's Russian sojourn, numerous FBI and Secret reports, etcetera. The 26 volumes were the butt of jokes, since they contained such bizarre items as Jack Ruby's mother's dental charts (which Mark Lane said wouldn't be relevant even if Ruby had bitten Oswald to death) as well as microphotographs of Oswald's pubic hairs (because the FBI was attempting to determine whether Oswald's rifle was in a particular blanket).

One of the most closely studied exhibits was Warren Commission Exhibit 885, black and white reproductions of frames of the Zapruder film, published two to a page, extending from frame 171 to 334.

Many researchers studied these frames—the only readily available way to study what the Zapruder film showed—and soon it was discovered that there was a splice in the film at frame 212. As I wrote in *Best Evidence*, "This was clearly observable on the sequence of individual Zapruder frames published as Exhibit 885. The [splice occurred] just as the President was about to disappear from view behind a highway sign, where the Commission said the first shot struck." The break was even obvious from the captions, which read: . . .205, 206, 207, 212, 213, etc.

As students of the case know, if one turns to page 19 of Volume 18, it is all readily visible: on the bottom is a frame captioned 212, showing a thick horizontal black line. When first viewing this frame, one does a double-take, because a tree grows up out of the ground, stops in midair, and then—shifted laterally—continues "growing" in the part of the frame above the splice line.

I bought my own set of the 26 volumes around May of 1965, at which time I was an engineering graduate student at UCLA (having already graduated from Cornell in Engineering Physics, Class of 1962). Having become quite interested in the Warren Report I began studying these frames in detail. I soon learned that one of the Warren Commission staff attorneys, Wesley Liebeler, was an assistant professor at the UCLA Law School.

On 12 October 1965, I walked over to the Law School, proceeded to Liebeler's office and introduced myself. It was immediately obvious that we had something in common—there, stretching across a bookshelf, was his set of the 26 volumes. It was, I said, as if were members of the same secret fraternity.

Liebeler, who died last year in a plane crash, was a very funny man—a University of Chicago Law School graduate who was somewhat right wing, politically (in 1964 language: a Barry Goldwater conservative) and a specialist in anti-trust law.

In *Best Evidence*, I wrote of that first meeting, and what happened when I took Volume 18 off the shelf, turned to page 19, and readily demonstrated that there was a splice in the published portion of the Zapruder film.

Liebeler was rather astonished

In the foreground of the field of view was the Stemmons Freeway sign, and I presented the splice as being possibly related to the hypothesis that a bullet had perhaps hit the sign. Looking back decades later, I no longer believe this, but it was eminently plausible at the time and seemed to support the general idea—a "hypothesis" if you will—that the splice had something to do with "hiding something" on Dealey Plaza. Specifically, since the sign appeared to have been moved and replaced after the assassination, it seemed reasonable, namely: that concealing filmed evidence of that impact—perhaps a bullet hole or other related damage—was what the splice was all about.

Meanwhile, Liebeler took a look at Volume 18, practically did a double-take, and then just stared at the page, at the clearly visible splice in frame 212 where a thick black horizontal line ran across the center of the frame where the film had been cut, frames removed, and the two ends spliced together. As I reported in *Best Evidence*, "My suspicions were so pronounced, however, that I was skeptical. How was it possible that a Warren Commission attorney could be unaware that the film was spliced? The information came from the Commission's own evidence. [So] I turned to Liebeler, who seemed quite taken aback and was studying the frames intensely, and asked him if he was acting, adding that it wasn't necessary to put on an act for my benefit. 'Honest, no!' he exclaimed, adding that he had definitely not known about the splice before.'"

Although much of our conversation centered on whether the sign had been hit by a bullet, Liebeler appeared concerned about something more fundamental.

How did it get there?

How come they hadn't been told about this? How could there be a splice in the official evidence? Clearly, the FBI knew: the FBI had numbered the frames, and the sequence of captions showed they were aware: "205", "206", "207", and then "212". So why was there no FBI report on this matter? No explanation?

Then came a touch of Liebeler's black humor. Again, from *Best Evidence*: "'The splice,' he remarked, was a 'very unlawyerlike' way of handling evidence, musing that if he were 'doing it,' he certainly would not have published the frame with the splice but simply omitted that one and renumbered the rest in sequence."

As I remember even to this day, Liebeler took the whole thing rather seriously. Again, from *Best Evidence*:

> Liebeler announced then and there he would write to J. Lee Rankin, the former U.S. Solicitor General who [had been] the Commission's General Counsel. He seemed genuinely concerned and even took my name and telephone number so he could contact me later, after he had heard from Rankin.

> "Yesterday afternoon," began Liebeler's letter of 13 October 1965, to J. Lee Rankin, "a graduate student in the [Engineering] Department here at UCLA walked into my office to discuss some work he [had] been doing on the Report. He had several interesting theories, supporting evidence for which he promised to provide in the future. He did make one point, however, during the course of the conversation that I think deserves some attention."

Liebeler then went into a detailed description of the splice, including a number of other, possibly related, facts I had shown him the day before. "If there is a ready explanation for the omission of the frames," his letter concluded, "I would certainly be relieved to know what it is. If there is none, I think it would be appropriate for us to raise this matter formally with the FBI."[5]

Some weeks later, when I visited his office again, he tossed some letters at me saying, "here, read these." The response had arrived—in the form of two replies to his letter. One was a detailed response from Norman Redlich, Rankin's special assistant during the Commission's investigation (to whom Liebeler had sent a copy of his letter); the other, a brief letter from J. Lee Rankin. The entire experience was fast becoming a crash course on how the Warren Commission had functioned, especially when evidence contrary to their lone-assassin conclusion arose.

Rankin's letter, just five sentences long, said he had seen Redlich's reply and ". . . [it] seemed to dispose of the matter to me. I confess I am reluctant to dig into the matter further. . ."[6] How had Redlich "disposed" of it? In the following, almost humorous, manner. The sign in the foreground, he wrote, could not have been hit by a bullet. And why was that?

Redlich dealt with each side of the sign separately. A bullet could not have struck the sign from the Depository side, he said, because Oswald had fired just three shots and the Commission had accounted for all of them. A bullet could not have struck from the grassy-knoll side because Oswald was firing from the other side, the side of the Texas School Book Depository.[7]

Such circular reasoning seemed comical enough, but Redlich carried it one step further as he addressed the more fundamental issue of the splice and four missing frames. He explained: "I would suspect that the frames you have in mind were deleted. . . because. . . they were of little value because during those frames the Presidential limousine was almost completely hidden by the sign."[8] He concluded that the issues raised in Liebeler's letter did "not warrant any request to the FBI for an investigation, either formal or otherwise." To my surprise Rankin closed his own letter with a gibe at Liebeler: "I am happy to learn that you are enjoying life as a law professor and I am looking forward to seeing some of your writing in the legal periodical when you find time to make contributions of that kind."[9]

My Attempt to Communicate with Herbert Orth

On 25 November 1965, I sent a telegram to the assistant head of photography at the *Life* Photolab, Herbert Orth. It was now the "second anniversary" of JFK's death, there was the usual commemorative activity, and I was hoping to get an answer from *Life* regarding the splices. A yellowed confirmation copy is still in my files:

Am graduate student UCLA engaged research Re Warren Report. Have deadline to meet. Must document this promptly.

Question 1: Was there any interruption in the sequence of frames of the color slide which you made up from the Zapruder film and gave to the Warren Commission?

Question 2: Were any copies of the Zapruder film that you gave to the WC spliced or damaged in any frames corresponding to those in the slide sequence?

Question 3: Was ending point of slide sequence 334 or 434? Reply night letter collect.

I didn't know what to expect, but I kept my eye peeled for an envelope from *Life* magazine.

To my surprise, an envelope did arrive—a plain envelope, without a return address—a most peculiar and unprofessional way to answer a citizen's inquiry—and inside on a plain white piece of paper (again, no letterhead) was a typed note:

26 November 1965

Dear Mr. Lifton:
I believe my testimony is a matter of public record. I am very sorry, but there is nothing further I can add.

Sincerely,
Herbert Orth

There was one problem with this response: Herbert Orth never testified. Although he was mentioned by FBI expert Shaneyfelt as having come to Washington and shown the staff the Zapruder film, he never appeared as a witness, so why say otherwise? And why the secrecy and evasiveness? Why not a letter on a *Life* letterhead, signed by Orth, at least stating something that was true?

As it turns out, the splice in what purports to be the original copy of the Zapruder film is *extremely* significant, but not for the reasons I thought in 1965 (a bullet hitting the sign). But going further with that discussion requires waiting until we reach 1969 (in our narrative) when it was discovered there was a *second* splice in the film, located in the earlier unpublished portion of the film, which is a discussion we will get to shortly.

Meanwhile, the plainly visible splice illustrates something very important about the JFK case: that often, significant evidence might be "hiding in plain sight." Readers of *Best Evidence* know this from my discovery in an FBI report (in the Commission's own files) the statement made by two agents who attended the Bethesda autopsy that, at the outset, it was "apparent" that there had been "surgery of the head area, namely, in the top of the skull."

In that case, the issue at hand was whether the President's wounds had been altered. Here, the issue was the cause and meaning of a splice in critical motion picture film evidence—a film utilized as a "clock". The splice apparently had gone unnoticed by the entire Commission staff and wasn't found until after the Report's publication when it was discovered by JFK researchers. Liebeler first heard about it from me, so no, I don't think Liebeler was acting. He and his fellow attorneys—and possibly even some in the FBI—did not realize the film had this splice, and so the matter was never properly investigated.

As I came to realize later—decades later, in fact—the splice is one of the more important indicators that the 8 mm film then held in a vault at *Life* was almost certainly a forgery and not the camera original.

1966: The opportunity to write for Ramparts

As I described in Chapter 2 of *Best Evidence*, the opportunity arose in the Spring of 1966 to write for *Ramparts* magazine, and my goal was to get a famous physicist to stand behind the headsnap

A friend of mine, Bruce Wintstein, attended Cal Tech and was a student of Dr. Richard Feynman. Bruce told Feynman about the Z film, and he consented to a meeting, which went on for about an hour.

When I told Feynman that JFK's head went backwards in response to the head shot, he took out a ruler to verify what I had said, and it was at that time that I learned I had made a small but significant error: that while the head indeed went to the rear *after* 313, it went forward by an inch or two between frame 312 (the last pre-impact frame, according to the film) and 313 (the first post-impact frame).

As a consequence, the notion of getting Feynman to stand behind the headsnap argument was no longer feasible.

The "double motion" on the Z film—the slight forward motion followed by a backwards slam—turns out to be important in understanding why certain researchers concluded that JFK had been struck in the head twice, once from behind and once from the front. [*Editor's note*: See the Prologue.]

Whether this is or is not valid ultimately depends on what the President's head wounds were immediately after he was shot; and that, of course, depends on the observations from Parkland Hospital (and Bethesda, too, if the wounds were unaltered).

As I came to realize years later, there was another explanation for that "small forward motion". If the film was altered—and specifically, if frames were deleted at that point (a subject to be discussed in detail soon)—then that "forward motion" was simply the result of film editing and frame deletion and had nothing to do with the impact of any bullet.

Meanwhile, another problem was nagging at me.

The Back of the Head

One after another after another, just about every Dallas doctor and nurse testified that (a) there was a wound at the back of the President's head, and (b) it was an exit. And yet . . . .

Amongst the published frames showing the head wounding was frame number 321 and 323, in which the back of JFK's head could be seen rather clearly, because it was facing the Zapruder camera. But there was little to see because the back of the head seemed all blacked out. In frame after frame, this seemed to be the case.

Fall of 1966: First Wave of Books

The fall of 1966 was a time when the conclusions of the Warren Commission were a subject of major public debate. The first books critical of *The Warren Report* had been published. *The Warren Report* was in the news with the same intensity as, say, the war in Iraq today. Every day there seemed to be another story about Dallas.

And it was about this time that Josiah Thompson, an assistant professor of philosophy at Haverford and certainly a skeptic of the Warren Commission conclusions, began working on the case and was employed by *Life* as a consultant.

1967: Life admits the splice.

In early 1967, *Life* magazine released a statement that accounted for the splice in the Zapruder film. I first heard about it when it was published in the *Newsweek* of 6 February 1967.

Gone was the serious reaction that I had personally witnessed in October 1965. Now Liebeler was telling Newsweek the following rather glib explanation:

Solved: The Mystery of the Missing Frames

The mystery of the missing frames in the published movie record of President Kennedy's assassination has been solved, according to a lawyer who served on the staff of the Warren Commission. Wesley J. Liebeler, now a UCLA law professor, says the frames (Nos. 208, 209, 210, 211), missing from Volume 18 of the commission report, were destroyed accidentally by *Life* magazine photo lab technicians working on the original film which *Life* bought from Dallas manufacturer and movie buff Abraham Zapruder.

Curiously, the technicians were never produced. Had *Life* produced such a person, had he made a statement, perhaps a tearful apology about the day he dropped the film and broke it, that would have been great. But that never happened.

Just consider a comparable situation in 2003. The cable networks would be vying for interviews, they would be walking alongside him as he left the Time-Life building in Rockefeller Plaza, they would want to know how he felt having broken the film. They would interview his superiors to find out if he was being fired, and if not, why not.

None of this happened in 1967. Absolutely nothing. *Life* put out the "explanation," and everybody simply accepted it.

But Time-Life held back another rather important fact: *that wasn't the only splice in the film*. There was another splice down at 155, but that wasn't part of the frames published by the Warren Commission and that wouldn't be discovered until 1969. More on that later.

1967: Life Refuses CBS Access to the Zapruder Film

In the fall of 1966, CBS began a study of *The Warren Report* which, when broadcast in June of 1967, was largely supportive.

It was now three years after the assassination, and CBS wanted the film—and was willing to pay for it.

But *Life* refused. Here, from the transcript of the fourth (and final) program, is what CBS's Walter Cronkite said about the situation:

> There is one further piece of evidence which we feel must now be made available to the entire public: Abraham's Zapruder's film of the actual assassination. The original is now the private property of *Life* magazine. A *Life* executive refused CBS News permission to show you that film at any price, on the ground that it is, "an invaluable asset of Time, Inc."

> And that, even though these broadcasts have demonstrated that the film may contain vital undiscovered clues to the assassination.

> *Life*'s decision means you cannot see the Zapruder film in its proper form, as motion picture film. We believe that the Zapruder film is an invaluable asset, not of Time, Inc., but of the people of the United States.

1967: Attempt to write about the forward high angle shot.

I don't want to bore the reader with the details, but back in 1967, I too viewed the Z film as "absolute truth" and sought explanations for everything in terms of Newton's laws. So how—if JFK was shot from the front—could one explain this forward motion of just an inch or two? I thought it was a clockwise rotation, wrote a paper about it, and distributed it to others. Paul Hoch published it as "The forward high angle shot?" in an anthology. No matter that I couldn't pinpoint where such a shooter might be located. I was dead serious about the physics: this was the only explanation. Or so it seemed. It wouldn't be for another few years before I realized that the Zapruder film wasn't sacrosanct; *that it had been edited*, which led to new explanations for that "forward motion" between 312 and 313; and also for the manner in which the President's head then snapped "violently backwards". It wasn't about bullets, but about deleted film frames.

1966-67: Meanwhile, back at UCLA: Liebeler's Memo to Warren

As described in *Best Evidence,* Liebeler taught a class on *The Warren Report* during the 1966-67 school year. In October, I had discovered the first evidence of JFK's wounds having been altered; and that resulted in Liebeler writing a memo to Chief Justice Warren, all other Commissioners and attorneys, plus the Justice Department and Kennedy family attorney Burke Marshall.

Although a devil's advocate in class, I was now in a most unusual position, because we were keeping a secret of sorts.

No matter that Liebeler's memo was apparently being ignored. The fact is Liebeler took it seriously, I could talk to him about it, privately (and did). Moreover, you don't go through something like this without it becoming an important learning experience, and that's what happened. It was as if I was getting tutored in various aspects of criminal law, and politics. It was a heady mix.

I must admit that I didn't fully comprehend the level on which Liebeler was reacting, either to the splice in the film or the evidence that the body had been altered. In both cases, my reaction had focused on the issue of a "second shooter"; Liebeler's, on the integrity of the evidence.

Take the situation with the sign, for instance, and the possibility it was struck. I'm sure Liebeler was interested in that (as a hypothesis), but there was a much deeper level on which he reacted, and it took me a while to understand.

Liebeler seemed focused on *the integrity of the evidence.* Essentially, if I can put words into his mouth, his was saying: "What the hell is a splice doing in our evidence?" Not, "Is there a second shooter?" or "Where is he firing from?" But: "This is evidence; who altered our record?"

He had had the same reaction regarding the business of altered wounds—based on the fact that the two FBI agents who attended the autopsy reported that it was "apparent" that there had been "surgery of the head area, namely, in the top of the skull." It wasn't that Liebeler necessarily believed it was true, simply because they wrote it, but *he wanted to know why any such thing was stated in that FBI report.* Why hadn't it been investigated; why had it sailed right by fellow staff attorney Arlen Specter, whose areas of responsibility was the autopsy? Moreover, even if it was true, it was clear that Liebeler didn't view it as evidence of a "second assassin.," but rather *evidence that the autopsy protocol had been falsified.*

For some six weeks after my initial discovery, I didn't have this perspective, and so I didn't "get it." My view was that of an assassination buff, not an attorney. Readers can read about my struggle to understand all this in *Best Evidence,* and it is analogous to the situation with the splice in the film or the wider issue of whether the film was altered.

Back in the fall of 1966, if someone asked me: "Well, what does it mean to change a wound?", I probably would have answered, "That's how they're hiding a second shooter!"

Putting aside the issue of just who "they" were, the point is that to me (and to many researchers), the "second shooter" *was* the conspiracy. The JFK conspiracy was a "conspiracy of shooters", a conspiracy evident to me but which had been willfully ignored by the Warren Commission. It took me a while to outgrow that view, which I now see as rather sophomoric, and I didn't do it completely on my own. Liebeler played a major role in my "education" in these matters, and so did others.

There was a very attractive woman in the law school of whom Liebeler was obviously fond. She was Susan Wittenberg. She and Liebeler fell in love and a year or two later they were married.

But at the time, Liebeler would "call Susan" the same way a President would call in a top advisor whenever he had a crisis. And so it was that Liebeler "called Susan" when I found the surgery statement. For a number of days, I didn't "get it." The engineer in me kept insisting on seeing "surgery" (the alteration of wounds) as the mechanical way to hide a second shooter, rather than *the overt act of a separate conspiracy, an "obstruction of justice" that went to the heart of the case.*

To this day, I have this image of Susan standing before me, next to Liebeler, with me prattling on about that second shooter, and Susan in effect saying, "Don't you understand what this means?!"

And frankly, I didn't. But they did. They *both* did.

Well then, *just what was it that they understood that I seemed not to?*

Gradually, it dawned. As lawyers, they understood. This was no longer about a "second shooter"; this was about the entire system; but primarily *fraud in the evidence.* Fraud in the evidence presented to a Presidential Commission, a Commission that had decreed that Oswald shot Kennedy. That conclusion was rooted in this autopsy, the Bethesda autopsy. It was a conclusion which—if these autopsy conclusions were false, if this was a "politically correct" autopsy—was at the heart of a storybook version of the assassination, one explaining the transition from Kennedy to Johnson in a manner largely denuded of political meaning.

But all this was untrue if there was fraud in the evidence. It was like buying a house and finding a plumbing problem in the bathroom. That might be repairable, but suppose fraud was discovered in the escrow? Then the whole deal would be off.

My very dear friend—the late Bernard Kenton, then pursuing his Ph.D. in physics— also shook his head at my initial inability to grasp all this. But he was politically radical. He had immediately understood the wider implications: *that if wounds were altered, it was no longer about a second shooter.* Who cared about that? Now it was about government involvement in altering evidence, in creating "false facts" for a legal inquiry. Whether it was about wounds being altered or a film being altered, the principles were the same.

So I had a number of friends perplexed at my inability to see the issue as they did, who in effect shook me by the shoulders and said, "Don't you get it? It's not about a second shooter—*anymore.*" Years later, I realized it was as if I had been swimming in the shallow end of the kiddie pool; and now it was time to grow up.

This was about the system, the society we lived in, it was about fraud in the evidence, and the political implications of that, and it took me a few weeks to "get it."

I mention this because of the almost completely analogous situation between the body and the film. The particulars are different, but the principle is the same. When one gets involved in fakery in the evidence, it is so easy to get sidetracked and to think the issue is some game of hide-and-seek with a second shooter—to miss what is actually at stake.

That's what happened to me—at least for a while. And I persisted in this naiveté for a few weeks before I finally caught on, before I realized that to a lawyer, everything had to do with *the process of fact finding* and the integrity of that process. It was similar to a student being judged on an examination. Often, the issue is not whether the correct answer has been produced, but how that answer was arrived at. To state it differently, I had a lot of trouble separating the substantive from the procedural. I was a detective, I thought; I wanted to know answers. Who cared about process?

I remember an important turning point in my own self education on these matters. I remember visiting another professor on the same floor, Litwin, who taught evidence. He had seen me in and out of Liebeler's office, so my being on that floor of the Law building was no big surprise.

Fraud in the Evidence

"Look," I said, "I don't understand something, and I'm coming into your office as a laymen, so you can explain this to me." I proceeded to lay out my confusion: "Hypothetically, suppose I go into the evidence cabinet of the police department, and suppose I take out the evidence and change it in some way. What law does that violate? Explain it to me."

I got back a brief but punchy lecture concerning a legal word to which I hadn't paid proper attention, and a new crime which (to me at least) I knew little: "obstruction of justice."

The body was evidence; and if the body was altered (i.e., if the wounds were altered), then the gun, the shells, etc.—all of it lost its "relevance." It no longer could be "connected up"—at least properly—to the evidence at the sniper's nest. So the integrity of the body was crucial, it served as a legal "connecting link" of sorts to the evidence on the sixth floor window. *If the body was altered, then the sniper's nest evidence was no longer "relevant".* A peculiar, neutral-sound term, but one loaded with meaning if the autopsy had been falsified. If that were so, then the key evidence against Oswald went down the drain. Why? Because it was no longer "relevant."

Litwin advised me to read books on evidence, and, because the current ones were all checked out by UCLA law students, I ended up educated myself by reading—indeed, studying—a classic, *Wigmore on Evidence.*

Moreover, from all this I also learned that *the crime of altering evidence might be catalogued as an "obstruction of justice";* also, that that "obstruction" might or might not be viewed as a central part of a conspiracy to murder someone.

So if someone altered a wound on JFK's body, that was a crime not because it violated some law about desecrating the dead but because such an alteration represented *an obstruction of justice.* That was the name, the legal name, for the larger issue involved.

Now I had a new word in my vocabulary, and a whole new series of concepts; and a new way of looking at the Warren Commission and its evidence, and the political process in which—implicitly at least—it was involved: sanctioning the legitimacy of the Presidency of Lyndon Johnson; verifying that the story told by the authorities as to the way JFK had met his death was true, that it really was all about "a man in a building who shot a man in a car". Nothing more than that.

Of central importance: the concept of "relevance" (in the legal sense) and that had to do with process—the process of fact-finding; of "connecting the dots" (to use layman's language); or, to use lawyer-talk, of "connecting" the murder on Elm Street with the evidence at the sniper's nest. For a while, I resisted. The scientist in me didn't think this way. I didn't think in terms of legal mumbo jumbo, of "relevance." I was like a detective and thought in rather concrete terms. I just wanted to know: Where are the shooters? Because to me "the shooters" defined the conspiracy.

As I came to realize, that wouldn't work. It wasn't adequate. To a legal fact finding situation, process is everything. The integrity of the process is related to the validity of the facts.

So I gradually came to understand Liebeler's thinking and even his vocabulary. To someone like Liebeler, you couldn't just have an unexplained splice show up in the film and say, "Ho hum. Oh well, what could have happened in 2/18ths of a second, anyway? Oh, maybe the sign was hit. Well, so what? What's the big deal?"

To state the matter somewhat differently, the issue wasn't: "Did a bullet hit the sign?" The issue was: "How the hell did a splice get into our evidence?! What's it doing there?"

And, unspoken at least: "What facts are being changed by this? Might this be an obstruction of justice?"

Moreover, as I would come to realize years later—indeed, decades later—these two splices in the so-called original Zapruder film almost certainly had nothing to do with "editing out" events on Dealey Plaza. If the film was altered, it had been edited optically. First it had been enlarged to 16 mm or 35 mm, the format in which professional editors worked (back in 1963); once in that format, it had been edited using standard techniques and equipment (an optical printer) employed by professional film editors in Hollywood, circa 1963. Moreover, the presence of these two splices were not connected with "concealing" anything on Dealey Plaza, but were part of the process of creating a bogus 8 mm "original."

Life's Zapruder Slides Are Brought to Los Angeles

Around 1967, Liebeler ordered the 4 x 5 inch slides from *Life* magazine for use by students in his class. They were to be held at the Beverly Hills office of Time-Life, and members of his class could go over and view them.

It had been bugging me that more detail didn't seem to be visible on the back of JFK's head, on the photos as published in *Life* magazine. Perhaps an editor airbrushed it out?

Now we had the actual slides, and so I looked at them and found, to my surprise, that they were black there, too! I had gotten one step closer to the source—the actual image on the 8 mm film. This darkness wasn't an artifact of the magazine's publication; it was that way on the source material. The question still remained: perhaps the slides had been altered, for some editorial reason, up at *Life*?

By this time I had learned what would be required to get to the bottom of all this: examine the original film on some kind of a viewing table, because I wanted to know, did the original film contain an actual mechanical splice or not? And I also wondered, was it possible that the so-called "original" contained just a picture of a splice (in which case it would be a copy)? So pursuing these matters, I realized the critical importance of having access to the original or (at least) a high quality copy made directly from the original.

But getting access to the original seemed out of the question. *Life* would never permit such an examination. As to examining a copy, the closest thing to that seemed to be these 4x5 inch transparencies that were now at the Beverly Hills office of Time-Life, which anyone in Liebeler's class could examine.

Josiah Thompson in New York

Meanwhile, in New York City, Josiah Thompson was having his own experiences with the film. Being employed as a *Life* consultant starting on 31 October 1966, he had the privilege of having access to 35 millimeter slides plus 4 x 5 inch transparencies from their Zapruder slide set, and he had an 8 mm copy of the film to examine as well. Thompson could study these materials in detail, and thoroughly understood how important they were to any analysis.

But as far as I can tell, Thompson had no interest in issues of authenticity. When it came to the Zapruder slides, that simply never occurred to him—nor, in fairness to Thompson, do I believe it occurred to any other researcher back then that any of this material derived from a doctored film. At least not in 1966. Back then, Thompson was concerned about a very practical matter. He wanted to get *Life's* permission to get some of these Zapruder fames published in his book. So, driven by the idea that "getting the truth out" was more important than the technicalities, Thompson set out on a daring course: he decided to secretly photograph the materials, which were kept "from time to time" (quoting court documents) in the desk of co-worker Ed Kearn. From the court documents:

> On November 18, 1966, Kern left his office at the end of the business day. Thompson was there and remained there alone after Kern had gone. Kern returned to his office in the late evening of the same day for some papers. It is undisputed that Kern then saw Thompson, alone, with his own camera making copies of Zapruder frames.

Subsequently, when Thompson couldn't obtain permission from *Life* to use frames for his book, an artist was employed to make fairly accurate sketches of what the frames showed. [*Editor's note*: See Appendix F.]

Looking backwards, I find this very interesting. Thompson was photographing the Zapruder film in the office of a *Life* editor, while I was having my own adventures with a hidden camera, and for similar reasons: in each case, someone had something we considered vital and that they would let us see privately, but not provide copies to disseminate publicly. In my case, it was the Liebeler Memorandum of 8 November 1966.

Liebeler had notified Chief Justice Warren, the former Warren Commission staff, and the Justice Department, via memorandum, of the surgery statement in the FBI report, but he wouldn't let me have a copy. So I had no way of communicating to others something I was most excited about: that based on meetings with me, and certain discoveries I had made, Liebeler had communicated to the Chief Justice of the United States, all former members of the Commission and the staff, plus the Justice Department and the Kennedy family attorney, the fact that the FBI report contained a statement that the President's head wounds had been altered. Liebeler was adamant: no, he would not give me a copy of the memo; but yes, he would let me look at it, alone, in his office.

I went to a camera store and rented a Minox camera, then kept my appointment with Liebeler. He locked me in his office, and went to teach a class. I took out the Minox and set to work photographing the memo that had just gone out to Chief Justice Warren with my name in it, just as Thompson, on the east coast, was clicking away photographing copies of *Life's* Zapruder's slides and transparencies.

There is a certain symmetry to the situation: On the east coast, up on the 30th floor of Rockefeller Center, Thompson was photographing slides of the Z film; on the west coast, I was copying Liebeler's memo. We were both dealing with the most important items of evidence in the case—me, with the body; Thompson, with the film—which, as it turns out, is truly important because it is a series of photographs of Kennedy's body, albeit taken at camera speed and at the time of his death.

For this, when his book appeared, he was sued, and essentially lost all the royalties of his book.

However, the Thompson lawsuit turned out to be important, because a number of documents concerning the sale of the film became a matter of court record. (and we will come back to these matters later). But it's because of Thompson's lawsuit that we have the *Life*-Zapruder contract, the one that reveals that Zapruder was paid $150,000, and in $25,000 annual payments that went out to January 1968.

Meanwhile, Liebeler's memorandum went to the Justice Department, and it became available under the Freedom of Information Act there (and is also available, I have learned, at the Gerald Ford Library and the Russell Library, since both Russell and Ford, as members of the Commission, were sent copies).

But back to Josiah Thompson. I bring Josiah Thompson into the story for another reason at this point. He is our compass to why so many (like him) were totally convinced—I am tempted to say, "seduced by the idea"—that the Z film was the closest thing to absolute truth, a veritable picture of reality unfolding before their eyes.

It was, after all, the vehicle by which they proved conspiracy.

And what conspiracy was that? The conspiracy of "multiple shooters", of course.

Thompson is one of those who typifies the view that the measure of "the conspiracy" is the number shooters, and here is the way he went about it—the way Josiah Thompson made a serious analytic error, one that many people make, and which is important to identify, if the evidence is to be properly analyzed.

November 1967, the publication of Six Seconds in Dallas

Thompson appreciated the film could function as a clock and wanted to make the argument that all of us now understood—that based on the available evidence, two shots had struck occupants of the limousine in less time than it took to fire the rifle twice. In "The Case for Three Assassins", a 30,000 word analysis I had written in July 1966, which became a *Ramparts magazine* cover story (January 1967 issue, with a big blue streamer on the cover), I had combined the timing issue with the head-snap analysis, noting that the "additional assassin" inferred in each case was located at entirely different locations (one to the front, the other to the rear) and came up with the snappy idea that "three assassins" killed JFK. Thompson traveled down the same path. But he simply ignored what had been published almost a year before, and *The Saturday Evening Post* of 2 December 1967 headlined, on its cover—and as if this was news—"Major New Study Shows Three Assassins Killed Kennedy".

How could an author permit the packaging of his ideas under the same headline as that used by another author and published eleven months before?

No matter. More important was something that appeared in Thompson's book: a drawing of the head wound as seen at Parkland Hospital by Dr. McClelland, a drawing based on Dr. McClelland's detailed medical description, and approved by McClelland prior to publication.

The wound was at the back of the head and about 5 x 7 cm (about 2-3/4 inches across).

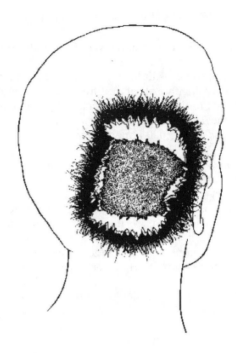

The McClelland diagram

It was of course completely different than what was observed at Bethesda.

By this time, of course, I was completely aware of the difference and was rather astonished at what Thompson made of it.

Apparently, he didn't understand that there was an anatomical difference between Parkland and Bethesda!

Instead, Josiah Thompson, a Ph.D. in philosophy and a man who writes well and has considerable analytic skills, made a major analytical gaffe. Instead of contrasting the two images, he combined them! And he wrote:

The pattern that emerges from this study of medical evidence is a dual one. From the Parkland doctors we get the picture of a bullet that struck the right front of the President's head. . . . ranged backward causing massive damage to the right brain hemisphere, sprung open the occipital and parietal bones, and exploded out over the rear of the limousine. From the Bethesda surgeons we get the picture of a bullet entering the rear of the President's head and driving forward. . . Putting the two pictures together we discern outlines of the double impact. First, a bullet from behind exploding forward, and in that same split second another bullet driving . . . [the] skull in the opposite direction.

As I wrote in *Best Evidence*: "This was the essence of the cross-fire theory to the head, but it was based on an analytic error. 'Putting the two pictures together' was incorrect. Both pertained to the same body, but to different times. Six hours separated those two observations."

To pursue this point a bit further. Just consider what would have happened if we had accurate medical photographs of the body in Dallas and Bethesda; and if, as the Dallas and Bethesda records indicate, these photographs depicted a completely different head wound at each of those locations. If Thompson viewed them side by side, and saw they were entirely different, would he—in that case—"put the pictures together" and conclude the President was the victim of a conspiracy of multiple shooters? Or would he say, "Hey, wait a minute! Who altered the head wounds? How come these two pictures are different?"

Its similar to the situation with the splice. When Liebeler first saw the splice, he was astonished. But his main concern was not (as mine was) whether the sign had been hit by a bullet; he was concerned with the larger issue of *who altered the evidence?*

In one of our conversations in late 1967, Liebeler expressed wonderment at the fact that Thompson didn't recognize the bifurcation between Dallas and Bethesda, that he could actually publish a diagram of the President's head wound in Dallas and not recognize the implications of it being different than the head wound at Bethesda! And so instead of asking, "Who altered the body?", Thompson focused on developing a theory about a cross-fire.

Using engineering language, I remember telling Liebeler, "He doesn't realize there's a time line here. He's left out the parameter of time."

Thompson's blunder

Liebeler and I had a somewhat contentious relationship, and although he wrote the memo to Warren, he never said he agreed with my theory. But every now and then he'd throw me a compliment; and on the occasion of my talking about Thompson's ignoring the time line, he did just that, flashing me a smile, and saying something like "exactly".

I understood; Liebeler understood. Josiah Thompson didn't.

And since Thompson's error is emblematic of the thinking of many to this day, its worth spelling out even further, because there's a whole history—in another area of human endeavor—of people who seemed unable to factor in the element of time. Biology.

It was as if Thompson was still living in this static universe in which facts stayed the way there were, were simply "gathered", and nothing changed with time. Dealing with Thompson in 1967 was something akin to a Darwinian attempting to deal with a pre-Darwinian biologist before 1859 and the publication of *The Origin of Species*. There were the birds and the bees and the flowers. They were simply there. Nothing had changed. And it was the job of the JFK researcher to simply collect and catalogue—bullets, wounds, the rifle, the wounds etcetera—and it apparently never entered his mind that the evidence—and here I am specifically referring to the body—might undergo some sort of fundamental change between the time of its "collection" or "original existence" and the time it was presented to the Warren Commission for a final accounting. Nothing had evolved from anything else. Everything was just *there*. That, by and large, was what I called "the 1967 view" of the evidence.

All this led to a failure to properly interpret conflicts in the record as important clues to obstruction of justice or falsification of evidence. Consequently, the tendency was to view *The Warren Report* as simply a pack of lies told about the evidence as collected by the Commission. That's how the truth had been hidden. No one had altered the data; Earl Warren had simply lied and concealed the obvious.

This "political" view persists to this day. On an appearance on The History Channel, Mark Lane—who likes to think of himself as *the senior* on these matters—was on the same program as I, and said, as in the tone of an elder giving a youngster some advice, that in this case, "There's no need to alter the evidence." To which Gerald Posner—who is fully familiar with my work and who absolutely understands the implications of what I have said—had a very different attitude and said, "You see, Mark, David is smart enough to understand that in order to have a conspiracy in this case, you must have altered evidence."

And that, essentially, is true; although I might modify it to this extent: to have a *politically significant* conspiracy, you probably have to have altered evidence and that is what altered wounds, splices, and planted bullets are all about—a plan to fabricate and alter facts connected with the JFK assassination.

Hollywood Valley Film Labs

Somewhere around late 1968 or early 1969, New Orleans' District Attorney Jim Garrison obtained a copy of the Zapruder film by subpoena from *Life* magazine. Violating the terms of the subpoena, he permitted a number of copies to be made. Someone brought one of those copies to Los Angeles and it was entrusted it to me for the purpose of getting still additional copies made. So I brought the 8mm copy to a company located near North Hollywood, specifically, to Hollywood Valley Film Lab.

While other customers were on line with their reels of family movies, I walked in with my little plastic reel containing my twenty-six seconds of film, went over to the counter, and handed it to the attendant.

"I'd like 100 copies, please," I said.

I remember those who knew what I had done being worried that the Government was watching and that I would be arrested or something.

When I came back a few days later, the counter-person pulled my order from the files, looked up at me and said: "Could you go into that office over there, please?"

"Why?" I asked.

"The owner would like to speak to you."

Oh, oh, I thought. Here we go. The government's found out what I've done.

So I opened the door and sat down with the owner. I don't remember his name, but I remember the subject of our talk, and it had nothing to do with the propriety of my having this film or of having copied it.

"I want to ask you something," he said, looking at me earnestly and obviously having studied the film I had brought in and exhibiting all the excitement of a new assassination buff, "Why do you think Jackie went out on the trunk?"

And he took out a projector, threw in an extra copy he had made for himself, and projected the image.

I breathed a sigh of relief. We had a brief but interesting conversation as to whether Jackie was trying to get out of the car or trying to retrieve a portion of her husband's head, an issue that to this day is the subject of considerable speculation and analysis.

I don't remember exactly what the bill was, but the duplicates came back on a long reel, one after another ("end to end") and I remember sitting at a table, cutting them, pasting on leaders, and preparing them for distribution.

It was in this manner that the "Zapruder film" was first distributed, bootleg fashion. Reports, researchers, anyone who wanted one, could get a copy for $10.00, postage prepaid.

Also, at the time, there was only one good way to see the film—to have an 8mm projector. So I bought one, a very good one, with "still frame", very slow speeds of "a frame at a time", and so forth.

The world of VHS was still a decade or more away, and there were of course no personal computers in 1969. Nor any Internet. Words like "J-Peg", "Tiff files", etcetera didn't exist. Photoshop meant a place where photos were developed, not a computer program. You had a projector with a stop frame feature, and you worried that the bulb would burn through the film.

In 1968, a film was, well, a "film", and if you wanted to show it, you had to project the "film" on a projector.

If you wanted your copy of the Zapruder film, you wrote David Lifton a letter, included your $10.00, and you got it back in the mail. And if you wanted to view it, you took out an 8mm projector and viewed it up on the wall. Or on a screen.

Today we see things very differently. I film can be digitized. It's digital image is composed of pixels. We worry about the hard drive and the speed of the computer. A photograph can be sent halfway around the word in an instant, as an attachment to an email. None of that was available in 1968.

But there was one fellow—a professor—who attempted to make a motion picture film directly from the poor black and white frames in the 26 volumes. In his own way, he was utilizing the principles I would, years later, come to know so well—the basic technology of the optical printer.

The Bob Gibbons Film

A motion picture film, of course, consists of the projection of individual frames; and Bob Gibbons, a professor at Southwest Missouri State University in St. Louis, showed some ingenuity in taking the frames of the Zapruder film in Volume 18 and turning them back into a motion picture film.

He took the pages of his Volume 18 and photographed them a frame at a time, with a motion picture camera—a camera which he set to "still frame" photography. He thus created a "motion picture" from the single frames in Volume 18. It was an interesting idea and a small example of what an optical printer—something I learned much more about in later years—could do.

It was also during this general period that a Los Angeles TV station broadcast the Zapruder film—the first known TV broadcast of which I am aware—as part of its general news coverage.

But back to the story of the 100 copies I made and was sending around the country, because it was around this time that a crucial discovery was made.

Counting Frames and Discovering a Second Splice

In Southern California, Fred Newcomb put the film on a moviola, and started counting frames. We were all wondering whether the copy subpoenaed by Garrison contained the same number of frames as the one given the Warren Commission. The Commission exhibit began at frame 171, and went out to frame 334. Was there a match?

Fred put the movie on a small 8mm moviola, and started counting frames. Yes, there was a match. So we had every reason to believe that the film subpoenaed from *Life* corresponded with that given to the Commission; but in the course of this frame-counting, Fred made an important—even sensational—discovery. By 1969, we all knew that there was a splice in the film where frame 207 was spliced to frame 212. In 1967, *Life* had explained that (with its story of the unnamed technician who accidentally broke the film). Now, an additional splice was discovered down in the 155-157 area! There it was—a horizontal thick ugly black line. What was *that* all about?

Had that poor film technician dropped the film a second time? Who was this hapless guy, anyway? And why hadn't *Life* said anything about this second splice, when it explained the first one? What the devil was going on here? Did *Life* employ technicians who accidentally broke historical evidence in multiple places, and who were never identified?

No one knew—and to this day, no one knows. Also, if both breaks had occurred at the same time, did that mean that the original Z film—at some point—was lying around in three pieces? Specifically, did the film, in its "broken" state, consist of three segments: Frame 1 out to frame 155; then 157 to 207, and then 207 on out to the end of the film? And had the film then been "restored"—stitched together again—by employing two splices, namely: by the splice at 155 and the second at 207?

And that conjured up another image: that the film for some reason had arrived in 3 pieces—segment A, segment B, and Segment C—and that these segments had been spliced together in a final step in the creation of the "original Zapruder film" and that that was the reason for the two splices. Very early on, I favored the multi-segment hypothesis, but had no idea *why* these multiple breaks might have occurred. More on all this later.

Another thing. There is an important difference between these two splices. The splice at 212 occurred in the segment of film that was given to the Warren Commission as an FBI exhibit. The splice at 155 was in an earlier section of the film—and so that wasn't discovered until the film was subpoenaed by Garrison and put on a movieola and examined frame by frame.

The splice at 212 was discovered around early 1965, when the 26 volumes were first available, and (as noted) I brought it to Liebeler's attention in October 1965. But the 155 splice wasn't discovered until 1969.

Over the years, I have seldom encountered anyone who viewed these splices as a pair.

Take Josiah Thompson, for instance. The 207/212 splice—and *Life's* explanation for it—is simply one that Thompson accepted and included in his book, while failing to mention the other splice in the 155-157 area. Surely he had to have seen the "other splice"? Or maybe he didn't notice. These things can be subtle and be "hiding in plain view" when you are not looking for them.

At the time, I wrote a memo about Fred's frame counting and what he had found. It is dated February 1969 and is entitled, "This is the Film That Was".

Meanwhile, contemplating what these splices might mean, I set out to develop an organized way to approach the analysis of this sort of evidence, a new methodology of sorts.

A Trifocal View of the Film Evidence

If the Zapruder film was altered, how might it have been done? And when? And where? These questions were entirely similar to those I had faced in considering the alteration of the body, and I had developed a consciously held methodology for dealing with the alteration of the evidence. I called it "the tri-focal view," meaning that, when evidence alteration was suspected, there were three contexts in which the situation had to be viewed in order to obtain a complete understanding:

Context 1: Was there a "before" and "after" situation ("before alteration" and "after alteration")? And if so, what was it? How would it be described?

Context 2: If something had been changed, then just what was being concealed or hidden?

Context 3: The "where" question: *How* had the evidence been intercepted and *where* had it been altered? Let's switch to legal language: If the evidence had been used in a trial, how would its provenance have been established? Was there a proper chain of possession? What was known about who possessed it, and what light did that shed on the issue of possible interception?

Consider the situation of JFK's body and, specifically, the throat wound. The "before" situation consisted of an entry at the front of the throat. The "after" situation—that it had been enlarged, and (at the autopsy) was designated an exit.

Posing the question, "What was being hidden?", the answer seemed to be a shot from the front. Finally, the "Where could it have been done?" question had led me to focus on the chain of custody of the body and to such things as the existence the decoy ambulance, the body bag, the second coffin, etcetera.

As we shall see, a similar situation exists here, only instead of dealing with coffins, we are dealing with film cans; but the principles are the same.

In the months following my first discovery of evidence that the wounds had been altered, I consciously developed this way of looking at evidence, this "tri-focal" view. In the case of the rifle, I noted that Oswald had mail-ordered one model from Klein's, yet another was found on 22 November 1963. I also applied it to the windshield. Early reports from those who saw it in Dallas said there was a hole; but the windshield sent to the FBI Lab months later had no hole. *Did these "conflicts in the record" represent innocent errors of observation? Or changes in the evidence?*

A favorite little book of mine in the area of problem solving was by the mathematician George Polya. He made the point that in solving a problem it was useful to work by analogy—when exploring some new area, try using the same method that had worked in another.

I began doing so in connection with the Zapruder film, and particularly, in attempting to tackle the problem of whether anything had been changed, and if so, just what it was. I asked myself the following questions:

Context 1: Was there a "before" and "after" situation—one before the Z film was altered; and another afterward? If so, just what was "before" and what was "after"?

Context 2: Exactly what was being hidden?

Context 3: Where could the film have been altered? What did I know about its chain of custody?

Sometime in the Spring of 1969 that I found a way to identify the "before" and "after" situation and, very likely, the crucial clue came from my reading of the very first page of the very first chapter of Sylvia Meagher's book, *Accessories After the Fact,* published in the fall of 1968.

Sylvia Meagher and the Car Stop

Meagher's book was a catalogue of divergences between what *The Warren Report* said versus what the underlying evidence indicated. Meagher entertained no theory about Z-film alteration; to the contrary, she found the idea impossible to believe. In 1969 correspondence with me, she asked, "How could such evidence be altered, when the final conclusions weren't available to know what to bring the evidence into conformity with?"

What a revealing statement. Meagher didn't grasp the essential fact that the person(s) who controlled the evidence could actually "alter the reality" of the investigation. In her world, there was—first of all—some false conclusion, politically arrived at, and then evidence was fabricated or lied about. She didn't seem to understand that fabricated evidence created a false reality all its own. Nonetheless, she was sensitive to divergences in the record and she began her book, on the very first page—with a provocative example entitled, "The Speed of the Limousine."

Meagher noted that a half dozen witnesses said the car stopped. She cited them one after another and then pointed out that, according to the Zapruder film, the car did *not* stop. So why mention this at all? Because, she wondered, why was the questioning of these witnesses so deficient? In short, Meagher was focusing on a deficiency in process—not the alteration of evidence. Yet, in doing so, she had focused on a fact that turned out to be very important: the speed of the car and whether or not it stopped. I believe that it was reading these passages that led to my own "aha" moment. Suddenly I became aware—very aware—that numerous witnesses reported the car had stopped and had said just that, often in passing, since that was not the central focus of their experience, but rather something that was part of a larger mosaic, something they simply took for granted. So there it was, embedded in the record.

Now I started to make lists. My friend and associate Pat Lambert, undertook to scan all news accounts and any other published material, as well as some 2000 pages of unpublished FBI reports. We laboriously sorted through all eyewitness accounts, from all sources. Working from my documents, but also from the list at the back of Thompson's book, Pat assembled a fairly thorough list of "car stop witnesses." [*Editor's note*: See Vincent Palamara's first chapter in *Murder in Dealey Plaza* (2000).]

To understand the importance of these statements, conduct the following thought experiment. Just consider the possibility that there was no Zapruder film. Then what?

What if there had been no film?

If there had been no Zapruder film and one had to rely on the witnesses, then clearly any legal or historical inquiry would have concluded—and rather matter of factly, it seems to me, by just relying on the eyewitness accounts—that during the assassination, the car had come to a complete (albeit momentary) halt. The reason people don't view the assassination that way is that the Zapruder film shows otherwise—there is no stop! To use legal language again, the film is considered the "best evidence" when it comes to ascertaining the car stop.

Analyzing the record in this fashion, and returning to my "tri-focal view," I now had answers to questions one and two:

Question number 1: Was there a "before" and "after" situation (which, in this instance, meant "the reality as witnessed" versus the reality as portrayed on the film)? The answer: *Yes, there was.*

Question number 2: What was being hidden? The answer (if the film had been altered): *The car stop.* At the very least, that's what this seemed to be all about. The witnesses said the car stopped; the film indicated otherwise. The film had been altered to conceal that fact.

But there was another way to view all this.

Velocity, Distance, and Elapsed Time

Every freshman physics student learns the simple formula, Rate x Time = Distance.

In applying this formula to Dallas, there were certain constants—"facts" if you will—that were unarguable and did not change. One was the distance between the spot on Elm Street where the assassination began and the Elm Street location where Mary Moorman raised her camera and took her famous picture. The elapsed time between the car's passing between those two points depended on its average velocity as it made the traverse.

As recorded on the Zapruder film, the elapsed time was roughly 5.6 seconds. However, if the car had actually been moving much more slowly—if many frames had been removed so as to "remove the stop" or to "speed it up"—then the elapsed time was, in actuality, longer.

The Zapruder film contained 486 frames. If the car had stopped, then the actual event—as originally filmed—contained more than 486 frames. How many more?

Common sense says the answer would depend on how much time was consumed by those events removed by film editing, for example, how long it took the car to decelerate to a complete halt and then speed up again.

JFK's limo weighed about two tons; it could not be stopped on a dime. Additional seconds were needed, both for the deceleration and the acceleration.

On 22 November 1963, Sheriff Bill Decker told the *Dallas Times-Herald* that he thought the assassination "took about 20 seconds." And that certainly seems reasonable, but why was this estimate important? Because the longer the actual elapsed time, the more obvious it was that the Secret Service was involved, and on two counts:

a. The slowing down of the car in the first place;

b. The failure of the agents to react.

Basically, an altered Z film implicated the Secret Service because the Secret Service had the Zapruder film. But the Secret Service also had the body, and the situations were roughly parallel.

The evidence suggesting the wounds were altered implied the Secret Service was involved—somehow—in the circumstances of the interception of the body (and that, in turn, implied involvement in altering the wounds and falsifying the autopsy, hiding facts about the shooting). Here, the Secret Service had the Zapruder film, evidence which recorded the deceleration of the car, as well as the agents' failure to react promptly. All this was hidden by altering the film and producing a "politically correct" assassination, an accidental security failure because everything happened "so fast"—what I have called the "We wuz caught by surprise" version of events.

Of course, the Secret Service had much other evidence, too. Beside the body and the Zapruder film, the Secret Service had the clothing, the car, the windshield from the car, the two large bullet pieces found in the car, etcetera. To anyone analyzing the event, the central role played by the Secret Service soon became obvious: that agency was instrumental in planning the trip, had the security function during the trip, and then possessed the key evidence afterward (which was then dutifully transmitted to the FBI).

So what it came down to was this: if the film or the body was altered, or both, then some Secret Service agents or officials were very likely involved—at the operational level—in the murder of JFK. (Why? Again: because they were the ones who had the evidence which needed to be altered to create the appearance that the JFK assassination was simply a matter of "a man in a building shooting a man in car.")

So those were the stakes, but *was* the film altered?

At this point, I must indulge the reader in an important aside—because in 1969, I had no idea how films could be altered and edited, and I set out to find answers, to obtain basic background information. In 1996, I shared my knowledge with the members of the ARRB, and what follows is sometimes verbatim from my June 1996 report.

A Technical Aside: Optical Printers

An optical printer is a device as basic to motion picture photography as the enlarger is to still photography. [*Editor's note*: See the chapter by David Healy above.]

An optical printer is a camera which makes a duplicate of a movie film by taking a picture of it (the "input" film) one frame at a time. In other words, the operator feeds in one film, and then, by photographing it one frame at a time, creates a second film (the copy film). Normally, we imagine cameras running at 16 or 18 or 40 frames per second. Optical printers can run at a fairly fast clip, but are basically designed for work one frame at a time. In that way, optical edits (an edit made by actually omitting frames on the copy, rather than cutting and pasting pieces of film together) can be made; titles can be inserted, film frames can be enlarged on the copy (called "reframing"), etcetera, and yes, one can "paint on" additional information via a process referred to as "insert matte photography"—in effect, projecting the film image onto a piece of glass, painting on additional information, and then re-projecting back to film.

The important concept: *films are edited not by pasting frames together with film cement, but by making a copy on which information is added or deleted optically.*

Regarding the motion of what is being filmed: optical printers can be used to slow down the action as well as to speed it up. For example: if you want to slow a film down, then you "step print" it. So, for a documentary about the motorcade, you might step print the Zapruder film 5:1, so that the output film has five frames per input frame; and then (when viewed) it moves down the street visibly more slowly; in the extreme, a step printed film might simply appear to be a sequence of stills, one blending into the next. Conversely, it would be possible to "speed up" the motion. Say, for example, there was a film of someone slowly walking. By eliminating every other frame (on the copy), the apparent velocity would be doubled (this is called an "EOF" for "every other frame" program).

Once I knew what an optical printer was, and what it could do, I became intensely aware that some 25 witnesses to the assassination said that the Presidential limo momentarily stopped during the shooting—yet the film showed no such stop. Were the witnesses wrong? Or had the car stopped? That, plus the Dallas observations regarding the head wounds, raised the same issue: whether or not the Zapruder film was the camera original or an 8mm forgery, produced by a complicated process of blowing it up, editing it, changing the information, and then reducing it back down to 8mm.

I learned something else: that altering the Zapruder film wouldn't be that easy. Putting aside the question of who might have intercepted the film and where the work might have been done, optical printers were not designed for home movies—not designed to accept 8mm film. Rather, they were designed for use by professionals making feature films and for special effects work. So they were designed to take 16mm (or 35mm) film. (In other words, going from 16 to 16, or 16 to 35, was a fairly standard operation on an Acme or Oxberry or Bell & Howell printer). However, there was a mitigating factor: information that Secret Service agent Sorrels (chief of the Dallas field office) had ordered (on Friday afternoon, 11/22/63) that the Zapruder film *not* be "slit"[10] and this made all the difference in the world. Here's why.

A Technical Aside: The Z Film

Although the Zapruder film was an 8mm film, it was originally "one-half" of a 16mm film, and that has implications regarding optical printing and the standard equipment available in 1963. To state the matter slightly differently: although "the Zapruder film" is an 8mm film, it did not go into the Zapruder camera in that format. In fact, it was one side (or "one half of", to use language loosely) of a 16mm film which contained sprockets on both sides. (This is called "double perf" or "double rank".)

A good analogy is a red and black typewriter ribbon. The red side is "side A"; the black side, "side B". The camera accepts a 25 foot cassette of 16mm film and then "side A" is first exposed; then the cassette is "turned over" and the other side ("side B") is exposed. After the film is processed (on standard 16mm equipment) the entire film is then slit down the middle and the two pieces pasted end-to end—as if the black and red sides of a typewriter ribbon were split apart and then pasted end to end. Thus, 25 ft. of 16mm becomes 50 ft. of 8mm. (See Healy chapter in this book for illustrations showing how all this is done.)

What was significant about the Sorrels testimony is that the original Zapruder film was *not* slit on Friday, 22 November 1963, and, in that unslit condition, it *could* in fact be put on a standard optical printer.

Whether or not that in fact occurred is a separate issue, but keeping the film "unslit" would have been essential—a pre-condition, if you will—to making it easy to "bump it up" to 16mm or 35 mm format.

Once in that format, standard editing equipment and techniques could be used, and the next "problem" peculiar to this situation—that the original was actually an 8mm film—would occur when it was time to "reduce back down" to 8mm format (which will be discussed later).

Special Effects Seminar

Some time around 1969 or 1970, I attended a one-evening seminar in West Hollywood on special effects. It had the quality of a magic show. An expert appeared who's profession was visual effects in movies, and he showed how films were altered and how the images we all took for granted were created. Numerous examples were given. One example in particular I remember concerned a scene from a movie with a famous actress (Audrey Hepburn, as I recall) and a lion. He demonstrated how the final scene—which showed Hepburn and the lion together—was actually a composite of two separate films—one with Hepburn, the other with the lion. So Hepburn and the lion were never together in reality; that was just an appearance created by combining two separate films. And there were many other examples provided.

In each case, the lecturer showed the individual film elements (projecting them separately) and then showed how they were combined. Prior to the final step, before all the elements were combined, the emerging film—the "work in progress"—would show the final composite scene in an outline form, but a big blackened out area would be located where another element (call it a "sub-movie", for want of a better term) would be designed to fit in the manner that a key fits into a lock. Once these "optical elements" were combined, the composite looked very convincing.

From my reading and the seminar, it was clear that one had to be well versed—at least as to the basics—to comprehend what might have been done to the Zapruder film and to realize that, just because the film shows "the car moving down Elm Street", that could well be a composite of two separate films: (1) a film showing the car, alone, moving down the street; and, (2) a separate film showing only "the bystanders." And indeed, many years later—decades later—I was exposed to diagrams and graphics at the Duluth Conference (May 2003), which addressed, in very specific terms, just how this might have worked. In short, how what we call "the Zapruder film"—which shows the car "coming down Elm Street"—could in fact have been created by combining two or more optical elements, where "the lawn with the bystanders" could be one element, "the car moving down the street" another.

1969: Marcus Swipes Newcomb's Film

Political movements are famous for breeding paranoia.

Upon hearing that Newcomb had a Zapruder film which contained a splice *besides* the one at 212, Marcus—who, back in 1965, had spent hundreds of hours analyzing poor black and white Z frames from Volume 18 of *The Warren Report*—grew agitated. The CIA, reasoned Marcus, was putting out disinformation. Ray arranged to visit Newcomb, who was sitting there, in his home, right at the kitchen table (as I recall) examining his film. It was a reasonably decent color copy made directly from the 8mm copy Garrison was provided when he subpoenaed the film from *Life* in New York.

Focusing on that splice at the 155 area (which he had persuaded himself had something to do with the CIA), Marcus made a decision. Clearly, he reasoned, this was disinformation put out by the CIA, false data intended to distract attention from the "real" splice.

Then he did it. Ray took Fred's precious film and ran out the door.

Within minutes, he was in his car and roaring off into the night. Ray felt he was saving "the movement" from "disinformation" put out by the CIA.

Fred was pissed—crestfallen is probably a better description—and I don't blame him.

Perhaps the clearest 8mm copy of the Zapruder film outside of that at *Life* in New York City, a precious "bootleg" from the Garrison trial, had been stolen by a fellow researcher, and there was nothing to be done about it.

Marcus didn't return Newcomb's copy for some 15 or 20 years, by which time it was totally irrelevant.

June 1970 : Life magazine and the Z film

By June 1970, the question of the Z film was becoming more important to my own work on the body. By that time, I had analyzed all the Dallas doctors' testimony and was convinced that the wounds had been altered. As to the "chain of possession", I had interviewed all the members of the military casket team that met Air Force One upon its Andrews arrival and learned of the ambulance chase that occurred after the body had arrived at Bethesda. Then there was the matter of the Zapruder film frames. These could be studied by taking one of my "bootleg copies" and peering at it through a magnifier.

During this same period, I met John ("Jack") Clemente, then about 65, an energetic roly-poly man who had been with the China Lake Naval Air Station. John knew all about lenses and optics, and we would spend hours using the (relatively) poor quality 8 mm film attempting to understand just what it showed. In connection with my writing a manuscript about the wounds (which became *Best Evidence*), one problem kept coming up: *what to do about the Z film?* I would look at the Zapruder frames and see the blackened out area at the back of the head and I wanted to know more. How to explain this? Was the back of the head just lying in shadow? Or had the area where the Dallas doctors seen the massive blowout been deliberately blacked out? And how could any of this be reasonably discussed without access to a good quality copy of the film—not some 8mm copy or terribly dark 35mm slides made from that copy, but the actual film.

One of the Southern California researchers—very likely it was Fred Newcomb—had a "friend of a friend" who knew cinematographer Haskell Wexler, who was politically "left of center" and decidedly anti-establishment. Sometime in the Spring of 1970, we were introduced and met at the office of Dove Films, his company. Haskell agreed to let his company letterhead be used for the purpose of writing a letter—a letter I helped draft—to *Life* magazine.

And so it was that Richard Pollard, Director of Photography for *Life*, received a letter stating that Wexler was considering using the Zapruder film in a movie, that he was considering buying the rights or maybe the film itself, and letting it be known that a price of $1 million might be paid.

The letter said that he would like to examine this film and have his appraisers take a look. The "appraisers" of course were going to be four Warren Commission researchers—me, Fred Newcomb, Jack Clemente, and a young law student, Dennis Roy.

A word about Pollard. In 1967, Josiah Thompson repeatedly sought Pollard's permission to publish various frames but was refused. Their publication without permission led to the lawsuit. Now things seemed to be different, but I have no idea why. To our collective astonishment, *Life* replied in the affirmative. Yes, they would be willing to ship the Zapruder film to the West Coast to the Beverly Hills office of Time-Life, under armed guard, to be examined in the manner we had proposed. The person from *Life* accompanying the film (besides the armed courier) would be Pollard's assistant, Ann Drayton.

From Pollard's response, I learned just what materials *Life* would be sending: not just an 8mm and a 16 mm copy (which, said *Life*'s letter, had been made by the "Watergate" method), and the 4 x 5 inch transparencies (which I had already seen under the auspices of Liebeler's class) but also certain "35 mm" films—not just individual 35mm slides, but an actual 35 mm filmed copy made directly from the 8mm original.

This was new: when had life converted an 8mm film to a 35 mm film?

And what was the "Watergate" method? That, it turned out, was the name for the optical printing method where a liquid—having the same index of refraction as the film emulsion—surrounded the frame as the optical printer did its work. The result: the scratches were made invisible or at least less visible. "Wet gate" printing was one of the advantages of duplicating a film on the optical printer (as opposed to simply using a contact printer).

Renting a Recordak

I had never thought of 35 mm film as being film that runs through a motion picture camera. To me, 35mm was the film size of *The New York Times*, which I often read on microfilm at the library, which inspired me to think: what better way to check the film—as a film—than to find a 35 mm Recordak microfilm reader, the same kind I used at the library? Why not pass any materials life sent us, 35 mm or 16 mm, through that reader? That way, I could examine it, frame by frame, as a film. This was important, because the two key question were: (1) What could be learned about the splices? and (2) What did the actual film show in the area of the head shot? What about frame 321 or 323? Those were the key frames that showed the *back* of the head. I knew it seemed blacked out on the magazine page and I also knew it appeared that way on the 4 x 5 inch slides. Was it blacked out on the actual film? I just didn't know, but I sure wanted to find out.

Officially, I was a consultant, an appraiser, and our intent was dead serious. But I also had a consciousness that it was all pretense—that we were, after all, involved in a sting of sorts. Here we were, supposedly appraisers, dealing with the very organization that now owned the Zapruder film, that had transported that film from New York to L.A. under armed guard. And yet we were four assassination buffs—me, Jack Clemente, Fred Newcomb, and Dennis Roy. We had fooled Time-Life, or so it seemed.

There were also serious tensions. Jack Clemente was my friend, but Newcomb— who had now learned what I was working on (the alteration of the wounds)—was making noise about publishing his own book, and I was furious. All this was submerged, however, as we set out trying to keep our eye on the ball, on our common interests. Posing as appraisers and exhibiting dead serious demeanors, the four of us were about to examine the most critical evidence in the case. Although I couldn't vouch for what the others were interested in, I (along with Jack Clemente, with whom I had shared my wound alteration theory) was focused on basically two things: the two splices and the appearance of the back of the head.

Within minutes of Ann Drayton's arrival, she opened a box and it was a researchers dream. Inside was a set of 4 x 5 inch transparencies, an 8mm film, a 16 mm film, and a 35mm film. Except for the original 8mm film itself, everything we could have wished to see was present,. Well, what did we want to do first?

We answered that we'd like to see the 16 mm projected.

Viewing the Film

So we saw it. It was the first time I had seen a truly high quality of the Zapruder film, the same quality that had been shown to Stewart Galanor at the National Archives—the same quality routinely available to *Life*'s editors and to Josiah Thompson when he had been briefly employed there.

Today, this kind of quality is taken for granted. People can go on the Internet and find the Zapruder film. They run it on their computers. Or they can buy the film on DVD. But not in 1970.

Back then, no one in the general public—except a few souls who had visited the National Archives—had ever seen anything like this.

The lawn was verdant green; the car, a dark, deep blue. Everything was so stunningly clear and vivid. Besides *Life*'s editors, some FBI and Secret Service officials, and those on the Warren Commission, only a few staff people at *Life* had seen film of this quality. And, of course, Josiah Thompson.

Suddenly we had been admitted to that small fraternity that was given a peek at this unique record of what Liebeler would have called "the reality of the event".

Although, from studying previous 8mm "bootleg copies", we were familiar with the basic sequence, this viewing experience was qualitatively different. Content-wise, it was the same film, but there was no comparison between the poor 8mm copies we had all previously studied and this spectacular 16mm copy.

We winced but tried to maintain our composure as we saw JFK flung to the rear.

We also noticed the lack of response of the Secret Service agents up front. The driver seemed to turn around twice, and the car slowed somewhat. The agent in the right front seat, Roy Kellerman, was apparently on the radio: the curly wire from the telephone or microphone in his hand was clearly visible. Overall, the film documented what seemed like a general lack of reaction. It was as if Kennedy was being slowly driven through a "free fire" zone and, *other than a few rearward glances, the two agents were doing absolutely nothing about it.*

But shocking though all this was, it was mere prelude, because then came the rest of what was inside box of materials. We split into two groups. Jack Clemente and I wanted to put the 16 mm film we had just viewed in the Recordak reader. Fred and Dennis started examining the transparencies on a lightbox.

To start, Jack and I slowly pulled the 16 mm through the reader, taking a closer look at the splicing down in the 155-157 area. It was really amazing because there was nothing subtle about it. There was the splice, plain as day. Thick black horizontal lines across the frame. I wondered: *How could Life have admitted to the 207/212 splice, in 1967, offering up the story about the technician who damaged the film, and say nothing about this very obvious second splice in the film?* And how could anything so graphic, so obvious, not been reported by the Secret Service or the FBI to the Warren Commission?

Then came another surprise as Jack and I pulled the film through the Recordak, and got to frames just past the head shot. Frames 321 and 323, which showed the back of the head (where the Dallas doctors saw an exit wound) all seemed "blacked out" just as they appeared on the page of *Life* magazine! So this phenomenon was clearly on the film itself; no one had cleaned up the plates at *Life* prior to publication. That theory was out the window. We were examining a splendid 35mm copy made directly from *Life's* actual original 8mm film, so this must be the way so-called original actually looked—it exhibited a persistent "blacking out", frame after frame, at the back of JFK's head.

Then, as we pulled the film a bit further through the Recordak, came still another surprise: for the first time, we were able to get a really good look, in color, at frames past frame 334 (where the Warren Commission exhibit of black and white frames had ended). Now, in vivid color, we saw frame 335 and frame 337—two frames showing the full JFK head in profile. Lo and behold, on the forward right hand side of the head, was a large whitish area that clearly was supposed to be a wound! It was enormous, occupying much of the forward right-hand side of JFK's head. But the problem was no one had seen any such thing when the President arrived at Parkland Hospital about 4 minutes later. Curiously, it had translucent quality: underneath the so-called wound, JFK's uninjured head was clearly visible—or so it seemed. Jack and I had the same reaction: this was art work. This "wound"—so called—must have been painted on. Just viewing it, it looked odd and it seemed preposterous that something of that size—if it was real—wouldn't have been visible, clearly visible, at Parkland Hospital.

But How Had Any of This Been Done?

I knew how the car stop had been eliminated—that was simply a process of periodic frame elimination. But what about all this? What about image alteration at the individual frame level? Was that possible? How was it done?

Meanwhile, Ann Drayton, the chaperone, had left the room for a moment—presumably to use the rest room or something—and I looked over and, to my considerable astonishment, saw Fred Newcomb, poised over a light box, a 35 mm camera in his hand, photographing one of the key frames.

This is exactly what Josiah Thompson had done at *Life* magazine, which had led to a lawsuit. [*Editor's note*: See Appendix F.]

"Put the damn camera away", I hissed. But Newcomb kept photographing. This was his great moment in the sun. (He had been hurt by Marcus; this was his chance. I was pissed.)

I approached Newcomb and we were arguing in low voices. I don't know who hit who first, but a shoving match quickly degenerated into the beginning of a fist fight. At least one punch was thrown, but it didn't get much beyond that because, at that moment, there was the sound of a doorknob turning and Ann Drayton re-entered the room. As fast as you could say, "Zapruder," our demeanor changed, as if we were players in a Groucho Marx comedy. As she entered the room, the camera had been put away, and it looked as we were just studio fellows who loved one another, in a harmonious relationship attending to business.

At some point, we took our "lunch break." We went to an inexpensive restaurant, and I remember ordering a hamburger. Ann Drayton asked: "Is Haskell really going to pay *Life* a million dollars for this?" Keeping a perfectly straight face, I replied: "Why of course. Why else are we eating hamburgers for lunch?"

During our second session (following lunch), much of the remaining time I remember going over and over the 35 mm film. That fascinated me—that the entire Zapruder film had been actually blown up to 35 mm. I just couldn't get over the clarity with which it had apparently been enlarged from 8 mm to 35 mm.

The splice at 155 was clearly visible and, in 35mm, the wounds had an even more bizarre look. I know it is subjective, but they just looked like they were painted on. *Somehow.*

And "somehow" was the key. How had any of that been done?

Then the afternoon came to an end. One by one, the items were put back into the *Life* box. The slides, the 16 mm film, the 35 mm slides, the 35 mm roll of film.

It was very depressing. We had just had an exquisite look at some priceless history, and now it was going back to the life vault in New York City—never to be seen again.

When we left, I felt depressed. The key materials went back into a box. We said our goodbyes and loaded the Recordak microfilm reader into one of our cars.

In Internet posts written about the event—and because of bad blood that developed between me and Newcomb—it was alleged that not all of *Life*'s materials had been returned. That is not true. Everything was returned. What was "taken"—to find a neutral term to describe it—was one or more photographs by Newcomb, pictures I understand still exist, but have not seen to this day.

In the aftermath of the *Life* visit, I puzzled about why there was a second splice and what the wound images meant.

I understood that the film was an 8mm but that actually that was one-half of a 16mm film. I also knew that the Secret Service had ordered that the film not be slit and that, because of this order, it was perfectly possible for the film to be put on a standard optical printer.

Now I went back to the library because I wanted to know more about image alteration—not how the velocity of the limo might have been changed, but how the actual images of the wounds on President Kennedy's head could have been changed.

Could that be done? If so, how?

Insert matte Photography

When I emerged from the Beverly Hills' office of Time-Life, I knew that I had to educate myself on the basics of how motion picture film imagery might be altered on a frame by frame basis. I knew next to nothing about the subject. My mind, as they say, was "tabula rasa"—a blank slate—when it came to this subject.

Living near UCLA, I did much work there, often using the libraries. So I went to Melnitz Hall, affiliated with the film school, and simply asked: who does this kind of work and are there books about this that I can read?

I soon learned still more about the "special effects" work that goes on in the world of motion pictures. Specifically, I learned how it was possible to introduce art work into an ordinary picture on a frame by frame basis, just as if one were putting a moustache on the Mona Lisa. In short, I learned about a field called, "Insert Matte Photography".

I acquired a rudimentary understanding of how it all worked and, for the first time, came to understand how it might be possible for the back of President Kennedy's head to have been blacked out and how it would also be possible to take a particular Zapruder frame (such as frame 335 or 337) and actually draw on what would appear to be—if one didn't look too closely—a passable "wound".

It wasn't easy to do these things, but it wasn't all that difficult, either. If the film had been "bumped to 35" and professionally edited, it would have been a rather straightforward procedure to employ a "matte artist" to draw pictures on what was already there and thus change the configuration of wounds of the head. And that technology provided an explanation of what the film appeared to show: a peculiar looking, almost translucent, Bethesda-like wound on the right side and/or top of JFK's head, which wasn't on the body when the body arrived at Parkland Hospital just a few minutes later.

Of all the things that had been done to the Zapruder film in the way of image alteration, perhaps this is the one that most stuck in my craw. Because, unless challenged, unless refuted, it in effect turned the Zapruder film into a false witness when it came to the wounds on the President's head. It had the effect of falsely informing a whole generation of researchers, who might look at those film frames, "See, the Dallas doctors were wrong. Here, take a look—there's the Bethesda wound, right there on the head, only the Dallas doctors didn't see it!"

On the surface, this was an absurd argument. How could the Dallas doctors miss a wound so large? But many researchers, I noticed, went down this path. They honestly believed that, since the Bethesda photographs showed a large flap connected with the head wound on the right hand side and since a few of the Zapruder frames appeared to show that same flap, that that's the way the head had looked in Dallas!

But I didn't believe that for a minute, because I trusted the Parkland Hospital observations—and no one in Dallas had seen any such thing. And then of course there was the wound's translucent quality—underneath it was what appeared to be the uninjured head!

So for me the stakes were high: if the Zapruder film was impeached as evidence when it came to the basic wound imagery, then the last obstacle to accepting the Dallas doctors' observations would have been removed.

But back to the notion of insert matte photography.

As I say, all this was just a hypothesis and the point of all this study was not to prove that it *had* been done—once we left the office that day, we no longer had the evidence, just our recollections—but to understand what *could* be done, to learn just what was within the realm of possibility.

At the time I was educating myself in these matters, it never occurred to me that the film might have actually gone to Hollywood, but that is something I have given serious consideration to in the years since. But, back then, the CIA was considered the source of all such magic. Consequently, at a time when I first conceived a hypothesis that really did deserve further investigation, my focus was misplaced. I was oblivious to the notion that the place to look for the someone with the resources to do all this film magic was my own town, the city of Los Angeles, and particularly Hollywood.

Nor did I notice something else at the time—something that would appear possibly relevant only decades later: that the person who had been made the most powerful man in the motion picture industry, Jack Valenti, had been an aide to LBJ. He had left the White House to be placed in charge of The Motion Picture Association of America in 1966.

But, as I say, it just never occurred to me to consider Los Angeles as a town where anything like that could have occurred—and this despite the fact that, sometime during this period, I distinctly remember attending the "special effects seminar" previously described. As to my forays onto the UCLA campus, the technology employed in editing and creating special effects were the subject of a magazine called *The American Cinemotrapher.* From time to time, I would simply go to the library and pour over old copies.

November 1971: Trip to Dallas

My maiden trip to Dallas as an assassination researcher occurred in November 1971 over the Thanksgiving weekend. Most people who visit Dallas go with a view to seeing how Lee Oswald shot the President or, if they don't believe the official version, verifying their own personal theory about the event.

When I went to Dallas in 1971, I too had ideas about the shots being fired from the grassy knoll, but I had a different purpose: I wanted to speak to people about their perception of the shooting, and see what they would say about the velocity of the car. And I wanted to hear this with my own ears and in their presence.

In 1971, there was no "Sixth Floor Museum"—just the old Texas School Book Depository.

I arrived at Dallas' Love Field with a friend, the late William Corrigan, and we rented a car at the airport and then proceeded into town along the same route President Kennedy's limousine had taken. It was Thanksgiving morning and Dallas was empty, like a stage set.

As I drove, Bill sat in the passenger seat and read aloud from the transcript of the radio log that day, recording the progress of the procession.

After we reached Dealey Plaza, we doubled back, explored the area, and I was lucky enough to be let up into the railroad tower, where we studied the view and took some photographs.

Then came the interviews, which was the most interesting part of all.

I was able to arrange interviews with Mary Moorman—with whom I spent an hour or two at her home in Dallas—and with Charles Franzen, who was standing on the south side of Elm with his wife and son; with Marvin Chism, the black man who can be seen running on the grassy knoll (near the Stemmons sign) with a child in his arms, immediately after the shots were fired; and with the Newmans, who had been standing right astride the limousine when the President was struck in the head.

With the exception of Mary Moorman—whose husband would not permit me to use a tape recorder—I taped all these interviews (and would subsequently donate copies of these materials to "The JFK Collection" at the National Archives during the life of the ARRB).

It was very clear from these interviews, that—at least according to these witnesses—the President's car had stopped (momentarily) during the shooting.

When the Newmans made statements to me about the car stopping right in front of them and when I told them that the film didn't appear to show any stop, they assured me that it did—that it didn't matter what the film showed. They were there. I didn't push the matter because I didn't want them to believe that I was entertaining a theory about film alteration (which of course I was). I was simply polite and friendly and discussed the event as if I basically agreed with everything they said.

I came away from these encounters with the firm impression that the witnesses believed the car had stopped—it wasn't some semantic thing, it wasn't an aberration. To them, it was a reality, an integral part of the reality of the event, as they recollected it.

After November 1971, I could say that I had conducted my own unusual inquiry: I had personally talked to the witnesses who said the car had stopped and also had the somewhat unique experience of having studied 35 mm prints of the Zapruder film.

I firmly believed the film had been altered. The question was, how could you prove such a thing? And when could it have happened? Didn't Zapruder sell the film directly to *Life* and didn't it go directly from Dallas to *Life* in New York City on Saturday, 23 November, the day after the assassination?

Speaking with Mrs. Zapruder

My story about how I came to speak with Mrs. Zapruder starts innocently enough. My Mom and Dad were in Mexico on a vacation around 1970, and my Mother—not exactly thrilled that I was so involved in pursuing the JFK murder—was in an elevator at a resort hotel when she heard another lady in the elevator referred to as "Mrs. Zapruder."

Wait a minute, she wondered. Wasn't that the name of the person who her son had been talking about—the fellow who had taken a film of the assassination?

So these two Jewish ladies started a conversation and that was how my mother ended up in conversation with "Mrs. Zapruder"—aka (to her family) as "Lillian".

My mom told Mrs. Zapruder how her son was always talking about her husband's film and how he would probably love to talk with her. Mrs. Zapruder—who along with Abe Zapruder—definitely did not like to talk about the film (especially about anything having to do with the money)—was probably not exactly thrilled by this elevator conversation, but it was the basis for my calling Mrs. Zapruder in November of 1971 when I was in Dallas.

As was my habit, I hooked up a tape recorder to the phone, because this conversation could be important—and so it was. This was not exactly a scene from James Bond, but I knew that my father—who was from Russia (as was Abe Zapruder)—was always very careful when speaking about money, and I expected that the same behavior would prevail here.

Every word would count.

To begin with, Mrs. Zapruder—whose first name was "Lilian"—really did not wish to speak with me. I could understand why, but some background is in order here.

Yiddish is a colorful language, and there is a word for what happened when old Abe, through pure serendipity, happened to end up falling into a pile of money, merely because he had taken a film and *Life* had paid so much for it.

The phrase is "schmaltz grub." "Schmaltz" means fat; "grub"—not meaning food, as in English—implied something along the lines of "honey pot". And the phrase might be used (as in the case of someone who didn't know she was going to meet a rich man), "She fell into a schmaltz grub."

People are not comfortable about talking about this sort of thing—and certainly not about the money.

When Mrs. Zapruder came to the phone, I introduced myself, reminded her how she had met my mother in an elevator somewhere in Mexico, and attempted to edge into the topic.

Almost immediately, I felt I was speaking to a character in the old Molly Goldberg TV show when she piously informed me, "I don't even have the details and I'm not at liberty to discuss it."

She also said she was on the way to her hairdresser. She was obviously anxious to get off the phone.

At which point, I pulled out my secret weapon—my ace-in-the-hole—the key document that I had obtained, courtesy of Josiah Thompson, from the *Life* magazine lawsuit that had cost him his royalties.

I casually mention to Mrs. Zapruder—as if I was dealing with nothing more significant than the weather—that I had a copy of their contract with *Life* magazine showing they had been paid $25,000 per year ($150,000 annually in today's money) and that the contract had netted them $150,000 (which would roughly correspond to approximately $900,000—nearly a million dollars—in today's equivalent).

By any definition, this was definitely a *schmalz grub* and not exactly the sort of thing that Mrs. Zapruder wanted to hear from a stranger over the phone.

So I casually said "I have a copy of the contract," which apparently got her attention—that was readily obvious—and she practically exclaimed, or almost snapped at me: "How did you get a copy of the contract?" And also: "What is your interest in all this? Are you writing a book?"

That particular response immediately evoked the image of a cousin of mine—Richard—who, whenever questioning got too personal on any matter, parried all inquiries by responding, "Are you writing a book?"

I adopted my most disinterested sounding demeanor and said, "Well, I was interested in the way it was handled with the business of the Secret Service getting involved in the sale of the film."

What Mrs. Zapruder said next floored me, because, if it is accurate, it means we really do not know what happened that afternoon. She said, *"They were not at all involved in it. I don't know where you got that idea from."*

(Well, I thought, how about Forrest Sorrels testimony? But I did not say that.)

At this point, my transcript reads, "both talking at once"—and perhaps someday an audio expert can disentangle my voice from hers and figure out what Mrs. Zapruder was saying.

Meanwhile, I was trying to backtrack, and I said "What I mean—" and Mrs. Zapruder interrupted me to say, "They handled it beautifully."

I was saying, "I mean, the business that the Government was immediately in the [transaction]—" and then Mrs. Zapruder said something that—again, if it was accurate—was truly important, which she said with considerable emphasis:

"Well, my husband gave—[he] *gave* them the film. He actually gave—he *gave* it to them. And so, they acted like gentlemen about the whole thing."

The implication of that statement is that the camera original left Zapruder's hands rather quickly.

After this part of the conversation, I tried to arrange a meeting.

No, said Mrs. Zapruder, she did not wish to meet with me.

"I couldn't give you anything; so there's really no point in getting together. I have no way of giving you anything."

" Do you have information on it?" I asked.

"No."

"All I have is news accounts," I opened, quoting that "Mr. Zapruder was out late at night, etcetera."

"Well, I'll tell you," she replied, "Any information that you want, really, if you want to take time—you read *The Warren Report*. And you—It, it's a complete report, as anything has ever done (sic). And if you really want to find out some real true facts, the true facts are in *The Warren Report*. So there's really nothing more to say, there's really nothing more to say." And: "I'm not at liberty to give you any information. Really I'm not. So there's really, there'd really be no point in getting together."

Mrs. Zapruder obviously wanted to get off the phone, and sooner than later, but I tried one more time:

"Are you surprised that the contract became a public document?" I asked, innocently, realizing she must have been horrified at the thought.

"I'm not surprised at anything," said. "I don't even know what's going on. I'll be very honest with you. As far as I'm concerned, at the moment, the subject is closed. Its absolutely closed. I have no interest in anything."

She sounded a bit rattled, and then said: "Listen, I'm on my way out to a dinner. I really can't give you very much time. If you want to call me again, go ahead; but really and truly, I don't think I'm going to have any time to talk to you."

And so we said our goodbyes.

Enter Barbara Bridges

As the record stood then—and as it stands today—here's the way it looks.

Zapruder went back to his office. There, according to his business partner (Erwin Swartz, who was not identified and questioned in detail until the mid-1990s [see Noel Twyman, *Bloody Treason*]), he was met by two policemen with guns, and they demanded that he turn over the film.

Old Abe refused—for which I am ever so grateful.

Then, at some point, Forrest Sorrels went over to his office, and after that point, Abe was in the hands of someone from the Secret Service and the rest is history: he was brought to the Kodak plant near Love Field, his film was processed, etcetera.

But before proceeding, who were the men with the guns? No Dallas Police officer filed a report saying he went to Zapruder's office with a shotgun or made any demand for the film. Yet this apparently happened as it is attested to by Erwin Swartz, Zapruder's business partner, who was present and who described it all in interviews in the mid-1990s with JFK researcher Noel Twyman.

Mr. Zapruder told Secret Service agent Max Phillips that afternoon—and he put it into his report—"According to Mr. Zapruder, the assassin was firing from behind Mr. Zapruder." When he testified, Zapruder said that the police "some of them were motorcycle cops. . . . they were running right behind me," which raised the question, "Which motorcycle cops?" (And when Zapruder testified, he volunteered, "They claim it was proven it could be done by one man. You know there was an indication there were two?" To which Liebeler, the examining counsel, replied: "Your films were extremely helpful to the work of the Commission, Mr. Zapruder."

In 1965, Zapruder was interviewed at his office by an extraordinary young lady, Barbara Bridges, and I have a tape of that interview. Barbara was young and beautiful and a UC Berkeley graduate student. I can just imagine the scene—the exotic and beautiful Barbara Bridges and old Abe, your typical Jewish uncle.

On the tape, two things stand out. First, when Zapruder talks about police who were running behind him, Barbara—genuinely confused as to what he was talking about—said to him, "By 'police', Mr. Zapruder—you mean police from the motorcade?"

Old Abe pauses and says, "Er, . . . well, . . . where else would they be from?"

And then a second interchange grabbed my attention. What was Abe doing closeted with the agents for so many hours?, asked Barbara. Why did they want to see his film so badly?

Abe shuffled and hemmed and hawed a bit and said, "Well, this was the way they knew that he was dead."

Somehow, that reminded me of the way my father might have answered an INS inspector at Ellis Island, but it just didn't sound credible. It just didn't ring true.

A proper conversion must be made to understand just how much money was involved. A *Money* magazine website gives the conversion chart: $25,000 in 1963 is equal to about $150,000 in today's money—and that $150,000 (the total over the 5 years) is the equivalent of $900,000. On Saturday, Abe had a deal for $50,000 (which, in today's money, would be about $300,000). By Monday, he had a contract for $150,000 and an arrangement involving yearly payments of $25,000 per annum starting in January 1964 and extending through 1968.

I must emphasize that I'm not only interested in what's on Abe Zapruder's film and how the deal was arranged, but what he may have seen—and not only through the viewfinder.

I don't begrudge Abe Zapruder his *schmalz grub*; I do worry, seriously worry, that we never got a true accounting of what he saw and of the exact circumstances of his sale of his film. And I sure would also like to know who were the police with guns who greeted him in his office—because no legitimate Dallas police ever filed a report stating any such thing and, given what Abe reports having seen in the area of the monument on the grassy knoll, that makes me decidedly uneasy.

The Sale to *Life*—Revisited

Most people think of *Life* magazine "as American as apple pie." But after being exposed to these many peculiarities and evidence suggesting the film was altered, the question becomes whether *Life's* acquisition of this extraordinary film was accidental or whether the entire transaction itself deserves much closer scrutiny.

Normally, rights are purchased so they may be exploited, where the word "exploit" is not meant in a pejorative sense: publishers must own rights in order to publish and distribute, whether it be a book, magazine or film. In this instance, *Life* behaved in a most extraordinary way: it failed to maximize the return on its investment.

In roughly chronological order, here's what is odd about the *Life* transaction:

1. *Life* failed to exploit the Zapruder film *as a motion picture film*. Why? As late as 1966, *Life* acted to keep it off the market, refusing even to let CBS show the film, a fact which CBS complained about, bitterly and rather loudly, in the fourth of its four part series about *The Warren Report* which aired in June 1967.

2. Why was so much additional money laid out between Saturday, 23 November, and Monday, 25 November—specifically to preclude it being used as a motion picture film? This is clear by comparing the agreement Zapruder signed on Saturday with the Monday contract. In the former case, he merely sold "print rights"; in the latter, "all rights". Something obviously changed over the weekend, and the Saturday/ Monday price difference ($100,000) would be, in today's money, the equivalent of $500,000. Was someone aware of the political dynamite represented by the head-snap?

3. When Zapruder returned to his office on Friday, 22 November, he was confronted by men "with guns" in Dallas police uniforms who demanded the film. Who were these gentlemen?

4. Regarding the participation of C. D. Jackson: he ought to have been a critical witness and quizzed regarding all circumstances leading to the decision to spend so much additional money to purchase film rights (and then not exploit those rights).

5. There was no explanation for why the payments to Zapruder were spread out over the course of four years—coincidentally, the length of the Johnson administration— or why, in 1975, he was given his film back for one dollar.

6. Who was so prescient, on 22 November 1963, as to order that the film to remain unslit? That paved the way for its subsequent alteration by enabling it to be edited on a standard optical printer. Was Forrest Sorrells, the Dallas Secret Service Chief, conversant in such details? If not, who was?

7. Stolley's description of the bidding is odd, to say the least, and suggests some element of pre-arrangement, namely: that the decision to sell the film to *Life* had already been made and that Zapruder may have been briefed prior to their first meeting. Stolley—who appears unwitting—began by offering Zapruder $5,000, at which time (he reports) Zapruder got a gleam in his eye, as if he well knew exactly how valuable was the asset he owned. Stolley then went up in $5,000 increments. When he reached $50,000 and Zapruder wanted still more, Stolley explained that he'd have to call his New York office. At that point, instead of saying, "OK, call your office", Zapruder capitulated and agreed to the deal. Why? Was this a genuine negotiation or some sort of charade?

8a. Reporting on the CBS radio network on November 25, Dan Rather said he had just seen the film and that, when the fatal shot struck, the President's head moved "violently forward". Was Rather looking at some earlier version? Or did he simply not report truthfully?

8b. The original written news release describing the film—disseminated via the wire services between 11/25 and 11/29—specifically described a forward motion after the head-shot.[10] That slight motion—not visible to the naked eye when the film is viewed in motion—is perceivable only if one studies the still frames carefully, and most researchers knew nothing about it until 1966. Who prepared these news releases? Who was so knowledgeable about the intricacies of the film at such an early hour?

The behavior of *Life* magazine, at the editorial level, is also peculiar.

a. Why, in the first edition using the film (29 November, which was "wrapped" on Sunday, 24 November, by noon) is no mention made of any impact to JFK's head? Why such silence on points that are, on the film we have today, really quite obvious?

b. Why the caption change in mid press run, in the 2 October 1964 issue? That change—made at great expense, obviously ordered by someone very high on the corporate ladder—implied that someone of importance was quite aware of and perhaps touchy about the public's perception concerning the backward movement of JFK's head in response to the fatal shot.

c. If *Life's* top executives really believed the story about Haskell Wexler possibly buying the film for $1 million and sent the film to the West Coast for that reason, then why was the film returned to Zapruder in 1975 for *one dollar*? Turning to 1975: if *Life*, for whatever reason, wanted to rid itself of this item, why didn't it give the film to the American people by donating it to the National Archives? Why return it to its original owner? No such provision was in the 1963 *Life*/Zapruder contract and its return to the Zapruder family only led to additional years where the film was generally unavailable, leading, still later, to a $16 million bonanza for the family.

The FBI's "Zapruder-frame booklet" (WCE 885)

The FBI prepared a booklet of black and white frames for the Warren Commission—"Commission Exhibit 885"—published in Volume 18. That booklet contains at least two significant anomalies. First of all, although revealing one splice (207/212), the existence of the other (at 155) is concealed, because the sequence starts at frame 171. Second: as previously noted, frames 314 and 315 were reversed, which would have confused any attempt at close analysis. Finally, the booklet stops at 334, one frame prior to the two frames which (in effect) "showcase" the large Bethesda head wound (frames 335 and 337). If studied closely, it would soon become apparent that this huge "Zapruder film head wound" conflicts (in size and location) with the "large" head wound described in the Bethesda autopsy report (which is situated towards the rear). The Warren Commission staff never studied any of this—and was very likely oblivious to these "conflicts in the record"—because frames past 334 weren't in their booklet of frames.

To recapitulate: Can we accept as *coincidence* that, with regard to the official FBI exhibit of the motion picture record, that (a) one of two splices was concealed, (b) the frames recording the impact of the fatal shot were reversed, and (c) key frames depicting the image of the fatal wound—335 and 337—were omitted because the sequence stopped at 334?

Having said all this, I would be the first to admit that, because this information became evident in piecemeal fashion over many years, the notion that there was something suspicious about all this—and, in particular, the film's sale to *Life*—took quite some time to develop.

Returning now to 1971 and the aftermath of my Dallas trip when I had individual interviews with bystanders Moorman, Brehm, John Chism, and Franzen. Although I was persuaded, based on these interviews, that JFK's limousine momentarily halted during the shooting and that in many respects the secret editing of the Zapruder film held the key to this affair, it was depressing so realize that this vital film evidence was, for all practical purpose, unavailable. Never again did I expect to see materials of the quality I had seen in June 1970 at the Beverly Hills office of Time-Life.

But I was wrong.

Fall 1972: I First Meet Robert Groden

Although living in Los Angeles, I made occasional trips to New York; and one such trip, made in August 1972, was for the purpose of briefing Dr. Cyril Wecht when he went to the National Archives to examine the Kennedy autopsy photographs and X-rays. (See Chapter 20 of B*est Evidence* for a detailed account of what transpired and Wecht's unwillingness to challenge the authenticity of the materials.)

After the visit, I was assigned the task of arranging Wecht's *New York Times* interview and was present when he was interviewed by Fred Graham. Wecht said JFK was shot twice from behind, mentioned nothing about inauthenticity, and then wrote an article for a forensics journal restating these beliefs. It was a depressing experience because, while in Washington, I managed to get Naval photographer John Stringer (who took the autopsy photos) on the phone—twice—and he insisted that the head wound he photographed was located at the *back* of the head in the "occipital area" (whereas the autopsy photographs showed no such thing). But Wecht brushed aside anything Stringer said, questioning his competence with anatomic language. To this day, Wecht refuses to deal seriously with matters of authenticity while simultaneously attempting to convey the illusion he stands at the forefront of the debate.

At that time, JFK researcher Jerry Policoff—aware of my intense interest in the medical evidence and the Zapruder film—told me I must attend a gathering he was having and meet a recent acquaintance of his. He stressed the person's identity would have to remain secret but assured me he possessed something very special: startlingly clear copies of the Zapruder film. Immediately, of course, my mind went back to June 1970 and what I had seen at the Beverly Hills office of Time-Life. Nobody could beat that for quality—of that I was certain.

So on a Saturday night I went to Policoff's apartment in Jackson Heights, Queens (New York City).A raucous party was in progress and it was on that occasion[11]—just days after spending time with Wecht at the Archives—that I first met "Robert", who held everyone transfixed by repeatedly projecting a copy of the Zapruder film. "Robert," of course, was Robert Groden, but would not reveal his true identity, a situation that persisted for about two years. That night, he was the center of attention, which he obviously enjoyed, as he projected his Zapruder film repeatedly against a wall or makeshift screen.

From the image quality, *it was immediately evident it was of the same quality I had seen in June 1970 at the Beverly Hills office of Time-Life.* As I recall, "Robert" had 16mm materials and perhaps 35mm materials there that night. Where, pray tell, had he obtained this from? And who in the world was this guy? He would only give me his first name, "Robert" and I dutifully carried him in my phone book, for some two years, as "Robert (Z)".

Of course, my curiosity knew no bounds, and I peppered him with questions. Groden—I will refer to him by his proper name here, even though I didn't know it then—was quite irritated with all my questions and particularly my persistent attempt to pinpoint what item (called an "optical element") had been the progenitor of these materials and where he had obtained them from.

It was a memorable experience because, against a background of loud voices partying and music that was either the Beatles or the Supremes, I was attempting to pose serious questions and obtain technical data. He could see I was not to be fobbed off with some cock and bull story and that I understood what an optical printer was; and, despite the noise and the general tumult, I was in fact questioning him rather seriously. This first encounter had a comic quality. After asking a question or two, and obtaining technical data from Groden, I would excuse myself and go to the bathroom, where I was making notes on tissue paper. Groden could see I was attempting to keep track of exactly what he was saying and he didn't like it one bit. It was an evening he never forgot.

Nevertheless, I did learn that night just how he had obtained prints of such clarity: there was a lab in New York City where *Life* had sent the film for enlargement in the late 1960s, and he had some connection with that lab. He would not provide any details, but this lab (I now realized) was the source of the extraordinary Z film materials I had seen at Time *Life's* Beverly Hills office in June 1970. This fellow "Robert" had worked there, obviously had had access to an optical printer at that facility, clearly knew how to oper-ate it; had "borrowed" a negative, and that was the source of his ultra-high quality prints. End of story or, at least, that's about how much I learned that night.

Either at this meeting or later, I learned what was special about this lab. Normally, optical printers are designed to work in professional format—either in 16mm or 35mm. But the owner (who it turned out was Moses "Moe" Weitzman) had made a special "shuttle" device, modifying his optical printer to accept 8 mm film. Consequently, around 1967, the 8mm original Z film (which *Life* purchased in November 1963) could be put into the standard optical printer and then blown up, magnified, in one step, to 35mm.

An important point needs to be made here. Weitzman had nothing whatever to do with the alteration of the original Zapruder film which occurred in November, 1963 in connection with its sale to *Life*—but Moe had *everything* to do (around 1967) with re-storing the film to this "oversized" or "magnified" format, one crucial to collecting data on which all theories of film alteration are based because only in such enlarged format is crucial detail visible and measurable.

Let me explain. To alter the Zapruder film initially, it was probably necessary to "bump it up" to 16mm and more likely 35mm. At that time, and after alterations were made, the edited film (altered in 16mm or 35mm format) would have to be "reduced" back down to 8mm. So *Life* was sold an 8mm film, which arrived either as an 8mm film, but possibly as a 16mm film, which had the assassination on "side 2".

For all practical purposes, once the film was slit (and then in 8mm format), it was impossible to study with precision. The images were just too small.

If I may introduce another analogy: a forger blows up a check, works on fabricating a signature in some enlarged format, then reduces the check back down to ordinary size. Years later, in connection with forensic investigation, it becomes useful to take the forgery and re-magnify it, to "blow it back up" to an oversized state. Why? Because various anomalies are most easily studied in that oversized format. That would be akin to what happened when *Life* sent its "original" to Moe Weitzman in 1967. He had noth-ing to do with the original (November 1963) alteration; but everything to do with creat-ing an enlarged version crucial for future study. And Robert Groden ended up with negatives and prints from that endeavor.

While it is true that Groden did some additional work on the film, the essential clarity of the film comes from Moe Weitzman's ingenuity, when he went from "8 to 35" in one step, and not from anything Groden did. It was as if Weitzman had climbed 90 percent of the way up Everest and Groden went the last 10 percent. Because of Weitzman's ingenuity, the jump from 8mm to 35mm had been made optically in one step. And once a 35mm optical negative had been created, the rest was standard operating procedure: creating 35mm prints; 16mm "reduction" prints; etcetera.[12]

From this first meeting, it was clear that Groden was connected with the lab to which *Life* had sent the original (around 1967), which had created the materials I had seen in June 1970. But just who was he? And what were his credentials?

Who is Robert Groden?

In what was to turn out to be a pattern of general evasiveness, I was never able to get straight answers to the question of who Groden was and exactly what training he had. But over the years, I acquired additional information. Of particular importance are the opening 30 pages or so of Groden's March 1975 Rockefeller Commission testimony. From it, we learn that he is a high school drop out, having left Forest Hills (Queens) High School in the 11th grade and joining the Army.

Although Groden claimed before the Rockefeller Commission that he completed high school (and had one year of college) in the Army, under questioning it was also revealed that he left the Army after only one year, because of a medically related discharge of a psychological nature. He then returned to the New York, worked for a record distributor and then, at some point, went to work as an optical technician making 35mm slides from pictures. Jumping ahead, I now know that he worked for extended periods at EFX Laboratories in New York run by Weitzman, and it was Groden's relationship with Weitzman and Weitzman's relationship with *Life* (back around 1967) that is crucial in understanding how Groden came into possession of so much JFK-related material—and why, during the years of the HSCA, he was entrusted with films by General Counsel Blakey, films Blakey would mail him and which he could then bring to New York—to Moe's lab, in fact—and copy.

1972-1973: Our "Early Years"

From six months or more after I first met Groden, all I had was his New Jersey phone number. I would repeatedly ask him—practically plead with him—if he could please make me a copy of what he had; he either demurred or stalled. As to questions of the film's authenticity, it became very clear that he was wedded to the idea that what he had was authentic—he couldn't conceive it were otherwise—and that posed another problem. Groden seemed threatened by any line of inquiry that implied inauthenticity. Finally, he parted with an 8mm copy, but it was useless. I needed a good 35mm copy, but that was out of the question: He wouldn't even part with a 16mm copy.

My correspondence file with Groden for the period 1972-75 reflects the story of two people who were friends, but reveals a growing tension in the relationship as well as a disillusionment, as I came to realize that Robert Groden was unwilling to make available his material to third parties and had the mentality of a juvenile collector, not an investigator. He was never going to part with the items that made him special: he felt he "owned" the materials he had and would not let anyone else have a negative or a print. His possession and access was unique—and he intended for it to stay that way.

On the other hand, I never told Groden about my theory of body alteration, because (a) I was in New York to complete my book and deemed him highly unreliable, almost juvenile; and (b) it was clear that he believed the autopsy photographs had been altered, while I didn't subscribe to that at all. Anyway, it was my theory of body alteration that that drove my interest in the possibility of the Z film having been altered. That subject— Z film authenticity—I openly discussed with him and he was adamant that the film could not have been altered! *Groden constantly emphasized that the Z film he saw had material between the sprocket holes. That could only occur on the original camera, he said. Therefore, the film had to be authentic, it could not be a dupe.* This particular point, which assumed greater importance years later, came up often and became a very sore point. All my efforts to get high quality 35mm material in order to make measurements were rebuffed or parried.

Groden viewed the assassination as a "shooting" and the conspiracy as a conspiracy of shooters. He was always talking about "firing points." He was particularly proud of dubbing sounds onto the sound track of a video copy, so you could hear the "bang bang bang" of shots. Dealing with Groden was like dealing with a teenager to whom the assassination was a video game, not a political event.

But I tried.

In 1971, Daniel Ellsberg became famous for releasing the Pentagon Papers. I repeatedly tried to flatter him, telling him that he could be the "Ellsberg of the Zapruder film". But to no avail. The fact is Groden had an incredible monopoly and was not about to give up the thing that made him "special" in the universe: sole access to high quality Zapruder film imagery, which in fact stemmed from his relatioinship with Weitzman.

Then something happened involving the Nix film, taken from the opposite side of Dealy Plaza. Early on, I realized that if the car stop had been removed from the Zapruder film, then it must have been removed from the Nix film as well. If the Nix film could be located, perhaps precise measurements of velocity could be made and compared with similar measurements made on the Zapruder film. I felt certain they wouldn't agree exactly and that that would provide further evidence of film alteration.

1973: The Nix Film and "Executive Action"

Oliver Stone's "JFK" was not the first feature film about Dallas. The first was "Executive Action", released in 1973. The screenplay, written by Donald Freed and Mark Lane, depicted a fictional plot instigated by wealthy Texas oil men assisted by high level government officials. JFK played himself—that is, news reel footage was utilized—and "the story" was built around that footage.

I was the film's researcher, formally employed by Wakeford-Orloff, the production company. As such, I could examine all incoming film materials from various New York City film libraries. So I could (and did) sit at a moviola and study clips with Oswald proclaiming his innocence: "I didn't shoot anybody, no sir!", etcetera.

At some point, I thought of an idea to obtain access to the Nix film: persuade producer Ed Lewis to utilize the Nix film in the movie. So I made the suggestion and requested that that a high quality Nix film be made and flown to California for inspection. I also suggested that UPI—which owned the film—should use EFX in New York. In short, my goal was to get UPI to do with the Nix film what *Life* had done in 1967 with the Zapruder film. The film would go to the lab where Groden worked, he would be at the controls, and I envisioned a situation in which we could both get excellent copies of the Nix film.

The production company gave the OK and the actual transaction was handled by film editor Ivan Dryer (another JFK researcher, later to become famous and wealthy as the inventor of the Laserium). Involved at the east coast end, according to my notes, was UPI executive Burt Rinehart, with whom I (or Ivan) had contact.

My notes to Wakeford Orloff editor Ivan Dryer dated 18 June 1973 reflect the arrangement for contacting UPI in New York, and what they were to be told:

1. EFX. Moe Weitzmann (212) 541 9220

2. Do NOT mention that they [EFX] did [the] Z [film] (How would Ivan know that?)

3. Technical superiority of EFX

- Best blow-up work in the world

- Full immersion liquid gate

My notes (from September 1973) reflect the detailed arrangements on the day the film went over; for example:

"The Deal"

"Between me and Bob"

"I get a Z (at least 16mm)"

"We both get 35mm Nix, in color"

"The Transaction:

"1. They (UPI) will call after 12."

"2. Will ask for Moe Weitzman"

"3. Robert will be at controls [of the EFX optical printer]"

"Full immersion liquid gate

"8 - 35; 1 step blow-up."

Page after page of my notes covers the phone calls back and forth, who should call who, exactly when the Nix film would arrive at EFX, etcetera.

As result of these cross country maneuverings, UPI did in fact send the Nix film to EFX (I was elated at that news) but then came a letdown: Groden told me (some days later) he had been unable to obtain access to it. At the time, I believed him, but years later, after many other experiences with Groden, I concluded this was false. Completely false. First of all, from that point forward, Groden seemed to have fantastic Nix imagery, comparable to what he had in the case of the Zapruder film. Second, he told at least one third party that the source of those terrific Nix images was the time he got the Nix film "in connection with *Executive Action*". So I feel confident that Groden ended up with the Nix imagery he has because of my efforts back in 1973.

But after this episode, my whole plan of comparing the car's velocity on two different films went down the drain. Groden claimed he had failed to catch the pass I had thrown him and he refused to share the Zapruder materials (beyond providing me with a truly terrible 8mm version of the film).

Years later, when I saw the extraordinarily high quality of the Nix film that Groden had, I became convinced that he in fact had access to a 35mm film element made directly from the original—though it is an open question with me as to whether he obtained such access at the time the Nix film went there in September 1973 or whether he in fact made such a Nix copy later, when he was with HSCA. Another related question is *whether he in fact now possesses the original Nix film* in view of the fact that it is missing.

CIRCA 1974: Growing Disillusionment

Jack Clemente, who had been at the Navy's China Lake air station, was well quali-fied to do optical work; and both he and I were chafing at the bit to make the kind of measurements on the Z film that could form the basis for a quantitative arguments concerning whether alteration had occurred. Yet we were hamstrung by Groden's un-willingness to make high quality film elements available.[14]

Clemente and I discussed this constantly and the file reflects our growing frustra-tion. Groden would often talk big about the legal risk he was taking. One memo, the basis for a talk I was going to have with him, reads:

"If you make a decision to be civilly disobedient, then at least do it with integrity. But you can't have it both ways. You can't, on the one hand, claim pure and high motives, and then, on the other, engage in the business of denying materials to researchers, such as myself, that are *absolutely essential* to their work."

One of the things that came up was this: what was the difference, really, between Groden's "monopoly" and that of the LMH company (the Z family legal entity that controlled the Z film)?

When push comes to shove in this case—legally speaking—the entire validity of your case, certainly morally—and perhaps legally—is going to depend on whether you have, in fact, practiced what you preach.

Have you?

And another quote from the same memo:

Have you in fact behaved, in such a way, as to deny access to key photographic blowup materials, so that your presence is always required in order to exhibit the Zapruder film?

I'm telling you Robert—and I speak as your friend—that this policy is wrong—morally wrong, and legally wrong.

If this thing goes to court. . . you are going to look ridiculous when you are a posturing virgin who, if pressed, will admit that she is a "little bit pregnant".

I told Groden he was behaving as "Son of Zapruder" and to cut it out. But it never did stop. I told him: "The Zapruder family has built a fence around this film, and all you have done is build a fence around their fence."

Groden's attitude towards the film was truly something to behold. As I came to see later, he believed he owned whatever he had enlarged. He had the same attitude to-wards enlarged images that an inventor had towards a new idea. If Groden enlarged it, why he owned it. That's the way he behaved, and it represented a most peculiar psychol-ogy.

Of course, in 1981, when *Best Evidence* was published and he finally learned what I had been working on—wound alteration, with all its ramifications, while he had a "com-peting hypothesis" which involved the alteration of photographs—the divergence be-tween us grew significantly. But more on that later.

1974 or 1975: Groden "goes public" with his Zapruder film

Around 1975, Groden went public. He went on a lecture tour with comedian Dick Gregory. In early March, 1975, he appeared on the Geraldo Rivera show, showing his "optically enhanced" Zapruder film on TV for the first time. I put the word "enhanced" in quotes, because I have always believed the so-called enhancement is overrated. What "enhances" Groden's copies—and is responsible for their startling clarity—is that Groden's film was made from a 35mm film element made *directly* from the 8mm original. So the issue was not the special optical work done by Groden, but rather *what he started with— the very special negative created by Weitzman.*

During this general period, Groden was an active lobbyist for the creation of a new investigation, showing his Zapruder film all over Capitol Hill. Please note, however, that during this entire period, whenever anyone wanted to see the film—whether it was a studio executive or a congressman or a student group—Groden would never part with a print. He never provided films to anyone. He insisted on being present and on projecting it himself. That meant Groden always had to be flown to wherever the location was. Those were the rules and that's how he maintained control over the film.

March 1975: Groden testifies before the Rockefeller Commission

The first 30 pages of the transcript of Groden's Rockefeller Commission testimony show the extent to which Groden was willing to evade legitimate questions under oath and hide behind a facade that he was protecting someone from harm. It also revealed how he responded when questioned about his credentials.

Groden testified that he dropped out of Forest Hills High School in the eleventh grade to enlist in the Army, and that he served "in New Jersey, in Georgia, and in Germany." But it turns out that he didn't serve the standard three-year hitch, at all.

OLSEN: Did you receive an honorable discharge?

GRODEN: Yes I did.

OLSEN: Was there any particular reason why your term of service was so short?

GRODEN: It was ill health and it related to that. I have never seen the exact records so I am not exactly sure how they termed it, *but it was an inability to cope with military life affecting my health.* (italics added)

ROETHE: An administrative discharge or [?]—

GRODEN: I don't know how to describe it. It was an honorable discharge but it was related to the fact that my health was suffering from the service.

OLSEN   It was medically related?

GRODEN   Yes, sir.

As I suggested to the ARRB (in quoting this material): "These facts, of course, ought to be verified." Then the questioning turned to Groden's work experience. Upon leaving the army, he testified, he took "various jobs": he worked at the New York World's fair, and "sold records for various record distributors for a period of a few years". As to how long he worked in jobs "unrelated to photography", he answered: "About three years", until 1968. He said that his first job that "had to do with photography" was in "June of 1969" at which time "I got my first employment as an optical technician."

OLSEN: By who?

GRODEN: I would prefer, if I may, not to identify any companies that I have worked for by name.

OLSEN   Well, it has a good deal to do with establishing what your qualifications are.

GRODEN: It does, but there may be an inference for anyone of the possible locations dealing with some of the photographic film evidence that I am submitting here and I don't wish to make any connections with them for their own sake.

OLSEN   Well, you will have to explain that to us. Why is it that you do not want to identify these employers?

GRODEN   It is a very general feeling. I have worked for five different optical houses in New York [*Author's note:* the whole issue turns on EFX, but Groden didn't want to say that, under oath]. I wish to not connect anyone of them with this case at all for their own sake and in this case perhaps even their own safety.

The fact is that Moe Weitzman would have become most embarrassed—professionally speaking—had it become known that his lab possessed all these copyrighted duplicate materials and had made them available to Robert Groden.

Meanwhile, an important discovery was made bearing on the chain of possession of the Zapruder film back in November, 1963.

CIA 450: Discovery by Paul Hoch

Around March 1976, JFK researcher Paul Hoch, perusing a batch of recently released CIA documents, discovered CIA item 450, a multi-page document with data arranged in tabular form, apparently devoted to an analysis of the Zapruder film and the creation of certain briefing materials requiring that 28 color photos be made from selected frames of a Kodachrome positive of the Zapruder film. CIA 450 established that "the film"—we'll discuss just "which" film (or copy) it was—had been at the National Photo Interpretation Center (NPIC) in Washington shortly after the assassination. NPIC is one of the most sophisticated photo labs in the world and played a major role in processing and interpreting U-2 spy plane films that played such a significant role in the Cuban Missile Crisis. Prior to Hoch's discovery, there was no reason to connect the Z film with NPIC.

The document apparently described the contents of four briefing boards—labeled "Panel 1", "Panel 2" "Panel 3" and "Panel 4"—each consisting of between six and eight Zapruder frames for a total of 28 frames. The prints, distributed amongst the four boards, were numbered from 1 through 28. (*Editor's note*: See Appendix C and the item entitled, "NPIC Typed Summary for Preparing a Briefing Board".)

These briefing boards were apparently used to illustrate some kind of presentation. Another sheet—apparently on legal size paper, again, with the same 28 frame numbers arrayed in multiple columns—was a shot and timing analysis as notes explaining the assassination in terms of several different 3 shot scenarios. One of these was labeled "Life Magazine" and the others were simply labeled "Other possibilities." In the *Life* column, two terse phrases used to describe the time intervals between shots—"74 frames later" and "48 frames after that" (each listed along with quotation marks)—were identical with phrases used in *Life* writer Paul Mandel's article, "End to Nagging Rumors: The Six Critical Seconds," which appeared in two issues of *Life*—the 6 December 1963 issue and the "JFK Memorial Issue" of 7 December 1963.

Was the CIA supplying *Life* with data? Or did the agency have the film later on, and was it reading *Life* for its information. (*Editor's note*: Again, see Appendix C, now the item entitled, "NPIC working notes related to a shot sequence analysis".)

Whatever the exact explanation, suffice it to say that previously unreported CIA possession of the Zapruder film was an important discovery. It raised the question of whether the CIA had the film prior to or in connection with its sale to *Life*.

1976: Groden Hired by HSCA

The HSCA was created in the fall of 1976 and at some point Groden was hired as a photo consultant. During this period, I had moved to New York City and was writing *Best Evidence*.

From time to time we spoke. Sometimes (but not very often) I visited. He was about an hour away. As I wrote the ARRB, "It was during this period that Groden had access to various items of photographic evidence; and, I believe, copied them at EFX Labs in NYC. I infer this from the film materials I later would see at his home, culminating with my contract with him to buy his entire collection (which I transferred to Betacam)." More on this later.

I always found it remarkable that Blakey hired Groden without the appropriate background investigation and then trusted him to duplicate this or that film. So Groden was in the position of having full access to any number of priceless originals, which he would bring to New York and duplicate at EFX on their optical printer. In this way, Groden developed a formidable film collection.

Fall 78: Groden testifies before HSCA

In the fall of 1978, Robert Groden testified before the HSCA, presenting the standard version of various arguments that had been in books and articles that President Kennedy had been shot by more than one assassin. Groden's films were very clear and provided the basis for much interesting conjecture. But in the final analysis, it was the autopsy report—and the medical documents from the Forensic Science Panel—that would shape the HSCA conclusions. So, in my view, Groden served as a convenient sparring partner for General Counsel Robert Blakey, who could create the appearance—by presenting Groden to the public—that he was a very open-minded fellow hearing all points of view, while in fact he was pursing a Mafia-did-it theory with considerable single-mindedness.

Meanwhile, Groden had his own agenda, which apparently revolved around increasing the size of his photo-collection.

Spring 1979: I visit Groden's home

Everyone remembers where they were when they first heard President Kennedy was assassinated. Similarly, I vividly remember the time when I first saw the photographs of President Kennedy lying in the morgue. That occurred in Robert Groden's home in Hopelawn, New Jersey, sometime in the Spring of 1979.

I became aware that he had these pictures and, since the book I was writing concerned the medical evidence, I very much wanted to see them. Groden repeatedly denied that he had them; he would look me straight in the eye and repeat these denials. I knew he was lying, but saw no way to get him to relent and show me the pictures.

Finally, on a visit to his home one evening, I bought his family some pizza and played along with his almost childlike game of capitulating to his claim—of reassuring him that I believed him and, further, that I didn't care, one way or the other, whether he had the pictures. It was then, while I was facing the TV set, either sitting next to his wife or one of his kids, that he came up behind me and just dropped this envelope in my lap.

I opened it, and there were the autopsy photos. As I recall, they were in black and white, and that is what I wrote in a footnote in *Best Evidence*.

As I later came to realize, I do not believe that Groden possessed what we call the "stare of death" photo, and this became an issue later on. I also believe that the only pictures I saw at that time were somewhat fuzzy black and whites.

I do recall Groden explaining to me—either then or on a subsequent visit—how he had obtained the pictures. He told me that, in connection with a request to Blakey to have authorization to photograph the autopsy photographs (in order to enlarge one and show Blakey or the Forensic Pathology Panel what he believed was a wound in the left temple), he had slipped an extra film roll into the camera, taken photographs using that roll, and walked out of the Archives (or the HSCA offices, I'm not sure which) with that roll, which he then developed privately.

I don't know whether that would be legally defined as "theft", but it was the first time I realized that Groden was in fact willing to cross the line and walk off with evidence while employed by the US government.

On one of these visits to Groden's home, I spent several hours helping him write his "Minority Dissent" to the HSCA's photo panel. In particular, the section titled "The Problem of Authenticity" (HSCA Volume 6, pp. 299-300) runs for two pages, and anyone who has read *Best Evidence* will recognize my writing style. I didn't believe that photo alteration explained what happened on 22 November 1963, but he was the proponent of that hypothesis and I lent a hand with my own writing skills so his argument would be stated with as much clarity and force as possible.

But now, back to the autopsy photographs. Groden had the pictures, and believed they were important because (he believed) they were fake. It is my belief that Groden then made the photographs available to Harrison Livingstone (with whom he was co-writing a book, *High Treason)* and that explains what happened next.

29 August 1979: Livingstone tries to sell the autopsy photos

On 29 August 1979, *The New York Times* carried a story revealing that Harrison Livingstone had possession of the autopsy photographs and was trying to sell them for one million dollars ("A Conspiracy Theorist Offers to Sell Pictures of 'Kennedy Autopsy'".)

Livingstone denied having stolen the photos. From *The New York Times'* story: "He says that he is selling them because he *and his group* need at least $800,000 'to prove the conspiracy in the murder of our President.'" Livingstone said that "he had asked for bids for the photographs, in both black and white and color, from the three television networks, two wire services, 10 newspaper including *The New York Times*, and two magazines. He said that he had received no bids as of late yesterday." (emphasis added)

Blakey, the General Counsel of the House Select Committee, then conducting its investigation of the JFK murder, was furious. The *Times* reported: "There are two things possible here, Mr. Blakey said. 'Either it's a fraud against the people who would purchase these pictures. Or it's an attempt to sell stolen property.'"

Continuing: "Reached at the office of his attorney in Baltimore, Mr. Livingstone said there was no fraud. 'I have five different pictures,' he said. 'They're legitimate. And they aren't stolen.'"

As I recall, that story caused Groden—who repeatedly claimed he was not Livingstone's source (but who became his co-author in writing *High Treason*, first published in 1989)—to go into a panic. It was obvious to me that Groden was Livingstone's source, but Groden would never admit it to me, explicitly. However, he later blamed me for getting him so fearful that, he said, he had destroyed his key negatives and all prints. In other words, in future dealings with Groden, it became a matter of "fact" that, supposedly, he no longer had the autopsy photographs. This "fact" remained in force only until the fall of 1982.

But the story is noteworthy because, years later, Groden would claim—as an excuse as to why he no longer had his original material—that a girlfriend had made off with key items from his precious collection. In other words, Groden had no problem creating fictions to explain his "non-possession" of items of physical evidence he was not supposed to have in the first place, or where his possession of whose items were in any event questionable.

30 August 1979: "Assassination Photos' Taken Off the Market"[15]

The text: "Copies of photographs purportedly made at the autopsy of President Kennedy were taken off the market yesterday by a conspiracy theorist who had said that he wanted to sell the pictures to finance a continuing investigation into Mr. Kennedy's death. 'I'm in a very dangerous and exposed position,' the theorist, Harrison Livingstone, said yesterday. He said that the photographs were not stolen, but that he feared that the Justice Department might take action against him anyway. 'The photographs,' he said, 'will not be available.'"

Livingstone also made this comment: that he had probably made a mistake by offering to sell the pictures to a variety of news organizations. "I didn't realize," he added, "that the Kennedy family didn't want these things made public."

At the time, and for many years later, Livingstone publicly blamed Groden as being the force behind these stories. That was not true. The source, as the story makes clear, was Livingstone himself. Also, when they later became co-authors, Groden would explain Livingstone's possession of the photographs in terms of strange and mysterious envelopes that had appeared, anonymously, in either his or Livingstone's mailbox. These stories were quite elaborate and told with great earnestness.

Best Evidence Nears Completion

As *Best Evidence* neared completion, I was acutely aware that I was operating in an environment where there were two sets of photographs, both in private hands.

First, there were the autopsy photographs, basically controlled by the Kennedy family.

Second, there was the Zapruder film, controlled by the Zapruder family.

I had now seen the very finest 35 mm version of the Z film, and I had seen rather low quality autopsy photographs—not particularly crisp or clear, but definitely of JFK.

My biggest concern lay in what to do about the Zapruder film and to what extent I was obligated to deal with miniscule imagery on the Zapruder film, when those frames weren't available for public debate.

I was well aware that the frames of the film—when viewed through a Recordak microfilm reader, as I had done some 9 years before—contained imagery of the back of the head and a weird looking so-called wound towards the front of the head. On the other hand, I could not properly present this issue without access to those frames of the film. I also believed, by this time, that the film was altered, but full well realized that a discussion of that was far beyond the scope of my book.

As any reader knows, it is a complicated topic. So I decided to discuss it in the form of an extensive footnote. The footnote basically raised the issue of Zapruder film alteration using two pieces of evidence: a letter that Wallace Milam had from Dallas Doctor Peters, who said the wound shown on the film was not the one he saw; and the existence of CIA document 450, which suggested that the CIA had the film before it went to *Life*.

The Zapruder Film Footnote

The main point of *Best Evidence*—to put the matter in legal terms—was to impeach the Bethesda autopsy as evidence by demonstrating that the President's wounds had been altered prior to autopsy. Because of a few film frames that appeared to show otherwise, the Zapruder film posed a potential problem to that thesis, but not one I could deal with directly, since the film wasn't available for a frame by frame discussion. So I wrote a footnote about the situation. The footnote, one of the longest in *Best Evidence*, ran some 750 words. My primary purpose was to attack the concept that the Zapruder film was necessarily the "best evidence" when it came to the imagery of the Dallas head wounds. It also had another purpose: to hark back to an opinion expressed earlier in the book (about the source of the fatal shot and the meaning of the small forward motion between frame 312 and 313) and inform the reader I had changed my mind:

"By this time, my view of the headsnap had changed considerably, and I no longer subscribed to the theory of a forward high-angle shot to explain the double motion. My revised view was inextricably linked to new information I had obtained bearing on the authenticity of the film.

"In 1971, I was permitted to study, in the L.A. offices of Time-Life, a 35 mm print made from what Time-Life called the 'camera original' of the Zapruder film. To my surprise, I found that those frames showed the large head wound situated toward the right front, not at the rear of the head as reported by the Dallas observers. The rear of the head gave the appearance of having been 'blacked out'—or of having been in deep shadow.

"I also discovered splices on the film which had never been mentioned by Time-Life. I then began exploring the possibility that the Zapruder film itself had been altered sometime before it became Warren Commission evidence in 1964, perhaps even before it went to *Life* on 23 November 1963. (*Life* purchased the film on 25 November 1963, for $150,000.) But alteration of the film required a film laboratory with the sophisticated apparatus normally used by Hollywood to create 'special effects'.

"Was the original Zapruder film at some point taken to such a laboratory? Obviously, the film went only from Zapruder to Kodak in Dallas, then to the Jamieson Film Company in Dallas, where three prints were made (two for the Secret Service, and one for Zapruder); then back to Zapruder, and then to the vault at *Life*. I suspected it had taken a secret detour, but I could find no direct evidence to prove that. [*Editor's note:* See Appendix D.]

"Then, in 1976, among records released by the CIA under the Freedom of Information Act, Paul Hoch found CIA item 450, a group of documents indicating that the Zapruder film was at the CIA's National Photo Interpretation Center (NPIC), possibly on Friday night, 22 November 1963, and certainly within days of the assassination. NPIC is one of the most sophisticated photo labs in the world.

"The CIA documents indicate that the film, when at NPIC, was not yet numbered as it was later by the FBI Laboratory. CIA tables of frame numbers arranged in a multi-column format bearing such headlines as 'frames on which shots occur' and 'seconds between shots' explores various three-shot interpretations of the film. One document refers to the existence of either a negative or a master positive—and calls for the striking of four pints from that item: one 'test print', and a second group of three prints. The total job, it indicated, would take seven hours. The making of four prints is significant—that number is exactly what existed in Dallas: an original, and three prints made from that original.

"In 1976, I interviewed Herbert Orth, the photo chief in *Life*. Orth believed the film never left his custody in 1963. Yet the CIA documents establish that it, or a copy, was worked on at the CIA's film lab in Washington. Indeed, the figures used in the CIA documents to describe the time intervals between shots—'74 frames later' and '48 frames after that'—are identical with those used in the second *Life* article about the film (*Life*, 12/7/63, 'End to Nagging Rumors: The Six Critical Seconds'). Was the CIA supplying *Life* with data? Or did the agency have the film late, and was it reading *Life* for its information?

"In my view, previously unreported CIA possession of the Zapruder film compromised the film's value as evidence: (1) the forward motion of Kennedy's head, for one frame preceding frame 313, might be the result of an altered film, and if that was so, it made the theory of a forward high-angle shot (See Chapter 2 [referring to *Best Evidence*]) completely unnecessary; (2) an altered film might also explain why the occipital area, where the Dallas doctors saw a wound, appears suspiciously dark, whereas a large wound appears on the forward right-hand side of the head, where the Dallas doctors saw no wound at all. Dr. Paul Peters, one of the Dallas doctors, quoted in his book, when shown color blowups made from the Zapruder film frames depicting these wounds, wrote: 'The wound which you marked . . . I never saw and I don't think there was such a wound. I think that was simply an artifact of copying Zapruder's movie. . . . The only wound I saw on President Kennedy's head was in the occipitoparietal area on the right side.'[13]"

January 1981: Best Evidence published

In promoting my book, the Zapruder film hardly came up. Remember, in 1981, the film was not available, so the issues raised by the Zapruder footnote in Chapter 24 never came to the fore. With regard to JFK's head wounds, it is often said that there were "no Dallas photographs", just the Bethesda autopsy photographs. In fact, there *were* some Dallas photographs—certain frames of the Z film (mainly 335 and 337) but until the advent of the Internet, no practical forum existed to publicly discuss, view, analyze and debate individual film frames.

So the issue lurked in the background.

Spring 1981: I come by the Autopsy Photographs

In the Spring of 1981, I saw excellent copies of the JFK autopsy photographs for the first time. Since my coming to possess good copies these pictures is entwined with how I came to possess a high quality 35mm copy of the Zapruder film, that story is worth relating.

It began with a letter from Maryland radio broadcaster Mark Crouch, introducing himself and saying that a retired Secret Service official (James Fox) lived nearby and he had these photos. Crouch suggested I come for a visit, and that we could go and see Fox together. Fox's general store (part bakery, fishing supply store, along with gas pump out front) was located in the Chesapeake Bay area. It was there that I first saw the JFK autopsy photographs. Fox was another person with a "collector" mentality—his major interest being World War II—and the way to reach him psychologically (explained Crouch) was to offer him some kind of World War II paraphernalia. So I brought along a tape recording of the hanging of the Nuremberg criminals, obtained some years before from the National Archives.

Skipping over many details, when I played the tape for Fox—the actual audio of Armed Forces radio recording the hanging—Fox grew quite excited. Like a race horse suddenly coming alive and wanting to go to a fire, he turned to me and said, "Do you want to see the Kennedy stuff?"

Well, I sure did, and as described in *Best Evidence*, he had the photos right there, in his bakery. Fox reached for an envelope that was propped up amongst some loaves of bread, opened it, and—with customers milling about saying such things as, "I'd like a sliced rye, please"—I first saw JFK's autopsy photographs. Subsequently Crouch persuaded Fox to loan him the pictures overnight and had them copied. That led to Crouch having a series of 35mm copy negatives which produced excellent prints—and that's how I obtained the JFK autopsy photos.

December 1982: Meeting at Groden's Home

Sometime after receiving these photos, I met with Groden, at his home in Hopelawn, New Jersey. From the report I wrote the ARRB :

At this meeting, I laid out my black and white set of autopsy prints; and Groden laid out his color set. Two things were apparent to me (for the first time):

1. The black and whites were crisp and clear; Groden's color set lacked definition (because, as I learned either that night, or perhaps back in 1979, I'm not sure which), Groden had made his set by photographing prints to which he had been given access by Blakey. But the black and white set were [copied] from a set of black and white negatives that Fox had made in the Secret Service lab.

2. Groden's set lacked the "stare of death" photo—the most important one in the collection (from a journalistic standpoint)."

Speaking of color, Groden was green with envy. I also knew, at that moment, that if I so much as turned my back, that photo would disappear. So I watched my set like a hawk, and eventually they went back into the envelope, which I held onto tightly for the remainder of my visit.

I proposed to Groden a "deal": that I make a set of black and whites for him, in return for a set of his color copies. I will never forget his answer. Groden said: "After all I've done for you [what??!], I would like you to make me a set of those prints, and in return you can have 'visiting rights' to my color set." I told Groden that that didn't work either in cases of child custody, or in autopsy photographs.

This meeting at Groden's home should dispel any doubt whatsoever that Groden, as of that date, had color prints of the autopsy photographs. (But I saw these materials still again in June 1989).

As to why he didn't have the stare of death photo, I do not know the answer to that. It may be that, in a panic after the 8/79 *The New York Times* stories, and ominous sounds from Blakey that the FBI might soon be knocking on Livingstone's door, that he actually destroyed a picture. It's also possible that, when copying them back when he was at HSCA, he simply froze, and wasn't able to copy the most important picture of all. . . .

But again: the whole incident sheds further light on the risks Groden was willing to take, as a collector, in walking off the premises with what in effect was stolen property. Also note: Groden didn't publish what he had until *after Best Evidence* published the Fox set of photographs in 1988; and he didn't publish the color photographs until years after that—and then, sold them to the *Globe* for $50,000. More on this later.

December 1982/January 1983

In December 1982 and then again in January 1983, I made trips to Dallas and showed the autopsy photographs to as many of the Dallas doctors and nurses with whom I could make appointments. Just about everybody said this was not the way the President's wounds looked when they saw the body. I made audio recordings of most of these interviews. When it was over, I had a fairly complete record of various Dallas observers, viewing the pictures, shaking their head from side to side, etcetera. But it was not clear to me when or where this material, a natural adjunct to the photos themselves, might be published.

Spring 1988: Publishing the photographs

In the Spring of 1988 with the 25th anniversary of the JFK assassination approaching, I had obtained another publisher for *Best Evidence*—Carrol and Graf in New York City. They proposed releasing *Best Evidence* in "trade paper" format and Kent Carrol asked if there was "anything new" I might have. Indeed there was, I said, informing him all about the autopsy photographs. After seeing some prints and learning they were not classified documents (albeit held at the National Archives), the decision was made to publish them in the new edition of *Best Evidence*, scheduled for release in the fall. Mark Crouch graciously sent me his negatives and new high quality prints were made at the UCLA Health Science Center.

Meanwhile, based on the material gathered from my December 1982 and January 1983 interviews, I wrote a detailed narrative. I also addressed the ethical issue: The body was the most important evidence in the case; yes, I said, I had concern for the feelings of the living, but that had to be balanced against "justice for the dead". The 1988 edition of *Best Evidence*, released about October 1988, marked the first time the autopsy photographs were published, and my detailed narrative describing the Dallas doctors' and nurses' reactions to this material was an "Afterword".

After publication, many people wrote requesting copies of the photographs. I decided not to sell the pictures and told anyone who asked to simply photograph the page of the book. I made a few exceptions: I sent Groden an entire set, *gratis*. Subsequently, I returned the negatives to Crouch, who subsequently sold them to researcher Walt Brown for several thousand dollars; and Brown, I am told, has made prints available for a modest price.

As it turned out, my possession of these very clear black and white copies of the autopsy photographs enabled me to get possession of the 35 mm copy of the Zapruder film—a completely unexpected (but most welcome) development.

1988: Opportunity knocks

In the Spring of 1988, several media events were planned for the upcoming "25th anniversary" of Dallas. One such project was a documentary by the PBS television program NOVA. I was approached producer Robert Richter, who wanted to interview me about my book. He also wanted access to the JFK autopsy photographs. Would I make them available for use on the program?

NOVA was special, and I thought Richter was fair-minded and a very nice guy. Somehow, during these conversations, the subject of the Zapruder film came up. The Zapruder family wanted a small fortune for permission to broadcast it. How was he going to deal with that, I asked? How did he propose to get around their budget-busting request for at least $50,000?

"I know Moe Weitzman," he said, simply and rather off-handedly.

"What?! You know Moe Weitzman?"

It was no problem, said Richter. He would just go over to Moe's office and get a 35mm copy from him. Moe had a whole drawer full of these 35 mm items (which the pros call "an optical element") and he would just pick the best of the lot, he said.

Suddenly a way around the Zapruder problem came into focus, and so I made a request. Sure, I would make available to him all my autopsy images—anything he wished—but what I wanted in return was a copy of that 35 mm item that Weitzman had.

Richter thought about it and told me he could not in good conscience actually give me a filmed copy of the 35 mm item. What he would do was make a fully professional magnetic transfer—on 1 inch stock—of the transfer he was making for his NOVA program, so I would have the film, but on magnetic tape.

Richter was a decent man; he obviously wanted to do what he could to please me, but also satisfy the requirements of his own conscience. So we agreed. I would give him all the autopsy images; he would give me a "one inch mag" of the Z film.

I had still another reason for cooperating with NOVA. It was always possible that the Kennedy family might take legal action against my publisher when the autopsy photos were published, but if at the same time they also appeared on NOVA, the premier PBS science program, I saw little chance of that happening. And it didn't.

Sometime over the summer of 1988, Richter came to my office along with a film crew, interviewed me in detail about *Best Evidence*, and I was pleased to learn that Walter Cronkite would be narrating. Clearly, times they were a-changin'. Cronkite was famous—or infamous—for having narrated four one-hour shows supporting *The Warren Report* in June of 1967. Now he would be narrating a full one hour documentary in which my work would be discussed extensively. I was under no illusion that NOVA would agree with me, but Richter assured me that I would get a fair hearing. (And I did.)

Shortly after the broadcast, I was provided a beautiful 1 inch magnetic transfer of Moe Weitzman's 35 mm internegative, with a number of special blow-up sequences made by NOVA for use during the program.

Meanwhile, Richter had to deal with the Zapruder family. Having seen the program, Henry Zapruder (son of Abe) wanted the usual pound of flesh, and Richter resisted. He was an old fashioned guy, maintained that his documentary was about educating the public, argued "fair use", and simply refused to pay any kind of exorbitant fee. I don't recall whether he gave the Zapruders $5,000 or possibly nothing at all, but I do remember there was quite a row and that, when it was over, having the feeling that Bob Richter had won.

Starting around the late fall of 1988, I used my newly acquired Z film in lectures. Word spread. I put the "one inch mag" on file at a professional duplicating house, and would call whenever I needed VHS copies. I sold hundreds of these items at $29.95 to students and researchers all over the country and the world. It is one of the clearest copies of the Zapruder film ever made. What any buyer was getting was Moe Weitzman's film, his 1967 "8-to-35" transfer, made directly from the original, on VHS, with additional blowup sequences, courtesy of NOVA. Moreover, jumping ahead some 13 years to the Spring of 2003, I learned that it was possible, using a digital computer and a "video capture" card, to reverse the film-to-tape transfer process and "re-capture", from the video, the individual frames of the 35mm film. But that technology wasn't available in 1988 and I am getting ahead of the story.

In 1988, what still eluded me was actual possession of a 35 mm copy of that 8mm film. Ultimately that's what I wanted, because I felt no serious analysis was possible without an optical element of that quality. Events culminating with my having access to one of the Weitzman 35 mm copies began unfolding in the summer of 1989.

Summer 1989: Breaking Groden's Monopoly

Moe Weitzman had some sort of weird father-son relationship with Groden, who had profited immensely from the film. Indeed, it was his whole life and, in a way, Groden actually controlled one critical facet of dissemination—the actual quality of the imagery that ended up on-screen.

If you were a documentary filmmaker or broadcaster and wanted to show the film, a stiff payment had to be made to the Zapruder family for "the rights" (to avoid a lawsuit), but that didn't guarantee you optical quality. If you cared about detail and, specifically, if you had some theory and needed truly clear imagery to make a point, then you had to hire Robert Groden. Groden had Moe Weitzman's 35mm negatives and even his equipment, which could generate vital blowups, imagery that would be at the heart of a program. So there was a symbiotic relationship of sorts between the Zapruders (who had film for sale) and Groden (who could highlight his own theory of cross-fire or of when a particular shot struck JFK or Connally). A producer with enough money could buy rights from the Zapruder family but, but only Groden could provide them with top quality opticals .

Groden was very proud of his films with their blowup sequences, even sending them into the U.S. Copyright office and taking out his own version of a copyright on the Zapruder film! This was of no legal merit, of course, but Groden would brandish this paperwork as if it were a valid enforceable copyright.

As I told the ARRB later, Groden sometimes reminded me of a character out of a Doonesbury cartoon, since he believed he owned anything he enlarged.

A typical transaction concerned TV station KRON-TV in San Francisco. KRON-TV is the NBC affiliate in San Francisco. Employed there—after leaving ABC network's 20/20—was producer Stanhope Gould and TV journalist Sylvia Chase. In the summer of 1988, Stanhope contacted me about doing a major documentary about *Best Evidence*, a project he had attempted to launch at 20/20.[16] I was hired as the chief consultant, and interviews were arranged with many of the *Best Evidence* witnesses as well as the Dallas doctors.

Then, Stanhope also visited with Robert Groden and, in what was a typical transaction, paid about $6,000 to $8,000 for "rights" to Groden's collection. At the time, Stanhope marveled at the clarity and extent of that collection; and it was about this time that it became apparent to me that, by contrast with the 1970s, Groden now had far more than the Zapruder film. He had Nix, Muchmore, Hughes, Bronson, Bell—one Dealey Plaza film after another. Indeed, just about every single one. It seemed obvious how he had acquired all this material: his past affiliation with the House Select Committee (HSCA) investigation (1976-1979).

I never directly questioned Groden as to whether he had taken any particular item off the premises, but whenever the matter came up, Groden said that anything he had done (and he conceded various films were taken off the premises and to Weitzman's lab in New York) was done with the full consent of General Counsel Robert Blakey.

I wasn't all that surprised. My general impression was that Blakey—who believed the Mafia was behind Kennedy's death (and interpreted just about all evidence that came his way in that context)—had found a cheap way to get film exhibits made for use in the public hearings: ask Robert Groden to do it and Groden could (and would) bring it to EFX in New York.

Naturally, being a collector, Groden would make a copy for himself, and his collector instinct didn't stop with images. On a number of occasions in connection with work for the HSCA, Groden had access to the actual original, and when I visited him at his home on one occasion, Groden proudly showed me a piece of film leader—approximately 4" long—that he had clipped off the original Zapruder film, as a souvenir. His whole attitude reminded me of a poacher who cuts off the ivory tusk of an elephant and can't resist bragging about his accomplishment.

What became important in years following—as when the original Nix film (for example) turned up missing or the original Muchmore couldn't be found—is whether Groden ever crossed the line and used his position to enhance his collection with irreplaceable originals.

In July of 1989, by which time I was living in Los Angeles, I had arranged to raise money in connection with creating a film partnership ("DSL Films") and sought to buy Groden's collection. I thought that maybe if I was nice enough to him and paid him enough, just maybe he would provide me with 35mm copies of the key films.

So, flying in from Los Angeles along with my good friend, Pat Valentino, we went to Groden's house (then in Boothwyn, Pennsylvania). Having rented fully professional Beta Cam equipment, we were prepared to pay him for permitting us to copy as much of his collection as possible.

Groden understood that he stood to make some thousands of dollars. Unfortunately, Groden—who had difficulty parting with anything—started laying down restrictions. Repeatedly, he would show us this or that item, but then tell us it was off limits. Finally, after doing this once too often—displaying something intriguing and immediately announcing that, for some mysterious reason, it was "restricted"—Valentino burst out and exclaimed sharply, "Is this *another* item we can't have?"

When it was finally decided just what we were to be allowed to copy, Groden cared not a whit about the formalities. He just wanted the money. He wanted the check. I couldn't believe his lack of sophistication. Yeah, I could copy this and that, but no paperwork was necessary. Having decided what he could part with, he was just drooling for the cash. That's what he wanted. The dough.

But that's not what I wanted. I wanted a record of all this, a list—and I wanted his signature on it.

I took out my computer and typed up a contract listing everything I was getting from Groden, item by item. Somehow we got it to work with Groden's printer and the record created that day, signed by Groden, became important. Because seven years later, when Groden was formally deposed as a witness, he denied—under oath—possession of things I had copied! Things I had paid for! But again, I am getting ahead of the story.

Groden signed the contract; my friend witnessed it.

Then, before copying anything, and in accordance with our agreement, I wrote him a check for $2,500. When our visit ended, I wrote him a second check—for $1,500. And on 20 July 1989, back in Los Angeles, I sent him a third check. By the time it was over, I had paid Robert Groden $5,000.

A year or two later came a very annoying downside and the process of dealing with Groden's version of reality began. Repeatedly, I heard that Groden was claiming to various third parties that he had never been paid. It was always the same story—Groden hadn't been paid; further of non-payment, he might lose his house.

So, I took to carrying around photocopies of the three checks, copied on both sides; my signature; his endorsement. Whenever I heard such stories, I produced the photocopies. Once, when I appeared on a TV show (and Groden was another guest), I carried them in my vest pocket, just in case. (It didn't come up.) I quipped that the only reason I didn't give Groden Xerox copies of the checks is that he might try to cash them.

Backtracking a bit: sometime in late 1989, when visiting Groden for some reason, I made a verbal slip, and it had serious consequences.

As I recall, Groden was bragging that he had every single 35 mm copy of the Zapruder film, that there were no other extant copies. He had every one, he assured me, and his manner was infuriating, because he was obviously taunting me: he had what I wanted—a 35 mm copy—and he knew why the issue was important (that it revolved around authenticity) but, like a spiteful child, he just wasn't going to cooperate. Period.

Rather fed up, I made a mistake. In the heat of one testy exchange, I shot back, "No, you don't have *every* copy of the film, Robert. There is one you *don't* have."

Which one was that? asked Groden.

"Bob Richter, the NOVA producer. *He* has a 35 mm copy."

As the words left my mouth, I just knew I should never have spoken them.

Groden blanched. It was as if I had kicked him in the solar plexus.

What? He didn't have *all* the copies? He didn't have every single copy? There was *one* he had missed?

It was as if I was speaking to a curator at a museum, and he was learning—to his shock and amazement—that something that was supposedly safe and sound and locked away in a vault was in fact not there.

I knew there was going to be trouble ahead.

And there was.

Groden went to Weitzman, solicited his cooperation, and then—as I learned soon thereafter directly from Richter—Groden actually showed up in Richter's New York office, with a letter from Weitzman, a letter claiming the 35mm negative that had been loaned Richter actually belonged to Robert Groden. Its return was demanded and legal action clearly threatened.

From the moment I heard of this, I pleaded with Richter not to return that 35 mm item, at least not right away. I explained the problem of Groden (which Richter had now experienced first hand) and how he had monopolized the imagery on the JFK case. I said that this 35mm copy of the film that Richter now possessed, made directly from the

8mm original back in 1967, was the last extant copy. If that item was returned, it would disappear forever into the Groden Black Hole. Don't let it happen, I urged. Please.

Richter was in a tight spot. He had to honor his commitment, but he also cared about truth and history and understood what I was saying. Just give it to me for a week, I pleaded. Let me bring it to a lab and work with it. Richter reached a Solomon-like solution. He wouldn't hand it directly to me, but would place it with a reliable optical lab in New York City. I could retain the lab to work with it and would have to pay the bill.

The lab Richter chose was Reel Effects, run by Jeff Kaplan, and after my first call, it was clear that the bill for an optical printer, with operator, would come to some $10,000. At least.

That day, I started calling everyone I knew who had any extra money and an interest in the Zapruder film. I formed what I called the "Save the Zapruder Film" committee. And who were we "saving" it from? We all knew. I distributed memos and material explaining the history of the film.

Everyone I spoke with had a shelf full of JFK assassination books; everyone was aware of the issue that the film had been possibly altered and the car-stop eliminated. Everyone also knew about the problem posed by Groden—his proclivity to monopolize and his hostility to any hypothesis that implied that the Zapruder film, which for years had been his claim to fame, might be inauthentic in any way. Here, finally, was a chance to do something about all this, but we had to work quickly.

I proposed to fly to New York shortly and do the work myself. How complicated could it be to operate such a printer? To each person, I promised a full 1" magnetic transfer, plus full 35 mm prints, plus a 16mm reduction print (for those with 16 mm projectors) plus a VHS. I needed about 5 people to put up $2,500 each.

The fact is, it was going to take some time to get the funds together. Meanwhile, I got my nearly 80 year old mother to pledge $10,000 to be able to pay the bill.

I flew to New York City and went to the lab.

At the New York Optical Lab

An optical printer is a big Rube Goldberg looking contraption. When I reported to the lab, I went into a room with the printer and the operator and sat next to it on a high chair, like a bar stool.

We loaded in Weitzman's 35 mm internegative, the one he had made back in 1967, directly from Zapruder's original.

A liquid—acetone—sloshed around in the apparatus actually containing the film (the "gate") the reason being that the liquid, which has the same index of refraction as the emulsion on the film, acts so as to eliminate scratches to the viewing lens.

The pungent aroma from the acetone—just inches from my face—was a major distraction. It would lead to choking and sneezing. I had to wear a cloth over my face.

But that wasn't the only difficulty. The other was the problem of simply "reading" the film.

Remember: the original Zapruder film was a positive. So when Moe Weitzman blew it up to 35 mm and on negative film, the resultant image was "reversed" and was a negative.

That meant all the colors were "reversed". So in addition to the smell of the acetone sloshing around inches from my nose, the Zapruder film, with which I was so familiar and bearing images that had been the center of my research for so many years, now appeared in "reversed color". Anyone who has ever taken snapshots is familiar with this. In the case of an ordinary black and white photo, "negative image" means that black becomes white, and vice versa. In color, an analogous situation prevailed. The three primary colors—red, blue and green—are "reversed": red becomes cyan, green becomes magenta, and blue becomes yellow. So the green lawn —now magenta—was a purplish color; blood, originally red, now looked aqua-marine, a greenish blue. Jackie's pink outfit was dark. Flesh tones no longer looked like flesh tones but were darker.

It was as if I was looking at Dealey Plaza through a weird night-scope.

Then came the issue of image content and wanting blowups. Anyone who has worked with the Z film knows how numerous questions emerge once the frames are examined, individually. Suddenly the film is a collection of hundreds of color photographs, each telling a story. To view different parts of each frame, one wheel (akin to a ships steering wheel) would be turned which controlled the "north-south" adjustment—up and down—and another which controlled east-west—right and left.

The operator, who also had to put up with the sloshing acetone, now had to put up with me as well. With my constant requests and instructions: "Could you frame that a little more to the left?. . . No. that's too far. There, just right! Now, move down about an inch." And so it went.

I could see he was getting a bit stressed. This was far from his normal routine. Finally, he said to me—"Look, why don't you operate this yourself? Its really not that complicated."

And so that's what happened. For several days, I had this incredible 35 mm color negative of the Zapruder film—Weitzman's 35 mm color internegative made in 1967 directly from the Life-owned 8 mm original—all to myself. Right there, visible through the lens, was the event which I had studied for so many years. I worked all day long, making sequences of blowups, focusing on different aspects on each pass: JFK, Jackie, the wounds, the Connallys, the reaction (or lack of it) of the men in the front seat.

When it was over, I had exposed a number of 35 mm interpositives (duplicates—in color positive—of what Weitzman had produced in 35 mm "color negative") plus 600 feet of special enlargement studies. All in 35mm.

The films were sent off to a New York processing lab.

A friend said I was like Ahab and I had finally gotten the whale. In 1970, at age 31, I had first seen material of this quality in the Beverly Hills office of Time-Life. Now, here I was, in 1990, 20 years later, with access to the special optical element that produced footage of such spectacular quality.

True enough, the material in the sprocket hole area was not captured on Weitzman's internegaive, but the quality of what *was* visible in the main body of the frame was just wonderful.

When my days at the optical printer were over, I paid the bill, and flew back to California.

Then came days of creating packages and mailing them, and cleaning up the financial situation. But it was over.

Once and for all, the Groden monopoly on the Zapruder film had been broken.

However, there was one important footnote to the story. A sequel of sorts.

I wanted to meet Moe Weitzman, and my initial contact with him was by phone in early August 1990.

How Weitzman Came to be Involved

Weitzman told me that the original work on the Zapruder film was done at a company called "Manhattan Effects"—that *Life* had gone to Oxberry (the makers of the famous Oxberry Optical Printer) and that Oxberry had referred them to him. He explained in detail how he modified the standard optical printer to accept an 8 mm film. First, he experimented by going from 8 mm to 16 mm and then found he could go "8 to 35" in one step. And why had he retained copies? How come everything wasn't returned to *Life*? Weitzman said these were test prints, that he made many such "test prints" and those had indeed remain in his custody. Later, when the company disbanded, he returned to clean up and retained possession of all such items (also called: "technicians copies"). "I kept the footage as a technical achievement," he said. "No other reason." He said he gave "no thought about the implications of what it was." He had promised Time/Life that he would not let the footage out of his hands, he said, and "I kept that promise for close to 6 or 7 years, at least. Nobody got to touch it; nobody had a copy of it."

Weitzman told me, "Robert Groden came to work for me in 1970, or 1969, and by happenstance he saw the footage that I had while I was showing it to someone as a sample of our blowup capabilities. And he went berserk over it. He wanted to see it. He wanted to use it. I made it clear to him that he couldn't have it. He could look at it but he couldn't duplicate it or take it away from the premises based on the commitment I had made to Time/Life."

Although Weitzman had one concept of what the rules were in dealing with Groden, Groden obviously behaved otherwise, because clearly he had that box full of material that he exhibited to me in the fall of 1972 at Jerry Policoff's apartment the night I first met him.

Weitzman then continued with this story of how Groden approached him—which, because of the mention of Dick Gregory, must have been in late 1974 or 1975—and it involved a hard-luck story: "Some years later he came to me telling me *that the material had disappeared*, and there was an opportunity to open the Warren Commission, would I make this footage available to Dick Gregory? I did do that. I felt it was for an official purpose; I didn't get any money for it. And that's where it stood. Till this day I have never made a single penny on the Zapruder footage or the other footage [the Nix film] that I did for UPI, which I regard as the more important footage." *In other words, to hear Weitzman tell it, Groden never took the film off the premises until the Dick Gregory lecture tour* (circa 1975, I think). Of course, based on Groden's appearance at the 1972 party at Policoff's, when I first met him, that is not what really happened.

Weitzman then went on to tell the story of his involvement with the Nix footage—which, unknown to him, I had played a role in routing to his laboratory. Weitzman talked of all the other films that Time-Life had gathered and which he had turned into 35mm film. "We did enough footage to do a feature film, as I remember," he told me. I reminded him that the Zapruder film was only 26 or 27 seconds long. He insisted he had done much more, "I made easily eight or nine thousand feet of film for them, of 35 mm." He said: "We didn't screen the footage, obviously, we just simply did it. The footage was all related. *They were gonna make a feature film on both Kennedy's assassination and his brother's assassination, I assume.*"

Weitzman told me all this work was done in the fall of 1967, when he was the "principal technician" (the senior technical person) at Manhattan Effects and before the summer of 1968, when he established EFX ("Effects Unlimited").

In considerable detail, Weitzman explained how he modified the Oxberry shuttle mechanism so that it would accept an 8mm film and also designed a "wet gate" which would work on an 8mm film frame.

He noted he had access to the Zapruder film around 1975 when CBS did their second major "Warren Report" documentary. However, Weitzman remembered it as a "20th anniversary" event, which would mean it was 1983. He feels that, because the technology was more refined and because a better film stock was available, the work he did on that occasion was "a tad sharper" than the work done the first time around.

Of central importance is that when Weitzman went from 8mm to 35mm "in one step", the product was a 35mm negative (exactly what I worked with in June 1990); and, to do anything with it, you had to learn how to read the Zapruder film "in reverse" (colorwise). And that was my experience—hour after hour!

I asked Weitzman how many such 35mm negatives had he retained. He replied: "I gave [Groden] a whole box of them. He might have 3, 4, 5 of them." He continued:

"I simply had them up on a shelf and they weren't being taken care of in any Archival manner. They were there for my amusement and viewing to show people, 'This is what I did X number of years ago.' Robert convinced me that it had Archival value, and he was gonna transfer it to high-definition and make laser discs."

We also discussed the issue of film authenticity. Weitzman was obviously an expert, but had never been exposed (by Groden) to the idea that evidence had been altered—be it the body or the film. I explained as best I could and also promised to send him my book.

Still another facet of my conversation—one not very pleasant—concerned my relationship with Groden. Something was apparently "wrong" between us, said Weitzman, because whenever my name came up, it was as if a "dark cloud" descended over Groden. It seemed evident Groden had done his usual number on me with Weitzman, and I finally decided to inform Weitzman about the kind of money Groden had been making from the films.

Weitzman was astonished. Until this conversation, he hadn't the faintest idea that Groden was engaged in business, selling access to negatives made using Weitzman's facilities to documentary film producers for thousands of dollars. He was "aggravated" and said, "I'm going to ask Robert to return what he has to me, and then I'll decide what I want to do with it."

As to the possibility that the film had been altered, Weitzman was extremely skeptical. He ticked off all the objections to anyone possibly having altered the film. Then I made the case that something might have happened, telling him about the car-stop witnesses, peculiarities concerning the chain of possession, and the issue of the darkening at the back of the head. I felt most complimented when he said, "I'm listening. I never paid any attention to all that. Obviously, you're very much immersed in it."

Indeed I was. And the way we left it was this: when I came to New York City (which I did in December), we would meet.

Also, I told him I knew Richter and would see to it that he got his film back. On this score, I urged him *not* to return the 35mm to Groden, suggesting that he (Weitzman) be the "neutral" archivist. If he truly didn't want to keep it, would he sell it? Might he be open to a financial offer from a group of researchers? I said that I would try to raise the money explaining the problem as I saw it: that Groden, as a collector, was refusing to let the research community have material that was essential to proving or disproving a theory, simply because he didn't subscribe to the theory.

All this was left undecided. What was eminently clear was Weitzman's astonish-ment at the extent of Groden's financial activity. I assured him it was true, and promised to send him my own contract with Groden for $8,000, with $5,000 already paid and cancelled checks to prove it.

I told him that there was a good side to Groden, but that we had become serious opponents and that "I have a problem with the fact that the very item of evidence I need to do legitimate scientific work with, he'll end up owning because of your good heartedness."

"Well, I'm gonna have to discuss this with Robert," replied Weitzman, who contin-ued:

If Robert's been profiting on the film all this while and I manufactured that film initially and made it available to him as non-profit, I think I'm gonna be a little upset about it. He doesn't own it. I'm getting rankled by the idea that Robert [thinks he] owns it. I've let him make use of it; he doesn't own it. . . . It's film physically that belongs to me. I don't own the image; the image belongs to. . . . Zapruder/Time/Life. The physical piece of negative belongs to me. And if Bob [Groden] has been making money on it, based on my letting him make use of it for scientific purposes, I'm gonna be a little irritated, because God knows I could use some money and I never charged anyone a nickel for it.

Based on the conversation, Weitzman said "I want to get Robert to give me back everything"—and by "everything" it was clear that he meant not only the Zapruder film negatives, but a bunch of other material as well. Then he would decide what to do.

Immediately after our conversation, I sent Weitzman a copy of my book and video, and also again asked that he not return the 35 mm negative to Groden. Again raising the possibility that—if he didn't want to be the "archivist"—then perhaps his 35 mm mate-rial might be purchased by a consortium of researchers.

I can *assure* you that a substantial number of researchers and other interested parties around the country feel exactly the way I do about this 35mm negative, and Groden's sole access to it; otherwise, I would not have been successful in being able to obtain a consensus and raise funds to prevent this from happening. Our concern has been very simple: preventing a single person with a particular view of this case from obtaining an unbreakable monopoly on the key negatives of the Zapruder film, a monopoly which would preclude the film, in its clearest form, from being available to students and researchers, and (important to me personally) preventing me from being able to do future work in the very serious area of authenticity—simply because Robert Groden disagrees with some of my ideas. (Lifton to Weitzman, 8/6/90)

I also pointed out:

I hope this situation is resolved so that. . . archival needs are met, and that authors and researchers who have contrary views on what the evidence may mean have access to data which may prove (or disprove) this or that hypothesis or theory. I am a bit uneasy over the fact that in order to open an honest line of communication with you, I find myself in the position of having to present you with facts that could be unpleasant news, vis a vis your prior relationship with Groden. I suppose I risk being seen as diabolical or Machiavallian. But I see no way around this. Just put yourself in my position: my life's work has—not by plan—ended up being devoted to this case. Yet when it comes to data, and a particular movie film, I have do deal with a monopolist (and believe me, I am being kind to put it that way), who has contrary views and absolute possession of certain key evidence; and uses that, in a sort of indirect way, to enforce his view.

As I have pointed out to a number of people, the reason the Z film enlargements possessed by Groden are so clear is not that he is some sort of genius, and that this is rocket science, but that the originally created 35 mm source material was so good to begin with—and he has had nearly unique access to that material. I have often told Robert: Zapruder has built a fence around this film; and now you have built a fence around Zapruder's fence.

The time has come to open that fence.

In fact, that 35 material should be available in every high school in this country; and whether this or that producer, researcher, or author, gets access to such vital historical materials should not be decided by the whim of Robert Groden.[17]

December 1990: Meeting with Moe Weitzman

Sometime around mid December, I met with Weitzman in New York City —at his offices then at Eastern Optical Effects, 321 W. 44th, New York City.

I wanted to begin a relationship with the man who had made this truly extraordinary 35mm negative, and seek his assistance in developing the evidence regarding inauthenticity. By that time, Weitzman had gotten back his 35mm negative from Richter and—being the sharp-eyed fellow he certainly was—noticed certain marks indicating that, when out of his possession, it had been copied. It was useless attempting to conceal what had happened. Thinking about Washington and the cherry tree, I simply confessed, acknowledging I had been involved in copying the film and restating some of the themes of my August letter as partial justification. There were some uncomfortable moments—and the issue of my having copied the film without his permission eventually became a major block to a further relationship—but on that day, we somehow got by all that and the visit proceeded rather smoothly.

Weitzman was about 60 years old and was a proud "techie". He reminded me of the Gene Hackman character in "The Conversation"—someone who respected, above all, expertise, technical expertise.

In considerable detail (and with considerable pride), Weitzman re-told the story of how he had come into possession of the original Zapruder film (and many other film originals that *Life* owned). *Life* had approached him with an 8mm film and asked if he could make a decent 16mm copy. Weitzman recalled his response: "I can do better than that: I can make you a 35mm copy". He then explained how he modified the film transport mechanism (called a "shuttle") on the optical printer, so it would accept a home movie with 8mm perforations. (Remember, by 1967 the original Zapruder film had been slit, so it was now truly an 8mm film).

Then, as I recall, Weitzman told how *Life* had possession of more than just the Zapruder film, and he was right quite correct about that. Their November 1967 issue described the great effort *Life* made to collect all films and marked the first publication of frames from the Bell, Paschall, and Dorman films as well as the Bond slides. Weitzman was apparently quite knowledgeable about *Life's* film collection effort.

At some point, our discussion turned to my concern that the Zapruder film was inauthentic and the two of us retired to another room, where he put the 35mm—clearly his pride and joy—on a Hazeltine Analyzer, a sophisticated moviola-type device for viewing the image with precision.

Traveling back and forth amongst the frames, Weitzman analyzed certain blur features and also focused on the black area at the back of JFK's head. At that meeting, he was thoughtful and obviously open to the idea that the film was not an original. He made any number of interesting technical observations, and I remember being very annoyed at not having thought to bring along a tape recorder. But I took notes. My ultimate goal was to get Weitzman to tell his remarkable story to a camera. He seemed open to the idea, but over the next few months, Robert Groden managed to patch up his differences with Weitzman, retrieved (or was perhaps permitted to retain, I'm not sure which) the priceless items which formed the heart of his collection, and I went into the dog house for having copied the film without his permission. Consequently, a future filmed interview became impossible.

In my files is an unmailed letter to Weitzman dated 2 March 1991, which refers to a conversation the day before in which I tried to explain my ethical justification for having copied the film without his permission.

I never did mail the letter and I never did patch up the situation with Weitzman.

1991: Oliver Stone and "JFK"

As I recall, Oliver Stone was well along on his movie project by 1990. The script called for the Zapruder movie to be projected, full screen, towards the end of the film.

Stone hired Groden, but Alex Ho, his associate, told me they were well aware of the "Groden problem"—i.e., that if they used Groden's existing materials, he would start making legal claims.

At issue was which problem to deal with: Groden, his spurious "copyright" and his claims of "ownership" of rights to the copies he had previously made, or the Zapruder family? He told me they had the film re-transferred to 35 mm—a 35mm item which Stone's company then owned—but it was never clear to me which 35mm negative was used as the source item. In any event, Stone then made a "movie rights" payment to the Zapruder family: $80,000 for the rights to use the Zapruder film in "JFK". Aside from the original Life contract, this was the largest single payment the Zapruder family had received.

Meanwhle, Groden—having sabotaged my relationship with Weitzman—now focused on Stone. He knew that Stone was furious that *The Washington Post* had published a long article by reporter George Lardner, based on the screenplay, attacking his yet-to-be-completed movie.

Where had Lardner gotten the screenplay? In fact, the source was author Harold Weisberg. Groden was close with Weisberg, didn't want any of this to surface, and so he now manufactured a story placing the onus on me. This was absurd, but Groden, who was working with Stone day to day on the set, repeated it often, and now the statement acquired a life of its own. One day I received a call from author John Newman, hired by Stone as a consultant. Newman, calling from the set, told me that actor Joe Pesci (who was hearing it from Stone) was saying, "Lifton leaked the screenplay." In fact, Groden had given the screenplay to Weisberg., who had given it to Lardner.

Meanwhile, Stone wanted to use the Nix film in the movie. Unfortunately, the original Nix film, which had passed through Groden's hands many times, had disappeared.

Still, there remained the matter of rights. Gayle Nix Jackson, Nix's granddaughter, owned the rights and was heartbroken over the fact that her grandfather's film had disappeared.

Somehow we met—over the telephone—and she told me that Stone's people—specifically, Jane Rusconi, a Groden pal—had offered her around $3,000. I told Gayle how valuable the Nix film was, noted that Warner Brothers was spending some $40 million dollars on the film, told her to screw up her courage and said she should ask—if not demand—around $50,000 and settle for $30,000. Gayle did exactly that—I actually helped her compose a letter—and within days, the matter was closed. She ended up getting somewhere around $20,000 for Warner's right to use her grandfather's film in Stone's extravaganza.

Returning to the screenplay matter, I wrote Stone a brief letter. It was short and sweet but I know that my final line got to him. With regard to the charge that I had leaked his script, I explained that (a) I didn't have his script, (b) had done no such thing. And then I said: "Oliver, I'm just a patsy."

I think that worked and after that, Stone dropped the notion that I was responsible for his problems with *The Washington Post*.

Oliver Stone's "JFK"

Oliver Stone's "JFK" was released in December 1991 and caused quite a sensation. It garnered major national publicity.

I happened to completely disagree with Jim Garrison—who I met several times back in 1967-68—or the thesis that New Orleans businessman Clay Shaw had anything whatsoever to do with the assassination; and it was a fact that, had Shaw lived, the film could not have been made.

But it was also a fact that—like it or not—Stone's film was focusing major attention on the JFK assassination, which, as far as most Americans were concerned, was an unsolved crime. It also involved John Newman's work—raising the possibility that the escalation of the Vietnam War was a motive for Dallas—and that part was excellent.

It was also a fact that Stone's film marked the first time that the Zapruder film was shown—full screen—in a movie theater. And anyone who purchased "The Director's Cut", on a laser disk, essentially could have the same view of the film, on a frame by frame basis, that I had by working with Weitzman's negative.

Again, audiences gasped as they saw the film replayed, with JFK's head being thrown back and to the left. The fact that I suspected that this was an artifact of an altered film didn't matter. I had to get used to the fact—and I did—that people went through phases in connection with immersing themselves in the evidence of the JFK case, and there was nothing wrong with that initial phase—when the headsnap, so shocking and brutal, was "evidence of a second shooter." (What bothered me about Groden, and others, was that they never got beyond that phase; never graduated to the point where they might have realized how absurd the headsnap really looked; and that it was almost certainly an artifact of an altered film; or, more accurately put, of an imperfectly altered film.)

Meanwhile, one major consequence of "JFK" was to create public pressure to release all withheld documents in the JFK case. That led to the passage of the JFK Records Act and to the creation of the Assassination Records Review Board (ARRB).

It was around this time that my full attention turned to Lee Harvey Oswald, the true mystery man in this entire affair, and I had to make a decision as to what to do with my own Zapruder research and insights.

The conclusion I arrived at was surprising—I would just give everything away. Film alteration was just too big a research area for one person to work on alone. I needed all the help I could get and now was the time to reach out to the new generation of researchers whose interest was sparked by Stone's movie and make them aware that this film, with its "six second" assassination and its "Bethesda type" wound imagery, was *not* the final word—that there was good reason to suspect this film was a fraud.

23 October 1992: ASK Convention in Dallas

I don't remember exactly what "ASK" stands for, but the group held several JFK research conventions in Dallas starting in 1991 and I attended several of them, including the one in 1992. At that time, I conducted a "Zapruder workshop," holding forth and educating the audience, as best I could, about the technology of optical printers, the story of Moe Weitzman, the car stop witnesses, how the Z film could have been altered, etcetera. I was assisted by JFK researcher Rick Anderson and my talk lasted several hours.

I had a selfish reason for doing so. From a memo in my own files:

I was sick and tired of hearing someone like Groden going on about how the film had to be original, while clinging to the very 35 mm materials necessary to prove it was a fraud. And the so-called "original" film appeared to show wounds that implied that all the Dallas doctors were wrong—the 35mm film showed no rear exit for the head wound and a huge so-called "wound" towards the front of the head.

So I welcomed the idea that other people would get involved in the controversy. To some extent, I felt I needed all the help I could get. I knew that if the Zapruder film could be impeached—definitively impeached—as evidence, then a major obstacle to the full and complete acceptance of my theory about the alteration of the President's body would be removed, namely: the notion that the Z frames showing the head wounding were authentic pictures of JFK's head wounds in Dallas. That figleaf had to be abandoned for the truth to emerge.

Everyone knows how obsessive authors are about protecting their turf until their work is published. But I now felt differently. I had the feeling that my own best interests would be served by sharing my knowledge, which I did.

Present in the audience—and quite enlightened by my presentation, it was obvious—were Noel Twyman, a San Diego businessman with a long string of inventions to his credit, and Harrison Livingstone. Livingstone went on to write about these ideas in his book(s) on the assassination, but his behavior has been bizarre, leaving all manner of threats—even death threats—on my answering machine, and even suing me for $50 million (in 2002), claiming I had been involved in a conspiracy to cause his demise.

Noel Twyman and I developed a warm relationship and he too wrote about the film as a forgery. Meanwhile, Groden moved forward with a plan to publish a coffee table book that would include the autopsy photographs and basically showcase his entire photo collection.

1993: Groden's Coffee Table Book

November 1998 marked the 25th anniversary of JFK's death, and Groden published a coffee table book, *The Killing of a President*. The book contained the key black and white autopsy photographs I had sent him in 1990, without any acknowledgement whatsoever. Indeed, Groden omitted *Best Evidence* both from his bibliography of books and video tapes at the end. But he did avail himself of key frames from a major San Francisco TV program, built around my work by award winning producer Stanhope Gould (who had handled the Watergate coverage under Cronkite). Under "recommended documentaries" Groden listed "JFK: An Unsolved Murder," which he knew was devoted primarily to *Best Evidence*. Wrote Groden: "The piece also includes an implausible theory that the President's body was stolen between Parkland and Bethesda Hospital."

Meanwhile, Groden had Weitzman to contend with, and the whole matter of the Zapruder film, as he now published many color frames from Weitzman's 35 mm negative. Telling an almost storybook version of that relationship and with one eye on the Zapruder lawyers, he now referred to Moe as "Mr. Weitzman" and wrote:

> I met Mr. Mr. Weitzman in 1969. The owner of a New York-based motion picture optical house that performed postproduction work on motion picture film, he had in his possession a legitimate, first-generation mechanic's copy of . . . Zapruder's film. . . . I went to work for Mr. Weitzman and quickly discovered our mutual interest in the . . . Kennedy killing. We spent many hours discussing the assassination, and I shared with him my personal investigations into the crime

Then came a version of how Groden had come into possession of the 35 mm material, which conveniently skipped over Groden's having taken the Zapruder material off the premises years before Weitzman was aware of what had happened:

"After several months, he showed me his pristine copy of this fim. . . Mr. Weitzeman gave me the film, also granting me access to an optical printer, a machine used to duplicate and enhance motion picture film. For the first time, I had an ultra-clear copy of Zapruder's film [well, at least he got that right!] access to the right equipment to clarify the film's images. . . .

"I created the first optically enhanced copies of the Zapruder film. . . I zoomed in, making the images larger within the frame. . . Now you could see, with a new clarity, what was really happening."

In his account, Groden spoke of how he had shown the film on national TV and the role he had played showing his film to various Congressmen, which surely helped launch the HSCA investigation. He said that his book was being published in response to "thousands of requests for copies of the photographic evidence in the Kennedy case; the photo collection contained in this book is the response to those requests. . . Many of these pictures are unpleasant and sensitive in nature but must be published in the interest of historical accuracy."

In fact, Groden's publication of the color photographs of JFK laid out in the morgue, absolutely infuriated Kennedy attorney Burke Marshall, who referred to Groden in terms that are normally not used in polite society.

But the real problem was that Moe Weitzman had created an absolutely unique resource—about a half dozen 35 mm prints of the Z film, made in 1967, every one of which belonged in the National Archives. Groden had them all and, despite his repeated statements about doing this or that "for history," the fact is that when it came down to the wire, Groden denied under oath having any such material.

But I am getting ahead of the story. The fact is, because of Oliver Stone's film, the entire political climate changed. I still followed everything about the Zapruder controversy as carefully, but from a distance. And I focused on my Oswald research. As to the Zapruder film, I had the best connection of all—Douglas Horne of the ARRB.

The ARRB

Whether you agree with Garrison or not (and I did not), the most enduring consequence of the movie JFK was the passage of The JFK Records Act and the creation of the Assassination Records Review Board (ARRB).

When the board was first created, I was invited to the "expert's conference" and met David Marwell and Jeremy Gunn for the first time. I learned that both had read my book but took different positions on questions of authencity of the evidence. Marwell, a friend of Gerald Posner, leaned more towards the "lone nutter" position; Jeremy Gunn seemed more open to such ideas as alteration of the body, Zapruder film inauthenticity, etcetera—which is not to say his beliefs accorded with mine in these areas, but that he seemed open to having such matters investigated.

Meanwhile, in what was a major break for me, Douglas Horne, a former Naval officer who was a strong supporter of my work, applied from Honolulu for a position with the ARRB and was accepted. Horne eventually became "Chief Analyst for Military Records"—a fairly high position at the ARRB—and his presence on the staff along with his dogged determination to further investigate many of the mysteries surrounding the autopsy, had a definite effect in shaping the ARRB's work in the medical area. New documents were located, witnesses whom I had interviewed were called to testify and, since the ARRB wanted to see some of my own materials, I had quite a bit of contact with the ARRB, often with Horne but also with Marwell and Gunn.

There were one or two occasions when the memos I prepared or phone calls I had were extensive enough that I felt I was an unpaid staff member. I was always glad to help and, in the area of the Zapruder film, I made a real difference—at least, I would like to think that was so.

The Zapruder film was going to be designated an "assassination record" and, although hearings were held on the matter, it seemed to me always a foregone conclusion. Meanwhile, the ARRB staff members didn't understand how motion pictures worked or how they were copied. In short, they knew nothing about optical printing—what such an apparatus was, how it worked, etcetera, nor did they know about Moe Weitzman, his company EFX, or the full scale of the activities of Robert Groden.

I set out to educate the ARRB in June of 1996 in what I thought would be an afternoon's worth of writing—I would just "dash off a memo" (or so I thought). As it turned out, my "afternoon project" grew like Topsy, and the result was a major document, "Memo To Jeremy Gunn, ARRB, 27 June 1996: My Experiences and Past Relationship With Robert Groden, 1972-93". (It is among the ARRB's papers at the National Archives.)

The memo—which, along with a cover letter, runs to almost 50 pages (single-spaced) and which has about six attachments—took at least a week to write. To create it, I found myself going into filing cabinets and storage boxes, examining journals, and retrieving letters that were 20 years or more old. It was a major project. One of my primary concerns was documenting the 35 mm items I knew Groden possessed and doing the best I could to explain the kind of "collector mentality" they would be up against in seeking to obtain such items for placement in the JFK Collection. From my memo:

> You may recall that when I appeared at the ARRB's April 1995 Experts Conference, I spent a good 10-15 minutes on the Groden problem—that problem being that I believe, based on my experiences with him over a 20 year period (from 1971–early 1990s), that he may well have original material, and/or irreplaceable and unique

original first generation negatives, made when he was employed at HSCA, or even earlier, due to a special relationship he had with EFX Film Labs in New York City. I am very concerned with what Groden has, and how he got it; and whether any of it is original material; and if so, what is to be done about it.

I then addressed the vital connection between the autopsy evidence and the head wound imagery appearing on certain Zapruder film frames. I wondered aloud whether Groden possessed "originals he may have obtained during the time he was employed at HSCA" or perhaps "copies that are unique—made from originals to which he had access at HSCA—and which ought to be designated as assassination records.[18]

If Groden is soon to be deposed. . . then I think it may be important that you know the background of my 22 year relationship with him and what I know about his unusual film collection. That relationship began in the fall of 1972, when we first met at the New York City apartment of a mutual acquaintance; was particularly active in the period of 1973, when (as the researcher on the movie "Executive Action") I played a key role in getting the original Nix film—owned by UPI—sent to EFX Labs, so that Groden would be able to make copies from the original, when it was duped for use in that movie; continued during the period he went public for the first time (by appearing with comedian Dick Gregory on the lecture circuit, and then on the Geraldo Rivera's show in March 1975); continued through his employment with the HSCA (1976-79), at which time I would often visit him at his Hopelawn, New Jersey home, where I first saw autopsy photos in Spring 1979; continued in 1980, when I paid him money for certain photos to be used in *Best Evidence*, published in January 1981; then continued into 1982, when I obtained the black and white autopsy photos from former Secret Service official James Fox, and, on a visit to Groden's place, compared them with Groden's color set; resumed again in fall of 1988 and spring of 1989, when I executed an $8,000 contract with him, made an initial payment to him of $5,000, and copied the bulk of his film collection, from his video masters onto professional Betacam.

The relationship between Robert Groden and me was always riddled with a certain tension—that between a collector and a researcher. Groden possessed crucial and unique photo materials; I had certain ideas and hypotheses. I needed his material to investigate my hypotheses. He disagreed with my ideas, and withheld material.

All this climaxed with much antagonism when I busted his "image monopoly" on the Zapruder film. That occurred in 1990, when I located and obtained complete access to—for about a 10 day period—the granddaddy of all the Zapruder negatives, a unique 35mm internegative that was originally created in 1967 by Moe Weitzman, the owner of EFX Labs, and Groden's "Godfather" of sorts.

I believe it is crucial that you have this entire story—this "global" view of Robert Groden—and so I have outlined all the major events as I know them, and will attempt to dash this off from memory (supplemented here and there by documents, such as are readily at hand).

Can I prove that Groden has original material? Not necessarily, but one could argue that surely that must be the case. Certainly, it is a question that deserves careful consideration.[19]

In phone calls with ARRB staffers, I noted that Groden seemed to think he owned anything he had copied, or enlarged. My memo ended with: "You are facing a formidable opponent. Good luck."

When it was over, the Review Board staff had in its possession a document that provided a complete bird's eye view of how motion picture duplication worked and the role Robert Groden and Weitzman's lab had played over the years in JFK assassination research. I was asked to testify to the ARRB in September 1996 at a public hearing in Los Angeles and, when the Washington hearing was held some months later and I turned on my TV to watch, I almost fell out of my chair when Judge Tunheim thanked all the citizens who had sent in helpful material and particularly singled me out and thanked me by name.

Meanwhile, the Board decided it was going to need expert assistance if it was to navigate the sticky wicket of certain film issues. The Board turned to Kodak for assistance. There are several matters that must be discussed—if only briefly—if one is to get a birds-eye view of the ARRB's work in the area of the bystander films taken in Dealey Plaza. Not necessarily in chronological order, they are:

- The ARRB and CIA Document 450;

- The ARRB deposition of Robert Groden;

- The ARRB and the matter of designating the Z film as an "assassination record";

- The ARRB's attempt to deal with the matter of authenticity;

- Zavada's investigation of the camera's "claw shadow", which led to his shooting certain test films

- Doug Horne's discovery, from Zavada's data, of the "full flush left" problem in May 1999, six months after the Board closed shop.

The ARRB and CIA Document 450

The reader will recall that back around 1976, Paul Hoch made the discovery of CIA Document 450, which suggested—at first sight—that the Zapruder film had gone to the CIA's National Photo Interpretation Center, prior to going to *Life*. Initially, the issue seemed to be whether NPIC had anything to do with processing the Zapruder film—which, if so, seemed rather peculiar, since the film had already been processed at the Kodak plant in Dallas. So that in turn, led to various hypotheses as to whether the NPIC photo lab in Washington perhaps had something to do with altering the film. The issues was whether it went to the NPIC in its pristine condition and was then altered or went there after it had been altered and, if so, what was it doing at NPIC at all?

As it turned out, alteration apparently had not taken place at NPIC. Two CIA employees were located who had been at NPIC—Homer McMahon, head of the NPIC color lab, and his assistant Ben Hunter—and the story behind the creation of the NPIC documents, which at first appeared so mysterious—gradually clarified the situation. The documents had nothing to do with the creation of a movie film, but rather with the processed of some 28 selected frames from a film positive (indeed, a 16 mm Kodachrome, supposedly the "original") which was brought to NPIC—either on Saturday or Sunday night on the assassination weekend—by a Secret Service agent who said he had just come from a classified film facility at Rochester run by Kodak, where the Kodachrome he was transporting had been processed.

The agent's name was "Smith", the ARRB was never able to identify who "Smith" was but the events described by McMahon definitely took place (according to McMahon) prior to the JFK's funeral, which would mean either Saturday night or Sunday night.

The NPIC lab was requested to make color prints from selected single frames—supposedly for use in creating "briefing boards". Twenty-eight frames were selected (according to McMahon's paperwork). Moreover, said McMahon, Agent Smith had said the entire matter was to be treated as "higher than 'top secret'" and that even his own supervisor was not permitted to know about this activity. ARRB interviews established that the film—as a motion picture film—had not been processed at NPIC in Washington and that a series of notations about processing times and the number of prints to be made was unrelated to motion picture photography but concerned the creation of a series of 28 color prints from selected motion picture film frames.

Although that mystery was resolved, the McMahon account raised serious questions about the chain of possession of the original film. That film—a 16 mm Kodachrome (with the assassination on Side B) had been processed at Kodak in Dallas on the afternoon of the assassination. Further, it had left Zapruder's possession on Saturday morning, when he made his initial deal with *Life* (in the amount of $50,000) and then turned over "the original" plus his third copy to *Life's* representative, Richard Stolly.

Yet here was McMahon reporting that Agent Smith had arrived with a Kodachrome, saying he had come from Rochester, where the film he was carrying had been processed at "Hawkeyeworks". Since the briefing boards prepared with McMahon's stills carry Zapruder frame numbers which are apparently from the film which (today) we call "the Zapruder film", the question arises as to whether the source item was the Kodachrome which McMahon was working with for several hours that long night and exactly what was its origin.

The Zapruder film—the actual Kodachrome film exposed in Zapruder's camera—had been processed at the Kodak plant in Dallas. Kodachrome required a very special processing plant. There were only some half dozen such Kodachrome facilities in the U.S., and the question had been: where could a Kodachrome copy of Zapruder's film—a Kodachrome which would subsequently be paraded about as an original, but which was in fact a copy—have been processed? Certainly not in Dallas.

Now a new possibility was emerging: that a Kodachrome processor was located either at Kodak's headquarters in Rochester or at Hawkeyeworks, precisely where the Kodachrome brought to MacMahon might have been processed.

McMahon was certain he had an original. From Horne's ARRB Report:

> Horne asked whether he was working with the original film or a copy, and McMahon stated with some certainty tht he was "sure we had the original filkm." Horne asked why,and he said that he was sure it was the original because it was Kodachrome, and because it was a "double 8"movie. Horne asked him to clarify whether the home movie was slit or unslit, and McMahon said that he was pretty sure the film was UNSLIT, because "we had to flip it over to see the image on the other side in the correct orientation. (Horne Call Report, 6/12/97; see Appendix C)

There was another twist. When Doug wanted to pursue the matter, pull 1963 records, and question people as to whether the Z film had been at Rochester, his requests were simply refused—*flatly refused*—and without explanation. Moreover, from multiple sources, I learned what occurred when the CIA found out that the word "Hawkeyeworks"—a classified term—had been mentioned by one of its employees in an ARRB interview: the order went out to change the record. The ARRB was notified that the name was still classified, so it would have to be expunged. Doug was given the job of editing the audio tape record of the interview and deleting any mention of the secret facility by its classified codename. This he did, writing the appropriate memo to make the fact a matter of record.

The ARRB's *Final Report* accurately reported the important fact that what was done in Washington, D.C., at NPIC's color lab was simply the creation of color stills, but left out the related drama of Hawkeyeworks and the CIA's insistence that the term be deleted. The *Final Report* said:

> Review Board Staff's Study and Clarification of Paul Hoch's FOIA Lead "CIA Document 450." The Review Board staff located and interviewed two former employees of the CIA' s National Photographic Interpretation Center (NPIC) and questioned them about " C I A Document 450," a 1970s Freedom Of Information Act release-original document undated-that indicates NPIC had a version of the Zapruder film, made "internegatives" and "copies," conducted a "print test," and performed a shot-and-timing analysis based on interpretation of the film's content.

The Deposition of Robert Groden

I had laid out chapter and verse pertaining to the amount of film material Groden had, the question of its origin, and the importance of the 35mm Zapruder copies he had obtained from Weitzman. At the end of my memo, I had written: "You are facing a formidable opponent. Good luck." Meanwhile, a friend of mine drew a cartoon—which I faxed to Jeremy—showing Groden, under oath, with an enormous dog—labeled "Groden's Dog"—sitting on a bunch of film cans and licking his chops. Groden was answering questions posed by the ARRB, and the cartoon showed him, right hand raised, saying, "I'm sorry Mr. Gunn. . . my dog ate it."

Groden was subpoenaed "duces tecum"—an order to produce certain specified items at the time of the examination. A location in Delaware was chosen because it was close to where Groden lived.

Doug Horne recalled some time later what it was like. "Groden showed up but he didn't have most of the items specified in the subpoena. Jeremy asked him if he possessed this or that. Groden made some positive admissions, and Jeremy told him—like a school teacher lecturing a child—that he must go home now and get them."

So later, the deposition resumed. As Doug recalled: "Groden was intent on playing a game, a tap dancing game with the government. Jeremy asked a series of technical questions; Groden's answers indicated he was a buffoon. That he was not trained in film. That he had no formal training, that he was using terms incorrectly. He was evasive during the whole deposition; either evasive, or pretending to be stupid.

"On the surface, he was friendly, and even unctuous; but underneath that veneer, was clearly someone who was playing a game, and either was evasive, or pretending to be ignorant at times."

Jeremy did pin down that Groden was a high school dropout and the negative circumstances under which he had left the Army.

Then came the hard questions—questions that addressed specifically things that Groden appeared to possess, either based on the book he published, or what was in the contract with me, and specifically any of the half dozen 35 mm Weitzman internegatives of the Zapruder film

No, said Groden, he didn't have that. As Doug remembered: "The main question we asked was whether he had this really high quality 35 mm; and whether he had taken any materials form the HSCA. And the whole experience was very frustrating. We felt like he was a prevaricator, but it was hard to tell whether he was lying or stupid."

From notes of a phone call later with Doug Horne: "With great specificity, we referenced the [35 mm] item you mentioned, and he denied having it." In this manner, the very valuable 35 mm internegative with which I had worked for days in 1990, and which had been the subject of such a struggle between Groden and myself simply disappeared, as far as the ARRB legal record was concerned.

A postscript to the Groden story occurred in December 1996, which concerned his involvement in the O. J. Simpson case as a photo expert, a situation that came close to resulting in ARRB General Counsel being called as a witness in order to testify about Groden's general character. In any event, it resulted in Gunn's statements about Groden becoming a matter of a court record.

Groden and the O.J. Simpson Case

I happen to live about two blocks from where the OJ murders were committed and, although OJ was acquitted in the criminal proceeding, he was then sued civilly. Suddenly, the case was being replayed, a key issue was whether OJ Simpson had been photographed in Bruno Magli shoes. The newspapers were reporting that the OJ team had an important witness who would prove these photographs of Simpson were all fakes—an expert who had appeared previously, and made important contributions, to the JFK case.

His name? Robert Groden.

I was astonished. Robert Groden was going to appear before a Los Angeles jury with his "credentials" from his days at the House Select Committee and testify (for a $10,000 fee, it turned out) in support of the proposition that photographs of Simpson showing him wearing the shoes were fake? *All fake?*

This was the same Groden who had argued that the Zapruder film was authentic, who had been an HSCA unpaid consultant, who had done so much to keep the consciousness of America rooted in the juvenile view that the key to the conspiracy was whether a shooter was hiding behind a wall or fence rather than on the authenticity of the film, which he denied was inauthentic in any way. And finally, this was the same Groden who claimed not to possess the key 35mm material from Weitzman which should have been located and made part of the JFK collection.

By this time, I had in my possession the June 1996 memo I had prepared on Groden and which had been instrumental in his being deposed before the ARRB; and I also had the contract that Groden had made with the tabloid *Globe* selling them the autopsy photographs for $50,000—photographs that included crisp black and whites he had obtained from me for absolutely nothing. By that time, I also had the experience of calling one of the major photo agencies in New York City to which Groden apparently sold the autopsy photographs. A young thing answered the phone and, hearing about my inquiry about the JFK autopsy photos and didn't they belong to the Kennedy family, earnestly informed me that the Kennedy family no longer controlled them. "They are owned by Robert Groden," she said.

I telephoned the plaintiff's attorney, Peter Gelblum. As it turned out, his office was just a few blocks from my own in West Los Angeles, just two blocks from where I had seen the man walking with the "fake pig."

Gelblum had no idea who I was, but his wife—as it turned out—was a big fan of my book, *Best Evidence*. So on a Sunday afternoon, I went over to his office and brought him a complete file of materials on Groden. This included contracts showing that Groden had sold the autopsy photographs—the clear prints he had received from me—to the tabloid *Globe* for $50,000!

As a result of the plaintiff's attorney having access to my ARRB memo—and other materials received from another JFK researcher—Groden was put through a rigorous cross examination. Groden was asked if he sold the JFK autopsy photographs to the *Globe*.

The examination between attorney Gelblum, representing the plaintiffs, and Groden, unfolded as follows and was illustrative of what had gone on when the ARRB had tried to pin Groden down with respect to his possession of various negatives and other photo materials. The entire interchange was similar to when President Clinton's deposition depending on the meaning of "is", as played out on 20 December 1996 in the Superior Court of California in Santa Monica:

Gelblum: In December 1991, sir, didn't you sell autopsy photographs of John F. Kennedy to the *Globe* tabloid?

Groden: I did not.

Gelblum: Okay. Did you enter into a contract with the "Globe" to sell autopsy photos of John F. Kennedy for $50,000, sir?

Groden: I did not.

Gelblum: Do you recognize what I'm putting in front of you now? (Witness is handed magazine.)

Groden::   Yes, I recognize it.

Gelblum   What is it?

Groden: It a copy of the "Globe" dated December 31, 1991.

Gelblum: And the cover story is about autopsy photos of John F. Kennedy, correct?

Groden: That is correct.

Gelblum: I'd like to mark next in order, a contract between you and the "Globe" for the sale of those photographs.

Gelblum: Is that what that is, sir?

(Witness reviews document.)

Q. (By Gelblum) Exhibit 2286, that's a contract between you and the "Globe" bearing your signature on page 2, for $50,000 to sell autopsy photographs of John F. Kennedy to the "Globe," isn't it, sir?

Groden: No, it is not.

Gelblum: Okay. Is your name on it?

Groden: Yes, it is.

Gelblum: Okay. And you're agreeing to sell some photographs for $50,000?

Groden: No, I'm not.

Gelblum: What are you agreeing to do, sir?

Groden:	To give them exclusive rights to a story about autopsy photographs being faked and to consult with them for the writing of such a story.
Gelblum:	Okay. And in the story?
Groden:	I allowed them to use the photographs in the story.
Gelblum:	You were paid $50,000 for that, right?
Groden:	Yes.
Gelblum:	So you didn't sell them the photos, you just sold them the right to publish the photos?
Groden:	I sold them the rights to the story and allowed them to use the photographs in the story to prove a point.
Gelblum:	Those are some of the photos you obtained from the House Select Committee when you were there?
Groden:	That's correct.
Gelblum:	Those are autopsy photos of John F. Kennedy, right?
Groden:	That's correct.[20]

At one point, counsel was asked to move forward for a conference with the judge, and the court transcript shows that Gelblum said Groden "is not playing with a full deck," that he was suspected of having made off with key assassination imagery, and that the attorneys were considering calling Jeremy Gunn in Washington to establish all this as fact. But the judge didn't want to proceed down that route and none of that was permitted to be stated before the jury.

On one of the days he was to appear, the plaintiff's lawyers wanted me to be there, in the audience, just to look at Groden while he testified.

Groden took the stand and we made eye contact.

Immediately, there was a problem. (A friend of mine said: "You're Groden's kryptonite," referring to the Superman story where that metal was his Achilles heel.)

The OJ lawyers stood up in court and appealed to the judge that I be ejected from the courtroom. It was clear they believed that my presence was disturbing to their client.

The judge went along with it and requested that I leave, which I did. On the way out, CNN—and one or two other stations—wanted to know what the fuss was all about, so I made several appearances before the press.

There I was, on national TV, explaining the problem of Robert Groden as a photo expert—and that night, I saw the very lovely Nancy Grace on "The Larry King Show", who had picked up on the theme: "Groden? Groden? He sold the autopsy photographs to the *Globe* for $50,000!"

Oink oink

And that is just about the final chapter of my dealings with Robert Groden who, these days, can be found on or near the grassy knoll, selling his wares; and who I hope some day will see to it that any negatives and other materials he may possess are placed in the JFK Records Collection at the National Archives, where they belong.

The Zapruder Family Gets $16 Million

The ARRB had to deal with the question, what to do about the Zapruder film? Surely, that would be designated an "assassination record"? Well, then, how much was it worth?

In 1996, I testified to the Board and made the decision to donate free of charge one of my Zapruder interpositives. Since I made this item myself, the question of whether the Zapruder copyright applied has always intrigued me. I think it would depend on the exact day when Weitzman did his work back in 1967. According to court records, the film wasn't copyrighted until 1967. So it would depend on the sequence. Did Weitzman make his 35mm copies before or after *Life* copyrighted the film, as a motion picture film? I don't know the answer.

Then came the matter of the Zapruder family. How much would they get?

When I testified, it still hadn't gotten through my head how much money was involved. I just knew, from personal experience, that the family, based on my experiences, tended to be greedy. I made a public plea that they simply donate the film.

An aside. Abe Zapruder was from Russia and so was my father. They both came to America about the same time.

I am Jewish but not all that observant, and I was out jogging one day a short while before I was to testify and was thinking about the time of the year it was. The Jewish High Holidays were at hand and the period between Roshashana, which was then followed, about ten days later, by Yom Kippur, the Day of Atonement. It is a special time. We are taught that God turns over a new page in *The Book of Life*, and that if you do a good deed, your past transgressions and misdeeds are forgiven. You can start anew. You are inscribed in *The Book of Life*.

It's a very lovely story

Just thinking about it and the importance of this film evidence in arriving at the truth about this event caused me to become somewhat emotional; and when I got home, I wrote out the passages that I wanted to say.

I had decided to donate to the National Archives one the very few high quality interpositive negatives I had made directly from the Moe Weitzman 35 mm item, which is what I did. I gave it lock, stock and barrel to the American Government, no strings attached. I began my testimony by explaining who Weitzman was and how he had enlarged the Zapruder film from 8 mm to 35 mm "in one fell swoop." I said the result was "stunning," referring people to the Laserdisk version of the movie, "JFK," and explaining what a "liquid gate" was. Then I talked about the 35 mm copies that Weitzman had retained.

"The very best very of these 35 mm negatives and interpositives were given to the customer, Time-Life, and I would hope the Review Board would attempt to locate these with all the resources you have available to you. They are a priceless record of our history. But, with regard to the 35mm negatives known as technician copies which Weitzman kept in his lab—these he gave to another researcher—and they remain, as they have always been, completely unavailable to the research community."

Then I turned to my own activity in having made beautiful copies from the 35 mm copy I used in the summer of 1990 and came my own donation.

"First, I supervised making high quality timed liquid gate contact interpositives; Then . . . rented the services of an optical lab in New York City. And for about a week,, I worked at the optical printer, taking the next step that would be necessary by any archivist in order to preserve that record and create a progenitor for all future 35mm prints: operating the printer myself, I also made high quality liquid-gate interpositives from the 35mm negative. Then, I made interpositive blowup sequences directly from that same 35mm internegative---some focusing on Kennedy, some on Connally, some on the two Secret Service agents in the front.

"I'm holding here one of those 35mm inter-positives—a timed liquid gate contact interpositive— which I am today donating to the ARRB for placement in the JFK Records Collection. From this archival item—this 35mm interpositive—it should be possible to make negative/positive pairs; that is, this 35mm interpositive can be the progenitor of many 35mm internegatives, and they, in turn, can be used to create 35mm positives, whether they be slides or motion picture film. Although I defer to Moe Weitzman, you call this item the Lifton interpositive made from the Weitzman internegative. . . .

"In regard to this item, I am donating this negative to the ARRB without any copyright claim whatsoever."

When I appeared before the Assassination Records Review Board, on 17 September 1996, I made a public plea that the Zapruders should do a mitzvah—a good deed— for the American people, and donate the original film to the American People, both the film and the copyright.

I would like to ask the Zapruder family (the LMH company) to donate the original Zapruder film to the JFK Collection in the National Archives. As mentioned before, they were paid $150,000 from 1963 through 1968. (Plus the contract indicates additional moneys from foreign and other sales). Then, about 1975, *Life* sold the film back to Zapruder for $1. Then the process started all over again. Tens of thousands of dollars have been flowing to the Zapruder family every time a significant Kennedy assassination anniversary rolls around—every time any producer or network or broadcast entity wants to do a film on this subject.

To the Zapruder family, I say: *When is enough, enough?* I have been in too many situations where people—serious researchers or producers—could not use this film because they could not afford it. I myself could not use the Zapruder film in the *Best Evidence* research video—a serious video dealing with issues pertaining to the autopsy, and distributed nationally by MCA—because of the extraordinary $1/cassette charge that Henry Zapruder, Abe's son, told me "sounded about right" for a royalty. And so we used a diagram instead.

And so I say to the Zapruder family: Donate this film to the National Archives. Not a copy, but the original. It is the Rossetta Stone for this case. And the issue now is authenticity. If the film has not been tampered with, then it is an accurate record of the wounds and is a time clock of the assassination. However, and more importantly, if the film *has* been tampered with in some way as many have alleged, then that matter must be investigated in the future—it represents an assassination record that has to be clarified—and that cannot be done properly by examining a copy of the film.

This is the week to do it, Mr. Zapruder. Inscribe yourself in *The Book of Life* forever. Donate your father's film to the JFK Collection at the National Archives. Remove all copyright constraints. It is the right thing to do.

These were very noble ideas, but all this was going to turn out to be useless.

Because the film was now being appraised; and when I heard the results, I was speechless.

The Zapruders had been paid $150,000 for the film and it had been returned to them, in 1975, for a dollar. Now, because it was feared—and rightly so—that some eccentric person would buy it—that this record of United States history would end up in some unknown private hands—the government had to step in to protect the imagery, for its contribution to discovering the truth about Dallas.

The appraisal was up in the tens of millions of dollars.

We were approaching the biggest oink oink moment of all.

The Zapruder family would get $16 mllion for the film taken by Abraham Zapruder but, as the final data to be discussed here indicates, there is serious question as to whether the film the government paid $16 million is authentic or whether that $16 million was paid for a forgery. To state the matter differently: going all the way back to the days of the Warren Commission, there has been a serious question as to whether the 8mm film—with its two splices—that was in *Life's* possession from late November 1963 onward and which was the basis for so much of the data in the FBI and Warren Commission investigation and which then was returned to Zapruder in 1975, the film for which the Government was now about to pay $16 million—was in fact the original (the "camera original") that had been in Abe Zapruder's camera on 22 November 1963. Or whether it was in fact an optically edited forgery.

The ARRB and the Matter of Z Film Authenticity

The ARRB faced a daunting task. The decision was made to turn to Kodak for technical advice, and Doug Horne was asked to draft a memo about Zapruder film inauthenticity by listing those specific reasons why some in the research community believed the Zapruder film was inauthentic. During that period, in connection with many requests being made of me by the ARRB, I had quite bit of contact with them. Back then, it seemed evident that Jeremy Gunn was open to the idea of Zapruder film inauthenticity; he seemed willing to see it properly explored. That's when I wrote my memo about Groden, and Doug joked that I was the ARRB's "unpaid consultant."

The Left Margin Issue—Initial Considerations

One of the arguments Groden had made was that the film had to be an original because there was "material between the sprocket holes." Although critical of Gorden in many area, I concede the man has spent many hours at an optical printer, and when I first heard this line of argument I had no ready answer.

In a nutshell: when an optical printer is used to make a copy, the area between the sprocket holes is normally masked. So a duplicate has the following appearance: a series of frames, one after another after another, with the sprocket holes off to one side.

So, if one were handed a film and asked whether it was a "camera original" or a duplicate, a quick determination could be made by simply checking whether there was image in the sprocket hole area. If so, that would suggest it was a camera original; if devoid of such image—if it was pitch black and just contained sprocket holes—then the film would appear to be a dupe.

Let's now turn the problem around view the problem posed by the intersprocket hole area to anyone attempting to create an 8mm forgery. If an optical printer normally creates a duplicate *without* material between the sprockets, then wouldn't the absence of image there be a dead giveaway? Yes, it would. So for it to appear to be an original, somehow and in some way, such intersprocket image would have to be created; otherwise, it would be obvious the film was a copy, and not an original.

What to do? Or, more accurately, what might have been done?

It should now be clear why the existence of this margin on the Zapruder film "which looks different" appeared so worthy of investigation. This intersprocket area is readily visible in the poor black and white reproductions that are in Volume 18 of the Warren Commission 26 volumes (Commission Exhibit 885). In frame after frame, the image extends well into the sprocket hole area, and the contrast is different, too. It's as if there was a piece of Magic Mending Tape running down the left hand side of the film. As to the actual original film—kept at the National Archives—Doug Horne had the opportunity to see it on more than one occasion and told me what it looked like in color: running down the edge, in the sprocket hole area, the film has a different tint.

So, from the outset, the "intersprocket area" became the focus of any study regarding authenticity.

Kodak Retained

Kodak was contacted by the ARRB and agreed to provide $20,000 of *pro bono* work, but a choice had to be made: would these resources go towards investigating the autopsy pictures or doing a full scale digital scan of the Zapruder film? The former was chosen; as to the film, it was far from ignored. Kodak assigned Rolland Zavada, a film chemist who was extremely knowledgable about 8mm photography to assist. Thus, from the ARRB's *Final Report*:

> *Eastman Kodak's Pro Bono Work for the Review Board Related to the Zapruder Film (and Autopsy Photographs).* The Review Board first met with the Eastman Kodak Company in June 1996 in Washington to discuss a wide variety of possible research topics related to a host of potential film issues. The Review Board . . . subsequently met with Kodak technical experts James Milch and Roland Zavada in Washington, D.C. At that meeting, the Review Board identified three major areas of interest, only one of which related to the Zapruder film: the possible digitization and enhancement of the Zapruder film, as well as edge print analysis of the original and first generation copies, and study of the optical characteristics of the Zapruder camera . . .in relation to perceived "anomalies" in the original film.

And shortly thereafter, appears this passage in the same *Final Report*, namely: that the ARRB received assistance from Kodak to "explain the relationship, if any, between the camera's operating characteristics and perceived 'anomalies' in the original film." Zavada got to work, setting out to investigate the "anomalies" in the left margin.

Rollie Zvada was nothing if not energetic. He went out and purchased five Zapruder-type cameras. As he explained to me later, he lucked out in one instance. A relative provided a camera that was 30 digits away from the serial number of Zapruder's. Rollie calculated that meant the camera was manufactured within an hour of Zapruder's. That was impressive.

Seeking to understand exactly how the camera worked, he took one of his five cameras and disassembled it. It was, as he liked to say in conversation, "in pieces." With the other four, he intended to do tests. Ultimately, Rollie's investigation ran several hundred pages, but there are three matters worth mentioning at this juncture.

Zavada's initial reaction to the Intersprocket Area

What pupports to be the Zapruder "out of camera" original is stored under the appropropriate refrigerated condition at the National Archives. Zavada got a good look at that actual original for the first time when he wanted to photograph it, in order to investigate the intersprocket area.

When the film was taken out, various senior Archive officials were present, because the Zapruder film was one of the most important artifacts stored at the Archives. Doug was standing right there and recently recounted to me Zavada's initial reaction upon examining the left margin area with its bluish tint.

"This really looks strange to me. I can't explain this," Rollie kept saying "This looks strange."

A man is entitled to change his opinion, which is part of the Rollie story, but Doug was a witness to his initial reaction.

Meanwhile, Zavada was hearing a lot from Doug concerning suspicions about inautheniticity and Rollie made one suggestion that was very important.

Zavada's Suggestion about "cutting into" one frame

Doug remembered that Rollie on more than one occasion mentioned "cutting into" the Zapruder film—snipping out one frame—and doing some kind of chemical test. His concern seemed to center around exactly what kind of film it was, said, Doug. "He kept talking 'kelvin', 'kelvin' 'kelvin'." Until October 2003, Doug didn't quite understand just what it was that Rollie was getting at. It concerns color balance, as designated by Kelvin temperature, a subject we shall revisit soon. (Outdoor film has a Kelvin temperature of 5600; indoor film, of about 3200). Suffice it to point out that Abe Zapruder filmed the assassination on Kodachrome "outdoor" film, known as "Kodachrome II." K-II has a film speed of ASA 25, and is color balanced for light from the sun. Kodachrome also makes an indoor film—Kodachrome IIA—which is ASA 40. More significantly, it is "color balanced" so it responds optimally to an artifical light source.

If the Zapruder film was a sophisticated forgery, then it would be likely—although not absolutely necessary—that Kodachrome-IIA would have been used to make the final forgery. That is, "indoor" film (K-IIA) rather than K-II would have been used—the reason being that the illumination when the final product was created would be the light bulb in an optical printer, not the sun.

For Zavada to even make such a suggestion shows that he is one very smart guy and, more important, apparently had some suspicions and engaged in enough thinking "outside the box" to come up with a "thought experiment" for a quick test to see if this kind of hanky panky was going on. The dyes in K-II and K-IIA are different, so Zavada had broached the suggestion (to Doug, at least) that a single frame of the film be snipped for use with a spectrometer. The frame Doug had in mind was one of the thirteen at the beginning of the film. It would not be history's loss if there was one less frame (than the thirteen already there) of Zapruder's secretary sitting in the pergola before the motorcade appeared.

Doug told me what happened. For David Marwell, it was completely out of the question and ridiculous. As for Gunn, he rolled his eyes in disbelief. The fact is that this test is perfectly sensible. If the emulsion and the dyes checked out, that wouldn't prove authenticity (because K-II might have been used with lighting adjustments), but should they be shown to be "indoor film," then that would constitute dispositive evidence of film forgery. It is truly unfortunate that "good Rollie" came up with this idea and yet doing it was deemed to be completely out of the question.

Meanwhile, Rollie had excellent reasons for his suspicions, which extended beyond some lunchtime conversation with Doug and were rooted in what he learned from his own interviews with those who had been on duty at Kodak when the "out-of-camera original" was processed.

Meanwhile, the Zapruder family was at work, creating a new product that would be available starting in the fall of 1998.

The LMH Project and the DVD Copy

The LMH Company is the name the Zapruder family used in setting up a legal entity to handle all business matters deriving from their ownership of the film, along with its copyright. ("LMH" comes from the names of family members: Lillian, Zapruder's widow, son Henry and daughter Myrna.)

Around 1997, when the handwriting was on the wall and the Zapruder family could see that there would be "a taking", that is—that the Government would legally take possession of their film—they undertook to create a commercial product, the legal strategy being to provide a yardstick as a basis for measuring the amount they could "recover." A Chicago firm was hired to produce this new product—a reconstructed film that could then be distributed to commercial markets on video tape, or via the new digital video disk ("DVD") format.

The first step was making a new master. In the ideal world, the Zapruder frames should have been scanned, digitally—but that was not done. The contractor hired by LMH took another route: they photographed the original film, frame by frame, using an ordinary view camera.

Doug Horne was present for several days, in the Archives, when the project went forward. The film was put on a table, with a hole in it, a "viewing hole," as it were. Beneath the hole was a very bright light source. Situated above the table, looking down, was a view camera. Illuminating the film from below, the company photographed the film—a frame at a time—from above.

This entailed "advancing" the film, one frame at a time, across the table. With each advancement, a single frame was positioned over the hole, then stabilized mechanically, then a picture taken; then on to the next frame, then another picture, and so forth— until the entire film had been photographed, a frame at a time, with the view camera. Then, the company took hundreds of photographs back in Chicago, digitized those photographs, and reassembled them into a motion picture film.

A disadvantage of this method is that it was *not* a digital scan. The 8 mm film itself was not scanned. The starting point were hundreds of "ordinary" photographs made with a view camera. Also, the film was not cleaned and, over the years, it has acquired a certain amount of dirt.

But one great advantage was that the company obtained an accurate image of the geometry of each 8mm frame, which would turn out to be important, when the DVD was issued in 1998.

Horne Requests Test with Original Camera

Doug Horne knew what needed to be done: that film should be run through the Zapruder camera in a test conducted at Dealey Plaza, preferably when the lighting was the same as it had been on 22 November 1963, and such test film be compared with the Zapruder film. It didn't take a photo expert to understand why this should be done: a match between the test film and the Zapruder film would be powerful evidence that the Zapruder film was a genuine original; contrarywise, any mismatch might be probative, even definitive, on whether the film in evidence was *not* taken by the Zapruder camera.

Neither David Marwell nor Jeremy Gunn wanted to do any such tests.

Marwell looked with complete disdain at the notion that the Zapruder film might be a forgery. He said he had experience in college, either on the newspaper or in a photography club, with contact printing, and he just didn't see how the film could be inauthentic. He kept bringing up the small size of an 8 mm film frame, saying: "You'd need engraving tools." As Doug observed later, he simply failed to inform himself about optical editing technology.

Gunn was a different matter. When Marwell left the ARRB and the problem was passed to Gunn, the problem was political. Gunn did not have good relations with the five Board members, who—Doug tells me—thought of him as a closet assassination buff (and, in some ways, he was). The Board members were essentially conservative, and Gunn knew they would never approve doing a test in Dealy Plaza. Their fear would be a *New York Times'* headline, "ARRB Suspects Zapruder Film Forgery".

Doug thought their fears were completely exaggerated. It was well within the rights of the ARRB to investigate the provenance of any assassination record. What "record" could be more important that the visual record of the Zapruder film?

When Marwell departed as Executive Director to take outside employment, Gunn became his successor as well as General Counsel. This was the autumn of 1997.

One day, Doug locked horns with Gunn on this issue.

"I insisted on a film test in Zapruder's actual camera in Dealey Plaza on November 22 at 12:30 PM," recalls Doug.

Gunn was cold, austere, distant, even hostile.

"What are your reasons for wanting to do this test?", he said.

"Film authenticity," replied Doug.

"And I said that the best way to test inauthenticity would be to see if the intersprocket sprocket image looked the same or not as the intersprocket image on the film at the Archives. That's exactly what I said."

"He then completely astounded me by saying 'Can you give me a reason to conduct this test that has nothing to do with authenticitiy?'"

"I was floored by his question," recalls Doug, "And I said, I literally exploded. 'I can't believe you're asking me that question. That's ridiculous. The only reason to do this test is authenticity.'"

Gunn said : "Let's call Rollie and put it to a vote."

And so, right on the spot, he called Rollie Zavada: How did he feel about conducting such a test—using Abe's camera, up on the white pedestal, on 22 November at 12:30 PM?

"I've already shot test film in Zapruder type cameras," replied Rollie, "and the only thing that Doug is proposing that's any different is to do it on 22 November at 12:30 P.M."

Then Rollie delivered the coup de grace: "I see no reason to do this test with Abe's original camera; it would be good enough to use any camera of the same make and model."

"And at that point, I knew I'd lost," recalls Doug. "I was devastated. Really, I was."

Gunn immediately proposed a compromise.

"We've got Tom Samoluk going to Dallas on other business around November 22 [1997]. Can you send us a Zapruder type camera filled with film, and we'll conduct the test that Doug wants, which is to do it on 22 November at 12:30 PM?"

"And Rollie said, 'Sure, I'll do that.'

"They thought they were doing a good thing," says Doug. "I was extremely disappointed, because: (1) a film pro wouldn't be conducting the test; (2) it wouldn't be Abe's camera."

Doug says that he knew that if Zapruder's actual camera wasn't used, then whatever anomalies were discovered would be attributed to camera-to-camera variations.

"Those were all the things running through my mind, so I was very disappointed," recalls Doug.

But it wasn't over—yet.

Samoluk Goes to Dallas

But let's return to Samoluk in November, 1997.

It was November, 1997 when Samoluk went to Dallas, tasked with the job of taking pictures from Zapruder's perch on 22 November, something he really didn't want to do, because Dealey Plaza can be a zoo on assassination anniversaries.

Meanwhile, Rollie had sent a camera via Federal Express—loaded with film and with directions—in a box to the ARRB in Washington; and now, in Dallas, Samoluk retired to his hotel room and opened the box.

He pulled out the camera, pressed the trigger, to make sure it would run, and nothing happened. He tried again. Nothing. Experimenting a bit in the hotel room, Samoluk became convinced that the camera was jammed and gave up on the project.

Upon returning to Washington, Doug ran over to him when he appeared at the ARRB offices and asked excitedly ("like a puppy dog," recalls Doug): "Did you conduct the test?"

"With a sheepish look on his face," recalls Doug, "he replied, 'No, I didn't, the friggin' camera jammed.'"

"What do you mean it jammed?" said Doug.

"Well, either it jammed or the batteries were no good!", replied Samoluk.

"What do you mean, batteries?" said Doug, growing increasingly upset. "This camera doesn't have batteries, you wind it with a big gigantic key that is on the side of the camera."

"And his jaw dropped open, his eyes got big, he got this 'Oh, shit!' look on his face."

Doug called Rollie and confirmed that there were no batteries and that Rollie had not wound the camera before he sent it to the Review Board.

Rollie had sent a long list of operating instructions, but nowhere did it say "Wind the camera."

"This was keystone cops, man, USG style," says Doug, reflecting on the experience.

The ARRB Completes Its Work

In Chicago, the Zapruder family was completing their work on reassembling the film as a motion picture film for public release, both on VHS and DVD, which occurred in the fall of 1998.

In September 1998, the ARRB was to go out of business. That meant there would be no ARRB after 30 September. No ifs, ands, or buts—the report had to be in. And Rollie Zavada was hard at work completing that report. He, too, had photographed selected frames from the Z film original on a light box at the Archives. These test frames would appear in his report as Figures 4-1 and 4-2, the first time Z frames had been published, in color, that extended out to the sprocket hole area.

In Washington, D.C., Doug was doing a myriad of things connected with the closing of shop.

On 30 September, the ARRB ceased to exist. There was a "sunset" news conference. Then it was over.

The Archives now had some 4 million pages, and one set of them would be "The Zavada Report".

In 1998, I posted a notice on the Internet. I did not feel like spending a small fortune at the Archives. So I did what I had done in the past, with other large documents. I would make copies for anyone who was interested.

My Conversation with Zavada: 14 October 1998

Zavada saw my notice on the Internet and wanted to clarify that I was not in violation of any regulations. He left a message on my answering machine and, on 14 October 1998, I called him and we had an extremely interesting conversation lasting for over an hour.

He seemed very precise, likable, competent. I asked him if he had really cleared up the matter of the left margin. Oh yes, he assured me, he had.

I asked him why the original camera hadn't been used. He said he asked for it three times and was refused. (Doug remembers Zavada being turned down by David Marwell).

I asked him if he had tested to see whether the film in evidence had been reframed—for example, whether the limousine in the film looked larger. He said he had never tested for that parameter.

Then I turned to the most important thing of all—the left margin area.

Rollie assured me that he had replicated everything in the intersprocket area, .

"Oh, there's no problem there," he assured me.

"Why is there no problem there?" I asked.

Zavada replied that it was all just "a camera characteristic."

He explained to me that his view had changed over the course of his work. He said that when he first approached the problem—the way the left margin looked—he was confused by its appearance. "It left me bewildered at first," he said, but then his puzzlement dissipated as he had studied it further.

"It really is just straightforward," he said, "and actually I was lucky and I got the head of the (Kodak) optics testing lab, and discussed it with him; and [then] I got the president of the of the Optics Division of Bell and Howell, and [even] the designer of the Zoom lens, [I] had lunch with them, and went through everything."

Well, OK, I thought. Rollie had lunch with a lot of important people. But what about the problem? Did he really solve it?

Rollie told me of what seemed unassailable evidence. He assured me that he had exposed test film—test film of his wife taken both in Rochester and in Dealy Plaza—and that there was no problem remaining. None at all.

My notes of the conversation continue:

DL Well, when you exposed film in whatever your substitute cameras were, did you get the same phenomena on the left?

RZ I got 'em all.

DL You got right out to the left margin (referring to all the anomalies)?

RZ Oh yes; and I also got *not* out to the left margin. Which you'll find in some of the Zapruder films also.

All in all, it was a very nice conversation. I liked Rollie Zavada. I thought he was thorough, competent, and that I could take whatever he said to the bank. I was sufficiently persuaded that I didn't bother to read the fine print, to really look at Rollie's pages. And, besides, I was preoccupied.

Around November 1998, the Archives released the Zavada report and I set out to duplicate about 30 copies, which went out to many people who were closely following the debate. The hardest part where the color pages.

Meanwhile, everybody but me, it seemed, had time to read it. Suddenly, I was in the role of shipping clerk. Doug had his own problems. He found new employment in Washington, D.C., and his new job started soon.

So the two of us put the issue of authenticity was put aside, and a major discovery, one made by Doug Horne, didn't occur until May 1999.

Horne Discovers the Full Flush Left Problem

In May of 1999, both Doug and I were interviewed at length by a German documentary outfit. Before leaving Germany, the producer interviewed me by telephone. What did I think of the Zapruder film?, she asked. I replied with my reasons for believing the film was very likely a forgery. She then telephoned Doug. What did he think? Well, he was more neutral on the issue, he said. It was a debate that could go either way, but if they wanted to discuss it further, he would retrieve his copy of the Zavada report and give it close study.

Doug did exactly that, and within a day, made a fundamental discovery. Turning to Figures 4-1 and 4-2, the Zapruder frames Rollie had photographed at the National Archives, it was clear that those frames went out full flush left. All the way to the left.

Then Doug compared those with the test shots Rollie made in Dealey Plaza, taken from Zapruder's perch, with one of his Zapruder-type cameras. One strip showed wife standing in the street, another showed a red truck passing through. Another test shot, his figure 4-26, showed his wife standing in front of their garage in Rochester. In each case, Rollie varied the telephoto setting and, as the zoom increased, the left margin moved somewhat to the left. But, contrary to what Rollie had told me, there was quite obviously a problem.

The test frames did not appear similar to those from the original Zapruder film, and it was a simple matter of geometry: Rollie's clearly did *not* go consistently full flush left. [*Editor's note*: See Doug Horne, "The Failures of the ARRB", *Kennedy Assassination Chronicles* (Spring 2000), pp. 21-22; and David W. Mantik, "Paradoxes of the JFK Assassination: The Zapruder Film Controversy", *Murder in Dealey Plaza* (2000), pp. 350-351.]

I was struck by the irony of the situation. The Zapruder film original sure did contain "material between the sprocket holes." The problem was there was too *much* material between the sprocket holes—*so much that these tests appeared to show the Zapruder film frames could not have been exposed in Zapruder's camera!*

Did it really matter that Rollie hadn't used the actual Zapruder camera for his tests? Rollie had assured Doug it didn't matter—that the camera he had used was for all practical purposes identical.

But, if so, then the frames in Zavada's own report—published not because he suspected anything about the geometry, but because he was investigating "claw shadow" and "claw flare"—revealed the terribly important fact that, based on geometry alone, they were not taken in Zapruder's camera. In effect, the "optical footprint" of the Zapruder lens was different than that employed to produce the frames of the so-called "original Zapruder film."

If these test results were replicated using Zapruder's actual camera, and with lighting conditions identical to 22 November, then they would constitute the proof that the film was not a "camera original".

The "Full Flush Left" Problem

(Captions and text by Doug Horne and David Lifton)

Zapruder Frames from The Zavada Report

Kodak consultant Rollie Zavada photographed these frames of the Zapruder film at the National Archives in 1996, using a single lens reflex 35 mm camera. (The Zapruder film frames being photographed were placed flat on a light box and illuminated from below.) In Zavada's report, these two film strips constitute Figures 4-1 and 4-2. The purpose of the photography was to record the nature and extent of the intersprocket images, which the ARRB had asked Rollie to study. Note that the intersprocket portions of each Zapruder film frame go virtually "full flush left," all the way to the edge of the sprocket holes, in these images.

Zapruder frames from "Image of an Assassination"

Superior reproductions of the "full flush left" phenomenon—better than those photographed by Rollie Zavada in 1996—can be found in the MPI DVD, "Image of an Assassination" (1998). The Zapruder frames on this DVD were photographed in the National Archives in 1997 by a contractor hired by the LMH Company, using Ektachrome color positive transparency film exposed in a 4" X 5" format view camera.

The Zapruder film frames were illuminated from below, and the view camera was mounted above the frames being photographed. These images are superior to Zavada's because the film that captured them was of a larger format, allowing better resolution, and the Zapruder film itself was better illuminated in this instance.

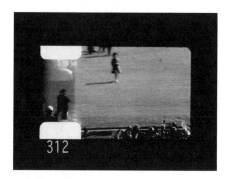 

These DVD images reveal that in most frames, the "full flush left" phenomenon not only goes all the way to the left of the sprocket holes, but actually extends a bit beyond the sprocket holes.

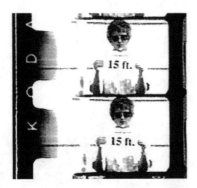

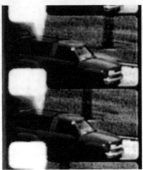

Zavada Test Frames

In at least three separate film tests, Kodak consultant Rollie Zavada exposed movie film in bright, sunny outdoor suroundings using the "full telephoto" setting—to maximize "intersprocket penetration"—on cameras identical to Zapruder's. Note that in none of the tests (shown here) could he replicate the continuous "full flush left" phenomenon seen on the previous two pages.

Since neither "full flush left" nor "beyond full flush left" intersprocket images could be consistently reproduced by Zavada on film shot in Bell and Howell cameras identical to Zapruder's, this strongly suggests that the film in the National Archives today known as the "Zapruder in-camera original" was not exposed in Zapruder's camera.

In any future test conducted under lighting conditions equivalent to those on 22 November 1963, failure to empirically reproduce the "full flush left" phenomenon in the actual camera used by Zapruder would constitute "dispositive evidence"—proof that the film in the National Archives purported to be the "original" Zapruder film is, in fact, a forgery: a film created in an optical laboratory setting or editing facility with optical equipment, rather than in Zapruder's camera. [*Editor's note*: The basic elements of optical printing are explained in the chapter by David Healy.]

Zapruder Frame versus Zavada Frame

Frame 269 of the Zapruder film at the National Archives clearly shows an image (motorcyclists) to the left of the left edge of the sprocket hole, which provides a good example of the "beyond full flush left phenomenon"—the extension of image to beyond the left edge of the sprocket holes. But film frames from the Zavada test film—exposed in a Zapruder-like camera—shows maximum intersprocket penetration of about 80%, not "full flush left" and certainly not "beyond." The Zavada test films establish what the left margin of a film exposed in Zapruder's camera *ought to* look like; the film in the Archives has quite a different "optical footprint" on the left, which strongly suggests that it could not have been exposed in Zapruder's camera.

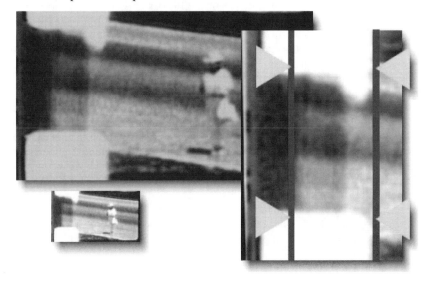

This discovery, for all practical purposes, went on the shelf. Both of us were involved in different issues. Also, in 1998, neither of us had checked the Zapruder DVD. Nontheless, a friend of mine tried to interest one of the major tabloids and briefly had contact with the editor, sending in color prints, but for some reason it didn't work out.

In 1999, Doug Horne made a 90 minute presentation at the JFK Lancer conference in Dallas. Towards the end, and in an "Oh, by the way" fashion, he presented the "full flush left issue" and clearly stated the implication (that the film might be a forgery) but no one seemed interested.

Full Flush Left—Circa, May, 2003 (at Duluth)

When Professor Fetzer asked me to make a presentation at Duluth, I decided to end with a report about this, which I illustrated with diagrams.

When he asked me to contribute to this book, I thought—mistakenly as it turns out—that the easiest way to illustrate the phenomenon would be with the frames of the 26 volumes.

That led to a problem. An effective visual presentation required that we compare "A" with "B". But we did not then have, on the computer, "B" (Rollie test frames) to compare with "A" (Zapruder frames). Also for "A" (Zapruder frames), we used copies of frames from the 26 volumes—and they came out dark on the left hand margin, due to multi-generational contrast buildup.

Meanwhile, Zavada responded.

Zavada's Statement of September 23, 2003

Zavada replied with a statement, posted on the Internet. He claimed his test shots proved the case—that his test shots proved full penetration of the intersprocket area— but they don't.

Zavada is in a somewhat untenable position. He initially found the intersprocket area as looking "strange" (he told me he was "bewildered"). He wanted to do a spectroscopic test—it was out of the question. He wanted to use the genuine camera—he was refused three times. Where his statement falls down is where he misrepresents what *his own tests* show.

"Can the Zapruder lens put an image on the film that is full flush left?", he quotes me as having asked. And he responds, "Under the correct circumstances of lens and light—yes, the image can fill the area between the sprockets. See my test shots."

But Rollie's test shots don't prove his point. And, as Doug has noted, "Saying something is so doesn't make it so."

Rollie tends to write in a technical and dense style. Repeatedly he talks as if film forgery is out of the question. He now writes of his ARRB work, "My knowledge of optical effects technology convinced me (at that time) that a dissertation on the probability of alteration was not needed."

A dissertation is perhaps not needed, but some very critical thinking is called for and there is important work that remains to be done. All the technical gibberish and appeal to authority (*his* authority) is no substitute for the tests which will generate definitive evidence one way or the other. It is useful to recall Zavada's initial reaction to seeing the left margin of this film: "This looks strange to me" and "I can't explain it." But that was then. Now, without having done the very tests he himself wanted to do, he says, "There is no detectable evidence of manipulation or image alteration on the 'Zapruder in-camera original'—and all supporting evidence precludes any forgery thereto."

Full Flush Left—The Current Situation

Meanwhile, Doug and I went back to our Zavada reports. In full color, Rollie's exhibits can be seen and arrangements made to capture those images as computer files.

More important, the film frames from the Zapruder DVD were checked. Doug Horne went frame by frame through the DVD. Lo and behold, it was even more dramatic: the frames clearly go out to the left margin, and even a little beyond. They are published in the illustrations in this edition, and on one page of a color insert.

For this edition of the book, we have selected several exhibits:

First, exhibits that show the Zapruder frames, as published in Zavada's report. Second, exhibits from the DVD that (again) show the leftward extent of the Zapruder frames. Third, the test shots from Zavada's report. Finally, a comparison between them.

David Healy—who has been in the film optics business for years—captured these images and has added frames with blowups. Now, a color panel has been prepared, showing the Zavada test frames. [*Editor's note*: See the color photo section, "Which Film *is* 'the Zapruder film'?"]

What does all this mean? In a nutshell—that, *based on these tests, the film in evidence (the Zapruder "original" at the National Archives) does not appear to have been exposed in Zapruder's camera.*

Is it possible that a test with Zapruder's camera would show anything different? By all means such a test should be conducted. In fact, I think the FBI should reclaim the camera from The Sixth Floor Museum, and that it should be the centerpiece of a future investigation, first, to determine whether this film was exposed in the camera; and, second, if the tests bear out what so far seems to be the case, then we must address the next question: who made this film—this fabricated version of what happened on 22 November 1963? The evidence presented here suggests that somebody created—and, in 1999, the government paid $16 million for—an optical forgery!

The consequences of all this for my book, *Best Evidence*, are also clear. If it can be shown definitively that the Zapruder film is an optically edited forgery, then the balance shifts as to which evidence is truly the most credible—the eyewitnesses or the film—and the door opens wide to the proposition that the Dallas eyewitness accounts are indeed better evidence than what appears on this doctored film. If the film is a forgery, then the imagery on the frames showing a "Bethesda-like" head wound on the President's body in Dealey Plaza—a wound not seen five minutes later at Parkland Hospital—is, once and for all, impeached as the "best evidence" of what JFK's head looked like in Dallas and the primacy of the Dallas doctors observations are restored.

In short, another piece of the disguise falls away, and it becomes clearer than ever that the body was altered, with the Zapruder film having been faked (among other reasons) to corroborate a false depiction of the wounds. In this way, film alteration and body alteration are integrally linked, historically. Both are parts of the same disguise.

Moreover, even if, because of film editing, we can't determine the truth about the details of the shooting—at least, not yet—we can now begin to understand the political significance of what is being hidden by determining the nature of the disguise employed to hide that truth.

Summary and Recapitulation

The preceding narrative reports my experiences with the Zapruder film from early 1965 when I was first shown the black and white frames in Volume 18 of the Warren

Report, through the ARRB years (1995-1998) and to the present. What follows are my personal opinions, because I consider Zapruder film research a "work in progress".

General Concepts

- The basic concept is that the assassination did not happen as set forth in *The Warren Report*—that basic facts were changed via the alteration of this film within hours of the shooting, its subsequent dissemination via *Life* magazine, and its use as key evidence in all subsequent investigations. It is highly probable that these alterations worked hand in hand with the alteration of the President's wounds (which became the basis for a false autopsy) to create the appearance of one assassin, shooting from behind. Certainly, by the time the President's body arrived at Bethesda, there was no evidence of a shot from the front. As far as the Zapruder imagery was concerned, key frames showed a large, white-ish, almost translucent blob (supposedly the Bethesda exit wound) on the forward right hand side of JFK's head, a wound not observed five minutes later by observers at Parkland Hospital, who reported an exit wound at the rear (where key Zapruder frames show a largely blacked-out area). Moreover, at the street location where most witnesses saw the car momentarily stop, no stop occurs; but, at that juncture, the President's head snaps violently backward (an artifact of film editing, I am convinced).

- Those newly arrived to this case view tend to think of the backward snap as powerful evidence of a shot from the front. Perfectly understandable, but one can't have it both ways: if the car stopped, then the backward snap is an artifact of an altered film. This doesn't mean that the President was not shot in the head from the front—based on the Dallas doctors observations of an exit wound at the back of the head, he certainly was. But that conclusion must rest on the Dallas medical data, not on the "backward snap" on the Zapruder film.

- The strongest circumstantial evidence that the Zapruder film must have been edited is the great majority of witnesses at or near the car who say it stopped, momentarily, whereas the car does not stop on the film. True, it slows down—somewhat—but it does not stop. And then it takes off. Rapidly. Moreover, Clint Hill's "race to catch the car" (readily visible on the Nix film) which he "overtakes" by frame 369 would be extremely difficult to accomplish in reality. When I was in Dallas in 1971, at age 32, I raced down the street at top speed, attempting to simulate "overtaking" an accelerating car. I advise anyone who thinks that what the films show Hill doing can be readily duplicated to try it.

- The car stop would imply that the assassination, from the standpoint of the Secret agents guarding the President, was not a six-second, "we wuz caught by surprise", affair, but rather an event lasting between 10 and 20 seconds (the elapsed time cited by Sheriff Decker), depending on the "length of the stop" in time, that is, on the time expended in the deceleration and then the acceleration of the car (time "lost" when the frames were deleted in the editing process and a "cinematic reality" substituted for what actually occurred).

- The removal of the car stop—which in effect means that events were speeded up—would account for the rapid snap backward of the President's head on the film. If the film was altered, that backward snap has little to do with a bullet impact but everything to do with film editing. It is an artifact of an altered film.

- The car stop implies the Secret Service was negligent, at least, and on two counts: actually stopping the car during the shooting and then failing to react to protect the President. Notably, it was the same agency—the Secret Service—that had custody of JFK's body that also quickly obtained control of the Zapruder film. So the potential exists here for the same officials who failed in their assigned duties then controlling the evidence that would have documented that malfeasance—and, perhaps worse, exposed its personnel to the charge of involvement in the assassination.

- The alteration of the film would explain why the head wound imagery shows wounds not visible at Parkland Hospital some five minutes later and why the one wound that was seen at Parkland—by most of the doctors and nurses—appears on the film as a blacked out area at the back of the head. Whether the primary purpose of film alteration was the car-stop, or the alteration of wound imagery, is debatable. Both seem to have occurred.

- In its very first issue carrying some 30 film frames (*Life*, 29 November 1963), the detailed caption copy failed to report any visible head impact at all. The caption text implies JFK suffered all his wounds when he was behind the highway sign. This of course changed in later issues, but raises the question of whether *Life* had been provided with some kind of "early edit" for that first issue.

- The fact that the FBI Exhibit given to the Warren Commission stops at Zapruder frame 334 contributed to the Commission not being aware that certain film frames (such as 335 and 337) contained striking head wound imagery clearly at variance with the head wound description in the autopsy report. [(Chapter 20 of *Best Evidence* develops this matter in detail, namely: that the autopsy report "head wound", albeit large, encompasses the *rear* of the head; whereas the head wound depicted in the autopsy photographs—and, for that matter, on frames 335 and 337 of the film, which appear to serve to "showcase" the head wound—extends towards the front.)]

- The Zapruder film was sold to *Life* magazine the day after the assassination under circumstances that were peculiar. When the bidding limit was reached, Zapruder went along with a price of $50,000 even though he wanted more. Stolley, the *Life* representative, does not seemed to be involved in this affair. He appears to have been the proverbial potted plant. *Life* publisher C. D. Jackson, whose name was on the contract, was a specialist in psychological warfare under Eisenhower, and a close friend of former CIA Director Allen Dulles. Jackson, as columnist Drew Pearson noted, was always pulling CIA chestnuts out of the fire, and this may be another example of that behavior. Most peculiar of all is that the film—purchased for around $900,000 in 2003 money—was not exploited as a motion picture film so as to maximize the return on the investment. Media companies don't normally operate that way.

- The importance of the film having been sold to someone so close to the CIA may mean that the time frame for alteration was more flexible, namely: that events pertaining to alteration or last minute substitution possibly occurred *after* the arrival of the film at *Life*. That is by no means a certainty. If a technical team was working on the film by Friday night (and the source for such special effects expertise was probably Los Angeles, although conceivably the film was not brought there but rather some experts were flown east), I see no reason why the job couldn't have been substantially completed by Sunday night. The result, of course, would have to be printed on Kodachrome stock (but couldn't be processed at Dallas, where the genuine original had already been processed) and that's why the experience of the CIA's Homer McMahon, as reported to the ARRB, is important. McMahon reports that it was Saturday or Sunday night when "Agent Smith" (of the Secret Service) showed up at the CIA's NPIC color lab carrying a 16 mm Kodachrome positive. Smith said he had just come from Rochester, that the item he was carrying (a Kodachrome positive) had been processed at Hawkeyeworks, a top secret Government lab run by Kodak, that "the subject matter was to be treated as 'above top secret'", and he was requesting NPIC's assistance in the creation of some 28 color blowups for briefing boards. (See Appendix C).

- Mrs. Zapruder told me in November 1971 that Abe "gave them the film," clearly implying he had parted with the original, and at an early hour. Local newspaper stories state that Abe Zapruder was closeted with "government agents" into the evening. Years later, *Life* representative Stolley said he couldn't find Zapruder at home until midnight Friday and that when he expressed his interest in viewing it as soon as possible, Zapruder begged off. He was tired, he had been driving around all night, he said; and would prefer seeing Stolley in the morning. Zapruder's business partner Erwin Swartz said he took two film cans to the Dallas Naval Air Station on Friday night. All this raises the question of whether Zapruder possessed the original on Friday night.

- On Saturday morning, with all other bidders excluded, Zapruder had a peculiar session with Stolley resulting in a sale—but only for print rights—for $50,000. At that point, Zapruder retained the "film rights", the right to sell his property as a motion picture, as long as he waited until 29 November. But by Monday, 25 November, that was precluded when more money was pledged and it became an "all rights" deal (with Zapruder retaining no film rights—indeed, no rights at all). The new sale price was $150,000 and the contract specified an annual payment schedule: $25,000 per annum, payable in early January 1964 through January 1968. The entire deal— $150,000—would correspond in today's money to about $900,000. (How and why the film was returned to the Zapruder family in 1975 for $1 has never been adequately explained.)

- The actual 8 mm film delivered to *Life* has two splices. The first—where frame 207 is spliced to frame 212—appears in the segment of the film published in Warren Commission Exhibit 885 in Volume 18 of the Commission's 26 volumes. That splice was discovered shortly after the 26 volumes were published in November 1964. As previously noted, in October 1965, at our very first meeting, I brought that splice to the attention of former Warren Commission counsel Wesley Liebeler. The next day he wrote his former colleague, attorney Norman Redlich, suggesting an FBI investigation. (See *Best Evidence*.) In January, 1967, *Life* "explained" the splice, claiming a technician had an "oops" moment and dropped the film. But *Life* never provided the name of the technician and, in nearly four decades since Dallas, no technician from *Life* has ever appeared to verify any of these assertions. Moreover, this January 1967 explanation failed to mention the existence of another splice, just as obvious, that existed in the unpublished portion of the film (around frame 155). This second splice was discovered in early 1969. *Life* never mentioned this second splice, nor did Josiah Thompson, who contracted to work with *Life* in 1966, and who made extensive use of these materials.

- The two areas of splicing in the original should not be considered indicative of the way the film was edited and altered (see next section for those details). The kind of editing being discussed would not have been done mechanically or in 8mm format. Almost certainly it was done optically (in 16 or 35 mm format), utilizing an optical printer. In short, the "editing" being considered here did not involve pasting 8mm film pieces together but was instead "optical editing" done in 16 or 35 mm format using an optical printer.

- The most reasonable hypothesis to account for the two splices in the so called "original Zapruder film" that ended up at *Life* is that the final reduction print (to 8mm)—an item which had "material in the sprocket hole area" (just as a camera original should)—was created in three segments (A, B, and C) and that before sending it off to *Life*, A was pasted to B, and then A-B to C. Why this happened probably concerns the "left margin" problem and will be explained below. But, in my opinion, the two splices pertain to some such peripheral "manufacturing" issue and have nothing to do with the actual editing of the film's content.

- The "blowup" of the 8mm Zapruder film, back to 35mm—an event important to *Life* and to the JFK research community—was the result of the ingenuity and craftsmanship of Moses Weitzman at EFX in 1967. That 1967 "re-enlargement" is unrelated to its original (1963) alteration. But that "re-enlargement" is valuable because it produced a copy of the "original" that was (after Weitzman's handiwork) then back in a format (35 mm) close to that in which the original alteration must have taken place. Consequently, all the anomalies on the 8mm (and which *Life* called its "original") were magnified on those 35mm "Weitzman copies" and are more readily visible, more easily measured, etcetera. But the general timeline must be kept firmly in mind here; specifically, one must distinguish between events taking place in 1963 (when any alteration was a criminal matter, and an obstruction of justice) from those taking place four (or more) years later, when *Life's* 8mm film, its so-called "original", was "re-captured" in—or "reenlarged to"—35 mm format. The 1967 re-enlargement probably occurred because someone on *Life's* staff (e.g., Director of Photography Richard Pollard) contracted with Weitzman's company, EFX, to do so.

- Because Robert Groden went to work at EFX around 1969, he learned of the existence of this 35 mm material sitting on a shelf or in a cabinet. Weitzman, rightly proud of his accomplishment in enlarging an 8 mm film to 35 mm, retained several copies, what he called "technician's copies." As Weitzman said, Groden then "pirated" a print off the premises, and that was how, in the early 1970s, Groden (a) obtained exclusive possession of material that was until that time only available in a vault at *Life* magazine and (b) became an assassination buff. Groden showed this film to many audiences, who were astonished at its breathtaking quality. Groden took much of the credit for work originally done by Weitzman and, as a consequence of his access to an optical printer in New York City, Blakey permitted him to have access to other films then acquired under the auspices of the HSCA. Groden's so called "film collection"—which indeed ranges far and wide—is undoubtedly related to his employment at the HSCA and his access to original materials, through this government position. The fact that key originals are missing in the aftermath of this affair is troubling, and may or may not be connected to the activities of this "collector."

- It is my personal opinion that no one should have been given access to these priceless and irreplaceable cinematic originals without a very serious background investigation; moreover, if General Counsel Blakey had done so in the case of Groden and, in particular, if Blakey had simply read what was in Groden's military file, he would not have been allowed unsupervised access to priceless photo materials. Groden's coffee table book is essentially a scrapbook demonstrating his unparalleled access to original imagery that, in some cases, is no longer available at the National Archives.

Method of Alteration

As a practical matter, the Zapruder film could only have been altered optically, that is, through the use of an Oxberry (or Acme) optical printer, the standard tool of the special effects profession. An optical printer re-photographs the original film, one frame at a time (but chugs along at full camera speed), and the result—if no editing is done—is a rather rapidly created duplicate. In connection with making that duplicate, various alterations can be made. A film can be re-framed to change the image size. Or sections can be omitted. Or frames can be periodically omitted (which would change the velocity of the car, for example). Finally, in a particular frame, additional imagery can be added (a "matte artist" can draw in or "paint on" additional information). This art would be crucial to understanding any changes in the head wound imagery. In effect, the "matte artist" can "draw on" the picture that is already there, much as a child draws lines on a poster. These are all the standard techniques in the tool box of the special effects person circa 1963. Films are not altered or edited that way today, when everything is done digitally. But that's how it was done then.

The Basic Problem

Although the Zapruder film—after processing—is an "8 mm film," that is not its configuration when inside the Zapruder camera. At that point, in its original format, it is a 16 mm film, with a "side A" and a "side B," akin to the red and black portions of an ordinary typewriter ribbon. One side is first exposed, then the film is "turned over" and the other side exposed. The result is processed as a 16 mm film, and then slit, after processing, with the two sides being pasted together—"end to end"—so that a 25 foot roll of this film produces a 50 foot film in 8 mm format. In order for the Z film to have been altered, it would be very useful if it remained *un*slit after being processed at Kodak in Dallas. I first discovered that the film was *not* slit—that it was unslit—when I saw records connected with the Thompson law suit in the early 1970s. Later, I learned from documents made that weekend that Dallas Secret Service Agent Forrest Sorrels ordered that the film, after processing, not be slit, i.e., remain *un*slit.

The chronology and semantics of "alteration"

"Alteration" does not mean that the film was altered at Kodak in Dallas, or anything of the kind (and certainly that was not the case). But the actual camera original was in fact processed at Kodak because Zapruder used Kodachrome film, Kodachrome requires a special processing plant, and Dallas was one of only a half dozen such plants in the nation where this was done.

Once the Secret Service—or any top-level officials of the U.S. Government became aware of what was on this film, and a decision was made to alter the film (to create a "politically correct" version of the assassination, for whatever reason)—it was necessary to obtain the camera original, to do that just as soon as possible, and to get it into the hands of a competent editor.

That original—the unslit 16mm film, after processing by Kodak in Dallas (a film that contained on "side B" the actual film record of what had happened)—had to be brought to someone with visual effects expertise. His job was to optically edit the event (per the instructions of some "producer"), and create a substitute (Kodachrome) original: a substitute 16 mm film with "side A" containing the family sequence and "side B" containing the altered Zapruder film.

Is such "early access" possible? Apparently so—certainly as a possibility. The original records of the Kodak lab establish that although the Zapruder film went through as film number 0183, and that—after returning from Jamieson with three Kodachrome II-A duplicates (which went through the processor as 0185, 0186, and 0187)—there is a missing number in the sequence, 0184. That number is unaccounted for. That means something went through the processor between the Zapruder original and the three copies. The matter is not trivial because only four film cans—the genuine original, plus the three copies exposed at Jamieson (then brought back to Kodak for processing)—are supposed to have existed. An additional copy raises the possibility of substitution—that early access was obtained to the original and a copy substituted, all of this occurring at a rather early hour.

Another matter. I have heard those unfamiliar with film processing wonder how it is that the film could be altered, since "there is more than one copy and the copies agree with the original." This is a weak argument. Only three copies were made—and two were in the custody of the Secret Service. So substitution in the case of those two would be easy. As to Zapruder's copy, that was given to *Life* along with the "original" when the initial sale was made on Saturday morning, November 23.

Viewed more generally, it cannot be ruled out that, by early evening on Friday, Abe Zapruder knew he was dealing with the government immediately after his film had been processed at Kodak and had been entreated to provide his film, being told it was needed for "national security." What his wife, Lillian, told me comports with that general theme. In 1971, she said: "My husband gave—*gave* them the film. He actually gave—he *gave* it to *them*." And: "They handled it beautifully. . . They acted like gentlemen about the whole matter."

So this is not just about optics; it is also about psychology and appeals to patriotism; and the same applies to *Life*. Someone there—probably someone high on the corporate ladder—has to be "witting" (to use the CIA term) and knowledgeable, in order for any late arriving (and edited) film to be substituted for something purchased from Zapruder. *Life's* caption text in its very first issue (29 November 63) is odd. Although supposedly possessing a film that clearly shows JFK being slammed to the rear, and publishing 31 frames from that film, it mentions nothing about any head impact being visible, and implies JFK sustained all his wounds when behind the Stemmons sign.

Here's the bottom line: however the "bookkeeping" was handled (or, retrospectively, is analyzed), once a new "original" was created, three corresponding "copies" would have been made from that master and substituted for those three "extant" prints made on 22 November. (I put "extant" in quotes because substitution would have been easy: of the three copies, two were already held by the Secret Service, and the third was at *Life*.)

A General Scheme For Fabrication of Original
and Substitution of Copies For the Zapruder film

Original Items:	*Forgeries:*
O (original)	O'
3 copies, made from O	3 copies made from O'
(duplicates made from O',	
or from same optical element	
which produced O')	
(C-1)	(C-1')
(C-2) go to the Secret Service	(C-2')
(C-3) retained by Zapruder	(C-3')
Transferred to *Life* on Monday, 11/25/63	

Let us now proceed to the next step.

The Actual Alteration of the Zapruder film: A Hypothesis

[*Author's note:* A word about terminology: I use the word "hypothesis" in recognition of the fact that not all elements of the Zapruder film alteration have been proven "beyond a reasonable doubt." However, in my opinion, enough evidence now exists to raise serious questions about the film being an original, and it is important to understand how alteration would have occurred in order to put that evidence in context.]

For the Zapruder film to have been altered, it had to be brought to someone who had expertise in the area of special effects—someone who worked day to day with an optical printer and who had access to the resources normally employed in special effects photography. Although I myself used to theorize that the film was "altered by the CIA," I no longer believe that to be so.

The CIA has wonderful expertise in the area of analysis—of looking at satellite photographs and interpreting them properly (for example, in analyzing how many trucks or missiles are on a boat, or on a dock) but that is "analysis" and quite different from the fabrication of a movie film. The CIA doesn't have a department to do that—it doesn't have a "special effects" department. On the off chance such skills were called for—say, for example, that it was necessary to fabricate a movie for some covert operation (say, to make it appear that a political figure was with a woman other than his wife)—then such work would almost certainly be "sub-contracted out" to the appropriate Hollywood facility. There is simply no reason to believe that the CIA maintained "in-house facilities" for any such work.

So if the Zapruder film was altered, the place to look is Los Angeles, not Langely. And what basically might have occurred is this. A politician (say, Johnson) would pick up the phone and entreat some friend in Hollywood—possibly a major studio head—with a talk that would be the equivalent (years later) of "Houston, we've got a problem." The "problem"? That there was a Castro plot to kill the President, that there had been a security failure (or some such thing), and that crucial facts had to be hidden to avoid a nuclear war. We know from documents and tapes available at The LBJ Library that Johnson was talking this way in order to control things politically after Dallas. This "World War III" story would have been used to recruit the appropriate film executive to get the appropriate personnel involved on an emergency basis to edit the film. (And the film would not necessary have to go west; an editor might be flown east). Without meaning to cast aspersions on any particular person, I note that all administrations have close ties with Hollywood, so for someone like a Lyndon Johnson to call up a film mogul and solicit his assistance would not be implausible. However, I would be the first to concede that, as of this writing, we do not have direct evidence of that conversation. Not yet, anyway. What we do have is a deliberately edited record of the radio tapes from *Air Force One*, the basic record of communications from Johnson to others between the time he arrived at Love Field until the time the plane landed. (It should be noted that within a year or two of Dallas, Johnson's closest aide, Jack Valenti, was basically put in charge of lobbying for the film industry and has been in that position now for almost four decades).

It is highly implausible, if the film was altered, that Valenti's Hollywood involvement is an accident. Would it be possible, if Hollywood expertise was brought to bear in this situation, that Valenti knows nothing about it, and that his prominence in such a position is purely accidental? Yes, that possible. And, in pointing out what is obvious—that Valenti ended up in such a powerful position in the film industry—I am certainly not offering that as evidence that he is directly involved in the alteration of any film from Dealey Plaza. Saying that something is "possible" does not mean that it is probable.

The technical problem faced by the team doing the alteration would be the rapid speed with which they would be required to work (*Life* had deadlines) and, most important, a rather critical (and yet to them, annoying) technical problem that would have occurred at the end of the process.

In whatever format they worked—and for ease of alteration, I would argue it was 35 mm)—at the end of the process, when the final optical negative (or, alternatively, interpositive) was created, the problem would have been to "reduce back down" to the 8mm format, which would then have to be placed on "Side B" of a 16 mm Kodachrome film (which would then have to be processed). Moreover, to pass as a camera original, there would have to be some image between the sprocket holes (as normally there would be, in film shot in Zapruder's camera).

This problem—that the film contain "material between the sprocket holes"— would *only* apply to the item (i.e., the putative "camera original") retained at *Life* and not to either of the Secret Service copies, or the third copy made by Zapruder and retained at *Life*.

Returning now to the putative original, which would have to be on Kodachrome and should also contain "image between the sprocket holes": This problem—essentially, a formatting issue—could not be ignored, because all the expertise in the world would be for naught if this factor was not taken into account and handled properly. The result would not look like a valid original.

For this Kodachrome to appear *not* to be a dupe, there had to be image— some image—in the sprocket hole area. Because that's what a "Kodachrome original" looks like.

As I noted previously, a film printer normally "masks out" that area.

So the problem faced by the special effects team (the optical forgers) would have been to create a duplicate—one which normally had the sprocket hole area masked out—but which would be made to look like an original by modifying the equipment so as to place some image in the sprocket hole area in this instance.

Because of the general appearance of these frames (and particularly, the way the left margin looks, as if there was a piece of magic mending tape running down the edge), I suspect that this problem was solved by making two passes through an optical printer—one for the main part of the film (what we view as the main body of the ordinary "film frame") and a second pass for the left hand margin (what would be called the sprocket hole area).

This would be somewhat similar (conceptually) to going to Kinko's and doing a copying job on a book where *two* passes were involved: first, positioning the page to get the main part of the text and then pressing the "scan" button once; then repositioning the original and pressing the scan button a second time; and then finally pressing the "print" button and getting the final product, which is in fact a composite of the two scans.

Another possibility is that a contact printer was used in some fashion to solve the "sprocket hole" problem. The principle would be the same—compositing two images—even though the hardware would be different.

I do not claim to know exactly how this was done—only that it was indeed accomplished and that, in doing so, in creating a 16 mm Kodachrome with "material between the sprocket holes," someone overdid it and "too much" image—*much too much* image—was put into this area, resulting in almost all the frames on the so-called "original" having image that (as shown on the DVD copy of the original film at the Archives) goes "beyond full flush left" and producing a result not attainable with Zapruder's camera.

A Word About Future Testing (I)

As noted above, this has been presented here as a hypothesis, but the matter need not remain in the realm of abstraction and conjecture. Investigating this matter will not confront us with political considerations that, for all practical purposes, may preclude an exhumation of JFK's body.

The Zapruder camera exists. The original film exists. Nothing is buried in a cemetery. Both the camera and the film are under the control of the government, so there is no reason why the appropriate testing cannot be done.

A definitive test, which would eliminate the possibility that Zavada's test films look the way they do because of camera-to-camera variation, would involve doing what Doug Horne wanted the ARRB to do in the first place: *run film through the actual Zapruder camera and compare that with the original.*

If these tests show what Zavada's test films show, then all remaining doubt is removed and the Zapruder film would then be proven to be an optical forgery, something that can not be produced by Zapruder's camera.

To remove still another variable—lighting—the test should be done when the lighting is identical to what it was on 22 November. That would mean either doing the test on 22 November or in late January, which would have the same lighting (as on 22 November) since it would be the same number of days on the "other side" of the Winter solstice.

It is for this reason that I think the appropriate investigative authority of the U.S. Government ought to repossess the camera currently at The Sixth Floor Museum, and place it either at the National Archives in Washington,or in an FBI vault.

The thought of any Sixth Floor Museum official—with that institution's huge vested interest in the legitimacy of the Zapruder—taking the camera down to Dealy Plaza and "experimenting", however, is simply too much to bear.

This camera ought to be the centerpiece of a future criminal investigation, the purpose of which would be to establish, officially and once and for all: *can the film in evidence have been made by the camera in evidence?* And if the answer is no—and that appears to be the case, based on the test films Zavada has exposed—then a second question must be addressed, namely: *who made this film?*

And if The Sixth Floor Museum wants a Zapruder camera for display purposes, then I suggest they go buy one—as Rollie did—either at a garage sale, for example, or on eBay.

Certain Other Matters

Hawkeyeworks—Revisited

After the final "politically correct" film had been created (probably in low contrast 35 mm format), the final step would have been to create an 8 mm copy of it. If done properly to mimic Zapruder's actual camera original, that copy would have had to have been placed on "side B" of standard 16 mm Kodachrome "double perf" film, resulting in a Kodachrome needing to be processed. *Somewhere.* And the problem would be where.

Kodachrome is special. It was created (primarily) for the civilian home movie market, required special processing, and there were only some half dozen processing plants in the U.S. equipped to handle such film.

Obviously, it could not be "processed" in Dallas (again), because the Zapruder film had *already* been processed there. Imagine Mr. Chamberlain, the supervisor at the Kodak plant in Dallas, asked by the government to process a Kodachrome film and seeing the Zapruder film emerging from the processor. ("But we already processed this last Friday!")

And yet some lab was needed. The Secret Service agent who identified himself as "Smith" and who brought the film to the NPIC color lab said he had just come from Rochester, where the film had been processed at Hawkeyeworks, the code name for a top secret facility in Rochester, New York, run by Kodak for the U.S. Government. Was there a Kodachrome processor there? McMahon's statement about what Smith told him doesn't prove the point—it could be considered hearsay—but the entire story is corroborated, not by what McMahon heard, but what he did. McMahon held in his hands the actual film: he worked with it for hours making some 28 color prints of specific frames and told the ARRB it was Kodachrome, with the assassination sequence on the second side.

The fact that Homer McMann says it was on 16mm double perf stock, that it was unslit and that he had to turn it "upside down" to view the image properly, further attests that this was a genuine Kodachrome. Yet the original Kodachrome was at *Life*, having been purchased for $50,000. So the implication is that a Kodachrome at NPIC must either have been a forgery or there was more than one "original". At the very least, McMahon's account, establishing that there was a second Kodachrome by Saturday or Sunday night, demonstrates the "official chronology" is seriously flawed.

Moreover, it should be noted what happened when Doug Horne found out about this situation and understood the implications of what Homer McMahon was saying during his 1997 ARRB interview—namely, that the Z film had been processed in Rochester—when Doug knew it had officially been processed in Dallas. Horne attempted to get his superiors at the ARRB to investigate further by requesting records for 1963, conducting interviews, etcetera.) His requests were flatly refused. So further inquiries were not made about this classified film facility. Then came another problem, concerning the name of the lab itself. When the CIA got wind of the fact that its former employee had used the name "Hawkeyeworks" in the taped interview with the ARRB, they went ballistic. The CIA liaison with the ARRB demanded that the reference to this code-named facility be removed. Consequently, Doug Horne was commanded to take the audio tape, duplicate it, and edit the duplicate to eliminate the spoken voice saying that word. Doug followed orders, writing a "memo for the record" of the deletion (and the original, unaltered tape, remains at the Archives, still sealed).

The Left Margin Problem and the Two Splices

Two phenomena are unique to the so-called "original" Zapruder film (the one that is today is in the National Archives): (1) The film contains two splices; and, (2) the left margin cannot be explained in terms of the optical system (the lens) of the Zapruder camera.

The existence of two splices in the so-called "original" Zapruder film is evidence that, however and wherever the work was done, when the final 8 mm product was produced, it was done in three segments. Call them A, B, and C. When the work was finished, two splices were required where A was pasted to B, and B to C. (In each case, frames were lost.) That those "missing frames" exist on the Secret Service copies implies the existence of a "master" from which all these film items were made.

But back to the splices: the existence of these splices were never mentioned by the FBI and were never brought to the attention of the Warren Commission investigation. As to the JFK research community, they learned about these splices not as a pair, but separately, and in events that were separated by roughly four years. An awareness of the first was developed in 1965 (as I have recounted above). In January, 1967, *Life* issued an explanation that a technician had broken the film by accident. Then, in 1969, when it was discovered that there was *another* splice, just as obvious—at frame 155—*Life* said nothing. Not a blessed thing. The second splice has never been explained, and it is my belief that the proper way to view these splices is to view them as a pair.

I don't know whether the sign was hit that day, but I no longer believe that a bullet striking the sign has anything to do with the existence of the first splice, the reason being that there is a second splice at frame 155; and in connection with that splice, there seemed to be just two frames missing, and what could have happened in just two frames (about 1/10 of a second) that *could* be hidden?

So I don't think these splices have anything to do with editing the content of the original Zapruder film; but rather must be viewed in another context: that they are somehow part of the process used to produce—for some reason in three segments—an 8 mm reduction print with material in the sprocket hole area.

Color Change Across the Splice

When Newcomb first did his frame counting back in 1969 he noticed —and demonstrated, to my satisfaction—that there was a slight change in color balance across the splice. Using the language of an artist, he said the change was from "warm" to "cool". One produced a background that was somewhat pink; the other, blue-ish. (The situation is akin to changing the "tint" control on a TV set). If there had been one uniform film, exposed in Dealey Plaza and then "accidentally broken" in two spots, where those those pieces were then cemented together, there would not be a change in the tint across the splice. Such a change suggests a slight change in the controls of a film printer from one segment to another and supports the hypothesis that what is called the 8mm Zapruder film "original" was in fact manufactured in three segments.

Turning Off the Edgeprinter (Dousing the Printer Lights)

Film is marked with various "edgeprints". The manufacturer puts edgeprints on the film stating the type of film. The processing plant turns on an edgeprinter to affix identification establishing *where* it was processed.

In interviews with those who had actually handled the film on 22 November—and these matters appear in one of Rollie's appendices—Zavada talked with John K. Anderson, who recalled that the Secret Service had come to the plant with the film. *He also remembers the Secret Service requesting that the edgeprinter be turned off for the Zapruder film processing.* Why? There can be no innocent explanation.

It would be similar to a situation at an autopsy where, before medical photography commenced, the key ID tags were removed. Not only was that request made but the Secret Service agents clearly didn't want anyone looking at what was on the film and also demanded that the safe lights be turned off!

Rollie Zavada's answer to these accounts is to cite the fact that, in the Secret Service copy, he can see the Dallas edgeprint. That doesn't prove a thing. In fact, Zavada is teetering on the edge of foolish circular reasoning. If the hypothesis being tested is whether the original is genuine (an out of camera original) or a forgery, and if the forgery would be made from some optical master—gussied up to look real—then Zavada cannot cite the secret Service copies in support of his argument. If the original is faked, then the copies were faked. They all come from the same progenitor. Its as simple as that.

What should concern Zavada—and us, too—is that within hours of the assassination, a Secret Service official overseeing the processing acted in a way to inhibit future authentication of the film.

Chemical Testing: the Reason Why

The assassination of President Kennedy took place outdoors. The "light source" was the sun. If the film was edited and a forgery created, then it is likely—not necessary, but likely—that Kodachrome indoor film was used at the final stage, when editing on some "master" was completed and the time came to "reduce back down" and produce, as a final product, an "8mm" film that would pass as a Kodachrome original.

Why? Because a film's dyes and chemicals are "color balanced" so as to be in agreement with the light source. The parameter used to describe this is the "Kelvin temperature" associated with the film. Indoor film is color balanced at 3200 degrees Kelvin; outdoor film at about 5600 degrees Kelvin.

The light source on an optical printer is *not* the sun; it is a bulb or other artificial light. Therefore, Kodachrome film that would most reasonably be used (for the purpose of making a forgery) would be Kodachrome II-A, the indoor version.

Of course, Kodak does not make "indoor film" for the purpose of making forgeries; it is made to shoot your child in a crib. But if a Kodachrome had to be chosen for use on a film printer, then the choice would be Kodachrome II-A (the indoor film) and not Kodachrome II.

Sometime after Zavada began his work—possibly after he saw the left margin area, and said to Doug "This is strange, I can't explain this"—Rollie suggested a test. He suggested cutting into the camera original film and destroying one frame in order to obtain a sample for a spectrometer. Such a spectro test would determine whether the film alleged to be the camera original is "Kodachrome II" (which it should be, since that's what Zapruder was using on 22 November) or "Kodachrome II-A", an indoor film, which is what would likely be used on an optical printer, since the light source is not the sun but an artificial source.

Doug knew that Marwell—who thought film inauthenticity was absurd—was unapproachable. But Horne did approach Gunn. Unfortunately, merely mentioning this test—which would have roiled the psyche of anyone at the Archives, where a museum mentality prevails—caused Jeremy to roll his eyes. It was obviously not going to happen and the matter was dropped.

As in any criminal case when "probable cause" makes someone is a suspect, additional tests are conducted seeking data to either establish innocence or make the case stronger. The probable cause in this case is Rollie's own test films. They do not match the Zapruder film at the left margin. As noted, the issue is geometry.

So I say there is probable cause to suspect an optical forgery and I therefore urge that the next step, doing the necessary spectro test, be underrtaken. The government has the authority to order such a test; and the results hold the potential of being definitive.

The greatest virtue of this test may be its elegance. Nobody has to be dug up at a cemetery. One insignificant frame of the film would be clipped off. Determining the truth is worth it.

The Kodachrome in evidence is marked "Kodachrome II" and has the edgeprint of an outdoor film. If the spectro test establishes it is indoor film, "Kodachrome II-A", the deception is proved and the ballgame is over.

Moreover, if the film fails the test, two things would be established: (a) that the film was exposed in a laboratory setting or that of an editing facility, and (b) someone went to the trouble of affixing a false manufacturing edgeprint (or cutting out the "A" in Kodachrome II-A) to create a film stock that would be used on an optical printer, but disguise it so that it appeared to be outdoor film.

The intent of affixing the false logo would be to deceive history. This test would end that deception, once and for all.

Other Films

I have previously argued that it is implausible—if not impossible—to believe that, if the Zapruder film was altered, that other films were not also altered. In making this statement, I am not saying it is a substitute for having direct evidence that other films were altered. It is not. And it must be recognized that, if events—basic aspects of what happened in Dealey Plaza—were altered on this optical record (if the car stopped and that was concealed, for example, as an especially obvious case), then the complete photographic record—many photos and films—had to be altered far beyond a single film.

It is a fact that within hours of the assassination, a net was thrown to obtain all films of the assassination. Notices were put in film cans that if anyone had film to notify the FBI. Of course, there is an official explanation doing this, but it is indicative of the sort of effort I am talking of to get all films. The point is that it was done. And it is absurd to believe that notices such as these were the conduit by which the Secret Service—and they seem to be the operative agency here—learned about the film. For example, Orville Nix's film ended up with Forrest Sorrels, and Nix told Mark Lane, back in 1965, that when he got his film back, it had splices. Again, splices: Hmmm.

One of my favorite examples concerning the government response to the existence of "another film" concerns a man in Canada, someone named Simpson. He called the Dallas Police Department and said he had been "passing through" and took a film of the shooting and got "the whole thing." Then, presumably, he returned to Canada. Sgt. Patrick Dean mentioned Simpson's call in his Warren Commission testimony. Back in 1965, when I was just starting out in my JFK research, and using the information operator, I located Simpson and telephoned him in Canada. He told me he had been drunk and just bragging—whether that is true, I have no way of verifying—but he told me that shortly after his call, the Royal Canadian Mounted Police were all over his property and into his life.

At first blush, that seems an admirable reaction. Our government doing its job. But just a minute: where are the records of such a search across the border in Canada? The short answer: *there is none*. In all my years, I have heard of no such records. No record in the files of the Secret Service or FBI or CIA of anyone going up to Canada to check out the Simpson allegation; yet Sgt. Dean testified about it, and I know from talking to Simpson that he had a rather intense experience after this call.

Researchers on the case must accept the fact that, if film alteration occurred which altered the velocity of the car, then more than one film had to have been altered. We must accept the fact that the story is more complex than the mere alteration of the Zapruder film, and we simply do not know the full story yet.

Film Alteration, Body Alteration, and "The Clock"

Everyone who has studied the JFK assassination has faced a "problem of authority" of sorts—that is, confronting the issue of whether the Warren Commission got it right and whether there is sufficient evidence to reject the official version. But what does it mean, really, if there was more than one shooter? Is that why we study this event—to count the shooters?

A rose is a rose is a rose, but the same is not true of conspiracies. If Oswald was truly a nut and an assassin,and it was then discovered that he was in league with "another nut," that would properly be called a "conspiracy," but would be entirely different than *if Oswald was not a nut at all, and had been carefully framed; or if there was fraud in the evidence and, for example, the autopsy was falsified.*

Not all conspiracies are equal—they do not have the same political significance. Two fringe characters who collude to kill the President qualify as a conspiracy, but a situation in which a group of officials collude to achieve the same goal is an entirely different matter.

I no longer view the Zapruder film as sacrosanct, and I certainly don't view "two shooters" as the gold standard for a conspiracy. As readers of *Best Evidence* know, my concern is the validity of the autopsy protocol: it is not who put the bullets *into* the President's body, but who took them *out*. Similar considerations apply to the film.

I am no longer concerned with whether there was a second shooter; my focus is on whether there was fraud in the evidence. That is the true measure of the extent and nature of a political conspiracy, such as the one which removed President Kennedy from office in 1963. Moreover, it is the mature way to look at this case. Tabulating lists of "firing points" is almost juvenile compared with the approach being suggested here.

To make this point clear: *the fraud is directed at denuding the assassination of political meaning by creating a false story about the death of the President, that it was all a quirk of fate, a man in a building who shot a man in a car.*

The fact is that there are tradeoffs. If the unaltered film showed a 20 second assassination and an absurdly non-reactive secret service, then JFK's murder was a political plot, and that problem would supercede in importance the "problem" of a "second shooter."

If a car-stop was removed, then almost certainly the "head snap" is an artifact of an altered film. If this film was altered, then we must redesign our concept of "conspiracy." It means Secret Service involvement, it means changed imagery in the area of wounds, it means other films being altered.

It means we really don't know what happened on Dealey Plaza on 22 November 1963.

But those details are perhaps not that important. What counts is the extent to which a disguise was employed at the time of the shooting and an effort made to conceal crucial details about JFK's murder to permanently alter the legal and historical record of the event and thus make it conform to a "storybook version" of the President's assassination: the man in the building who shot a man in a car. That "innocent" story paved the way for a politically stable transition and conferred legitimacy on the administration that succeeded his.

2003: Pig on a Leash

As one who has studied the assassination for several decades, I often think of the scene of President Kennedy's limousine proceeding down Houston Street that sunny day in Dallas, and towards the red brick building which was (then) the Texas School Book Depository, and which is today called "The Sixth Floor Museum".

Those of us who have studied the case in depth—who have spent years of our lives writing articles and books and attempting to tell the world that our particular theory is the correct view of Dealey Plaza and of this event—have a particular stake as to how the past is represented at this institution.

For many years, it was just a building—the place where it all had occurred—but there was no museum, no bookstore, and it would have been a fluke if one could even get into the building. I remember how privileged I felt when, for the first time—in 1990—because I was connected with a TV documentary, I was allowed to go up to the sixth floor and could walk around and examine the "sniper's nest."

There I was, standing near the window from which Oswald was supposed to have shot the President. I didn't believe any of it for a single minute, but it was a good feeling to be up there, on that floor, and crouching behind that window; to realize that, as Professor Litwin had explained to me some decades ago, the reason the sniper's nest could "be connected" to the crime in the street below was through alterations made on the body of the President; that it all came down to two virtual "arrows", two trajectories reported in a Navy autopsy report based on a body containing altered wounds.

Meanwhile, those of use who spent time on this case have gone on with our lives, and have grown older and wiser and richer (or poorer) as the case may be and have learned that much of what happens is connected with money.

And now a must unusual situation has developed. Because, with the creation of The Sixth Floor Museum, there has developed a politics of sort. The Sixth Floor Museum is run by people with a specific point of view, namely: that *The Warren Report* was right and that Lee Oswald shot the President from that sixth floor window, just as it alleged.

They don't care about this or that theory. The government's account is good enough. And it's not about scholarship; it's also a marketing decision. It's much more convenient to run a business that way than to start having to worry about who is right and who is wrong.

Meanwhile, people are drawn to the site and to that building, not just because it was the site of a great American tragedy, but because of the unanswered questions left in its wake and because of questions raised by books written by persons like myself.

This is not just another building. Tens of thousands—indeed hundreds of thousands—of people now visit The Sixth Floor Museum. It is a major attraction in Dallas, and now the museum has become even more powerful because the Zapruder family has given The Sixth Floor Museum the copyright to the Zapruder film.

So now we have a situation in which a Museum which perpetuates a false history of the event controls the copyright of an altered film on which that false history is based. Who could have ever anticipated such a situation?

It is truly bizarre. Back in 1963, a number of gunmen, well hidden at various locations in Dealey Plaza, shot the President to death. Now, different authors compete for the right for their book to be carried in the book store to determine what history shall say about all of this—about whose version shall prevail.

The situation reminds me in some ways of *Animal Farm*. In that situation, the pigs were originally the outsiders, but then they took over. Like the pigs on Manor farm, there is an ongoing struggle for power, and different cliques now control what is distributed at The Sixth Floor Museum Book Store.

One thing is certain: conspiracy is not welcome.

Even the Zapruder film is edited for presentation at The Sixth Floor Museum—over and beyond whatever criminal editing was done in connection with the actual murder—to eliminate the head shot and further sanitize the event! It would be as if the Arizona Memorial at Pearl Harbor was missing the U.S.S. Arizona. I once asked Gary Mack why the film was edited and was told that it was to make it more amenable for the visiting families.

I have a suggestion. Let The Sixth Floor Museum set up a kiddie room, a kindergarten, where those who are too young or who don't want to face the brutality of a President's death watch the sanitized event in the kindergarten. But for the rest of us, I prefer an unedited version of the film—thank you—and certainly not one edited by The Sixth Floor Museum.

And, oh yes, the Museum has put a webcam up at the sniper's nest, so the whole world—from New York to Timbuktu—can appreciate the "view from the sniper's nest."

That, too, now is part of the global village in which we live—thanks to The Sixth Floor Museum.

So pardon me, but when I think of JFK's limo going north on Houston, and approaching the building, I now see all the different competing authors, especially those whose books are now promoted in the book store, poking their heads out of different windows—the ones that are involved in promoting the Oswald version or perhaps a conspiracy that does not involve the alteration of any evidence.

Got a theory about Dealey Plaza? Want to write about it in a book, or present it in a video? Need some Zapruder frames to make your point? You'll have to speak to The Sixth Floor Museum about that.

President Kennedy was a student of history, and I think he would have appreciated the irony—that the building that played such a major role in his death would become a museum, that a key factor in the plot that took his life involved the alteration of certain photographs, and that that institution would control the copyrights to altered photographs which perpetuate a false view of his murder.

In some ways, it is as if the pigs have taken over the institution, but I'm not sure it is in any better shape than if the building had simply been demolished. At least, in that case, the false history would live on, but only in various libraries and not on Dealey Plaza itself.

As my friend, Professor Larry Haapanen, has said, if The Sixth Floor Museum wants to have a webcam, why don't they go one step further? Why not create an interactive video, so that people—from all over the world—can get behind a rifle in the sixth floor window and take virtual shots at cars that are traveling down Elm Street and see if they can duplicate Oswald's feat?

And, as he has suggested, perhaps—if they fail—a notice could appear on the computer screen, saying, "Sorry, you took 13 seconds!"

Consider what happened on a recent documentary shoot in Dealy Plaza. Here was an important issue for The Sixth Floor Museum which controls both the Moorman copyright as well as the Zapruder. Mary Moorman was being interviewed for a documentary to be broadcast on a national network.

Mary told major media interviewers as recently as a few years ago how she stepped into the street to take President Kennedy's picture and then, after the shots were fired, stepped back up onto the grass. She was most specific about these two events: the step into the street, the step back up onto the grass. Here are her exact words:

Moorman: Uh, just immediately before the presidential car came into view, we were, you know, there was just tremendous excitement. And my friend who was with me, we were right ready to take the picture. And she's not timid. She, as the car approached us, she did holler for the president, "Mr. President, look this way!" *And I'd stepped out off the curb into the street to take the picture.* And snapped it immediately. And that evidently was the first shot. You know. I could hear the sound. And. . . .

Jones: Now when you heard the sound, did you immediately think "rifle shot?"

Moorman.   Oh no. A firecracker, maybe. There was another one just immediately following which I still thought was a firecracker. *And then I stepped back up on to the grassy area.* I guess just, people were falling around us, you know. Knowing something was wrong. I certainly didn't know what was wrong.

The trouble is the Zapruder film shows no such thing. And if this actually happened, then Mary's account is further evidence—just like the car stop—that the film was altered through professional optical editing, where Mary was put up on the grass.

But now, some years later, at a time when The Sixth Floor Museum controls Mary's copyright, she is being interviewed by the Museum's Gary Mack. Mary has learned she should not say she stepped into the street, but she still says she stepped forward. And she says so again and again, on each successive take. The problem is: Mary doesn't even do that on the Zapruder film. She just stands there.

And Mary apparently remembers something else—how slowly the car was moving, just the way she told me when I visited with her back in November 1971 and she told me that it stopped. Now she simply says it "wasn't going that fast."

The film shoot stops.

Mack cuts in. He turns to the cameraman and says, "That's it", indicating the camera should be turned off.

Someone says "going that fast". Gary Mack looks down at the grass and fidgets at Mary's blooper. He turns to Mary and says, "They will or will not use that. That's OK."

A senior producer walks over, in a casual matter. "Wasn't going that fast?" he says, mimicking her.

Then he continues, "Mary, you're so cute!" The implication is clear. She should be careful about what she says and stick to the script.

Mary Ann puts her head in her hands, like a child who has made a mistake.

Mack says, "We're going to do one more take. We'll have it go 'slowly'."

Meanwhile, before the shoot resumes, Mary keeps saying that she "stepped forward". This is clearly a troublesome phrase, because if Mary "stepped forward" that raises all sorts of problems, one being that she must then "step back" when the Zapruder film shows neither.

During one take, the one actually broadcast, Mary tells it this way and uses the troublesome phrase:

I just stepped to the, uh, to the edge here, and Jean is hollering, 'Look Mr. President, look our way!" and then I snapped the picture, which was at the same instant, evidently, as the bullet hit him, not realizing that 's what had happened. But I did hear a noise.

[And then I stepped back , and then, two more noises,] and then I could see people around me falling to the ground, or running, and doing—and that let me to know that something was happening.

I put the ten words in brackets above because—as actually broadcast—these particular words were deleted. As actually broadcast, Mary's account was as follows:

But I did hear a noise, and then I could see people around me falling to the ground, or running, and doing—and that let me to know that something was happening.

By the deletion of the words ("and then I stepped back, and then, [I heard] two more noises"), two critical matters were omitted from Mary's account, namely: (1) the implication that she had stepped forward, very possibly into the street, especially if she was already standing at the edge; and (2) the fact that Mary Mooman believes that she heard three shots—the first as she took her picture *and then two more!*

This is quite different than the official version, but it is the one Mary has always given as her version of this event. Mary always says that in her various interviews—both during this filming and elsewhere—and it's plain as day that what she calls the "first shot" occurred the instant she took her picture, and then there were two more. But that raises complications and contradicts the official version, so the problem was dealt with by making a silent edit (omitting the bracketed words above). Obviously, when the witness' account came up against the official version, there was no contest—it was the official version that prevailed.

Discovery Channel personnel say, with reasonable self-mocking wit, that they are not scholars and historians but popularizers, that their specialty is "history–lite". But I wonder if this even qualifies in that category. It seems to me it is simply false, and manipulative—and all of it is happening under the auspices of an interview being conducted by someone from The Sixth Floor Museum. Is this valid history? I would like to see a full dress interview of Mary Moorman by an objective investigator in which no attempt is made to edit or guide her, and the matter of when it was first pointed out to her that she should be careful about this issue of whether or not she "stepped forward" is discussed in detail. *Who communicated to her the fact that, her memory notwithstanding, the Zapruder film showed something else, so perhaps she should tailor her story accordingly?*

At another point, the matter of Mary's medical bills comes up. Something that costs almost a thousand dollars. In what appears to be perfectly innocent small talk, Mack says that she'll be able to take care of that easily in view of the payment being made to her that day. Then they all get down to business.

The whole thing is so unsavory. It's not even that there is a deliberate effort to promote lies, but certain people have made up their minds as how what happened has to be presented—how many shots were fired, whether the car stopped, whether Mary stepped into the street, etcetera—and that provides a criterion for what is acceptable, for what should or should not be said. For what is and is not correct. Politically correct.

I don't know exactly what to call this, but its certainly not the proper way to approach documentary film making in the area of history.

This is just one example.

What we have going on here now is the politics of the perpetuators of the false version. The vying for position. Who will The Sixth Floor Museum allow to grace its shelves at its book store?

As for the Zapruder film, I don't have the latest price list, so I don't know how much The Sixth Floor Museum will charge this year for the sequence showing the President being shot. Or what happens if you want to pause and comment on the blood that is supposed to be coming out of the front of the huge wound at the front of JFK's head, when the wound seen at Parkland four minutes later is at the rear. Or how much they will want for the Nix film. And I don't know if they will permit the use of the Moorman photograph in conjunction with the Zapruder film, because that's one combination that, depending on how data is employed, can be used to argue for inauthenticity. I don't know all the financial details, but I do know how I feel about all this.

I think its outrageous.

Gary Mack—who is extremely genial, very well organized, and used to be a familiar propent of conspiracy—once told me why so many people who took pictures that day have entrusted their photos and copyrights to the museum. "The pictures will be taken care of, and they'll get a comfortable income."

My suggestion: if someone wants a "comfortable income," then let them buy bonds. I simply fail to see that any of this is legitimate. I don't know the legalities, but if the Zapruder film was falsified, then here is the situation as I see it:

1. The Zapruder family became the transmission belt for placing a false film record before the American public. In 1963, Abe Zapruder signed a contract for $150,000 ($900,000 in today's money) and hid the true facts with an incorrect news release, claiming he only received $40,000 and then gave $25,000 of that to Officer Tippit.

2. On the first week of every new year through the Johnson presidency, the Zapruder family was paid $25,000, an annual payment that is the equivalent (in today's money) of $150,000 per payment.

3. In 1967, a copyright was taken out by *Life* on this film, which was allegedly exposed by Zapruder in his camera, but which, based on the optics, was manufactured by unknown third parties. Should the film be proved a forgery, the Zapruder lawyers will undoubtedly argue that, bogus or not, it represents a "derivative work", albeit one made without their permission. It will be interesting to see how a court would treat such a claim.

4. Around 1975, the Zapruders were given back the film for the sum of $1 and a new round of commercial exploitation began.

5. Throughout, the Zapruders have protected the copyright to this altered evidence, this forgery, with a zealousness that has restricted public debate. The film is really only available to those people or companies willing to fork over substantial sums of cash. I personally experienced this in 1989, when I could not afford to use the film in my nationally distributed video to illustrate the head snap. Although the government and *Life* are responsible for the film not being widely available in the first years of the Johnson administration, the Zapruders took over that role once the film was returned. Anyone wishing to utilize the Zapruder film after 1975 had to contend with the likes of Zapruder attorney Jamie Silverberg, who has made the protection of the Zapruder copyright his life's work and who—whether he knows it or not—has been deeply involved in controlling the distribution of altered evidence. And for a tidy profit. Having hit the jackpot with the $16 million payment for the film itself, the family has turned the copyright—which ought to have been obtained by the ARRB, along with the film, for the American people—over to The Sixth Floor Museum. So now that institution heads the effort to protect this cash cow. Silverburg no longer works for the Zapruders—his client has become The Sixth Floor Museum.

6. In 1991, the Zapruders were paid $80,0000 for the use of the film in Oliver Stone's movie—a consequence of which was the passage of The JFK Records Act and the creation of the ARRB. Their film was then declared an assassination record and "taken" by the government, and they ended up with $16 million "in just compensation"—sixteen million for a film which, according to the optics, could not have been exposed in old Abe's camera. Moreover, because the ARRB fumbled and did not declare the "third duplicate" (the copy provided *Life* in 1963 and returned to Zapruder in 1975 along with the original) as an assassination record (which they should have) the Zapruders were able to arrange a tax shelter for this windfall. And how did they do that? By arranging to "donate" that copy to the Museum, and take a write-off which would soften the tax liability on the windfall they *did* receive for the one legally "taken" by the government.

7. Moreover, in the midst of this hub bub and with millions of dollars changing hands, the ARRB—read, General Counsel Jeremy Gunn—proceeded in a rather careless and high-handed fashion and failed to "take" the copyright along with the film for the American people. So, contrary to all promises made to the public about securing the copyright, the public still has to pay!

8. In the aftermath of this entire fiasco, the Zapruders turned the copyright over to The Sixth Floor Museum, where the politics of perpetuation is being played out, and a

book store now exists which only favors books that are basically supportive of the official version or of innocuous conspiracies that don't involve the alteration of key evidence.

9. As an institution, The Sixth Floor Museum now perpetuates the myth of the lone assassin, and controls the copyright of altered films on which that myth is based.

As people debate the assassination and need this or that film to make this or that point, Zapruder frames are needed, or perhaps a sequence of frames depending on the buyer.

Producers worry about alienating the management at The Sixth Floor. Two have told me why they have to be careful about expressing themselves. "We don't want the museum to cut us off," they say, specifically naming one or two of the top officials there.

It's as if Dealey Plaza suddenly has a gatekeeper, now living in the building from which President Kennedy was supposedly shot.

I am reminded of the situation at Manor Farms.

From Orwell's *Animal Farm*: "Squealer consoles the animals saying: 'Do not imagine, comrades, that leadership is a pleasure. On the contrary, it is a deep and heavy responsibility. No one believes more firmly than Comrade Napolean that all animals are equal. He would only be too happy to let you make your decisions for yourselves. But somehow you might make the wrong decisions, comrades, and then where should we be?'"

The debate goes on. The cash register rings.

Now the money goes to the Sixth Floor Museum, who are the owners—once removed—of this *schmalz grub*.

The pig is still on the leash.

Notes

1. "Court documents" refer to documents connected with lawsuit between Time-Life and Bernard Geis (also referred to as "Josiah Thompson lawsuit"), available on the Internet.
2. *Rush to Judgement*, p. 55.
3. *Drew Pearson Diaries*, 1949-1959, Holt, Rinehart, and Winston, 1974, pp. 461-62.
4. Author's files.
5. Letter, Liebeler to Rankin, 10/13/65, as quoted on p. 25 of *Best Evidence*, original Macmillan edition (or 1988 Carrol & Graf edition, which has identical pagination).
6. Letter, Rankin to Liebeler, 10/21/65, as quoted in *Best Evidence*, p. 26.
7. Letter, Redlich to Liebeler, 10/18/65, as quoted in *Best Evidence*, p. 26.
8. *Ibid.*
9. Letter, Rankin to Liebeler, 10/21/65, as quoted in *Best Evidence*, p. 26.
10. Either Zapruder's testimony or Sorrel's testimony.
11. In July 2003, Policoff and I discussed the month and year of this meeting. He thinks it was 1971, which would mean Jan. 1971, my only trip to New York City that year. However, my Groden correspondance file contains letters by me written in the spring 1973, and again in 1975, which refer to our first meeting as having been in the fall of 1972.
12. One does not print directly from a 35mm negative (of the fine grained kind employed in this case). Because it is considered an archival item, one first makes a 35mm interpositive and from that makes a "printing negative"—and then a positive. (See Figure 1.)
13. Letter, Dr. Paul Peters to Wallace Milam, 4/14/80.

14. An example of this was whether the film indicated the car stopped during the shooting. In November 1971, I went to Dallas for the first time and tape recorded interviews with Bill and Gayle Newman, who were directly to Kennedy's right when he was struck in the head and who insisted that the car came to a momentary halt, right in front of them. If this occurred, then the giveaway on the Zapruder film would be one or more frames in which there was no blur—either in the background (bystanders) or in the foreground (car or occupants), an impossibility if the car was moving (in which case one or the other or both had to exhibit some blur). In short, the existence of a perfectly "blurless" frame would be circumstantial evidence that the car had stopped and that the film was an optical print, in which the stop had been edited out. Obviously, the blur measurements had to be made on the finest copy of the film, where a copy several generations downstream, or in 8mm, would be useless (because the error resulting from graininess and smallness of the image precluded any meaningful measurements.) This kind of work simply could not go forward if Groden wouldn't give us a clear 16 or, better yet, a 35mm copy, which he would not do. [*Editor's note*: Compare Costella's work on the impossible frame 232.]

15. *The New York Times*, 8/30/79, p. 16, column 1.

16. Stanhope met me in the aftermath of the publication of *Best Evidence* in 1981 and pushed hard for "20/20" to do a show on the book. He tried again in the fall of 1983. As I recall, there was major resistance from Roone Arledge, who is a friend of Ethel Kennedy.

17. When I called Moe Weitzman, I was entering what, for Groden, was hallowed ground. This was Groden's most special relationship—the man who was his enabler; who had made it all possible, who permitted Groden to have access to an optical printer, very likely at no charge, and who, because of the role his lab played, was responsible for Groden's access to certain key assassination materials. I don't know what went on between Weitzman and Groden after my August 1990 conversation with Weitzman. All I know is what Weitzman told me he was going to do, namely: ask for all his materials back. How Groden managed to get himself back again into Weitzman's good graces I do not know. But I presume his approach would go along these lines: "Moe, you're not involved in the assassination as an issue, but I am." Or "I'll see that this is properly preserved."

18. Letter, David Lifton to Jeremy Gunn, June 28, 1996, JFK Records Collection.

19. *Ibid*.

20. Reporter's Daily Transcript, 12/20/96, Superior Court, State of California, Rufo et al (Plaintiffs), vs Orenthal James Simpson, NO. SC031947.

*David Lifton
presenting at the
Zapruder Film Symposium,
Duluth, Minnesota
11 May 2003*

UNITED STATES GOVERNMENT

Memorandum

TO   : Mr. Mohr   DATE: November 23, 1963

FROM   : C. D. DeLoach

SUBJECT: ASSASSINATION OF PRESIDENT KENNEDY
          8 MILLIMETER COLOR FILM
          TAKEN AT SCENE OF ASSASSINATION

       We have received inquiries from "Time" magazine, "Telenews,"
"The New York Times" and a number of other communications outlets relative to
several minutes of 8 millimeter color film which was reportedly taken at the scene
of the assassination by one Abraham Zapruder. Zapruder is the owner of a women's
wear shop called "Jennifer Juniors" in Dallas. "Time and Life" magazine have
allegedly promised Zapruder the sum of $40,000 if he will turn the film over to them.
Zapruder has been quoted as stating "The FBI has this film and will not give it back
to me."

       Ed Guthman and Jack Rosenthal of the Department have received similar
requests from the same news outlets.

       I called SAC Shanklin at Dallas to ask him if we had this film. After
checking, Shanklin called me back and stated that the Secret Service had first obtained
this film from Zapruder. Shanklin stated he believed that Zapruder had later offered
a copy of the film to us. He stated he would have to check further regarding the
matter; however, he knew that we had this film and was having it processed at the
present time at a commercial shop in Dallas. Shanklin stated he did not believe the
film would be of any evidentiary value; however, he first had to take a look at the film
to determine this factor.

       After checking, I called Shanklin back and told him not to pay any
attention to any contacts that were made with him by news outlets. I stated he should
continue his processing of the film and should then determine whether the film was of
any evidentiary value or not. Shanklin stated he had received calls from Movietone
News requesting the film. I told him that after he had taken a look at this film, he
should get back in touch with us. Shanklin stated that since talking to me the first
time, he had ascertained that the film had not been received from Zapruder but to the
contrary the Secret Service had obtained the film from Zapruder and had turned it over
to us late last night. He stated that to his knowledge the Dallas Agents had not made
contact with Zapruder.

       I informed Guthman of the Department regarding this matter and told
him that the Secret Service had first obtained the film and then turned it over to us.
I told Guthman also that despite the pressure that was being put on by the news outlets
this matter would have to be treated strictly as evidence and later on a determination
would be made as to whether the film would be given back to Zapruder or not.

       For information.

*This, the first of two internal FBI memoranda of 23 November 1963 from
Cartha DeLoach to John Mohr discussing the "Zapruder film", was discovered by
Roy Schaeffer. It not only reports that the film's owner, Abraham Zapruder, had
been quoted as saying, "The FBI took my film and will not give it back to me", but
that the FBI would make a determination "later on" whether to return it,
which by itself undermines chain-of-possession arguments for authenticity.*

Epilogue

Distorting the Photographic Record:
"Death in Dealey Plaza"

James H. Fetzer, Ph.D.

[*Editor's note*: On 26 February 2003, and again on 1 March 2003, the Discovery Channel broadcast a sixty-minute program on events in Dealey Plaza during 22 November 1963. Although ostensibly about the photographers and the photographs they had taken, this program immediately promoted itself as "a search for new clues hidden in these frames of shocking evidence", implying that it was aiming at the discovery of new evidence in the photographic record, which would have been thematic with the channel's own name. When the program itself receives criticial scrutiny, however, it becomes obvious that it betrayed that objective and promoted a covert agenda to cover up those hidden clues.]

A Discovery Channel television program entitled, "Unsolved History", featured a segment on the assassination entitled, "JFK: Death in Dealey Plaza", narrated by Kathleen Kern. As the credits explain, the program was under the control of Gary Mack, the Archivist for The Sixth Floor Museum, which is located on the sixth floor of the Book Depository from which Lee Oswald allegedly took three shots, killing the President while wounding the Governor of Texas. The televised program ran 60 minutes, including 44 minutes of the production and 16 minutes of advertising, promotions, and the like. For consistency, I shall refer to specific events on a time-line that includes all 60 minutes.

The Sixth Floor Museum and its Archivist do not enjoy a good reputation among many members of the assassination research community. Black Op Radio, for example, which has a weekly broadcast dealing with recent research on the assassination and related issues, has a web page devoted to The Sixth Floor Museum and its policy of excluding serious studies that support the existence of a conspiracy and cover-up from those it makes available for sale to the public. These include Noel Twyman, *Bloody Treason* (1997), Stewart Galanor, *Cover-Up* (1998), and my *Assassination Science* (1998) and *Murder in Dealey Plaza* (2000). The odds that it will carry the book you are reading are not good.

427

The program displays high production values. I have viewed it many times now, one of which was in the company of a Hollywood producer, who observed at several points during the program that a lot of money had been spent on technical aspects of the film to make it polished and smooth. My concerns, however, had to do with the content of the program itself, which I suspected would gloss over crucial evidence in the specific photographs and films that it discussed, leaving the false impressions (1) that the photographic record appears to be consistent and seamless and (2) that this record supports the conclusion that JFK was killed by three shots fired by a lone gunman.

During the first two minutes of the program—between 01:15 and 01:30, in particular—Kathleen Kern intones, "Now, 'Unsolved History' turns Dealey Plaza into a high-tech laboratory and searches for new clues in these frames of shocking evidence. We will photographically reconstruct this 45 seconds that changed the world on 'Unsolved History'." This sounds quite promising, especially the idea of looking for "new clues" in the photographic record. The actual program, however, contradicts this promise by repeatedly ignoring or suppressing evidence that had to be familiar to its creators.

By 01:50 into the program, for example, David Wiegman, who was then a White House photographer, relates how he heard three shots: "Bang . . . bang . . . bang—just about like that", creating the indelible impression that Wegman was there, Wiegman was positioned to know, and that there had been only three, evenly spaced shots. But the flat bed-truck that ordinarily came before the President's limousine had been cancelled. The reporters and photographers had been consigned to ride to the rear of the motorcade. Wiegman was not in a good position to know and even admits he was "about seven cars back".

This means that he was still on Houston, while the limousine was well down Elm, when the shots began to be fired. He claims to have "felt compression on his cheek" from one of the shots, but that is most unlikely if the shots had been fired from more than sixty feet above him. It is less unlikely, however, if he felt a shot fired from the second floor of the Dal-Tex Building, which I suspect was the source of three shots—the miss that hit James Tague, the hit to the back of Jack's head, and the miss that hit the chrome strip—which may have been fired by a Mannlicher-Carcano and been the only shots fired with an unsilenced weapon.

More importantly, Wiegman is the only source the program presents on this question, which creates a highly misleading impression. There were more than 200 witnesses in Dealey Plaza, who offered very different opinions about the number and source of the shots. The HSCA, for example, reviewed the statements of 178 persons who were in the plaza, with the following results: 21 (11 percent) thought the shots came from the grassy knoll; 49 (27 percent) from the Book Depository; 78 (44 percent) could not tell; and 30 (17 percent) thought they had originated elsewhere. (See *The Final Assassinations Report* 1979, p. 95.)

As though this were not bad enough, Stewart Galanor has analyzed the data on which these statistics were based and has discovered bias. After reevaluating the testimony of 216 witnesses available to the Warren Commission, he found that 70 (32 percent) were not asked for their opinion. Of the remaining 146, 54 (37 percent) thought the shots had come from the vicinity of the grassy knoll; 46 (32 percent) thought they had come from the Book Depository; 35 (24 perecent) could not tell; and 6 (4 percent) thought they had come from both the grassy knoll and the Book Depository. Only 5 (3 percent) believed they had originated elsewhere (Stewart Galanor, *Cover-Up* 1998, p. 72, and his appendix, "216 Witnesses").

By 04:05, Kathleen Kern is reporting, "John Fitzgerald Kennedy was rushed to Parkland Hospital, where he was pronounced dead from a devastating gunshot to the head. Within an hour, after an intensive manhunt, 21-year-old Lee Harvey Oswald was arrested." A backyard photograph is displayed. By 04:20, she says, "Oswald worked in the Texas School Book Depository, where many claim the shots came from." But of course, many made different claims, which are never mentioned, much less discussed. And by showing but not talking about the backyard photograph, the impression is left that it is authentic and incriminating, when it has been faked and thus exonerates him.

Eric Hamburg, an author, and Daniel Martinez, an historian—neither of whom, to the best of my knowledge, is an expert on the assassination—offer general remarks about the event. By 04:50, Gary Mack has been introduced with some comments on traumatic occurrences in American history. By 05:30, Kathleen is asking whether Lee Oswald was the lone assassin and, by 06:00, she is observing, "Others claim that the physical evidence suggests another assassin, firing from the front. The hypothetical person waited behind the fence on the infamous grassy knoll. Were any of these gunmen captured on film?", which at this point in time becomes the program's focus.

Many photographs and films are shown, none of which, according to the program, offers any support for any conspiracy theory. Even when those photographs include features that have drawn an immense amount of attention from students of the case, these are never pursued, other than by dismissive remarks from Gary Mack, who suggests that they could be studied forever and never reveal anything conclusive about the possibility of other gunmen. What is most deceptive about such claims is that, while none of this evidence may be conclusive, it is certain fascinating and includes striking indications of the possible presence of multiple gunmen, where none of these indications is identified, much less discussed, during this program.

Motorcade turning onto Main

By 07:00, Kathleen Kern is describing the "crack investigative team" that will pursue all of these important questions, including "Gary Mack, assassination historian; Mark Wagg, Dallas photographer; Steve McWilliams, cinematographer; and Douglas Mark, graphic designer". I am sure I am not the only viewer who noticed that this "crack investigative team" is strong on photographers, cinematographers, and graphic designers but short on anyone knowledgeable about the assassination of JFK—apart from Gary Mack. This is a Mack production, as the evidence displays. I shall discuss samples of his work in accord with the real-time sequence of those events in Dallas.

Motorcade turning onto Main

At 58:30, we see the motorcade turn onto Main Street as it begins the long stretch en route to Dealey Plaza. This scene, which appears without discussion, indicates that the motorcade was proceeding in violation of Secret Service policies for the protection of the President. Observe the crowds spilling out into the street and the row of open windows.

You do not have to be an expert on security to understand that the failure to control the crowd and to secure the windows placed the President at great jeopardy. There were more than fifteen indications of Secret Service complicity in setting up JFK for the hit, as *Murder in Dealey Plaza* (2000) explains and as many other authors have observed. Yet it was not worth a mention in the television production, "Death in Dealey Plaza" (2003).

Photograph of Book Depository

At 17:30, we watch the Hughes film of the motorcade turning from Main onto Houston, with the sixth floor window of the Book Depository clearly in view. If someone is there about to shoot, it is not evident here, as Gary Mack wistfully remarks that, if Hughes had only continued filming, he should have caught the shooter. "Several witnesses saw a gun sticking out the window and saw the shots", he observes, almost in passing. I found this remark so stunning that I asked him to identify his sources in a request that I have sent to him. To

the best of my knowledge, that is simply not the case. Although I am aware of rumors that prisoners incarcerated at a nearby jail were in the position to make such observations, I am not aware that their observations have ever been recorded. Gary Mack has yet to reply to my inquiry.

Turn from Houston onto Elm

At 00:22, we see the photograph taken by Jim Towner as the limousine turns from Houston onto Elm. The interesting features here include the laundry van and the enormous silver van behind it. There has been speculation that the larger van could have been a command center for communication-and-control of the assassination. Since it could also have been a shooting location for an assassin, its presence at this vulnerable intersection should be a matter of keen interest for a program of this kind, which proclaims that it is devoted to the dicovery of "new clues" in the photographic record. Neither here nor elsewhere are any "new clues" found that deserved to be mentioned during this program.

Photograph of the grassy knoll

At 07:07, we see a Willis photograph, which was taken toward the grassy knoll and has several features of immense interest, including the Zapruder pedestal and two subjects of special concern, the Umbrella Man and Black Dog Man. By 24:40, we have returned to the Willis photo, where Mack is again wistfully remarking, "What is so tantalizing about the Willis picture is that, if there was a grassy knoll gunman, he's got to be in there somewhere. You could look at this picture every day for the rest of your life and you may or may not see anything." But the features I am identifying are well-known to the research community. Here is a slightly earlier Hugh Betzner phottgraph from Robert Groden, *The Killing of a President* (1993).

"Black Dog Man"

Robert Groden, The Killing of a President *(1993), p. 192*

The question is not whether Black Dog Man, for example, is a shooter or Umbrella Man is an assassination coordinator, as many students believe, but that, during this program on the photographic evidence, crucial features of photographs are not mentioned, much less discussed, even though they are completely familiar to the research community of which Mack has been an active member in the past. It is impossible that the Archivist for The Sixth Floor Museum is not thoroughly familiar with the leading collection of photographs on the assassination, which has been in print since 1993, ten years prior to this program. So not only are no "new clues" discovered but numerous "old clues" are ignored.

The Nix assassination film

By 18:45, we see the Nix film, which was taken facing the grassy knoll. As Jack White has observed, there are many interesting features of this film, including that many of its frames appear to have been blacked in. More importantly, there is the image of what many have taken to be a shooter, who even appears to follow the limousine as it passes through the plaza, which I have circled here. The question is not whether this is or is not a shooter, in fact, but that it looks very much like a shooter and surely ought to have been identified and discussed during a program ostensibly devoted to exploring the film and photographic record for indications of shooters. At several points in the program, the general area across the top where this image is present are lightened up, which has the effect of obscuring the very features of greatest interest to students of the case.

Nix frames blacked-in

Edges of sloppy retouching are clearly seen around car top.

Jack White, "N is for Nix . . . knoll frames blacked-in"

The Moorman Polaroid

A Polaroid photo taken by Dealey Plaza witness Mary Ann Moorman shows the President within half a second after being shot in the head. In the background are several ambiguous shapes, one of which appears to be a man in a police uniform standing behind the stockade fence at the top of the Grassy Knoll. Ruth Stapleton, sister of former President Carter, was the first to identify one of the shapes as a man. Though he appears to be dressed in the uniform of a Dallas policeman, the "officer" wore no hat. This man was discovered independently years later by Fort Worth researchers Jack White and Gary Mack, who named him Badge Man (see page 200).

Robert Groden, The Killing of a President *(1993), p. 200 and p. 204*

By 25:40, an extended discussion of the Moorman has commenced that runs longer than that of any other photo. Anyone who still doubts that Gary Mack has been circumventing information about the contents of these photographs should have those reservations laid to rest by his discussion of the Moorman, which somehow neglects to mention the image of Badge Man. As Groden's caption represents, Badge Man was discovered by Jack White in collaboration with Gary Mack! The only excuse for not discussing Badge Man would have been his personal ignorance. But he cannot be ignorant of a discovery that he made; and if he were as ignorant as his presentations throughout the program suggest, then he was incompetent to produce it. The pretensions of this program of satisfying even the most minimal standards of objectivity are thereby conclusively shattered!

Other omissions occur with the apparent complicity of Daniel Martinez. In one scene that occurs at 16:00, Mack and Martinez are seen walking away from what is no doubt supposed to be "the sniper's nest". Yet, as Larry Swanberg has pointed out to me, this cannot be "the sniper's nest", because a Plexiglass window has been erected around it in The Sixth Floor Museum. Unless the floor was rebuilt for the purpose of this program, the scene appears to be a simulation. Since this production has all of the properties of a misleading attempt to create the impression of an objective and thorough consideration of the film and photographic record, it thus appears to be a fake scene in a fake program about a fake film, the lack of authenticity of which has been the subject of this book in its entirety. The ironies abound.

The shooter in camouflage

Back of a man's head and possibly a rifle behind the retaining wall on the Knoll.

Robert Groden and Harrison Livingstone, High Treason *(1989)*

More importantly, at 48:38, Mack and Martinez are busily reviewing the Zapruder film together and, at frame 413, Martinez asks Mack about two figures in the background he claims not to have noticed before. The stunning feature of the frame, however, shows up in the foreground—a man in military camouflage who appears to be sighting a rifle—which receives no attention at all, even though its presence was publicized as long ago as Robert J. Groden and Harrison Edward Livingstone, *High Treason* (1989), which discusses it and even provides a print of the frame, which is reproduced here. One might almost think that this was a deliberate act of distraction, which obviously contradicted the avowed objective of searching for possible shooters in the film and photo record. Perhaps that was not the purpose of this program.

Zapruder's TV interview

At 46:08, we are observing Abraham Zapruder during an interview at a television station at a time when, I presume, he ought to have been looking after his film. As the frame makes apparent, Zapruder described a massive blow-out to the right/front of the President's head. This, in my opinion, is the most striking evidence that Zapruder may have been a knowing participant in the assassination. The evidence that is presented in the Prologue makes it apparent that X-rays have been altered, some in what appears to have been an effort to create the impresssion of a blow-out to the right/front of the head that would be consistent with a high-velocity shot from behind. If the "blob" was painted in and no such wound occurred, then Zapruder appears to have been playing a prescribed role in covering up the true causes of death of JFK.

Either Mack was competent to produce this film or he was not. If he was competent, there was a lot of material to work with, material that was familiar to assassination experts. Consider, for example, his commentary about the Nix film that occurs around 18:45: "If his film had been lighter—*if, if, if*—there might have been a clear image of the grassy knoll to know for sure if there was another gunman there or not." Here he is clearly playing with words. There *is* an image—one that has caught the attention of many students of the crime—that is at least sufficiently clear to deserve identification and discussion. Yet none occurs. Which speaks volumes about the motives and concerns that brought this production to television with the cooperation of The Sixth Floor Museum.

By 53:50, Mack is observing that, during this event, "Virtually every second was captured by a camera somewhere", which, in my opinion, is the theme that viewers are supposed to absorb. Virtually every second may have been captured, but that, alas!, does not mean that the present photographic record contains every frame or photo that was taken during that interval of time. As this book has explained, that appears to be far from the truth, where those who know no better are left at the mercy of this man who would have them believe things that are not true about the death of John F. Kennedy. It is a sad commentary that a program ostensibly devoted to clarifying the photographic record should have been used instead for its obfuscation.

Windshield A:
The windshield in the Altgens photograph of 22 November 1963. (See Murder in Dealey Plaza *2000, p. 149.)*

Ford Motor Company   Washington Office
Intra-Company Communication   December 18, 1963

TO: R.W. Markley, Jr.
FROM: F. Vaughn Ferguson
Re: Changes in White House "Bubbletop"

On November 23rd, the day following the President's assassination, I went to the White House garage in response to a telephone call to my home from the Secret Service. When I arrived about 10:00 a.m., the White House "Bubbletop" was in a stall in the garage with two Secret Service men detailed to guard it. A canvas cover was over the unit. I was permitted only to see the windshield of the car and then only after the guards had received permission from higher ranking Secret Service personnel. Examination of the windshield disclosed no perforation, but substantial cracks radiating a couple of inches from the center of the windshield at a point directly beneath the mirror. I was at the garage only about one hour that day, but while I was there Morgan Geis contacted the Secret Service and told them to have me make arrangements to replace the windshield.

Windshield B:
The windshield observed by F. Vaughn Ferguson on 23 November 1963. (See Murder in Dealey Plaza *2000, p. 431.)*

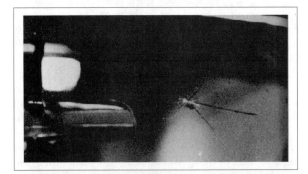

Windshield C:
The windshield later produced by the Secret Service and published as Warren Commission Exhibit 350. The Secret Service was playing a shell game. (See Assassination Science *1998, pp. 142–144.)*

Windshield D:
Jim Lewis has fired a high-powered rifle through a windshield at 200 yards and hit a dummy in the neck, evidence in support of Windshield A. (See Murder in Dealey Plaza *2000, p. 149.)*

Appendix A

Murder in Dealey Plaza:
A Critical Mass of Evidence

George Costello

[*Editor's note*: The following review appeared in *The Federal Lawyer* 48/4 (May 2001), pp. 52–56 (formerly: *The Federal Bar News and Journal*), a publication for attorneys who work for the federal government, who practice before federal agencies, or who appear before federal courts. It was selected for *The Federal Lawyer*'s 2002 "Outstanding Book Review" award for "Excellence in Journalism". The views presented here are those of the author and not of the Congressional Research Service.]

There has always been strong evidence of multiple gunmen in the assassination of President Kennedy—strong evidence that the official story presented in *The Warren Report*,[1] and in large measure ratified by the report of the House Select Committee on Assassinations (HSCA),[2] is false. Conspiracy evidence, however, has always run up against autopsy evidence that substantiates the official story that shots hit the President only from behind.[3] Ordinarily, the autopsy is the best evidence of how a murder was accomplished, but the Kennedy assassination has proven to be the exception to the rule. *Murder in Dealey Plaza* pulls the props from under the autopsy report, and gives us good reason to believe that the report, along with accompanying X-rays and photos, was falsified to hide evidence of frontal shots.

Murder in Dealey Plaza is aptly subtitled "What We Know Now that We Didn't Know Then About the Death of JFK." For years, key evidence in the case was kept secret by the federal government. Thanks to the work of the Assassination Records Review Board (ARRB), however, we now have much more information than we did before about the assassination of President Kennedy, and about the cover-up orchestrated from within the government.[4] Thanks to the dedication and persistence of people like Professor James Fetzer, Dr. Gary Aguilar, Dr. David Mantik, and Douglas Horne—contributors to *Murder in Dealey Plaza*—we now have a better idea about what really happened.

Soon after the ARRB released its report in 1998, supporters of the Warren Commission's conclusion that Lee Harvey Oswald was the lone assassin were quick to provide sound bites proclaiming that there were no "smoking guns" in the released files. This was true only in the very literal sense that the actual murder

437

weapons and assassins were not identified.[5] There is explosive material in the newly released files—evidence that helps establish that the autopsy report was misleading on critical points, that supporting X-rays and photographs relied upon by the HSCA were falsified, and that the government has never revealed the true nature of the President's wounds.

Murder in Dealey Plaza, building on knowledge that has been gained over the years,[6] sets forth much of the new information and explains its import.[7] The principal focus is on the medical evidence, but there are also interesting chapters on the Presidential limousine, the failure of Secret Service protection, the authenticity of the Zapruder film, the failure of professional historians to probe behind the cover-up, and Dallas Police Chief Jesse Curry's files on the case. A perceptive 1964 essay by Bertrand Russell rounds out the book.[8]

Among the book's findings are the following:

- Contrary to conclusions in the HSCA's report, witnesses to the Bethesda autopsy confirmed, rather than contradicted, the Dallas doctors' assertions that there was a large hole in the back of the President's head.[9] Such a hole would ordinarily signify an exit wound, not an entrance wound, and is therefore indicative of a shot from the front.

- Autopsy X-rays were forged, probably shortly after the autopsy, to make it appear that there was a round metallic object, 6.5 mm in diameter, lodged in the back of the President's skull near the alleged bullet entry site identified by the HSCA. (Accused assassin Lee Harvey Oswald's rifle used 6.5 mm ammunition.)

- Not all of the photos and X-rays taken at the autopsy remain in the collection at the National Archives. ARRB interviews with autopsy doctors, photographers, and X-ray technicians reveal that some photographs and X-rays taken during the autopsy are missing from the collection at the National Archives, and that some of the photographs now in that collection were not taken during the autopsy.

- As a follow-up to the autopsy there were two separate brain examinations of two different brains. The first examination, evidently of President Kennedy's brain, was probably conducted on the morning of Monday, 25 November, prior to the President's funeral. The second examination, conducted about a week later, was of a different brain—a brain that showed damage consistent with the official story of a head shot from the rear.

Among the conclusions that can be drawn from these and other findings are the following:

- President Kennedy was shot at least twice in the head. At least one shot to the head came from the front.

- Autopsy photos and X-rays were falsified to conceal the true nature of President Kennedy's wounds, and to create images consistent with the official version of the shooting. The autopsy report was deliberately misleading.

- The second brain examination, evidently of a brain not the President's, was conducted in order to create a record of a brain specimen that was consistent with the official story that President Kennedy had been shot from behind.

- All of the official investigations of President Kennedy's assassination relied on falsified or misleading medical data to reach their conclusions.

The new findings about the medical evidence cannot be set forth in full detail in a book review of this length. Some elaboration here, however, should help convince the reader that the medical essays in *Murder in Dealey Plaza* are both thorough and persuasive with respect to their principal findings, and that the book merits serious attention.

The Autopsy Witnesses

One of the most shocking revelations in the ARRB's releases is the fact that the HSCA misrepresented the basic thrust of statements made to Committee staff by witnesses to President Kennedy's autopsy at Bethesda.[10] According to the HSCA report, "In disagreement with the observations of the Parkland doctors are the 26 people present at the autopsy. All of those interviewed who attended the autopsy corroborated the general location of the wounds as depicted in the photographs; none had differing accounts . . . . [I]t appears more probable that the observations of the Parkland doctors are incorrect." [11]

The autopsy photographs referred to by the HSCA report show the back of the head apparently intact, the hair free of blood, with only a small red spot near the cowlick.[12] By contrast, doctors at Parkland Hospital in Dallas who treated the mortally wounded President, including neurosurgeons, described a large, gaping wound in the back of the head, with brain tissue from the cerebellum as well as the cerebrum extruding. (The cerebellum, located low in the back of the brain, has a very distinctive appearance that no doctor should mistake for the cerebrum.)

The autopsy report, although it wrongly concluded that President Kennedy was shot only from behind, also clashed directly with these photographs. The report describes a large hole "involving chiefly the parietal bone, but extending somewhat into the temporal and occipital regions."[13] This is a description of a hole that extends well into the back of the head.[14] Any large hole in both the parietal and occipital bones should have been readily apparent in a photograph of the back of the head, at least if there was a corresponding loss of scalp.

According to Dr. Aguilar, it is simply not true that the autopsy witnesses interviewed by the HSCA staff corroborated the autopsy photos. Staff summaries of the witnesses' statements, locked up for 30 years until being released through the ARRB, reveal that all 13 of those interviewed (only half of those present at the autopsy) corroborated the observations of the Parkland doctors that there was a large wound in the back of the head. Many Warren Commission witnesses had also described a large wound in the back of the head. Dr. Aguilar reports that, between Parkland and Bethesda, there were more than 40 witnesses—including the autopsists themselves—whose original observations attested to a right-rearward skull wound.[15]

Thus, it is no longer a matter of Parkland doctors and other Dallas witnesses being contradicted by the autopsy photographs and all of the autopsy witnesses. Rather, it appears that the current autopsy photographs were contradicted by virtually all interviewed witnesses at the Bethesda autopsy as well as at Parkland. As Dr. Aguilar contends, it is difficult to imagine how there could have been near unanimity among so many people—many of them highly trained professionals— and how all of them could have been wrong about so basic a matter as the location of a large head wound recognized by all as the fatal wound.

Incomplete and Altered Autopsy Photos

How can it be that the autopsy photographs conflict so starkly with the observations of the 13 autopsy witnesses who described a large hole in the back of the President's head? With the exception of one confusing photo of the inside of the skull,[16] the collection of autopsy photographs at the National Archives does not verify a large defect in the back of the head. In fact, as mentioned above, the extant photos of the exterior of the back of the head show it to be intact. The explanation appears to be that the original autopsy photos were replaced with subsequently made and probably fabricated photos that were intended to be consistent with the official story of shots from behind.

Through interviews with the autopsy doctors, photographers, X-ray technicians, autopsy witnesses, and a technician who developed autopsy pictures, the ARRB helped to establish that there were key photographs taken during the autopsy that are not now present in the collection at the National Archives. Various discrepancies emerged. For example, particular angles and views that were photographed during the autopsy are not now represented (e.g., the inside of the chest cavity, the inside and outside of the skull where the beveling of a bullet entry is revealed). The number of exposures supposedly taken during the autopsy exceeds the number of pictures in the collection. Photos now in the collection were taken with film that was not used by the autopsy photographer, and that was not developed at the Naval Photographic Center, where apparently the original autopsy photos were developed.

Another strong indictment of the authenticity of the extant photo showing a blood-free and intact back of the head is the reaction to this photo by the two FBI agents present at the autopsy: "this looks like it's been doctored in some way" and "it looks like it could have been reconstructed or something".[17]

The HSCA's account of authentication of the photographs is almost as troubling as its misrepresentation of the statements of the autopsy witnesses. The Committee reported that the autopsy photographs were authenticated, although it claimed that the Department of Defense "had been unable to locate" the camera and lens that had been used at the autopsy. HSCA files released in 1997, however, revealed that DOD had indeed identified the camera and sent it to the Committee, but that the Committee's photographic experts, rather than raising embarrassing questions of authenticity, chose instead to conclude that the camera and lens had not been the one used to take the autopsy photographs existing in 1977.[18]

Forgery of the Autopsy X-Rays

There are two aspects of the extant autopsy X-rays that Dr. Mantik believes are forged. One is the round, 6.5 mm fragment mentioned above, apparently lodged in the back of the skull and visible on the frontal X-ray. The other is the intact back of the skull seen on the lateral X-rays. Dr. Mantik, a radiation oncologist who is board-certified by the American College of Radiology and who also has a Ph.D. in physics, relies on optical densitometry measurements to confirm the forgeries.

The round 6.5 mm object that appears to be lodged in the back of the skull was apparently not present on the X-rays taken the night of the autopsy.[19] When questioned under oath by the ARRB, the three autopsy doctors had no recollection of the object, and no witness to the autopsy has ever described it. A major objective of autopsy X-rays is to identify bullets and bullet fragments present in the body so that they can be removed and preserved as evidence. Other much smaller bullet fragments were removed from the President's head during the autopsy, and it stands to reason that this largest of all objects would also have been spotted and removed. The fact that this object was not identified and removed the night of the autopsy is by itself strong evidence that it was not there. In addition, irregularities in optical density measurements led Dr. Mantik to conclude that the object was not a bullet fragment at all, but had been placed on the X-ray film through use of a composite.[20]

The lateral X-ray shows an impossibly dense area within the posterior skull—so dense, in fact, that Dr. Mantik concluded that if it were bone it would have to be nearly solid bone from one side of the skull to the other. Also indicative of forgery is the fact that there is no corresponding dense area visible on the frontal X-ray, as one would expect if there were something that dense within the skull.[21] Dr. Mantik concludes that this X-ray also appears to be a composite created by double exposure.[22]

Another aspect of the skull X-rays bears emphasis, although it is not indicative of forgery. Visible on the lateral X-ray is a trail of tiny metallic particles extending from near the hair line on the right forehead most of the way back across the top of the skull. This trail of particles does not line up with either of the bullet entry sites identified by government inquiries. The trail clearly could not have resulted from a bullet that entered low on the back of the skull near the external occipital protuberance (the site identified by the autopsy pathologists). In fact, the autopsy report misplaces this trail by over 10 cm, an astonishing error that the pathologists could not explain to the ARRB. Nor does the trail line up with the much higher site posited by the HSCA. The trail of particles does align, however, with a possible bullet entry site near the hairline on the forehead.[23]

The Two Brain Examinations

If the discovery by ARRB staffer Douglas Horne that there were two brain examinations of two different brains following President Kennedy's autopsy does not constitute a "smoking gun", it is hard to imagine what would. Horne set forth his findings in a staff memorandum released to the public in 1998, and summarized by Horne in a chapter in *Murder in Dealey Plaza*.[24]

Horne based his conclusions on "three sets of indicia": (1) conflicting evidence, drawn mostly from ARRB interviews with participants, as to the timing of what was initially assumed to be one brain examination; (2) conflicting evidence as to the type of film and photographic techniques used to photograph the brain(s); and (3) differences between the appearance of the brain at autopsy and in photographs of the (second) brain examination.

As for the timing, both autopsy doctor J. Thornton Boswell and autopsy photographer John Stringer told both the HSCA and the ARRB that the brain exam was conducted 2 or 3 days after the autopsy. President Kennedy was killed in the early afternoon of Friday, 22 November 1963, his body was flown back to Washington that afternoon, and the autopsy was conducted that evening. The brain exam that was conducted 2 or 3 days after the autopsy most likely occurred on the morning of Monday, 25 November, the day of the funeral, there having been pressure to complete the autopsy procedures in time to bury the brain with the body.

There was other evidence, however, of a later brain exam. Dr. Pierre Finck of the Armed Forces Institute of Pathology, the third doctor present at the autopsy (and a meticulous record keeper), wrote in a 1965 memo to his superior that Dr.

Humes had called him on 29 November 1963 about the need to examine the President's brain, and that he had subsequently attended such an examination. Dr. Finck reaffirmed to the ARRB that the brain examination he attended could not have been as soon as 2 or 3 days after the autopsy. Relying on this information as well as interviews with other key people, Horne concluded that Dr. Finck had been excluded from the first brain exam, and was then called in to observe the second.[25]

The brain observed at autopsy and the photographed brain were grossly disparate. The right hemisphere of the photographed brain was disturbed, but virtually all of the brain matter was present. The recorded weight was 1500 grams, near the upper limit for a male brain (the average is reportedly 1350 to 1400 grams).[26] But by all accounts a significant amount of the President's brain was blown away when he was shot in the head.[27] Witnesses at Parkland and at the autopsy said that at least a third of the brain was gone, and the extant autopsy X-rays show a complete absence of brain in the front of the head. These major discrepancies alone could have justified Horne's conclusion that the brain that was photographed and described could not have been that of President Kennedy.

Conclusion

What does all of this mean? Any one of the findings summarized above would be troubling by itself. Together, these findings form a critical mass of evidence indicating that President Kennedy's autopsy was falsified, and help establish a compelling case that people within the federal government covered up evidence of frontal shots—and hence of multiple gunmen and conspiracy in the assassination of President Kennedy. Because it pulls this evidence together in one place, *Murder in Dealey Plaza* is one of the most important books to date on the Kennedy assassination.

The new evidence turns the tables. No longer can defenders of the lone assassin theory hide behind the autopsy evidence and claim that it trumps all the other evidence. The weight of this other evidence now trumps the autopsy report. Lone assassin theorists must address and explain the new evidence if they wish to regain credibility.

It is time for people of integrity who were involved in the official investigations—especially the professionals—to take a good-faith look at the new evidence and confront the likelihood that their conclusions were based on falsified data. *Murder in Dealey Plaza* may not be the last word on the medical evidence, but it should be the starting point for a fresh look—not only at the medical evidence, but also at the assassination and its implications.

Endnotes

1. *The Warren Report* is the popular name of the *Report of the President's Commission on the Assassination of President John F. Kennedy*. The Warren Commission was established on 29 November 1963 by E.O. 11130, and charged with evaluating the evidence developed by the FBI, with making such further investigation as the Commission finds desirable, and with reporting findings and conclusions to President Johnson. The Commission's report, delivered to President Johnson on 24 September 1964, concluded that Lee Harvey Oswald, acting alone, and firing three shots from a sixth floor window of the Texas School Book Depository above and behind the presidential limousine, killed President Kennedy and wounded Governor Connolly, and that Jack Ruby, acting alone, killed Oswald two days later.

2. The House Select Committee on Assassinations was formed in 1976 to review the evidence relating to the assassinations of President Kennedy and Rev. Martin Luther King, Jr. The Committee devoted much of its limited resources to assembling panels of experts to examine and evaluate the evidence, and conducted only a limited new investigation. See Gaeton Fonzi, *The Last Investigation* (1993). The Committee's report, issued in 1979, agreed with the Warren Commission that the President was killed by Lee Harvey Oswald, who fired three shots from the sixth floor of the Texas School Book Depository. The Committee also, however, found a high probability that a second gunman fired at the motorcade, but missed, from behind the picket fence atop the grassy knoll to the front and right of the Presidential limousine.

3. According to the official story formulated by the Warren Commission and agreed to by the HSCA, two of the three shots fired by Lee Harvey Oswald from the sixth floor sniper's nest in the Texas School Book Depository building struck President Kennedy. Under this scenario the first shot to strike the President hit him in the upper back and exited his throat just below the Adam's apple. This same bullet (later dubbed the single bullet or magic bullet), then allegedly struck Governor Connolly, seated in front of the President, and caused all of the Governor's wounds. Both official accounts agreed that the second shot to strike the President was fatal, and entered the back of the head. They strongly disagreed, however, as to the location of the bullet entry hole on the back of the head. The Warren Commission, relying on the findings of the autopsy doctors, concluded that this bullet entered low on the skull slightly above and to the right of the external occipital protuberance. The HSCA, however, relying on autopsy photographs and X-rays, placed the entry hole about four inches higher, near the cowlick.

4. The ARRB was established pursuant to the President John F. Kennedy Assassination Records Collection Act of 1992, Pub. L. 102-526. The Board's mission was to obtain all government records relating to the assassination, and to the fullest extent possible release those records to the American people. The Board was not charged with investigating the crime or with making findings as to who was responsible for the President's murder. The Board was authorized, however, to pursue issues related to the completeness of assassination records and the possible destruction of records; relying on this authority, the Board conducted extensive interviews relating to the autopsy and other medical records.

5 In the Prologue to *Murder in Dealey Plaza* (*MIDP*), Fetzer identifies 16 smoking guns revealed by the new evidence.

6 A number of researchers have contributed to deciphering the medical evidence. Among the more significant books on the subject have been Harold Weisberg, *Post Mortem* (1975); Charles Wilber, *Medicolegal Investigation of the President John F. Kennedy Murder* (1978); David Lifton, *Best Evidence* (1980); Noel Twyman, *Bloody Treason* (1997); Harrison Livingstone, *High Treason II* (1998); and James Fetzer, editor, *Assassination Science* (1998).

7 *MIDP* is a sequel to Fetzer's 1998 book *Assassination Science*. Both books are collections of essays by assassination researchers probing different aspects of the case. The *MIDP* chapters on the medical evidence are thorough summaries that cover the new evidence and bring the essentials together in one place.

MIDP does not replicate what is found in *Assassination Science*, however, and is well supplemented by the earlier work.

8   This review's emphasis on the medical evidence is not intended to minimize the significant contributions of Vince Palamara's analysis of the Secret Service performance in Dallas and its aftermath, of Douglas Weldon's research into the post-assassination disposition of the presidential limousine, or of David Mantik's analysis of the Zapruder film. All of these chapters in *MIDP* are well worth the reader's attention.

9   After the shooting in Dealey Plaza, President Kennedy was taken to Parkland Hospital in Dallas, where a team of doctors attempted unsuccessfully to save his life. During the course of treatment, these doctors observed two wounds: a small puncture wound of the throat and a large hole in the back of the head. After President Kennedy was pronounced dead, his body was forcibly removed from Parkland Hospital, in disregard of Texas law requiring that the autopsy be performed there, and transported to the National Naval Medical Center at Bethesda, Maryland. The autopsy was performed at Bethesda under the direction of Dr. James Humes, of the Naval Medical Center, and with the assistance of Dr. J. Thornton Boswell, also of the Naval Medical Center, and Dr. Pierre Finck, from the Armed Forces Institute of Pathology.

10 That HSCA staff kept the witness statements and their import from its own panel of forensic pathology experts is also shocking. When Dr. Aguilar showed these statements in 1995 to Dr. Michael Baden and Dr. Cyril Wecht, both members of the HSCA panel, they both said they had never seen them before. *MIDP*, p. 188.

11 *Report of the House Select Committee on Assassinations*, 95th Cong., 2d Sess., vol. 7, at 37–39 (1979), as quoted and emphasized in *MIDP*, pp. 197–98.

12 That red spot was later identified by HSCA experts as the bullet entry hole. This represented a major upward shift of about four inches from the entry point identified by the autopsy doctors, just to the right and just above the external occipital protuberance (EOP). With the exception of one occasion when Dr. Humes seemed to waver on the issue under questioning by the HSCA, the three autopsy doctors Humes, Boswell, and Finck have consistently maintained that the bullet entry hole was at the lower site, near the EOP.

13 In 1996 Dr. Boswell reconfirmed these observations by drawing just such a large hole on a skull as an illustration for the ARRB, *MIDP* pp. 235–37.

14 The two parietal bones cover much of the top and sides of the skull, from the coronal suture in front, where they meet the frontal bones, to the lambdoid suture in the back, where they meet the occipital bone. The back of the head is thus comprised of parietal bone on top and occipital bone below. Note as well that the occipital bone overlies the area of the brain that contains the cerebellum, and that the Parkland doctors reported seeing tissue from the cerebellum extruding from the wound in the back of the head.

15 The emphasis on original statements is important. Soon after the autopsy Secret Service agents visited the Parkland doctors in an effort to get them to revise their statements. Some of them did back off their initial statements, both with

respect to the head wound and with respect to the wound in the front of the throat, which they had initially described as a likely entry wound.

16 Confusing to the layman, that is. Dr. Mantik contends that this picture, properly oriented and interpreted, shows the damage to the back of the head and also reveals the proper placement of a bone fragment found at the assassination scene in Dealey Plaza.

17 Sworn statements of Francis X. O'Neill and James W. Sibert, respectively, to ARRB counsel Jeremy Gunn, as reproduced in *MIDP*, p. 208. Dr. Robert Grossman, a neurosurgeon who attended President Kennedy at Parkland Hospital, had a similar reaction to the picture when interviewed by ARRB staff. See *MIDP*, p. 201.

18 Whether the lens in the camera had been changed between 1963 and the HSCA's examination in 1977 remains unknown.

19 It is probably not coincidental that the size of this fragment precisely matched the 6.5 mm ammunition used by Oswald's rifle. Nor is it likely to be coincidental that spatially compatible images of the 6.5 mm object are visible on the lateral and frontal X-rays (the object is round on the frontal view, and narrow on the lateral view, and in both views appears at the same spot on the back of the skull). A random artifact might appear on one or the other views, but not both, or a speck-on-the-lens artifact could appear in identical shape and size on both images, but the odds of the spatially compatible but distinctly differently shaped images appearing by random on two different X-rays at the same spot on the skull are indeed remote.

20 Dr. Mantik also quotes Larry Sturdivan, the HSCA's ballistics expert, who states unequivocally that this object could not possibly be a sheared-off cross-section of a bullet or bullet jacket. Never in his experience, Mr. Sturdivan explained, had he seen a bullet that had sheared off in this manner after striking a body.

21 A forger's objective would have been to simulate an intact skull, not to create a suspiciously dense area inside the skull, so the need to fabricate the frontal X-ray would probably not have been anticipated.

22 This finding is summarized by Dr. Fetzer as Smoking Gun #7 in the Prologue to *MIDP*, and was described in more detail by Dr. Mantik in *Assassination Science*. An effect of the composite was to leave the frontal skull looking unusually dark, a feature that puzzled even Dr. Humes when interviewed by the ARRB.

23 No government inquiry has identified a bullet entry hole at this site, but Tom Robinson, the funeral home employee who restored the body after the autopsy, described a wound at that location. *MIDP*, p. 250. This trail of particles, incidentally, is more characteristic of an exploding bullet than of the full metal jacketed bullets used by Oswalds weapon. See *MIDP*, Prologue, Smoking Gun #4.

24 The complete staff memorandum was printed in *Probe*, vol. 7, No. 4 (May–June 2000). *Probe*, now discontinued, was a research journal produced by Citizens for Truth About the Kennedy Assassination.

25 It may seem incredible that Drs. Humes and Boswell could have participated in such a deception. Note, however, that John Stringer, the autopsy photographer, when asked by the ARRB why he signed a false statement verifying the

completeness of the photographic record, responded that he was ordered to. Perhaps Dr. Humes had similar orders. There were instances when Dr. Humes was less than candid about what transpired the night of the autopsy. For example, Dr. Humes had told the Warren Commission and the HSCA that he had burned his autopsy notes because some of the President's blood was on them and he did not want them to be the subject of morbid curiosity. He also, however, burned a first draft of the autopsy report that could not have been stained with the President's blood. See *Final Report of the ARRB*, p. 122, and *MIDP*, pp. 268-71. Also, Dr. Humes initially claimed that he was not aware that there was a bullet wound in the throat until he talked by phone with Parkland doctors the next morning, and that it was only then that he realized that the throat wound must have been the point of exit for the bullet that entered the back. (The small bullet hole in the throat observed by Parkland doctors had been cut through to insert a breathing tube during resuscitation efforts.) This story was contradicted in 1992 by Dr. Robert B. Livingston, who was Scientific Director for two of the National Institutes of Health in 1963. Dr. Livingston recounted that he had called Dr. Humes the afternoon of the assassination, before the body arrived at Bethesda, and had alerted him that news reports from Dallas indicated there was a bullet entry wound in the throat. See *Assassination Science*, p. 162. Even Dr. Boswell confirmed to the ARRB that the autopsy doctors were aware of the throat wound during the course of the autopsy.

26 Oddly, no brain weight was recorded on the autopsy report.

27 Occupants of the Presidential limousine, as well as the motorcycle policeman riding to the left rear of the limousine, were splattered by blood and brain matter. (In one of several incredible episodes of destruction of evidence, the limousine was washed down at Parkland Hospital soon after the assassination, prior to the inspection that later took place in the White House garage. As a result, there is no complete photographic record of the limousine crime scene in the collection at the Archives. For a full account, see Douglas Weldon's chapter, "The Kennedy Limousine: 1963", in *Murder in Dealey Plaza*. Weldon also presents evidence suggesting that the original windshield, in which several witnesses saw a through hole, was replaced by one containing no perforation, but only cracks consistent with a hit from the rear.)

```
Date: Sun, 27 Jul 2003 15:52:12 -0500
From: jfetzer@d.umn.edu
To: GaryM@jfk.org
Subject: A question and a request

Gary,

About 17:30 into "Death in Dealey Plaza", you state, "Several witnesses
saw a gun sticking out the window and saw the shots fired". Could you
please provide me with your sources? This is quite a remarkable claim.

In addition to illuminating me on this question, could you please send
me a list of the books that are carried for sale by The Sixth Floor Mus-
eum? I would like to make sure that any statements I make are accurate.

Thanks.

Jim
```

Email to Gary Mack from James H. Fetzer

Appendix B

The Zavada Summary:
Dissecting the Zapruder Bell & Howell 8mm Movie Camera

Roland J. Zavada

[*Editor's note*: This study resulted from a request from the ARRB to Kodak, which asked that film tests using a Model 414 PD Bell & Howell Zoomatic Director Series camera be conducted in order to determine whether various recognized anomalies in the Zapruder film held by the National Archives are borne out by actual tests. The following presentation was given before the Movie Machine Society during its Toronto Conference held 24 October 1998. A useful discussion of the Zavada Report by David S. Lifton may be found in Appendix H.]

This presentation is based on a report prepared for Kodak and submitted to the Assassinations Records Review Board, which concerns technical information on the image capture characteristics of the Bell & Howell Model 414PD 8mm roll film camera to the MMS. A Model 414PD camera was used by Abraham Zapruder to film the assassination of President John F. Kennedy. The National Archives intends to make the full report public in the near future, perhaps including a web-accessible version. This piece thus provides only a brief synopsis and outline and should not be construed as a substitute for the original.

Introduction

Just after noon on 22 November 1963, Mr. Abraham Zapruder, a woman's clothing manufacturer, climbed onto a small concrete pedestal in Dealey Plaza with his 8mm movie camera. After President Kennedy's motorcade came into view and passed, Mr. Zapruder's 26 second film record of the assassination became the most significant amateur recording of a news event in history.

The Bell & Howell 414PD 8mm camera was, in 1963, a top of the line, high quality 8mm amateur movie camera. The optics were outstanding, the drive mechanism provided consistent long-run exposure time per wind, the automatic exposure mechanism was of award winning design that yielded excellent results and the camera had a power zoom lens. The "P" in the model reference stood for

"Power Zoom" and the "D" for "Dual Electric-Eye". The image formed within the standardized projectable area had no flaws or faults. Why then have we made an extensive study of the camera's image capture characteristics?

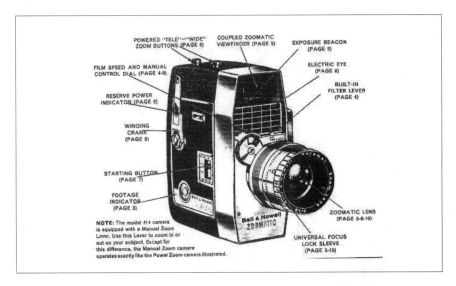

The camera used is not untypical of several models that position the film with its claw moving in an aperture cutout area adjacent to the image forming picture area. Consequently, scene information falls into this unmasked area due to the excess (circular) imaging area produced by the lens. For normal home movie projection this additional recorded scene information would be of no consequence as the projector aperture would hold back or mask-out this area.

We have the typical camera aperture area (i.e. the images that would be viewed by standard projection), and an additional area where the image extends into the area between the perforations and adds to the total scene content. To some students of the assassination, the Zapruder original film contains several image anomalies—almost all being related to the scene information recorded or imaged into the area between the perforations. (See the sample frames below, shot in Dealey Plaza.)

There is great significance attached to this area by various researchers who speculate that the anomalies may represent not the peculiar optics of Zapruder's Bell & Howell camera but, rather, evidence of film alteration. It is important, therefore, to understand how the camera optics record images in this area and why certain anomalies are present—which is part of the objective of this study.

Overview of Image Anomalies

The image characteristics that have been identified as "those of concern" are inconsistencies; i.e. they are not the same density, color, and quality as those contained in the primary image area. The cause of those inconsistencies thus provides a focus for our review of camera characteristics. A look at a few frames from the Zapruder "in camera" original, provide a "picture" of the image characteristic that will be the bases of detailed discussions. (See photo from the Warren Commission Exhibit.)

Image anomalies or characteristics addressed:

Claw Shadow: Between the perforations there is a broad bar where the image has more density (darker) than the primary image area.

Claw or Aperture Flare: Sometimes adjacent to the dark (claw shadow) bar and between it and the primary image is a "streak" lighter than the dark bar and the adjacent image.

Multiple Exposure Areas Adjacent to Perforation: Sometimes there appears a lighter image area resembling images of perforation holes.

Ghost Images: Sometimes there appear to be "ghost" images such as a motorcycle fender. These are real images, which because of the design of the claw cutout area occur simultaneously above and below the perforation holes of the primary image being formed.

First Frame Overexposure: Occurs in the Zapruder original with his first exposure of the motorcade and at least twice in his filming of the first half of the roll. The possible causes of the fogged or lesser density first frame are reviewed, to the best extent possible—recognizing the limitation that we could not conduct a practical test with the Zapruder B&H 414 PD camera.

The camera mechanism includes a negator spring motor drive which, when released by a pivotal movement of a control arm from its position (by pushing down on the start button), serves to rotate a scroll gear to drive a worm (gear). This worm serves to rotate a film footage indicator dial, and to rotate a gear carrying a crank pin to oscillate a shuttle or film pulldown claw and rotate a shutter, as well as drive a governor, and to rotate gears. The shuttle is urged by spring (pressed against the film) toward feeding engagement with the film (i.e., to engage the perforation holes) in a position between an aperture plate incorporating an exposure aperture (area) and a pressure plate (to hold the film flat and motionless during exposure). The shuttle is pivoted on a pin. The gear also carries a known disc segment type of shutter which covers the aperture during frame-by-frame feed of the film and when the camera is stopped.

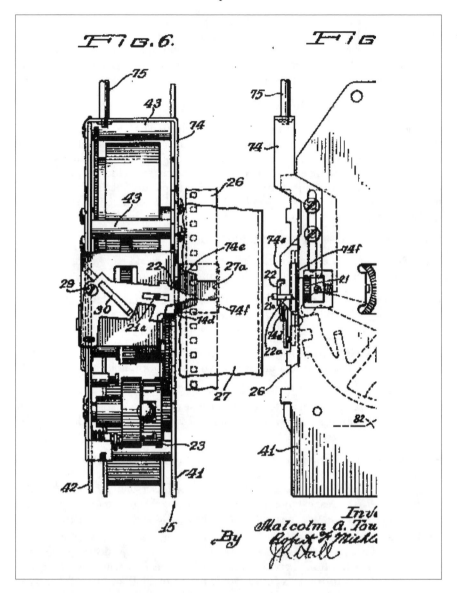

Film Intermittent

In the ratchet type, the claw is normally brought into contact with the film by the action of a light spring. The claw can reciprocate (out of one perforation into the next) in a single plane because its upper edge is tapered so that it will ratchet or cam out of engagement with a perforation at the beginning of the upward movement. The claw will ride along the surface of the film through its entire upward or return stroke until it drops into the succeeding perforation hole. This type of mechanism is the simplest form of the two mentioned, and is the type employed in the Bell & Howell 414PD Camera. (See Drawing.)

Camera Aperture

The drawing shown provides the representative dimensions of the aperture, which limits image height, inside edge and shows the cutout for the intermittent claw. The characteristics of the aperture cutout are directly related to our study of image anomalies. Note the size and location of the cutout for the pulldown claw adjacent to the Standardized (0.192 in. nom. width) image area. Note that the height of the opening for the claw movement is necessarily greater (0.263 inch) than the perforation pitch (0.150 inch) plus one perforation height (0.050 inch). The significance of the size of this opening will be emphasized when we discuss Multiple Exposure Areas.

Shutter/Exposure Time

The shutter, for the great majority of motion picture cameras, employs a rotating disc with an open sector to allow light from the lens to reach the film during its stationary exposure period. During the period when the opaque sector of the shutter obscures the light from the lens, the next frame of the film is moved and relocated by the intermittent. The Bell & Howell 414PD camera uses a shutter having an open sector the equivalent of about 165° to 170° resulting in an exposure time of 0.025 second (or 1/40th of a second) per frame.

Motor/Governor

Early spring wound movie cameras were limited by their clock-spring wind-up motors which were a challenge to designers to maintain constant torque to transport the film at a uniform velocity because of inertial (acceleration) effects from the start of the clutched spring motor. Their run time was relatively short. In the late 1950s and early 1960s a major change occurred for the high-end cameras with the introduction of the negator spring. The B&H 414 Camera series was the first of the Bell & Howell line to incorporate the negator spring. The negator spring motor provided an almost constant torque throughout its effective run time and essentially "negated" transport speed effects. Further, the run time was extended significantly. The differences in run time were in the order of double, from 25–30 seconds to more than a minute (15 feet of film).

Film Velocity/Frame Rate

The question of frame rate of the Zapruder camera was an important technical consideration of the FBI in their investigation of the timing of the three shots. The FBI reported that their studies showed the camera to be operating at 18.3 fps, or 2.3 fps fast according to the (then) published standard and the reference in the owner's manual.

Evolution of Standards to Higher Frame Rates: It has been acknowledged that Bell & Howell's and Eastman Kodak's engineering practice for cameras moved toward 18 fps in the late 1950s, and that this velocity was not uncommon in USA practice. The committee action to change standards takes time. The published standard for camera velocity in use in 1963 issued in 1954. Standards reflect practice and the evolutionary change to the higher frame rate of 18 frames per second was subsequently recognized in American National Standards issued in October of 1964, for Camera and Projector Usage—PH22.21 and PH22.22. Bell & Howell testing confirmed that the Zapruder camera operated at slightly faster than 18 fps—meeting the requirements of the revised standard.

Optical/Image Characteristics

Varamat Zoom Lens

The 3:1 zoom lens of the 414 camera series had eleven elements and reported to be of excellent quality. That quality position was confirmed in correspondence from the former Director of Engineering of the Optical Division, Mr. Rudolf Hartmann. He related: "the Varamat had an unusually flat resolution curve across its picture format (9 field position, 3 focal lengths, full aperture), yielding more than 60 lp/mm (line pairs per millimeter) resolution. Visual (air-image) resolution was 225 I/mm min. at any test position."

Any attempt on my part to provide details on the lens or the zoom mechanism would be redundant. Dr. Cox and Mr. Mellberg confirmed that their patents, Cox #3074317 and Mellberg #3059533, are directly applicable to the 414 camera series.

"Windows" of the Lens

In simplest terms the entrance window of a lens defines the area of the object we are looking at; and the image in the lenses following it is called the exit window, since this defines the area of the image seen. To determine if the exit window size varied, the aperture plate was removed and a light was imaged through the lens onto frosted acetate to observe (as close as possible to the film plane) any change in exit window size with changes in focal length. We observed that there were changes. Although the full exit window remained almost the same, the effective illumination area changed by the presence of dark peripheral rings at the wide angle through normal lens setting. These dark rings began at a diameter slightly greater than the image area diagonal.

Electric Eye and Iris Diaphragm

An article, "A Direct Drive Automatic Iris Control", by LaRue, Bagby, Bushman, Feeland and MacMillin was published in the September 1958 issue of the *SMPTE Journal* and gives the reader design and engineering details on the automatic exposure system. The exposure sensing is achieved by feedback from two photo-voltaic (Se) cells, one sensing overall scene illumination and the other sensing paraxial luminance for backlight compensation. (Hence the "D" in 414PD relates to dual electric eye.)

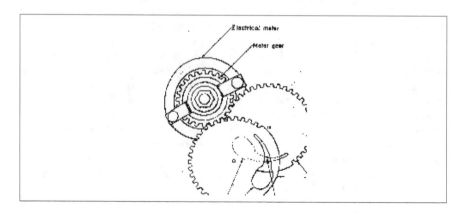

The iris diaphragm in the 414 camera series uses two overlapping disks each of which has a wedge shaped angular slot. The intersection of the two slots forms the variable aperture. Gear teeth are formed on the periphery of the disks that engage a gear mounted on the meter coil. (See drawing above.)

Unusual Iris Shapes

Because the cut of slots in the two iris blades are not linear (as shown), unusual patterns can be formed as seen from the series of photographs of aperture openings. The subject of iris patterns and its effect on the resulting image is well documented in the literature on optical physics. Its significance here is the question of whether or not the possible unusual patterns yielded image artifacts. If the subject is not in focus, inversion, multiple images, etc. can and do occur. However, if the image is focused properly, the iris pattern makes no difference. The question presents itself: are Mr. Zapruder's images in focus? By examination they appear to be. Did an unusual pattern contribute to any of the artifacts seen? In my opinion, I doubt it.

Recognized Image Anomalies in the Zapruder Original Film

Image Penetration between the Perforations

The characteristics and depth of the image penetration are not always seen as the same but do follow a consistent and repeatable pattern. The pattern is directly related to the effective image area from the exit window of the Varamat lens, the focal length of lens and in some cases, the aperture setting. We can show and conclude that:

The telephoto lens setting consistently produces the maximum image penetration into the perforation area;

Normal lens focal length produces some but not full penetration into the perforation area; and

Wide-angle lens focal length produces the least penetration into the perforation area.

Claw Shadow

One of the image anomalies seen is a darker (higher density) band or wide bar in the image area between the perforations. This anomaly can be noted in the Zapruder frames as well as my practical test photos. This higher density (band or streak) can be explained as being caused by the shadow of the intermittent claw (and its supporting arm) as it moves upward over the film to engage the following perforation and pull down the next frame. The pull-down is with the shutter closed, but the upward movement of the claw out of the perforation, over the area between the perforations, into the next perforation hole is done while the shutter is open and the film is being exposed. The claw movement over the area between the perforations reduces the amount of light reaching the film causing more density. (Less light is more density on a reversal film.) The reduction in exposure to the area behind the claw is not linear. The claw functions with a shutter crank pin engaging the claw slot giving a sinusoidal time relationship to the pulldown ratchet re-entry action.

Claw or Aperture Flare

Claw flare appears to be a very real image anomaly often, but not always, seen adjacent to the dark bar caused by the claw shadow and the normal image area. In addition, when the 8mm image is viewed normal, the bottom of the upper perforation may show some flare-like density difference. It is this perforation that "sees" the bottom of the claw arm as it enters the perforation hole and pauses before beginning its rapid positioning stroke.

Multiple Exposure Areas—Perforation-Like Images

Within the perforation area, adjacent to a perforation above or below or both, an image occurs that resembles a perforation. The images simply represent multiple, i.e. double exposure of the area of the "excess" aperture cutout for the intermittent claw action. Above the upper and below the lower perforation hole, the excess aperture cutout allows an image to be formed concurrent with the primary image. When the succeeding image is formed it adds light to that previously formed causing multiple or double exposure. The shape that this image area takes, and importantly whether it exists at all, is directly dependent on the size of the exit window of the lens based on the chosen focal length together with the influence of scene content. Not all exposure conditions produce the phenomena; however, telephoto in bright lighting conditions does. With blank frames between some test target exposures, the phenomenon is visible and multiple exposures adjacent to the perforations are easily seen. (See photo below.)

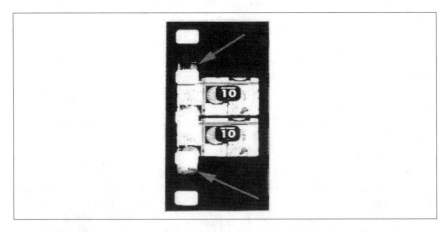

Ghost Images

In the Zapruder motorcade scene, below the perforation, one case see a white object heading toward a bystander in the primary image. This so-called ghost image has caused a lot of speculation and questions from many that examined the Zapruder film. Now, by our understanding of the multiple exposure around the perforations explained above, it is reasonable to conclude the cause as simple double exposure of a primary image superimposed on the excess image of the preceding frame. (See ghosting on test chart below.)

First Frame Over-Exposure

The first frame of the advance motorcade scene shows an over-exposure condition, known as "first-frame-overexposure." In my discussions with M. E. Brown, former Manager of the 16mm and 8mm Department at Eastman Kodak, the condition was undesirable and a development/design problem to be avoided, but a not uncommon occurrence.

Mr. Zapruder's camera appears to have been prone to the problem. The Secret Service copies of his family pictures show two other occurrences of first frame over exposure. With my test cameras, I had one, #3, that consistently had a noticeable first-frame over-exposure by about one-third of a stop. We were not given the opportunity to run a practical test with Zapruder's camera to determine if the first-frame artifact was a consistent problem or unique to the assassination film roll.

Conclusion

It is my conclusion that all the inter-perforation image anomalies identified can be explained by the design and image capture characteristics of the Bell & Howell 414PD Camera.

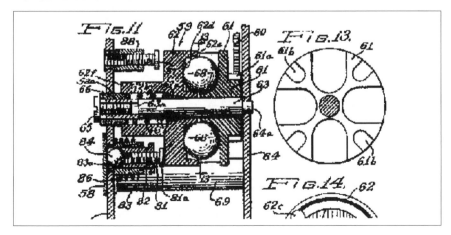

Appendix C

The NPIC Report:
The Zapruder Film
in November 1963

Douglas P. Horne

[*Editor's note*: In June and July of 1997, the ARRB interviewed two former CIA employees of the NPIC (National Photographic Interpretation Center), Homer McMahon and Bennett Hunter, who were involved in processing a movie of the death of JFK the weekend of the assassination. The Secret Service agent who couriered this film to the NPIC told them that the film was developed by Kodak at Rochester, NY, contrary to the existing documentary record, which indicates that the film and three copies were processed in Dallas, TX. David Healy has conjectured that this may be missing copy #0184 and that it may have been taken to Rochester as a negative and turned into a positive before being brought to the NPIC. (See the Preface.) This appendix is drawn from a chapter of *Murder in Dealey Plaza* (2000), where the complete document may be found.]

CALL REPORT: PUBLIC

Document's Author: Douglas Horne/ARRB   Date Created: 06/12/97

The Players
Who called whom?   Dave Montague and Douglas Horne called Homer A. McMahon of
Witnesses/Consultants

Description of the Call
Date: :.   06/12/97
Subject: **Dave Montague and Douglas Horne Called Homer A. McMahon (Modified on June
13, 1997)**

Summary of the Call:
[See Contact Profile for details on how this individual was located.]

Dave Montague located Mr. McMahon and initiated telephonic contact on June 9, 1997; I was invited to participate in the interview as the staff member most interested in, and most familiar with, the NPIC working notes of their analysis of the Zapruder film.

The following is a summary of the independent recollections of Mr. McMahon made during ARRB's cursory, initial assessment interview. Comments are not verbatim unless in quotations:

-He was the Head of NPIC's color lab in 1963. At that time NPIC was no longer in NW Washington above Steuart Motors (where it was during the Cuban Missile Crisis), but had relocated to BLDG 213 in the Washington Navy Yard, following a quick 90-day renovation of a warehouse with no windows directed by Robert Kennedy. McMahon was careful to clarify that he was an employee of NPIC in 1963, not the CIA, and that the CIA only "paid his salary."

-McMahon did recall the Zapruder film analysis in some detail, and confirmed ARRB's understanding that the analysis (of which frames in which shots struck occupants of the limousine) was performed at the request of the Secret Service. He recalled that a Secret Service agent named "Bill Smith" personally brought the film over to NPIC, and that the personnel involved in the analysis were himself (McMahon), Bill Smith of the USSS, and a third person whose name McMahon would not reveal to us during the interview "because he is still current."

-TIMING: McMahon thought that the analysis had occurred only "1 or 2 days" after the assassination; he also recalled that there was a great sense of urgency regarding the desired product, and that he had to "work all night long" to complete the required work (described below). At one point he said he thought he had gone into work about 1 A.M. to commence the analysis; later he corrected himself and said that perhaps it was more like 8 P.M., but that in any case he was sure that the work occurred after normal working hours, required him to return to work, and that the analysis went on all night long.

-McMahon never used the name Zapruder film during the interview; he repeatedly referred to the film in question as an "amateur movie" of the assassination brought to NPIC by the Secret Service.

-PROVENANCE OF THE FILM: McMahon stated that Secret Service agent Bill Smith claimed he had personally picked up the film from the amateur who had exposed it, had flown it to Rochester for developing, and had then couriered it to Washington, DC to NPIC for analysis and for the creation of photographic briefing boards, using still photographic prints enlarged from selected individual frames of the movie. After twice mentioning Rochester as the site where the film was developed, Dave Montague (in an attempt to specify whether McMahon was referring to R.I.T., or Kodak) asked whether he meant Kodak, and McMahon emphatically said "I mean Kodak at Rochester." I asked him how firm he was that this is what the Secret Service agent told him, and he said he was "absolutely certain."

-REASONS FOR ANALYSIS AT NPIC VICE ANOTHER LOCATION: McMahon said that USSS agent Bill Smith told him the reason the film had been couriered to NPIC was because NPIC had special, state-of-the-art enlarging equipment which Kodak did not have at Rochester. McMahon said that after the analysis of where shots occurred on the film was completed, many frames were selected ("perhaps as many as 40, but not more than about 40") for reproduction as photographic prints, and that NPIC's special "10-20-40 enlarger" was used to magnify each desired image frame "40 times its original size for the manufacture of internegatives." McMahon said that the internegatives were then used for the production of multiple color prints of each selected frame. He said that the color lab at NPIC where he worked did not prepare the actual briefing boards, but that he assumed the briefing boards were prepared somewhere else at NPIC, in some other department.

-In response to clarification questions by Horne, McMahon said that *at no time was the amateur movie copied as a motion picture film* ,and that the only photographic work done at NPIC was to make color prints. He could not remember whether the prints were 5" X 7" format, or 8" X 10" format.

-Horne asked whether he was working with the original film or a copy, and McMahon stated with some certainty that he was "sure we had the original film." Horne asked why, and he said that he was sure it was the original because it was Kodachrome, and because it was a "double 8" movie. Horne asked him to clarify whether the home movie was slit or unslit, and McMahon said that he was pretty sure the film was UNSLIT, because "we had to flip it over to see the image on the other side in the correct orientation." He said that the movie was placed in an optical printer, in which the selected frames were then magnified to 40 times their original size for the production of internegatives. He said a "liquid gate" process was used (on the home movie frames) to produce the internegatives.

-Prior to the production of internegatives and color prints for briefing boards, he said he recalled an analysis "to determine where the 3 shots hit." He said he would not share the results of the analysis with us on the telephone. The film was projected as a motion picture 4 or 5 times during the analysis phase, for purposes of determining "where the 3 shots hit."

-At this point Horne informed Mr. McMahon that CIA's HRG had deposited a surviving briefing board and the original working notes in the JFK Collection in 1993 for access by the public, and that they were not classified. Montague promised to send McMahon an information package explaining the JFK Act and the Review Board's mandate, and Horne and Montague asked Mr. McMahon is he would be willing to submit to a formal, in-depth, recorded interview at Archives II with the briefing board and the working notes available to him during the interview. He agreed.

-McMahon explained that the working notes were "prepared jointly by the 3 of us working on the project that night." END

CALL REPORT

Document's Author: Douglas Horne/ARRB   **Date Created:** 06/26/97

The Players

Who called whom?   Douglas Horne called Morgan Bennett Hunter (Ben Hunter) of CIA

Description of the Call

Date: 06/26/97
Subject: **Doug Horne Called Ben Hunter**

Summary of the Call:
   I spoke briefly with Ben Hunter to say that the July 2, 1997 interview of Mr. McMahon had been cancelled (at his--Ben Hunter's--request) and that Mr. McMahon had rejected the tentative rescheduled interview date of July 11 (for the same reason Hunter had been unavailable on July 2--vacation). I told him there was no scheduled date now for our interview with Homer McMahon, and that my instructions were to interview Homer McMahon as soon as practical, at a time convenient to Mr. McMahon. I told him that if he (Ben Hunter) was available at that time, we would include him; otherwise, we would schedule a second viewing of the briefing board panels for him subsequent to the McMahon interview.

   Following discussion of these logistical details, Mr. Hunter said that he had been thinking about the events at NPIC which he discussed with us, and wished to amend his previous comments as follows:
   -He said he now recalls that a Secret Service agent did deliver the materials to NPIC;
   -He said he now believes it was the Secret Service agent who said "don't discuss this with anyone, and if people persist in knowing what you were doing, refer them to Captain Sands;"
   -He said he now is fairly certain that Captain Sands was a high-ranking employee in NPIC's management structure, possibly the second or third highest ranking member of the organization. He does still recall that Sands was present during the NPIC event he discussed with us--the manufacture of internegatives and prints from selected frames of the Zapruder film.

   Mr. Hunter said that he still wants to talk with Homer McMahon, even if they cannot view the photographic briefing board panels together due to schedule conflicts. I told him this was fine, but that we wanted to interview Mr. McMahon first, and promised to pass McMahon's telephone number to him *after* ARRB had concluded its discussions with McMahon. END

PANEL I		PANEL II		PANEL III		PANEL IV	
Print No.	Frame No.	Print No.	Frame No.	Print No.	Frame No.	Print No.	Frame No.
1	188	7	225	15	266	21	310
2	198	8	226	16	274	22	311
3	206	9	230	17	289	23	312
4	213	10	239	18	290	24	313
5	217	11	242	19	291	25	314
6	222	12	246	20	292	26	322
		13	256			27	334
		14	257			28	384

(Undated) NPIC typed summary for preparing a "briefing board"

MEETING REPORT

Document's Author: Douglas Horne/ARRB   **Date Created:** 07/15/97

Meeting Logistics

Date: 07/14/97
Agecny Name: Witnesses/Consultants
Attendees: Homer McMahon, Jeremy Gunn, Doug Horne, Michelle Combs, and Marie
                     Fagnant
Topic: **ARRB Interviewed Homer McMahon**

Summary of the Meeting

ARRB staff followed up its June 9, 1997 telephonic initial assessment interview of Mr. McMahon with an in-depth, in-person interview at Archives II during which the original working notes from NPIC and a surviving photographic briefing board could be used as exhibits to test the recollections of the witness. The interview was audiotaped; therefore, this meeting report will only recount substantive highlights of the interview. (All statements which read as if they were "facts" are actually Mr. McMahon's recounting of events as he remembers them in 1997.)

Mr. McMahon was manager of the NPIC (National Photo Interpretation Center) color lab in 1963. About two days after the assassination of President Kennedy, but before the funeral took place, a Secret Service agent named "Bill Smith" delivered an amateur film of the assassination to NPIC and requested that color prints be made of frames believed associated with wounding ("frames in which shots occurred"), for purposes of assembling a briefing board. Mr. Smith did not explain who the briefing boards would be for, or who would be briefed. The only persons who witnessed this activity (which McMahon described as an "all night job") were USSS agent Smith, Homer McMahon, and Ben Hunter (McMahon's assistant). Although no materials produced were stamped with classification markings, Smith told McMahon that the subject matter was to be treated as "above top secret;" McMahon said that not even his supervisor was allowed to know what he had worked on, nor was his supervisor allowed to participate. Smith told McMahon that he had personally picked up the film (in an undeveloped condition from the man who exposed it) in Dallas, flown it to Rochester, N.Y. (where it was developed by Kodak), and then flown it down to NPIC in Washington so that enlargements of selected frames could be made on NPIC's state-of-the-art equipment.

After the film (either an unslit original or possibly a duplicate) was viewed more than once on a 16 mm projector in a briefing room at NPIC, the original (a double-8 mm unslit original) was placed in a 10X20X40 precision enlarger, and 5" X 7" format internegatives were made from selected frames. A full-immersion "wet-gate" or liquid gate process was used on the original film to reduce refractivity of the film and maximize the optical quality of the internegatives. Subsequently, three each 5" X 7" contact prints were made from the internegatives. He recalled that a minimum of 20, and a maximum of 40 frames were duplicated via internegatives and prints. All prints, internegatives, and scraps were turned over to Bill Smith at the conclusion of the work. Some working notes were created on a yellow legal pad, and they were turned over also. At the conclusion of the work, McMahon said he knew that briefing boards were going to be constructed at NPIC from the prints, but he did not participate in that, and did not know who did. McMahon stated definitively that at no point did NPIC reproduce the assassination movie (the Zapruder film) as a motion picture; all NPIC did was produce internegatives and color prints of selected still frames.

Although the process of selecting which frames depicted events surrounding the wounding of limousine occupants (Kennedy and Connally) was a "joint process," McMahon said his opinion, which was that President Kennedy was shot 6 to 8 times from at least three directions, was ultimately ignored, and the opinion of USSS agent Smith, that there were 3 shots from behind from the Book Depository, ultimately was employed in selecting frames in the movie for reproduction. At one point he said "you can't fight city hall," and then reminded us that his job was to produce internegatives and photographs, not to do analysis. He said that it was clear that the Secret Service agent had previously viewed the film and already had opinions about which frames depicted woundings.

At one point in the interview, Mr. McMahon described in some detail various health-related memory problems which he claims to suffer from. Details are on the tape.

Toward the end of the interview, McMahon was shown the NPIC working notes and the surviving briefing board (there are four panels), which are both in the JFK Collection in flat # 90A.

NPIC Working Notes: McMahon recognized the half-sized sheet of yellow legal paper containing a handwritten description of briefing board panel contents, and on its reverse side containing a description of the work performed that night and how long each step took, as being written in his own handwriting (and partially in Ben Hunter's). He said that three other full-length yellow legal pad pages of notes (containing three possible 3-shot scenarios, a 16 FPS and 18 FPS timing analysis, and additional timing computations) were not in his handwriting, and were not made by him or previously seen by him.

Briefing Board Panels (4): McMahon looked at the 28 photographs on all four briefing board panels, and said that he had made all of them; he also said that some were missing. I asked him which types of images that he had produced he thought were missing, and he said he thought motorcade images from prior to frame 188 (i.e., earlier in the motorcade, before the limousine disappeared behind the roadsign) were the photographs he produced which were not on the briefing board panels. He said it looked to him like the prints he had produced had been trimmed, i.e., made smaller. END

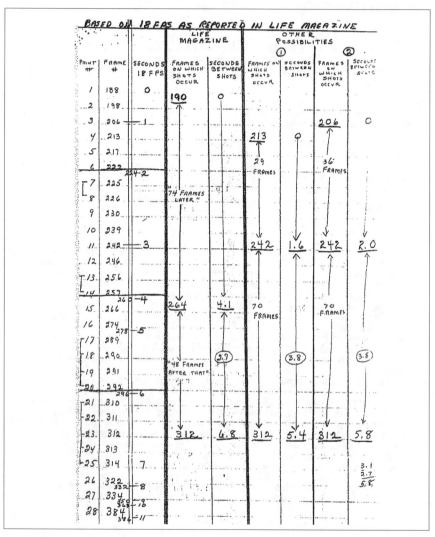

(Undated) NPIC working notes related to a shot sequence analysis published in Life.

Appendix D

The Twyman Chronology

DATE/TIME	EVENT	REFERENCE/SOURCE
November 22, 1963 12:30 p.m.	Abraham Zapruder films assassination; returns to his office in state of shock.	
November 22, 1963 about 2:00 p.m.	Secret Service agent Forrest Sorrels meets with Zapruder and requests copies of film.	W.C. Vol. VII, p. 352, testimony of Sorrels. No mention of Jamison Film.
November 22, 1963 12:30 p.m. to 9 p.m., approx.	Dallas police arrive at Zapruder's office with shotguns. Zapruder refuses to give film to police; insists on government representative. Forrest Sorrels arrives at Zapruder's office. Four film positives developed at Eastman Kodak after three reversal duplicates developed at Jamison Film Company, using Kodachrome II camera stock furnished to Jamison by Eastman Kodak.*	Interview of Swartz by Richard Bartholomew and Noel Twyman, 11/21/94 in Dallas; interview with Bruce Jamison 12/26/94.
November 22, 1963 about 10 p.m.	Zapruder and Swartz deliver one copy of the film to Secret Service office in Dallas with understanding that it was to be sent immediately to FBI headquarters in Washington, D.C., by courier jet plane.	Interview with Swartz, 11/21/94 in Dallas; also Richard B. Stolley in *Esquire*, 11/1/73, cited by Shackelford.
November 22, 1963 (evening)	H. L. Hunt purchases "first copy" of film through his security guard, Paul Rothermel, Jr.	Russell, p. 581 (interview of Rothermel).
November 22, 1963 midnight	Richard B. Stolley of *Life* magazine contacts Zapruder; asks to meet to view film; Zapruder agrees to meet at 9 a.m. Saturday.	*Columbia*; Richard B. Stolley Essays, Oct. 1988, pp. 54-58; confirmed by Erwin Swartz 11/21/94 interview.
November 23, 1963	One copy of film obtained by Secret Service inspector Thomas Kelley from Sorrels. Kelley then loaned it to the FBI on November 27. It was returned to the Secret Service office in Dallas on December 4, 1963, where it was retained.	Shackelford citing memo of Sorrels to Thomas J. Kelley; and National Archives document released 6/12/94.
November 23, 1963 8 a.m.	Stolley meets with Zapruder one hour early to view film, along with Secret Service agents.	*Columbia*; Richard B. Stolley Essays, Oct. 1988, pp. 54-58.

*Bruce Jamison told me that the three copies were made using the contact printing process, and that all of the information from the original would be exactly duplicated on the copies, including edge images and film stock symbols. Unless unique optical and film editing techniques were used, the only way in which the original would differ from the copies

DATE/TIME	EVENT	REFERENCE/SOURCE
November 23, 1963 10 a.m.	Stolley negotiates with Zapruder to purchase print rights to film for $50,000. Zapruder turns "original" over to Stolley for *Life* magazine.* (*Life* later purchases all rights for a total of $150,000.)	Richard B. Stolley in *Esquire*; cited by Martin Shackelford 7/12/93.
November 23, 1963 3:00 p.m.	"Original" sent by courier to *Life*'s Chicago office where it is studied on a Moviola projector. Ten black-and-white prints made. *Note:* Shackelford cites Richard Stolley in *Esquire* that Stolley took Zapruder's original *and* a copy when he left Zapruder's office at 10 a.m. on November 23.	Loudon Wainright, 1/1/86 cited by Martin Shackelford, 7/12/93; also Richard Stolley in *Columbia*, Oct. 1988, p. 57, *Four Days in Dallas.*
November 24, 1963 9:00 to 9:30 a.m.	While "original" was in Chicago, duplicate was shown to Time-Life executives in New York including C.D. Jackson, *Life*'s publisher (ex-CIA, friend of Allen Dulles and contact with CIA). Jackson was "so upset" by head wound sequence that he proposed all rights be purchased from Zapruder and withheld from public viewing.	Richard Stolley in *Esquire* 11/1/73, cited by Martin Shackelford 7/12/93; also Loudon Wainright, 1/1/86.
November 29, 1963	*Life* publishes issue showing selected frames from Zapruder film. Not shown were any of the frames in the segments under question in this book (frames 302, 303, 315, 316, 317).	
September 1964	Warren Commission publishes its report, showing all frames from 171 to 334,** but in poor black-and-white quality; very difficult to see rapid head turns or detect frame removal at 302, 303, 315, 316, 317.	
October 2, 1964	*Life* publishes issue showing fatal head shot, but again not showing frames 302, 303, 315, 316, 317.	

would be in the film stock I.D. printings on the film edge: the copies would almost certainly have two sets of I.D. printings—the original printings and the printings of the camera stock used to make the reversal duplicates. This undoubtedly gave the forgers grave problems in preserving the original printing. Dr. David Mantik is researching this aspect. His work is scheduled to be published in 1997 in a new book, *Assassination Science: Experts Speak Out on the Death of JFK*, ed. James H. Fetzer.

*Erwin Swartz disagrees with Stolley here. In a 11/21/94 interview, Swartz said he personally delivered the original to Stolley at the Adolphus Hotel in Dallas on either November 26 or 27. Stolley may have been given a copy on November 23 and then the original on November 26 or 27, although Swartz does not remember Stolley getting a copy on November 23.

**Not shown in the September 1964 issue were frames missing while the limousine was behind the freeway sign, explained as an inadvertent break in the film while handling by *Life* lab technicians.

Exhibit 12-2A. Chain of Possession of the Zapruder Film—Key Events.

Noel Twyman, Bloody Treason *(1997) pp. 134–135*

Appendix E

The DellaRosa Report

Rich DellaRosa

[*Editor's note*: Rich DellaRosa moderates the *JFKresearch.com* forum, which has been the most productive of the Internet groups by a considerable margin. New research finds its way to this forum with surprising regularity and few discoveries appear elsewhere without first undergoing critical scrutiny there. Rich is one of two persons I know who have seen another and more complete film of the assassination in Dealey Plaza, which cannot be "the Zapruder film", as we have discovered, but which tells us a great deal about why evidence of Secret Service complicity had to be removed and a cover film created. He sent this to me on 27 April 2003 shortly before the second Zapruder Film Conference.]

Within the JFK research community on the Internet, there are some half dozen of us who have seen a different film of the assassination. Each of us has viewed it independent of the others. I have described it in a post that appears [on another page] of the message archives. However, I will repost it here at the conclusion of this post.

To those who reject the possibility of another film having been taken, or those whose sensibilities are offended by the suggestion of the Z film having been altered, I wish to reiterate that I am not in doubt about what I saw—and I saw it on three occasions.

Also I wish to definitively state that I am not lying about it. I have no reason to lie or be less than truthful. I have nothing to profit from talking about it—I am not charging lecture fees, I am not peddling any books. If anyone chooses not to believe any of us, I don't give a damn.

Various researchers have stated, intimated, whispered or accused us of either (1) being confused about what we saw or (2) are lying for some reason. To them I say, "Think what you like, I care not." Ironic that for many years I was terribly apprehensive about telling anyone what I saw because it was painfully apparent that the film in question is one which accurately depicts the assassination (the extant Z film does not) and is one which the powers behind the assassination and cover-up do not want us to see.

Do not request me to produce the film. If I could, I would do so gladly and willingly if for no other reason than to prove the doubters wrong. Here, then, is a repost of my previous message.

Repost

Someone asked me to repost my description of the other film. Here goes, for the umpteenth time.

I viewed the other film on three occasions: once in 1974, again in 1976, and once in the 1990s. In 1974 and 1976 I was a part-time student at the University of Maryland at College Park, while I was still in the US Air Force stationed at Andrews Air Force Base. I'm not disclosing the details of the third occasion for the time being.

The film was, as best I can recall, 16 mm. As I mentioned in another post, the first occasion pre-dates the showing of the extant film on "Goodnight America" by Robert Groden and Geraldo Rivera. As such, I had nothing to compare the film to—but the details were so graphic, they remained with me from then on.

By the second occasion, I had seen the Z film on TV but only on that one occasion. I felt they were not the same but I could not be more specific. One thing was certain: the quality of the other film was much better than what was shown on TV.

By the third occasion I had viewed the extant film many, many times and had it on CD ROM and had virtually memorized every frame. When I then saw the other film, the differences just seemed to jump out at me. I simultaneously realized that I had seen the other film before AND that it was not the Zapruder film.

Here is what I remember from viewing the other film:

- the film shows the limo making the turn onto Elm Street (in other words, there is no [gap] in the film betwen the initial motorcycles and the limo).

- the limo had difficulty making the turn. Greer swung wide and had some difficulty regaining control. As such, the limo was in the curb lane at the top of Elm, and gradually moved toward the center as it continued. If you look closely at the extant Z film, you can see evidence of this.

- just prior to the headshot(s) the limo stops (not slows but stops)—the occupants of the limo are jostled as the car comes to a sudden stop. In my opinion. JFK was hit in the head by a shot from the rear. Bill Greer turns around and looks directly at JFK. Just as he does, the exploding headshot occurs as if on cue—clearly fired from the front, with blood and brain matter splattering to the left rear—very graphic. Greer then turns back around and the limo lurches forward. The stop lasted maybe three or four seconds. (I believe that Greer stopped the limo in response to a signal being given from someone along the curb.)

- the limo rapidly accelerates as it approaches the underpass. The lead car appears as an obstacle and eventually pulls over allowing the limo to pass it.

I have always believed that the camera angle was similar, but not identical, to Zapruder's, causing me to conclude that the other film was taken by someone else, perhaps a concealed cameramn using high quality 16 mm equipment. The photo that Ed O'Hagan posted with the red dot showing the placement of a camera and tripod is very significant because it is in a position that I would have chosen as the position of the concealed cameraman. [*Editor's note*: That position lies within the pergola and may be seen in the photos displayed as Figure 31 and Figure 32 of John Costella's first chapter.]

That concludes my recollections of the other film.

But what about Zapruder?

In short, I believe that Zapruder was a paid decoy. What could cause a man who claimed to have a bad case of vertigo to climb up on that pedestal? Answer: $$$$$$$$$

Zappy was a personal friend of H. L. Hunt (very likely the person who commissioned the other film). Zappy was born a White Russian—aka anti-communist. His buddy H. L. believed that JFK was a communist—perhaps Zappy agreed.

Zappy bought himself a new Bell & Howell movie camera just prior to the assassination.

Zappy immediately sought to profit from his film—selling it to *Life* magazine in less than 24 hours for $150,000 but announcing that he only received $25,000, which he donated away.

Although his employee described him as being distraught and hysterical after the shooting, he appeared at the WFAA TV studios shortly after, appeared on camera and was quite calm and collected.

Why was a decoy needed? In short, to distract attention from the presence of the concealed cameraman. If anyone were asked if they had seen anyone taking a movie of the motorcade, they would absolutely remember Zapruder—being very conspicuously perched on his pedestal doing the waltz with Marilyn Sitzman. That being so, there would be no desire to look any further—we know because it has worked for over 30 years.

Did Zapruder actually shoot a movie? I believe he did. And I believe that it was sold to Time-Life, and that it was edited, altered, rotoscoped, screwed, blewed, and tatooed by any number of public and private entities, and then dangled in front of the public when the time was deemed right, both to quell the rising demands of researchers and to assist those who had seen the other film into forgetting what they saw.

Believe it or not.

Someone travelled to Mexico City from 26 September to 3 October 1963 posing as Lee Oswald, as Robert Groden, The Search for Lee Harvey Oswald *(1995), has explained. This person visited the Cuban Embassy attempting to obtain a visa to visit Cuba. The CIA took many surveillance photographs of the man calling himself "Lee Harvey Oswald", one of which was provided to the Warren Commission. That someone was impersonating Lee Oswald in Mexico City provides very strong evidence that he was being set up as the patsy.*

Appendix F

The Thompson AARB
Statement

Josiah Thompson, Ph.D.

[*Editor's note*: There are several interesting aspects to Josiah Thompson's statement to the ARRB. The most important concerns the central role he attributes to the film on his presumption that it is authentic, which I have discussed in the Preface. Beyond that, he describes himself as having stolen a copy of the film from Time-Life, his employer at the time. *Life* filed a suit against him for using sketches of frames in *Six Seconds in Dallas* (1967). We agree on at least one point: not a penny should have been paid for the film.]

Before the ARRB, 2 April 1997

13   Next, we will hear from Mr. Josiah Thompson,
14 who is an author, one of the early authors of a widely
15 read book on the assassination, "Six Seconds in
16 Dallas," I believe.
17   Mr. Thompson, thank you for joining us today.
18   STATEMENT OF JOSIAH THOMPSON
19   MR. THOMPSON: Thank you, Mr. Chairman, Dr.
20 Marwell, distinguished members of the panel. I do not
21 have a prepared statement but sitting here, I have had
22 a few thoughts, on two basic points. One concerns the

61

1 anomalies concerning this film in private hands, which
2 I had much experience of in the 1960s and '70s. And
3 secondly, a question that was just asked, what is the
4 central, enormous research importance of this film. I
5 could and will give you some reasons for the centrality
6 of the film.
7   Friday afternoon, November 22nd, and Forrest
8 Sorrels is in Abraham Zapruder's office. Abraham
9 Zapruder gets his camera out of the safe. Had Forrest
10 Sorrels said, "Mr. Zapruder, I am taking that camera

11 and that film as evidence in this homicide," we might
12 still be here today, but we wouldn't be here with this
13 particular problem.
14   Forrest Sorrels did not do that. I think he
15 made a mistake. And because he did not do that, in
16 August of 1966, when I came to this very building and
17 saw the Zapruder film for the first time, what I was
18 permitted to see was a copy of a Secret Service copy.
19 In the summer of 1966, that was the only way any
20 ordinary citizen in this country could see a copy of
21 the Zapruder film, coming to the Archives, registering,
22 and having Marian Johnson screen a copy of a copy. I

62

1   did that. It was a miserable copy, a miserable copy.
2   I had heard through the grapevine that *Life*'s
3   original, and *Life*'s copies made from that original,
4   4-by-5 transparencies, were remarkably clear. Through
5   brute luck, two months later I ended up being hired to
6   co-direct Life Magazine's assassination investigation
7   and was permitted to see copies made from the original
8   4-by-5 transparencies made from the original.
9   Everything I had been told was correct, they
10 were remarkably clear. One could see the hit on
11 Connally, which was completely unclear on the copy in
12 the Archives. Dallas, November 1966. We have 4-by-5
13 transparencies. The *Life* team is made up of three or
14 four members. One of those members ends up either
15 stealing or destroying four of those frames, very, very
16 important frames. As a young professor of philosophy,
17 I had not a clue what was going on, but I knew
18 something was going on.
19   So three weeks later, I snuck a camera into
20 the Time-Life building and made a copy of the Zapruder
21 film against specific orders of my employer, *Life*
22 Magazine. I did that for two reasons. The film was in

63

1   private hands and private custody. I figured, I had no
2   idea what was going on at *Life* Magazine, figured it was
3   a power struggle of some sort and thought for posterity
4   it would be very useful to have a copy outside those
5   private hands.
6   In addition, I wanted to make certain
7   measurements on the film concerning the movement of the
8   President's head, measurements that were finally

9   published in "Six Seconds," which would give some
10 notion as to whether impressed forces on the President
11 at the time of the head shot could be interpreted as
12 either one shot or two shots. I was not permitted to
13 take the film out of the building, hence, to do that I
14 had to make a copy, I had to steal a copy.
15   The following June, we made an offer to Time,
16 Inc., my publisher and I made an offer, which was we
17 would turn over all commercial interests in the book to
18 Time, Inc., in exchange for the right to use selected
19 parts of certain Zapruder frames. We were turned down
20 flat, and on advice of counsel went forward and
21 published artists' renderings. We were sued. I lost
22 all of the earnings of the book. But we won.

64

1   Judge Enzer B. Wyatt of the Southern District
2   ruled in a summary judgment that we had used the film
3   as a fair use. That particular judgment mentioned by
4   Jim Lesar was in fact an enormously important expansion
5   of the doctrine of fair use where First Amendment
6   privilege is involved.
7   That is the way things stood. In other
8   words, what I am trying to explain here is that with
9   the film in private hands, all sorts of anomalies
10 occurred. The necessity of me trying to act for the
11 public good to steal a copy of the film, which is a
12 rather extraordinary event.
13   Why is this film important? It is enormously
14 important. If you want to know what happened in Dealey
15 Plaza, this film shows you, as much as any film can.
16 How could it be used by the research community? Well,
17 there have been certain quibbles about the authenticity
18 of this film. I have no doubt that it is authentic,
19 but that can be proven, that can be shown. All queries
20 and challenges to the authenticity, if this film is in
21 government hands, remains in government hands, can be
22 satisfactorily overcome. When that is done, this film

65

1   then becomes a baseline for all additional studies for
2   what happened in Dealey Plaza.
3   For example, the medical evidence. There
4   have been many claims of extra autopsies, faking of
5   autopsy photos, et cetera, et cetera. If the medical
6   evidence does not match what you see on the Zapruder

7   film, then you might have cause to challenge that sort
8   of evidence. Evidence of other films could be compared
9   against this film as a baseline. If they match, fine.
10 If they don't match, you know something is wrong. Much
11 more importantly, of course, is the deduction of
12 trajectories and ultimately, firing points, which can
13 only be done by great precision by using the most
14 resolved copy of the film available.
15   All of that can be done only if this film
16 remains in government hands. In 1964, J. Edgar Hoover
17 said this case would be forever open. In 1977-78, the
18 House committee judged that a conspiracy was involved
19 in the Kennedy assassination, was, in fact, probable.
20 We now know that the case really is still open at this
21 time, and as Jim Lesar pointed out, there may be a
22 federal prosecution in the future. For all those

66

1   reasons, this central evidence in the case should
2   remain in government hands, as it is now, and the legal
3   arguments, I think, that Mr. Lesar and the professor
4   offered should sustain you in your judgment to take the
5   film.
6   JUDGE TUNHEIM: Thank you Mr. Thompson. Are
7   there questions from the board?
8   I have a question for you. In terms of the
9   future needs and uses of this film by researchers, do
10 you think that copies made now, particularly copies
11 that might be — the complete frame, including the
12 sprocket, copies that are digitalized, do you think
13 that serves the same purpose for the sake of
14 researchers who are examining this film, assuming you
15 that can guarantee that they do come from the original?
16   MR. THOMPSON: Yes, I don't think any
17 researchers should be fiddling around with the
18 original. I think there should be a protocol
19 established as for how a digitized copy is made with
20 the state of the art equipment, state of the art
21 techniques, state of the art algorithms, et cetera.
22 That digitized copy, which is then fully authenticated,

67

1   should then be the basis of all research in the future.
2   The original would simply be held as a kind of
3   reference mark that would continually be available to
4   justify the copy as a foundational copy.

5   MR. GRAFF: You seem to water down a little
6   bit in your last statement — I realize that you don't
7   have a piece of paper in front of you — the importance
8   of holding on to the original. Suppose you had a team
9   saying this is an accurate, true copy of the original.
10   Why would the possession of the original by the
11   government be essential?
12   MR. THOMPSON: Well, because we don't know
13   whether the techniques that we use tomorrow and the
14   protocols and algorithms we would use tomorrow to make
15   the most highly resolved copy we could make, we don't
16   know that five years from now we can't do better or ten
17   years from now we can't do better.
18   JUDGE TUNHEIM: With respect to the question
19   that Dr. Hall asked Mr. Lesar, is there a ceiling on
20   the amount that the taxpayers should pay for this film,
21   in your view?
22   MR. THOMPSON: I don't think the taxpayers

68

1   should pay a penny for this film. I should add that
2   the figure $150,000 that the Zapruder family received
3   from *Life* Magazine, I know from working at *Life*, did
4   not include the licensing rights. *Life* then sold the
5   Zapruder film to Der Stern, Paris Match, et cetera, et
6   cetera. The Zapruder family also had an interest in
7   those licensing rights. So, I have no idea whether Jim
8   Lesar's estimate as under a million dollars is
9   accurate. In my opinion, it could run as far as 3 to
10   $5 million at this point.
11   JUDGE TUNHEIM: Thank you very much, Mr.
12   Thompson. We appreciate your joining us today.

When the Warren Commission reenacted events in Dealey Plaza, it employed the simple expedient of using the Secret Service Cadillac in lieu of the Presidential Lincoln limousine, fabricating evidence and depriving it of forensic significance.

Appendix G

The Mack ARRB Statement

Gary Mack

[*Editor's note*: About a year before he became the Archivist for The Sixth Floor Museum, Gary Mack made an eloquent presentation to the ARRB. He suggested at least eight lines of inquiry for the ARRB to pursue, including securing transcripts of Secret Service radio transmissions; KLIF radio station broadcast recordings; enhancements of the Moorman photograph; a series of photographs taken by one Cap Field; Army Signal Corps photographs of the autopsy; recordings made over the Dallas Police Department radio channels; a series of still photographs taken by Carl Dockery, M.D.; and of multiple confessions. Unlike "Death in Dealey Plaza", his performance in this instance reveals rather than conceals many potentially valuable lines of research. (See the Epilogue.)]

Before the AARB, 18 November 1994

MR. MARWELL: The next witness will be Gary Mack.

CHAIRMAN TUNHEIM: Good morning, Mr. Mack.

MR. MACK: Good morning.

I trust you have a copy of the letter that I sent. The areas that I have worked on since the mid-1970s are primarily media and photographs, and I have run across some things that I have yet to find answers for, and I listed some of them here.

The first one I want to ask you about and urge you to poke around as much as you can, recordings of the Secret Service radio channels in the motorcade. There were at least two, perhaps three. There is a reference, and I am sorry I don't recall exactly where, but there is a reference that the Dallas Police broadcasts were also monitored by the Secret Service. They had a center set up at the Adolphus Hotel. It was then fed back to Air Force One out at Love Field and then monitored back in Washington.

Those recordings have never surfaced. There is an indication in the testimony from one of the Secret Service agents in the Kennedy car that he had referred to a transcript. Well, a transcript tells me that there must have been a recording somewhere. So I would urge you to check with the Signal Corps or its successor agency or agencies to find out what happened to those transcripts and recordings.

471

One of the reasons I suggest that is, the agent in question, Agent Kellerman, testified that he had his microphone on when the final shot or shots were fired. It would be theoretically another recording of at least part of the shooting.

Number two on my list first came to my attention in Mark Lane's book *Rush To Judgment* in the mid-'60s where he quoted Joe Long of KLIF radio, one of the most popular stations in Dallas at that time, and Joe said that the Secret Service confiscated some of their recordings and never returned them. I have confirmed that with several personnel at other stations that recall in the weeks immediately following the assassination numerous visits by Secret Service agents who asked for specific things, and in those days the material, films, audiotapes and videotapes were turned over without receipts, and the recollection of the people in charge is that not everything they loaned to the Secret Service was returned. To my knowledge, there is no specific listing of material, and I think that should be pursued.

When a film of Robert Oswald meeting with his brother Lee Harvey Oswald in custody is known to have been shot and has never surfaced that concerns me. There is no indication that it was a sound film, but the fact that a film like that could vanish is very troubling to me.

Number three on the list, attempts to conduct photo enhancements and blowups of one or more amateur photographs shot by witness Mary Moorman, despite some of the accounts that have appeared in print, at the end of the day Mary Moorman went home with her photographs. They were not confiscated from her, but they were borrowed while she was being questioned the day of the assassination.

In the following months, she loaned the picture to the FBI at least four times. She retained signed receipts for those. She did get a letter to appear before the Warren Commission. She asked for a delay. She had twisted her ankle and could barely walk, and the Warren Commission indicated that they would recontact her and she never heard from them again. So that is the only reason she did not testify.

But she did loan her picture to the FBI and they had told her it was for the Warren Commission and for their investigation. There is nothing in the record that indicates that the FBI or Warren Commission ever did anything with her picture of the assassination. It is the only one known to exist that shows the Grassy Knoll at the time of the head shot, and it is astounding to me that a photograph like that could exist, was known to exist within minutes of the assassination, and yet there is no official interest in that photograph as far as the available documentation shows.

We do have reports of other films and photographs that drew some interest right away, but not this one, and her recollection is, and it is support by a friend of hers named Jean Hill, their recollection is that at some point in the days or weeks following, they were exhibited a giant blowup of one of the other pictures she took in the sequence, and this picture was of the School Book Depository moments before the assassination, and they were looking at windows and trying to see if there were any figures in the windows. Their memory is that they never did see anything, but that tells me that there was official interest, at least, on the part of the Secret Service, that they did some work on one or more of those pictures, and the record is blank. I know of no such documentation and it must be somewhere.

Number four, Secret Service or FBI efforts to locate Cap Field who may have photographed the assassination. That name came from a document that was released in the late '70s, and I tried to follow up on that at that time, contacting the college up in Denton, North Texas State University, and we went through records and just could not find any reference to this guy named Cap Field. There is just no way to tell where that trail went, but there is one document indicating that Cap Field may have taken one or more pictures that day.

Number five, Army or Signal Corps motion pictures of the JFK autopsy at Bethesda. I am not an expert in this area, but I have been told by a person that was familiar with the Bethesda room that there were mountings for a motion picture camera. It was a teaching institution, at least that room was, and a standard autopsy procedure would certainly include an audio recording of the comments, and I have never seen any reference to either one of those, and I would think that somewhere there have to be some recordings of what exactly was said, and I think pun intended that would certainly be the best evidence about what they observed in Washington.

Number six, broadcast recordings of the Dallas Police radio channels. Several radio stations in Dallas at the time did monitor the police broadcasts. Whether they recorded them or not, I have not been able to determine. Without getting into any great detail on the acoustics evidence, it is the belief of Dr. Barger who did the work for the House Assassinations Committee that those Dictabelts in evidence are not the originals, and it is the one mistake he admits to. He says that he has told me and he has told others that when the House Committee showed him those dictabelts they said these are the originals and they did not question that.

After the controversy arose, his studies indicated that they have two hum tones and that tells him that they are not the originals. This was a theory of mine that I followed as closely as possible without being a scientist. Dr. Barger, I believe, is an honest, decent man, and he stands by his work. His basic observation that was ignored by the National Academy of Sciences study is that the Dallas Police radio system at the time was an FM system.

When I called Dr. Louis Alvarez, who was the one on the National Academy of Sciences panel most involved with this, I asked him, was it an AM system or an FM system? He said, well, it was AM, they were all AM in those days. I said, I am sorry, it was an FM system. It was a relatively new system, how would that affect your findings? He said, Gary, if that is true, we would have to start all over again. He asked me if I could document that, I cannot. The paperwork is gone, but I do know the names and phone numbers of some of the City of Dallas radio engineers who designed the system and installed it and maintained it.

The acoustics issue, despite the difficulties, is far from a dead issue. It needs to be pursued because, as far as I am concerned, while it is great that everybody is releasing documents, and what you are doing has truly great value, at the end of all this work, your documents are going to give us bits and pieces of information, but I just am not convinced that it is going to solve the crime. I don't think it is going to tell us whether there was or was not a conspiracy to kill the President, but the acoustics evidence can certainly do that.

The other element about the acoustics evidence is that one area where Warren Commission member David Belin and House Committee Staff Counsel Bob Blakey agree is that the acoustics evidence should be pursued. In other words, the same analysis that was applied to the Grassy Knoll shot should be applied to the other three shots. If you trace the source of those shots, just like the Grassy Knoll shot, either it is going to lead to that window or it is going to lead to some illogical place, and that would be the way to settle this issue. It would be a real shame if the acoustics thing was just left hanging because it is one of the very few pieces of hard evidence left.

Number seven, numerous still photographs of the Oswald emergency work shot by Dr. Carl Dockery. I first learned about Dockery's pictures from Mike Coleto's book *The Oswald File*, and I called Dockery and he confirmed it. His memory was that he had his camera with him. He shot an entire roll of film documenting what the autopsy surgeons or what the doctors were doing. He ran out of film and he borrowed a camera from someone out in the hallway, apparently a news photographer, and he has something like six or seven rolls of film with him. As best Dockery could remember, he shot a good 150 photographs.

I have no idea where those are. He has never seen them. They were confiscated by Parkland security and ultimately went to, I believe it was J.C. Price, and I made that phone call, either to him or one other person, and they claimed they did not recall that. So, again, these may be in FBI files. There is an FBI document indicating they were aware of this. I don't know that there is anything of any significance as far as changing history, but I think it is proper to document it, and they are certain there were no other photographs taken in the Oswald emergency work.

Finally, number eight, the numerous confessions in recent years by people who claim to have been involved with some aspect of the assassination. This has been a very frustrating area for me in that I have spent a lot of time working on legitimate issues in this case, as have many other researchers. Since 1990, I have found that I have spent an awful lot of time trying to correct the historical record with some of these phony stories that are coming out, and without going through a list or maybe I could provide you a list sometime in the future, the most significant story in recent years was Ricky White, the Rosco White story. That story and I could give you a stack of stuff this big, a friend and I have spent hundreds and hundreds of hours on this thing. It is a complete fabrication. It is my personal belief that everybody involved with that story knew it.

I will give you an example. A few days after the 6 August 1990, news conference, a friend of mine noticed a document in the office of Bud Fensterwald, who was the head of the Assassination Archives Records Center in Washington. Fensterwald had a report on his desk, an interview that had been conducted by Kevin Walsh with a man named Philip Jordan. Philip Jordan was the mysterious Mr. X who Ricky White kept referring to. Philip Jordan was in a position to know whether that story was true or not, and what he told Kevin Walsh was the story was not true. Yet Fensterwald and others stood by as Ricky White claimed that his father killed Kennedy. It is just absolutely outrageous to me that these kind of things go on.

I am not sure there can be legislation to prevent it, but if that is part of your work, I would very, very highly, strongly urge you to come up with some legislation that would provide some criminal penalties for these people who come up with these phony stories.

I was on a museum retreat for the past week-and-a-half down in South Texas, and I got a call from one of the Fox stations with another one. Now we have four gunmen up in the Book Depository. It is just—it is never ending. These people get attorneys to find out whether they are going to be in trouble so they know exactly what they should or should not say, and it is just mind-boggling.

On the one hand, those of us who research this case and who are amateurs, don't have any formal training in this, we tend to think outside the borders, which I think overall is good for this case because we are not locked into a certain way of studying something. But, on the other hand, there are some profiteers and others who like the limelight, and that kind of thing. It is just mind-boggling what is going on in the research community when these stories come out.

And those of us who know how to research and know how to look things up and know how to ask questions, when we look into this and say, you have serious problems with this story, we are then painted as disinformation agents. Some of these people, and I don't wish to cast the research community with such a wide brush, but they want to seek the truth but you had better find the right truth or you are in trouble. Well, I am not locked into those people, and I wanted to at least offer my assistance with some of these phony stories because you will have a lot of work before you, and I would hate to see you get derailed with stuff that leads nowhere.

I think I will leave it at that, and I will follow this up with a written.

CHAIRMAN TUNHEIM: Thank you, Mr. Mack.

Any questions?

MR. MARWELL: It would be helpful in your written submission if you give us some details on the issues that you have mentioned today.

MR. MACK: Absolutely. I would be happy to.

CHAIRMAN TUNHEIM: Mr. Mack, the reference to Cap Field that you mentioned in your number four, is that in an FBI record that you saw the name?

MR. MACK: Yes, it was, and I believe it was in one of the documents that was released along with, and it might be the same one, that came out in late '77/early '78 that identified Charles Bronson as having taken a film of the assassination. That document went to Earl Golz of the *Dallas Morning News*. Earl found Mr. Bronson, but Cap Field, and my memory is Cap Field is on that list, and that is the only documentation.

What I have found living here and talking with people is that there are a lot of people in the Dallas area who, for one reason or another, just would prefer not to come forward. I learned a story just a few weeks ago. A retired Kodak executive remembered that while they were processing Abraham Zapruder's film out in the Dallas office out by Love Field, that a woman had come in, and this was a woman in her late 30s, a brunette, who had taken a picture at the assassination scene, and her picture was the first one out of the processor, and they were working on this because it was quicker to do stills than it was moving film.

He didn't catch her name, but he stood next to her while she was explaining her story to some of the Federal investigators who were already there. She was running from Main Street up to Elm Street across the grass, realized she wasn't going to get there close enough, stopped and took a picture. In the foreground were some people standing on the south curb of Elm Street. The Kennedy limousine was directly behind them, directly behind the limousine was the Book Depository Building. When the picture came out of the processor, the first thing they noticed was the exposure was terrific but the focus was way, way off. It was virtually useless, and she was told that. Well, she apparently went home and whether anyone even got her name or that is unknown.

If this story is true, and I have no reason to doubt it, the man—we sought him out, he did not seek us out, today if we can locate that slide, and this is a color slide, computer enhancement can return it literally to almost the best clarity you could have had at the time. Of course, back in those days nothing like that existed. The Kodak executive's name is Jack Harrison. Jack said they were pushing the technicians very hard to do whatever you can to sharpen this picture and approve it, and they just said, hey, there is nothing we can do.

So here is a woman with a potentially important photograph, a still photograph. What is especially interesting to me is that from the description of her position, what the picture showed, she may very well be the real Babushka Lady.

That is an area in the research community that is very controversial at this point, and without going into any great detail, I do not believe that Beverly

Oliver is the Babushka Lady, or, let me rephrase that, she certainly could be but the rest of the story is a fabrication. That is my personal belief based on the work I have done.

What has happened, though, apparently, is the story from Jack Harrison that this woman existed, she has a photograph that could have some important answers. It is probably sitting in a shoe box somewhere in her closet and she has no idea, and how do you find a woman like that. How do you get people to come forward. Maybe your work will do that.

DR. HALL: Mr. Chairman, I have a question for Mr. Mack.

Do you have any knowledge, Mr. Mack, given the time and effort you have put in to this enterprise of any former public officials who took with them materials related to the assassination that are now held in private hands that would otherwise be deemed public documents?

MR. MACK: I have to think. It seems to me, yes. I don't know of any original materials, if that is what you are asking. Several police officers kept copies of things, mostly photographs. I don't know of any original material, but I would have to think about that.

DR. HALL: Could I ask, Mr. Chairman, that, Mr. Mack, as part of the statement that you provide to us, if you would speak to that issue, I would be most appreciative.

MR. MACK: I would be happy to. That is an interesting thought.

DR. NELSON: I think just to clarify your point that we are looking for documents and might miss some of these questions, actually under the statute the term document is very widely interpreted, and it means in some ways information that emerges in whatever form, whatever form of the media, so that, in fact, photographs in this instance would be regarded as proper material.

I just thought I would clarify that point because —

MR. MACK: One comes to mind. A local photographer who worked for the NBC affiliate named Jimmy Darnell filmed the loading of the President's casket on to Air Force One. He filmed it from close range, and after he was done, a Dallas Police officer came up to him and said, you shouldn't be doing that, that is sacrilegious, give me your camera. Jimmy had just joined the station and hadn't been in the business very long and he did turn over the camera or gave him the film, and the officer—Jimmy knew the officer's name and he told me the officer's name, and I don't recall it. It will come to me in a minute.

I called him and he had no knowledge of such a film and didn't recall doing that, but was not really surprised, it was not the kind of thing he would be enthusiastic to admit. He said that if he had done that, he would have given it to Chief Curry, which means it would have gone to the FBI, so the TV station filed a Freedom of Information Request right away and got an answer within like four days that their files do not have any such film.

Since there is such controversy, and legitimate controversy, I should add, about the condition of the President's body in Dallas versus the body in Washington, I would doubt very highly there would be anything significant in this film of loading the body onto Air Force One, but you never know, and what else was on that film that has also vanished.

It is just one that comes to mind.

CHAIRMAN TUNHEIM: Other questions?

[No response.]

CHAIRMAN TUNHEIM: Thank you, Mr. Mack. We appreciate your testimony.

MR. MACK: Thanks.

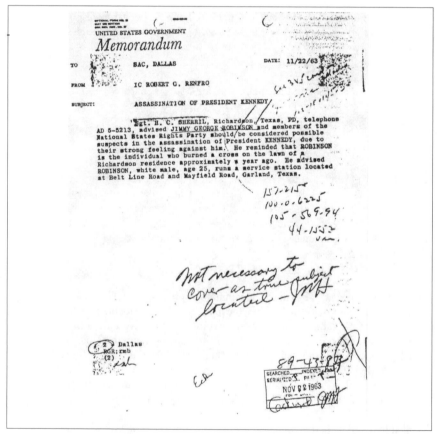

According to J. Edgar Hoover, Director of the FBI, it was not necessary to investigate other possible suspects, because the "true subject" had already been arrested. Oswald was not presumed innocent until proven guilty.

Appendix H

Lifton on the Zavada Report

David Lifton

[*Editor's note*: David Lifton here provides an objective description of the organization and contents of "The Zavada Report", which Zavada summarized in Appendix B. Lifton's response to the report supports the inference that it was a serious study that should be helpful in understanding the camera and its properties. As he observes, while Zavada explains away certain anomalies associated with the film as predictable properties of the ordinary operation of the Bell & Howell camera, he does not take a stand on the question of the authenticity of the film's content, which, as he has acknowledged in correspondence with me, he considers to lie beyond the scope of his professional competence.]

The Zevada Report

In 1996, the ARRB contacted some top people at Kodak in connection with conducting a study of (what purports to be) the original Zapruder film, plus the two Secret Service copies.

I say "purports to be" because many researchers, including myself, entertain serious doubts that it is the camera original; and that issue, in fact, is a major focus of the work that the ARRB asked Kodak to do.

The primary work was done by Roland J. Zavada, now retired, but formerly Standards Director for Imaging Technologies, for Eastman Kodak. (His past responsibilities included coordinating the activities of the Consumer Video and Broadcast Telecine Television Evaluation Laboratories. He was also a product engineer on reversal motion picture film, and a principal member of the Kodak team that introduced Kodachrome II, Ektachrome Commerical and Kodachrome Print film, and also developed the "Super 8" system.

The Zavada Report (he titled it "Analysis of Selected Motion Picture Evidence") consists of seven sections and totals (approximately) 470 pages.

This is not a government-sponsored study as to whether an assassin can be seen hiding behind a fence. Based on my own first reading, this is a serious attempt to bring some first rate talent to bear on the question of whether (a) there are unexplainable anomalies in this film and (b) —and this is implied, but not spelled out—whether they constitute circumstantial evidence of film forgery.

The Zavada Report does not have a set of conclusions, and he does not come down on one side of the issue or another. He just investigates, and reports what he finds. The readers will be the jury. At least, this is the way I read it.

As students of this area of the case know, the official story goes like this: Z filmed the motorcade; then went to Kodak and processed his film; then went to Jamieson Film Company in Dallas with his camera original and had 3 copies printed on Ektachrome; and then took his 3 copies back to Kodak where they were processed. Thus, at the end of this procedure, Mr. Z had four film cans—an original plus 3 copies. Then, supposedly, he gave two of the copies to the Secret Service and, the next morning, sold the original (along with his remaining copy—called the "Dallas copy") to Time-Life. Although Zapruder told the press he got $40k for the film (and donated $25k to the family of Tippit), in fact his deal was for $150k, consisting of 6 $25k payments—one that weekend, and then 5 more $25k payments, on the first of each year, out to 1968). So much for background—admittedly oversimplified; now back to the Zavada report.

Lurking in the background are these issues:

Issue 1

Is the original Z film at the Archives—the one that was the subject of a "taking" by the ARRB—really the camera original?

Issue 2

Are each of the two Secret Service copies at the National Archives actually made from that camera original?

What we have here is a very complicated "chain of possession" story, intertwined with some very complex technical issues relating to how the original camera worked, what a "camera original" should look like; and what the copies should look like.

Here is the way Zavada organized his work:

The first section—23 pages in length—gives Zavada's background, an overview of the project, a table of contents for all the sections; and a table of contents for all the attachments.

Then come four sections—labeled "Study 1", "Study 2", "Study 3" and "Study 4" (which are 30, 14, 33, and 55 pp. respectively). These sections deal with the question of how the Jamieson printer that made the Secret Service copies works (and whether there are anomalies in the edge printing); the second two deal with the actual Zapruder camera, and how it works, and whether or not there are anomalies on what purports to be the original at the National Archives.

The "objective" of each of these studies—as described by Zavada himself—are:

Study 1

(30 pp., which includes 8 pp. with color illustrations; close-up color shots of film strips, to show how edge markings work)

Objective: Write a technical report on the exact meaning of the edge print and date-code found on the Zapruder films at the National Archives designated as "out of camera" original and the two first-generation Secret Service copies; and, address to the extent possible, what the edge and date codes, and unique numerical codes either punched into the films or photographically copied, reveal about each film's pedigree. (Per ARRB request.)

Study 2

(14 pp., which includes 10 pp. of color; includes color Nix, Muchmore)

Objective: Analyze the 35mm "blow-up" motion picture prints and determine to the fullest extent possible when they were printed, and on what film product, and the vintage of the print and/or print-through of the intermediate stock. (Per ARRB request.)

Study 3

(33 pp., which includes 7 pp. of color; includes some color film strip showing previously unpublished "family" scenes)

Objective: Our goal is to analyze the printing characteristics of the copies of the Zapruder "out-of-camera" original film made by the Jamieson Film company 11/22/63, and to document, to the best of our ability, how these copies were produced.

Study 4

(55 pp., which includes 10 pp. with color; no Z frames; just photos illustrating how the claw on the camera works)

Objective: Conduct film tests using a Model 414 PD Bell & Howell Zoomatic Director Series camera to determine whether the recognized anomalies in the Zapruder film theoretically attributed to claw flare, claw shadow, development turbidity, first frame inertial effect, and the design of the photo-electric cell [*Author's note:* These are the "innocent explanations" for some of the oddities observed on what purports to be the camera original"] are borne out by actual tests with film—i.e., create a "control" against which to compare the film identified in the Archives as the "out-of-camera original". Subsequently, write a report evaluating the likely meaning of similarities and/or differences observed between the newly created "control" film and the film in the archives designated as the "out-of-camera original". (Per ARRB.)

In summary: To provide a thorough understanding of the specific image capture characteristics of the camera used by Mr. A. Zapruder to film the assassination of president Kennedy in 1963.

Attachments

Next come four "Attachments" (or appendices) containing all kinds of useful documentation from how the camera work;, how an optical printer works; correspondence between Zavada and the ARRB; correspondence between Zavada and other technical people (e.g., Moses Weitzman).

These Attachments are titled:

Attachment for Study 1

Edge Print Analysis of the Zapruder Original Movie Film and Secret Service Copies (78 pp.)

Very interesting correspondence and ARRB memos, including a wonderful first person account of the processing of Z's film at Kodak, by the fellow who ran the lab.

Attachment for Study 2

Edge Print Analysis and Supporting Technical Information of two 35mm films provided to the ARRB by Robert Groden. (17pp.)

Analysis of films provided under oath by Robert Groden, and Zavada's attempts to deal with Groden's claims that this is all he had, and its vintage was 1972/73.

Attachment for Study 3

Initial Motion Picture Printing of the Zapruder 8 mm Original Movie Film (101 pp.)

("everything you ever wanted to know about the printer that made the two Secret Service copies. . . ")

Attachment for Study 4

Bell & Howell Director Series 414PD 8mm Movie Camera. (118 pp.)

("Everything you ever wanted to know about the Z camera ....")

A word about color:

Each of the four main sections of the report has certain color reproductions (some from hitherto unprinted frames of the Z film—e.g. the "family" scenes, which were on "side A"). These color graphics are of extremely high quality, and quite beautiful to behold. Often, an entire "strip" of film is printed, to illustrate a point about edge printing.

This report is primary source material for anyone who is a serious student of the authenticity question regarding the Z film.

Jim Fetzer and David Lifton at the Zapruder Film Symposium, Duluth, Minnesota, 9–11 May 2003. (Photograph by Jack White)

Appendix I

The Hoax becomes The Joke:
MPI's "Image of an Assassination"

John P. Costella, Ph.D.

[*Editor's note:* After the ARRB secured the "camera original" Zapruder film as an assassination record, it heeded Josiah Thompson's suggestion (Appendix F) that a state-of-the-art digitized reference be created, to obviate the need for any further handling of the $16,000,000 strip of film. But when MPI released "Image of an Assassination" (1998), it became clear that this historically crucial task had not been conducted competently, with missing frames leading a long list of elementary and inexcusable mistakes. As John Costella describes in this appendix, even the "making of" section on the MPI DVD *itself* appears to be a fraud, suggesting the entire project may have been a form of disinformation—a spoof—in which "mistakes" were carefully crafted in the hope of confounding researchers with the intent of hindering the study of the film for decades to come.]

As described in my first chapter, I was initially astounded to learn that the reference digitization of the Zapruder film had been botched in so many elementary ways. [*Editor's note*: See the color section, "Which film *is* "The Zapruder Film"?"] As a scientist, the story was simply unbelievable: they weren't sending man to Mars, or building a nuclear fusion reactor—all they had to do was enlarge a few hundred photographs, and scan them into a computer. Given access to professional photographic equipment, a high school student could almost do it.

Very quickly, I realized that these "mistakes" were just the latest examples of obfuscation and disinformation. But it wasn't until I subsequently obtained a copy of the MPI DVD itself, hoping to scour the "making of" section for clues as to what had really happened, that I realized that I was watching a spoof—a parody, full of "in" jokes that, to a layman, would just seem to be the technical gobbledygook, but which to the initiated would be hilarious if they weren't so evil.

At first, I thought I was just witnessing the inaccuracies that can often creep into professional television productions—accuracy sacrificed for fancy graphics and simple explanations. Before I even took the shrink-wrap off the DVD box, I noticed that the film strip shown on the cover was a fake—it was made up of the same frame repeated over and over. "Artistic license," I muttered.

But this excuse soon wore thin. Just 03:10 into Title 1, a slick animation purports to explain how Double 8 mm film is exposed in the Zapruder camera. First we see what is described to be a length of 16 mm film, complete with sprocket holes. The exposure of the first half of the film is then illustrated, snaking down the left of the 16 mm film—but the "exposures" shown include *extra*, small sprocket holes, which simply do not exist. The exposure of right half of the film is then shown—still with non-existent extra holes, and moreover in the wrong direction. What should clarify and educate instead simply confuses and misinforms.

The technical "jokes" and the obvious hoax

At this point, it is worth jumping to Chapter 6 of Title 1 (at 28:11), which continues the technical explanation of how the project was carried out. At 30:30, we are told that a special transport mechanism was built, "that would hold the entire length of the 25-foot film." But why? Only six feet of the film actually contains images—the rest is made up of leaders and blank tape. At 30:40 we are told that the film is stored in a special vault, held at 25°F—but shown is a temperature recording chart, at 50°F. More "artistic license"?

At 31:05 we get to see how they kept track of the frame numbers: they were printed onto a separate strip of plastic. This was placed next to the film in the protective polyester sleeve: we can see the technician trying to align the two. But at 31:10 we can see the *end* of the particular strip of numbers used for this part of the film, jiggled around by the technician. The numbers, not quite distinct, are clearly in the hundreds (perhaps in the 340's).

In other words, there was not one strip of numbers for the entire film, but rather separate pieces. But how on Earth could the technician match the number up with the correct film frame? To the naked eye (even magnified), many frames would look identical. Is this "scientific", let alone "state of the art"? Surely it would be sensible to have one long strip of numbers, aligned with the length of the film? And where is the special "transport mechanism" that moves the two, simultaneously, through the camera? Is it any wonder that frames were missed altogether?

At 31:12 we are told that the protective sleeves were *removed* when the film was under the camera. How was this achieved? Some of the highly magnified images clearly show "rings", which to a physicist means that two transparent surfaces were not in perfect contact. Some are even out of focus, which implies a complete gap in the contact.

At 31:13 we see the film under the camera, being held down by hand! It appears to be sitting on a sheet of plastic (presumably for protection—is this the "transport mechanism"?) which is itself buckled! At 31:30, the photographic expert, Joseph Barabe, describes the steps taken to maintain consistency from frame to frame: the film emulsion, the bulb used, and the exposure time. Scientifically, this sounds excellent: keep it in mind.

At 32:05, Barabe explains that he used a precise photographic timer for the exposures. At the same time, we see him timing a test exposure *by looking at his watch and pressing a manual shutter lead button*. At this point, the penny drops. The entire production is a spoof—a joke. One can just imagine the chuckles: "Did you catch the joke about the precision timing?"

But let us persevere. At 32:09 we see some of the transparencies. Clearly, they photographed the frames before Z-001 (of Sitzman and the Hesters) that are still on the "original" film. From the numbering, there appear to be 14 such frames, because Z-001 is visible, and labeled "015". (Much of this footage seems to have disappeared; Groden shows a copy of it on his *Assassination Films* video.) None of these important "pre-motorcade" frames made it past the cutting room floor: they do not appear on the film sequences.

At 32:19 we are told that the entire width of the film was reproduced (as seen on the transparencies), from film edge to film edge. This is also denied to researchers: the widest film sequence cuts off the left edge through the middle of the edge printing, and the other three edges of each frame are tightly "cropped", destroying vital calibration and continuity information.

At 32:39, James Silverberg, the Zapruder film attorney, describes the fundamental importance of the project: reproducing the image between the sprocket holes. But the imagery shown during his voice-over is the *only* high-quality imagery we have of these regions: no other magnified view appears on the DVD.

At 34:02 we are shown the processed transparencies being checked for flaws. Clearly, there were problems: one transparency is out of sequence—presumably a "re-shoot". How were the numbers re-aligned for such "re-shoots"?

The real "fun" begins at 34:25, with Todd Murphy of "There TV", who was apparently completely responsible for the digital imaging. Another "in" joke: a Microsoft Windows mouse-pad, sacrilegious in any all-Mac environment such as that shown. Another at 35:21: the transparency goes into the scanner perfectly mounted and aligned, but the scan on the screen is crooked. But how? *It's a hoax!*— the calibration marks and frame numbers, along either side of the transparency, *are not there on the screen!* The "making of" section appears to be an elaborate deception!

At 35:36 we see Todd trying to "register" (align) an image. What scientific process was employed? He just shifts them around, until they look like they agree with each other. What an appalling fraud! Would the National Archives really leave this historic digitization in the hands of such an amateur? The answer is obvious.

The *coup de grace* occurs at 36:20. Remember the apparent care taken to maintain absolutely consistent light and color reproduction in making the photographic transparencies? Todd decides that he doesn't like the changes in lighting as the camera pans down Elm Street. So we see him fiddling the light and color controls, *frame by frame*, just moving things around with the mouse, until it looks good to him, "which I think looks much better than the original footage"—which might be the right attitude if this were a television advertisement.

At 36:50 we are told that most of the "dust and scratches" on the original film were removed. Again: Why? How? But we are shown marks on the film that Gary Mack insists is mold—and he has claimed that NARA have since removed a good fraction of it. So what *are* those marks: scratches or mold?

At 37:21 we are assured that the images are archived at their "original resolution". But they are not: no high-resolution scan of an entire frame is contained on the DVD at all. We are also left in the dark as to why the sequences are all shown with stretched or compressed frames. The ultimate "joke" or insult: the very first frame shown in the "Digital Reproductions" section is not frame Z-001 at all. It is Z-002.

What about the other sections of the DVD?

If we return to 04:04 of Title 1, we see the only known photograph of Abraham Zapruder actually using his camera—which he seems to be holding uncomfortably, no doubt because his eye is not actually looking through the viewfinder! Following this we begin to be treated to some interviews that are "courtesy of the Sixth Floor Museum". (Contemplate David Lifton's description of Mary Moorman's treatment "courtesy of the Sixth Floor Museum"!)

At 08:05 we see a segment of Zapruder's interview at WFAA-TV (more of which can be seen in the "historical footage" section of the DVD). There are several remarkable features of this footage. Zapruder's depiction of a blow-out of the President's right *temple* has been described by Jim Fetzer (*Editor's note*: See his chapter on "Distorting the Photographic Record"). What strikes one on the DVD version is the amazing *clarity* of the footage—because this was purportedly a *videotape* recording of a live broadcast.

This videotape seems to be better defined than any other videotape taken on the day of the assassination—superior, even, to that of Walter Cronkite. Indeed, it rivals the clarity of the footage taken on film—which would imply that it were staged at a later date. Could it be?

It is a surprisingly simple yet compelling scenario to contemplate: Zapruder's description of the head wound; his description of just three shots; the newsman's story of *also* hearing three shots; of seeing people down on the grass near the Triple Underpass, which he presumes included Zapruder, to which Zapruder confirms, "Yes, I was." The problem is that no film or photograph of Dealey Plaza after the assassination shows Zapruder there.

Also shown is a photo of the sixth floor window—at which Zapruder remarks that he "must have been in the line of fire". But the "Zapruder" film shows all the shots finishing before the President even *passes* Zapruder. Either Zapruder was there, and the shots occurred further down Elm Street (and hence the film is a hoax) or else he was not there filming at all (and the filmer is a hoax as well).

But isn't this also the interview where Zapruder purportedly breaks down, overwrought by what he remembers seeing? At first sight, it appears so. He says he feels sick—but he doesn't look very convincing, and he stays on to continue the discussion.By 13:20 we are seeing an interview with Richard Stolley of *Life*, describing his negotiations with Zapruder, which had led to the purchase of the film.

David Healy has noted that Stolley's story makes no sense at all. Firstly, he paints Zapruder as a shrewd businessman, but then notes that he did not allow *any* of the other media (banging at the door) to make competitive bids. Then, when Stolley's bid got to $50,000, and he said, "Mr. Zapruder, this is truly as high as I can go without calling New York, for authorization to go higher," Zapruder suddenly decided to accept that amount—despite having been told, in effect, that Stolley *would* go higher!

By Monday, *Life* had bought the motion picture rights as well, for an additional $100,000. At 18:38, we see a contract signed by Abraham Zapruder. The only problem is that this signature is incompatible with an "Abraham Zapruder" signature appearing in an attachment to the Zavada Report (the 'A' is written clockwise in the latter, but anticlockwise in the former), and completely different from an "Abraham Zapruder" signature shown in Trask's *Pictures of the Pain* (the 'p', in particular, loops down then up in the latter, but up then down in the former).

Although changes in signature can occur over time, such fundamental changes in the way one hand-writes letters is impossible. (Try it yourself!) This, in itself—from either a scientific *or* a legal point of view—must surely cast the most serious doubt on the innocence of Abraham Zapruder's involvement in the Hoax of the Century.

*Of all the witnesses to the tragedy, the only unimpeachable one
is the 8-mm movie camera of Abraham Zapruder.*
— Quote from *Life* on the cover of MPI's
"Image of an Assassination" (1998)

Index

G

H

David Healy
at the Zapruder Film Symposium,
Duluth, Minnesota, 9–11 May 2003.
(Photograph by Jan Fetzer)

Acknowledgments

This collection of new studies originated with the Zapruder Film Symposium held on the campus of the University of Minnesota, Duluth, 9-11 May 2003. My first debt of thanks goes to Pauline Nuhring, for her exceptional enthusiasm, dedication, and competence. This is our second conference together, and I find working with her a pleasure. The speakers, Jack White, David Healy, John P. Costella, David W. Mantik, and David Lifton provided important—even extraordinary—new information about the Zapruder film, which made it apparent that a third edited volume on this subject would make a valuable addition to our understanding of the conspiracy and cover-up that ended the life of our 35th President.

One of the first results of the Zapruder Film Symposium was the discovery that the films available to the public, including David Lifton's "Z Film" (undated), the Macmillan CD, "JFK Assassination: A Visual Investigation" (1993), Robert Groden's "The Assassination Films" (1995), and MPI's "Image of an Assassination" (1998), all differ significantly in the amount of information they provide. Even the best, MPI's "Image of an Assassination" (1998) does not include frames 155 and 156; does not include frames 208, 209, 210, and 211; has reversed frames 331 and 332; and also does not include (what ought to be) frames 341, 350, and (even) the final frame, 486.

John P. Costella, Ph.D., has produced a fresh version of the film, which overcomes all of these deficiencies and introduces improvements never before seen in any Zapruder film, namely: corrections for pincushion and aspect ratio distortion; inclusion of the so-called "ghost panels"; and masking open sprocket holes to make information more accessible. In the interest of advancing the frontiers of knowledge, education, research, science, and inquiry—with the expert technical assistance of Scott A. Lederer—this new, improved version is being made available to the public free and without charge at the internet web site:

www.assassinationscience.com.

I am also grateful to George Costello, Roland Zavada, Douglas P. Horne, Noel Twyman, and Rich DellaRosa for their important contributions. Each of the authors of the chapters of this book retains the copyright of his work as follows:

"Fraud and Fabrication in the Death of JFK" © 2003 James H. Fetzer
"Which Film *is* 'the Zapruder film'?" © 2003 James H. Fetzer
    and Scott A. Lederer
"Mysteries of the JFK Assassination" © 2003 Jack White
"Technical Aspects of Film Alteration" © 2003 David Healy
"A Scientist's Verdict: The Film is a Fraud" © 2003 John P. Costella
"Was Mary Standing in the Street?" © 2003 Jack White
"Mary Moorman and Her Polaroids" © 2003 John P. Costella
"The Dealey Plaza Home Movies" © 2003 David W. Mantik
"Pig on a Leash: A Question of Authenticity" © 2003 David S. Lifton
"Distorting the Photographic Record" © 2003 James H. Fetzer

Contributors

JOHN P. COSTELLA, Ph.D., of Narre Warren, Victoria, Australia. After graduating at the top of his class with honors degrees in both electrical engineering and the sciences from the University of Melbourne, he completed a Ph.D. in theoretical physics, specializing in high energy physics, Einstein's theory of relativity, and classical electrodynamics, which is the mathematical analysis of the physics of moving objects and the light they emit. After three years of postdoctoral research and lecturing at the University, he took a position as a teacher of Mathematics, Physics, and Information Technology at Mentone Grammar, a leading private boys' high school in suburban bayside Melbourne. He has undertaken the most sophisticated analyses of the Zapruder film in the history of the study of the assassination, where he is making exremely important scientific discoveries.

JAMES H. FETZER, Ph.D., of Duluth, MN. McKnight University Professor of Philosophy at the University of Minnesota, where he teaches on its Duluth campus, he received his A.B. *magna cum laude* from Princeton and his Ph.D. in the history and philosophy of science at Indiana. He has published 20 books and more than 100 articles in philosophy of science and on the theoretical foundations of computer science, artifical intelligence, and cognitive science. He has chaired or cochaired four conferences on the death of JFK (Minneapolis 1999, Dallas 2000, Dallas 2001, Duluth 2003) and edits an electronic journal for advanced study of the death of JFK, *assassinationresearch.com*. A frequent guest on radio talk shows (with more than 250 appearances), he edited *Assassination Science* (1998) and *Murder in Dealey Plaza* (2000). He maintains a web site at *assassinationscience.com*.

DAVID HEALY of Las Vegas, NV. Healy has spent more than thirty years in television and film production and post-production and has an extensive background using a wide variety of special effects cinematographic techniques. He has shot tape or film for all three of the national networks and for many other outlets in areas other than advertising. Healy engineered, designed, and built two editing facilities and has field tested ENG news camera packages for a camera manufacturer. For the past thirteen years, his specialty has been video

498

post-production for Silicon Valley high-tech corporations and some other Fortune 500 companies. His works have been nominated for and have won major industry awards. David filmed and produced a documentary record of the second Zapruder Film Symposium.

DAVID S. LIFTON of Los Angeles, CA. A graduate of Cornell University's School of Engineering Physics, he was a UCLA graduate student and working at North American Aviation on Project Apollo when JFK was assassinated. In 1966, after composing a classic essay on the medical evidence for *Ramparts* magazine, he discovered data suggesting that the body had been altered prior to the autopsy. His research led to the publication of *Best Evidence* (1980), a comprehensive investigation elaborating the secret interception of the body and falsification of the autopsy. His book was a *New York Times'* bestseller and a Book of the Month selection. Writer and producer of "Best Evidence Research Video" (1989), a unique filmed record of the experiences of autopsy technicians from Bethesda Naval Hosptial, Lifton collaborated with the Assassination Records Review Board and was a witness at one of its hearings. He is currently completing a biography of Lee Oswald.

DAVID W. MANTIK, M.D., Ph.D., of Rancho Mirage, CA. He received his Ph.D. in physics from Wisconsin and his M.D. from the University of Michigan. A Board Certified Radiation Oncologist, he has done pioneering work studying the autopsy X-rays with densitometry, a type of investigation never before performed, which led to the discovery that the autopsy X-rays have been altered and has pulled the rug out from under the government's previous investigations. The leading expert on the medical evidence in the world today, his classic studies of the X-rays and of the alteration of the film appear in *Assassination Science* (1998) and in *Murder in Dealey Plaza* (2000).

JACK WHITE of Fort Worth, TX. A leading expert on photographic aspects of the assassination of JFK, he produced *The Continuing Inquiry* for the celebrated investigator, Penn Jones, with whom he worked for three years. He served as an advisor on photographic evidence for the House Select Committee on Assassinations during its reinvestigation of 1977–78 and for Oliver Stone in producing his motion picture, "JFK". He has produced many documentaries on the assassination, including his own video, "The Great Zapruder Film Hoax", which includes an interview of William Reymond by Jim Marrs in which Raymond describes another—more complete—film that he has seen. His research on the photographic record appears in *Assassination Science* (1998) and in *Murder in Dealey Plaza* (2000).